Business, Government, and Society

A Managerial Perspective, Text and Cases

Eleventh Edition

George A. Steiner

Harry and Elsa Kunin Professor of Business and Society and Professor of Management, Emeritus, UCLA

John F. Steiner

Professor of Management California State University, Los Angeles

McGraw-Hill Irwin

Boston   Burr Ridge, IL   Dubuque, IA   Madison, WI   New York   San Francisco   St. Louis
Bangkok   Bogotá   Caracas   Kuala Lumpur   Lisbon   London   Madrid   Mexico City
Milan   Montreal   New Delhi   Santiago   Seoul   Singapore   Sydney   Taipei   Toronto

 **McGraw-Hill**
Irwin

BUSINESS, GOVERNMENT, AND SOCIETY:
A MANAGERIAL PERSPECTIVE, TEXT AND CASES
Published by McGraw-Hill/Irwin, a business unit of The McGraw-Hill Companies, Inc., 1221 Avenue of the Americas, New York, NY, 10020. Copyright © 2006, 2003, 2000, 1997, 1994, 1991, 1988, 1985 by The McGraw-Hill Companies, Inc. All rights reserved. No part of this publication may be reproduced or distributed in any form or by any means, or stored in a database or retrieval system, without the prior written consent of The McGraw-Hill Companies, Inc., including, but not limited to, in any network or other electronic storage or transmission, or broadcast for distance learning.

Some ancillaries, including electronic and print components, may not be available to customers outside the United States.

This book is printed on acid-free paper.

2 3 4 5 6 7 8 9 0 DOC/DOC 0 9 8 7 6

ISBN-13: 978-0-07-299442-1
ISBN-10: 0-07-299442-8

Editorial director: *John E. Biernat*
Senior sponsoring editor: *Kelly H. Lowery*
Editorial assistant: *Kirsten L. Guidero*
Senior marketing manager: *Lisa Nicks*
Producer, Media technology: *Mark Molsky*
Project manager: *Marlena Pechan*
Production supervisor: *Gina Hangos*
Coordinator freelance design: *Artemio Ortiz, Jr.*
Photo research coordinator: *Lori Kramer*
Photo researcher: *David Tietz*
Media project manager: *Betty Hadala*
Supplement producer: *Gina F. DiMartino*
Developer, Media technology: *Brian Nacik*
Cover design: *David Seidler*
Typeface: *10/12 Palatino*
Compositor: *TechBooks/GTS, York, PA*
Printer: *R. R. Donnelley*

Library of Congress Cataloging-in-Publication Data

Steiner, George Albert, 1912-
    Business, government, and society : a managerial perspective, text and cases / George A. Steiner, John F. Steiner.—11th ed.
        p. cm.
    Includes bibliographical references and index.
    ISBN 0-07-299442-8 (alk. paper)
    1. Industries—Social aspects—United States. 2. Industrial policy—United States. I. Steiner, John F. II. Title.
HD60.5.U5S8 2006
658.4—dc22

                                                                                    2005041785

www.mhhe.com

We dedicate this book to the memory
of Jean Wood Steiner

Brief Table of Contents

Table of Contents

Preface

The Eleventh Edition of *Business, Government, and Society* continues our long effort to tell the story of how these three great human entities interact to shape our world. As always, since the last edition a stream of events has dictated the need for wide, and sometimes deep, revision. Accordingly, we have updated each chapter to include new ideas, laws, personalities, and publications.

While current events move rapidly over the surface of our subject matter, the underlying principles and relationships at its core lie undisturbed. As in every edition, we accommodate the flow of ephemera, but we also continue the work of building insight into the basic nature of the discipline. So, while current events will play havoc with the look of this edition, we believe that under the surface, discussions about the plain nature of business, government, and society interrelationships are stronger and will longer endure than in our previous editions.

We carry on our effort to give more prominence to global and comparative aspects of the subject matter. In the new edition we travel to nations on every continent and focus on international efforts to define corporate duties. Although we emphasize current events, we continue to provide historical background in the belief that it helps us to understand why things are as they are. We explain the ancient origins of the tension between wealth and virtue, discuss how great industries have shaped nations, and study personalities from the past to show how they have left their imprint on the world. Often, what is fresh in our memory is but the periodic display of an enduring phenomenon.

With the Eleventh Edition we also continue a strong and spirited collaboration between father and son extending now over twenty-five years.

THE CHAPTERS

The new edition brings many changes. Key updates and additions in the chapters include the following:

- Chapter 1, which introduces the subject matter, retains its pragmatic approach to the field based on four models of the business–government–society relationship. The discussion of capitalism is deepened to describe its historical development and the enduring attacks on its flaws.
- Chapter 2, on the business environment, is revised and updated to reflect recent events and the progress of trends.
- Chapter 4, on critics of business, extends discussion of business criticism in the United States back to the colonial era, and includes a new section on socialism and a new discussion of the tactics used by business critics.
- Chapter 5, on corporate social responsibility, updates readers on recent developments in codes of conduct and other initiatives to define the social responsibilities of transnational corporations.
- Chapter 6, on implementing social responsibilities, continues to focus on the tools and levers available to managers who want to create responsible corporations.

It contains a new discussion of stakeholder engagement and an updated treatment of corporate social reporting.

- Chapter 7, on business ethics, is revised to cover the recent outbreak of corporate fraud and includes new discussion of the individuals, companies, and prosecutions involved.
- Chapter 9, on business in politics, is revised to show how the new campaign reform law passed in 2002 affected corporate electoral activity in the 2004 elections.
- Chapter 10, on regulation, includes a new discussion of regulation in foreign nations.
- Chapter 12, on multinational corporations, has updated commentary on the growing size and power of multinationals and the expansion of global trade.
- Chapter 16, on consumerism, has extended explanation of the historical growth of consumerism and a revised discussion of product liability.
- Chapter 17, on the changing workplace, contains a new section on the difficult task of balancing worker protection with the need to allow flexibility in workforce adjustment.
- Chapter 19, on corporate governance, is revised to discuss reforms related to recent corporate scandals and passage of the Sarbanes-Oxley Act.

THE CASE STUDIES

Every chapter, with the exception of Chapter 1, concludes with a case study. The cases illustrate one or more central themes in the chapter. Main issues in the cases have pro and con sides and will generate classroom debate and controversy.

Our philosophy of case writing is based on a few key beliefs. We believe that cases should raise sharp and, if possible, multiple issues. We believe that these issues should be developed, but not in exhausting detail. So our cases are of moderate length. We believe that cases should be written to generate questions rather than answer them. Therefore, we try to open lines of inquiry and we list central questions at the end. And we believe that, except for historical incidents, cases should be current. Therefore, we have updated cases carried over from the last edition.

Five new cases are added to the Eleventh Edition.

- "A Campaign against KFC Corporation." People for the Ethical Treatment of Animals was successful in pressuring some fast-food restaurant and supermarket chains to change the treatment of food animals by their suppliers. But KFC refuses to give in. The case explores the tactics of activist critics and the defensive actions of the target corporation.
- "Mark Kasky versus Nike Inc." Kasky, a jogger, believed that Nike profited from abused Asian workers who made its shoes and clothing—and then lied about their working conditions. He sued Nike for consumer fraud, leading to novel and surprising court rulings.
- "The Trial of Martha Stewart." Was she guilty of a serious crime or was she a victim of overzealous government attorneys? Her story illustrates how the criminal prosecution of a corporate executive works.

- "Westar Goes to Washington." Westar, an electric utility in Kansas, had no political strategy until a dynamic new leader asked Congress to help him succeed in a diversification strategy. The leader turned out to be a crook and Congress showed itself to be a pragmatic institution.
- "Cendant Shareholders Attack Executive Pay." Henry Silverman created Cendant and made it one of the nation's largest and most profitable corporations. After a disastrous merger his strategic insight put the company back on a growth course. Even so, some of the shareholders think he is paid too much.

CHAPTER-OPENING STORIES

As in past editions, we begin each chapter with a true story about a company, a biographical figure, or a government action to introduce the forthcoming material. Five new stories are added to this edition.

- "Mary 'Mother' Jones." Mother Jones was a labor leader. Now largely forgotten, she was one of the most famous women in America at the turn of the twentieth century. She understood how to use power and she used it to attack corporations.
- "The Fall of Arthur Andersen." Arthur Andersen was once noted for its high ethics. It fell to practices that would have shocked its founder. Had it retained its integrity it might have blunted some of the biggest accounting fraud scandals.
- "Public Law 108-357." How does a bill become a law? This is the story of a mammoth tax bill that became a business lobbyist's paradise. It is a story that departs from high school civics texts.
- "Ted Turner Attacks Media Giants." The billionaire takes a maverick position among telecommunications executives on growing concentration in the industry.
- "Harvey W. Wiley." Wiley was the nation's first great consumer crusader. Like Ralph Nader many years later, he worked hard for legislative gains only to be defeated by the deep political power of corporations.

SUPPORT MATERIALS FOR INSTRUCTORS

An *Instructor's Resource CD/ROM* includes sample course outlines, chapter objectives, case study teaching notes with answers to the case questions, term paper topics for each text chapter, and a test bank covering chapters and case studies, including multiple-choice, true/false, fill-in, and essay questions.

A set of *PowerPoint® slides* highlighting chapter topics is available for use in classroom lectures.

A *Computerized Test Bank* contains all of the questions in the print test bank. It is a powerful system that allows tests to be prepared quickly and easily. Instructors can view questions as they are selected for a test; scramble questions and answers; add, delete, and edit questions; create multiple test versions; and view and save tests.

A book-specific *Online Learning Center* features resources for both instructors and students. The site offers downloadable supplements for instructors and interactive exercises and self-quizzes designed to enhance student understanding of text material. Go to: www.mhhe.com/steiner11e.

Acknowledgments

We are sincerely indebted to the many authors who have informed us and to colleagues and friends who have been with us over the years. Where appropriate we cite their work. Many others have been helpful with their contributions and suggestions during the writing of this edition. We are especially grateful to Larry Holloway, Kansas Corporation Commission; David Lee, Ramsey-Shilling Company; Brenda O' Connor, Department of Justice; Ian Stirton, Federal Election Commission; Randolph Tritell, Federal Trade Commission; Melinda Warren, Center for the Study of American Business; and J. Fred Weston, University of California at Los Angeles.

The following reviewers helped us to set our revision goals and gave us many valuable suggestions about the text. They are

Florence Alberts
San Francisco State University

Abe Bakhsheshy
University of Utah

Myrna L. Gusdorf
Linn-Benton Community College

Sharon Hama-West
University of South Florida

Carnella Hardin
Glendale Community College

Douglas G. Heeter
Ferris State University

Heejoon Kang
Indiana University

Marilyn R. Kaplan
University of Texas at Dallas

Susan Key
University of Alabama at Birmingham

Marsha Matson
University of Miami

Gary Shields
Wayne State University

John M. Stevens
Pennsylvania State University

Raymond W. Vegso
Canisius College

At California State University, Los Angeles, we thank G. Timothy Haight and Kern Kwong for their support. George Jacobson, Philip Lohman and Bahram Mahdavian made many helpful comments and suggestions. We also thank Alan Stein at the John F. Kennedy Memorial Library for continuing advice and assistance on the research process.

We are deeply indebted to our outstanding editorial team at McGraw-Hill/Irwin, including sponsoring editor Kelly Lowery, editorial assistant Kirsten Guidero, and project manager Marlena Pechan. The skill and effort of each has left an imprint on the book. It was our good fortune that they chose to introduce Peter de Lissovoy, a copy editor with insight and sure judgment, to the project.

Finally, we are grateful to Deborah Luedy for her graceful and generous support of our work.

That the book exists at all is, as always, a small wonder. That it may have improved in quality since the last edition is possible because of the efforts of those named here.

About the Authors

George A. Steiner

is one of the leading pioneers in the development of university curriculums, research, and scholarly writings in the field of business, government, and society. In 1983 he was the recipient of the first Sumner Marcus Award for distinguished achievement in the field by the Social Issues in Management Division of the Academy of Management. In 1990 he received the Distinguished Educator Award, given for the second time by the Academy of Management. After receiving his B.S. in business administration at Temple University, he was awarded an M.A. in economics from the Wharton School of the University of Pennsylvania and a Ph.D. in economics from the University of Illinois. He is the author of many books and articles. Two of his books received "book-of-the-year" awards. In recognition of his writings, Temple University awarded him a Litt.D. honorary degree. Professor Steiner has held top-level positions in the federal government and in industry, including corporate board directorships. Past president of the Academy of Management and co-founder of *The California Management Review,* he is Harry and Elsa Kunin Professor of Business and Society and Professor of Management, Emeritus, Anderson School, UCLA.

John F. Steiner

is Professor of Management at California State University, Los Angeles. He received his B.S. from Southern Oregon University and received an M.A. and Ph.D. in political science from the University of Arizona. He has co-authored two other books with George A. Steiner, *Issues in Business and Society* and *Casebook for Business, Government, and Society.* He is also the author of *Industry, Society, and Change: A Casebook.* Professor Steiner is a former chair of the Social Issues in Management Division of the Academy of Management and former chair of the Department of Management at California State University, Los Angeles.

Chapter **One**

The Study of Business, Government, and Society

Exxon Mobil Corporation

On stage at the 2001 annual shareholders meeting, Lee Raymond, age 62, chairman and CEO of ExxonMobil, was in control. On the floor Radhi Darmansyah, an Indonesian villager, stood before a microphone ready to issue a challenge.

"While you made $26 million . . . last year Mr. Raymond, more than one thousand six hundred of my people were killed, maimed, or tortured around your facilities in Aceh. I am here to ask for your help."

In Aceh Province, Radhi's home, the company extracts natural gas from beneath a rain forest, generating billions of dollars in revenue for itself and for the Indonesian government. Aceh is also the base of a guerilla movement and without the government soldiers who patrol the 500-square-mile field, Exxon workers would be in danger. The soldiers have a history of brutalizing the villagers, who fish and grow rice under the tropical sun and who sympathize with the rebels. In faltering English, Radhi continued.

"They are murdering my brothers and sisters. They are raping and keeping school-girls as sexual slaves. I ask you today to please issue a public statement that you will not return to Aceh until my land is free of human rights abuses, and until my people are free . . . "

"I believe your time is up," interrupted Lee Raymond after a chime signaled the end of the two minutes allocated for comments.

Radhi continued speaking.

"I'm sorry you'll have to come back another time." Raymond ordered the microphone cut off.

Radhi tried to go on but security guards moved in to return him to his seat.[1]

---

[1] Thaddeus Herrick, "CEO's Controversial Views Lead to Tough Summer for ExxonMobil," *The Wall Street Journal,* August 29, 2001, p. B1.

Lee Raymond, Chairman of the Board and CEO, Exxon Mobil Corporation. Source: © Exxon Corp./AP Photo.

Lee Raymond is a commanding figure. After growing up in Watertown, South Dakota, he left for college on the advice of his father, a railroad engineer, who saw in him a greater future than the small town had to offer. He eventually got a doctorate in chemical engineering from the University of Minnesota and, after marrying his high school sweetheart, joined Exxon in 1963.[2] He spent 30 years on Exxon's corporate ladder, learning to manage, working around the world, absorbing the company culture, and moving up. In 1993 he became CEO of the world's largest oil company.

ExxonMobil is a massive organizational force, shaping international markets, pushing against competitors, and influencing governments. Although it is headquartered in Irving, Texas, and most people regard it as an American company, 70 percent of its sales, which were $237 billion in 2003, are in other countries. Its main business is discovering, producing, and selling oil and natural gas and it has a long record of profiting more at it than its rivals. In 2003, it got a remarkable 21 percent return on capital employed.[3]

World demand for energy is insatiable and rising, putting ExxonMobil on a treadmill of constantly finding new oil and natural gas supplies to compensate for declining production in existing fields. Output from a mature field drops 5 to 8 percent a year. To maintain profitability the company pursues new reserves wherever they are located, taking political risks and at times abiding unrest and corruption. In Venezuela and Iran its assets were expropriated. In Chad, Angola, Nigeria, and Equatorial Guinea it has paid dictators for access to oil. It accepts protection from the Indonesian troops accused of battering Radhi Darmansyah's villagers. "You kinda have to go where the oil is," says Lee Raymond.[4]

ExxonMobil cannot be well understood apart from its history. It descends from the Standard Oil trust incorporated in 1882 by John D. Rockefeller as Standard Oil of New Jersey. Rockefeller was a brilliant strategist and organizer who destroyed competitors. He believed that the end of imposing order on a youthful, rowdy oil industry justified the use of ruthless means. As Standard Oil grew, Rockefeller's values defined the company's culture, that is, the shared assumptions, both spoken and unspoken, that animate its employees. If the principles of a founder such as Rockefeller are effective,

---

[2] Steve Liesman and Allanna Sullivan, "Mystery Man: Mobil Merger Positions an Enigma at Oil Giant's Helm," *The Wall Street Journal,* December 1, 1999, p. A1.

[3] Figures in this paragraph are from Exxon Mobil Corporation, Form 10-K, filed with the Securities and Exchange Commission, March 15, 2004.

[4] Quoted in Daniel Fisher, "Dangerous Liaisons," *Forbes,* April 28, 2003, p. 84.

they become embedded over time in the organization. Once they are widely shared, they tend to be exceptionally long-lived and stable.[5] Rockefeller emphasized cost control, efficiency, centralized organization, and suppression of competitors. And no set of principles was ever more triumphant. At one time Standard Oil controlled more than 90 percent of the American oil industry.

Its power so offended public values that in 1890 Congress passed the Sherman Antitrust Act to outlaw its monopoly. In 1911, after years of legal battles, the trust was finally broken into 39 separate companies. After the breakup, Standard Oil of New Jersey continued to exist, and although it had shed 57 percent of its assets to create the new firms, it was still the world's largest oil company. Some companies formed in the breakup were Standard Oil of Indiana (which was later renamed Amoco), Atlantic Refining (ARCO), Standard Oil of California (Chevron), Continental Oil (Conoco), Standard Oil of Ohio (Sohio), Chesebrough-Ponds (a company that made petroleum jelly), and Vacuum Oil and Standard Oil of New York (which were reunited as Mobil). In 1972 Standard Oil of New Jersey changed its name to Exxon, and in 1999 it merged with Mobil, to form ExxonMobil.

Today Rockefeller's influence is invisible. But ExxonMobil's actions remain consistent with his nature. Lee Raymond's first day at the company came more than 70 years after Rockefeller stepped aside from its day-to-day management. Yet he became CEO only after 30 years of apprenticeship in the firm's culture and he drives the firm in ways that echo the founder's beliefs. Under Raymond's leadership it has a centralized and authoritarian culture. Cost control, capital productivity, and strict financial controls are emphasized in operations. The overriding performance criterion is return on capital. Industry rivals regard ExxonMobil as a fierce competitor. The company itself recently noted that it "employs all methods of competition which are lawful and appropriate."[6] Nevertheless, ExxonMobil exists in a more difficult environment than did Rockefeller's dominating trust.

Markets are more contested. ExxonMobil pumps only 5.6 percent of the world's daily output of oil. It competes not only with other investor-owned energy companies but with large government-owned firms and with the Organization of Petroleum Exporting Countries (OPEC), which has 40 percent of world output.

Governments are more powerful and relations with them more complex. ExxonMobil's operations are restricted by the laws and regulations of each country in which it does business. In the United States alone there are about 300 federal regulatory agencies, most of which impose rules and standards on the company. Only a handful of these existed in Rockefeller's day. In foreign countries ExxonMobil faces import and export restrictions, price controls, and regulations to protect nature. In 2003 it supported governments by paying $75 billion in taxes worldwide, a sum exceeding the combined revenues of Procter & Gamble and Microsoft. Governments also subsidize ExxonMobil in various ways. The U.S. Army Corps of Engineers, for example, dredges harbor channels for its supertankers.

ExxonMobil faces a demanding social environment. Energy is the fuel of society. The energy industry is the world's largest and most important because it makes

---

[5] See, for example, Edgar H. Schein, *The Corporate Culture Survival Guide* (San Francisco: Jossey-Bass, 1999), part one.

[6] Exxon Mobil Corporation, Form 10-K, March 15, 2004, p. 2.

economies run. So ExxonMobil provides a vital resource; however, because it is such a big company and because of the physical nature of its products, its activities are closely scrutinized by environmental, civil rights, labor, and consumer groups—many of which are hostile.

Lee Raymond agitates environmentalists. In a 1997 speech he rejected the scientific case for global warming. Alone among major oil company executives, he calls investment in renewable energy "a complete waste of money."[7] Two groups have formed to attack the company. In Europe, where it uses the Esso brand, a coalition of activists called Stop Esso is running a boycott until ExxonMobil takes action against climate change. In the United States, religious groups started Campaign ExxonMobil to convince investors that Raymond's positions jeopardize their returns.

In 1999, when Exxon merged with Mobil, it infuriated gay rights advocates by revoking Mobil's policy of domestic partner benefits for gay and lesbian employees. Ever since, gay rights groups have organized boycotts and sponsored resolutions at shareholder meetings calling for same-sex partner benefits. Although support for the gay rights position rose from 8 percent in 2000 to 27 percent in 2003, Raymond does not support change. Explaining its position, the company argues that it is guided by the law, and federal law defines a spouse so that only heterosexual couples are included.[8]

In 1989 a company supertanker, the *Exxon Valdez,* spilled 11 million gallons of oil into Alaskan waters. Its captain, having consumed enough whiskey "to make most people unconscious," grounded it on a charted reef in Prince William Sound.[9] The disaster brought serious legal, political, and image problems for the firm. Relations became tense and bitter with the State of Alaska and several federal agencies, including the Environmental Protection Agency. Congress passed a punitive federal law, the Oil Protection Act of 1990. One provision barred the *Exxon Valdez* from ever again entering the sound where the oil spill occurred.

ExxonMobil spent $2.5 billion to clean up the spill, $1.1 billion to settle criminal lawsuits by the State of Alaska and the federal government for harm to the environment, and $300 million to pay damage claims by people and businesses. Lee Raymond went to Alaska to direct the cleanup. He negotiated much of the criminal settlement in person. But he refused to settle a civil case brought by local fishers and Natives. In 1994 a jury gave them $5 billion in punitive damages, then the largest such award in history. The company called the sum outrageous and, on Raymond's decision, has fought a long string of appeals in federal courts to have it reduced. It argues that since the spill was an accident rather than a deliberate act of negligence, no punitive damages are justified and that, in addition, the amount is so excessive it violates the due process clause of the Fourteenth Amendment. Meanwhile, the fishing industry in the sound has yet to recover from the spill. People in the picturesque fishing towns live with anger at a corporation that for 10 years has fought paying a penny of the $5 billion award.

---

[7] "The Unrepentant Oilman," *The Economist,* March 15, 2003, p. 64.

[8] "ExxonMobil's Anti-Discrimination and Domestic Partner Policies," and Lee Raymond, "Very Clear Policies Against Discrimination," both at www.exxonmobil.com. Mobil employees with domestic partner benefits retained them in the merged company.

[9] *In re: the Exxon Mobil,* 270 F.3d 1238.

Scientists have found persistent environmental damage caused by the oil, including long-term declines in marine populations. So also have sociologists reported on how the disaster created "corrosive" communities. Just after the spill, Exxon paid generously for local labor to help with the cleanup. Soon the areas' small towns swelled with opportunists, straining roads, schools, and services. The tiny fishing port of Valdez grew from 2,500 residents to 10,000. Many people quit low-paying jobs, enticed by the $16.00 an hour Exxon paid, but this destabilized work patterns in the local economies. Friendships and families frayed as Exxon offered some fishers windfall contracts to use their boats in the cleanup. Others, whose boats were not hired, endured a poor fishing season in the blighted local waters. Jealousy arose. Those who accepted the company's money were called "spillionaires" and "Exxon whores."[10]

Eventually, the Exxon money dried up. Damage to marine populations in the sound remained, crippling the local fishing industry. Prolonged litigation against Exxon created uncertainty. Financial hardship, alcohol abuse, and divorce grew more frequent. A study of Cordova fishers six years after the spill found "more than one-third suffered from depression or post-traumatic stress disorder."[11] When the mayor of Cordova killed himself, his ashes were cast out at Bligh Reef where the tanker had run aground.[12]

The *Exxon Valdez* award is not the end of ExxonMobil's legal problems. In 2001 the company was hit with a $1 billion punitive damages award in New Orleans for contaminating land with radiation. It is appealing. In 2003 an Alabama jury convicted it of fraud for avoiding payments owed to the state on natural gas leases, imposing a $12 billion award. An appeals court judge reduced the sum from $12 billion to $3.6 billion, but wrote that "Exxon engaged in a carefully planned scheme, conceived and approved at the highest echelons of its corporate offices, to keep nearly $1 billion in easy money."[13] Exxon is appealing. It denies any wrongdoing and calls the award grossly excessive and unconstitutional.

ExxonMobil funds worldwide programs to benefit nature, the arts, education, health, and communities. These range from an $11 million campaign to save the world's tigers from extinction, an appropriate project since the tiger is the company's brand symbol, to sponsorship of free poetry readings in Singapore, where the company has a chemical plant. In 2003 ExxonMobil gave $103 million to a range of arts, science, education, health, nature, and civic projects. This is a large sum from the perspective of an individual. However, for ExxonMobil it was one-twentieth of 1 percent of its $237 billion revenues that year, the equivalent of a person making $1,000,000 a year giving $500 to charity. Does this giving live up to the elegant example of founder John D. Rockefeller, the great philanthropist of his era?

Lee Raymond is now near retirement. ExxonMobil's directors asked him to postpone his departure to consolidate the 1999 merger with Mobil. Replacements for him

---

[10] Duane A. Gill and J. Steven Picou, "Technological Disaster and Chronic Community Stress," *Society & Natural Resources,* December 1998, p. 795.

[11] Catalina M. Arata, "Coping with Technological Disaster: An Application of the Conservation of Resources Model to the *Exxon Valdez* Oil Spill," *Journal of Traumatic Stress* 13, no. 1 (2000), p. 34.

[12] Ashley Shelby, "Whatever It Takes," *The Nation,* April 5, 2004, p. 16.

[13] Circuit Judge Tracy McCooey, cited in Phillip Rawls, *The Legal Intelligencer,* April 2, 2004, p. 4.

are under scrutiny by Raymond and the board. All are internal candidates, so even if his eventual successor does not share Raymond's blunt style, that person will nevertheless reflect deep-seated values in the company culture.

The story of ExxonMobil illustrates the importance of interactions between one large corporation, governments, and society. Such interactions are innumerable. In this first chapter we attempt to bring some order to the universe of these interactions by introducing four basic models of the business–government–society relationship. We also define basic terms and explain our approach to the subject matter.

The ExxonMobil story raises questions about the role of corporations in society and how to evaluate their actions. When can we say a corporation is socially responsible? What actions are ethical or unethical? How responsive must a corporation be to its critics? How can managers make corporations more responsible? We defer extended discussion of the answers until later in the book, but we raise these central questions here.

WHAT IS THE BUSINESS–GOVERNMENT–SOCIETY FIELD?

In the universe of human endeavor, we can distinguish subdivisions of economic, political, and social activity—that is, business, government, and society—in every civilization throughout time. Interplay among these activities creates an environment in which businesses operate. The business–government–society (BGS) field is the study of this environment and its importance for managers.

To begin, we define the basic terms.

business
Profit-making activity that provides products and services to satisfy human needs.

Business is a broad term encompassing a range of actions and institutions. It covers management, manufacturing, finance, trade, service, investment, and other activities. Entities as different as a hamburger stand and a giant corporation are businesses. The fundamental purpose of every business is to make a profit by providing products and services that satisfy human needs.

government
Structures and processes in society that authoritatively make and apply policies and rules.

Government refers to structures and processes in society that authoritatively make and apply policies and rules. Like business, it encompasses a wide range of activities and institutions at many levels, from international to local. The focus of this book is on the economic and regulatory powers of government as they affect business.

A *society* is a network of human relations that includes three interacting elements: (1) ideas, (2) institutions, and (3) material things.

society
A network of human relations composed of ideas, institutions, and material things.

Ideas, or intangible objects of thought, include values and ideologies. *Values* are enduring beliefs about which fundamental choices in personal and social life are correct. Cultural habits and norms are based on values. *Ideologies*—for example democracy and capitalism—are bundles of values that create a certain world view. They establish the broad goals of life by defining what is considered good, true, right, beautiful, and acceptable. Ideas shape every institution in a society.

Institutions are formal patterns of relations that link people together to accomplish a goal. They are essential to coordinate the work of individuals who have no personal relationship with each other.[14] In modern societies, economic, political, cultural, legal, religious, military, educational, media, and familial institutions are

[14] Arnold J. Toynbee, *A Study of History,* vol. XII, *Reconsiderations* (London: Oxford University Press, 1961), p. 270.

FIGURE 1.1
How Institutions Support Markets

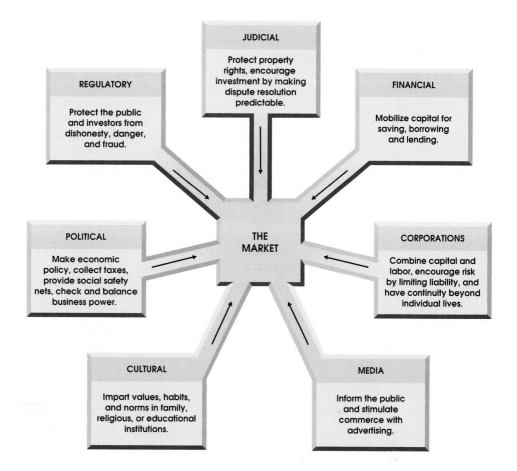

idea
An intangible object of thought.

value
An enduring belief about which fundamental life choices are correct.

ideology
A bundle of values that creates a particular view of the world.

institution
A formal pattern of relations that links people together to accomplish a goal.

salient. There are multiple economic institutions including financial institutions, the corporate form, and markets. Collectively, we call these business.

Figure 1.1 shows how a range of institutions support markets. Capitalism as an economic system shows wide variation in the nations where it exists because supporting institutions grow from unique historical and cultural roots. In developed nations these institutions are highly evolved and mutually supportive. Where they are weak, markets work in dysfunctional ways. An example is Russia, which introduced a market economy after the fall of communism.

Institutions that had evolved under Soviet political repression and state planning were ill-suited to support a free market. The story of labor is an example. In the old system workers spent lifetimes in secure jobs at state-owned firms. There was no unemployment insurance and, since few workers ever moved, housing markets were undeveloped. A free market economy requires a strong labor market, so workers can switch from jobs in declining firms to jobs in expanding ones. But in Russia the development of a labor market was arrested. The government did not yet provide unemployment benefits to idled workers, so there was no safety net. And housing markets were anemic. Company managers, out of basic humanity, were unwilling to lay off workers who got no benefits and who would find it difficult to move elsewhere.[15] As a result, restructuring in the new Russian economy was torpid. The lesson is that institutions are vital to markets.

Each institution has a specific purpose in society. The function of business is to make a profit by producing goods and services at prices attractive to consumers. A business uses the resources of society to create new wealth. This justifies its existence and is its priority task. All other social tasks—raising an army, advancing knowledge, healing the sick, or raising children—depend on it. Businesses must, therefore, be managed to make a profit. A categorical statement of this point comes from Peter Drucker: "Business management must always, in every decision and action, put economic performance first."[16] Without profit, business fails in its duty to society and lacks legitimacy.

material things
Tangible artifacts of a society that shape and are shaped by ideas and institutions.

The third element in society is *material things,* including land, natural resources, infrastructure, and manufactured goods. These shape and, in the case of fabricated objects, are partly products of ideas and institutions. Economic institutions, together with the extent of resources, largely determine the type and quantity of society's material goods.

The BGS field is the study of interactions among the three broad areas defined above. The primary focus is on the interaction of business with the other two elements. The basic subject matter, therefore, is how business shapes and changes government and society, and how it, in turn, is molded by political and social pressures. Of special interest is how forces in the BGS nexus affect the manager's task.

WHY IS THE BGS FIELD IMPORTANT TO MANAGERS?

To succeed in meeting its objectives a business must be responsive to both its economic and its noneconomic environment.[17] ExxonMobil, for example, must efficiently discover, refine, transport, and market energy. Yet swift response to market forces is not always enough. There are powerful nonmarket forces to which many businesses, especially large ones, are exposed. Their importance is clear in the two dramatic episodes that punctuate ExxonMobil's history—the 1911 court-ordered breakup and the 1989 *Exxon Valdez* oil spill.

In 1911 the Supreme Court, in a decision that reflected public opinion as well as interpretation of the law, forced Standard Oil to conform with social values favoring open, competitive markets. With unparalleled managerial genius, courage, and perspicacity, John D. Rockefeller and his lieutenants had built a wonder of efficiency that spread fuel and light throughout America at lower cost than otherwise would have prevailed. They never understood why this remarkable commercial performance was not the full measure of Standard Oil. But beyond efficiency, the public demanded fair play. Thus, the great company was dismembered.

---

[15] Joseph E. Stiglitz, *Globalization and Its Discontents* (New York: W. W. Norton, 2002), p. 140.

[16] *Management: Tasks—Responsibilities—Practices* (New York: Harper & Row, 1973), p. 40.

[17] For discussion of this distinction see Jean J. Boddewyn, "Understanding and Advancing the Concept of 'Nonmarket,'" *Business & Society,* September 2003.

In Alaska a sudden crisis changed ExxonMobil's political and social environments, leading to billions of dollars of sanctions. Today ExxonMobil operates its tanker fleet with extreme care. It has new environmental safeguards and randomly tests crew members for drugs and alcohol. Remarkably, it is now so disciplined that it measures oil spills from its fleet of tankers in teaspoons per million gallons shipped. In 2003 it reported losing less than one teaspoon per million gallons.[18]

Recognizing that a company operates not only within markets but within a society is critical. If the society, or one or more powerful interests within it, does not accept a company's actions, that firm will be punished and constrained. A basic agreement or *social contract* exists between the business institution and society. This contract defines the broad duties that business must perform to retain society's support. It is partly expressed in law, but it also resides in social values.

social contract
An underlying agreement between business and society on basic duties and responsibilities business must carry out to retain public support. It may be reflected in laws and regulations.

Unfortunately for managers, the social contract is not as clear-cut as are the economic forces a business faces, as complex and ambiguous as the latter often are. For example, the public believes that business has social responsibilities beyond making profits and obeying regulations. If business does not meet them, it may suffer. But precisely what are they? How is corporate performance measured? To what extent must a business comply with ethical values not written into law? When meeting social expectations conflicts with maximizing profits, what is the priority? Despite these questions, the social contract contains the expectations of society, and managers who ignore or violate it are courting disaster.

FOUR MODELS OF THE BGS RELATIONSHIP

Interactions among business, government, and society are infinite and their meaning is open to interpretation. Faced with this complexity, many people use simple mental models to impose order and meaning on what they observe. These models are like prisms, each having a different refractive quality, each giving the holder a different view of the world. Depending on the model (or prism) used, a person will think differently about the scope of business power in society, criteria for managerial decisions, the extent of corporate responsibility, the ethical duties of managers, and the need for regulation.

The following four models are basic alternatives for seeing the BGS relationship. As abstractions they oversimplify reality and magnify central issues. Each model can be both descriptive and prescriptive; that is, it can be both an explanation of how the BGS relationship does work and, in addition, an ideal about how it should work.

The Market Capitalism Model

The market capitalism model, shown in Figure 1.2, depicts business as operating within a market environment, responding primarily to powerful economic forces. There, it is substantially sheltered from direct impact by social and political forces. The market acts as a buffer between business and nonmarket forces. To appreciate this model, it is important to understand the history and nature of markets and the classic explanation of how they work.

[18] Exxon Mobil Corporation, "All Ahead Safe," *National Journal,* March 20, 2004, p. 888 (advertisement).

FIGURE 1.2
The Market Capitalism Model

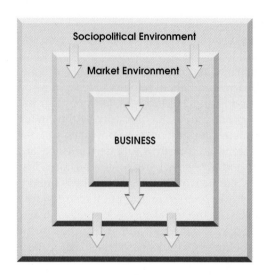

Markets are as old as humanity, but for most of recorded history they were a minor institution. People produced mainly for subsistence, not to trade. Then, in the 1700s, some economies began to expand and industrialize, division of labor developed within them, and people started to produce more for trade. As trade grew, the market, through its price signals, took on a more central role in directing the creation and distribution of goods. The advent of this kind of *market economy,* or an economy in which markets play a major role, reshaped human life.

market economy
The economy that emerges when people move beyond subsistence production to production for trade and markets take on a more central role.

capitalism
An economy in which private individuals and corporations own the means of production and, motivated by the desire for profit, compete in free markets under conditions of limited restraint by government.

The classic explanation of how a market economy works comes from the Scottish professor of moral philosophy Adam Smith (1723–1790). In his extraordinary treatise, *The Wealth of Nations,* Smith wrote about what he called "commercial society" or what today we call *capitalism.* He never used that word, which was adopted later by the socialist philosopher Karl Marx (1818–1883), who contrived it as a term of pointed insult. But it caught on and soon lost its negative connotation.[19] Smith said that the desire to trade for mutual advantage lay deep in human instinct. He noted that the growing division of labor in society led more people to try to satisfy their self-interests by specializing their work, then exchanging goods with each other. As they did so, the market's pricing mechanism reconciled supply and demand, and its ceaseless tendency was to make commodities cheaper, better, and more available.

The beauty of this process, according to Smith, was that it coordinated the activities of strangers who, to pursue their selfish advantage, were forced to fulfill the needs of others. In Smith's words, each trader was "led by an invisible hand to promote an end which was no part of his intention," the collective good of society.[20] Through markets that harnessed the constant energy of greed for the

---

[19] Jerry Z. Muller, *The Mind and the Market: Capitalism in Modern European Thought* (New York: Knopf, 2002), p. xvi.

[20] Adam Smith, *The Wealth of Nations,* ed. E. Cannan (New York: Modern Library, 1937), Book IV, chap. II, p. 423. First published in 1776.

Full Production and Full Employment under Our Democratic System of Private Enterprise, ca. 1944, a crayon and ink drawing by Michael Lenson, an artist working for the Works Progress Administration Federal Art Project. Lenson focuses on the virtues of market capitalism. Source: Courtesy of The Library of Congress.

public welfare, Smith believed that nations would achieve "universal opulence." His genius was to demystify the way markets work, to frame market capitalism in moral terms, to extol its virtues, and to give it lasting justification as a source of human progress. The greater good for society came when businesses competed freely.

In Smith's day producers and sellers were individuals and small businesses managed by their owners. Later, by the late 1800s and early 1900s, throughout the industrialized world, the type of economy described by Smith had evolved into a system of *managerial capitalism*. In it the innumerable, small, owner-run firms that animated Smith's marketplace were overshadowed by a much smaller number of dominant corporations run by hierarchies of salaried managers.[21] These managers had limited ownership in their companies and worked for shareholders. This form of capitalism has now spread throughout the world. Nowhere does it work exactly like Smith's theory. Nevertheless, the market capitalism model continues to exist as an ideal against which to measure practice.

The model incorporates important assumptions. One is that government interference in economic life is slight. This is called *laissez-faire*, a term first used by the French to mean that government should "let us alone." This stood for the belief that government intervention in the market is undesirable. It is costly because it lessens the efficiency with which free enterprise operates to benefit consumers. It is unnecessary because market forces are benevolent and, if liberated, will channel economic resources to meet society's needs. It is for governments, not businesses, to correct social problems. Therefore, managers should define company interests narrowly, as profitability and efficiency.

Another assumption is that individuals can own private property and freely risk investments. Under these circumstances, business owners are powerfully

managerial capitalism
A market economy in which the dominant businesses are large firms run by salaried managers, not smaller firms run by owner-entrepreneurs.

laissez-faire
An economic philosophy that rejects government intervention in markets.

---

[21] Alfred D. Chandler, Jr., "The Emergence of Managerial Capitalism," *Business History Review,* Winter 1984, p. 473.

motivated to make a profit. If free competition exists, the market will hold profits to a minimum and the quality of products and services will rise as firms try to attract more buyers. If one enterprise tries to increase profits by charging higher prices, consumers will go to a competitor. If one producer makes higher-quality products, others must follow. In this way, markets convert selfish competition into broad social benefits.

Other assumptions include these: Consumers are informed about products and prices and make rational decisions. Moral restraint accompanies the self-interested behavior of business. Basic institutions such as banking and laws exist to ease commerce. There are many producers and consumers in competitive markets.

The perspective of the market capitalism model leads to these conclusions about the BGS relationship: (1) government regulation should be limited, (2) markets discipline private economic activity to promote social welfare, (3) the proper measure of corporate performance is profit, and (4) the ethical duty of management is to promote the interests of shareholders. These tenets of market capitalism have shaped economic values in the industrialized West and, as markets spread, they do so increasingly elsewhere.

There are many critics of capitalism and the market capitalism model. As promised by its defenders, capitalism has created material progress. Yet there are trade-offs. It is argued that capitalism creates prosperity only at the cost of rising inequality. Karl Marx believed that owners of capital exploited workers and used imperialist foreign policies to spread markets. Others believe that markets erode virtue. The avarice, self-love, and ruthlessness that energize them are base values that drive out virtues such as love and friendship. Another enduring fear is that markets place too much emphasis on money and material objects. Pope John Paul II, for example, has cautioned against a "domination of things over people."[22] Critics see these problems as inherent to markets. Still other criticisms focus on the flaws that sometimes, perhaps inevitably, appear in them. Without correction they may reward conspiracies and monopoly. Also, the profit motive has led companies to pollute and plunder the earth.

All these criticisms of capitalism are pronounced today, but none are new. They represent a series of recurrent attacks that wind through the Western philosophical tradition. Adam Smith himself had some reservations and second thoughts. He feared both physical and moral decline in factory workers and the unwarranted idolization of the rich, who might have earned their wealth by unvirtuous methods. In his later years, he grew to see more need for government intervention. But Smith never envisioned a system based solely on greed and self-interest. He expected that in society these traits must coexist with restraint and benevolence.[23] The ageless debate over whether capitalism is the best means to human fulfillment will continue.[24] Meanwhile, we turn our discussion to an alternative model of the BGS relationship that attracts many of capitalism's detractors.

---

[22] Encyclical Letter, *Centesimus annus*, May 1, 1991, p. 16.

[23] *The Theory of Moral Sentiments*, ed. E. G. West (Indianapolis: Liberty Classics, 1976), pp. 70–72. Originally published in 1853.

[24] Muller, *The Mind and the Market: Capitalism in Modern European Thought*, pp. x–xiv.

The Dominance Model

The dominance model is a second basic way of seeing the BGS relationship. It represents primarily the perspective of business critics. In it, business and government dominate the great mass of people. This idea is represented in the pyramidal, hierarchical image of society shown in Figure 1.3. Those who subscribe to the model believe that corporations and a powerful elite control a system that enriches a few at the expense of the many. Such a system is undemocratic. In democratic theory, governments and leaders represent interests expressed by the people, who are sovereign.

Proponents of the dominance model focus on the defects and inefficiencies of capitalism. They believe that corporations are insulated from pressures holding them responsible, that regulation by a government in thrall to big business is feeble, and that market forces are inadequate to ensure ethical management. Unlike other models, the dominance model does not represent an ideal in addition to a description of how things are. For its advocates, the ideal is to turn it upside down so that the BGS relationship conforms to democratic principles.

In the United States, the dominance model gained a following during the latter half of the nineteenth century when large trusts such as Standard Oil emerged, buying politicians, exploiting workers, monopolizing markets, and sharpening income inequality. Beginning in the 1870s, farmers and other critics of big business rejected the ideal of the market capitalism model and based a reform movement called populism on the critical view of the BGS relationship implied in the dominance model.

This was an era when, for the first time, on a national scale the actions of powerful business magnates shaped the destinies of common people. Some displayed contempt for commoners. "The public be damned," railroad magnate William H. Vanderbilt told a reporter during an interview in his luxurious private railway

FIGURE 1.3
The Dominance Model

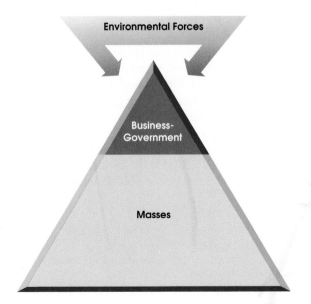

Environmental Forces

Business-Government

Masses

This 1900 political cartoon illustrates a central theme of the dominance model, that powerful business interests act in concert with government to further selfish money interests. Although the cartoon is old, the idea remains compelling for many. Source: © Bettmann/**CORBIS**

IN THE HANDS OF HIS PHILANTHROPIC FRIENDS.

car.[25] The next day, newspapers around the country printed his remark, enraging the public. Later, Edward Harriman, the aloof, arrogant president of the Union Pacific Railroad, allegedly reassured industry leaders worried about reform legislation, saying "that he 'could buy Congress' and that if necessary he 'could buy the judiciary.'"[26] It was with respect to Harriman that President Theodore Roosevelt once noted that "men of very great wealth in too many instances totally failed to understand the temper of the country and its needs."[27]

The populist movement in America ultimately fell short of reforming the BGS relationship to a democratic ideal. Other industrializing nations, notably Japan, had similar populist movements. Marxism, an ideology opposed to industrial capitalism, emerged in Europe at about the same time as these movements, and it also contained ideas resonant with the dominance model. In capitalist societies, according to Karl Marx, an owner class dominates the economy and ruling institutions. Many business critics worldwide advocated socialist reforms that, based on Marx's theory, could achieve more equitable distribution of power and wealth.

[25] "Reporter C. P. Dresser Dead," *New York Times,* April 25, 1891, p. 7. In fairness to Vanderbilt, the context of the remark is unclear. See Ashley W. Cole, "A Famous Remark," *New York Times,* August 25, 1918, p. 22 (letter to the editor).

[26] Quoted from correspondence of Theodore Roosevelt in Maury Klein, *The Life & Legend of E. H. Harriman* (Chapel Hill: University of North Carolina Press, 2000), p. 369.

[27] Ibid., p. 363.

FIGURE 1.4
The Counter-
vailing Forces
Model

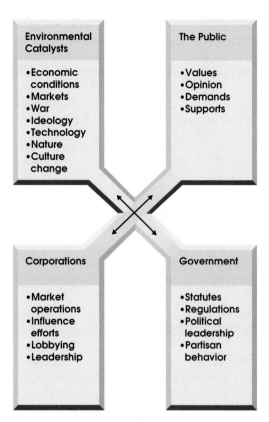

Critical attitudes about business power in society live on. Ralph Nader, declaring his 2000 candidacy for president, spoke the language of the dominance model.

> Over the past twenty years, big business has increasingly dominated our political economy. This control by corporate government over our political government is creating a widening "democracy gap." . . . The unconstrained behavior of big business is subordinating our democracy to the control of a corporate plutocracy that knows few self-imposed limits to the spread of its power to all sectors of our society.[28]

In the United States the dominance model may have been most accurate in the late 1800s when it first arose to conceptualize a world in which corporate power was more brazen and politicians openly represented industries. However, it remains popular. In recent years the fear of transnational corporations has given it new life in a global context.

The Countervailing Forces Model

The countervailing forces model, shown in Figure 1.4, depicts the BGS relationship as a flow of interactions among the major elements of society. It suggests complex exchanges of influence among them, attributing dominance to none.

---

[28] "Statement of Ralph Nader," in *The Ralph Nader Reader* (New York: Seven Stories Press, 2000), pp. 3 and 4.

This is a model of multiple or pluralistic forces. Their strength waxes and wanes depending on factors such as the subject at issue, the power of competing interests, the intensity of feeling, and the influence of leaders. The countervailing forces model reflects the BGS relationship in industrialized nations with democratic traditions. It differs from the market capitalism model, because it opens business directly to influence by nonmarket forces. Many important interactions implied in it would be evaluated as negligible in the dominance model.

What overarching conclusions can be drawn from this model?

1. Business is deeply integrated into an open society and must respond to many forces, both economic and noneconomic. It is not isolated from its social environment, nor is it dominant.

2. Business is a major initiator of change in society through its interaction with government, its production and marketing activities, and its use of new technologies.

3. Broad public support of business depends on its adjustment to multiple social, political, and economic forces. Incorrect adjustment leads to failure. This is the social contract at work.

4. BGS relationships continuously evolve as changes take place in the main ideas, institutions, and processes of society.

The Stakeholder Model

stakeholder
An entity that is benefitted or burdened by the actions of a corporation or whose actions may benefit or burden the corporation. The corporation has an ethical duty toward these entities.

primary stakeholders
Entities in a relationship with the corporation in which they, the corporation, or both are affected immediately, continuously, and powerfully.

The stakeholder model in Figure 1.5 shows the corporation at the center of an array of mutual relationships with persons, groups, and entities called *stakeholders*. Stakeholders are those whom the corporation benefits or burdens by its actions and those who benefit or burden the firm with their actions. A large corporation has many stakeholders. These can be divided into two categories based on the nature of the relationship.

Primary stakeholders are a small number of constituents for which the impact of the relationship is immediate, continuous, and powerful on both the firm and the constituent. They are stockholders (owners), customers, employees, communities, and governments and may, depending on the firm, include others such as suppliers or creditors.

Secondary stakeholders include a possibly broad range of constituents in which the relationship involves less mutual immediacy, benefit, burden, or power to influence. Examples are activist groups, trade associations, and schools.

Exponents of the stakeholder model debate how to identify who or what is a stakeholder. Some use a broad definition and include, for example, natural entities such as the earth's atmosphere, oceans, terrain, and living creatures because corporations have an impact on them.[29] Others reject this broadening, since these natural entities are represented by conventional stakeholders such as environmental groups. Some include competitors because, although they do not work to benefit the firm, they have the power to affect it. At the furthest reaches of the

---

[29] See, for example, Edward Stead and Jean Garner Stead, "Earth: A Spiritual Stakeholder," *Business Ethics Quarterly,* Ruffin Series no. 2 (2000), pp. 321–44.

FIGURE 1.5
The
Stakeholder
Model

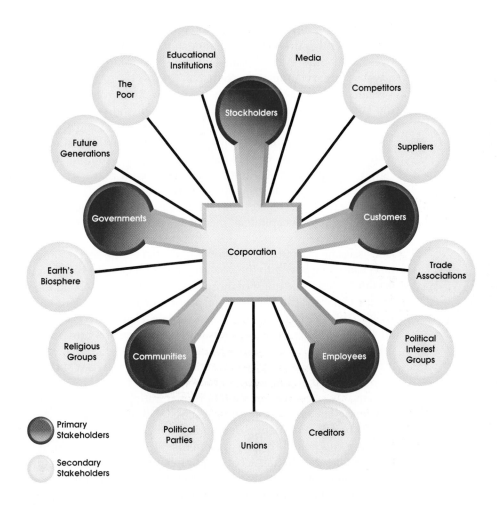

secondary stakeholders Entities in a relationship with the corporation in which the effects on them, the corporation, or both are less significant and pressing.

stakeholder idea lie groups such as the poor and future generations. But in the words of one stakeholder advocate, "[s]takeholder theory should not be used to weave a basket big enough to hold the world's misery."[30] If groups such as the poor were included in the stakeholder network, managers would be morally obliged to run headlong at endless problems, taking them beyond any conceivable economic mission.

The stakeholder model reorders the priorities of management away from those in the market capitalism model. There, the corporation is the private property of those who contribute its capital. Its immediate priority is to benefit one group—the investors. The stakeholder model, by contrast, is an ethical theory of management in which the welfare of each stakeholder must be considered as an end.

---

[30] Max Clarkson, *A Risk-Based Model of Stakeholder Theory* (Toronto: The Centre for Corporate Social Performance & Ethics, 1994), cited in Robert Phillips, *Stakeholder Theory and Organizational Ethics* (San Francisco: Berrett-Koehler, 2003), p. 119.

Stakeholder interests have intrinsic worth; they are not valued only to the extent that they enrich investors. Managers have a duty to consider the interests of multiple stakeholders, and because of this, "the interests of shareowners . . . are not always primary and never exclusive."[31]

Stakeholder management, then, creates duties toward multiple constituents of the corporation—duties not emphasized in the practice of market capitalism, which tends toward domination of the environment and enrichment of shareowners. Management must raise its gaze above profits to see and respond to a spectrum of other values. One group of scholars, for example, urges that corporations "should adopt processes and modes of behavior that are sensitive to the concerns and capabilities of each stakeholder constituency."[32] The stakeholder model is intended to redefine the corporation. It rejects the shareholder-centered view of the firm in the market capitalism model as "ethically unacceptable."[33]

Not everyone agrees. Critics of the stakeholder model argue that it is not a realistic assessment of power relationships between the corporation and other entities. It seeks to give power to the powerless by replacing force with ethical duty, a timeless and often futile quest of moralists. In addition, it sets up too vague a guideline to substitute for the yardstick of profits for investors. Unlike traditional criteria such as return on capital, there is no single, clear, and objective measure to evaluate the combined ethical/economic performance of a firm. According to one critic, this lack of a criterion "would render impossible rational management decision making for there is simply no way to adjudicate between alternative projects when there is more than one bottom line."[34]

Some puzzles exist in stakeholder thinking. It is not clear who or what is a legitimate stakeholder, to what each stakeholder is entitled, or how managers should balance competing demands among a range of stakeholders. Yet its advocates are compelled by two arguments. First, a corporation that embraces stakeholders performs better. A corporation better sustains its wealth-creating function with the support of a network of parties beyond shareholders. Second, it is the ethical way to manage because stakeholders have moral rights that grow from the way powerful corporations affect them. Irrespective of academic debates, in practice many large corporations have adopted methods and processes to analyze their stakeholders and engage them. This trend is discussed in Chapter 6.

OUR APPROACH TO THE SUBJECT MATTER

Discussion of the business–government–society field could be organized in many ways. The following is an overview of our approach.

---

[31] James E. Post, Lee E. Preston, and Sybille Sachs, *Redefining the Corporation: Stakeholder Management and Organizational Wealth* (Stanford, CA: Stanford University Press, 2002), p. 17.

[32] Clarkson Centre for Business Ethics, *Principles of Stakeholder Management* (Toronto: Clarkson Centre for Business Ethics, 1999).

[33] Post, Preston, and Sachs, *Redefining the Corporation,* p. 16.

[34] John Argenti, "Stakeholders: The Case Against," *Long Range Planning,* June 1997, p. 444.

Comprehensive Scope

This book is comprehensive. It covers many subjects. We believe that for those new to the field seeing a panorama is helpful. Because there is less depth in the treatment of subjects than can be found in specialized volumes, we suggest additional sources in footnotes.

Interdisciplinary Approach with a Management Focus

This field is exceptionally interdisciplinary. It exists at the confluence of a fairly large number of established academic disciplines, each of which contributes to its study. These disciplines include the traditional business disciplines, particularly management; other professional disciplines, including medicine, law, and theology; the social sciences, including economics, political science, philosophy, history, and sociology; and, from time to time, natural sciences such as chemistry and ecology. Thus, our approach is eclectic; we cross boundaries to find insight.

strategic management
Actions taken by managers to adapt a company to changes in its market and sociopolitical environments.

The dominant orientation, however, is the discipline of management and, within it, the study of *strategic management,* or actions that adapt the company to its changing environment. To compete and survive, firms must create missions, purposes, and objectives; the policies and programs to achieve them; and the methods to implement them. We discuss these elements as they relate to corporate social performance, illustrating successes and failures.

Use of Theory, Description, and Case Studies

theory
A statement or vision that creates insight by describing patterns or relationships in a diffuse subject matter. A good theory is concise and simplifies complex phenomena.

Theories simplify and organize areas of knowledge by describing patterns or regularities in the subject matter. Theories are important in every field, but especially in this one, where innumerable details from broad categories of human experience intersect to create a new intellectual universe. Where theory is missing or weak, scholarship must rely more on description and the use of case method.

No underlying theory to integrate the entire field exists. Fortunately, the community of scholars studying BGS relationships is building theory in several areas. The first is theory describing how corporations interact with stakeholders. The second is theory regarding the ethical duties of corporations and managers. And the third is theory explaining corporate social performance and how it can be measured. Theory in this area focuses on defining exactly what a firm does to be responsible in society and on creating scales and rulers with which to weigh and measure its actions. A growing body of scholarship in all three areas shows increasing sophistication and wider agreement on basic ideas.

Despite the lack of a single theory to unify the field, useful theories abound in related disciplines. For example, there are economic theories about the impact of government regulation, scientific theories regarding industrial pollution, political theories explaining corporate power, and legal theories on subjects such as negligence applied by courts to corporations when, for example, industrial accidents occur. When fitting, we discuss such theories; elsewhere we rely on descriptions of events. We also use case studies at the end of each chapter to raise issues for discussion.

Global Perspective

Rising international trade and investment mandates a global focus. Although every business has a home country, a few transnational corporations have more sales, employees, and investment outside their home borders than within them. Among American firms examples are ExxonMobil with 70 percent of its sales in foreign countries, Coca-Cola with 63 percent, IBM with 59 percent, Dow Chemical with 58 percent, and Hewlett-Packard with 58 percent. Among non-U.S. firms examples include Nestlé of Switzerland with 68 percent, Unilever of the Netherlands and the United Kingdom with 61 percent, Sony of Japan with 67 percent, and Toyota Motor of Japan with 55 percent.[35] Growth of global markets also has a profound impact on governments, which find their economic and social welfare policies judged by world financial markets. And on a societal plane, the consequences of commerce for wars, plagues, nature, human rights, and income equality challenge international institutions. Therefore, in this book the focus is often global.

Historical Perspective

history
The study of phenomena moving through time.

History is the study of phenomena moving through time. The BGS relationship is a stream of events, of which only one part exists today. Historical perspective is important for many reasons. It helps us see that today's BGS relationship is not like that of other eras; that current ideas and institutions are not the only alternative; that historical forces are irrepressible; that corporations both cause and adapt to change; that our era is not unique in undergoing rapid change; and that we are shaping the future now. When appropriate, we examine the antecedents of current arrangements.

---

[35] United Nations Conference on Trade and Development, *World Investment Report 2003* (New York and Geneva: United Nations, 2003), annex table A.I.1.

Chapter Two

The Dynamic Environment

Royal Dutch Shell PLC

scenario
A plausible projection of the future based on assumptions about how current trends might evolve.

Royal Dutch Shell is the world's second-largest private energy company. In the 1970s it pioneered a method of analyzing its environment using scenarios. A *scenario* is a plausible projection of the future based on assumptions about how current trends might evolve. Carefully written scenarios challenge managers to think in original ways. They are mental wind tunnels in which environmental forces are shifted around the form of the company to see how it "flies."

In 1971 Shell's planners developed a scenario in which oil-rich countries cut their oil exports to raise prices. The conventional wisdom of that day held this to be improbable. Nonetheless, thinking about such an event changed Shell's planning, and when the first OPEC oil embargo occurred in 1973, Shell was the only major oil firm prepared for it. Its reward was higher profits for years afterward.

Today historically unprecedented economic, technological, and geopolitical trends sweep the global business environment. Shell has a complex structure in which geographically separate companies with separate product lines operate with great autonomy in more than 130 countries. The company believes that its scenarios help it to find a unifying strategic direction and make better planning decisions in a turbulent world.

liberalization
An economic policy of lowering tariffs and other barriers to encourage trade.

In the early 1990s Shell planners formed a theory of change in the global business environment. They saw three dominant forces shaping the future: *liberalization* (meaning relaxation of trade restrictions and regulations), globalization, and technology. These forces were inescapable, so businesses must adapt to them. Shell's planners bottled this belief in a phrase, "THERE IS NO ALTERNATIVE," and used its acronym, TINA, as shorthand for the three forces and their unrelenting nature. According to Shell, "TINA is a rough, impersonal game, involving stresses and pressures akin to those of the Industrial Revolution."[1] How will TINA shape history? Shell has used a sequence of scenarios to examine the possibilities. Typically, these scenarios set forth two futures that are in conflict.

[1] Shell International Limited, *Global Scenarios 1995–2020,* Public Scenarios PX96-2, 1996, p. 2. Abbreviated versions of all the scenarios discussed can be found at www.shell.com.

- In 1995 a set of scenarios examined the central question of how the world would adapt to liberalization, globalization, and technology. A *Just Do It* scenario, named after the Nike ad slogan, predicted the rise of flourishing U.S.-style free markets, individualism, aggressive competition, and materialism. The alternative *Da Wo* scenario, named after a Chinese proverb, was based on an Asian ideal of community welfare opposed to the excesses of Western individualism.
- In 2001 a set of scenarios explored the social consequences of the three forces out to the year 2020. In *Business Class* the United States leads the world toward tighter economic integration. A global, urban elite in business, government, entertainment, and international organizations shapes attitudes and policies. The contrasting *Prism* scenario sets forth an intriguing world in which splintered regional, ethnic, religious, and national values confound the growth of a monochrome global culture. Many versions of modernity and prosperity flower.

Shell develops all the scenarios at length; each fills a separate volume. Much in them focuses on the future of the energy industry. Current scenarios contrast two energy futures, one a state of gradual evolution from oil and gas to renewable energy sources (or possibly nuclear energy), the other a radical alternative in which societies switch to hydrogen economies as a result of advances in fuel cells.

"Businesses, by definition, put ideas into practice," says Ged Davis, the Shell executive in charge of scenarios.[2] But despite intense study of the world around it, Shell has made mistakes. In 1997 it tried to dispose of an obsolete oil drilling platform by simply sinking it in the North Sea, then had to back down after an ugly confrontation with environmental activists.[3] Soon, its reputation suffered again when human rights activists associated it with abuses by troops guarding its Nigerian oil fields. Most recently, Sir Philip Watts, its executive chairman, disgraced the company by lying about the size of proved oil and gas reserves. Caught, Watts resigned, leaving the credibility of the company motto—"You can be sure of Shell"—in tatters.[4] Given that Shell's scenarios have explored the rise of environmental and human rights values and the importance of public trust, there is room to wonder about the connection between scenario learning and company action. It is not unusual for corporate exemplars to suffer inexplicable lapses. Rather than invalidating the use of good management practices, these events simply confirm the fallibility of human nature.

In this chapter we identify deep historical forces that create change and risk in the business environment. Then, we discuss key dimensions of this environment, describing major trends and challenges. Much of this discussion focuses on subjects at the heart of Shell's scenarios.

---

[2] "Scenarios: Exploring Societal Problems," speech to the World Conservation Union, August 27, 2002, p. 1.

[3] John F. Mahon and Richard A. McGowan, "Corporate Reputation, Crises, and Stakeholder Management," *Global Focus* 11, no. 3 (1999), pp. 45–47.

[4] "Humiliation," *The Economist*, April 24, 2004, p. 14.

VOLATILITY IN THE BUSINESS ENVIRONMENT

In 1844 Philip Hone, the mayor of New York City, was baffled by the volatility of his environment. "This world is going on too fast," he wrote.

> Improvements, Politics, Reform, Religion—all fly. Railroads, steamers, packets, race against time and beat it hollow. Flying is dangerous. By and by we shall have balloons and pass over to Europe between sun and sun. Oh, for the good old days of heavy post-coaches and speed at the rate of six miles an hour.[5]

Hone's views reflect what people have experienced throughout history, including today. From ancient to modern times, environments have been volatile and generally unpredictable. For example, the Black Death in the middle of the fourteenth century killed one-third of the population of Europe and completely changed that world. The industrial revolution in the eighteenth century in England was unforeseen and threw the world into a new trajectory of progress and environmental volatility.

Throughout history, managers who have been inattentive to environmental change have, at best, lost opportunities for profit and, at worst, led their companies to failure. Take the Baldwin Locomotive Works. Matthias W. Baldwin, a watchmaker, started the firm to build steam locomotives. His first engine, "Old Ironsides," built in 1832, was a mechanical masterpiece. Baldwin drove his company to advance and perfect steam technology. He delighted in the changing times, once writing that "not to go ahead nowadays is to go behind very fast."[6] Baldwin died in 1866, but his company prospered, growing with the railroad industry and dominating worldwide sales of steam locomotives. At its zenith in 1918 it rolled out 3,580 locomotives from a 600-acre Philadelphia plant that could dock and load five ships at a time to serve foreign customers. But the company's managers were so fixated on steam that they were blindsided by the revolutionary diesel engine that competitors introduced in the 1930s. When they finally caught on, their first diesels were heavy and uneconomical, unable to compete with better units made by General Motors. In 1956, Baldwin made its last locomotive (ironically, a diesel), leaving the field to General Motors, which went on to dominate global sales.

Today's changing conditions in the United States and around the globe bewilder people in and out of business with their volatility and scope. For instance, worldwide markets exist for the first time in many industries. Product innovations are so quickly seen and copied that seizing an advantage over competitors is difficult. And societal expectations about the ethical duties of corporations dictate new, elevated performance standards. What insights exist to help us make sense of such pervasive change?

[5] Quoted in John Steel Gordon, "When Our Ancestors Became Us," *American Heritage*, December 1989, p. 108.

[6] Quoted in John K. Brown, *The Baldwin Locomotive Works: 1831–1915* (Baltimore: The Johns Hopkins University Press, 1995), p. 4.

UNDERLYING HISTORICAL FORCES CHANGING THE BUSINESS ENVIRONMENT

historical force
An environmental force of unknown origin and mysterious action that provides the energy for events. The discussion divides this force, somewhat artificially, into nine separate but related forces causing distinct chains of events.

We believe that, in a broad sense, order can be found in the swirling patterns of current events; that there is a deep logic in the passing of history; and that change in the business environment is the result of elemental historical forces moving in roughly predictable directions. Henry Adams defined a *historical force* as "anything that does, or helps to do, work."[7] The work to which Adams refers is the power to cause events. Change in the business environment is the work of nine deep historical forces or streams of related events discussed below.

The Industrial Revolution

The first historical force is the industrial revolution. It is a powerful force that grips the imagination of humanity. The term *industrial revolution* refers to transforming changes that turn simple economies of farmers and artisans into complex industrial economies. Such change requires specific conditions, including a sufficiency of capital, labor, natural resources, and fuels; transportation; strong markets; and the ideas and institutions to combine effectively these ingredients. These conditions first arose in England during the late eighteenth century, then spread to Western Europe and the United States during the nineteenth century. Japan and Russia took off in the first half of the twentieth century, and other Asian nations, including Taiwan, South Korea, and China, followed in the second half. Industrialization continues to spread as less developed nations try to create the conditions for it.

industrial revolution
Transforming changes that turn agricultural economies into industrial economies. This transformation occurs in the presence of certain economic, technological, political, and philosophical conditions.

Industrial growth remakes societies. It elevates living standards, alters life experiences, and shifts values. Since institutions built on older ideas change more slowly than people's lives, industrialization generates huge strains in the social fabric. It continues today to generate these strains in both developing and developed economies. The striking thing about economic growth is its astounding size and acceleration in the twentieth century. The total amount of goods and services produced in the twentieth century exceeds all that produced in recorded human history. Indeed, as Figure 2.1 shows, output for just the second half of the century, from 1950 to 2000, exceeds all that came before.

Inequality

From time immemorial, status distinctions, class structures, and gaps between rich and poor have defined societies. Inequality is ubiquitous, as are its consequences—envy, demands for fair distribution of wealth, and doctrines to justify why some people have more than others. The basic political conflict in every nation, and often between nations, is the antagonism between rich and poor.[8]

---

[7] In the essay "A Dynamic Theory of History (1904)," in Henry Adams, *The Education of Henry Adams* (New York: Modern Library, 1931), p. 474; originally published in 1908.

[8] Mortimer J. Adler, *The Great Ideas* (New York: Macmillan, 1992), pp. 578–79.

FIGURE 2.1
World GDP Growth in 50-Year Intervals

Source: Bradford J. DeLong, "Estimating World GDP, One Million B.C.–Present," available at http://econ161.berkeley.edu.

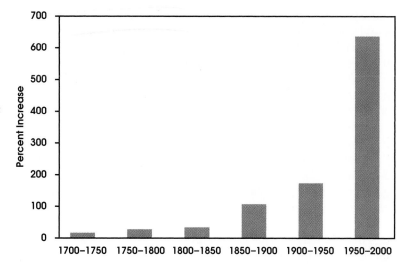

Gini index
A statistical measure of inequality in which 0 is perfect equality (everyone has the same amount of wealth) and 100 is absolute inequality (a single person has all wealth).

The industrial revolution accelerated the accumulation of wealth without solving the persistent problem of its uneven distribution. Explosive economic growth widened the gap between rich and poor around the globe. Global income inequality is measured by the *Gini index,* a statistic in which 0 percent stands for absolute equality, that is, a theoretical situation in which everyone has the same income, and 100 percent represents absolute inequality, where one person has all the income. Using this measure, inequality becomes greater as the percentage figure rises toward 100.

Figure 2.2 shows that by 1820, when the industrial revolution was spreading from England to western Europe, global income inequality was already very high. The Gini index of 50 percent in 1820 climbed to 61 percent in 1910, as economies in

FIGURE 2.2   **World Poverty and Income Inequality Since 1820**

Sources: François Bourguignon and Christian Morrisson, "Inequality among World Citizens: 1820–1992," *American Economic Review,* September 2002, table 1; UNDP, *Human Development Report 2003,* p. 39; and U.S. Census Bureau, "Total Midyear Population for the World: 1950–2050," April 2004.

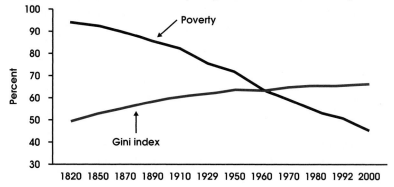

industrializing nations rapidly expanded. After that, the rise continued, but more slowly, as populous Asian countries holding the bulk of the world's poor began to industrialize and catch up. The Gini index reached 64 percent in 1950 and continued its decelerating rise to 66 percent in 2000.[9] This represents an extreme level of inequality across the world population, so high that it is exceeded within only a handful of the world's most aristocratic nations today. The cause is the diverging economic fortunes of nations.

Contrary to popular opinion, economic growth does not itself increase income inequality within modernizing nations. During industrialization the incomes of the poorest people rise in proportion to the rise in average income for the country as a whole.[10] The cause of most of the rise in world income inequality is a growing gap between the peoples of rich and poor nations, not a growing separation of rich and poor within nations.

Today about 2.8 billion people live in poverty, defined as having an income of less than $2 a day.[11] This is more poor people than at any time in history, an enormous pool of misfortune constituting 46 percent of world population. Yet in 1820, near the beginning of the industrial revolution, 94 percent of the world's population lived in poverty. The great and steady retreat in the poverty percentage for almost two centuries, in the face of vaulting population growth, is testimony to the wealth-creating power of industrial development. Even as economic growth has widened the gap between rich and poor it has dramatically reduced the proportion of the poor in the total population.

Although the Gini index line in Figure 2.2 seems to rise only modestly on the graph and lacks the drama of the high GDP growth during the same years, it in fact represents a striking confluence of progress and tragedy. If world distribution of income had not become more unequal after 1820, economic growth would have reduced the number of people living in poverty today by 80 percent.[12] Instead, as the wealth divide between nations opened further with each passing year, the distribution of income grew ever more unequal. Yet even as inequality worsened, the drop in the poverty line shows how economic growth led to a continuous, sharp reduction in privation.

The vast majority of the world's 2.8 billion poor people live in economies not yet transformed by industrial growth. Their presence creates expectations that the ethical duties of global corporations include helping the poor and equitably distributing the fruits of commerce. The lesson of almost two centuries is that if corporations are harnessed to create economic growth, the poor will benefit.

---

[9] Figures are from François Bourguignon and Christian Morrisson, "Inequality among World Citizens: 1820–1992," *American Economic Review,* September 2002, pp. 731–32; and United Nations Development Programme, *Human Development Report 2002* (New York: Oxford University Press, 2002), p. 19.

[10] David Dollar and Aart Kraay, "Spreading the Wealth," *Foreign Affairs,* January/February 2002, p. 128.

[11] United Nations Development Programme, *Human Development Report 2003* (New York: Oxford University Press, 2003), pp. 40–41.

[12] Bourguignon and Morrisson, "Inequality among World Citizens," p. 733. The $2-a-day figure represents what could be purchased in the United States for $2, not what could be purchased in local currency.

The Human Development Index

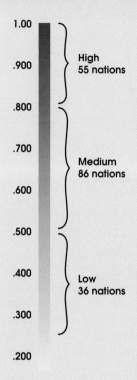

The Human Development Index (HDI) is a statistical tool used by the United Nations for measuring the progress of humanity. It is based on the theory that income alone is not an adequate measure of the standard of living, let alone a rich and fulfilling life. If this theory is correct, discussions of inequality based on income differences within and between nations do not give a complete picture of differences in human welfare.

The HDI is a scale running from 0 to 1, with 1 representing the highest human development and 0 the lowest. It measures the development of nations as an average of scores in three equally weighted categories.

- *Longevity,* or life expectancy at birth.
- *Knowledge,* or the adult literacy rate plus the ratio of students enrolled in school as a percentage of the population of official school age.
- *Income,* or gross domestic product per capita (in equivalent U.S. dollars).

Of the 177 nations in the 2002 Human Development Index, 55 have high index values of 0.800 or above, 86 are in the medium range with values of 0.500 to 0.799, and 36 fall in the low range with values below 0.499. Norway is highest ranked with an index value of 0.956. Sierra Leone is lowest at 0.273. The United States ranks eighth with 0.939.[13]

Historical HDI index values show enormous increases in human welfare since the late nineteenth century, as a consequence mainly of declining mortality and economic growth. In 1870 the United States had an HDI value of 0.467, a score that would today put it close to Nigeria in the low human development category. In 1913 it had an HDI value of 0.730 that would today rank it slightly below Iran deep in the medium human development category.[14]

Since 1950 the absolute gap between the highest- and lowest-rated countries has narrowed substantially, showing that inequality in living standards around the world, as measured by the HDI, is declining even while income inequality, as measured by per capita GDP, is rising. Thus, inequality is greater if measured only by monetary income and less if longevity and education, two traditional measures of a good life, are taken into consideration.

Although the HDI reveals dramatic human progress, the world average index value (0.722 in 2002) is now rising more slowly. Since 1990 the HDI has been falling in 21 countries. Such a broad fall is unprecedented. It is caused by the spread of the HIV/AIDS epidemic in Sub-Saharan Africa, which shortens life spans and harms economies by disabling workers, and by dramatic income declines in the Russian Federation and some Eastern European nations.

[13] United Nations Development Programme, *Human Development Report 2004* (New York: Oxford University Press, 2004), pp. 139–42.

[14] Nicholas Crafts, "Globalization and Growth in the Twentieth Century," IMF working paper, WP/pp/44 (Washington, DC: International Monetary Fund, March 2000), pp. 6–7.

Population Growth

The basic population trend throughout human history is upward. As shown in Figure 2.3, world population inched ahead for centuries, then grew somewhat more rapidly beginning about 10,000 years ago when large-scale crop cultivation

FIGURE 2.3
Historical
World
Population
Growth and
Projections to
2300

Sources: U.S. Bureau
of the Census,
"Historical
Estimates of World
Population,"
available at
www.census.gov/
ipc/www/worldhis.
html; and United
Nations, *World
Population 2300,* p. 2
and table 2.

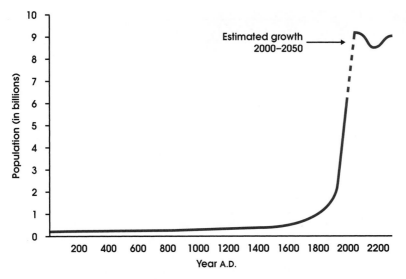

was introduced. After eight more centuries, population growth began a rapid new acceleration in the late 1800s which turned into a skyrocketing rise through the twentieth century. It took until 1825 for the world population to reach one billion; then each billionth additional person was added faster and faster—first in 100 years, then in 35, then 15, then only 12.[15] This astonishing growth had two causes, both related to the industrial revolution. First, advances in water sanitation and medicine reduced deaths from infectious disease, and second, mechanized farming expanded the food supply.

Figure 2.4 shows the same rise in population, but depicts it in relation to GDP growth over the same period to dramatize the latter. In the initial stages of industrial revolution economic progress stimulated population growth, but it is now primarily a brake on it because it has led to declining fertility. In developed societies having fewer children frees women to attend school, hold rewarding jobs, and increase income. In the United States, Europe, and Japan fertility rates have dropped below the replacement rate of 2.1 births per woman. Fertility remains above the replacement rate in less developed continents and regions, but even there overall rates are falling as the world economy expands.

The world population reached 6.1 billion persons in 2000 and it continues to rise. But the rapidity of growth is slowing now primarily because of declining fertility. Despite a continued drop in fertility rates, population experts predict that the world population will grow to a peak of 9.2 billion in 2075. Then, it will decline over a century to 8.3 billion in 2175 before slowly rising to 9 billion in 2300.[16] This is a captivating look at the distant future, but for the immediate future, in the years

---

[15] Clive Ponting, *A Green History of the World* (New York: Penguin Books, 1991), p. 240.

[16] United Nations, *World Population in 2300* (New York: United Nations Department of Economic and Social Affairs, 2004), p. 2.

FIGURE 2.4
**World
GDP and
Population
since 1750**

Source: Bradford J.
DeLong, "Estimating
World GDP,
One Million B.C.–
Present," available
at http://econ161.
berkeley.edu.

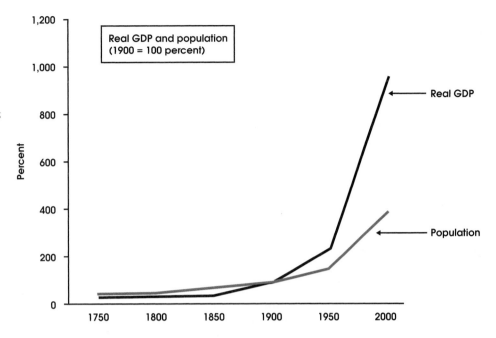

2000 to 2050 represented by the broken line in Figure 2.3, rapid growth will remain the dominant trend in the business environment.

Fastest growth to 2050 is expected in the least developed regions, where fertility remains high. Africa will grow 127 percent, despite the HIV/AIDS epidemic. High-income regions will grow, but more slowly. The populations of Asia and North America will each rise by 42 percent and Latin America by 48 percent. Only Europe's population will not grow; it will decline by 13 percent to be only 6 percent of world population.[17] Because people will live longer, populations everywhere will age. In 2000 the average age was 26, but by 2050 it will be 37 (and 48 in Europe).[18]

These population trends have many implications. First, although overall growth is slowing, it will be highest in less industrialized regions, widening further the wealth gap between high- and low-income countries. Second, growth will continue to strain the earth's ecosystems, especially as industrial activity spreads. Third, the West is in demographic decline compared with other peoples. In 1900 Western nations held 30 percent of the world's population and had colonial rule over another 15 percent. But today they are stripped of their former colonies and hold only 13 percent of the world's population.[19] In the future, growing non-Western peoples will be stronger economically, militarily, and politically and will push to

[17] Ibid., tables 2 and 3.
[18] Ibid., table A.24.
[19] Samuel P. Huntington, *The Clash of Civilizations and the Remaking of World Order* (New York: Simon & Schuster, 1996), p. 84.

expand their influence. This can be seen today in Islamic societies, which have young, rapidly growing populations. Although Western market values and business ideology seem ascendant now, they may be less widespread in the future as the numerical basis of Western civilization declines. In such ways will population trends alter the business environment and create new societal expectations for corporate behavior.

Technology

Throughout recorded history new technologies and devices have fueled commerce and reshaped societies. In the 1450s the printing press was an immediate commercial success, but its impact went far beyond the publishing business. Over the next 100 years the affordable, printed word reshaped European culture by creating a free market for ideas that undermined the doctrinal monopoly of the Catholic Church. Printed pamphlets spread Martin Luther's challenge to its scriptural dogma and brought on the Protestant Reformation. Galileo was placed under house arrest in Florence for holding heretical views about astronomy, but his theories prevailed because they were published in Protestant Holland. A Europe opened to the exchange of new ideas based on experience and observation was primed for the scientific revolution.

The invention of the steam engine in the late 1700s and its widespread use beginning in the early 1800s, along with increased use of the waterwheel and new iron-making methods, triggered the industrial revolution. As Figure 2.5 shows, this was the first of five waves of technological revolution. In each wave innovations spread, stimulating economic booms of increased investment, rising productivity, and output growth. The shortening of successive waves reveals faster technological innovation.

New technologies foster the productivity gains that sustain long-term economic progress, and they promote human welfare. However, like the printing press, they also can agitate societies. For example, before the 1860s a transatlantic voyage on a sailing ship took a month, cost a year's wages for a European worker, and was risky. About 5 to 10 percent of passengers died due to sinkings and shipboard transmission of diseases. Then steamship technology cut the cost of passage by

FIGURE 2.5   Waves of Innovation since the Beginning of the Industrial Revolution

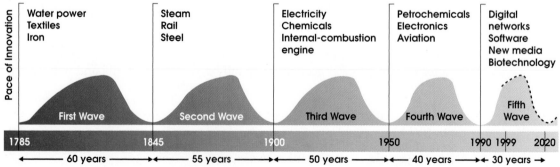

90 percent and reduced travel time to one week, cutting mortality to less than 1 percent. As a result, European immigrants poured into the American east, creating labor gluts that led to wage depressions and fueling political movements against big companies, financiers, and the gold standard.[20] In this way, steamship technology strained American political stability.

During the rise of industrial societies over more than two centuries, technology has altered human civilization by stimulating economic and population growth to sustained rises unimaginable in previous recorded history. New things have created many benefits, including higher living standards and longer life spans, but because technology changes faster than human beliefs and institutions, it also imposes strains.

Globalization

Globalization occurs when networks of economic, political, social, military, scientific, or environmental interdependence grow to span worldwide distances.[21] In the economic realm, globalization refers to the development of an increasingly integrated commercial system based on free markets in which nations are open to foreign trade and investment. The current rise of such a system began after World War II, when the victor nations lowered trade barriers and loosened capital controls. Over the next 50 years, international negotiations led more nations to open themselves to global flows of goods, services, and investment until today no national economy of any significance remains isolated from world markets.

Today's economic globalization is the leading edge of a long trend. For thousands of years the human community has, in fits and starts, become more tightly knit. According to historians J. R. McNeill and William H. McNeill, in prehistoric times humans interacted in a loose worldwide web through which genes and inventions such as language and the bow and arrow were slowly exchanged by migrations between relatively isolated bands. Beginning about 12,000 years ago with the growth of agricultural societies, stable and expanding populations formed the first cities. Over time, these cities grew into nodes that tied regions together. Still, there was little interaction between civilizations on different continents. Then, about 500 years ago, China sponsored oceanic voyages to extend its power.[22]

Soon Portugal and Spain followed and over the next 250 years mariners connected even the most remote places to the great centers of civilization. By the late 1700s the world was knit together with the exchange of trade goods, currencies, and ideas. The consequences of this initial globalization are similar to those arising from the current globalization. Economic activity rapidly increased. Mines in Bolivia exported such quantities of silver that nations around the world adopted silver currencies, smoothing international trade. Trade expansion increased inequality among nations. Cultures changed, as when, for example, Spanish conquistadors introduced horses to the Plains Indians. Infectious diseases spread. In

---

[20] Robert William Fogel, *The Fourth Great Awakening & The Future of Egalitarianism* (Chicago: University of Chicago Press, 2001), p. 54.

[21] Joseph Nye, Jr., "Globalization's Democratic Deficit," *Foreign Affairs,* July–August 2001, p. 2.

[22] *The Human Web* (New York: W. W. Norton & Company, 2003), intro. and chap. VI.

little more than a century microbes endemic to Europe killed 50 to 90 percent of the population of the Americas from Cape Horn to the Arctic.

Since this initial tying together of societies in the late 1700s, the trend toward integration has continued. Globalization has been accelerated by new technologies, particularly those based on electricity, but also sometimes slowed by national rivalries and wars.

Transnational corporations, especially a few hundred of the largest headquartered in developed nations, are the central forces of current economic globalization. Their rising levels of investment outside home countries make them the modern equivalents of the intrepid mariners who opened trade routes in the 1400s. Many of these firms have more resources than the governments of smaller nations. However, globalization complicates their management. By operating in many countries they multiply the number and kind of stakeholders to which they must respond. Their actions create strains and anxieties that lead to heightened expectations of responsible behavior. In addition, there is a strong anticorporate movement supported mainly by groups in rich nations that see the growing velocity of trade with alarm because it clashes with their values on the environment, human rights, and democracy. These groups seek to restrain and regulate the activities of transnational corporations and they have had some success.

Nation-States

The modern nation-state system arose in an unplanned way out of the wreckage of the Roman Empire. The institution of the nation-state was well-suited for Western Europe, where boundaries were contiguous with the extent of languages. However, the idea was subsequently transplanted to territories in Eastern Europe, Southwest Asia, and the Middle East, partly by force of colonial empires and partly by mimicry among non-Western political elites for whom the idea had attained high prestige. Where it was transplanted, nations were often irrationally defined and boundary lines split historic areas of culture, ethnicity, religion, and language.

The nation-state is the unit of human organization in which individuals and cultural groups can influence their circumstances and future. This is its paramount function and the reason it has survived over centuries. Today the world is a mosaic of independent countries, and the dynamics of this system are a powerful force in the international business environment. Conflict between nations seeking to aggrandize wealth and power is frequent, though because of economic globalization its nature has changed.

In the past, nations increased their power by seizing territory from other nations. With more territory they acquired new natural resources, agriculture, and labor. Hence, in the 1930s Japan colonized South Asian countries to gain access to oil and bauxite. Now, however, the wealth of high-income nations is based on the operation of global corporations that use flows of capital and knowledge to provide goods and services in many nations. Seizing the headquarters or a few manufacturing facilities of one of these corporations would not enable the aggressor nation to take advantage of the value chain in the firm's worldwide operations, particularly where wealth creation was based on brainpower. So nations today increasingly prefer to aggrandize themselves through trade, where they can build wealth more efficiently than through traditional warfare designed to seize land and stocks of material resources.[23]

Although economic trends discourage war to seize resources, conflict between ethnic and religious groupings across nation-state boundaries is prominent today. For example, the nationalistic feelings of Palestinians have affected global companies in many industries, from oil firms caught in Middle East conflicts to airlines losing passengers afraid of terrorism.

Dominant Ideologies

Thought shapes history. An ideology is a set of reinforcing beliefs and values that constructs a worldview. The industrial revolution in the West was facilitated by a set of interlocking ideologies, including capitalism, but also constitutional democracy characterized by protections for rights that allowed individualism to flourish; progress, or the idea that humanity was in upward motion toward material betterment; Darwinism, or Charles Darwin's finding that constant improvement characterized the biological world, which reinforced the idea of progress; social Darwinism, or Herbert Spencer's idea that evolutionary competition in human society, as well as the natural world, weeded out the unfit and advanced humanity; and the Protestant ethic, or the belief that hard work, saving, thrift, and honesty led to salvation.

Ideologies are highly competitive and there is a Darwinian competition among them. Vibrant pluralism of belief existed for most of recorded history, but many doctrines have perished as a result of globalization. As ideas diffuse through trade, travel, missionary work, and conquest, they often clash. A centuries-old culling process in the marketplace of ideas has eliminated and marginalized many historical belief systems and favored the ascendancy of a few.[24] Hundreds of local religions and regional languages have died out. Cultural styles in entertainment, dress, sports, and food now converge in urban societies. In the political sphere monarchy and dictatorship are fighting an end game against democracy. After two centuries of contention the economic ideology of capitalism has marginalized its rival socialism. This sifting of ideas accelerated in the twentieth century as a result of rising literacy and innovations that spread information, from magazines and radios in the early part of the century to jet aircraft and computers later.

Great Leadership

Leaders have brought both beneficial and disastrous changes to societies and businesses. Alexander imposed his rule over the ancient Mediterranean world, creating new trade routes on which Greek merchants flourished. Adolf Hitler of Germany and Joseph Stalin in the Soviet Union were strong leaders, but they unleashed evil that retarded industrial growth in their countries.

There are two views about the power of leaders as a historical force. One is that leaders simply ride the wave of history. "Great men," writes Arnold Toynbee, "are

[23] This thesis is elaborated in Richard Rosecrance, *The Rise of the Virtual State* (New York: Basic Books, 1999).
[24] J. R. McNeill and William H. McNeill, *The Human Web,* pp. 269–76.

precisely the points of intersection of great social forces."[25] When oil was discovered in western Pennsylvania in 1859, John D. Rockefeller was a young man living in nearby Cleveland, where he had accumulated a little money selling produce. He saw an opportunity in the new industry. His remarkable traits enabled him to domineer over a rising industry that reshaped the nation and the world. Yet is there any doubt that the reshaping would have occurred had Rockefeller decided to stick with selling lettuce and carrots?

A differing view is that leaders themselves change history rather than being pushed by its tide. "The history of the world," wrote Thomas Carlyle, "is at bottom the History of the Great Men who have worked here."[26] It was John Jacob Astor of the American Fur Company who established a presence in the wild lands of the American continent, exploring them, knitting them together, and thwarting the efforts of other nations to occupy them. The United States map might today be different absent the effects of Astor's singular lust for fur riches. It was James B. Duke of the American Tobacco Company whose solitary marketing genius turned cigarette smoking from a local custom confined largely to the American South into a worldwide health disaster continuing now for more than a century.

Cases and stories of business leaders in this text provide instances for debate about the role of business leaders in changing the world.

Chance

Scholars are reluctant to use the notion of chance, accident, or random occurrence as a category of analysis. Yet some changes in the business environment may be best explained as the product of unknown and unpredictable causes. No less perceptive a student of history than Niccolò Machiavelli observed that fortune determines about half the course of human events and human beings the other half. We cannot improve on this estimate, but we note it. Its significance is that managers must be prepared for the most unprecedented events and have faith in Machiavelli's counsel that when such episodes arrive those who are ready will prevail, as fortune "directs her bolts where there have been no defenses or bulwarks prepared against her."[27] No doubt Machiavelli would think Shell's scenarios are praiseworthy.

SEVEN KEY ENVIRONMENTS OF BUSINESS

Figure 2.6 shows the seven most important environments affecting business today. In each one powerful forces create change in the relationships between businesses, governments, and societies. These forces are often related and major changes in one area rarely occur in isolation. Here we give thumbnail sketches of each key environment. We will dig more deeply into them throughout the book.

[25] *A Study of History,* vol. XII, *Reconsiderations* (London: Oxford University Press, 1961), p. 125.

[26] In "The Hero as Divinity," reprinted in Carl Niemeyer, ed., *Thomas Carlyle on Heroes, Hero-Worship and the Heroic in History* (Lincoln: University of Nebraska Press, 1966), p. 1. This essay was originally written in 1840.

[27] Niccolò Machiavelli, *The Prince,* trans. George Bull (New York: Penguin Books, 1961), chap. XXV, p. 73.

FIGURE 2.6
The Seven Key
Environments
of Business

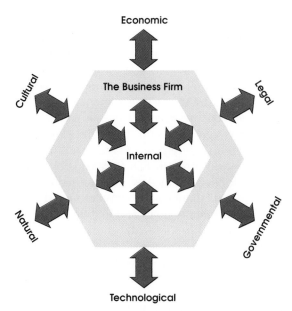

The Economic Environment

The economic environment consists of forces that influence market operations, including overall economic activity, commodity prices, interest rates, currency fluctuations, wages, competitors' actions, technology change, and government policies. Today the global economic environment is driven by continuing long-term growth in output and investment that is related to tightening integration of actors.

World GDP tripled in the twenty years between 1982 and 2002, rising from $10.8 trillion to $32.2 trillion.[28] Growth slowed in 2001 and 2002 because of the economic repercussions of the September 11, 2001, terrorist attacks on the World Trade Center and the Pentagon and of the SARS (sudden acute respiratory syndrome) epidemic in Asia. However, in 2003 the growth rate in the world economy picked up again, led by economic recovery in the United States and rapid expansion in Asia, particularly in China and India. Underlying this strong and continuing overall economic growth are two basic subtrends.

trade liberalization
A philosophy in which nations promote trade by easing restrictions, including both tariff and nontariff barriers. This philosophy, sometimes referred to as simply *liberalization,* is the bedrock of economic globalization.

The first is rising trade. Three years after the end of World War II, in 1948, the global sum of all merchandise exported was only $58 billion. In 2002 it was $6.3 trillion, an increase of more than 1,000 percent.[29] This spectacular rise has been enabled by a trading system created at the end of World War II. Nations entering the system have been encouraged to lower tariffs and other trade barriers because other member nations promised to reciprocate this openness. The system has evolved into an institution called the World Trade Organization (WTO), which embodies an ongoing process of negotiation and *trade liberalization* in which 142 nations now

[28] United Nations Conference on Trade and Development, *World Investment Report 2003* (New York: United Nations, 2003), table I.1.

[29] World Trade Organization, *International Trade Statistics 2003* (Geneva: WTO, 2003), table II.2.

participate. In addition, several hundred regional trade agreements promote freer exchange among countries that are parties to them.[30] Other causes of rising trade are long-term growth of consumer demand in high-income countries and lower transportation costs.

foreign direct investment
Capital investment by private firms outside their home countries.

The second subtrend underlying continued economic growth is a major expansion of foreign direct investment (FDI) by transnational corporations. *Foreign direct investment* is capital investment by private firms outside their home countries. Over the twenty years between 1982 and 2002, global FDI inflows rose from $59 billion a year to $651 billion, a 1,100 percent increase.[31] There are almost 65,000 transnational corporations and through FDI they control about 900,000 foreign businesses. Many of these foreign businesses are obtained by merger and acquisition and between 1997 and 2002 there was an unprecedented burst of cross-border merger activity both in the number of deals and in their dollar value.[32] Expanding FDI and merger activity reflects a fundamental change in the competitive circumstances of corporations.

Rising trade and increasing affluence have rapidly expanded markets. To remain competitive corporations have expanded with markets and restructured for efficiency. They invest to enter growing markets or to increase their power in them. Many larger transnational firms have also restructured, creating "global factories" in which production takes place across geographically dispersed networks. These networks seek to duplicate at a global level the efficiencies of specialization and outsourcing often seen at the national level. They are now so extensive that nearly two-thirds of the world's exports move within them.

It would be hard to understate the importance and impact of FDI by transnational corporations on regions, nations, and the global economy. As large firms expand in faraway areas, they affect businesses, labor markets, tax bases, politics, and the fiscal affairs of nations. Discussions of corporate responsibility, and the anxieties of antiglobalists, most often center on environmental protection and a spectrum of issues related to human rights. International codes listing corporate duties in these areas have proliferated. There is far less discussion and code development with respect to economic impacts, yet these are the most consequential and they grow continuously larger as FDI rises.

The Technological Environment

Today new scientific discoveries create a business environment filled with mind-boggling technology. For example, semiconductor manufacturing can create microchips with components the size of 1 ten-millionth of a meter. *Nanotechnology* allows scientists and engineers to manipulate objects the size of atoms and make tiny machines invisible to the naked eye. When this ability is harnessed to manufacturing, it will create chips of astonishing computing power that operate on an atomic scale comparable to the process of photosynthesis in plants. Users with

nanotechnology
Technology that is developed on the scale of a nanometer, which is one-billionth of a meter.

---

[30] International Monetary Fund, *World Economic Outlook* (Washington, DC: IMF, April 2004), box 1.3.

[31] UNCTAD, *World Investment Report 2003,* table I.1.

[32] For the six years of 1997 through 2002 there were 633 deals worth $2.4 trillion as compared to the previous six years, including 1991 through 1996, with 134 deals worth $290 billion. Ibid., table I.7.

such a circuit could store all information in the Library of Congress in the space of a sugar cube.[33] Human genome mapping promises new biogenetic products that will cure intractable diseases. Fuel cells and methods of harnessing renewable energy may dramatically reduce use of fossil fuels. Digital telecommunications technology links a global network of computers, software, and electronic devices that promises to reshape life and work. Forces generated by these new technologies will shake the foundations of the most secure businesses and alter consumer choices, standards of living, the fortunes of industries, and the ethical duties of corporations.

New technologies create both threats and opportunities and the track record for seeing them is uneven. Often, companies focus on the immediate commercial and strategic possibilities of a technology and find it difficult to predict ultimate significance. For example, Western Union was the dominant communications company of the nineteenth century, but it was so confident in the telegraph that it rejected the telephone.

When Alexander Graham Bell invented the telephone in 1876, it had only a three-mile range. Western Union considered hooking telephones into its lines, but decided that such a short range device was only a toy. So Bell formed his own company. When engineers lengthened the range of the phone by using wires made of copper instead of iron, Western Union saw its mistake and rushed into the business with a phone device of its own. The mighty company used "every devious and underhanded method," including political pressure and bribes, to prevent towns and cities from adopting the Bell phone.[34] But in 1878 it lost a patent infringement suit brought by Bell's company and had to drop the business. The tiny Bell Telephone Company grew into AT&T, one of the great firms of the twentieth century. Today the Internet has created a similar strategic junction in telecommunications. Companies rise and fall based on new ideas about its application, and it may be many years before its implications are well understood.

New technologies have unforeseen consequences for society when they are put into widespread use for commercial gain. Sometimes these implications are unanticipated. The cigarette rolling machine was invented before the dangers of smoking were discovered. The manufacturing technologies that mixed asbestos into hundreds of common materials were developed long before the morbid effects of asbestos fibers became clear.

Commercially harnessed technologies can have both good and bad consequences. Corporations have a duty to avoid harming their stakeholders. So they must carefully weigh not only the strategic impact of technologies on their business models, but also the stresses and strains they may impose on people.

The Government Environment

Business is simultaneously encouraged and constrained by governments. There are now two long-term global trends in the government environment of major importance to business.

---

[33] Philip Bond, quoted in Ronald Bailey, "The Smaller the Better," *Reason*, December 2003, p. 47.

[34] Page Smith, *The Rise of Industrial America*, vol. 6 (New York: Penguin Books, 1984), p. 115.

FIGURE 2.7
The Rise of Democratic Regimes

Source: UNDP, *Human Development Report 2002*, p. 15 and fig. 1-1 (based on Polity IV. 2002 database, University of Maryland).

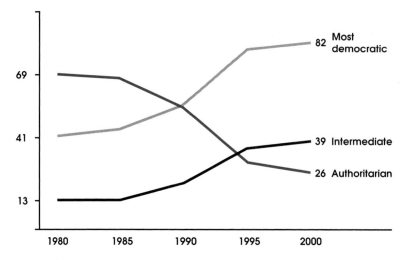

First, government activity has greatly expanded. One way of measuring this is by the size of government expenditures relative to gross domestic product, and around the world this has been rising. In the United States, for example, government spending in 1913 was 8 percent of GDP, but by 1998 it had risen to 33 percent.[35] The increases have been higher in European countries and lower in less developed nations, but broadly the trend is up because governments have taken on new functions. For one, governments have taken on social welfare roles and make huge transfer payments to their citizens. This role grew importantly in the years between the two world wars when there was a wave of democratization and many nations expanded their electorates. The new voters included women and the less privileged, groups that voted to enlarge government by supporting assistance programs. The other main source of growth in government is expanded regulation of domestic industries to protect citizens against abuses. In the United States, for example, there is today practically no aspect of business that governments cannot and will not regulate if the occasion arises and popular support exists. New laws, added to past laws, result in more constraints on business than ever before.

democracy
A form of government requiring three elements— popular sovereignty, political liberty, and majority rule.

The second long-term trend is that more governments are becoming open and democratic. In 1900 no nation was a full democracy with multiparty elections and universal suffrage. The United States and Britain were close, but both lacked female suffrage, and the United States additionally lacked black suffrage. Yet by 1950 there were 22 democracies and by 2002 there were 121.[36] Figure 2.7 shows the dramatic rise of democratic regimes in the last years of the twentieth century. The cause of this rise is complex. Democracy is associated with economic growth, expanding education, and rising use of new information technologies. It is both

[35] International Monetary Fund, *World Economic Outlook 2000* (Washington, DC: IMF, May 2000), table 5.4.

[36] Figures are from *Democracy's Century: A Survey of Global Political Change in the 20th Century* (Washington, DC: Freedom House, 2001), p. 2 and from figure 2.7.

preceded and accompanied by development of an independent media, sound rule of law, a professional civil service, and an independent judiciary. However, these factors may be either causes or effects, or possibly both. For business, the consequence of more openness to popular majorities is that governments increasingly respond to public demands for corporate social performance.

The Legal Environment

The legal environment consists of legislation, regulation, and litigation. There are five enduring trends in this environment, all working to constrain business behavior. First, laws and regulations have steadily grown in number and complexity. Second, corporations have expanding duties to protect rights of stakeholders, including employees, consumers, the public, and even competitors. These rights are set forth and protected by a flow of laws and court decisions on, for example, discrimination, sexual harassment, advertising, antitrust, the environment, product liability, and intellectual property. Third, globalization has increased the complexity of the legal environment by exposing corporations to international law and laws of foreign nations. In addition, advocacy groups promoting human rights and environmental causes push corporations to adopt so-called *soft law,* or voluntarily adopted codes of conduct that set forth rules for corporate behavior based on emerging international standards of conduct. These rules often exceed requirements in specific laws of nations. Fourth, although the requirements of ethical behavior and corporate social responsibility go beyond legal duty, they are continuously plucked from the voluntary realm and encoded into law. For instance, saving money by firing a long-time employee the week before he or she qualified for a pension was always ignoble. In 1974 the Employee Retirement Income Security Act made it illegal as well.

soft law
Voluntarily adopted codes of conduct setting forth rules about corporate behavior. Guidelines are often derived from emerging international conduct standards.

Finally, the law is constantly evolving. Because of technological change, for example, corporations need to anticipate emerging causes of liability. In this respect, the old *T. J. Hooper* case is still good reading for corporate counsel. On a sunny day in March 1928 the tugboat *T. J. Hooper* hauled a coal barge out to sea. Two days later it hit stormy weather off New Jersey, and the barge sank with its load of coal. The owners of the coal cargo sued, claiming that the tug was unseaworthy because it had no receiving radio. Lacking a radio, the *T. J. Hooper* missed a weather broadcast that caused other ships to put into a harbor before the gale hit. Although no law required a radio and there was no industry custom of installing them, the eminent judge Learned Hand held that "there are precautions so imperative that even their universal disregard will not excuse their omission."[37]

The tug owners were found negligent and paid for the coal cargo because they had not adopted a cutting-edge technology. Moving ahead to the present, a parallel example is the existence of cardiac defibrillators. No Federal Aviation Administration rule yet requires airlines to carry them on passenger jets, but their availability opens any airline that does not to charges of negligence by the survivors of a heart-attack victim.[38]

[37] *In re The* T. J. Hooper *et al.,* 60 F.2d 737 (1932), at 740.

[38] Milton Bordwin, "Your Company and 'THE LAW,'" *Management Review,* January 2000, p. 58.

The Cultural Environment

culture
A system of shared knowledge, values, norms, customs, and rituals acquired by social learning.

A *culture* is a system of shared knowledge, values, norms, customs, and rituals acquired by social learning. No universal culture exists, so the environment of a transnational corporation includes a variety of cultures, each with differing peoples, languages, religions, and values.

On one level, this variation causes conflicts of business custom, and managers in foreign countries must absorb both subtle and striking differences in employee loyalty, group versus individual initiative, the place of women in organizations, ethical values, norms of giving and gratuities, attitudes toward authority, the meaning of time, and clothing worn in business settings. The consequences of cultural differences are often trivial, even humorous. Thus, a consulting firm that helps American managers avoid social blunders in foreign countries counsels them not to force the custom of name tags at business meetings on Europeans, who feel they are being treated as schoolchildren when wearing them.[39] However, consequences can be serious too. In France, the notion is widespread that American fast food causes obesity and, worst of all, is bad tasting and insults the refined French palate. President Jacques Chirac said that national ways of eating should be preserved in the face of an assault by cross-Atlantic invaders; and a minister of agriculture once said that the United States was "home to the world's worst food."[40] For McDonald's, these cultural feelings turned deadly. A mob wrecked one of its restaurants and another was bombed, killing an employee.

On a deeper level, although no uniform world culture exists there is a fundamental divide between the culture of Western economic development and the rest of the world's cultural groupings. The culture of the advanced West promotes a core ideology of markets, individualism, and democratic government. It is sustained by Western nations that dominate international organizations, contain the most powerful corporations, and have the strongest militaries. However, although developing nations tend to adopt elements of Western culture, some nations and cultures have resisted its spread. Islamic nations and China see spreading Western values as a form of cultural aggression. They have resisted adopting them, particularly participatory forms of government.

Over the last half of the twentieth century, some cultural values in developed nations began to shift, creating changes in the global business environment. In these societies, beginning in the 1960s, traditional values based on historical realities of economic scarcity were transformed. In their place came what are called *postmodern values*, or values based on assumptions of affluence. For example, in older industrializing societies materialism was a dominant value. People sacrificed other values such as leisure time and environmental purity to make money and buy necessities, then luxuries. While consumption is still a powerful value in developed nations, their affluent citizens grow more concerned with quality of life and self-expression.

postmodern values
Values based on assumptions of affluence, for example, quality of life and self-expression.

The World Values Surveys, a series of surveys in 75 countries now spanning 25 years, show that the rise of postmodern values has uniformly shifted the social,

[39] Lalita Khosia, "You Say Tomato," *Forbes,* May 21, 2001, p. 36.
[40] John-Thor Dahlburg, "To Many French, Ugly American Is McDonald's," *Los Angeles Times,* April 22, 2000, p. A10.

political, economic, and sexual norms of rich countries. Despite some resistence in non-Western cultures, surveys show the rise of these norms in all modernizing nations. Among the Chinese public, for example, there is "surprisingly high" support for values linked to democracy.[41] And support for democratic ideals in eleven Muslim societies has grown to equal that in Western societies.[42]

Postmodern norms are a strong influence in the operating environments of multinational corporations. To illustrate, there is a powerful global movement to promote fundamental human rights by stamping out racism, sexism, authoritarianism, intolerance, and xenophobia. This movement is energized by West-dominated coalitions of individuals, advocacy groups, governments, and international organizations such as the United Nations. Similar and interrelated movements have risen to promote sustainable development and humanitarian assistance to poor areas. This global tide of morality, based on the postmodern values of the West, elevates expectations about the behavior of multinational corporations. Increasingly, they must follow proliferating codes and rules developed by moral reformers and must define their basic purposes as promoting human welfare above narrow profit making.

The Natural Environment

Economic activity is a geophysical force with power to change the natural environment. Just as it has strained the ability of human institutions to adapt, so also has it overwhelmed the ability of ecosystems to cleanse and regenerate. Economic productivity in the twentieth century depleted mineral resources, reduced forest cover, killed species, released molecules not found in nature, unbalanced the nitrogen cycle, and probably triggered climate change by altering the chemistry of the earth's atmosphere. The Living Planet Index of the World Wildlife Fund, which measures the health of the earth's biosphere, declined by 33 percent between 1970 and 2000, meaning that in contrast to the phenomenal economic growth of these years the earth has lost about a third of its natural capital.[43] Figure 2.8 shows how this decline compares with growth in world real GDP and population.

Attitudes about the relationship of economic activity to nature are now rapidly changing. When the twentieth century began, dominating and consuming nature was justified by a variety of doctrines, not the least being capitalism, which values nature as a production input. At its end, thinking moved toward preservation of nature. Managers must adapt to this changed thinking. With growing frequency environmental criteria enters into judgments of their performance.

The Internal Environment

In a corporation, the internal environment consists of four groups, as shown in Figure 2.9. Each group has different objectives, beliefs, needs, and functions that managers must coordinate to achieve overall company goals. In this process, a corporate culture that transcends the values of any single internal group is created.

---

[41] Richard Inglehart, "Globalization and Postmodern Values," *Washington Quarterly,* Winter 2000, p. 19.

[42] Ronald Inglehart and Pippa Norris, "The True Clash of Civilizations," *Foreign Policy,* March/April 2003, pp. 64–66.

[43] World Wide Fund for Nature, *Living Planet Report: 2002* (Gland, Switzerland: WWF International, 2002), p. 3.

FIGURE 2.8
Rates of Change of GDP, Population, and Living Planet Index

Sources: Bradford J. DeLong, "Estimating World GDP, One Million B.C.–Present," available at http://econ161.berkeley.edu; and World Wide Fund International, *Living Planet Report: 2000* (Gland, Switzerland: WWF International: 2000).

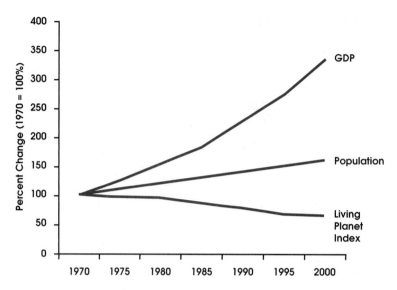

Forces in external environments have recently reduced the power of these internal groups. Managers are limited in their decisions by government and forced to accommodate a range of outside stakeholders having the power or claiming the right to influence them. Employees are losing power over management because of globalization of labor markets that puts them in competition with lower-wage workers elsewhere. In the United States, new financial regulations designed to protect shareholders from dishonest managers have given boards of directors more power and greater independence from top management. However, there is also some erosion of shareholder power by external groups demanding socially responsible actions that conflict with profit maximization.

FIGURE 2.9
A Depiction of the Internal Business Environment

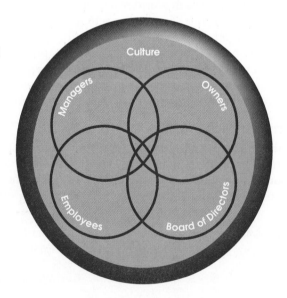

CONCLUDING OBSERVATIONS

The environments of business have profound implications for managers. Figure 2.10 summarizes the chapter discussion by illustrating the dynamic interconnection of business with historical forces and current environments. The deep historical forces act to shape the seven key environments, while the actions of business constantly influence not only current environments but, in addition, the deeper course of history. As the arrow running from the corporation to the world in Figure 2.10 indicates, business is not simply a passive entity that moves with historical and environmental forces like a billiard ball reacting to impacts. On the contrary,

FIGURE 2.10   **The Dynamic Interaction of Historical Forces, Business Environments, and Corporate Actions**

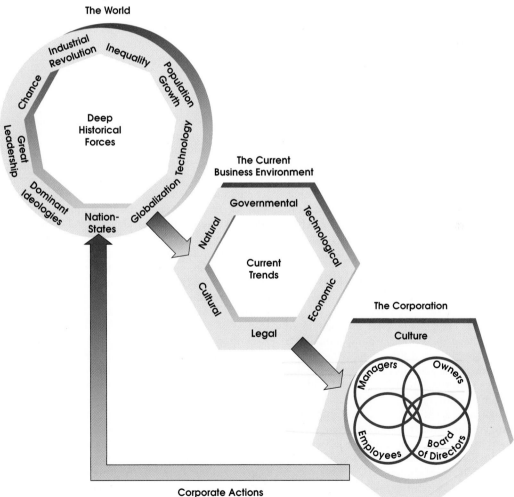

although strongly constrained by its environment, business has a powerful capacity to shape society and change history in ways small and large.

For example, when Eastman Kodak wanted to display the speed of its fast film and Flashmatic shutter in 1940, it ran magazine ads showing pictures of "Kodak Moments" when people blew out candles on their birthday cakes. The ads so popularized this charming rite that it became universal among Americans.[44] In contrast to such a small cultural change, the story of the automobile illustrates how industries can rearrange whole societies. Perhaps no twentieth century industry created more intentional and unintentional change. It was a prime mover of the American economy and once accounted directly or indirectly for one of every eight jobs. It encouraged an expansive highway system, brought decline to the railroads, depleted oil reserves, created pollution, altered cities, entrenched the idea that status was conferred by ownership of material objects, and changed patterns of courtship and crime.

[44] James B. Twitchell, *Lead Us Not into Temptation* (New York: Columbia University Press, 1999), p. 26.

The American Fur Company

The American Fur Company was a relentless monopoly built in the climactic era of the fur trade. It was created in 1808 by John Jacob Astor, a striving German immigrant, in an environment so favorable that over vast North American territories it had more power than the fledgling American government. In its time, this company shaped the destiny of a young nation. It made Astor the richest American of his day. Yet by the 1830s its situation had so changed that it and the 300-year-old trade in furs collapsed.

ASTOR ARRIVES IN A YOUNG NATION

In 1763 Astor was born to a butcher and his wife in the German village of Waldorf. Young John Jacob found village life dull, so at the age of 15 he left for London, working four years there to save money for an ocean voyage to the New World. In 1783, at the age of 20, with no education, little money, and speaking poor English, he set sail on a merchant ship. During the long voyage, a fur trader taught him how to appraise and handle skins. These lessons gave Astor knowledge he needed for an occupation. He would soon show himself an apt student.

At this time, the fur trade on the North American continent was almost 300 years old. It had begun early in the sixteenth century after Spanish and French explorers made contact with native forest dwellers, and it soon included the British. The Europeans wanted beaver, martin, ermine, mink, otter, bear, deer, muskrat, wolf, racoon, and other animal skins for fashionable hats and clothing. The Native Americans, who had not yet entered the age of metal, were anxious to get even the simplest manufactured goods such as knives, mirrors, ornaments, and buttons. This simple mutual advantage proved durable over time.

Indians were the fur industry's production workers. Fur traders usually depended on them to trap animals, then negotiated with them to buy pelts in exchange for trinkets. Indian women skinned and prepared the hides. Overhead costs for traders were low. Instead of wages, Indians took trade goods worth a fraction of a fur's ultimate value. Since furs were light and compact, they could be transported economically by mules, barges, and ships to eastern ports and thence to Europe. Profits on furs were enormous.

Fur trading had transforming effects on society because it promoted settlement. Traders worked on the edges of Euro-American habitation. Over time, fur production in these frontier areas always declined. Populations of fur-bearing animals such as beaver, having slow breeding cycles, were steadily depleted. The reliability of Indian trappers fell as their tribal cultures buckled under the strains of new values and diseases. When productivity in an area fell, fur traders pushed over the horizon. In their wake arrived settlers using fresh maps and trails. Farms and towns sprouted. Indians were killed or dislodged. This unsentimental cycle of the fur trade, repeated over and over, generated the waves of migration that settled much of the United States.

ASTOR ENTERS THE FUR BUSINESS

Astor made his way to New York where he got a job selling bakery goods. He invested most of his $2-a-week pay in small trinkets and in his spare time prowled the waterfront for Indians who might have a fur to trade. Within a year he had picked up enough skins to take a ship back to London, where he established connections with fur-trading houses. This was a phenomenal achievement for an immigrant lad of 21 who had been nearly penniless on his arrival in America, and it revealed Astor's deadly serious and hard-driving personality.

Astor worked briefly with a fur dealer in New York City during which time he trekked into the forests of upstate New York to bargain for furs. He soon left his employer and by 1787 was working solely for himself. He demonstrated sharp negotiating skills in trading trinkets for furs and soon built up an impressive business. One neighbor said:

> Many times I have seen John Jacob Astor with his coat off, unpacking in a vacant yard near my residence a lot of furs he had bought dog-cheap off the Indians and beating them out, cleaning them and repacking them in more elegant and salable form to be transported to England and Germany, where they would yield him 1,000 percent on the original costs.[1]

Astor made great profits and expanded his business but, like other Americans, he was blocked from harvesting furs in the forests of the Northwest Territory. The Northwest Territory was the huge unsettled area between the Ohio River and the Mississippi River bounded on the north by the Great Lakes. After the Revolutionary War, Great Britain had ceded this area to the United States but continued to maintain forts and troops there because the American government was too weak to enforce its rights. British fur-trading companies exploited the area and incited Indians to attack traders and settlers who dared enter.

This British audacity pushed Congress near to declaring war. To avoid hostilities, England agreed to a treaty in 1794[2] that required removal of British troops and gave both British and Americans trading rights in the Northwest Territory. "Now," said Astor on hearing this news, "I will make my fortune in the fur trade."[3] But he was stunned when President George Washington proposed befriending the Indians by setting up government fur-trading posts to be run with benevolent policies. These posts would compete with Astor and other private traders. Congress approved the plan, which required that trade goods be sold at cost, prohibited the use of liquor, and required payment of fair prices for furs.

The government trading posts infuriated Astor, who moved quickly to undercut them. He saturated the territory with his agents, instructing them to buy every fur they could get their hands on before competitors did. He bought trade goods in huge quantities to lower the cost, and his agents paid for furs with these trinkets. And he allowed liquor to flow freely during trade negotiations, creating an advantage the government could not match.

Astor had great success with these tactics. The government lacked his nimbleness and commitment, and he outwitted other rivals. In less than 10 years he was the second-richest man in America (after only Stephen Girard, the shipping magnate and banker). Having accumulated deep resources, the Astor juggernaut turned toward the West.

THE LOUISIANA PURCHASE

In 1803 the territory of the United States more than doubled with the Louisiana Purchase. President Thomas Jefferson agreed to purchase from France for $15 million approximately 800,000 square miles of land between the Mississippi River and the Rocky Mountains and running north from New Orleans to the forty-ninth parallel, which is now the Canada–U.S. boundary. At the time, little was known about the area called the Louisiana Territory. No accurate or complete maps existed; even its exact boundaries were vague. But Louisiana was beautiful in its mystery.

---

[1] A "Gentleman of Schenectady," quoted in John Upton Terrell, *Furs by Astor* (New York: Morrow, 1963), p. 55.

[2] The treaty was negotiated for the United States by John Jay and is known as Jay's Treaty.

[3] Terrell, *Furs by Astor,* p. 93.

Some geographers thought it was largely an arid desert. Others predicted a lush, fertile land over which Jefferson's ideal of an agrarian republic could spread. Rumors of geological wonders, horrific animals, and strange natives circulated, including the story of a tribe of bow-hunting, man-hating female savages in which the archers had their right breasts removed to keep them from interfering with the bowstrings.[4]

Jefferson himself had a clear vision of how to use the new territory. He did not believe it could be settled right away, and until it could, he wanted to populate it with Indians and fur traders. In his 1803 message to Congress, he proposed to relocate into Louisiana eastern tribes getting in the way of American settlers, and over the next 50 years this occurred many times.[5] He also ordered an Expedition of Discovery headed by Meriwether Lewis and William Clark to explore on foot the unknown territory.

A primary purpose of the Lewis and Clark expedition was to determine the suitability of Louisiana for the fur trade. The adventurers set out on a round-trip march between St. Louis and the Pacific Ocean, going where no white American had gone before, and on their return in 1806 reported a wondrous land "richer in beaver and otter than any country on earth."[6] They also reported that most Indian tribes in the territory were friendly to Americans and the fur trade. These discoveries were not lost on fur traders, among them John Jacob Astor.

THE AMERICAN FUR COMPANY IS BORN

The Lewis and Clark expedition was a catalyst for fur-trading in the new territory. Beaver production in the Northwest Territory was already beginning to fall off. Beavers reproduce slowly, and their populations quickly decline when trapping begins, especially when no restraint is practiced, as was the case in those days. Immediately, the North West Company, Astor's

[4] Ben Gilbert, *The Trailblazers* (New York: Time-Life Books, 1973), p. 18.

[5] For a list of 24 relocations, see Cardinal Goodwin, *The Trans-Mississippi West (1803–1853)* (New York: Appleton, 1922), plate following p. 88.

[6] Quoted in David J. Wishart, *The Fur Trade of the American West (1807–1840): A Geographical Synthesis* (Lincoln: University of Nebraska Press, 1979), p. 19, citing the original journals of the trip.

main competitor in the old Northwest Territory, began to move down from Canada to trade for beaver skins with Great Plains Indians. Its intent was to harvest the newly discovered fur resources in the Louisiana Territory as rapidly as possible.

However, it had to reckon with Astor, who wanted the prize himself. In his distant New York City study, Astor pored over maps of the fur-rich areas discovered by Lewis and Clark, hatching a vast and daring plan for a new company that would string trading posts over a 2,000-mile route.

In those days, state legislatures had exclusive power to create a company by issuing a charter that listed the conditions of its existence. So he approached the governor and legislature of New York seeking to charter a company to be known as the American Fur Company.

To sell the idea, he cloaked his mercenary scheme with a veil of patriotism. He argued that most of the furs taken from the Louisiana territory went to Canadians and British, thereby depriving America of trade revenue. His new company would drive the foreigners out. He would join with 10 or 12 other wealthy entrepreneurs to capitalize the new company, which would then issue stock to others. The new company would enhance U.S. security by establishing a strong presence of American citizens over unpopulated areas. And finally, Astor promised that his company would deal honestly with the Indians and drive out smaller, irresponsible traders. The legislators of New York, responding more to Astor's open pocketbook than to the credibility of his arguments, passed a charter setting up the American Fur Company. Soon President Jefferson wrote a letter to Astor giving his blessing to the new company also.

Astor proceeded to take on four partners and establish a board of directors for the American Fur Company as the charter required. However, he retained 99.9 percent of the stock, elected himself president, and subsequently declared dividends whenever he wanted to compensate himself. The partnership was a fiction; Astor never intended to share either the proceeds of the company or any portion of the fur trade that he could control.

In 1810 he made his first move. His ship, the *Tonquin*, sailed to the mouth of the Columbia River on the Pacific Coast and set up a trading post named Astoria. At this time, Britain and the United States contested the wild area known as Oregon territory, consisting of present-day Oregon and Washington. Astor got diplomatic support for his trading post by arguing that its presence established an American claim to the territory. Secretly, however, he hoped to form a new nation called Astoria and make himself king.

Meanwhile, he would make Astoria one end of a vise that would squeeze competitors out of the new fur areas. Furs taken in the west would come to Astoria and then be shipped to China, which was a major fur market, or to New York. By this time, Astor owned a fleet of ships with which to do this. The other end of the vise would be St. Louis. Furs from Astor's planned string of trading posts on the eastern slopes of the Rocky Mountains would come down the Missouri River system to St. Louis and from there go overland to New York or on to the port of New Orleans to be shipped to Europe. It was a megalomaniac scheme, and no one but Astor had both the nerve and the resources even to attempt it. But it was too grandiose. Only part of it was to work, and the rest worked only until the fur trade fell apart.

THE ROAD TO MONOPOLY

In 1813 Astor's plan suffered a great reversal when he was forced to sell Astoria to the British during the War of 1812. He sold out at a fraction of its value because British soldiers were in a position to seize it as a war prize. Without Astoria as a foothold in the Oregon territory, he was unable to compete with British and Canadian fur companies. And 61 of Astor's employees died pursuing the settlement, along with hundreds of natives they came in conflict with.[7] Unbowed, Astor later commissioned Washington Irving, the best-selling author of the day, to write a book about the intrepid adventurers and himself as the great mind behind them.[8]

Despite the loss of Astoria, Astor nonetheless predominated. In 1816 his lobbying succeeded in getting Congress to pass a law forbidding foreigners from trading furs in U.S. territories. This prevented Canadian and British companies from operating in the Northwest Territory, and Astor immediately bought out their interests, giving him a monopoly in furs east of the Missouri River. Blocked from the Pacific Coast trade by the British presence, he turned his attention to the upper-Missouri fur trade.

Astor bided his time as other fur companies pioneered trading in the northern Great Plains and then, after discovery of rich valleys of beaver, in the Rocky Mountains. By 1822 Astor had established a presence selling trade goods and buying furs in St. Louis, but he waited as other companies sent expensive expeditions of traders and mountain men up the Missouri, absorbing heavy losses of men and money. Despite losses, these pioneering companies found tremendous reserves of beaver in Rocky Mountain valleys, mapped new routes, and discovered advantageous locations for trading posts.

Then he crushed the competition. In 1826 he merged with Bernard Pratte & Company, an established firm, using it as an agent. He bought out and liquidated another competitor, Stone, Bostwick & Company. In 1827 he broke the Columbia Fur Company by building his own trading posts next to every one of theirs, engaging in cutthroat price competition for furs, and plying Indians liberally with whiskey. His trappers shadowed Columbia Fur Company trapping parties to discover where the rich sources of beaver were, then muscled into the areas. Using similar tactics, he bankrupted Menard & Valle. Now, according to Astor's biographer Terrell:

> Competition on the Missouri River was all but nonexistent. What remained was inconsequential, and might have been likened to a terrier yapping at a bear. The bear lumbered on, ignoring the noise until it became aggravating. Then with the sudden swipe of a paw, the yapping was forever stilled.[9]

Astor made astonishing profits. He would buy, for example, a 10-pound keg of gunpowder for $2, or 20 cents a pound, in London and transport it to his trading posts using his ships. He paid himself a 2 percent commission for buying the trade goods, or $.04 cents on the keg of gunpowder. He paid himself a freight charge for carrying the gunpowder on his ship to New Orleans. From there the keg was transported up the Missouri using the inexpensive labor of his hired trappers and traders. The gunpowder was valued at $4 a pound to the Indians, who were not allowed to pay money for it but got it only by exchanging furs or on credit. In the 1820s Astor charged one 2-pound beaver skin for each pound of gunpowder, getting 10 skins weighing 20 pounds for the keg of gunpowder. These skins were transported back to

---

[7] Axel Madsen, *John Jacob Astor: America's First Multimillionaire* (New York: Wiley, 2001), p. 163.

[8] *Astoria; or, Enterprise beyond the Rocky Mountains* (New York: The Century Co., 1909); originally published in 1839.

[9] Terrell, *Furs by Astor,* p. 391.

Portrait of John Jacob Astor. © Bettman/Corbis.

were often just as good. Trade goods, however, had mystical significance beyond their utility or monetary value. Their allure lay in magical, spiritual qualities. Indians believed that the future could be seen by looking in a reflection of the self. Because manufactured mirrors gave a clearer reflection than water they were a wondrous advance in prophecy. They thought guns had supernatural properties, because they created thunder, an event associated with the spiritual world. They thought pots and kettles were alive, because they rang or sang out when hit. Thus, Indians found supernatural qualities in trade goods that were lost on Europeans.[11]

Astor encouraged Indians to take trade goods on credit. As a result, some tribes—the Winnebagos, Sacs, Foxes, Cherokees, Chickasaws, and Sioux—were hopelessly mired in debt, owing the American Fur Company as much as $50,000 each. Since trinkets had sky-high markups, Astor could not lose much even if tribal debts grew, but indebtedness forced tribes to trade furs with him rather than with competitors.

His traders and trappers fared no better. He marked up trade goods heavily before selling them to traders. Often, traders were in debt to Astor or had mortgaged their trading posts to him and were forced to mark up goods heavily themselves before selling them to Indians and trappers. Trappers employed by the American Fur Company were ruthlessly exploited. They worked unlimited hours in hazardous conditions and extreme weather, but when Astor achieved dominance in an area, he cut their salaries from $100 a year to $250 every three years. They had to buy trade goods and staples at markups that were higher than those charged Indians to get furs. Whiskey costing $.30 a gallon in St. Louis was diluted with water and sold to them at $3 a pint. Coffee and sugar costing $.10 a pound was sold for $2 at trading posts up the Missouri. Clothing was marked up 300 to 400 percent.

Astor had contrived a lucrative, pitiless system that amplified his fortune by diminishing those caught in its workings. Though never venturing out West, he was in touch, working long hours, his shrewd mind obsessed with the most minor details and with squeezing out the smallest unnecessary expenses. In 1831 his son William estimated American Fur Company

London, where they were worth $7 a pound or $140. From the $140 Astor deducted a 5 percent commission, or $7, for brokering the sale of the furs. Astor also subtracted 25 percent, or $35 from the $140, for the estimated costs of transportation and wages.

All told, this left a net profit for the American Fur Company of $97.96, or 4,900 percent on the original $2 investment.[10] And Astor owned over 99 percent of the company's shares. This profitable arithmetic was repeated on a wide range of trade goods. The value of trade goods lay not in their utility, but in Indian beliefs. Indians coveted them so much that they considered whites foolish to exchange even the smallest trinkets for beaver skins that were abundant in the forests. The idea of material acquisition beyond basic needs was foreign to most Indian cultures. The Arikaras, for example, believed that a person who had more possessions than needed to survive ought to give the excess to others. Offering money to Indians did not motivate them to trap and process furs; they were indifferent to accumulating currency.

Trade goods such as rifles, knives, clothing, blankets, beads, and trinkets were useful, making them attractive to the Indians, but native-made equivalents

---

[10] These calculations are based on figures in ibid., pp. 397–98.

[11] Richard White, "Expansion and Exodus," in Betty Ballantine and Ian Ballantine, eds., *The Native Americans: An Illustrated History* (Atlanta: Turner, 1993), chap. 14.

revenues of "not less than $500,000" yearly.[12] Astor was by now the richest man in America. He began to buy real estate in and around New York City.

ASTOR RACES ON

In the early 1830s it seemed nothing could slow Astor. Men who hated the American Fur Company started competing firms, but few lasted. Astor destroyed them by underbidding for furs and debauching the Indians with alcohol.

In 1832 Congress prohibited bringing alcohol into Indian territories, but the law was mostly ignored. Astor never favored using alcohol. It raised costs. However, many competitors saw inebriation as their only hope of seducing Indians with furs away from him. Astor, obsessed with defeating his rivals, let the spirits flow despite sad consequences.

Alcohol was unknown in native cultures; Indians developed a craving for it only after European traders introduced intoxication into fur price negotiations. Some thought that spirits occupied their bodies when they drank. Among Indians who took to whiskey, a new desire was created, a desire that motivated them to produce furs. A few tribes, notably the Pawnee, Crow, and Arikara, never imbibed. Most did, however, and some were so debilitated that their fur production fell and traders moved on.

Astor smuggled liquor as needed past Indian agents. He ordered construction of a still at the confluence of the Yellowstone and Missouri rivers, producing enough spirits to keep tribes in several states in a constant drunken state. Congress could not enforce its will because the federal government had almost no presence in vast areas of the West. Statutes were meaningless where no authorities stood to enforce them. In Indian country, the only law was the will of leaders of trading companies and brigades of trappers who wore self-designed, military-style uniforms and could rob, cheat, and murder both Indians and whites with impunity. An 1831 report to Lewis Cass, Secretary of War, stated:

> The traders that occupy the largest and most important space in the Indian country are the agents and engagees of the American Fur Trade Company. They

entertain, as I know to be the fact, no sort of respect for our citizens, agents, officers of the Government, or its laws or general policy.[13]

Government officials such as Cass were disinclined to thwart Astor in any case since they were frequently in his pay. Cass, who was the federal official in charge of enforcing the prohibition law, was paid $35,000 by the American Fur Company between 1817 and 1834.[14] At one time, Astor even advanced a personal loan of $5,000 to President James Monroe. Over the years, the Astor lobby achieved most of its objectives in Washington, DC, and state capitals, including heavy tariffs on imported furs and abolition of the government fur-trading posts so beloved to Washington and Jefferson. Under these circumstances, it is not surprising that the government failed to regulate the fur trade.

In 1831 Astor introduced a new technological innovation, the steamboat *Yellowstone*, which could travel 50 to 100 miles a day up the Missouri, transporting supplies to his posts. Keelboats used by competitors made only twenty miles upriver on a good day and exposed men pulling them with ropes from the bank to hostile Indian fire. Upriver Indians were awestruck by the *Yellowstone* and traveled hundreds of miles to see the spirit that walked on water. Some tribes refused to trade with the Hudson Bay Company any longer, believing that because of the *Yellowstone* it could no longer compete with the American Fur Company.

THE ENVIRONMENT OF THE FUR TRADE CHANGES

Although the American Fur Company was ascendant, unfavorable trends were building that would bring it down. Demand for beaver was falling as the fashion trends that made every European and American gentleman want a beaver hat waned. Silk hats became the new rage. Also, new ways of felting hats without using fibrous underhair from beaver pelts had developed, and nutria pelts from South America were entering the market.

These were not the only problems. In 1832 trade came to a near standstill during a worldwide cholera epidemic because many people thought the disease was spread on transported furs. Beaver populations were depleted by overtrapping. The fur companies made no

[12] Gustavus Myers, *History of the Great American Fortunes* (New York: Modern Library, 1936), p. 102; originally published in 1909.

[13] Report of Andrew S. Hughes, quoted in ibid., p. 99.

[14] Myers, *History of the Great American Fortunes,* p. 103.

conservation efforts; the incentive was rather to trap all beaver in an area, leaving none for competitors. In the 1820s the Hudson Bay Company tried to prevent Astor from moving into Oregon territory by exterminating beaver along a band of terrain to create a "fur desert" that would be unprofitable for Astor's trappers to cross.

Losses of human life rose as mountain men entered the shrinking areas where beaver were still abundant, leaving behind somewhat friendly Indians such as the Snake and Crow to encounter more hostile tribes such as the Blackfeet, who poisoned their arrows with rattlesnake venom and conducted open war against trappers.[15] One study of 446 mountain men actively trapping between 1805 and 1845 found that 182, or 41 percent, were killed in the occupation.[16]

Astor knew that the fur industry was doomed. Beaver pelts that had fetched $6 a pound in 1830 brought only $3.50 a pound by 1833. In that year he liquidated all his fur-trading interests. He spent the rest of his life accumulating more money in New York real estate. For a time, the American Fur Company continued under new owners, but the industry environment continued to worsen. In 1837 the firm's steamboat *St. Peters* carried smallpox up the Missouri, killing more than 17,000 natives, and an agent observed that "our most profitable Indians have died."[17] By 1840 the firm had withdrawn from the Rocky Mountains and focused on buffalo robes, which remained profitable for some time.

ASTOR'S LAST YEARS

Astor lived on in New York, wringing immense profits from rents and leases as the city grew around his real estate holdings. By 1847 he had built a fortune of $20 million that towered above any other of that day. This sum has been estimated to be the equivalent of $78 billion today, more than the wealth of Microsoft's Bill Gates.[18] In his last years he was weak and frail and exercised by having attendants toss him up and down in a blanket. Yet despite his physical deterioration, he remained focused on getting every last penny from his tenants, poring over the rents for long hours behind the barred windows of his office.

Astor gave little to charity, and social critics attacked him for his stinginess. When he died in 1848, his major gift to society was $460,000 in his will for building an Astor Library. In addition, he left $50,000 to the town of Waldorf, Germany, his birthplace; $30,000 for the German Society of New York; and $30,000 to the Home for Aged Ladies in New York City. This totaled, in the words of one commentator, less than "the proceeds of one year's pillage of the Indians."[19] The rest of his wealth went to his heirs. As to how America felt about him, one obituary minced no words.

> No doubt he had many fine, noble qualities, but avarice seemed to hold an all-conquering sway.... [W]hat a vast amount of good he might have rendered the world! But how reverse is the case—he dies and no one mourns! His soul was eaten up with avarice. Charity and benevolence found not a congenial home in his cold and frigid bosom![20]

THE LEGACY OF THE FUR TRADE

For 300 years the fur trade shaped the economic, political, and cultural life of both native and European inhabitants of the raw North American continent. Its climactic era has often been depicted as a progressive and romantic period when trading posts represented "civilization which was slowly mastering the opposition of nature and barbarism."[21] According to historian Dan Elbert Clark:

> The fur traders, with all their faults and shortcomings, were the pathfinders of civilization. They marked the trails that were followed by settlers. They built trading posts where later appeared thriving towns and cities. They knew the Indians better than any other class of white men who came among them.[22]

[15] Trappers also attacked Blackfeet without provocation. See Osborne Russell, *Journal of a Trapper* (Lincoln: University of Nebraska Press, 1955), pp. 52, 86.

[16] William H. Goetzmann, "The Mountain Man as Jacksonian Man," *American Quarterly,* Fall 1963, p. 409.

[17] Jacob Halsey, a clerk at Fort Pierre, quoted in Wishart, *The Fur Trade of the American West,* p. 68.

[18] This is the estimate of Michael Klepper and Robert Gunther in "The American Heritage 40," *American Heritage,* October 1998, p. 56.

[19] Myers, *History of the Great American Fortunes,* p. 149.

[20] "John Jacob Astor," *Appleton's Journal of Literature, Science and Art,* June 1, 1848, p. 116.

[21] Arthur D. Howden Smith, *John Jacob Astor: Landlord of New York* (Philadelphia: Lippincott, 1929), p. 131.

[22] Dan Elbert Clark, *The West in American History* (New York: Thomas Y. Crowell, 1937), p. 441.

The American Fur Company and its competitors greatly advanced geographical knowledge and blazed trails. The fur industry reinforced central American values such as rugged individualism, the frontier spirit, and optimism about the inevitability of progress. Yet there is also a dark side to the story. Traders undermined Indian cultures by introducing new economic motivations. Tribal societies were destroyed by alcohol, smallpox, and venereal disease. "The fur trade," according to Professor David J. Wishart of the University of Nebraska, "was the vanguard of a massive wave of Euro-American colonisation which brought into contact two sets of cultures with disparate and irreconcilable ways of life."[23]

The industry also left extensive ecological damage in its wake. It slaughtered animal populations and denuded riverside forest areas to get steamboat fuel. Astor's mentality of pillage set a destructive standard. Argues Wishart: "The attitude of rapacious, short-term exploitation which was imprinted during the fur trade persisted after 1840 as the focus shifted from furs to minerals, timber, land, and water."[24]

The American Fur Company, now largely forgotten, was the main actor in a global industry with enormous geopolitical power. The firm's operation was like a test-tube experiment on the social consequences of raw, unrestrained capitalism. It would be many years before the American nation gave thought to the lessons.

[23] Wishart, *The Fur Trade of the American West*, p. 215.
[24] Ibid., p. 212.

Questions

1. How would you evaluate Astor in terms of his motive, his managerial ability, and his ethics? What lesson does his career teach about the relationship between virtue and success?

2. How did the environment of the American Fur Company change in the 1830s? What deep historical forces are implicated in these changes?

3. What were the impacts of the fur trade on society in major dimensions of the business environment, that is, economic, cultural, technological, natural, governmental, legal, and internal?

4. Who were the most important stakeholders of the nineteenth-century fur industry? Were they treated responsibly by the standards of the day? By the standards of today?

5. On balance, is the legacy of the American Fur Company and of the fur trade itself a positive legacy? Or is the impact predominantly negative?

6. Does the story of the American Fur Company hint at how and why capitalism has changed and has been changed over the years?

7. Do one or more models of the business–government–society relationship discussed in Chapter 1 apply to the historical era set forth in this case? Which model or models have explanatory power and why?

Chapter **Three**

Business Power

James B. Duke and the American Tobacco Company

On December 23, 1856, the first cries of new life swelled from a North Carolina farmhouse, their source a baby boy named James Buchanan Duke. The lad would have far more impact on the world than the failed president his name was intended to honor.

Soon, the Civil War displaced the Duke family from its land. On returning home in 1865 little James's father built a small factory to manufacture a brand of chewing tobacco named Pro Bono Publico (a Latin phrase meaning "for the public good"). James helped. He was a precocious, energetic boy who became the driving force behind the business.

By his late teens, James had visions of grandeur for the little factory. But the presence of a rival firm, the Bull Durham Co., thwarted them. Its chewing tobacco was so dominant that head-on competition seemed hopeless. In a major gamble he committed the company to a lesser product—the cigarette. This was a venturesome move, because few people smoked then. Most tobacco users were rural men and they associated cigarettes with degenerate dudes and dandies in cities.

In 1881 Duke brought 10 Russian immigrants to his North Carolina factory and set them to work rolling cigarettes. Each made about 2,000 per day. At first he had trouble selling them. Tobacco shops refused to order his Duke of Durham brand because customers never asked for them. But Duke was a merchandising genius. In Atlanta, he put up a billboard of a famous actress holding Duke cigarettes in her outstretched hand. The use of a woman to advertise cigarettes created a sensation and, along with it, demand. In St. Louis, Duke confronted extreme prejudice against cigarettes. Tobacco shop proprietors simply would not place orders. He had his agents hire a young, redheaded widow to call on the tobacconists, and she got 19 orders on her first day.

By this time a Virginia engineer, James Bonsack, had invented a machine capable of rolling 200 cigarettes per minute. He offered it first to the largest tobacco companies, but they turned him down, believing that smokers would reject newfangled, machine-rolled cigarettes. Duke saw the significance of the technology and jumped at it.[1] In 1883 he negotiated an exclusive agreement to operate the device and his competitors never recovered. With the new Bonsack machines, Duke simultaneously

[1] Patrick G. Porter, "Origins of the American Tobacco Company," *Business History Review,* Spring 1969, pp. 68–69.

Duke lured men to try his new cigarette brands by putting picture cards in packs. The first cards were stage actresses in poses that were provocative for that day. Later card series included Indian chiefs, perilous occupations, ocean and river steamers, coins, musical instruments, flags, fish, ships, and prize fighters. Source: Emergence of Advertising in America, 1850–1920: Selections from the Collections of Duke University, Rare Book, Manuscript, and Special Collections Library, Duke University.

cut manufacturing costs from $.80 per thousand to $.30 and multiplied factory production by many times.[2]

To find new markets for this swollen output, Duke first went to New York City, where he rented a loft and set up a small cigarette factory. Then he moved to create demand. He was tireless, working twelve hours a day in the factory, then making the rounds of tobacco shops at night. He gave secret rebates and cash payments to friendly dealers. He hired people to visit tobacco shops and demand his new machine-rolled Cameo and Cross Cuts brands. Immigrants were welcomed with free samples as they emerged from the New York Immigration Station to set foot in America for the first time. Ingeniously, he put numbered cards with glamour photos of actresses in his cigarette packs, encouraging men to complete a collection. Late at night he haunted the streets, picking up crumpled cigarette packs from sidewalks and trash cans, creating a crude sales count.

Overseas, Duke's minions were also at work. One great conquest was China. At the time a few Chinese, mostly older men, smoked a bitter native tobacco in pipes. Cigarettes were unknown. Duke sent experts to Shantung Province with bright leaf

[2] John K. Winkler, *Tobacco Tycoon: The Story of James Buchanan Duke* (New York: Random House, 1942), p. 56.

from North Carolina to cultivate a milder tobacco. His sales force hired "teachers" to walk village streets showing curious Chinese how to light and hold cigarettes. He installed Bonsak machines in four huge manufacturing plants that soon ran 24 hours a day. And he unleashed on the Chinese a full range of promotional activities. At one time his cigarette packs contained pictures of seminude American actresses, which were a big hit with Chinese men. In this way, Duke turned China into a nation of smokers.

Back home his tactics wore down competitors. He carefully observed John D. Rockefeller's conquest of the oil industry and saw that Rockefeller's methods could be applied to the tobacco industry. In 1884, at the age of 26, he engineered a combination of his firm and other large firms into a holding company known as the American Tobacco trust. As president, Duke built the trust into a monopoly that controlled 98 percent of the domestic cigarette market in 1892, a year in which 2.9 billion cigarettes were sold.[3] Not content with domination alone, he worked tirelessly to expand the tobacco market. By 1903, more than 10 billion cigarettes were sold in the United States.[4] Over two decades his combination ruthlessly swallowed or bankrupted 250 firms until it dominated the cigar, snuff, and smoking tobacco markets too.

Duke used a simple method to strangle competitors. Instead of selling its output at wholesale prices, Duke's company "consigned" its products to dealers. The dealers had to pay full retail price for tobacco goods sent to them "on consignment" and do so within ten days of receipt. Three months later, the company paid the dealer a "commission," which was the dealer's profit. Dealers who sold competitors' brands were not eligible to receive this "commission," so they could not make a profit on the brands that the vast majority of their customers wanted. Duke's combination used detectives to spy on dealers and enforce this scheme. Many dealers disliked this arrogant, coercive system, but they had to play along or wither away.

Duke's monopoly lasted until 1911, when the Supreme Court ordered it broken up.[5] Duke himself figured out how to divide the giant firm into four independent companies: Ligget & Myers, P. Lorillard, R. J. Reynolds, and a new American Tobacco Company. After the breakup he retired from the tobacco industry to start an electric utility, Duke Power & Light. He also gave money to a small North Carolina college, which became Duke University. He died of complications from pernicious anemia in 1925.

Duke's career illustrates the power of commerce to shape society. He made the cigarette an acceptable consumer product and spread it around the world. His monopoly destroyed rivals and defined the structure of the tobacco industry. Its influence checked the early efforts of antitobacco leagues to publicize health hazards. His bribes to legislators blocked antismoking laws. And, owing largely to Duke's ingenuity, growing tobacco trade revived the crippled post–Civil War southern economy. Eventually, he ran into a hard check on power when the Supreme Court dismantled his colossus, but his work endures in the roll call of smokers across 130 years.

[3] "Iron Heel of Monopoly," *New York Times,* December 28, 1892, p. 10.
[4] "The Caesar of Tobacco," *The Wall Street Journal,* June 27, 1903, p. 6.
[5] *United States v. American Tobacco Company,* 221 U.S. 106 (1911).

THE NATURE OF BUSINESS POWER

Business has tremendous power to change society, and the extent of this power is underappreciated. In past eras, companies in ascending industries changed societies by altering all three of their primary elements—ideas, institutions, and material things. This effect is visible in the stories of dominant companies such as the American Tobacco Company, the American Fur Company, and the Standard Oil Trust. The cumulative power of all business is a massive, irrepressible shaping force. In this chapter we explain the underlying dynamics of this power to change society. We then discuss its limits.

WHAT IS POWER?

power
The force or strength to act or to compel another entity to act.

Power is the force or strength to act or to compel another entity to act. It exists on a wide spectrum ranging from coercion at one extreme to weak influence at the other. Its use in human society creates change. Although power is sometimes exerted to prevent change, such resistance is itself a force that alters history. There are many sources of power, including wealth, position, knowledge, law, arms, status, and charisma. Power is unevenly distributed, and all societies have mechanisms to control and channel it for wide or narrow benefit. These mechanisms, which are imperfect, include governments, laws, police, cultural values, and public opinion. Also, multiple, competing formations of power may check and balance each other.

business power
The force behind an act by a company, industry, or sector.

Business power is the force behind an act by a company, industry, or sector. The greater this force, the more the action creates change or influences the actions of other entities in society. Its basic origin is a grant of authority from society to convert resources efficiently into needed goods and services. In return for doing this, society gives corporations the authority to take necessary actions and permits a profit. This agreement derives from the social contract.

legitimacy
The rightful use of power. Its opposite is tyranny, or the exercise of power beyond right.

The social contract legitimizes business power by giving it a moral basis. *Legitimacy* is the rightful use of power. The power of giant corporations is legitimate when it is exercised in keeping with the agreed-upon contract.[6] The philosopher John Locke wrote that for governments the opposite of legitimacy is tyranny, defined as "the exercise of power beyond right."[7] Corporations breach the social contract, exercising "power beyond right," when they violate social values, endanger the public, or act illegally.

Business power is legitimate when it is used for the common good. The grounds of legitimacy vary between societies and over time. Child labor, once widespread in the United States, is no longer permitted, but it exists in other nations. As we will see in subsequent chapters, the definition of the common good that business must serve has expanded throughout American history and is now expanding globally.

---

[6] For an effort to stipulate social contract norms that should guide business behavior, see Thomas Donaldson and Thomas W. Dunfee, *Ties That Bind: A Social Contracts Approach to Business Ethics* (Boston: Harvard Business School Press, 1999).

[7] John Locke, *The Second Treatise of Government* (New York: Bobbs-Merrill, 1952), p. 112; originally published in 1690.

LEVELS AND SPHERES OF CORPORATE POWER

Corporate actions have an impact on society at two levels, and on each level they create change. On the *surface level,* business power is the direct cause of visible, immediate changes, both great and small. Corporations expand and contract, hire and fire; they make and sell products.

On a *deep level,* corporate power shapes society over time through the aggregate changes of industrial growth. At this level, corporate power creates many indirect, unforeseen, and invisible effects. Multiple lines of events converge and interact in complex networks of cause and effect. At this deep level, the workings of corporate power are unplanned, unpredictable, and slow to appear, but they are far more significant. Corporate power "is something more than men," wrote John Steinbeck. "It's the monster. Men made it, but they can't control it."[8] This is a poetic but accurate description of business power at a deep level.

On both the surface and deep levels, business power is exercised in spheres corresponding to the seven business environments set forth in Chapter 2.

- *Economic power* is the ability of the corporation to influence events, activities, and people by virtue of control over resources, particularly property. At the surface level, the operation of a corporation may immediately and visibly affect its stakeholders, for example, by building or closing a factory. At a deeper level, the accumulating impact of corporate economic activity has sweeping effects. For example, over many years corporations have created enough wealth to raise dramatically living standards in industrialized nations.

- *Technological power* is the ability to influence the direction, rate, characteristics, and consequences of physical innovations as they develop. On a surface level, in 1914, assembly lines run by new electric motors allowed Henry Ford to introduce transportation based on the internal combustion engine. Using this method, he turned an expensive luxury of the rich into a mass consumer product. But at a deeper level, as the auto took hold in American society it created unanticipated consequences. One juvenile court judge in the 1920s called the automobile a "house of prostitution on wheels," something that the puritanical Henry Ford doubtless never intended to create.[9]

- *Political power* is the ability to influence governments. On the surface, corporations give money to candidates and lobby legislatures. On a deeper level around the world industrialization engenders values that radiate freedom and erode authoritarian regimes.

- *Legal power* is the ability to shape the laws of society. On the surface, big corporations have formidable legal resources that intimidate opponents. On a deeper level, the laws of the United States—including constitutional, civil, and criminal laws—have been shaped by the consequences of industrial activity.

[8] *The Grapes of Wrath* (New York: Viking Press, 1939), p. 45.

[9] Frederick Lewis Allen, *Only Yesterday: An Informal History of the 1920s* (New York: Harper & Brothers, 1931), p. 100.

American Landscape, a 1930 oil painting, depicts Ford Motor Company's River Rouge plant. Here artist Charles Sheeler makes a comment on the power of business to change and shape society. Outwardly, this vista seems to beautify and ennoble the architecture of industry, making it appear almost pastoral. Yet on another level the painting provokes anxiety. Factory buildings run nature off the scene, dominating a landscape that is now, but for the sky, entirely artificial. A tiny human figure in the middle ground is overwhelmed and marginalized by the massive complex; its movement is limited and regimented by the surrounding industrial structure. Here, then, art reveals emotions about industrial growth in a way that words cannot. This theme is found in other Sheeler paintings and photographs. Source: Charles Sheeler, *American Landscape.* 1930. Oil on Canvas, 24″ × 31″ (61 × 78.8 cm). The Museum of Modern Art, New York. Gift of Abby Aldrich Rockefeller. © The Museum of Modern Art. Licensed by SCALA/Art Resource, NY.

- *Cultural power* is the ability to influence cultural values, habits, and institutions such as the family. John Wanamaker, founder of a department store chain and a master of advertising, started Mother's Day in the early 1900s. He ran full-page ads in the *Philadelphia Inquirer* about a woman mourning for her mother, creating the sentiment that gratitude for mothers should be expressed by a gift on a special day.[10] At a deeper level, the cumulative impact of ads has altered American society by reinforcing values selectively, for example, materialism

---

[10] Richard Wolkomir and Joyce Wolkomir, "You Are What You Buy," *Smithsonian*, May 2000, p. 107.

over asceticism, individualism over community, or personal appearance over inner character.

- *Environmental power* is the impact of a company on nature. On the surface, a power plant may pollute the air; on a deeper level, since the seventeenth century, emission of gases in the burning of wood, coal, and oil to power industry has altered the chemistry of earth's atmosphere. One study found that since 1882 the Standard Oil Trust and its successor companies have contributed between 4.7 and 5.2 percent of worldwide carbon dioxide emissions.[11]
- *Power over individuals* is exercised over employees, managers, stockholders, consumers, and citizens. On the surface, a corporation may determine the work life and buying habits of individuals. At a deeper level, industrialism sets the pattern of daily life. People are regimented, living by clocks, moving in routes fixed by the model of an industrial city with its streets and sidewalks. Their occupation determines their status and fortune.

Activity in the economic sphere is the primary force for change. From this, change radiates into other spheres. The story of the railroad industry in the United States illustrates how an expanding industry with a radical new technology can change its environments.

THE STORY OF THE RAILROADS

When small railroads sprang up in the 1820s, most passengers and freight moved by horse and over canals. The railroad was a vastly superior conveyance and was bound to revolutionize transportation. Tracks cost less to build than canals and did not freeze in winter. Routes could be more direct. For the first time in history, people and cargo traveled overland at faster than the speed of a horse. The trip from New York to Chicago was reduced from three weeks to just three days. And the cost of moving goods and passengers was less; in a day a train could go back and forth many times over the distance that a canal boat or wagon could traverse once.

The initial boom in railroading came at mid-century. In 1850 trains ran on only about 9,000 miles of track, but by 1860 more than 30,000 miles had been laid down. During that decade, 30 railroad companies completed route systems, which had significant consequences for the financial system. Tracks were expensive, and each of these enterprises was a giant for its day. Many needed $10 to $35 million in capital, and the smallest at least $2 million. Companies in other industries did not approach this size; only a handful of textile mills and steel plants had required capitalization of more than $1 million.[12]

The call for this much money transformed capital markets. The only place such huge sums could be raised was in large northeastern cities. Since interest rates

---

[11] Friends of the Earth International, *Exxon's Climate Footprint* (London: FOEI, January 2004), p. 5. See also Richard Heede, *Exxon Mobil Corporation Emissions Inventory: 1882–2002* (London: Friends of the Earth Trust Ltd., December 17, 2003).

[12] Alfred D. Chandler, Jr., *The Visible Hand: The Managerial Revolution in American Business* (Cambridge, MA: Belknap Press, 1977), pp. 83, 86, and 90.

were a little higher in Boston at the time, New York became the center of financial activity and has remained so to this day. Railroads sold bonds and offered stocks to raise capital, and a new investment banking industry was created. The New York Stock Exchange went from a sleepy place, where only a few hundred shares of stock might change hands each week, to a roaring market. Speculative techniques such as margin trading, short-selling, and options trading appeared for the first time. Later, the financial mechanisms inspired by railroad construction were in place when other industries needed more capital to grow. This changed American history by accelerating the industrial transformation of the late 1800s. It also put New York bankers such as J. P. Morgan in a position to control access to capital.

At first the railroads ran between existing trade centers, but as time passed and track mileage increased, they linked ever more points. The 30,626 miles of track in 1860 increased to 93,267 miles by 1880 and 163,597 miles by 1890.[13] This required enormous amounts of wood, and led to extensive clear-cuts where forests were harvested to make ties and stoke fires in early steam locomotives. A deeper consequence of extending the tracks was a society transformed.

Before tracks radiated everywhere, the United States was a nation of farmers and small towns held together by the traditional institutions of family, church, and local government. Since long-distance travel was time-consuming and arduous, these towns often were isolated. Populations were stable. People identified more with local areas than with the nation as a whole. Into this world came the train, a destabilizing technology powered by aggressive market capitalism.

Trains took away young people who might have stayed in rural society but for the lure of wealth in distant cities. In their place came a stream of outsiders who were less under the control of community values. Small-town intimacy declined, and a new phenomenon appeared in American life—the impersonal crowd of strangers. Trains violated established customs. Sunday was a day of rest and worship, so many churchgoers were angered when huffing and whistling trains intruded on services. But new capital accounting methods used by railroad companies dictated using equipment an extra day each week to increase return on investment. This imperative trumped devoutness. In early America, localities set their own time according to the sun's overhead transit, but this resulted in a patchwork of time zones that made scheduling difficult. An editorial in *Railroad Age* argued, "Local time must go."[14] For the convenience of the railroads, a General Time Convention met in 1882 and standardized the time of day, though not without resistance from holdouts who felt that "[s]urely the world ran by higher priorities than railroad scheduling."[15]

As the railroads grew, they spread impersonality and an ethic of commerce. Towns reoriented themselves around their train stations. Shops and restaurants

[13] Bureau of the Census, *Statistical Abstract of the United States,* 77th ed. (Washington, DC: U.S. Government Printing Office, 1956), table 683.

[14] Bill Kauffman, "Why Spring Ahead," *The American Enterprise,* April–May 2001, p. 50.

[15] Ibid., p. 50, quoting Michael O'Malley, *Keeping Watch: A History of American Time* (Washington, DC: Smithsonian Institution Press, 1996).

sprang up nearby so that strangers would spend money before moving on. The railroads gave more frequent service to cities with commercial possibilities and bypassed small towns or let them wither from less frequent service. This speeded urbanization and the centralization of corporate power in cities. Rural areas were redefined. Once the cultural heartland, they now were seen as backward and rustic—places best used for vacations from urban stress.

The railroads also changed American politics. On the surface, their lobbyists could dominate legislatures. On a deeper level, the changes were more profound. Congress had always selected nominees before presidential elections, but now trains brought delegates to national party nominating conventions, changing the way candidates were picked. Trains enabled all sorts of associations to have national meetings, and the rails spread issues that might in an earlier era have remained local. The movement to give women the vote, for example, succeeded after Susan B. Anthony took trains to all parts of the country, spreading her rhetoric and unifying the cause.[16]

At first government encouraged and subsidized railroads. All told, federal and state governments gave them land grants of 164 million acres, an area equal to the size of California and Nevada combined.[17] But later the challenge was to control them. When Congress passed the Interstate Commerce Act in 1887 to regulate railroads, the approach of the statute, with all its strengths and weaknesses, set the example for regulating other industries later.

Many other changes in American society are traceable to the railroads. They were the first businesses to require modern management structures. The need for precise coordination of speeding trains over vast reaches caused railroads to pioneer professional management teams, division structures, and modern cost accounting—all innovations later adopted in other industries.[18] Railroads lay behind Indian wars. For the plains Indians, the tracks that divided old hunting grounds were the main barrier to peace.[19] Thousands of laborers came from China to lay rail, and their descendants live on in communities along the lines. Railroads changed the language. The word *diner,* meaning a place to eat, appeared after the introduction of the Pullman Palace Car Company's first dining car in 1868. And social values changed. Big-city commercial values rumbled down the tracks, jolting traditions along rural byways.

TWO PERSPECTIVES ON BUSINESS POWER

There is agreement that business has great power. There is considerable disagreement about whether its power is adequately checked and balanced for the public good. Views about business power cover a wide spectrum, but there are two basic and opposing positions.

[16] These and other social and political changes are treated at length in Sarah H. Gordon, *Passage to Union* (Chicago: Ivan R. Dees, 1996).

[17] Page Smith, *The Rise of Industrial America*, vol. 6 (New York: Viking Penguin, 1984), p. 99.

[18] Chandler, *The Visible Hand*, chap. 3.

[19] Smith, *The Rise of Industrial America*, p. 89.

dominance theory
The view that business is the most powerful institution in society, because of its control of wealth. This power is inadequately checked and, therefore, excessive.

pluralist theory
The view that business power is exercised in a society where other institutions also have great power. It is counterbalanced and restricted and, therefore, not excessive.

On one side is the *dominance theory,* which holds that business is preeminent in American society, primarily because of its control of wealth, and that its power is both excessive and inadequately checked. Corporations can alter their environments in self-interested ways that harm the general welfare. This was the thesis of Karl Marx, who wrote that a ruling capitalist class exploited workers and dominated other classes. The dominance theory is the basis of the dominance model of the business–government–society relationship set forth in Chapter 1.

On the other side the *pluralist theory* holds that business power is exercised in a society in which other institutions such as markets, government, labor unions, advocacy groups, and public opinion also have great power. Business power is counterbalanced, restricted, controlled, and subject to defeat. Adam Smith was convinced that largely through market forces, business power could be disciplined to benefit society. The pluralist theory is the basis of the countervailing forces model in Chapter 1.

The Dominance Theory

In industrializing societies, business organizations grow in size and concentrate wealth. According to the dominance theory, business abuses the power its size and wealth confer in a number of ways. The rise of huge corporations creates a business elite that exercises inordinate power over public policy. Asset concentration creates monopoly or oligopoly in markets that reduces competition and harms consumers. Corporations wield financial and organizational resources unmatched by opposing interests. For example, they use campaign contributions to corrupt politicians, hire lobbyists to undermine the independence of elected officials, employ accountants and lawyers to avoid taxes, and run public relations campaigns that shape opinion in their favor. Moreover, large corporations achieve such importance in a nation's economy that elected officials are forced to adopt probusiness measures or face public wrath. "If enterprises falter for lack of inducement to invest, hire, and produce," writes one advocate of the dominance theory, "members of the political elite are more likely than those of the entrepreneurial elite to lose their positions."[20] We will discuss further the growth in size and wealth of corporations and the presence of elites in the American context.

Corporate Asset Concentration

The idea that concentration of economic power results in abuse arose, in part, as an intellectual reaction to the awesome economic growth of the late nineteenth century. Until then, the United States had been primarily an agricultural economy. But between 1860 and 1890, industrial progress transformed the country. Statistics illustrating this are striking. During these 30 years, the number of manufacturing plants more than doubled, growing from 140,433 to 355,415; the value of what they made rose more than 400 percent, from $1.8 billion to $9.3 billion; and the capital invested in them grew 650 percent, from $1 billion to $6.5 billion.[21]

[20] Charles E. Lindblom, *The Market System: What It Is, How It Works, and What to Make of It* (New Haven: Yale University Press, 2001), p. 247.

[21] Figures in this paragraph are from Arthur M. Schlesinger, *Political and Social Growth of the United States: 1852–1933* (New York: Macmillan, 1935), pp. 132–44.

This growth did more than create wealth; it also concentrated it. At the end of the century, between 1895 and 1904, an unprecedented merger wave assembled dominant firms in industry after industry. Since then, there have been other great merger waves, but this was the first. It made a definitive impression on the American mind, and its legacy is an enduring fear of big companies.

Merger waves are caused by changes in the economic environment that create incentives to combine. The main stimulus for the 1895–1904 wave was the growth of the transcontinental railroads, which reduced transportation costs, thereby creating new national markets. Companies rushed to transform themselves from regional operations to national ones. Combinations such as James Duke's American Tobacco Company gorged themselves, swallowing competitors. They crowded into formerly isolated markets, wiping out small family businesses. The story was repeated in roughly 300 commodities, including oil, copper, cattle, smelting, and such items as playing cards and tombstones. A 1904 study of the 92 largest firms found that 78 controlled 50 percent of their market, 57 controlled 60 percent or more, and 26 controlled 80 percent or more.[22]

At the time, the public failed to see the growth of huge firms as a natural, inevitable, or desirable response to the new economic incentives. Instead, it saw them as colossal monuments to greed. Companies of this size were something new. They inspired a mixture of awe and fear. In 1904, when the United States Steel Corporation became the first company with more than $1 billion in assets, people were astounded. Previously, such numbers applied in the realm of astronomy, not business.

In the twentieth century, corporations continued to grow in size, but the marked rise in asset concentration slowed and leveled off. By 1929 the 200 largest nonfinancial corporations in the United States (less than 0.7 percent of all nonfinancials) controlled nearly 50 percent of all corporate wealth.[23] But by 1947 the nation's top 200 corporations had 46 percent of corporate wealth, and this fell to 34 percent in 1984. After that, asset concentration rose only slightly to a high of 36 percent in 1996.[24]

Today there is a trend toward globalization of production. As a result, the number of transnational firms and the scale of their activity has grown. There are approximately 65,000 transnationals, up from only about 35,000 as recently as 1990. Assets and sales of the largest of these firms are rising. In the decade between 1990 and 2000, assets of the 100 biggest transnationals increased by 107 percent and sales by 53 percent.[25] However, despite heightened global merger activity, the

[22] John Moody, *The Truth about Trusts: A Description and Analysis of the American Trust Movement* (New York: Greenwood Press, 1968), p. 487; originally published in 1904.

[23] Adolph Berle and Gardner C. Means, *The Modern Corporation and Private Property*, rev. ed. (New York: Harcourt, Brace & World, 1968), p. 33.

[24] J. Fred Weston, Kwang S. Chung, and Juan A. Siu, *Takeovers, Restructuring, and Corporate Governance*, 2d ed. (Upper Saddle River, NJ: Prentice Hall, 1998), p. 116. See also J. Fred Weston, "Mergers and Economic Efficiency," in *Industrial Concentration, Mergers, and Growth*, vol. 2 (Washington, DC: U.S. Government Printing Office, June 1981). These figures allow rotation of new firms into the top 200 firms. If the same 200 firms had been followed over the years, asset concentration would have fallen even faster.

[25] United Nations Conference on Trade and Development (UNCTAD), *World Investment Report 2003* (New York: United Nations, July 2003), box table I.1.1; and UNCTAD, *World Investment Report 1993* (New York: United Nations, July 1993), table I.1.1.

largest global firms do not show signs of concentrating international assets the way that large American firms have concentrated domestic assets. In fact, the foreign assets of the largest 100 transnationals fell from 13 percent of estimated global assets in 1999 to 11 percent in 2003.[26] And these 100 firms are still only a small part of world economic activity. For the decade 1990–2000, their economic activity as a share of world GDP grew from 3.5 percent to only 4.3 percent.[27]

Despite this, adherents of the dominance theory believe that the increasing size and financial power of global corporations will be converted into the same old abuses. But the link between market power and abuse remains to be seen. Larger transnational firms in many industries do not necessarily even have increased market power because they face formidable competitors, emerging competition from new industries, enlarged market boundaries, and more aggressive antitrust enforcement. In the sociopolitical dimension, these firms face growing global pressures to act responsibly.

Also, no corporation, no matter how large, is assured of prospering. Over time, poor management, competition, and technological change have continuously revised the roster of America's biggest companies. Of the 100 largest corporations in 1909, only 36 remained on the list until 1948. Between 1948 and 1958, only 65 of the top 100 held their place. Only 116 company names remained on the Fortune 500 list of industrial corporations from its inception in 1955 to 1994. By 2003 only 71 of the original 500 were still there.[28] Many firms dropped from the list were, of course, acquired by other firms. Among the 100 largest transnational corporations there were 28 American firms in 1990, but that number had declined to 23 by 2000.[29] The lesson is that, with a very few exceptions, the power of uncontrollable competitive forces exceeds the power of even the largest corporations to maintain their dominance.

Elite Dominance

Another argument that supports the dominance theory is that there exist a small number of individuals who, by virtue of wealth and position, control the nation. The members of this elite are alleged to act in concert and in undemocratic ways. There is a long history of belief in an economic elite dominating American society. In the debates preceding adoption of the Constitution in 1789, some opponents charged that the delegates were wealthy aristocrats designing a government favorable to their businesses. Later, farmers suspected the hand of an economic elite in the probusiness policies of Alexander Hamilton, George Washington's secretary

[26] Figures are from UNCTAD, *World Investment Report 2000*, p. 71; and UNCTAD, *World Investment Report 2002* (New York: United Nations, July 2002), p. 85.

[27] UNCTAD, *World Investment Report 2002,* box table IV.1.2. These figures are based on a value-added calculation (the sum of salaries, pretax profits, and depreciation and amortization) for TNCs.

[28] Figures in this paragraph are from Neil H. Jacoby, *Corporate Power and Social Responsibility* (New York: Macmillan, 1973), p. 32; John Paul Newport, Jr., "A New Era of Rapid Rise and Ruin," *Fortune*, April 24, 1989, p. 77; Carol J. Loomis, "Forty Years of the 500," *Fortune,* May 15, 1995, p. 182; and Julie Schlosser and Ellen Florian, "Fifty Years of Amazing Facts!" *Fortune*, April 3, 2004, p. 159.

[29] UNCTAD, *World Investment Report 2002,* p. 93.

The Rise and Decline of Powerful Corporations

In 1896 journalist Charles H. Dow created a list of 12 companies as an index of stock market performance. Each firm was a leader in an important industry and represented its fortunes. As America's industrial structure changed over the years, companies came and went; and the list, today called the Dow Jones Industrial Average Index, grew from 12 to 30. The most recent additions and deletions were made in 2004.

The leading firms in 1896 reflect a different world. Farming was much more important in the American economy, and four firms dealt in agricultural products. They included James B. Duke's American Tobacco Company, cotton and sugar producers, and a company that made livestock feed. Other firms represented the prominence of industrial technologies based on iron, lead, and coal. U.S. Leather made a product in the shadow of imminent obsolescence, leather belts used for power transmission in factories. General Electric, which made electric motors, was the technology company of that era. Chicago Gas and Laclede Gas Light Co. of St. Louis were utilities supplying natural gas for new gas streetlamps in cities. North American Co. ran streetcars.

1896	2004	
American Cotton Oil	Allied Signal	J. P. Morgan
American Sugar Refining	Aluminum Co. of America	Johnson & Johnson
American Tobacco	American Express	McDonald's
Chicago Gas	American International Group	Merck
Distilling & Cattle Feeding	Boeing	Microsoft
General Electric	Caterpillar	3M
Laclede Gas Light	Coca-Cola	Pfizer
National Lead	DuPont	Philip Morris
North American	ExxonMobil	Procter & Gamble
Tennessee Coal & Iron	General Electric	SBC Communications
U.S. Leather	General Motors	Travelers Group
U.S. Rubber	Hewlett-Packard	United Technologies
	Home Depot	Verizon Communications
	IBM	Wal-Mart Stores
	Intel	Walt Disney

The 2004 list registers the rise of new technologies and sectors of the economy providing services and consumer products. General Electric is the only company that was on the 1896 list, and it was removed for nine years between 1898 and 1907. Of the other 11 original firms, 2 (American Tobacco and North American) were broken up by antitrust action, 1 (U.S. Leather) was dissolved, and 8 continue to operate as less important companies or as parts of other firms that acquired their assets.

As a biography of American industry, the index dramatizes the rise and fall of powerful companies and industries. Over more than a century, 100 different firms have been listed. The index teaches that dominance of even the largest firms is transient.

of the treasury, who had many ties to wealth and commercial power. Since the colonial era, charges of elitism have surfaced repeatedly in popular movements opposed to big business.

power elite
A small group of individuals in control of the economy, government, and military. The theory of its existence is associated with the American sociologist C. Wright Mills.

The modern impetus for the theory of elite dominance comes from the sociologist C. Wright Mills, who wrote a scholarly book in 1956 describing a "power elite" in American society. "Insofar as national events are decided," wrote Mills, "the power elite are those who decide them."[30] Mills described American society as a pyramid of power and status. At the top was a tiny elite in command of the economic, political, and military domains. Mills was never specific about its numbers, but said it was small. Just below was a group of lieutenants who carried out the elite's policies. They included professional managers of corporations, politicians beholden to the elite for their election, and bureaucrats appointed by the politicians. The large base of the pyramid was composed of a mass of powerless citizens, including feeble groups and associations with little policy impact. This image of a pyramid corresponds to the dominance model in Chapter 1.

Mills did not believe that America was a democracy and thought that the elite simply used government "as an umbrella under whose authority they do their work."[31] Although he never suggested that the economic segment of the elite was dominant over the political and military, he noted that "the key organizations, perhaps, are the major corporations."[32]

The Power Elite is a book in which there is more speculation than substantiation. It is based on cursory evidence. There is none of the statistical research that would be required to support such sweeping generalizations in a similar work of sociology today. Yet the book contained a powerful new explanation of economic power and came out just as many American leftists were becoming disenchanted with Marxism. Mills's vision of a small ruling elite caught on and has been popular with the anticorporate left ever since. Mills would have been pleased. In correspondence, he once expressed indignation about the power of "the sons of bitches who run American Big Business."[33]

Scholars inspired by Mills have pressed the study of elites and are less reluctant to suggest business dominance. One is G. William Domhoff, who has for more than 30 years researched a "governing class" in American society.

> There is a social upper class in the United States that is a ruling class by virtue of its dominant role in the economy and government. . . . This ruling class is socially cohesive, has its basis in the large corporations and banks, plays a major role in shaping the social and political climate, and dominates the federal government through a variety of organizations and methods.[34]

[30] C. Wright Mills, *The Power Elite* (New York: Oxford University Press, 1956), p. 18.

[31] Ibid., p. 287.

[32] Ibid., p. 283.

[33] In a letter to his parents quoted by John B. Judis, "The Spiritual Wobbly," *New York Times Book Review,* July 9, 2000, p. 9.

[34] G. William Domhoff, *Who Rules America Now? A View for the 80s* (Englewood Cliffs, NJ: Prentice Hall, 1983), p. 1.

In an effort extending over 25 years political scientist Thomas R. Dye has tried to identify precisely which individuals constitute an American elite. Believing that power comes from leadership roles in corporations, government, and other large organizations, he defines a "national institutional elite" composed of

> individuals who occupy *the top positions in the institutional structure of American society.* These are the individuals who possess the formal authority to formulate, direct, and manage programs, policies, and activities of the major corporate, governmental, legal, educational, civic, and cultural institutions in the nation. . . . For purposes of analysis we have divided American society into ten sectors: (1) industrial (nonfinancial) corporations, (2) banking, (3) insurance, (4) investments, (5) mass media, (6) law, (7) education, (8) foundations, (9) civic and cultural organizations, and (10) government.[35]

Applying this method, Dye identified 7,314 elite positions and found that they were held by 5,778 individuals (because some persons held more than one position). This is a much larger elite than that suggested by Mills, but it is still only about three-thousandths of 1 percent of the population.

Elites formed from some combination of wealth, ability, position, and social status are inevitable. Their existence is a challenge to the validity of democratic governance in that it divides citizens into a small number who rule and a vast majority who are ruled. But elites are not necessarily sinister, oppressive, or conspiratorial. They can be sources of talent and expert leadership. The American business elite comes from the ranks of top corporate executives and directors, and those who hold these positions do so based overwhelmingly on ability. Turnover is frequent. However, those selected at these rarified levels come from a narrow range of backgrounds. Every study of them finds that disproportionately they are male, white, and Christian; that they come from upper-class families; and that they graduate from a few prestigious universities. Evidence suggests that inclusion of blacks, Latinos, and women is based on their similarity in background and thinking to the existing elite.[36] In conclusion, the presence of an American elite, one perhaps dominated by business interests, troubles a nation with such a deep commitment to equality. Yet some argue that its actions are adequately checked and balanced. This view is taken up in the next section.

Pluralist Theory

pluralistic society
A society with multiple groups and institutions through which power is diffused.

A *pluralistic society* is one having multiple groups and institutions through which power is diffused. Within such a society no entity or interest has overriding power, and each may check and balance others. The countervailing forces model in Chapter 1 illustrates how, in such a society, business must interact with constraining forces in its environment. It may have considerable influence over some of them; but over most it has limited influence, and over a few none at all. Several features of American society support its pluralism.

---

[35] Thomas R. Dye, *Who's Running America? The Bush Restoration*, 7th ed. (Upper Saddle River, NJ: Prentice Hall, 2002), p. 8; emphasis in the original.

[36] Richard L. Zweigenhaft and G. William Domhoff, *Diversity in the Power Elite: Have Women and Minorities Reached the Top?* (New Haven: Yale University Press, 1998).

J. P. Morgan and the Panic of 1907

In the first decade of the twentieth century, J. P. Morgan (1837–1913), head of J. P. Morgan & Co. in New York, was often called the most powerful man in the country. He specialized in buying competing companies in the same industry and merging them into a single, monopolistic firm. He joined separate railroads into large systems. He combined smaller electrical concerns into General Electric in 1892 and then pulled a collection of manufacturers into the International Harvester Company, which started with 85 percent of the farm machinery market. In 1901 he created the first billion-dollar company when he merged 785 separate firms to form the United States Steel Company with capitalization of $1.4 billion.

Morgan and two of his close associates together held 341 corporate directorships. His power was very independent of government controls since at the time antitrust laws were unenforced, there was no national bank to regulate the money supply, and existing securities and banking laws were rudimentary. One awestruck biographer said that Morgan "was a God" who "ruled for a generation the pitiless, predatory world of cash."[37] His critics were less kind. Senator Robert W. La Follette once called him "a beefy, red-faced, thick-necked financial bully, drunk with wealth and power."[38]

In October 1907 panic swept Wall Street and stocks plummeted as frantic investors sold shares. Soon a number of banks suffered runs of withdrawals and were on the verge of failure. Liquidity, or the free flow of money, was fast vanishing from financial markets, and the nation's banking system teetered on the verge of collapse. So influential was Morgan that he commanded the New York Stock Exchange to stay open all day on October 24 to maintain investor confidence. To support it, he raised $25 million of credit.

The federal government could do little to ease the crisis. President Theodore Roosevelt was off hunting bears in Louisiana, an ironic pursuit in light of the crashing stock market. Without a national bank, the government had no capacity to increase the money supply and restore liquidity. Powerless, Secretary of the Treasury George B. Cortelyou traveled to New York to get Morgan's advice.

On the evening of October 24, Morgan gathered members of the New York banking elite at his private library. He played solitaire while in another room the assembled bankers discussed methods for resolving the crisis. Periodically, someone came to him with a proposal, several of which he rejected. Finally, a plan was hatched in which $33 million would be raised to support the stock exchange and failing banks. Where would this money come from? The secretary of the treasury was to supply $10 million in government funds, John D. Rockefeller contributed $10 million, and Morgan the remaining $13 million.

This action stabilized the economy. Perhaps it demonstrates that elite power may be exercised in the common good. It should be noted, however, that the panic of 1907—and other panics of that era—came after Morgan and other titans of finance repeatedly choked the stock exchange with the colossal stock offerings needed to finance their new combinations.

Morgan was widely criticized for his role in ending the panic of 1907. Conspiracy theorists, suspicious of so much power resident in one man, attacked him. Upton Sinclair, for example, accused him of inciting the panic for self-gain, a wildly erroneous accusation. In 1912 Morgan was the focus of congressional hearings by the Pujo Commission, which concluded that he led a "money trust" that controlled the nation's finances and that this was unfortunate. Death claimed him in 1913 just before Congress passed the Federal Reserve Act to set up a central bank and ensure that no private banker would ever again be sole caretaker of the money supply.

[37] John K. Winkler, *Morgan the Magnificent* (New York: Doubleday, 1950), p. 3; originally published in 1930.
[38] Jean Strouse, *Morgan: American Financier* (New York: Random House, 2000), p. x.

First, it is infused with democratic values. Unlike many nations, America has no history of feudal or authoritarian rule, so there is no entrenched deference to an aristocracy of wealth. In colonial days, Americans adopted the then-revolutionary doctrine of natural rights, which held that all persons were created equal and entitled to the same opportunities and protections. The French aristocrat Alexis de Tocqueville, who toured America and wrote an insightful book about American customs in the 1830s, was forcibly struck by the "prodigious influence" of the notion of equality. Belief in equality, he wrote, ran through American society, directing public opinion, informing the law, and defining politics. It was, he wrote, "the fundamental fact from which all others seem to be derived."[39] Thus, in America laws apply equally to all. All interests have the right to be heard. To be legitimate, power must be exercised for the common good.

Second, American society encompasses a large population spread over a wide geography and engaged in diverse occupations. It has a great mixture of interests, more than some other countries. Economic interests, including labor, banking, manufacturing, agriculture, and consumers, are a permanent fixture. A rainbow of voluntary associations (whose size, longevity, and influence vary) compete in governments at all levels.

Third, the Constitution encourages pluralism. Its guarantees of rights protect the freedom of individuals to form associations and freely to express and pursue interests. Thus, business is challenged by civil rights, environmental, and other groups. The Constitution diffuses political power through the three branches of the federal government and between the federal and state governments and to the people. This creates a remarkably open political system.

In addition, business is exposed to constraining market pressures that force a stream of resource allocation decisions to center on cost reduction and consumer satisfaction, forces that can fell even the mighty. Henry J. Kaiser seemed unerring in business. The son of German immigrants, he worked his way up from store clerk to owner of 32 companies, including seven shipyards that launched one finished ship a day during most of World War II. When he started an auto company in 1945, nobody thought he would fail. Eager customers put down 670,000 deposits before a single car was built.[40] But his cars, the Kaiser and the Frazier, were underpowered and overpriced, and the market eventually rejected them. The venture failed. Kaiser never got costs under control; he had to negotiate the prices of many parts with competing auto companies that made them. Toward the end, he built a model that was sold at Sears as the Allstate. This was a terrible mistake because it gave the car a low-quality image with consumers.

In sum, predictable and strong forces in a pluralistic, free market society limit business power. Wise managers anticipate that, despite having considerable influence on governments, markets, and public opinion, their power can be restricted, challenged, or shared by others. Overall, there are four boundaries on managerial power.

[39] Alexis de Tocqueville, *Democracy in America* (New York: New American Library, 1956), p. 26; originally published as two volumes in 1835 and 1850.
[40] Robert Sobel, "The $150 Million Lemon," *Audacity,* Winter 1997, p. 11.

FIGURE 3.1
**Boundaries of
Managerial
Power**

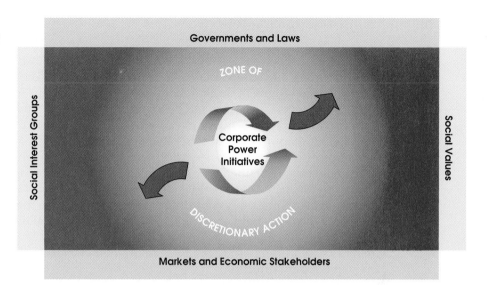

1. *Governments and laws* in all countries regulate business activity. Governments are the ultimate arbiters of legitimate behavior and can act forcefully to blunt the exercise of corporate power that harms the public. Laws channel and restrict operations.
2. *Social interest groups* represent every segment of society and use many methods to restrain business, including product boycotts, lawsuits, picket lines, media campaigns, and lobbying for more regulation. Historically, labor has been the great antagonist and counterweight to business power, but also prominent in recent years are environmental, civil rights, religious, consumer, and public interest groups.
3. *Social values* are transmitted across generations, reflected in public opinion, and embedded in the law. Managers internalize them in schools and churches. Social values include norms of duty, justice, truth, and piety that can direct a manager's behavior as powerfully as laws. For example, in the 1960s shifting generational values gave film studios license to experiment with brazen nudity and violence, but Walt Disney never did. No financial incentive was enough to make him forsake his own values about the importance of morality, family life, and the small-town decency he saw in his Kansas boyhood.[41]
4. *Markets and economic stakeholders* impose strong limits. Stockholders, employees, suppliers, creditors, and competitors influence corporate decisions. The marketplace also registers the great waves of technological change that can sweep away even the largest corporations.

Figure 3.1 illustrates the boundaries of managerial power. Just as in the solar system the planets move freely within but cannot escape their gravitational fields, so major corporations in American society move within orbits constrained by plural interests.

[41] Richard Schickel, *The Disney Version,* 3d ed. (Chicago: Ivan R. Dee, 1997), p. 39.

CONCLUDING OBSERVATIONS

In a recent poll, 72 percent of Americans felt that "too much power is concentrated in the hands of a few large companies."[42] Are they correct? The answer requires perspective and judgment. In this chapter we break down the idea of corporate power into patterns, categories, and theories to allow critical thinking. We explain how corporate power is a strong force for change and how, at a deep level, economic growth shapes society in sweeping, unplanned ways.

We also set forth two opposing perspectives. The dominance theory holds that inadequately restrained economic power is concentrated in large corporations and in the hands of a wealthy elite. The pluralist theory holds that many restraints in an open society control corporate power. These theories are locked in perpetual conflict. Both are molds into which varieties of evidence must be fitted. Both contain insights, but neither has a lock on accuracy. And both attract adherents based on inner judgments about whether market capitalism moves society in the right direction.

If corporate power remains generally accountable to democratic controls, society will accord it legitimacy. If rule by law and a just economy exist, corporate power will broadly and ultimately be directed toward the public welfare, this despite the habitual breakouts of deviltry that inflame critics.

[42] Karlyn Bowman and Todd Weiner, *Attitudes Toward Business* (Washington, DC: American Enterprise Institute), August 2002, table B-21.

John D. Rockefeller and the Standard Oil Trust

This is the story of John D. Rockefeller, founder of the Standard Oil Company. It is the story of a somber, small-town boy who dominated the oil industry with organizational genius, audacity, and ruthless, methodical execution. He became the richest man in America and, for a time, the most hated.

Rockefeller's life spanned 98 years. At his birth Martin Van Buren was president and settlers drove covered wagons over the Oregon Trail. He lived to see Franklin Roosevelt's New Deal, watch the rise of the Nazi party in Germany, and hear Frank Sinatra and *The Lone Ranger* on radio.

The historical backdrop of this lifetime is an economy gripped by the fever of industrial progress. Rockefeller built his fortune in an era that lacked many of today's ethical norms and commercial laws, an era in which the power of a corporation and its founder could be exercised with fewer restraints.

THE FORMATIVE YEARS

John Davison Rockefeller was born on July 8, 1839, in a small village in southern New York. He was the second of six children and the oldest boy. His father, William Rockefeller, was an itinerant quack doctor who sold worthless elixirs and engaged in a wide variety of businesses. He was jovial, slick, and cunning and made enough money to keep the family in handsome style until he had to flee and live away from home to avoid arrest on a charge of raping a local woman. After that, he visited only in the dark of night. But he taught young John D. and his brothers lessons of business conduct, especially that sentimentality should not influence business transactions. "I cheat my boys every chance I get," he once said. "I want to make 'em sharp."[1]

[1] David Freeman Hawke, *John D.: The Founding Father of the Rockefellers* (New York: Harper & Row, 1980), p. 13.

John D.'s mother was a somber, religious woman who gave the children a strict upbringing, emphasizing manners, church attendance, and the work ethic. She preached homilies such as "Willful waste makes woeful want." And she taught charity to the children; from an early age John D. made regular contributions to worthy causes.

Young John D. was not precocious in school. In high school he was an uninspired student, little interested in books and ideas, but willing to work hard. He grew into a somber, intense lad nicknamed "the Deacon" by his classmates because he faithfully attended a Baptist church and memorized hymns. In the summer of 1855 he attended a three-month course at a business college in Cleveland, Ohio, and then set out looking for a job. In addition to his formal schooling, he carried the contradictory temperaments of his parents—the wily, self-assured boldness of his father and the exacting, pietistic character of his mother. He internalized both, and the combination was to prove formidable. Here was a man with the precision of an accountant and the cunning of Cesare Borgia.

EARLY BUSINESS CAREER

Rockefeller's first job was as a bookkeeper at a Cleveland firm where he meticulously examined each bill submitted and pounced on errors. He also recorded every cent he earned and spent in a personal ledger. Its pages show that he was parsimonious and saved most of his $25-a-month salary but that he still gave generously to the Baptist church and the poor. In 1859 he formed a successful partnership with two others in the produce business in Cleveland and proved himself an intense negotiator, described by an acquaintance as a person "who can walk right up on a man's shirt bosom and sit down."[2] The business boomed from supplying food to the Union army during the Civil War. Although in his early 20s at the time, the steady, unemotional lad was never touched by patriotic fervor. In those days, the law permitted any man of means to pay someone else to serve in his place, and this he did.

[2] Jules Abels, *The Rockefeller Billions* (New York: Macmillan, 1965), p. 35.

BEGINNINGS OF THE OIL BUSINESS

Profits from the produce business were high, and John D. looked around for a promising new investment. He soon found one—a Cleveland petroleum refinery in which he invested $4,000 in 1863. At the time, petroleum production and refining was an infant industry. A new drilling technology had led to an 1859 oil strike in nearby Pennsylvania, followed by a frenzied boom in drilling and refining. Soon Rockefeller devoted himself full time to the oil business, and he began to apply his principles of parsimony. One basic principle was to avoid paying a profit to anyone. For example, instead of buying barrels and paying the cooper $2.50 each, Rockefeller set up his own barrel-making factory and made them for $.96. He purchased a forest to make staves from his own trees. Another basic principle was methodical cost cutting. Lumber for barrel staves was kiln-dried before shipment to the cooperage plant. Water evaporated from the wood, making it lighter and lowering transportation costs.

Though obsessed with details and small economies, Rockefeller also proved aggressive in larger plans. He borrowed heavily from banks to expand the refinery. The risk scared his partners, so he bought them out. In 1865 he borrowed more to build a second refinery. Soon he incorporated an export sales company in New York, making the world his market.

DYNAMICS OF THE OIL INDUSTRY

During this early period, the new industry was in a chaotic state. A basic cause was overproduction in the Pennsylvania oil regions, which were the only source of crude oil. The price of crude fluctuated wildly, but was in long-term decline. Each drop in the price of crude oil encouraged construction of new refineries and by the late 1860s refining capacity was three times greater than oil production. This caused vicious price wars. Some refiners tried to stay in business by selling products at a loss to raise cash for continued debt payments. In doing so, they dragged down profit margins for all refiners.

Rockefeller had the insight to invest in large-scale refineries and, because he cut costs relentlessly, his refineries made money. Yet despite disciplined cost control, the market forces of a sick industry ate away at his net earnings. He believed it was time to "rationalize" the entire industry and stop destructive competition.[3] His method for doing this would be monopoly, his tactics hard-nosed.

ROCKEFELLER'S COMPETITIVE STRATEGIES

Rockefeller used a range of competitive strategies. He was a low-cost, high-volume producer. He used debt financing to expand. He attempted to make his refined petroleum products of high and consistent quality, since fly-by-night refiners turned out inferior distillates. Cheap kerosene with a low ignition point had burned many a home down after exploding in a wick lamp. When he incorporated the Standard Oil Company of Ohio in 1870, the name suggested a "standard oil" of uniformly good quality. He engaged in vertical integration by making wooden barrels. As time when on, he also bought pipelines, storage tanks, and railroad tank cars.

Critical to his success, however, was the art of strong-arming the railroads. In this, Rockefeller was the master. Transportation costs paid to railroads were important to refiners, who shipped in crude oil and then shipped out products such as kerosene or lubricating oil. In the 1860s railroads were highly competitive and often altered shipping rates to attract business. No law prohibited this and published rates were only the starting point of negotiations.

Railroads often granted *rebates* to shippers; that is, they returned part of the freight charge after shipment. These rebates were usually secret and given in return for the guarantee of future business. Large volume shippers, including oil refineries, got the biggest rebates. Standard Oil was no exception.

At this time, Rockefeller has been described by biographers as a prepossessing man with penetrating eyes who drove a hard bargain. He would take the measure of a person with a withering stare, and few were his match. He was formidable in negotiations because he was invariably informed in detail about the other's business. And he was still a pious churchgoer who read the Bible nightly before retiring.

Late in 1870 Rockefeller hatched a brazen plan for stabilizing the oil industry at the refining level. In clandestine meetings, he worked out a rebate scheme between a few major refiners and the three railroads going into the Pennsylvania oil regions. They gave this scheme an innocent-sounding name, the South Improvement Plan. In it, the railroads agreed to increase published rates for hauling oil. Then Rockefeller's Cleveland refineries and a few others would get large rebates on each barrel shipped. For example, the regular rate between the oil regions and Cleveland would be $.80 a barrel and between Cleveland and New York $2.00 a barrel. It would cost a total of $2.80 per barrel for any other refinery in Cleveland to bring in a barrel of crude oil and ship a barrel of refined oil to New York for sale or export. Rockefeller and his accomplices, on the other hand, would be charged $2.80 but then get a rebate of $.90.

In addition, the refineries participating in the South Improvement Plan received *drawbacks*, or payments made on the shipment of oil by competitors! Thus, Rockefeller would be paid $.40 on every barrel of crude oil his competitors shipped into Cleveland and $.50 on every barrel of refined oil shipped to New York. Under this venal scheme, the more a competitor shipped, the more Rockefeller's transportation costs were lowered. While competitors were charged $2.80 on the critical route (Pennsylvania oil regions–Cleveland–New York), Rockefeller paid only $1.00. Moreover, the railroads agreed to give the conspirators waybills detailing competitors' shipments; a better espionage system would be hard to find.

Why did the railroads agree to this plot? There were several reasons. First, it removed the uncertainty of cutthroat competition. Oil traffic was guaranteed in large volume. Second, the refiners provided services to the railroads including tank cars, loading facilities, and insurance. And third, railroad executives received stock in the participating refineries, giving them a stake in their success.

The consequences of the South Improvement Plan were predictable. Nonparticipating refiners faced bloated transportation costs and would be uncompetitive. They had two choices. Either they could sell to Rockefeller and his allies, or they could stand on principle and go bankrupt. When they sold, as they must, the flaw in industry structure would be corrected. Rockefeller intended to acquire them, then close them or limit their capacity. This would give him market power to stabilize the price of both crude

---

[3] Ron Chernow, *Titan: The Life of John D. Rockefeller, Sr.* (New York: Random House, 1998), pp. 130 and 149–52.

oil and refined products. And the rebates would be a formidable barrier to new entrants.

THE CONSPIRACY PLAYS OUT

In February of 1872 the new freight rates were announced. Quickly, the full design was revealed, causing widespread, explosive rage in the oil regions. Although it broke no laws, it overstepped prevailing norms. People believed that since railroads got their right-of-ways from the public they had a duty to serve shippers fairly. Volume discounts might be justified, but this shakedown was extortionate. Producers and refiners in the oil regions boycotted the conspirators and the railroads. Rockefeller, seen as the prime mover behind the South Improvement Plan, was vilified in the industry and the press. His wife feared for his life. Yet he never wavered. "It was right," he said of the plan. "I knew it as a matter of conscience. It was right between me and my God."[4] As journalist Ida Tarbell noted, Rockefeller was not squeamish about such business affairs.

> Mr. Rockefeller was "good." There was no more faithful Baptist in Cleveland than he. Every enterprise of that church he had supported liberally from his youth. He gave to its poor. He visited its sick. He wept with its suffering. Moreover, he gave unostentatiously to many outside charities. . . . Yet he was willing to strain every nerve to obtain himself special and unjust privileges from the railroads which were bound to ruin every man in the oil business not sharing them with him.[5]

Within a month, the weight of negative public opinion and loss of revenue caused the railroads to cave in. They rescinded the discriminatory rate structure. All appearances were of a Rockefeller defeat, but appearances deceived. Rockefeller had moved quickly, meeting one by one with rival refiners, explaining the rebate scheme and its salutary effect on the industry, and asking to buy them out. He offered the exact value of the business in cash or, preferably, in Standard Oil Company stock.

By the time the railroads reset their rates, Rockefeller had bought out 21 of his 26 Cleveland competitors. Some acquisitions were simply dismantled to reduce surplus capacity. He now dominated Cleveland, the country's major refining center, and controlled more than a quarter of U.S. capacity. In secrecy, he negotiated a new rebate agreement with the Erie Railroad. Of these actions, Ida Tarbell noted sardonically: "He had a mind which, stopped by a wall, burrows under or creeps around."[6] Regardless of methods, he had, indeed, corrected structural flaws in the oil industry. It would attract more capital. If any circumstance cast a shadow over this striking victory, it was that public opinion had turned against him. From then on, he was reviled as an unfair competitor, hatred of him growing apace with his burgeoning wealth. He never understood why.

ONWARD THE COURSE OF EMPIRE

Rockefeller, now 33, was wealthy. Yet he drove on, compelled to finish a grand design, to spread his pattern over the industry landscape, to conform it to his vision.

He continued the strategy of horizontal integration at the refinery level by absorbing more and more of his competitors. As the size of Standard Oil increased, Rockefeller gained added leverage over the railroads. Like an orchestra conductor he played them against each other, granting shares of the oil traffic in return for rebates that gave him a decisive advantage.

Some competitors stubbornly clung to their businesses, partly out of hatred for Rockefeller. He made them "sweat" and "feel sick" until they sold.[7] The fleets of tank cars that he leased to railroads were often "unavailable" to ship feedstock and distillates to and from such refiners. Rockefeller concealed many of his acquisitions, disguising the full sweep of his drive to monopoly. These companies were the Trojan horses in his war against rival refiners. They seemed independent but secretly helped to undermine Standard's competitors. Often they were at the center of elaborate pricing conspiracies involving code words in telegrams such as "doubters" for refiners and "mixer" for railroad drawbacks. The phantoms bought some refiners who refused in principle to sell out to

---

[4] Peter Collier and David Horowitz, *The Rockefellers: An American Dynasty* (New York: New American Library, 1976), p. 11.

[5] Ida M. Tarbell, *The History of the Standard Oil Company*, vol. 1 (Gloucester, MA: Peter Smith, 1963), p. 43.

[6] Ibid., p. 99.

[7] Abels, *The Rockefeller Billions*, p. 35.

Standard Oil. Their existence confronted independents with a dark, mysterious force that could not be brought into the light and fought.

THE STANDARD OIL TRUST

By 1882 Rockefeller's company was capitalized at $70 million and produced 90 percent of the nation's refining output. Its main product, illuminating oil, was changing the way people lived. Before the sale of affordable illuminating oil of good quality, most Americans went to bed with darkness. They could not afford expensive candles or whale oil and feared using the unstable kerosene made by early, small refiners. With the rise of Rockefeller's colossus, they had reliable, inexpensive light and stayed up. Their lives, and the life of the nation, changed.

Rockefeller reorganized Standard Oil as a trust.[8] His purpose was to make state regulation more difficult. Soon other large companies followed his lead, adopting the trust form to avoid government restrictions. Inside Standard Oil, Rockefeller's organizing skills were extraordinary. Working with a loyal inner circle of managers, he directed his far-flung empire from headquarters at 26 Broadway in New York City. As he absorbed his competitors, so had he co-opted the best minds in the industry and much of Standard's success is attributable to this stellar supporting cast. Though dominant, Rockefeller delegated great responsibility to his managers. High-level committees controlled business operations. He circulated monthly cost statements for each refinery, causing fierce internal competition among their managers that led to high performance. He set up a network of informants around the globe. Critics called them spies, but they functioned as a well-organized information system. A perfectionist, he insisted on having a statement of the exact net worth of Standard Oil on his desk every morning. Oil prices always were calculated to three decimals. He was so dogged about efficiency and recycling that his Standard Oil plants might win environmental awards were they operating today. At night he prowled the headquarters turning down wicks in oil lamps.

His management style was one of formal politeness. He never spoke harshly to any employee. Once, when a manager leaked information to the press, Rockefeller said to his secretary: "Suggest to Mr. Blank that he would do admirably as a newspaper man, and that we shall not need his services after the close of this month."[9] Compared with other moguls of that era, he lived simply. He had two large estates, in Cleveland and New York, but neither was too ostentatious. He read the Bible daily, continued regular attendance at a Baptist church, and gave generously to charities.

Rockefeller's organizing skills were critical to his success. Discussions often focus on his ethics, but the key to Standard Oil's long-term domination lay elsewhere. The company was an immense, organized force opposed only by smaller, less united adversaries. Its success came from centralized, coordinated effort. Compromising methods, to the extent they were used, were of far less importance.[10]

EXTENDING DOMINATION

By the 1880s Standard Oil had overwhelming market power. Its embrace of refining activity was virtually complete, and it had moved into drilling, pipelines, storage tanks, transportation, and marketing of finished products. By now the entire world was addicted to kerosene and other petroleum products, and Standard's international sales grew.

Rockefeller's dominating competitive philosophy prevailed. His marketing agents were ordered to destroy independent suppliers. To suppress competition, his employees pioneered fanatical customer service. The intelligence-gathering network paid competitors' employees to pass information to Standard Oil. Railroad agents were bribed to misroute shipments. Standard workers climbed on competitors' tank cars and measured the contents. Price warfare was relentless. A stubborn competitor often found Standard selling kerosene to its customers at a price substantially below production cost.

Rockefeller himself was never proved to be directly involved in flagrant misconduct. He blamed

---

[8] A trust is a method of controlling a number of companies in which the voting stock of each company is transferred to a board of trustees. The trustees then have the power to coordinate the operations of all companies in the group. This organizing form is no longer legal in the United States.

[9] Quoted in "A Great Monopoly's Work: An Inner View of the Standard Oil Company," *New York Times,* February 27, 1883, p. 1.

[10] David M. Chalmers, ed., "Introductory Essay," in Ida M. Tarbell, *The History of the Standard Oil Company, Briefer Version* (Mineola, NY: Dover, 2003), pp. xvii–xviii.

criminal and unethical actions on overzealous subordinates. His critics thought the strategy of suffocating small rivals and policies such as that requiring regular written intelligence reports encouraged degenerative ethics among his minions.

Rockefeller saw Standard Oil as a stabilizing force in the industry and as a righteous crusade to illuminate the world. How, as a good Christian devoted to the moral injunctions of the Bible, was Rockefeller able to suborn such vicious behavior in commerce? One biographer, Allan Nevins, gives this explanation:

> From a chaotic industry he was building an efficient industrial empire for what seemed to him the good not only of its heads but of the general public. If he relaxed his general methods of warfare . . . a multitude of small competitors would smash his empire and plunge the oil business back to chaos. He always believed in what William McKinley called "benevolent assimilation"; he preferred to buy out rivals on decent terms, and to employ the ablest competitors as helpers. It was when his terms were refused that he ruthlessly crushed the "outsiders." . . . It seemed to him better that a limited number of small businesses should die than that the whole industry should go through a constant process of half-dying, reviving, and again half-dying.[11]

THE STANDARD OIL TRUST UNDER ATTACK

Standard Oil continued to grow, doubling in size before the turn of the century and doubling again by 1905.[12] Eventually its very size brought a flood of criticism that complicated operations. Predatory monopoly was at odds with prevailing beliefs about individual rights and free competition. The states tried to regulate Standard Oil and filed antitrust suits against it. Overwrought muckrakers lashed out at Rockefeller. Because of him, wrote one, "hundreds and thousands of men have been ruined."[13] Rockefeller was the personification of greed in political cartoons. Politicians not suborned by his bribery lambasted him.

Rockefeller, by now the richest American, was shaken by public hatred. He hired bodyguards and slept with a revolver. Pinkerton detectives were present at church on Sundays to handle the gawkers and shouters who appeared. He developed a digestive ailment so severe that he could eat only a few bland foods, and upon his doctor's advice he stopped daily office work. By 1896 he appeared only rarely at 26 Broadway. Soon he was afflicted with a nervous disorder and lost all his hair.

As attacks on Rockefeller grew, the vise of government regulation tightened on his company. A swarm of lawsuits and legislative hearings hung about it. Finally, in 1911, the Supreme Court ordered its breakup under the Sherman Antitrust Act, holding that its monopoly position was an "undue" restraint on trade that violated the "standard of reason."[14] The company was given six months to separate into 39 independent firms. The breakup consisted mainly of moving the desks of managers at 26 Broadway and was a financial windfall for Rockefeller, who received shares of stock in all the companies, the prices of which were driven up by frenzied public buying. Before the breakup kerosene sales had buoyed the company. However, just as electric light bulbs were replacing oil lamps, the automobile jolted demand for another petroleum distillate—gasoline. Rockefeller, who was 71 at the time of the breakup and would live another 26 years, earned new fortunes simply by maintaining his equity in the separate companies.

Rockefeller remained a source of fascination for the American public. As *The Wall Street Journal* noted, "[t]he richest man in a world where money is power is necessarily a fascinating object of study."[15] This being so, it was his enduring misfortune that muckraking journalist Ida Tarbell turned her gaze on him. Tarbell wrote two unflattering character studies and a detailed, two-volume biography of Rockefeller, all serialized in the widely read *McClure's Magazine* between 1902 and 1905. Her unsentimental words were no less ruthless than the actions of the old man himself. Although admitting that Rockefeller and Standard Oil had some measure of "legitimate greatness," she was obsessed with his flaws. In one essay she found "something indefinably repulsive" in his

---

[11] Allan Nevins, *Study in Power: John D. Rockefeller,* vol. 2 (New York: Scribner, 1953), p. 433.

[12] Ibid., app. 3, p. 478.

[13] Henry Demarest Lloyd, "Story of a Great Monopoly," *The Atlantic,* March 1881, p. 320.

[14] *Standard Oil Company of New Jersey v. United States*, 31 U.S. 221. It was an 8–1 decision.

[15] "Incarnate Business," *The Wall Street Journal*, June 26, 1905, p. 1.

appearance, writing that his mouth was "the cruelest feature of his face," and that his nose "rose like a thorn."[16] Such ad hominem attacks lacked merit but, in addition, Tarbell delved deeply into Rockefeller's career, producing narratives of exquisite detail. The thesis she conveyed to the public was that by his singular example, Rockefeller was responsible for debasing the moral tone of American business. She believed his story incited legions of the ambitious to use cold-blooded methods, teaching them that success justifies itself. Like the master, the junior scoundrels often cited biblical verse to support their actions.

Few public figures have a nemesis such as Ida Tarbell. Her relentless pen, along with others, deprived him of some public adulation he may have craved and her scholarship permanently defined him. Her intricate period research cannot be duplicated and subsequent biographers, even more friendly ones, must go to it for insight. Rockefeller may or may not have deserved such a definitive hand. He called her a "poisonous woman."[17]

THE GREAT ALMONER

Since childhood Rockefeller had made charitable donations and, as his fortune accumulated, he increased them. After 1884 the total was never less than $100,000 a year, and after 1892 it was usually over $1 million and sometimes far more. In his mind, these benefactions were linked to his duty as a good Christian to uplift humanity. To a reporter he once said:

> I believe the power to make money is a gift from God—just as are the instincts for art, music, literature, the doctor's talent, yours—to be developed and used to the best of our ability for the good of mankind. Having been endowed with the gift I possess, I believe it is my duty to make money and still more money and to use the money I make for the good of my fellow-man according to the dictates of my conscience.[18]

Over his lifetime, Rockefeller gave gifts of approximately $550 million. He gave, for example, $8.2 million

John D. Rockefeller at age 65. This photograph was taken shortly after a disease, generalized alopecia, caused him to lose his hair. Courtesy of the Library of Congress.

for the construction of Peking Union Medical College in response to the need to educate doctors in China. He gave $50 million to the University of Chicago. He created charitable trusts and endowed them with millions. One such trust was the General Education Board, set up in 1902, which started 1,600 new high schools. Another, the Rockefeller Sanitary Commission, succeeded in eradicating hookworm in the South. The largest was the Rockefeller Foundation, established in 1913 and endowed with $200 million. Its purpose was "to promote the well-being of mankind throughout the world." Rockefeller always said, however, that the greatest philanthropy of all was developing the earth's natural resources and employing people. Critics greeted his gifts with skepticism, thinking them atonement for years of plundering American society.

In his later years, Rockefeller lived a secluded, placid existence on his great Pocantico estate in New York, which had 75 buildings and 70 miles of roads. As years passed, the public grew increasingly fond of him. Memories of his early business career dimmed, and a new generation viewed him in the glow of his huge charitable contributions. For many years, he

[16] Ida Tarbell, "John D. Rockefeller: A Character Study," *McClure's*, August 1905, p. 386.

[17] Chernow, *Titan: The Life of John D. Rockefeller, Sr.*, p. xxii.

[18] Quoted in Abels, *The Rockefeller Billions*, p. 280.

carried shiny nickels and dimes in his pockets to give to children and well-wishers. On his 86th birthday he wrote the following verse.

> I was early taught to work as well as play,
> My life has been one long, happy holiday;
> Full of work and full of play—
> I dropped the worry on the way—
> And God was good to me every day.

He died in 1937 at the age of 97. His estate was valued at $26,410,837. He had given the rest away.

Questions

1. With reference to the levels and spheres of corporate power discussed in the chapter, how did the power of Standard Oil change society? Was this power exercised in keeping with the social contract of Rockefeller's era?

2. How does the story of Standard Oil illustrate the limits of business power? Does it better illustrate the dominance theory or the pluralist theory discussed in the chapter?

3. Did Rockefeller himself ever act unethically? By the standards of his day? By those of today? How could he simultaneously be a devout Christian and a ruthless monopolist? Is there any contradiction between his personal and business ethics?

4. In the utilitarian sense of accomplishing the greatest good for the greatest number in society, was the Standard Oil Company a net plus or a minus? On balance, did the company meet its responsibilities to society?

5. Did strategies of Standard Oil encourage unethical behavior? Could Rockefeller's vision have been fulfilled using "nicer" tactics?

Chapter **Four**

Critics of Business

Mary "Mother" Jones

In the early years of the twentieth century Mary Jones (1837–1930), known as Mother Jones, was one of the most notable women in America. Emerging from personal tragedy, she created a singular persona and hurled herself with great force against big corporations and the capitalist system that sustained them. Hers was an era of great change, dissent, and conflict. It was the ideal stage for a defiant performance.

She was born in 1837 as Mary Harris in Cork, Ireland. When she was eight years old, a fungus blighted the nation's potato crop, causing a terrible famine. She emigrated with her family to Toronto and there grew up, graduated from a convent school, and became a schoolteacher. In 1860 she left for a teaching job in Michigan, but within a year she moved to Chicago and took up dressmaking. After a few months, she moved to Memphis and married an iron molder named George Jones. Between 1862 and 1867 they had four children. She devoted herself to cooking, cleaning, and sewing for the family. Then yellow fever struck.

The deadly epidemic came in the fall of 1867. As mortality rose, rich families left town, leaving those who could not afford travel to become victims. The sounds of death carts taking bodies away filled neighborhoods. Mary Jones describes what happened to her.

> All about my house I could hear weeping and the cries of delirium. One by one, my four little children sickened and died. I washed their little bodies and got them ready for burial. My husband caught the fever and died. I sat alone through nights of grief. No one came to me. No one could.[1]

She nursed the sick until the plague ended, then returned to Chicago to set up a dressmaking business. She often worked for wealthy society matrons.

> I had ample opportunity to observe the luxury and extravagance of their lives. Often while sewing for the lords and barons who lived in magnificence on the Lake Shore Drive, I would look out of the plate glass windows and see the poor, shivering wretches, jobless and hungry, walking along the frozen lake front. The contrast of their condition with that of the tropical comfort of the people for whom I sewed was painful to me. My employers seemed neither to notice nor to care.[2]

[1] Mary Field Parton, ed., *The Autobiography of Mother Jones* (Chicago: C. H. Kerr, 1925), p. 12.
[2] Ibid., chap. 1, p. 13.

Several years passed, then in 1871 the Great Chicago Fire burned her business and left her destitute. After the fire she attended evening meetings of the Knights of Labor, an early union, and became engrossed in the fight of industrial workers for better wages and conditions. The perspective of class war began to dominate her view of society. She felt that workers were enslaved by corporate employers and by the corrupt politicians and judges who did their bidding. She believed that only by overthrowing capitalism could the laboring class end its bondage and usher in a new day of socialism, so she joined a small socialist political party.

For almost two decades Mary Jones worked in obscurity for labor causes and during this time she created the persona that would make her powerful and famous. Mary Jones became Mother Jones. The loss of her own family had freed her to take on another, to adopt the downtrodden. In an era when women had no vote, held no leadership positions, and received no encouragement to speak up, she would use this metaphor of motherhood to give her power.

She rose to prominence as an organizer for the United Mine Workers. Horrible working conditions prevailed in coal mines. Miners worked 10- and 12-hour days in damp, dusty, cramped, dangerous tunnels. Wages were so low that to get by mining families put their children to work. Boys as young as eight years old toiled six or seven days a week, some spending so many hours in cramped shafts that their bones grew irregularly and they could not stand straight as adults. Textile mills were built near mining towns to employ the miners' wives and daughters. The United Mine Workers wanted to unionize the miners, but the coal companies viciously resisted. Organizers were followed and observed. Miners who shook an organizer's hand were fired. Hired thugs beat up troublemakers. Companies had friendly judges convene lunacy hearings and commit pro-union employees to asylums. The miners wanted unions, but they were intimidated.

In the late 1890s Mother Jones arrived in Pennsylvania coal country. At 60 years old she looked like a grandmother. She stood five feet tall with silver hair and sharp blue eyes. With great energy she worked the coal towns. She was an explosive orator with a vocal range from shrill cries to a forceful, low pitch that mesmerized listeners. She knew the miners' language and spoke in colorful terms, calling mine owners "a crew of pirates," "a gang of thieves," and "cowards." She called the men her "boys" and as their "mother" told them to stand up to the companies.

During a bitter strike in 1900 when some miners were losing their nerve she organized marches of the miners' wives. The women paraded to work sites wearing aprons, waving mops, and banging pans. Laughing company guards saw no danger from the comical processions and let them through, not realizing how Mother Jones had cleverly dramatized the role of aggrieved wives and mothers fighting for the welfare of their families. She scolded the men, telling them they were shamed if their wives stood up to the companies and they did not.

Mother Jones used ironic wit to puncture establishment pretensions. In 1902 she was arrested in West Virginia after the coal companies got an injunction against union organizing. In court, the judge suspended her sentence, but advised her that because she was a woman it would be "better far for her to follow the lines and paths which the Allwise Being intended her sex should pursue." She appreciated the advice, she said, adding that it was no surprise he was taking the company's side,

Mary "Mother" Jones. Source: Courtesy of the Library of Congress.

since experience had taught her that "robbers tend to like each other."[3] When asked by a Princeton professor to address his class, she brought with her a stooped and pale 10-year-old boy. "Here's a textbook on economics," she said. "He gets three dollars a week . . . [working] in a carpet factory ten hours a day while the children of the rich are getting higher education."[4] She had a favorite story for audiences: "I asked a man in prison once how he happened to get there. He had stolen a pair of shoes. I told him that if he had stolen a railroad he could be a United States Senator."[5]

Eventually, Mother Jones fell out with the United Mine Workers because she was more militant than its leadership. She became a lecturer for the Socialist Party, but in time she renounced socialism. She was a doer, not an ideologue, and she lacked patience with hairsplitting doctrinal debates among intellectuals who led comfortable lives. However, in 1905 she helped launch the International Workers of the World (IWW), a radical union dedicated to overthrowing American capitalism. By 1911 she had returned to the front lines in mining regions. Later, she marched with striking

[3] Gene R. Nichol, Jr., "Fighting Poverty with Virtue," *Michigan Law Review,* May 2002, p. 1661.

[4] Quoted in Marilyn Jurich, "The Female Trickster—Known as Trickstar—As Exemplified by Two American Legendary Women, 'Billy' Tipton and Mother Jones," *Journal of American Culture,* Spring 1999, p. 69.

[5] "Mother Jones Speaks to Coney Island Crowd," *New York Times,* July 27, 1903.

garment and streetcar workers in New York City. In 1916 she started a riot by two hundred wives of streetcar workers with an inflammatory speech, telling them: "You ought to be out raising hell."[6]

By the 1920s Mother Jones had grown disillusioned with unions. She quit the IWW saying it was more interested in symbolic displays than in concrete victories. Other unions had grown comfortable with the corporate establishment. She had contempt for union leaders motivated by their own status and importance in society and called John L. Lewis, president of the United Mine Workers, a "pie counter hunter."[7] She retired from public life, speaking out now and then, and died in 1930 at the age of 92.

Today Mother Jones is little remembered. Her time passed and the specific labor abuses that enraged her are mostly ended. Perhaps her invective is unmatched today. She defined "monster capitalism," as a "robber system" supported by the "national gang of burglars of Wall Street." The corporations she attacked had "snake brains"and were run by "idiots" and "commercial pirates." But her ideas live on. Although her life was unique in its tragedy and drama, her attacks were based on enduring values that recycle through time. We may forget Mother Jones, but we hear her in today's business critics. In this chapter we explore the birth and life of these values.

ORIGINS OF CRITICAL ATTITUDES TOWARD BUSINESS

There are two underlying sources of criticism of business, one ancient and the other modern. The first is the belief that people in business place profit before more worthy values such as honesty, truth, justice, love, piety, aesthetics, tranquillity, and respect for nature. The second is the strain placed on societies by economic development. During industrialization and later, when market economies grow large and complex, business has a range of problematic impacts on societies. We will discuss both fundamental sources of criticism. We begin in the ancient Mediterranean world.

The Greeks and Romans

agrarian society
A society with a largely agricultural economy.

The earliest societies were agrarian in nature. An *agrarian society* is a preindustrial society in which economic, political, and cultural values are based on agricultural experience. In these societies, most people worked the land for subsistence. No industrial centers or mass markets existed, so business activity beyond barter and exchange was a tiny part of the economy. The activities of merchants were often thought unprincipled because their sharp trading practices clashed with the traditional, more altruistic values of family and clan relations among farmers. Merchants typically had lower class status than officials, farmers, soldiers, artisans, and teachers.

The extraordinary civilizations of ancient Greece and Rome were based on subsistence agriculture. Economic activity by merchants, bankers, and manufacturers was limited. The largest factory in Athens, for example, employed 120 workers

---

[6] "Car Riot Started by 'Mother' Jones," *New York Times,* October 6, 1916, p. 1.

[7] Quoted in Elliot J. Gorn, *Mother Jones: The Most Dangerous Woman in America* (New York: Hill and Wang, 2001), p. 249.

making shields.[8] Commercial activity was greater in Rome, but it was still mainly an agrarian society. Perhaps because industry was so limited in both societies, inaccurate economic doctrines arose to explain commercial activity.[9] For example, the desire for riches was suspect due to the popular belief that the amount of wealth was fixed. If so, an individual accumulated wealth only by subtracting from the share of others. This is believable logic in an agrarian society because the land on which the economy is based is fixed in amount.

Philosophers moved into this realm of intellectual error, reasoning that profit seeking was an inferior motive and that commercial activity led to excess, corruption, and misery. Their views are of lasting significance because, as with many topics of discourse in Western civilization, they first defined the terms of debate over the ranking of profit relative to other values. In particular, both Plato and Aristotle articulated the fundamental indictment that casts an everlasting shadow over business.

Plato believed that insatiable appetites existed in every person. These could be controlled only by inner virtues painstakingly acquired through character development. The pursuit of money was one such appetite, and Plato thought that when people engaged in trade they inevitably succumbed to the temptation of excess and became grasping. In a society, as with an individual, wealth spawned evils, including inequality, envy, class conflict, and war. "Virtue and wealth," he argued, "are balanced against one another in the scales."[10] Rulers of the utopian society he conceived in *The Republic* were prohibited from owning possessions for fear they would be corrupted and turn into tyrants. So troubled was he about this that they were forbidden even to touch gold or silver.

Aristotle believed there was a benign form of acquisition that consisted of getting the things needed for subsistence. This kind of acquisition was natural and moderate. However, after trading and monetary systems arose, the art of acquisition was no longer practiced this simple way. Instead, merchants studied the techniques of commerce, figuring out how to make the greatest profit, seeking not the necessities, but unlimited pools of money. Aristotle thought this was a lower form of acquisition because it was activity that did not contribute to inner virtue.

For Aristotle, happiness is the ultimate goal of life. It comes to those who develop character virtues such as courage, temperance, justice, and wisdom. He called these virtues "goods of the soul" and held them superior to "external goods," which he defined as possessions and money. Aristotle believed that the amount of happiness a person gained in life was equal to the amount of virtue accumulated in the soul. Since material possessions beyond those needed for subsistence added nothing to the store of virtue in the soul, it followed that they contributed nothing to happiness; thus, it was a waste or "perversion" of any virtue to apply it toward the acquisition of excess. "The proper function of courage, for example, is not to produce money but to give confidence," he wrote.[11]

---

[8] Will Durant, *The Life of Greece* (New York: Simon & Schuster, 1939), p. 272.

[9] John Kenneth Galbraith, *Economics in Perspective* (Boston: Houghton Mifflin, 1987), pp. 9–10.

[10] *The Republic,* trans. F. M. Cornford (New York: Oxford University Press, 1945), p. 274.

[11] In *Politics,* trans. Ernest Barker (New York: Oxford University Press, 1962), book I, chap. X, § 17. See also book VII, chap. 1, §§ 1–10.

Thus, both Plato and Aristotle relegated the profit motive to the sphere of lower or base impulses, a place from which it would not escape for centuries and then only partially. Soon, Roman law would forbid the senatorial class from making business investments (and the law would be widely circumvented). Likewise, the Stoic philosophers of Rome, including Epictetus and Marcus Aurelius, taught that the truly rich person possessed inner peace rather than capital or property. "Asked, 'Who is the rich man?' Epictetus replied, 'He who is content.'"[12] These sages looked down on merchants of their day as materialists who, in pursuit of wealth, sacrificed character development. Of course, this did not deter the merchants from accumulating fortunes and neglecting the study of ideals. The scornful ethos of the philosophers, though potent enough to endure and to beget perennial hostility, has never had enough power to suppress the tide of commerce.

The Medieval World

During the Middle Ages, the prevailing theology of the Roman Catholic Church was intolerant of profit seeking. As the Christian religion arose, its early practitioners had been persecuted by the wealthy and corrupt ruling class of Rome. The Church, then, rejected a focus on wealth and sought special status for the poor. Saint Augustine, the towering figure of early Church doctrine, accepted the idea that material wealth was fixed in supply. To become rich, a person necessarily sinned by accumulation that violated the natural equality of Creation. Moreover, the love of material things was a snare that pulled the soul away from God.[13]

The Church's most definitive theologian, St. Thomas Aquinas, was greatly influenced by the ideas of Aristotle when he set forth Church cannon about the ethics of profit making and lending money. Merchants were exhorted to charge a *just price* for their wares, a price that incorporated a modest profit just adequate to maintain them in the social station to which they were born. The just price stands in contrast to the modern idea of a *market price* determined by supply and demand without any moral dimension. Today we hear echoes of medieval theology when consumers complain that high prices for a scarce product are unjust. Catholicism also condemned *usury*, or the lending of money for interest. By the twelfth and thirteenth centuries, however, the money supply and economic activity had greatly expanded and interest-bearing loans were commonplace. "Commercial activity," notes historian Will Durant, "proved stronger than fear of prison or hell."[14] In time, the Church backed away from the dogma of just price and usury. It was a slow process. Church teaching making lending money for interest a sin was not officially renounced until 1917.

The Modern World

As business activity accelerated during the Renaissance, new theories arose to justify previously condemned practices. Two are of great importance. First, is the rise of the *Protestant ethic* in the sixteenth century. The Protestant reformers Martin

market price
A price determined by the interaction of supply and demand.

usury
The lending of money for interest.

Protestant ethic
The belief that hard work and adherence to a set of virtues such as thrift, saving, and sobriety would bring wealth and God's approval.

[12] *The Golden Sayings of Epictetus,* trans. Hastings Crossley, in Charles W. Eliot, ed., *Plato, Epictetus, Marcus Aurelius* (Danbury, CT: Grolier, 1980), p. 179.

[13] Saint Augustine, *The City of God,* trans. Gerald G. Walsh, et al. (New York: Image Books, 1958), book XIX, chap. 17. This work was completed in A.D. 426.

[14] *The Age of Faith* (New York: Simon & Schuster, 1950), p. 631.

Luther and John Calvin believed that work was a means of serving God and that if a person earned great wealth through hard work it was a sign of God's approval. This confronted the Church's antagonism toward commerce with a new doctrine that removed moral suspicion of wealth. It contradicted the belief that pursuit of money corrupted the soul. Second, in 1776 Adam Smith published his theory of capitalism, writing that free markets harnessed greed for the public good and protected consumers from abuse. This defied the Church's insistence on the idea of a just price. Moreover, visible wealth creation in expanding economies forcefully countered the notion that only a more or less fixed amount of wealth existed in a society. These developments ended the domination of doctrines that made business activity seem faintly criminal and released new energies into commerce. But the broom of doctrinal reform failed to make a clean sweep, and many business critics clung to the old approbations of the Greek philosophers and of the Church.

In addition, just when old strictures were loosening, the industrial revolution created new tensions that reinforced critical attitudes about business. These new tensions arose as inventions and industries transformed agrarian societies and challenged traditional values with modern alternatives. During industrialization, rural, slow-paced, stable societies are swiftly and dramatically altered. They become urban and fast-paced. More emphasis is placed on material things and people's values shift. Wealth creation overwhelms self-restraint. Consumption supplants thrift and saving. Conquest of nature replaces awe of nature.

THE AMERICAN CRITIQUE OF BUSINESS

As societies modernize, the antiquarian values of Greece live on in the charges of critics who are troubled by these changes. Always, the fundamental critique is altered to fit changed circumstances. We will see how this happened in the United States.

The Colonial Era

The American nation was first settled by corporations. The colonists who landed at Jamestown, Virginia, in 1606 were sponsored by investors in the London Company, who hoped to make a fortune by discovering gold in the New World. Instead, the colonists found a mild strain of native tobacco that caused a sensation in England (and became the basis for the plantation economy that would rise in the South). The Pilgrims who came in the *Mayflower* to Cape Cod, Massachusetts, in 1620 had fled persecution to set up a religious colony. But their voyage was financed by the Plymouth Company, whose backers sought to make a profit. To repay their debt and to buy manufactured goods they exported furs and forest products such as timber, tar, and turpentine. In this way the early colonists became lively traders.

As international trade in coastal regions expanded, settlers moved inland, creating a broad agrarian base for the economy. These frontier farms seethed with profit-oriented activity. Unlike European peasants, American farmers owned their land and this turned them into little capitalists. Most tried to make money by raising crops for market. Some were land speculators. Others built and ran grain mills and in other ways employed their capital like the traders and merchants in towns.

The popular theoretician of the rising capitalist spirit was Benjamin Franklin (1706–1790). Franklin began a business career at the age of 22 by opening a printing shop. He then bought several newspapers and retired rich at the age of 42. During travels in Europe he became acquainted with Adam Smith, who shared parts of the manuscript for *Wealth of Nations* with him. Franklin came to accept Smith's then-radical views on the superiority of laissez-faire markets. Writing prolifically, Franklin gave form to a new American business ethos. In 1732 he published the first annual *Poor Richard's Almanack*, an eclectic book of facts, information, and self-help advice. Over many years the *Almanack* carried aphorisms and maxims about the road to success in business, a road open to all who practiced virtues such as hard work, thrift, and frugality. "The sleeping Fox catches no Poultry." "Lost Time is never found again." "Diligence is the Mother of Good Luck." "The Art of getting Riches consists very much in Thrift."[15] Unlike the Old World theologians who taught that commercial success was slightly sinful, Franklin taught that God would approve the pursuit of self-interest and wealth. "God gives all things to Industry."[16] He made business activity synonymous with traditional virtues and released it from moral suspicion. His teaching resonated with the American condition and he became the prophet of a vibrant economy. Not surprisingly, his *Almanacks* were bestsellers.

The Young Nation

The amalgam of a new land, a new people, and new thinking generated an early emphasis on business activity and material progress. Yet not everyone felt this was either inevitable or proper and dissent soon emerged. After independence in 1783 business interests were important in the new nation but not to the extent that they would be in time. There were few large companies. The economy was 90 percent agricultural, so the interests of farmers and planters dominated those of infant industry. A major debate arose over the direction of the economy, one that would define subsequent debate between business and its critics in America. It was played out in a bitter rivalry between two members of President George Washington's cabinet who differed both in temperament and ideas.

Alexander Hamilton (1755–1804), the first Secretary of the Treasury, was young, ambitious, brilliant, and inclined to action. He believed that industrial growth would increase national power and designed a grand scheme to promote manufacturing and finance. He was an arrogant, aloof leader who mistrusted the wisdom of common citizens. Having once said that "the people is a great beast," he favored rule by an economic elite.[17] Hamilton got Congress to approve his plans for taxation, debt financing, tariffs to protect infant industry, and creation of a national bank, setting a policy of industrialization in motion.

He was opposed by Secretary of State Thomas Jefferson (1743–1826), one of America's most original and philosophical minds. Jefferson was a shy man who

---

[15] Quotations are in *Poor Richard's Almanack,* 1749, and "The Way to Wealth," Preface to *Poor Richard Improved,* 1758, in Nathan G. Goodman, ed., *The Autobiography of Benjamin Franklin and Selections from his other Writings* (New York: Carlton House, 1932), pp. 198, 206, 207.

[16] Ibid., "The Way to Wealth," p. 207.

[17] Quoted in Vernon Louis Parrington, *Main Currents in American Thought,* vol. 1 (New York: Harcourt, Brace, 1958), p. 300; originally published in 1927.

avoided conflict. His thinking achieved great depth, but he was less a man of action than Hamilton. His weakness as a manager is summed up in a revealing statement. "We can only be answerable for the orders we give, and not for their execution."[18] He had grown up in sparsely populated frontier areas of Virginia, never having seen a village of more than 20 houses until he was 18 years old. Deeply impressed by the common sense and resourcefulness of the settlers he knew, he formed the opinion that an agrarian economy of landowning farmers was the ideal social order.

Reading books as much as fifteen hours a day, he gathered arguments to reinforce his convictions. According to Jefferson, America should aspire to spread farming over its immense, unsettled territory. He wrote that God placed "genuine virtue" in farmers, His chosen people. Manufacturing as an occupation "suffocates the germ of virtue," leads to venality, and corrupts the "manners and principles" of those who work at it.[19] He believed that an agrarian economy would prevent the rise of subservience to the wealthy and bring a state of equality, basic justice, and concern for the common good. Jefferson was well-read in Greek philosophy and it was no coincidence that he echoed the admonitions against commerce found in Plato and Aristotle. Even as he restated the Greeks, he laid the ground for more than two centuries of American business critics to follow.

Jefferson did not prevail. His agrarian ideal was fated to exist in the shadows of industrial growth. His theory of a nation of small farmers was somewhat nebulous and idealistic. As a policy it was no match for the more concrete design that Hamilton sold to Congress with great energy, a design that was surely more in tune with economic forces afoot in the young nation. With the support of business leaders, Hamilton carried out a bold, visionary program to stimulate the growth of manufacturing. His actions prepared the ground for the unexampled industrial growth that roared through the next century. He so angered Jefferson that the two rarely spoke even as they served together in George Washington's cabinet. Each had many followers and the conflict between their positions created not only the basis for subsequent criticism of business, but the basic cleavage that has prevailed in the American two-party system to the present.

1800–1865

The first half of the nineteenth century saw steady industrial growth. This aroused critics who clung to the values and life of the agrarian society fading before their eyes. Early in the century banking and manufacturing expanded. Markets were opened by tens of thousands of miles of new turnpikes. Completion of the 350-mile-long Erie Canal in 1825 inspired another 4,400 miles of canals to transport goods over water.[20] Railroads started to run in the 1830s. Immigrants arrived and cities grew. Business boomed.

---

[18] Letter to Baron F. W. von Steuben, March 10, 1781, quoted in Stanley Elkins and Eric McKitrick, *The Age of Federalism* (New York: Oxford University Press, 1993), p. 206.

[19] Quotes are from *Notes on Virginia*, in Adrienne Koch and William Peden, *The Life and Selected Writings of Thomas Jefferson* (New York: Random House, 1944), p. 280; first published in 1784.

[20] James Oliver Robertson, *America's Business* (New York: Hill and Wang, 1985), p. 81.

As the force of events put capitalism in control, agrarian romantics were pushed to the side, having only the power to object as cherished values were eroded. "Commerce," complained Ralph Waldo Emerson in 1839, "threatens to upset the balance of man and establish a new, universal Monarchy more tyrannical than Babylon or Rome."[21] Later, his friend Henry David Thoreau wrote to belittle a society in which this commerce smothered the poetry and grace of everyday life.

> This world is a place of business. What an infinite bustle! I am awakened almost every night by the panting of the locomotive. It interrupts my dreams. There is no sabbath. It would be glorious to see mankind at leisure for once. It is nothing but work, work, work. I cannot easily buy a blank-book to write thoughts in; they are commonly ruled for dollars and cents. . . . I think that there is nothing, not even crime, more opposed to poetry, to philosophy, ay, to life itself, than this incessant business.[22]

Among those who rejected capitalism, some tried to create alternative worlds. Beginning in the 1820s there was a frenzy of utopia building. Small bands of people who disdained the values prized in industrial society—materialism, competition, individualism, and tireless labor—built model communities intended to act as beacons for a better way. The largest was New Harmony, Indiana, founded in 1825 by Robert Owen (1771–1858), an English industrialist. Owen ran a large cotton mill in Scotland that had become a model for fair treatment of workers. Yet he believed that human values were corrupted by factory work and life in capitalist societies. He aspired to show that a society based on principles of equality, charity, cooperation, and moderation could flourish. At New Harmony money was abolished and the residents shared the fruits of communal labor. An educational system was designed to instill collective thinking in both children and adults.

Owen called his creation a "socialist" system and in the 1820s the term "socialism" first came into widespread use as a reference to Owen's philosophy. He started several other socialist communities and his ventures inspired others to form utopias based on socialist principles. More than 100 such communities appeared between 1820 and 1850.[23] A few were successful. The Oneida Community in New York lasted thirty-one years from 1848 to 1879. But most floundered, on average in less than two years.[24]

New Harmony emptied after only four years. Like other utopias it required businesslike activities for subsistence, but it attracted more loafers than skilled farmers and artisans who, in any case, could command higher material rewards in the outside world. After their initial zeal wore off, the sojourners tired of spartan living, regimentation, and rules to enforce cooperation. Most communes had programs to infuse socialist values into human natures tainted by capitalist schooling. Rarely did this work. One indication is that pilfering of supplies from common storehouses was common.

[21] Quoted from Emerson's *Journals,* vol. V, pp. 284–86, in Parrington, *Main Currents in American Thought,* vol. I, p. 386.

[22] "Life without Principle," *The Atlantic Monthly,* October 1863, pp. 484–85.

[23] W. Fitzhugh Brundage, *A Socialist Utopia in the New South* (Urbana: University of Illinois Press, 1996), p. 6.

[24] Joshua Muravchik, *Heaven on Earth: The Rise and Fall of Socialism* (San Francisco: Encounter Books, 2002), p. 51.

The agrarian and socialist communes failed utterly as alternatives to the bustling capitalism beyond their margins. Although a few new ones appeared as late as the 1890s, by the 1850s the idea had run its course. It failed in practice because it was based on romantic thinking, not on sustaining social forces. A series of withered utopias and a growing consensus on capitalist values adjourned the experiments. Socialism would return, but it awaited a new day and new ideas.

Populists and Progressives

At the end of the Civil War in 1865, America was still a predominantly rural, agrarian society of small, local businesses. But explosive industrial growth rapidly reshaped it, creating severe social problems in the process. Cities grew as farmers left the land and immigrants swelled slum populations. Corrupt political machines ran cities but failed to improve parlous conditions. Companies merged into huge national monopolies. These changes were the raw material of two movements critical of big business.

populist movement
A political reform movement that arose among farmers in the late 1800s. Populists blamed social problems on industry and sought radical reforms such as government ownership of railroads.

The first was the *populist movement,* a farmers' protest movement that began in the 1870s and led to formation of a national political party, the Populist Party, which assailed business interests until its decisive defeat in the presidential election of 1896. The movement arose soon after the Civil War, when farmers experienced falling crop prices. The declines were due mainly to overproduction by mechanized farm machinery and to competition from foreign farmers exploiting new transport technologies. Farmers overlooked these factors and blamed their distress on railroad companies, the largest businesses of the day, which frequently overcharged for crop hauling, and on "plutocrats" such as J. P. Morgan and other eastern bankers who controlled the loan companies that foreclosed on their farms.

In a typical tirade, Mary Lease, a populist orator who whipped up crowds of farmers at picnics and fairs, explained:

> Wall Street owns the country. It is no longer a government of the people, by the people and for the people, but a government of Wall Street and for Wall Street.
> The great common people of this country are slaves, and monopoly is the master.
> The West and South are bound and prostrate before the manufacturing East.[25]

To solve agrarian ills, the populists advocated government ownership of railroad, telegraph, and telephone companies and banks, a policy dagger that revealed their fundamental rejection of capitalism. They demanded direct election of U.S. senators, who at the time were picked by state legislatures corrupted with money from big business. And to ease credit they sought to abandon the gold standard and expand the money supply.

Historian Louis Galambos believes that despite the populist critique, there existed a great reservoir of respect for and confidence in business until the late 1880s.[26] After that, analysis of newspaper and magazine editorials shows mounting

---

[25] In John D. Hicks, *The Populist Revolt* (Minneapolis: University of Minnesota Press, 1931), p. 160.

[26] Louis Galambos, *The Public Image of Big Business in America, 1880–1940* (Baltimore: Johns Hopkins University Press, 1975), chap. 3. Galambos examined 8,976 items related to big business that were printed in newspapers and journals between 1879 and 1940, using content analysis to reconstruct rough measures of opinion among certain influential groups.

Art Y
radica
ist of
gressi
had a
ability
highli
excess
indust
This ca
typical
then d
Young
others,
appear
1912.

Was President McKinley the Wizard of Oz?

The Wonderful Wizard of Oz is one of the all-time best-selling children's books.[27] It was written by Lyman Frank Baum (1856–1919), an actor, sales clerk, and small-town newspaper editor who loved creating stories for children. On the surface, the book is a magical adventure in a fairyland where children are as wise as adults. However, the book has a deeper dimension. It is a parable of populism.[28]

The Wonderful Wizard of Oz satirizes the evils of an industrial society run by a moneyed elite of bankers and industrialists. "Oz" is the abbreviation for ounce, a measure of gold. It and the Yellow Brick Road allude to the hated gold standard. The main characters represent groups in society. Dorothy is the common person. The Scarecrow is the farmer. The Tin Woodsman is industrial labor. His rusted condition symbolizes factory closings in the depression years of the 1890s, and his lack of a heart hints that factories dehumanize workers. The Cowardly Lion is William Jennings Bryan, the defeated Populist Party candidate, whom Baum regarded as lacking sufficient courage. The

Wicked Witch of the East is a parody of the capitalist elite. She kept the munchkins, or "little people," in servitude. At the end of the Yellow Brick Road lay the Emerald City, or Washington, DC, where on arrival the group was met by the Wizard, representing the president of the United States. At the time Baum wrote the book, William McKinley was president, having defeated Bryan in 1896. Populists reviled McKinley because he had the backing of big trusts and he supported the hated gold standard.

At the conclusion, Dorothy melted the Wicked Witch of the East, the Wizard flew off in a balloon, the Scarecrow became the ruler of Oz, and the Tin Woodsman took charge of the East. This ending is the unrealized populist dream.

Baum's first motive was to be a child's storyteller, not to write political satire for adults. He never stated that the book contained populist themes, leading to debate over whether finding such symbolism is fair. Yet Baum lived in South Dakota while populism was emerging and he marched in Populist Party rallies. *The Wonderful Wizard of Oz* was written in 1898, at the height of ardor for reform. Therefore, it seems reasonable to think that Baum's tale was inspired by the politics of the day.

[27] L. Frank Baum (Chicago: Reilly & Britten, 1915), first published in 1900.

[28] The classic interpretation of symbolism is by Henry W. Littlefield, "The Wizard of Oz: Parable on Populism," *American Quarterly,* Spring 1964.

hostility toward large trusts. Soon the populists succeeded in electing many state and local officials, who enacted laws to regulate the railroads and provided the political groundswell behind creation of the Interstate Commerce Commission in 1887 to regulate railroads.

The populist movement was a diverse, unstable coalition of interests, including farmers, labor, prohibitionists, antimonopolists, silverites, and suffragists. These groups were held together for a time by a common, deep-seated hostility toward big companies. Ultimately, the populists failed to forge an effective political coalition and the movement was moribund after 1900 when William Jennings Bryan, the Populist Party's presidential candidate, was decisively defeated for a second time.

However, the populists refined a logic and lexicon for attacking the business system. They blamed adverse consequences of industrialization on monopoly, trusts, Wall Street, "silk-hatted Easterners," the soulless "loan sharks" and shameless "bloodhounds of money" who foreclosed on farms, and on corrupt politicians who worked as errand boys for the "moneybags" in a system of "plutocracy" (or

Recent anticorporate assaults have attracted widespread attention via the Internet and the 24-hour news cycle. But such campaigns are not new. In the 1800s a remarkably similar advocacy network led the global antislavery campaign.[55] In the 1970s powerful international campaigns against Nestlé and other infant-formula makers led to reforms of infant-formula marketing practices in less developed countries. And in the 1980s a powerful human rights coalition coerced large corporations to leave apartheid-era South Africa.[56]

The progressive left movement is highly articulated and specialized. It has a network structure that includes leftist philanthropic and legal foundations; research institutes; publications; mutual funds; pension funds; unions; and groups of environmental, human rights, and labor advocates. These elements are knit together not only by shared ideology, but by flows of funding, program sponsorships, shared directorships, overlapping membership, information exchange, and coalition agreements.[57] Entities in the movement are specialized to engage in a form of organizational symbiosis. Some groups use lawsuits to challenge business; others engage in civil disobedience. Some groups write conduct codes for industries; others train inspectors to enforce codes. Some groups rate corporations on their social responsibility; others form mutual funds to invest in socially responsible companies. Figure 4.3 shows various parts of the progressive left that combine in the fight to impose corporate responsibility.

Attacks on corporations marshal a range of devices that create pressure. Following is a list, hardly exhaustive, of widely used tactics.

- *Consumer boycotts.* A boycott is a call to pressure a company by not buying its products and services. In recent years, there have been hundreds of boycott calls by advocacy groups. Here are some current examples: People for the Ethical Treatment of Animals is boycotting PETCO for mistreatment of animals sold in its stores; a broad coalition is boycotting ExxonMobil over its denial of global warming.

- *Shareholder proposals.* Rules permit shareowners of public companies to sponsor resolutions on which all stockholders may vote at annual meetings. If passed, they put pressure on management to comply. Religious groups have led in sponsoring resolutions in line with the progressive agenda. The Interfaith Center on Corporate Responsibility coordinates more than 200 religious orders and denominations that put more than 200 proposals a year before stockholders. Examples (with the percentage of the shareholder vote they received in 2004) are a proposal asking MetLife to limit its CEO's pay to no more than 100 times the average pay of nonmanagement workers (2 percent) and one asking Pfizer to issue an annual report on all corporate political contributions and lobbying expenditures (11 percent).

[55] Margaret E. Keck and Kathryn Sikkink, *Activists Beyond Borders* (Ithaca, NY: Cornell University Press, 1998), pp. 8–12.

[56] S. Prakash Sethi and Oliver F. Williams, *Economic Imperatives and Ethical Values in Global Business: The South African Experience and International Codes Today* (South Bend, IN: University of Notre Dame Press, 2001).

[57] For details on network dynamics see Jarol B. Manheim, *Biz-War and the Out-of-Power Elite: The Progressive-Left Attack on the Corporation* (Mahwah, NJ: Lawrence Erlbaum, 2004), pp. 38–40.

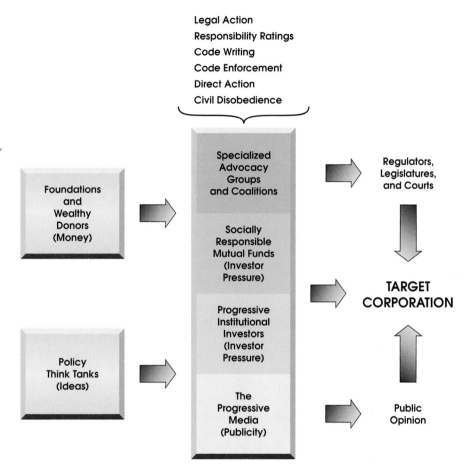

FIGURE 4.3
How the Progressive Network Attacks a Corporation

Source: Adapted from Jarol B. Manheim, *Biz-War and the Out-of-Power Elite* (Mahwah, NJ: Lawrence Erlbaum, 2004), fig. 10.2. Reprinted with permission of Laurence Erlbaum Associates, Publishers.

- *Harassment.* When Citigroup employees used booths on college campuses to market credit cards, activists upset with the big bank over its credit practices set up booths right next to them, warning students away. Forms of harassment are limited only by the imagination. Activists bring lawsuits based on clever charges such as racketeering. They disrupt the lives of executives and their families by picketing their homes, protesting at their children's schools, and interrupting services at their churches. They attract attention by climbing corporate buildings to unfurl banners.
- *Codes of conduct.* Some advocacy groups develop codes of conduct that essentially enact progressive agendas. Corporations are pressured to sign on to these codes. If they sign, they generally must submit to compliance monitoring done by specialized organizations with connections to activists. An example is Social Accountability 8000, a detailed code created by organizations in the worldwide campaign against sweatshop labor. The code sets forth principles for ethical treatment of workers consistent with the progressive ideology. It requires that corporate signers meet many conditions to achieve certification and then submit

to periodic monitoring by examiners trained to enforce the code. An organization named Verité, which has ties in the progressive network, was set up to verify that companies have met code requirements.

- *Corporate campaigns.* A corporate campaign is a broad, sustained attack on a corporation, usually by a coalition of groups, that employs a wide range of tactics.[58] They are a primary means of mobilizing activists for coordinated warfare against the targeted firm. The campaign depicts the firm as engaging in antisocial behavior to make a profit while representing the advocacy groups as crusaders for the public interest. A large transnational corporation has enormous financial resources, strong influence in government, and frequently a trusted brand name. Activists typically have slender financing, little political influence, and low public recognition. However, they have one key source of strength: the tendency of the public to perceive an environmental, religious, or human rights group as selfless and acting in the public interest. Using this perception, activists seize the ethical high ground and engage the corporation with an assault that might be likened to warfare because the action sometimes stretches or breaks the bonds of civil society.

As an example of a corporate campaign, a few years ago a coalition of environmental groups began targeting Home Depot for selling wood harvested from endangered old-growth forests. Home Depot was picked because as the world's largest home improvement chain it sells enormous amounts of lumber around the world. The coalition, which included Rainforest Action Network, Earth First!, Greenpeace, Sierra Club, and other groups, then organized an extraordinary assault. Organizers got more than 250,000 people to sign petitions, send postcards, or call the company asking it to desist. Elementary school children recorded a song about forest preservation that was sent to Home Depot's CEO. When the company tried to build new stores, activists fought zoning permits. At its annual meeting, progressive shareholders presented resolutions that management was forced to oppose. A team of climbers hung a five-story banner on the company's head offices in Atlanta reading, "HOME DEPOT: STOP SELLING OLD GROWTH."

Over two years there were more than 600 demonstrations outside Home Depot outlets. Inside, activists prowled the aisles and put stickers on products made from old-growth wood. One activist in a bear costume tied himself to the rafters over the cash register in a Canadian Home Depot, remaining there for several hours to address customers below. An Indian named Qwatsinas, the hereditary chief of a Canadian rainforest tribe, entered Home Depot's flagship store in Atlanta to engage in "ethical shoplifting." He took Red Cedar lumber believed to have been illegally logged from his native land and turned it in to the FBI as stolen property.[59]

Escalating pressure led Home Depot to announce that it would phase out purchase of wood from endangered forests by the end of 2002. It agreed to begin using wood certified by the Forest Stewardship Council, a group that verifies sustainability in wood harvesting using criteria inspired by environmentalists.

---

[58] For an extended discussion, see Jarol B. Manheim, *The Death of a Thousand Cuts: Corporate Campaigns and the Attack on Corporations* (Mahwah, NJ: Lawrence Erlbaum, 2001).

[59] Jill Krill, "Felling the Lumbering Giants," *Multinational Monitor,* January–February 2001, p. 17.

When Home Depot's resistance collapsed, Lowe's, a smaller competitor, soon announced that it would match Home Depot's policies. After putting up stubborn resistance Boise Cascade caved in a year later.[60]

Activist coercion of forest products companies will continue. Over the past twenty years there have been hundreds of like campaigns and many other "victories."[61] For example, since 1995 about 30 companies have left the Burmese market because of pressure from the human rights activists in the Free Burma Coalition.[62]

Corporate campaigns challenge traditional notions of democracy. Advocacy groups have limited memberships and are not constrained to represent more than a narrow splinter of the political spectrum. Unlike representative legislatures, they are not accountable to any broad base of voters even as they claim that their ideas about everything from healthy forests to executive pay represent the public interest. They are unwilling to accept as responsible corporate behavior that is guided merely by statutes or by the choices of individual consumers as registered in markets. Instead, they argue that since corporations have corrupted governments and manipulated consumers, they are justified in taking action to impose standards of "responsibility," "justice," "equity," and "rights" as defined by the progressive vision. This vision is not uncontroversial. Once into a campaign, progressive advocates tap the deep cynicism in public opinion to build anger against the corporate target. When the target capitulates and changes its policies, the activists have, in effect, appropriated its power and assets to further their policy agenda. And this may have been accomplished by an end run around democratic institutions and regulators.[63]

CONCLUDING OBSERVATIONS

We have narrated a history in which basic criticisms of business are repeated over and over. Each era brings new personalities, new targets, and some new issues, but the fundamental language and substance of criticism remain the same. The history of business criticism is at root a dialogue between critics and defenders of capitalism. Imagine a dinner party at which Aristotle, St. Augustine, Thomas Jefferson, and Ralph Nader sat at one table and Adam Smith, Benjamin Franklin, Alexander Hamilton, and Ronald Reagan at another. Imagine the harmony among table mates as contrasted with the gulf between the two groups.

There is no question that industrial capitalism is a historical force for continuous, turbulent social change; it is, as the economist Joseph Shumpeter wrote in 1942, "a perennial gale of creative destruction" that strains institutions and challenges

---

[60] Jim Carlton, "Boise Cascade Turns Green," *The Wall Street Journal,* September 3, 2003, p. B6.

[61] See, for example, Kevin Danaher and Jason Mark, *Insurrection: Citizen Challenges to Corporate Power* (New York: Routledge, 2003); and "Lessons from Winning Campaigns," *Multinational Monitor,* January–February 2004.

[62] Debora L. Spar and Lane T. La Mure, "The Power of Activism: Assessing the Impact of NGOs on Global Business," *California Management Review,* Spring 2003, p. 78.

[63] See Gary Johns, "The NGO Challenge: Whose Democracy Is It Anyway?" conference paper, American Enterprise Institute, Washington DC, June 11, 2003.

existing authority.[64] The defense of capitalism is that, for the most part, the changes it brings represent progress, a condition of improvement for humanity. All the while that critics have been objecting, it has steadily improved living standards for millions. In the United States, it operates in a democratic political system that has reformed its greatest abuses over the years. As against promoting greed and avarice, it has instead promoted positive cultural values such as imagination, innovation, cooperation, hard work, and the interpersonal trust necessary to conduct millions of daily business transactions. In the words of one defender, market capitalism is triumphant in the face of ageless criticism.

> If the principles of commerce and technology, on which America is founded, are in some ways less noble than those of the ancient world, they are also more realistic and more practical. Moreover, they have produced not just material but also moral progress: the abolition of slavery, the elevation of countless people from poverty to comfort, the relief of suffering produced by disease, humanitarian campaigns against torture and famine all over the world, and a widely shared conception of human rights, human freedom, and human dignity.[65]

In the end, a broad spectrum of criticism is an important check on business power. Many legitimate criticisms demand attention. If criticism is properly channeled, it can preserve the best of the business institution and bring wide benefit. In Ralph Nader's words: "Whenever, in our nation's history, people successfully challenge the excessive power of commercial interests, whether over workers, child labor, minorities, consumers and the environment, the country became better and the economy stronger."[66]

[64] *Capitalism, Socialism and Democracy* (New York: Harper & Row, 1976), p. 143; originally published in 1942.

[65] Dinesh D'Souza, *The Virtue of Prosperity* (New York: Free Press, 2000), pp. 186–87.

[66] "Human Need Trumps Corporate Greed," *The Wall Street Journal,* October 25, 2000, p. A22.

A Campaign against KFC Corporation

The formal declaration of war came on January 6, 2003. In a press release, People for the Ethical Treatment of Animals (PETA), a militant animal rights group, announced it was beginning a pressure campaign against KFC Corporation, the world's largest chicken restaurant chain. PETA held KFC responsible for the "cruel treatment" of poultry raised and slaughtered for its restaurants. It asked KFC to introduce new and more humane practices.[1]

KFC responded by posting a statement on its Web site in which it "dismissed allegations made by PETA" and claimed its chickens were treated humanely.[2] KFC does not raise any chickens. In the United States it buys them from 18 independent companies that operate 52 growing and rendering facilities and from similar suppliers in other nations. PETA is angry about the management of chickens by these suppliers, but such small, independent facilities make difficult targets. KFC, a widely known brand, is vulnerable to attack. By assaulting its brand image PETA hoped to force KFC into using its leverage over suppliers. This strategy has been successful against other restaurant and supermarket chains.

[1] "Company Stonewalls on Animal Welfare Reforms," press release, People for the Ethical Treatment of Animals, January 6, 2003, available at www.peta.org.

[2] "KFC Denies PETA Claims," press release, KFC Corporation, January 7, 2003.

PETA's initial effort was a campaign against McDonald's in 1999. After less than a year of exposure to a boycott, restaurant demonstrations, and the group's mccruelty.com Web site the company succumbed, imposing stricter animal welfare standards on its suppliers as a condition for ending the campaign. Among other measures, McDonald's required roomier cages for layer hens, surprise slaughterhouse inspections, and more effective stunning of chickens before they were killed. Chicken growers and rendering plants regarded these measures as unnecessary and onerous, but because of McDonald's buying power they were forced to comply. After McDonald's capitulated, its smaller rivals followed. Burger King introduced animal welfare guidelines after a five-month campaign. Then Wendy's buckled. Safeway lasted only three months. Albertson's and Kroger's each required only one week in 2002.

PRELUDE TO CONFRONTATION

The PETA campaign was no surprise to KFC. It found out about the group's intentions in April 2001, when KFC President Cheryl Bachelder received a letter from Bruce Friedrich, the director of PETA's restaurant campaigns. In the letter, Friedrich asked why KFC, knowing of PETA's actions against its competitors, was doing "nothing at all" to improve the lives of chickens grown for its restaurants. Friedrich asked what KFC intended to do, offered to put the company in touch with animal welfare experts, and pointedly stated that "we are looking ahead to our next target."[3]

Over the next several weeks Friedrich had a series of phone calls and meetings with Cheryl Bachelder, president of KFC, and David Novak, CEO of its parent corporation Yum! Brands. Yum! Brands was created in 1997 when Pepsico spun off its KFC, Pizza Hut, and Taco Bell chains as a separate corporation (initially called Tricon Global). In 2002 the new firm acquired the Long John Silver's and A&W chains. The KFC brand traces its origins to the Kentucky Fried Chicken restaurant franchise started by the avuncular Colonel Harlan Sanders in 1952. Today, KFC operates 13,000 restaurants in 80 countries as a subsidiary of Yum! Brands. Both are headquartered in Louisville, Kentucky.

The dialogue revealed a wide gulf between the company and its interlocutor. Friedrich was told that

KFC included humane treatment guidelines in its poultry supplier contracts. But he accused the company of using only inadequate industry standards that permitted horrendous treatment of chickens and considering their welfare only at the point where deaths from abuse lowered profits. He explained that the suffering of chickens was an ethical issue that went beyond financial considerations.[4] KFC said it was setting up an animal welfare panel staffed by outside experts to review its guidelines for suppliers. It also promised to keep PETA informed.

In the months that followed, KFC took several actions. It convened an Animal Welfare Advisory Council composed of outside academic and industry experts. It started unannounced audits of growers and slaughterhouses. It worked with industry associations that were developing new poultry welfare guidelines. However, its efforts were unsatisfactory to PETA because they did not introduce the specific and more extensive changes the organization sought. These included:

- *Introduction of gas killing.* KFC chickens are stunned by electrical shock before immersion in scalding water (to loosen feathers) and then exposed to mechanical blades that slit their throats. PETA believes that gas killing is preferable because it ensures that chickens are insensate before these painful procedures, whereas electrical stunning is less reliable.

- *Installation of cameras in slaughterhouses.* Cameras would supplement audits and make oversight more reliable.

- *Introduction of mechanized chicken-catching.* Hand-catching crews gather KFC chickens from grower buildings. PETA believes that the crews treat the birds roughly and that mechanical catching systems are less likely to result in bruises and broken bones.

- *A timetable for introducing new genetic strains of chickens.* The chickens eaten in KFC restaurants, known as "broilers," are bred to gain weight rapidly over their brief lives. However, the "broiler breeders" used to produce the flocks of chickens slaughtered for restaurant meals live longer. They exhibit the rapid weight-gain characteristic of all broiler strains, but their skeletons and joints do not grow

---

[3] The letter is available at www.kfccruelty.com/letter-042501.asp.

[4] Letter of May 14, 2001, from Bruce G. Friedrich to Jonathan D. Blum, senior vice president, Tricon Global Restaurants, available at www.kfccruelty.com/letter-052401.asp.

commensurate with their overall weight and they are prone to painful joint conditions as they age. PETA requested introduction of leaner genetic strains that did not exhibit skeletal deficiencies.

- *Elimination of forced growth.* Broiler strains bred for rapid weight gain under forced growth regimens suffer from metabolic pathologies and excess mortality. Slowing growth means longer upkeep of chickens before slaughter, but it reduces premature deaths.

- *Provision of more room for birds to move around.* PETA requests that KFC give its chickens at least two to three times more space per bird and give them sheltered areas and perches in the warehouselike buildings where they are raised.

- *Allowance for instinctive behavior of chickens.* PETA believes that birds raised in captivity suffer from chronic stress and boredom induced by suppression of natural behaviors. Among other measures, it suggests that they get whole green cabbages to peck and eat.[5]

The debate between the antagonists was dysfunctional. In letters written for the record, PETA addressed the corporation in the tone of a parent scolding an errant child. It was "extremely concerned" that the firm "has no interest in making real progress to stop animal cruelty," adding that "we have pressed you to take action on this issue, yet you have done nothing."[6] KFC, on the other hand, wrote to PETA "[i]n the spirit of open communications," but kept it at arm's length, giving only brief and general information about conducting audits, holding meetings, and working on animal welfare standards with industry groups.[7] PETA believed that KFC was dragging its feet.

PEOPLE FOR THE ETHICAL TREATMENT OF ANIMALS

PETA is dominated by its founder, Ingrid Newkirk, who became an animal rights activist after a formative experience. In 1972 she was living in Maryland, training to become a stockbroker, when a neighbor moved, abandoning cats that soon bred litters of

kittens on her property. She gathered them up and took them to a nearby animal shelter, believing they would receive care. A short time later she asked to see the cats and learned that they had been killed. This news generated a visceral change in her. She talked her way into a job at the shelter and left the broker training program. At the shelter she observed brutal treatment of animals and began to arrive early in the morning to kill them in a humane way before the others came. "I must have killed a thousand of them," she says, "sometimes dozens every day."[8]

From the shelter Newkirk moved on to work as a deputy sheriff on animal cruelty investigations and then headed a commission to control animal disease. She was inspired to form PETA after reading a book, *Animal Liberation,* by philosopher Peter Singer.[9] In this book and in subsequent writing, Singer argues that animals have moral rights. Moral rights are strong entitlements to dutiful treatment by others—in this case human beings. Singer asserts that the traditional, absolute dominion of humans over animals is an unfair exploitation. Because animals are living, sentient beings capable of suffering, their interests are entitled to equal consideration with human interests. In his words: "No matter what the nature of the being, the principle of equality requires that its suffering be counted equally with the like suffering . . . of any other being."[10] Thus, he argues, animals have an unalienable right to have their needs accommodated by humans. Denial of this right is speciesism, or the prejudicial favoring of one species over another. Speciesism, according to Singer, is an evil akin to racism and sexism because it restricts moral rights to one species just as racism and sexism have restricted them to one race or sex. The PETA Mission Statement, Exhibit 1, reflects the inspiration Newkirk found in this philosophy.

Newkirk has a combative attitude about animal rights. "The animals are defenseless," she says. "They can't talk back, and they can't fight back. But we can. And no matter what it takes, we always will."[11] After reading about a Palestinian bomb put on a donkey

[5] Letter of August 6, 2002, from Bruce G. Friedrich to Jonathan D. Blum, available at www.kfccruelty.com/letter-080602.asp.

[6] Ibid.

[7] Letter of July 17, 2002, from Jonathan Blum to Bruce G. Friedrich, available at www.kfccruelty.com/petakfc.asp.

[8] Quoted in Michael Specter, "The Extremist," *The New Yorker,* April 14, 2003, p. 56.

[9] New York: Avon Books, 1975.

[10] Ibid., p. 8.

[11] Quoted in Specter, "The Extremist," p. 54.

**EXHIBIT 1
PETA's
Mission
Statement**

Source: Courtesy
of People for the
Ethical Treatment of
Animals (PETA).
www.peta.org/
about/mission.asp
(2004).

People for the Ethical Treatment of Animals (PETA), with more than 800,000 members, is the largest animal rights organization in the world. Founded in 1980, PETA is dedicated to establishing and protecting the rights of all animals. PETA operates under the simple principle that animals are not ours to eat, wear, experiment on, or use for entertainment.

PETA focuses its attention on the four areas in which the largest numbers of animals suffer the most intensely for the longest periods of time: on factory farms, in laboratories, in the fur trade, and in the entertainment industry. We also work on a variety of other issues, including the cruel killing of beavers, birds and other "pests," and the abuse of backyard dogs.

PETA works through public education, cruelty investigations, research, animal rescue, legislation, special events, celebrity involvement, and direct action.

and detonated by remote control she wrote to Yasir Arafat requesting that innocent animals be left out of the Arab-Israeli conflict. Her will stipulates that when she dies the meat on her body is to be cooked for a human barbeque, her skin used to make leather products such as purses, and her feet made into umbrella stands.[12]

In the fight for animal rights PETA uses a broad range of tactics. Because most people give no thought to animal rights, its actions are designed to attract attention, even at the expense of offending potential supporters. Perhaps the mildest attention-getting tactic is the use of theater. For example, PETA demonstrators have dragged themselves down streets with their feet in leg traps to publicize the evils of fur trapping. Another tactic is that of the outrageous act. To protest pictures of women wearing fur in *Vogue* magazine, activists went to the expensive Manhattan restaurant where its editor was having lunch and threw a dead racoon on her plate. Young ladies at county fairs are crowned as Pork Queens only to have pies thrown in their faces by PETA members. The group has asked Wisconsin, the "Dairy State," to change its state beverage from cows' milk to soy milk. And it deliberately tries to create controversy. An exhibit of eight-foot panels called "Holocaust on Your Plate" juxtaposes photographic images of Nazi concentration camps with images of factory farms and slaughterhouses, making the point that both represent similar injustices. The exhibit asks: "Decades from now, what will you tell your grandchildren when they ask you whose side you were on during the 'animals'

holocaust?'"[13] The suggestion of a moral equivalency between Nazis and animal farmers is inescapable.

PETA freely uses sexuality to make its message attractive. The group has former *Playboy* Playmates wearing bikinis made of lettuce hand out "veggie dogs" outside the American Meat Institute's Annual Hot Dog Lunches put on in Washington, DC, for government officials. A representative for the trade group accused PETA of contradicting itself for fighting animal exploitation by exploiting women, noting that trade association members didn't need to take off their clothes to get people to eat their food. PETA fired back that the Playmates had volunteered to host the veggie-wagon, "which is the opposite of exploitation—it's using your success to take a stand for compassion."[14]

PETA often uses celebrities to present its message. Famous and glamorous people attract wide admiration and media coverage. Their use endows a view that might otherwise be widely regarded as silly or arrogant without the celebrity's aura of success and legitimacy. Finally, PETA is adept at using the Internet to broadcast its message. It sets up multiple Web sites for campaigns and issues such as zoos, circuses, and animal testing. There is even a site for children. The network of sites is easy to navigate and entertaining. There are facts, games, pictures, video clips, humor, celebrities, and fund-raising pitches.

All these tactics have been employed in the fight against KFC.

---

[12] Ibid., pp. 57, 58.

[13] The exhibit is at a PETA Web site, www.masskilling.com.

[14] Richard Leiby, "Bring Condiments!" *Washington Post,* July 20, 2004, p. C3.

THE CHICKENS

At the center of the conflict are the chickens. Chickens are gallinaceous birds; that is, their species is part of the order Galliformes, which includes turkeys, pheasants, grouse, and partridges. Galliformes are heavy-bodied, short-duration fliers that feed on insects and seeds, nest on the ground, and hatch precocial (self-caring) young. They are social birds that communicate with each other and establish complex hierarchies in flocks.

The earliest wild chickens, members of the species *Gallus gallus,* inhabited the jungles of southeast Asia, where they were hunted by the natives. About 4,000 years ago they were domesticated, and besides being a source of food they were objects of religious sacrifice. From Asia the domesticated chicken, *Gallus domesticus,* spread across the globe. In ancient Greece they were valued for the sport of cockfighting, and in imperial Rome prophets read the future in their entrails. Chickens had such a hold on the superstitious Romans that generals kept special flocks in the belief that their behavior could foretell victory or defeat in battle. In the hours before combat, hardened legionnaires crowded around flocks seeking portents. As the legions marched, they spread *Gallus domesticus* across the extent of their empire. Centuries later, the earliest European settlers brought chickens to the North American continent.

In the United States, large-scale chicken production developed slowly. As late as the 1920s large chicken farms had flocks of only about 500 free-ranging birds. Today the industry is highly specialized, with some farms in egg production and others raising broilers (or chickens slaughtered for meat; literally, chickens that can be broiled—or baked or fried). Flocks are now raised in warehouselike buildings that use automated equipment to maintain up to 100,000 birds. Consumption of chicken has risen. In 1955 only a little more than 1 billion broilers were raised, or 6.5 chickens for each American; by 2002 there were 8.6 billion raised, or 30 per American.[15]

Chickens, like other animal species, adopted a repertoire of behaviors to permit survival in an ecological niche. Descriptions of the activities of chickens in natural environments suggest certain instinctive behaviors designed to satisfy basic needs. They are social animals that live in flocks of approximately ten members and establish dominance hierarchies called pecking orders. The dominant bird in a flock can peck any other bird, and that bird will yield. Status in the pecking order is communicated by sounds such as crowing or cackling, aggressive or passive postures, spacing, access to more or less desirable nesting sites, and activities such as running at or away from rivals. In mixed-sex flocks there are two pecking orders, one for cocks and one for hens, but the hen hierarchy is completely subordinate. All hens yield to even the lowest cock. This is a genetically predisposed trait essential for species survival because a cock will not mate with a dominating hen. Pecking orders have survival value. Once dominance is established, fighting ceases and energy is used in socially productive ways.

Chickens are omnivorous, eating plants, insects, and small animals such as lizards. Hens are secretive and build hidden nests, preferably on the ground. During the day chickens spread out to forage, but at dusk they reduce the spaces between them. At night they often roost in trees. According to PETA, chickens are "inquisitive and interesting animals" and "as intelligent as mammals like cats and dogs and even primates." In nature, they are individuals with "distinct personalities" that "form friendships and social hierarchies, recognize one another, love their young, and enjoy a full life, dust-bathing, making nests, roosting in trees, and more."[16]

Life in high-density growing environments frustrates these natural behaviors. Crowding or confinement in cages makes it hard to group into small flocks and establish pecking orders. Without a complete pecking order, individuals may not yield to threat displays, and physical attacks occur as birds compete over space, food, and water.[17] Weaker animals have no place to hide and may be assaulted repeatedly until they die. In addition, crowded chickens are unable to engage in a range of preferred foraging, grooming, nesting, brooding, and roosting behaviors. Critics claim that such deprivation violates the right of an animal to satisfy its needs through natural behaviors.

---

[15] *Statistical Abstract of the United States 1956,* 77th ed., tables 1 and 857; and *Statistical Abstract of the United States 2003,* 123d ed., tables 1 and 851.

[16] "The Hidden Lives of Chickens," at www.peta.org/feat/hiddenlives/.

[17] T. R. O'Keefe et al., "Social Organization in Caged Layers: The Peck Order Revisited," *Poultry Science,* July 1988, p. 1013.

THE CAMPAIGN

With the start of the campaign, PETA sought to inflict damage on the KFC brand and harass company executives. In the following months it conducted hundreds of demonstrations at KFC restaurants around the world. Protesters dressed like chickens and locked themselves in cages. They handed out "Buckets of Blood" containing "Psycho Col. Sanders" figures, toy chickens with slit throats, and fake blood, bones, and feathers. When Yum! Brands CEO David Novak appeared at the opening of a restaurant in Germany, two activists doused him with the blood and feathers. According to Friedrich: "There is so much blood on this chicken-killer's hands, a little more on his business suit won't hurt."[18]

KFC issued a statement calling the attacks "corporate terrorism" that "crossed the line from simply expressing their views to corporate attacks and personal violence."[19] In Paris, Ingrid Newkirk and celebrity Chrissie Hynde of The Pretenders led activists who stormed into a busy KFC restaurant at the noon hour. They smeared red paint symbolizing chicken blood on the front window and went around talking to customers until security guards threw them out. Outside the protest blocked traffic on a boulevard for two hours. Back in the United States, PETA put up roadside billboards depicting Col. Sanders hacking a chicken with a bloody knife under the slogan "Kentucky Fried Cruelty. We do chickens wrong." Outdoor sign firms in some locations considered the ads so offensive that they refused to put them up.[20]

Although the main effort of the campaign went into publicly associating the KFC brand image with cruelty toward chickens, another focus was on pressuring KFC and Yum! Brands executives. After several months of the campaign KFC President Cheryl Bachelder failed to keep what Ingrid Newkirk thought was a commitment to call her. So Newkirk called Bachelder at her home in Louisville, Kentucky, on a Saturday evening to discuss KFC's progress in meeting PETA's demands. Bachelder objected to being

Yum! Brands CEO David Novak after being splattered with blood at a demonstration in Hanover, Germany, on June 23, 2003. Source: AP Photo/PETA Deutschland, HO.

called at home. Newkirk responded with a letter that read, in part:

> Of course you would rather not be disturbed in the privacy of your own home, but the animals you torture and slaughter pay for that home with their misery and their very lives yet have nothing remotely like a life or even a nest of any kind. . . . It is merely an accident of birth that you are not one of them.[21]

Newkirk wrote to both Bachelder and CEO Novak at their homes, posting the letters with their home addresses on PETA's kfccruelty.com Web site. It enlisted former Beatle Paul McCartney to write to Novak. His letter, which requested an end to "the egregious forms of abuse endured by chickens," ran as a full-page ad in the Louisville *Courier-Journal*. A KFC spokesperson responded that "PETA should follow one of Sir Paul's songs and just 'Let It Be.'"[22]

[18] Quoted in Jay Nordlinger, "PETA vs. KFC," *National Review,* December 22, 2003, p. 28.

[19] Cited in "Animal Rights Activists Spray KFC Chief with Fake Blood and Chicken Feathers," The Associated Press State & Local Wire, June 23, 2003.

[20] "Finger-Lickin' Foul?" *Houston Press,* December 18, 2003, p. 2.

[21] Letter of March 24, 2003, from Ingrid E. Newkirk to Cheryl Bachelder, available at www.kfccruelty.com/petakfc.asp.

[22] Mark Naegele, "McCartney Accuses KFC of Fowl Play," *Columbus Dispatch,* July 25, 2003, p. 2C.

PETA also wrote to friends and neighbors of Yum! Brands and KFC executives, requesting to speak with them. This was followed by door-to-door neighborhood visits describing KFC's brutality to chickens. Bachelder's home was picketed. Pickets also came one Sunday to the Louisville church attended by Novak and another top executive. Outside the service, PETA parked its "Reality TV" truck which displayed big-screen images of slaughterhouse abuses.[23] On Christmas Eve and Christmas day 2003 Friedrich dressed up as Santa Claus and blocked a sidewalk outside the church. He also demonstrated at the suburban home of a KFC senior vice president, leading to his conviction for trespass and a court order to stay away from the executive and his home.[24]

Early in the campaign, actor Jason Alexander, who played George Costanza on "Seinfeld," was appearing in KFC commercials. PETA attempted to set up a meeting with him, but he refused to return calls. Learning that he was about to open in a Los Angeles production of "The Producers," PETA said that unless there was a meeting, it would have pickets at the theater accusing him of complicity in KFC's cruelty to animals. Alexander then met with Newkirk, and afterwards called KFC President Bachelder to discuss PETA's propositions. After talking with Alexander, Bachelder flew to Norfolk, Virginia, for a meeting with Newkirk at PETA's headquarters.[25]

At this meeting Bachelder agreed to install cameras in slaughterhouses that supply KFC chickens, to provide more stimulation for chickens, to use mechanized chicken-gathering equipment, and to increase the space given to each bird. In return, PETA agreed to scale back its campaign for 60 days.[26] However, the agreement fell apart when Newkirk accused Bachelder of not following through. KFC responded that no new commitments had been made and that the actions agreed to were already in the works and not contingent on PETA pressure or deadlines. Within months Alexander was dropped from KFC commercials and replaced by NASCAR driver Dale Earnhardt Jr.

PETA also took advantage of procedural and legal mechanisms to attack KFC. Members of the group appeared at the Yum! Brands 2003 annual shareholders meeting in Louisville to speak. After they spoke, Novak called on the group to end its campaign, saying, "We don't want to be abused, just like you don't want the chickens to be abused."[27] When Bruce Friedrich tried to speak again, Novak cut him off, stating that the company did not like to be threatened. In 2004 PETA took the steps needed to qualify a shareholder resolution for voting. The resolution described a perceived gap between Yum! Brands official animal welfare guidelines and continued cruelty toward chickens. It called on the company to publish a report on actions being taken to close this gap.[28] But when the votes of Yum! Brands shareholders were counted it had only 7.6 percent.

In July 2003 PETA sued Yum! Brands alleging that in response to PETA's charges KFC had made false and misleading statements on its Web site and in fielding calls from customers. It claimed that consumers relied on these statements in deciding whether to eat at KFC restaurants. As deceptions "that conceal from the public the horrific suffering by chickens raised and killed for KFC," the statements violated California's unfair business practice and false advertising laws.[29] Two months later, PETA withdrew the suit when KFC agreed to remove offending statements from its Web site and to change the scripts its customer service representatives used in response to questions about animal welfare. If the case had gone further, PETA's attorneys could have made KFC release internal documents. A trial would have been a publicity bonanza for PETA because the company would have been forced to prove the validity of eight classes of statements set forth in the lawsuit.

[23] Scott Sonner, "PETA Steps Up Campaign against KFC Farm, Slaughter Practices," The Associated Press State & Local Wire, September 19, 2003.

[24] "Christmas Protests Net Conviction for PETA Exec," *Restaurant Business,* May 18, 2004, online at restaurantbiz.com.

[25] Marc Kaufman, "For One Actor, No More Chicken Parts," *Washington Post,* July 6, 2003, p. D1.

[26] Wesley J. Smith, "PETA-Fried," *National Review,* July 11, 2003, p. 25.

[27] Bruce Schreiner, "Protesters Spice Yum! Shareholders Meeting," The Associated Press State & Local Wire, May 15, 2003.

[28] Yum! Brands, Inc., *Proxy Statement,* March 26, 2004, pp. 31–32.

[29] Complaint, Superior Court of California, County of Los Angeles, *People for the Ethical Treatment of Animals v. KFC Corporation,* filed July 7, 2003, available at www.kfccruelty.com.

A MUTED REACTION FROM KFC AND YUM! BRANDS

Throughout the PETA campaign, KFC and Yum! Brands have tried to maintain a low media profile while working to elevate animal welfare standards. This reticence is characteristic of the animal agriculture, food, and restaurant industry generally when food animal management is attacked. In settings of mass production and slaughter some pain for animals is inevitable. Altering production to address basic sources of chicken discomfort, injury, and behavioral deprivation raises costs. For example, Temple Grandin, a faculty member at Colorado State University and a member of KFC's Animal Welfare Advisory Council, estimated that conversion to gas killing of chickens, a more humane method of rendering them insensate than electrical shock and the method preferred by PETA, would cost $2 million per slaughter plant.[30]

Most consumers are ignorant of factory farming methods and fail to make a connection between a supermarket cellophane pack or KFC meal and the life experience of the creature in it. Despite PETA's efforts, there is no groundswell of public opinion for more humane treatment of chickens. This vacuum of knowledge and interest sustains industry calculations balancing poultry welfare against costs. For example, pending industrywide guidelines that KFC indicates it will adopt stipulate that electrical "stunning should be effective at [a] minimum of 98% of birds in [a] 500-bird sample."[31] This standard may be defined as humane, but ten conscious chickens out of every 500 will be plunged in a tank of scalding hot water to loosen their feathers before further "processing." Such compromises in chicken welfare to avoid higher costs are tacitly accepted by people who dine at KFC restaurants, but they are difficult to defend in a media debate. PETA's greatest source of power is the desire of average people to think of themselves as humane and decent.[32] The impossibility of defending a standard that allows chickens to be boiled alive makes cautious nonconfrontation a better policy than frontal attacks on PETA.

When newspaper reporters call KFC seeking reactions to restaurant demonstrations, the company issues a brief statement from its Web site reading in part: "KFC is committed to the well-being and humane treatment of chickens." The company emphasizes that it follows Animal Welfare Guidelines developed by its Animal Welfare Advisory Board. It claims to have taken a leadership role in new guidelines being formed by two industry trade associations, the Food Marketing Institute and the National Council of Chain Restaurants. Since 2001 these associations have worked with the eight major animal trade associations (including the American Meat Institute, the National Pork Board, the National Chicken Council, and the National Turkey Federation) to develop voluntary animal welfare guidelines applicable across the animal agriculture industry. Once the guidelines are final, industry facilities will be audited and the results of those audits placed on a Web site where buyers such as KFC can evaluate them. There will be no passing or failing scores; buyers can decide where to set their animal welfare purchasing standards.[33]

Meanwhile, since 2000 KFC has followed the Yum! Brands Animal Welfare Guiding Principles (Exhibit 2) and a more comprehensive set of Poultry Welfare Guidelines covering breeding, chicken houses, catching, transport, holding, stunning, and slaughter of chickens. These guidelines require each supplier to set up an animal welfare program, designate a program leader, train employees, and keep records. KFC audits facilities for compliance.

Now and then KFC and Yum! Brands allow strong feelings about the PETA campaign to show. Four months after the start of PETA's attacks a KFC spokeswoman promised that "just like the U.S. government, we will not negotiate with corporate terrorists."[34] In July 2004 Gregg Dedrick, who had replaced Bachelder as president of KFC, attacked PETA in a news conference about an undercover video of a West Virginia slaughterhouse released by PETA activists. In the video workers at the plant, which supplied chickens to KFC, were shown kicking chickens like footballs, spray painting them in the face, and throwing them

---

[30] Cited in Schreiner, "Protesters Spice Yum! Shareholders Meeting."

[31] FMI-NCCR Animal Welfare Program, *June 2003 Report,* at www.fmi.org, p. 2.

[32] Eric Dezenhall, *Nail 'Em* (Amherst, NY: Prometheus Books, 2003), p. 80.

[33] Joe M. Regenstein, "Animal Welfare Reform—The Quiet Revolution?" *Food Technology,* October 2003, p. 108.

[34] Paul Holmes, "If KFC Wants to Combat PETA, Using Similar Over-the-Top Rhetoric Isn't the Best Method," *PR Week,* April 5, 2004, p. 7.

EXHIBIT 2
Yum! Brands
Animal
Welfare
Guiding
Principles

Source: www.yum.
com, (2004).

Food Safety: Above all else, we are committed to providing our customers with safe, delicious meals and ensuring that our restaurants are maintained and operated under the highest food safety standards. This commitment is at the heart of our entire operations and supply chain management, and is evident in every aspect of our business—from raw material procurement to our restaurant food preparation and delivery.

Animal Treatment: Yum! Brands believes treating animals humanely and with care is a key part of our quality assurance efforts. This means animals should be free from mistreatment at all possible times from how they are raised and cared for to how they are transported and processed. Our goal is to only deal with suppliers who provide an environment that is free from cruelty, abuse and neglect.

Partnership: Yum! Brands partners with experts on our Animal Welfare Advisory Council and our suppliers to implement humane procedures/guidelines and to audit our suppliers to determine whether the adopted guidelines are being met.

Ongoing Training and Education: Yum! Brands recognizes that maintaining high standards of animal welfare is an ongoing process. Training and education has and will continue to play a key role in our efforts. Yum! Brands will continue to work with experts to ensure our quality assurance employees and suppliers have the training and knowledge necessary to further the humane treatment of animals.

Performance Quantification & Follow-up: Yum! Brands' animal welfare guidelines are specific and quantifiable. Yum! Brands measures performance against these guidelines through audits of our suppliers on a consistent basis.

Communication: Yum! Brands will communicate our best practices to counterparts within the industry and work with industry associations such as the National Council of Chain Restaurants and the Food Marketing Institute to implement continuous improvement of industry standards and operations.

---

into walls.[35] Dedrick called the tape "appalling" and said KFC had stopped purchasing from the plant until it met strict conditions for reinstatement. But he said that the press had fallen for PETA's mischaracterization of the plant as a "KFC facility," when in fact it supplied both KFC and its competitors. He said that the press was "a pawn used by PETA" which had "distorted the truth time and time again" in its "campaign of harassment, invasion of privacy and what I'd call 'corporate terrorism.'"[36]

As the campaign moved through its second year, KFC stood firm. The PETA recommendation to boycott KFC restaurants has had an unclear effect.

Quarterly sales reports show fluctuations, but no clear up or down trend in KFC sales, while overall Yum! Brands sales have risen. Supporters give KFC encouragement. Wesley J. Smith, writing in *National Review,* evoked the era of the Holocaust, but drew a far different lesson from it than PETA: "As history so clearly teaches, appeasement against totalitarians, far from bringing an end to conflict, results in an ever-escalating set of demands." He encouraged KFC to "stand firmly against activists' intimidation whenever and however it occurs—even if it means that their presidents' homes are picketed, their stockholder meetings disrupted, and their executives' business suits stained by fake blood and pies in the face."[37]

[35] Stephanie Simon, "Video Sparks Inquiry into Apparent Chicken Abuse," *Los Angeles Times,* July 21, 2004, p. A10.

[36] "Press Conference Comments by KFC President Gregg Dedrick," July 21, 2004, www.kfc.com, p. 2.

[37] Wesley J. Smith, "PETA–Fried," *National Review,* July 11, 2003, p. 25.

Questions

1. Do you support KFC Corporation or People for the Ethical Treatment of Animals in this controversy? Why?

2. What are the basic criticisms that PETA makes of KFC? Are they convincing? Are its criticisms similar to timeless criticisms of business mentioned in the chapter?

3. What methods and arguments has KFC used to support its actions? Is it conducting the best defense?

4. Is the range of PETA's actions acceptable? Why does the group use controversial tactics? What are its sources of power in corporate campaigns?

5. Do animals have rights? If so, what are they? What duties do human beings have toward animals? Does KFC protect animal welfare at an acceptable level?

Chapter **Five**

Corporate Social Responsibility

Merck & Co., Inc.

Corporate social responsibility takes many forms. The story that follows stands out as extraordinary.

For centuries river blindness, or *onchocerciasis* (on-ko-sir-KYE-a-sis), has tortured humanity in tropical regions. The disease is caused by a parasitic worm that lives only in humans. People are infected by the worm's tiny, immature larvae when bitten by the female black fly, which swarms near fast-moving rivers and streams. The larvae settle in human tissue and form colonies, often visible outside the body as lumps the size of tennis balls, where adults grow up to two feet long. Mature adults live for 7 to 18 years coiled in these internal nodes, mating, and releasing tens of thousands of microscopic new worms. These offspring migrate from the internal nodes back to the skin, where they cause disfiguring welts, lumps, and discoloration along with an insistent itch that has driven many sufferers to suicide. Eventually, they move into the eyes, causing blindness. The cycle of infection is renewed when black flies bite a person with onchocerciasis, ingesting blood containing tiny worms, then bite uninfected individuals, passing on the parasite.

More than 18 million people have the disease, most of them in the river regions of some of the poorest African nations. Among these people, 500,000 have impaired vision and 350,000 are blind. The disease saps economies by blinding and enervating workers and by driving farmers away from fertile, riverside land.

Until recently, no practical treatment for river blindness existed. Thirty years ago the World Bank began pesticide spraying to kill the black fly, but it was a frustrating job. Winds can carry flies up to 100 miles from wet breeding grounds. And scientists estimate that the breeding cycle has to be suppressed for 14 years to stop reinfections.

In 1975 scientists at Merck discovered a compound that killed animal parasites. By 1981 they had synthesized it and introduced it as a veterinary drug. But they had a strong hunch it also would be effective in humans against *Onchocerca volvulus,* the river blindness parasite.

Merck faced a hard decision. It cost an average of $230 million to bring a new drug to market and more to manufacture it later.[1] Yet the people who had the disease

 [1] David Bollier, *Merck & Company* (Stanford, CA: Business Enterprise Trust, 1991), p. 5.

In countries ravaged by river blindness, the blind sometimes hold sticks and follow the lead of children. Merck commissioned this bronze sculpture for the lobby of its New Jersey headquarters, where top executives pass by each day. It symbolizes Merck's commitment to make medicine for the good of humanity. Because of Merck's unprecedented donation of a river blindness drug, such scenes are no longer common. Photo courtesy of Merck & Co., Inc.

were among the world's poorest. Their villages had no doctors to prescribe it. Should Merck develop a drug that might never be profitable? The company chose to go ahead, largely because humanitarian and scientific goals motivated its researchers, and restraining them in a corporate culture that prized innovation was awkward. Managers reasoned that donations from governments and foundations could pay much of the cost later.

Clinical trials of the drug, called ivermectin, confirmed its effectiveness. A single low dose calibrated to body weight and taken once a year dramatically reduced the population of the tiny worms migrating through the body and impaired reproduction by adult parasites, alleviating symptoms and preventing blindness.[2]

Eventually, it became clear that neither those in need nor their governments could afford to buy ivermectin. So in 1987 Merck decided that it would manufacture and ship it at no cost to areas where it was needed for as long as it was needed to control river blindness. The company asked governments and private organizations to set up distribution programs.

Since then, Merck has given away more than 1 billion tablets in treatment programs put together by the United Nations and the World Bank.[3] One program in the 11 African nations where the disease is most endemic is estimated to have prevented 600,000 cases of blindness so far and returned millions of acres of fertile land to production. In the Nigerian state of Ebonyi, for example, the infection rate dropped from 65 percent in 1997 to only 10 percent in 2004.[4] Because the black fly is so persistent and adult parasites in the body survive yearly doses of ivermectin, river blindness will not soon be eliminated.[5] But within the next decade the Merck donation program will protect millions of people from new infection and blindness.

For a drug company to go through the new drug development process and then give the drug away was unprecedented. However, Merck's management believes that although developing and donating ivermectin has cost hundreds of millions of dollars, humanitarianism and enlightened self-interest vindicate the decision.

Few corporations have such a singular opportunity to drive evil from human life and the mind-set to take advantage of it, but most firms today go beyond normal business to enrich society in some way. Merck's donations of medicine are a stellar

[2] Mohammed A. Aziz et al., "Efficacy and Tolerance of Ivermectin in Human Onchocerciasis," *The Lancet,* July 24, 1982.

[3] James B. Russo and Albert I. Wertheimer, "Pharm Aid," *Pharmaceutical Executive,* April 2004, p. 40.

[4] Chinedu Eze, "Ebony Records Reduction in River Blindness," *This Day,* March 2, 2004, p. 1.

[5] "River Blindness," *The Lancet,* July 20, 2002, p. 182.

example of old-fashioned philanthropy the way it has been done in America since the rise of big companies. The program also pioneered a form of global social action in partnership with other nations, international organizations, and civil society groups. In this chapter we define the idea of corporate social responsibility and explain how it has expanded in meaning and practice over time. The next chapter explains more about how corporations carry out their social responsibilities.

THE EVOLVING IDEA OF SOCIAL RESPONSIBILITY

corporate social responsibility
The duty of a corporation to create wealth in ways that avoid harm to, protect, or enhance societal assets.

Corporate social responsibility is the duty of a corporation to create wealth in ways that avoid harm to, protect, or enhance societal assets. The term is a modern one. It did not enter common use until the 1960s, when it appeared in academic literature. It has no precise, operational meaning. It is primarily a political theory, not a management or economic theory, because its central purposes are to control and legitimize the exercise of corporate power.

The fundamental idea is that corporations have duties that go beyond carrying out their basic economic function in a lawful manner. Here is the reasoning. The social contract dictates that the overall performance of a firm must benefit society. Because of imperfections in the market, the firm will not fulfill all its duties, and may breach some, if it responds single-mindedly to free market forces. Laws and regulations will correct some market flaws, more in developed nations, fewer in the less developed. But a zone of discretion inevitably remains and the firm must, therefore, voluntarily take additional actions to meet its full obligations to society. What additional actions must it take? These have to be defined in practice by negotiation with stakeholders. In doing so there is often a struggle between corporations, their critics, and a range of stakeholders.

Over time, as we will explain, the doctrine has evolved to require more expansive action by companies largely because stakeholder groups have gained more power to impose their agendas, but also because the ethical and legal philosophies underlying it have matured to support broader action by managers. The story of corporate social responsibility begins with Adam Smith.

Social Responsibility in Classical Economic Theory

Throughout American history, classical capitalism, which is the basis for the market capitalism model in Chapter 1, has been the basic inspiration for business. In the classical view, a business is socially responsible if it maximizes profits while operating within the law, because an "invisible hand" will direct economic activity to serve the good of the whole.

This ideology, derived from Adam Smith's *Wealth of Nations,* is compelling in its simplicity and its resonance with self-interest. In nineteenth century America, it was elevated to the status of a commandment. However, the idea that markets harness low motives and work them into social progress has always attracted skeptics. Smith himself had a surprising number of reservations about the market's ability to protect human welfare.[6] Today the classical ideology still commands the

---

[6] Jacob Viner, "Adam Smith and Laissez-Faire," *Journal of Political Economy,* April 1927.

Andrew Carnegie's Philanthropy

After selling United States Steel for $250 million, Carnegie retired to devote his life to what he called "scientific philanthropy." He found this to be hard work. Every day he received hundreds of requests for money. So he developed a set of priorities for giving, listing the areas of worthy projects in order of their importance to him.[7]

1. Universities
2. Free libraries

3. Hospitals
4. Parks
5. Concert and meeting halls
6. Swimming baths
7. Churches

Eventually, Carnegie wore out and set up a philanthropic foundation in New York, endowing it with $125 million presided over by a staff paid to cull through the supplicants.

[7] Alex Groner et al., *The History of American Business and Industry* (New York: American Heritage, 1972), p. 206.

economic landscape, but, as we will see, ethical theories of broader responsibility have worn down its prominences.

The Early Charitable Impulse

The idea that corporations had social responsibilities awaited the rise of corporations themselves. Meanwhile, the most prominent expression of duty to society was the good deed of charity by business owners.

Most colonial era businesses were very small. Merchants practiced thrift and frugality, which were dominant virtues then, to an extreme. Benjamin Franklin's advice to a business acquaintance reflects the penny-pinching nature of the time: "He that kills a breeding sow, destroys all her offspring to the thousandth generation. He that murders a crown, destroys all that it might have produced, even scores of pounds."[8] Yet charity was a coexisting virtue, and business owners sought respectability by giving to churches, orphanages, and poorhouses. Their actions first illustrate that although American business history can be pictured as a jungle of profit maximization, people in it have always been concerned citizens.[9]

Charity by owners continued in the early nineteenth century, and grew as great fortunes were made. Mostly, the new millionaires endowed social causes as individuals, not through the companies that were the fountainheads of their wealth. One of the earliest was Steven Girard, a shipping and banking tycoon. When he died in 1831, the richest person in the nation, he made generous charitable bequests in his will, the largest of which was $6 million for a school to educate orphaned boys from the first grade through high school.[10] This single act changed

[8] In "Advice to a Young Tradesman [1748]," in *The Autobiography of Benjamin Franklin and Selections from His Other Writings,* ed. Nathan G. Goodman (New York: Carlton House, 1932), p. 210. A crown was a British coin on which appeared the figure of a royal crown.

[9] Mark Sharfman, "The Evolution of Corporate Philanthropy, 1883–1952," *Business & Society,* December 1994.

[10] The school became known as Girard College, which the senior author of this book attended. It still exists in Philadelphia.

Andrew Carnegie (1835–1919). Courtesy of the Library of Congress.

social Darwinism
A philosophy of the late 1800s and early 1900s that used evolution to explain the dynamics of human society and institutions. The idea of "survival of the fittest" in the social realm implied that rich people and dominant companies were morally superior.

the climate of education in the United States because it came before free public schooling, when a high-school education was still only for children of the wealthy.

Following Girard, others donated generously and did so while still living. John D. Rockefeller systematically gave away $550 million over his lifetime. Andrew Carnegie gave $350 million during his life to social causes, built 2,811 public libraries, and donated 7,689 organs to churches. He wrote a famous article entitled "The Disgrace of Dying Rich" and argued that it was the duty of a man of wealth "to consider all surplus revenues . . . as trust funds which he is called upon to administer."[11]

However, Carnegie's philosophy of giving was highly paternalistic. He believed that big fortunes should be used for grand purposes such as endowing universities and building concert halls like Carnegie Hall. They should not be wasted by paying higher wages to workers or giving gifts to poor people; that would dissipate riches on small indulgences and would not, in the end, elevate the culture of a society. Thus, one day when a friend of Carnegie's encountered a beggar and gave him a quarter, Carnegie admonished the friend that it was one of "the very worst actions of his life."[12]

In this remark, Carnegie echoed the doctrine of *social Darwinism,* which held that charity interfered with the natural evolutionary process in which society shed its less fit to make way for the better adapted. Well-meaning people who gave to charity interfered with the natural law of progress by propping up failed examples of the human race. The leading advocate of this astringent doctrine, the English philosopher Herbert Spencer, wrote the following heartless passage in a best-selling 1850 book.

> It seems hard that a laborer incapacitated by sickness from competing with his stronger fellows should have to bear the resulting privations. It seems hard that widows and orphans should be left to struggle for life or death. Nevertheless, when regarded not separately, but in connection with the interests of universal humanity, these harsh fatalities are seen to be full of the highest beneficence—the same beneficence which brings to early graves the children of diseased parents and singles out the low-spirited, the intemperate, and the debilitated as the victims of an epidemic.[13]

[11] Andrew Carnegie, *The Gospel of Wealth* (Cambridge, MA: Harvard University Press, 1962), p. 25; originally published in 1901.

[12] Quoted in Page Smith, *The Rise of Industrial America,* vol. 6 (New York: Penguin Books, 1984), p. 136.

[13] Herbert Spencer, *Social Statics* (New York: Robert Schalkenbach Foundation, 1970), p. 289; first published in 1850, p. 289.

Herbert Spencer (1820–1903). Spencer attempted a synthesis of human knowledge based on the unifying idea of evolution. When he visited the United States in 1882 a grand dinner attended by 200 leading Americans was held for him at Delmonico's in New York.
© Hatton-Deutsch Collection/CORBIS.

ultra vires
A Latin phrase denoting acts beyond the powers given the corporation by law.

Spencer approved of some charity, though only when it raised the character and superiority of the giver. Still, the overall effect of Spencer's arguments was to moderate charity by business leaders and retard the growth of a modern social conscience.

More than just faith in markets and social Darwinism constrained business from undertaking voluntary social action. Charters granted by states when corporations were formed required that profits be disbursed to shareholders. Courts consistently held charitable gifts to be *ultra vires*, that is, "beyond the law," because charters did not expressly permit them. To use company funds for charity or social works took money from the pockets of shareholders and invited lawsuits. Thus, when Rockefeller had the humanitarian impulse to build the first medical school in China, he paid for it out of his own pocket; not a penny came from Standard Oil. Although most companies took a negative view of philanthropy, by the 1880s the railroads were an exception. They sponsored the Young Men's Christian Association (YMCA) movement, which provided rooming and religious indoctrination for rail construction crews. Yet such actions were exceptional.

As the twentieth century approached, classical ideology was still a mountain of resistence to expanding the idea of business social responsibility. A poet of that era, James Russell Lowell, captured the spirit of the day.

Not a deed would he do

Not a word would he utter

Till he's weighed its relation

To plain bread and butter.

Social Responsibility in the Late Nineteenth and Early Twentieth Centuries

Giving, no matter how generous, was a narrow kind of social responsibility often unrelated to a company's impacts on society. By the late 1800s it was growing apparent to the business elite that prevailing doctrines used to legitimize business defined its responsibilities too narrowly. Industrialization had fostered social problems and political corruption. Farmers were in revolt. Labor was increasingly violent. Socialism was at high tide. A growing number of average Americans began to question unfettered laissez-faire economics and the heartless doctrine of social Darwinism. Business feared calls for more regulation, was terrified of socialist calls for appropriation of assets, and sought to blunt the urgency of these appeals by voluntary action.

During the Progressive era, three interrelated themes of broader responsibility emerged. First, managers were *trustees,* that is, agents whose corporate roles put them in positions of power over the fate of not just stockholders, but of others such as workers, customers, and communities. This power implied a duty to promote the welfare of each group. Second, managers had an obligation to *balance* these

trustee
An agent of a company whose corporate role puts him or her in a position of power over the fate of not just stockholders, but of others such as customers, employees, and communities.

**service
principle**
A belief that
managers
served society
by making
companies
profitable and
that aggregate
success by
many managers
would resolve
major social
problems.

multiple interests. They were, in effect, coordinators who settled competing claims. Third, many managers subscribed to the *service principle,* a near-spiritual belief that individual managers served society by making each business successful; if they all prospered, the aggregate effect would eradicate social injustice, poverty, and other ills. This belief was only a fancy reincarnation of classical ideology. However, many of its adherents conceded that companies were still obligated to undertake social projects that helped, or "served," the public.[14] These three interrelated ideas—trusteeship, balance, and service—expanded the idea of business responsibility beyond simple charity. But the type of responsibility envisioned was highly paternalistic, and the actions of big company leaders often showed an underlying Scroogelike mentality.

One such leader was Henry Ford, who had an aptitude for covering meanness with a shining veneer of citizenship. In the winter of 1914 Ford thrilled the public by announcing the "Five-Dollar Day" for Ford Motor Co. workers. Five dollars was about double the daily pay for manufacturing workers at the time and seemed very generous. In fact, although Ford took credit for being big-hearted, the $5 wage was intended to cool unionizing and was not what it appeared on the surface. The offer attracted hordes of job seekers from around the country to Highland Park, Michigan. One subzero morning in January, there were 2,000 lined up outside the Ford plant by 5:00 A.M.; by dawn there were 10,000. Disorder broke out, and the fire department turned hoses on the freezing men.

The few who were hired had to serve a six-month apprenticeship and comply with the puritanical Ford Motor Co. code of conduct (no drinking, marital discord, or otherwise immoral living) to qualify for the $5 day. Many were fired on pretexts before the six months passed. Thousands of replacements waited outside each day hoping to fill a new vacancy. Inside, Ford speeded up the assembly line. Insecure employees worked faster under the threat of being purged for a younger, stronger, lower-paid new hire. Those who hung on to qualify for the $5 wage had to face greedy merchants, landlords, and realtors in the surrounding area who raised prices and rents.

Ford was a master of image. In 1926 he announced the first five-day, 40-hour week for workers, but with public accolades still echoing for this "humanitarian" gesture, he speeded up the line still more, cut wages, and announced a program to weed out less-efficient employees. These actions were necessary, he said, to compensate for Saturdays off. Later that year, Ford told the adulatory public that he had started a social program to fight juvenile delinquency. He proposed to employ 5,000 boys 16 to 20 years old and pay them "independence wages."[15] This was trumpeted as citizenship, but as the "boys" were hired, older workers were pitted against younger, lower-paid replacements.

A few business leaders, however, acted more consistently with the emerging themes of business responsibility. One was General Robert E. Wood, who led Sears, Roebuck and Company from 1924 to 1954. He believed that a large corporation was more than an economic institution; it was a social and political one as well. In

[14] Rolf Lunden, *Business and Religion in the American 1920s* (New York: Greenwood Press, 1988), pp. 147–50.

[15] Keith Sward, *The Legend of Henry Ford* (New York: Rinehart & Company, 1948), p. 176.

Inventor and industrialist Henry Ford (1863–1947). The public made him a folk hero and saw him as a generous employer. But he manipulated workers to lower costs. Courtesy of the Library of Congress.

the Sears *Annual Report* for 1936, he outlined the ways in which Sears was discharging its responsibilities to what he said were the chief constituencies of the company—customers, the public, employees, sources of merchandise supply, and stockholders.[16] Stockholders came last because, according to General Wood, they could not attain their "full measure of reward" unless the other groups were satisfied first. In thought and action, General Wood was far ahead of his time.

Nevertheless, in the 1920s and after that, corporations found various ways to support communities. Organized charities were formed, such as the Community Chest, the Red Cross, and the Boy Scouts, to which they contributed. In many cities, companies gave money and expertise to improve schools and public health. In the 1940s corporations began to give cash and stock to tax-exempt foundations set up for philanthropic giving.

1950–The Present

The contemporary understanding of corporate social responsibility was formed during this period. An early and influential statement of the idea was made in 1954 by Howard R. Bowen in his book *Social Responsibilities of the Businessman.*[17] Bowen said that managers felt strong public expectations to act in ways that went beyond profit-maximizing and were, in fact, meeting those expectations. Then he laid out the basic arguments for social responsibility: (1) managers have an ethical duty to consider the broad social impacts of their decisions; (2) businesses are reservoirs of skill and energy for improving civic life; (3) corporations must use power in keeping with a broad social contract, or lose their legitimacy; (4) it is in the enlightened self-interest of business to improve society; and (5) voluntary action may head off negative public attitudes and unwanted regulations. This book, despite being 50 years old, remains an excellent encapsulation of the current ideology of corporate responsibility.

Not everyone accepted Bowen's arguments. The primary dissenters were conservative economists who claimed that business is *most* responsible when it makes money efficiently, not when it misapplies its energy on social projects. The best-known advocate of this view, then and now, is Nobel laureate Milton Friedman.

> There is one and only one social responsibility of business—to use its resources and engage in activities designed to increase its profits so long as it stays within the rules of the game, which is to say, engages in open and free competition, without deception or fraud. . . . Few trends could so thoroughly undermine the very foundations of our free society as the acceptance by corporate officials of social responsibility other than to make as much money for their stockholders as possible. This is a fundamentally subversive doctrine.[18]

[16] James C. Worthy, *Shaping an American Institution: Robert E. Wood and Sears, Roebuck* (Urbana: University of Illinois Press, 1984), p. 173.

[17] New York: Harper, 1954.

[18] *Capitalism and Freedom* (Chicago: University of Chicago Press, 1962), p. 133.

Friedman argues that managers are the employees of a corporation's owners and are directly responsible to them. Stockholders want to maximize profits, so the manager's sole objective is to accommodate them. If a manager spends corporate funds on social projects, he or she is diverting shareholders' dollars to programs they may not even favor. Similarly, if the cost of social projects is passed on to consumers in higher prices, the manager is spending their money. This "taxation without representation," says Friedman, is wrong.[19] Furthermore, if the market price of a product does not reflect the true costs of producing it, but includes costs for social programs, then the market's allocation mechanism is distorted.

The opposition of Friedman and other adherents of classical economic doctrine proved to be a principled, rearguard action. In theory the arguments were unerring, but in practice they were inexpedient. At the time they were expressed there was a power struggle going on between corporations and critics seeking to control the excesses of capitalism and reduce externalities such as pollution. In this struggle, Friedman's position incited critics and invited retaliation and more regulation should the business community openly agree with it. Moreover, the idea that corporations could undertake expanded corporate social responsibility had enormous utility for business. If corporations volunteered to do more it would calm critics, forestall regulation, and preserve corporate legitimacy. Not surprisingly, Friedman's view was decisively rejected by business leaders, who soon articulated a vision of expanded duty. In 1971 the Committee for Economic Development, a prestigious corporate leadership group, published a bold statement of the case for expansive social responsibility. Society, said the report, has broadened its expectations outward over "three concentric circles of responsibilities."[20]

- An *inner circle* of clear-cut responsibility for efficient execution of the economic function resulting in products, jobs, and economic growth.
- An *intermediate circle* encompassing responsibility to exercise this economic function with a sensitive awareness of changing social values and priorities.
- An *outer circle* that outlines newly emerging and still amorphous responsibilities that business should assume to improve the social environment, even if they are not directly related to specific business processes.

Classical ideology focused solely on the first circle. Now business leaders argued that management responsibilities went further. The report was followed in 1981 by a *Statement on Corporate Responsibility* from the Business Roundtable, a group of 200 CEOs of the largest corporations. It said:

> Economic responsibility is by no means incompatible with other corporate responsibilities in society. . . . A corporation's responsibilities include how the whole business is conducted every day. It must be a thoughtful institution which rises above the bottom line to consider the impact of its actions on all, from shareholders to the society at large. Its business activities must make social sense.[21]

[19] "The Social Responsibility of Business Is to Increase Its Profits," *New York Times Magazine*, September 13, 1970.
[20] Committee for Economic Development, *Social Responsibilities of Business Corporations* (New York: CED, 1971), p. 11.
[21] New York: Business Roundtable, October 1981, pp. 12 and 14.

After these statements from top executives appeared, the range of social programs assumed by business expanded rapidly in education, the arts, public health, housing, the environment, literacy, employee relations, and other areas. However, although the business elite formally rejected "Friedmanism," corporate cultures, which change only at glacial rates, still promoted a single-minded obsession with efficiency and financial results. The belief that a trade-off existed between profits and social responsibility was (and still is) widespread and visible in corporate actions. The newer, expanded theory of corporate social responsibility protected the legitimacy of the large corporation, though it failed to counter public cynicism or activist discontent. And Friedman's views remain an article of faith for many economic conservatives.[22]

Friedmanism
The theory that the sole responsibility of a corporation is to optimize profits while obeying the law.

BASIC ELEMENTS OF SOCIAL RESPONSIBILITY

Three principle elements of social responsibility are market actions, externally mandated actions, and voluntary actions. Figure 5.1 illustrates the relative magnitudes of each one, how they have changed over historical eras, and how change will progress if the trend toward expansion of the idea of corporate social responsibility continues. To be socially responsible, a corporation must fulfill its duties in each area of action.

Market actions are competitive responses to forces in markets. Such actions have always dominated and this will continue. When a corporation responds to markets, it fulfills its first and most important social responsibility. General Motors, for example, creates several hundred thousand jobs, pays billions of dollars in taxes to governments, and makes valuable products. The impact of every large business in this basic area is of far greater significance than the voluntary actions it may undertake. Some critics believe that certain businesses, for instance, gambling, defense, tobacco, animal agriculture, and alcohol, are irresponsible no matter how profitable. Such judgments do not invalidate the general rule that the overriding impact of a corporation on society (therefore, the greatest test of responsibility) originates in normal market operations.

Mandated actions are programs required either by government regulation or by agreements negotiated with stakeholders, such as union contracts or codes of conduct. For corporations in developed nations, the size of this element grew significantly in the twentieth century and it is now slowly expanding in international operations.

The third element is *voluntary actions*, or actions that go beyond legal, regulatory, or negotiated mandates. Some voluntary actions can be described as "legal plus" because they exceed required mandates. An example would be cutting pollution below legally permitted levels. Other actions are unrelated to mandates, but respond to public consensus. Charitable giving is an example. A few companies have acted beyond public consensus in ways that they believed were responsible. For example, Benetton Group once ran an anti–death penalty ad campaign in the

[22] See, for example, David Henderson, *Misguided Virtue: False Notions of Corporate Social Responsibility* (Philadelphia: Coronet Books, 2001). Henderson is a former chief economist at the Organization for Economic Cooperation and Development.

FIGURE 5.1
Principal
Elements
of Social
Responsibility
and Their
Evolving
Magnitudes

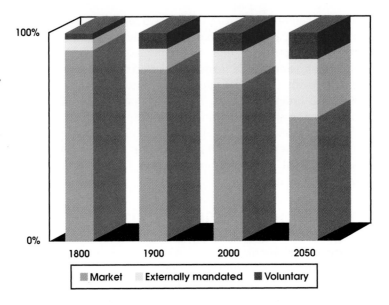

United States. Ads showing the faces of murderers on death row were intended to provoke debate on the death penalty. They did, but they also led Sears, Roebuck to drop Benetton clothing from its stores and ignited a boycott of Benetton outlets by relatives of murdered children.[23]

GENERAL PRINCIPLES OF CORPORATE SOCIAL RESPONSIBILITY

No universal rules for social responsibility apply to every company. Managers must decide what their firms will do. The following are general principles to guide them.

- *Corporations are economic institutions run for profit.* Their greatest responsibility is to provide economic benefits. They should be judged primarily on economic criteria and cannot be expected to meet purely social objectives without financial incentives. However, corporations must incur short-run costs to correct social problems that threaten long-term sustainability. And solving social problems can sometimes be profitable.

- *All firms must follow multiple bodies of law,* including (1) corporation laws and chartering provisions, (2) the civil and criminal laws of nations, (3) bodies of regulation that protect stakeholders, and (4) international laws. However, obeying the law is a minimum. Law is reactive and lags behind emerging norms and duties.

- *Corporations have a duty to correct the adverse social impacts they cause.* They should try to internalize *external costs,* or costs of production borne by society. A factory dumping toxic effluent into a stream creates costs such as human and animal disease imposed on innocents, not on the company or its customers.

external cost
A cost not paid
by a firm or its
customers, but
by members of
society.

[23] Jerry Della Famina, "Benetton Ad Models Are Dressed to Kill Sales," *The Wall Street Journal,* March 20, 2000, p. A34.

- *Social responsibility varies with company characteristics* such as size, industry, strategies, marketing techniques, locations, internal cultures, stakeholder demands, and managers' values. Thus, a global pharmaceutical company such as Merck has a far different impact on society than a local insurance company, so its responsibilities are both different and greater.

- *Managers should try to meet legitimate needs of stakeholders.* Studies report general agreement by managers that their primary responsibilities are to three groups: customers, stockholders, and employees, with governments and communities also recognized but given lesser emphasis.[24] However, the multiple demands of stakeholders sometimes conflict, and each company must set priorities. Research suggests that the effort made by companies to respond to various stakeholders varies significantly between firms and among industries.[25]

- *Corporate behavior must comply with norms in an underlying social contract.* To understand this contract and how it changes, managers can study the direction of national policies and global norms as evidenced in legislation, regulations, treaties, trade agreements, declarations, and public opinion.[26]

- *Corporations should accept a measure of accountability toward stakeholders and publicly report* on their market, mandated, and voluntary actions. Reporting is most effective when it is transparent, that is, when it is verifiable by parties outside the firm.

ARE SOCIAL AND FINANCIAL PERFORMANCE RELATED?

Scholars have done many studies to see if companies that are more socially responsible are also more profitable. A recent review of 95 such studies over 30 years found that a majority (53 percent) showed a positive relationship between profits and responsibility. However, 24 percent of them found no relationship, 19 percent a mixed relationship, and 5 percent a negative relationship.[27] Overall, these studies generally support the thesis that social responsibility and profits go together. Yet since many studies have mixed, inconclusive, or negative findings, this conclusion cannot be stated with the highest confidence.

[24] This is the order of priority revealed in surveys of 220 CEOs of large U.S. companies. See Linda D. Lerner and Gerald E. Fryxell, "CEO Stakeholder Attitudes and Corporate Social Activity in the Fortune 500," *Business & Society,* April 1994, table 2. See also Steven F. Walker and Jeffrey W. Marr, *Stakeholder Power* (Cambridge, MA: Perseus, 2001), pp. 24–25 and 156, for reinforcing survey results.

[25] Catherine Lerme Bendheim, Sandra A. Waddock, and Samuel Graves, "Determining Best Practice in Corporate Stakeholder Relations Using Data Envelopment Analysis: An Industry-Level Study," *Business & Society,* September 1998. This study includes the environment as a stakeholder and not government.

[26] Lee E. Preston and James E. Post, *Private Management and Public Policy: The Principle of Public Responsibility* (Englewood Cliffs, NJ: Prentice Hall, 1975), p. 57; Sandra Waddock, "Creating Corporate Accountability: Foundational Principles to Make Corporate Citizenship Real," *Journal of Business Ethics* 50 (2004).

[27] Joshua Daniel Margolis and James Patrick Walsh, *People and Profits: The Search for a Link between a Company's Social and Financial Performance* (Mahwah, NJ: Lawrence Erlbaum, 2001), p. 10. See also Jennifer J. Griffin and John F. Mahon, "The Corporate Social Performance and Corporate Financial Performance Debate," *Business & Society,* March 1997.

The inconsistency of results from study to study is not surprising given the difficult problems of method that researchers face. To begin, there is no universal definition of social responsibility that fits every firm. Therefore, an objective ranking of corporations as more or less responsible is impossible. Many studies have used social responsibility rankings of companies done by progressive organizations such as the Domini Social Equity Fund, a social responsibility investment fund. Others rely on social responsibility rankings made by executives of Fortune 500 companies, who have a more conservative perspective.

As opposed to the subjectivity of a corporation's social performance it might seem that financial performance can be gauged more objectively; but among measures of profitability such as return on assets, earnings per share, or net income, which is best? In the above-mentioned review of 95 studies, the authors report that researchers drew on 27 different information sources to rate social performance and used 70 different methods of calculating financial performance. This ensures that the findings of one study will not be exactly comparable to the findings of others.

Thus, while most academic studies suggest that more responsible companies are more profitable, there are still enough methodological questions to reserve final judgment. Yet it seems fair to say that corporations rated high in social responsibility are no less profitable than lower-rated firms and are probably doing a little better.

CORPORATE SOCIAL RESPONSIBILITY IN GLOBAL CONTEXT

By the end of the twentieth century the doctrine of corporate social responsibility had been widely accepted in industrialized nations, particularly the United States, but also in Europe, Japan, Australia, and a few developing nations such as India and the Philippines. Wide consensus over its meaning, extent, and execution existed within the developed economies. However, recent events have fueled new debate over the duties of corporations in their international operations. In the 1980s and 1990s trade increased as free markets spread and governments lowered trade barriers. Dominant corporations in developed nations became larger and more transnational. As they did, critics and observers perceived the exercise of too much power and too little restraint in their foreign operations.

The perception that transnationals eluded proper controls was rooted in several observations. First, international law is weak in addressing social impacts of business. It strongly protects commercial rights, but norms protecting cultures, human rights, and nature are less codified. Second, giant corporations are subject to strong laws and regulations in their home countries, but restraints often diminish in foreign operations. Regulation is uneven in less developed nations with insular norms and rudimentary laws and institutions. Sometimes rules are underdeveloped or only feebly enforced. Some governments have overly bureaucratic agencies that become riddled with corruption. Some have incompetent leaders. And still others are undemocratic, run by elites that syphon off the economic benefits of corporate investment and neglect public needs. Third, in adapting to global economic growth corporations have used strategies of joint venture, outsourcing, and supply chain extension that create efficiencies, but sometimes also distance them from direct accountability for social harms. And fourth, more national regulation of multinational corporations is unlikely. The governments of emerging nations fear, correctly, that stricter rules and regulations will deter foreign investment.

Developed countries have highly evolved, expertly enforced domestic regulations. Yet these do not apply outside their borders. The reason is that enforcement is problematic. In international law, *extraterritoriality* is the exercise of jurisdiction by one nation over actions that occur within the borders of another nation. Treaties that Western colonial nations forced on subject countries in the 1800s often gave them extraterritorial rights within a colonized country, so that the doctrine today has a bad taint. If the United States were to enforce the Clean Air Act on American oil company facilities in African nations it would be regarded as an arrogant violation of the sovereign rights of those regimes, even if it led to cleaner air. In addition, less-developed nations might fight higher regulatory standards, fearing they would scare away foreign investors. And problems of gathering data or evidence in distant countries make extension of domestic regulation impractical.

In a world where regulation is uneven some corporations, such as Merck, have operated with high standards across nations. But there are indications that some others have compromised their standards in permissive host country environments. Many reports are accusations by progressive left critics.[28] The docket of cases brought under a singular law, the *Alien Tort Claims Act,* opens a window into allegations of the most serious kind. This law allows foreign citizens to bring civil actions in American courts for violations of international law occurring anywhere in the world.

The original intent of the Alien Tort Claims Act, an old law passed in 1789, was to bring justice to pirates on the high seas.[29] But it was rediscovered by progressive and labor movement lawyers who saw it as a way to sue corporations in U.S. courts for actions in violation of international law anywhere in the world. Since the early 1990s there have been more than 50 such lawsuits, most alleging human rights abuses and environmental crimes. So far, none of them have led to judgments against a corporation. The cases bring up grave charges. For example, Pfizer was accused of injuring Nigerians by secretly administering an experimental antibiotic, Coca-Cola of complicity in the murder of a union leader trying to organize a bottling plant in Columbia, Adidas America of using Chinese prisoners to make soccer balls, the British mining firm Rio Tinto of exposing New Guinea villagers to toxic chemicals, and Unocal of cooperation with a Burmese military that kidnapped and forced citizens to labor on a gas pipeline project.[30]

extra-territoriality
A term used in law for application of one nation's laws within the borders of another. It also refers to the immunity commonly granted to foreign diplomats.

Alien Tort Claims Act
A 1789 law permitting foreign citizens to litigate alleged violations of international law in federal district courts.

---

[28] See, for example, issues of the *Multinational Monitor,* a magazine of the progressive left.

[29] The entirety of this statute is a brief clause in the Judiciary Act of 1789 providing that "the district courts shall have original jurisdiction of any civil action by an alien for a tort only, committed in violation of the law of nations or a treaty of the United States."

[30] See *Abdullahi v. Pfizer, Inc.,* 01 Civ. 8118, 2d Cir. N.Y. (2003); *Sinaltrainal v. Coca-Cola Company,* 256 F. Supp. 2d 1345 (2003); *Ge v. Peng,* 201 F. Supp. 2d 14 (2000); *Sarei v. Rio Tinto Limited,* 221 F. Supp. 2d 1116 (2002); and *Doe I v. Unocal,* 100 F. Supp. 2d 1294 (2000). *Doe I v. Unocal* was settled in 2004 when Unocal agreed to fund projects to improve the living conditions of Burmese living near the pipeline.

Companies in the apparel and toy industries have been targeted by progressive and union activists during antisweatshop campaigns. Adidas, Disney, The Gap, Levi Strauss, Mattel, Nike, and Reebok all have codes focused on labor and human rights practices along their global chains of suppliers and contractors. Such companies obsessively cultivate brand images, and loss of brand reputation among consumers is disastrous. All companies that promote consumer brands are similarly vulnerable to brand attacks. To protect its brand, Starbucks has both "Coffee Sourcing Guidelines" that set forth environmentally friendly growing practices for coffee farms and a "Supplier Code of Conduct" designed to prevent human rights, labor, and environmental abuses elsewhere along the supply chain. Rolls-Royce, an especially venerable brand, has a code of conduct for its "supplier/partners" to set forth "minimum" ethical, human rights, and labor standards for contractors in countries with "different legal and cultural environments." The Rolls-Royce code contains a "snowball clause," or a requirement that contractors use their power over firms in their own supply chains. This clause, which is frequently used by powerful companies at the center of large supply networks, extends the reach of a code.

snowball clause
A clause in a conduct code requiring or exhorting the corporation to use its power over contractors to make them comply with code standards.

A few companies have invested heavily in making their codes work. The Gap created a vendor compliance department where 100 employees monitor application of a code of conduct in contractors' workplaces around the world. At Nike, a staff of 80 works to check on supplier compliance with its code of labor and environmental practices.[34] Many other firms undertake extensive activity related to their codes. Yet, to be effective codes must satisfy attentive stakeholders. Activists and academics are highly critical of most efforts. They say the codes are filled with high-minded intentions, but methods for fulfilling them in daily operations are not specified. Companies do not commit themselves to compliance with international norms such as those set forth in the *Universal Declaration of Human Rights*.[35]

Universal Declaration of Human Rights
A declaration recognizing the "equal and inalienable rights of all members of the human family" adopted by the General Assembly of the United Nations in 1948. It contains thirty articles that catalog basic human rights. It is not legally enforceable but has status as a benchmark in judicial proceedings.

Most companies reject rigorous monitoring by outsiders and simply check on themselves, a practice not designed to instill trust in those with a cynical view of corporate behavior, precisely the audience the code is intended to reassure. Even where monitoring occurs, it is often undisclosed or reported only in company-written reports. But such reports are not, in the language of academics, "transparent." That is, the facts cannot be independently verified outside the company. In a statement that sums up the feelings of many observers, S. Prakash Sethi writes:

> To date, MNCs have a poor record of implementing their own codes. . . . A review of MNC efforts, and those of their trade associations, in the sphere of codes of conduct over the past 15+ years indicates that MNCs, in general, do not see codes of conduct as an opportunity to improve their overseas performance with regard to labor, environment, and other related issues. . . . Instead, these codes are viewed as a necessary evil and an inconvenient nuisance, which should be handled with minimum cost and as little effort as possible.[36]

[34] Dara O'Rourke, "Outsourcing Regulation: Analyzing Nongovernmental Systems of Labor Standards and Monitoring," *Policy Studies Journal*, February 2003, p. 1.

[35] Penelope Simons, "Corporate Voluntarism and Human Rights: The Adequacy and Effectiveness of Voluntary Self-Regulation Regimes," *Industrial Relations*, January 2004, p. 101.

[36] S. Prakash Sethi, *Setting Global Standards: Guidelines for Creating Codes of Conduct in Multinational Corporations* (New York: John Wiley & Sons, 2003), pp. 83–84.

Industry Codes

When an industry is besieged by critics, it sometimes creates an industrywide code. The argument for doing this is that companies in the industry face similar competitive forces and external pressures. Therefore, to create a level playing field in which no company is disadvantaged by following costly social responsibility standards, a common code is desirable. In addition, a single code avoids the disorder of multiple codes. An unspoken advantage is that the industry-backed organization that executes the code will be lenient with member companies. Again, the industries most likely to have international codes are those in which companies have sensitive brand images or have been the targets of pressure campaigns. These include the toy, banking, carpet, apparel, sugar, chemical, and extractive industries. Here are two examples.

- The Equator Principles are guidelines adopted by 20 large banks that lend to finance development projects such as dams and pipelines. They were adopted in 2003 by bankers under pressure from activists attacking such loans for disrupting indigenous peoples and causing pollution and deforestation. The nine principles adopt lending criteria used by the World Bank. They require loan recipients to study and mitigate adverse impacts. Activists have complained that compliance with the principles cannot be verified.

- The Free Labor Association (FLA) Workplace Code of Conduct is joined by 13 well-known, large apparel and footwear companies and more than 500 contractors. It consists of nine general principles along with a document of standards and monitoring procedures. Its origins were troubled. In 1996 President Clinton, responding to concerns of unions and human rights groups about sweatshop working conditions, convened meetings between companies, unions, and human rights groups to negotiate principles for workplaces in Asia and Latin America. Eventually, the companies broke away from the discussions and, meeting in secret with a few of the less fervent human rights groups, came up with their own standards in 1998. The FLA code has been criticized as lax.[37] For example, it allows employers to require 60-hour workweeks and permits paying local minimum wage rates even if these are below a living wage. Standards are largely qualitative and allow auditors considerable leeway in determining violations. Violations are not made public.

Global Compact
A set of 10 voluntary principles based on international norms administered by the United Nations. Member companies are to follow the principles in every country in which they do business.

global corporate citizenship
A metaphorical term that compares multinational corporations operating in the world economy to citizens living in a nation. The implication is that, like citizens, corporations have both rights and duties.

Industry codes invite compromises fatal to credibility. To succeed they must include most companies. But this invites compromise to bring in companies that are less enthusiastic about high standards. Leading companies that might gain competitive advantage by introducing higher standards are stuck with the common denominator.[38] However, despite dismissal by highly critical activists, industry codes are often effective shields against consumer perceptions of inaction. And they set a precedent for use of a code.

The United Nations and the Global Compact

One of the most important of the collaborative codes is the *Global Compact*, a set of 10 principles to guide corporate action set forth by the United Nations. The United Nations promotes the idea of *global corporate citizenship*, meaning that transnational

[37] See, for example, ibid., chap. 8.
[38] See the discussion in ibid., pp. 85–89.

The OECD Guidelines for Multinational Enterprises

GENERAL POLICIES

Enterprises should take fully into account established policies in the countries in which they operate, and consider the views of other stakeholders. In this regard, enterprises should:

1. Contribute to economic, social and environmental progress with a view to achieving sustainable development.

2. Respect the human rights of those affected by their activities consistent with the host government's international obligations and commitments.

3. Encourage local capacity building through close co-operation with the local community, including business interests, as well as developing the enterprise's activities in domestic and foreign markets, consistent with the need for sound commercial practice.

4. Encourage human capital formation, in particular by creating employment opportunities and facilitating training opportunities for employees.

5. Refrain from seeking or accepting exemptions not contemplated in the statutory or regulatory framework related to environmental, health, safety, labour, taxation, financial incentives, or other issues.

6. Support and uphold good corporate governance principles and develop and apply good corporate governance practices.

7. Develop and apply effective self-regulatory practices and management systems that foster a relationship of confidence and mutual trust between enterprises and the societies in which they operate.

8. Promote employee awareness of, and compliance with, company policies through appropriate dissemination of these policies, including through training programmes.

9. Refrain from discriminatory or disciplinary action against employees who make *bona fide* reports to management or, as appropriate, to the competent public authorities, on practices that contravene the law, the *Guidelines* or the enterprise's policies.

10. Encourage, where practicable, business partners, including suppliers and sub-contractors, to apply principles of corporate conduct compatible with the *Guidelines*.

11. Abstain from any improper involvement in local political activities.

Source: Organisation for Economic Co-operation and Development, *The OECD Guidelines for Multinational Enterprises: Revision 2000* (Paris: OECD, 2000). Reprinted with permission.

2,300 companies have formally committed themselves to the Charter's principles. The ICC provides no standards or guidelines for implementing them and does no enforcement. It sees the standards as a framework for building an environmental management system that incorporates other, more actionable codes, for example, the International Organization for Standardization's 14000 and 14001 standards for certifying the environmental performance of facilities.

- The OECD Guidelines for Multinational Corporations is the only comprehensive global code of corporate conduct endorsed by governments. The OECD, or the Organization for Economic Co-operation and Development, is a group of 30 nations in Europe and North America formed in 1961. Its main purpose is to boost economic growth of its members by expanding trade. However, the Guidelines emphasize that corporations must act responsibly if global economic progress is to continue. Eight non-OECD nations have adopted the guidelines, bringing the number of countries to 38, including those that are home to nearly all large transnationals. The Guidelines consist of 11 general policies (see the box) that are then supplemented with more detailed guidance statements. Governments are charged with receiving complaints of violations and mediating settlements.

- The Calvert Women's Principles were set forth in 2004 by the Calvert Group, the largest social responsibility mutual fund family in the United States. The six-principle code with 40 action steps commits corporations to promote gender equality in pay, train and promote women, and protect women from discrimination and violence. The Preamble states that women are the majority of low-level global production workers and 70 percent of those living on $1 or less a day. The code is designed to make corporations the "vehicles for addressing gender inequalities and advancing the global empowerment of women."[42] Calvert plans to use it for evaluating its investments and will develop audit procedures for signatory companies.

- The CERES Principles are a set of 10 principles for corporate environmental responsibility. CERES stands for the Coalition for Environmentally Responsible Economies, an alliance of progressive environmental groups, investors, and religious orders. These groups were galvanized by the *Exxon Valdez* oil spill to create the code in 1989. About 60 companies have signed on, including Bank of America and General Motors, but most are smaller firms. Many larger firms approached by the coalition have refused to sign.

Assessing the Codes

Corporate conduct codes are in an early stage of development. Their ultimate utility and form are not clear. But they are now a fundamental mechanism of the global drive for corporate social responsibility. The conduct code idea has flowered because it has important advantages for both corporations and their would-be reformers.

For corporations, codes protect brands, reputations, trade liberalization, and capitalism with voluntary, flexible action instead of regulation. For activists, codes hold the promise of making corporations more responsible in a period when added government regulation is unlikely. Codes also build recognition for global norms of commerce. As these norms jell, dodging them is harder for corporations.

Codes have been criticized for the arrogance of promoting mainly standards of the developed world and holding these superior to different political and social customs in other regions. For example, codes based on norms from International Labor Organisation protocols give workers the basic right of collective bargaining. In some countries, such as China, the government does not recognize this right. The Sullivan Principles denied the right of racial repression asserted by the South African government. Yet events in South Africa illustrated the general rule that values about basic rights in growing economies converge on international standards given the exposure to them.

[42] *The Calvert Women's Principles: A Global Code of Conduct for Corporations* (Bethesda, MD: The Calvert Group, Ltd., 2004), p. 1.

Codes are based on the agendas of the entities that create them. This is the reason for their proliferation. The current overgrowth of codes causes confusion and "code fatigue." For example, an Asian factory making clothing or shoes for a number of U.S. and European companies might need to certify compliance with standards in at least four widely used industry and multi-stakeholder codes plus additional standards based on specific corporate codes. More codes are under development. But eventually a few strong and widely supported codes are likely to emerge from a Darwinian competition among the current contenders. Winning codes will be those that involve multiple stakeholders, focus on reasonable and measurable actions, and satisfy activist demands for transparency.

Finally, the rise of codes and the international expansion of the corporate social responsibility doctrine has failed to placate critics. For 30 years Milton Moskowitz published first a newsletter and then a journal focused on social responsibility. At first he believed that corporate leaders were serious about a new gospel of virtue in business. Recently he has come to perceive that the actions of its executive advocates and of the companies that embodied it masked the conduct of business as usual.

> Words, words, words. Looking over the history of corporate social responsibility, I can see it has consisted of 95 percent rhetoric and 5 percent action. Companies are adept at drawing up high-sounding mission statements. Changing the way they do business? That's something else.[43]

Christian Aid, a British NGO, recently published a report about the state of corporate social responsibility. It was highly critical. The report included case studies of three corporations—Coca-Cola, Shell, and British American Tobacco—that contrasted each firm's commitment to high principles with reports and allegations of behavior that did not live up to them. It concluded that codes and voluntary responsibility initiatives were inadequate.

> In simple terms, companies make loud, public commitments to principles of ethical behaviour and undertake "good works." . . . The problem with CSR, we say, is that it is unable to deliver on its grand promises. [It] . . . is a completely inadequate response to the sometimes devastating impact that multinational companies can have in an ever-more globalised world—and . . . it is actually used to mask that impact. . . . Whatever responsible initiatives companies choose to carry out on their own behalf, binding international standards of corporate behaviour must be established to guarantee that the rights of people and the environment in developing countries are properly protected.[44]

CONCLUDING OBSERVATIONS

Historically, corporations have been motivated primarily by the central focus on profits in classical economic ideology. However, as they have grown in size and power, they have been exhorted and pressured to alter this single-minded focus. This is because (1) the idea of corporate social responsibility has continuously expanded in meaning and (2) the power of stakeholders to define corporate duty has increased.

---

[43] "What Has CSR Really Accomplished?" *Business Ethics,* May/June and July/August 2002, p. 4.

[44] Christian Aid, *Behind the Mask: The Real Face of Corporate Social Responsibility* (London: Christian Aid, 2004), pp. 2, 3, and 4.

FIGURE 5.2 **The Evolution of Corporate Social Responsibility**

Although the term corporate social responsibility is of recent use, the idea it represents has been under construction for more than two centuries. This timeline shows how various elements changed to expand the idea. The duty to serve society by making a profit has remained constant. Philanthropy has been a constant duty of business owners and later of corporations themselves. The duty to comply with regulation has grown since the first restrictive statutes in the late 1800s. And the theory of social responsibility has evolved from the cruel denials of Herbert Spencer to broad expectations on transnational corporations today.

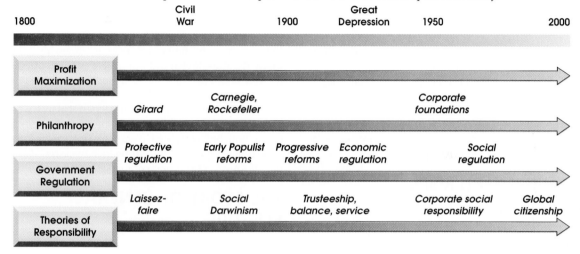

Whereas only a short time ago the norms and power equations of individual nations defined the responsibilities of corporations, the explosive growth of global trade and global corporations created new standards and practices of social responsibility tied to global norms. The rise of these new standards and expectations is reflected in proliferating corporate codes of conduct. If history is any guide, the doctrine will continue to expand.

In this chapter we focused on defining and explaining the idea of corporate social responsibility and its evolution. Figure 5.2 summarizes this evolution. In the next chapter we look at the methods corporations adopt to ensure that they carry out their responsibilities to society.

The Jack Welch Era at General Electric

In April 1981 John Francis "Jack" Welch, Jr., became chief executive officer of General Electric. He held the position for 20 years until retiring in September 2001. During that time, he transformed GE, taking a solidly profitable manufacturing company and turning it into an exceptionally profitable conglomerate dominated by service businesses. If you had invested $100 in GE stock when Welch took the reins and held it for 20 years, it would have been worth $6,749.

Welch is lauded for his creative management style and became a national business hero. A fawning *BusinessWeek* article called him "America's #1 Manager."[1] *Fortune* magazine gushed that GE under Welch was "the best-managed, best-regarded company

[1] John A. Byrne, "Jack: A Close-Up Look at How America's #1 Manager Runs GE," *BusinessWeek*, June 8, 1998, p. 91.

in America."[2] Yet the intense, aggressive Welch made fortunes for GE shareholders using methods that had mixed impacts on employees, unions, communities, other companies, and governments. As a result, not everyone sees the GE performance as a model for corporate social responsibility. Upon Welch's retirement, the *Multinational Monitor,* a progressive magazine founded by Ralph Nader, devoted an entire issue to making "The Case Against GE." The lead editorial branded Welch as a corporate titan opposed to rules of society and said that his actions were "disastrous" for workers and communities.[3]

Did General Electric under Jack Welch carry out the full range of its duties to society? Did it fall short? Readers are invited to assess how closely the company's actions conformed to ideals of corporate social responsibility found in the definitions, examples, and guidelines from this chapter.

JACK WELCH RISES

Most top executives come from backgrounds of wealth and privilege. Jack Welch is an exception. He was born in 1935 to working-class Irish parents in a small Massachusetts town. His father was a quiet, passive man who endured as a railroad conductor punching tickets on a commuter train. Welch's mother was a dominating woman who caused her husband to wilt but instilled a powerful drive in her son. Welch was an outstanding student at the University of Massachusetts at Amherst and went on to get a doctorate in chemical engineering at the University of Illinois.

After graduating, he started working at a GE plastics factory in 1960. His tremendous energy and ambition were very apparent. He was so competitive in weekend softball games that his aggressive play alienated co-workers and he stopped going. After one year, he threatened to quit when he got the same $1,000 raise as everyone else. His boss cajoled him into staying and as the years and promotions flashed by he never again wavered.

As he rose, Welch exhibited a fiery temperament and expected those around him to share his intensity. He was blunt, impatient with subordinates, and

emotionally volatile. He loved no-holds-barred discussions in meetings but frequently put people on the spot, saying, "My six-year-old kid could do better than that."[4] With every promotion, he sized up his new staff with a cold eye and purged those who failed to impress him. "I'm the first to admit," he says, "I could be impulsive in removing people during those early days."[5]

This was just preparation for the big leagues to come. GE had a polished corporate culture reflecting the eastern establishment values of its leadership over many decades. Welch did not fit. He was impatient, frustrated by the company's bureaucracy, and lacking in deference. With this mismatch GE might have repulsed Welch at some point, but his performance was outstanding. Several times he got mixed reviews for a promotion, but because of exemplary financial results he was never blocked. In 1981 he took over as CEO of one of America's singular companies.

THE STORY OF GENERAL ELECTRIC

The lineage of General Electric goes back to 1879 when Thomas Alva Edison (1847–1931), with the backing of banker J. P. Morgan, started the Edison Electric Light Company to make light bulbs and electrical equipment. Although Edison was a great inventor, he was not a far-sighted manager and the company lost ground in the market for electrical equipment. So in 1892 Morgan took charge, engineering a merger with a competitor and plotting to reduce Edison to a figurehead in the new company.

Morgan disposed of Edison's top managers and dropped the word Edison from its name so that the firm became simply General Electric Company. Morgan sat as a commanding figure on the new company's board. Although Edison was also a director, he attended only the first meeting and never appeared again.[6]

After the merger, GE went on to build a near-monopoly in the incandescent bulb market. Over the years, other products emerged from the company. Early in the twentieth century, its motors worked the

[2] Jerry Useem, "It's All Yours, Jeff. Now What?" *Fortune,* September 17, 2001, p. 64.

[3] "You Don't Know Jack," *Multinational Monitor,* July–August 2001, p. 5.

[4] Jack Welch, *Jack: Straight from the Gut* (New York: Warner Books, 2001), p. 43.

[5] Ibid., p. 43.

[6] Thomas F. O'Boyle, *At Any Cost: Jack Welch, General Electric, and the Pursuit of Profit* (New York: Knopf, 1998), p. 55.

Panama Canal locks, powered battleships, and ran locomotives.[7] GE's research labs bred a profusion of new electrical appliances, including fans, toasters, refrigerators, vacuum cleaners, ranges, garbage disposals, air conditioners, and irons. At first these new inventions were very expensive, but as more people used them production costs fell and they became commodities within the reach of every family. By 1960 GE was credited with a remarkable list of other inventions, including the X-ray machine, the motion picture with sound, fluorescent lighting, the diesel-electric locomotive, the jet engine, synthetic diamonds, the hard plastic Lexan, and Silly Putty.[8]

As it added manufacturing capacity to build these inventions, GE grew. By 1981, when Jack Welch took the reins, the company had $27 billion in revenues and 404,000 employees. It was organized into 50 separate businesses reporting to a layer of six sector executives at corporate headquarters in Fairfield, Connecticut, who in turn reported to the CEO. To make it run, a large and strong staff of researchers and planners created detailed annual plans setting forth revenue goals and other objectives for each business.

THE WELCH ERA BEGINS

Welch believes that managers must confront reality and adapt to the world as it is, not as they wish it to be. As he studied GE's situation in the early 1980s, he saw a corporation that needed to change. GE's manufacturing businesses were still profitable, but margins were shrinking. The wages of American workers were rising even as their productivity was declining. International competition was growing, particularly from the Japanese, who had cost advantages because of a weak yen. Although GE seemed healthy on the surface, ominous forces were gathering in the environment. In addition, Welch saw GE bloated with the layers of bureaucracy that had infuriated him by slowing decisions and frustrating change. The company, as currently operated, could not weather the competitive storms ahead. It would have to change.

Welch articulated a simple guiding vision. Every GE business would be the number one or number two player in its industry. If it failed this test it would

[7] For more on the history of GE see John Winthrop Hammond, *Men and Volts: The Story of General Electric* (Philadelphia: J. B. Lippincott, 1948).

[8] Thomas F. O'Boyle, "'At Any Cost' Is Too High," *Multinational Monitor,* July–August 2001, p. 41.

Jack Welch (1935–). © Bob Daemmrich/CORBIS.

be fixed, closed, or sold. In addition, Welch said that all GE businesses would have to fit into one of three areas—core manufacturing, technology, or services. Any business that fell outside these three strategic hubs was a candidate for sale or closure. This included manufacturing businesses that could not sustain high profit margins.

In the next five years, Welch executed his strategy by closing 73 plants, selling 232 businesses, and eliminating 132,000 workers from GE payrolls.[9] As he conformed GE to his vision, he also bought hundreds of other businesses large and small. Within GE businesses he eliminated jobs through attrition, layoffs, and outsourcing. In the largest acquisition of that period, Welch acquired RCA in 1985. RCA was a giant electronics and broadcasting conglomerate with a storied history as the company that had developed radio technology. After paying $6.7 billion for RCA, Welch chopped it up, keeping NBC and selling other businesses one by one, in effect, destroying the giant

[9] Frank Swoboda, "GE Picks Welch's Successor," *Washington Post,* November 28, 2000, p. E1.

company as an organizational entity. As jobs vanished, Welch got the nickname "Neutron Jack," comparing him with a neutron bomb that left buildings standing but killed everyone inside.

Welch also attacked the GE bureaucracy. One problem was its size. There were too many vice presidents, too many layers, and too many staffs with authority to review and approve decisions. A second problem was the bureaucratic mentality in which headquarters staff practiced a "superficial congeniality" that Welch interpreted as smiling to your face and getting you behind your back.[10] He demolished the hierarchy by laying off thousands of central staff in strategic planning, personnel, and other areas. Then he set out to change GE's culture by promoting the notion of a "boundaryless" organization, or one in which ideas were freely exchanged so that organizational learning could rapidly occur. Welch compared GE to an old house:

> Floors represent layers and the walls functional barriers. To get the best out of an organization, these floors and walls must be blown away, creating an open space where ideas flow freely, independent of rank or function.[11]

Later, Welch introduced the practice of "workout" sessions in which employees in every GE business had an opportunity to confront their bosses to express frustration with bureaucratic practices and suggest more efficient alternatives. Managers in these sessions sat in front of a room filled with subordinates and had to agree or disagree on the spot to carry out suggestions. Thousands of such sessions were held to drive out the bureaucratic mentality. Welch also used Crotonville, the company's campus-like training center on the Hudson River, to meet with managers and instill his vision. He invited candid discussions, and gradually the company culture became more informal and open.

Welch introduced other initiatives that transformed GE. In 1986 he emphasized globalization. The manager of each GE business was held responsible for globalizing that business. This worked so well that by 1998 GE ranked number one in foreign assets among transnational corporations.[12] In 1990 the idea of "best practices" was introduced. GE businesses

were encouraged to share ideas so that something that worked well in one part of the company could be spread to all parts. In 1996 Welch adopted companywide a statistical program called Six Sigma to eliminate defects. Finally, in 1999 he digitized GE, requiring every manager to incorporate the Internet into their operations.

DIFFERENTIATION

Welch is convinced that having the right people in management positions is the single most important cause of success in a business. Early in his career, he developed a colorful vocabulary to differentiate between players. Inept managers were "turkeys" and "dinks," standouts were called "all-stars." As CEO he reinforced strategic initiatives with a system of "differentiation" that generously rewarded managers who achieved performance goals and got rid of those who missed them. In this system, every year each GE business was forced to evaluate its managers and rank them on a "vitality curve" that differentiated among As, Bs, and Cs. The As were committed people, filled with passion for their jobs, who took initiative and exceeded performance goals. They had what Welch called "the four Es of GE leadership":

> very high *energy* levels, the ability to *energize* others around common goals, the *edge* to make tough yes-and-no decisions, and finally, the ability to consistently *execute* and deliver on their promises.[13]

The vitality curve was Darwinian. The As were the top 20 percent, Bs were the middle 70 percent, and Cs were the bottom 10 percent (see Exhibit 1). The As received salary increases, promotions, and stock options. Welch followed their careers closely. He kept large loose-leaf notebooks containing evaluations of the top 750 of GE's 4,000 managers. Bs were considered vital to the success of the company and were coached so that some would become As. Cs were not worth wasting time on and were dismissed. The process was repeated annually, and each time the bottom 10 percent had to go. The curve applied to every GE business. No business leader could claim that his or her group was an exception, though some tried. Filling the A, B, and C categories forced difficult decisions. If 20 managers were evaluated, 2 had to be placed at the bottom and their careers at GE ended. After several years of getting rid of low performers,

---

[10] Welch, *Jack*, p. 96.

[11] Ibid.

[12] United Nations Conference on Trade and Development, *World Investment Report 2000* (New York: U.N., 2000), table III.1.

[13] Welch, *Jack*, p. 158.

EXHIBIT 1
The Vitality Curve

Source: Jack Welch, *Jack: Straight from the Gut* (New York: Warner Books, 2001), p. 95. © 2001 by John F. Welch, Jr. Foundation. Reprinted by permission of Warner Books, Inc.

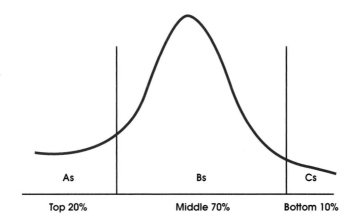

As	Bs	Cs
Top 20%	Middle 70%	Bottom 10%

the leaders of GE businesses resisted classifying anyone as a C, but Welch was relentless. If they didn't identify the bottom 10 percent, he refused to carry out stock option and salary recommendations for the entire group until they did. In this way, the bar of performance was continually raised.

Welch compared people to plants. "If they grow, you have a beautiful garden," he said. "If they don't, you cut them out."[14] He disagreed with those who found the system heartless:

> Some think it's cruel or brutal to remove the bottom 10 percent of our people. It isn't. It's just the opposite. What I think is brutal and "false kindness" is keeping people around who aren't going to grow and prosper. . . . The characterization of a vitality curve as cruel stems from false logic and is an outgrowth of a culture that practices false kindness.[15]

AN ASSESSMENT OF THE WELCH YEARS

With Jack Welch at the helm GE sustained exceptionally high rates of profitability, and shareholders were enriched. Even with five stock splits, earnings per share rose from $.46 in 1981 to $1.07 in 2000, his last full year as CEO, and total return on GE shares averaged 21.5 percent.[16] In 2000 GE reported a net operating margin of 19 percent and earned 27 percent

on invested capital.[17] These are high figures for a large transnational corporation.

Welch also reshaped GE. He continuously bought and sold businesses both large and small. During his last four years alone he made more than 400 acquisitions. One underlying reason for the increasing profitability of GE is that through this churning of businesses GE's center of gravity shifted from manufacturing to services. The GE he inherited earned 85 percent of its revenues from manufacturing; the GE he created got 70 percent of its revenues from services.[18] Exhibit 2 shows the main business segments of GE and their contribution to revenues. The bulk of service revenue comes from GE Capital Services, but manufacturing businesses also engage in services; for example, the company not only makes aircraft engines, it services them over their lifetimes. Welch wrung profits from GE by creating a performance culture. Managers were energized. Plants grew more efficient. For instance, when Welch became CEO, GE's locomotive plant in Erie, Pennsylvania, needed 7,500 hourly employees to make 350 locomotives a year. By 2000 productivity had improved so much that only 4,000 workers could make 900 locomotives a year.[19]

The story of the Welch years has the elements of legend. An ambitious son of working-class parents rises through hard work to command a mighty company, inspire managers everywhere, and become rich

---

[14] Quoted in Carol Hymowitz and Matt Murray, "Raises and Praise or Out the Door—How GE's Chief Rates and Spurs His Employees," *The Wall Street Journal,* June 21, 1999, p. B1.

[15] Welch, *Jack,* p. 162.

[16] Swoboda, "GE Picks Welch's Successor," p. E1; Julie Schlosser, "Jack? Jack Who?" *Fortune,* September 17, 2001, p. 52.

[17] General Electric Company, *GE Annual Report 2000* (Fairfield, CT: General Electric Company, 2001), p. 42.

[18] James Flanigan, "New Boss's Challenge: To Keep GE Together," *Los Angeles Times,* August 26, 2001, p. C1.

[19] "Dignity and Defiance: An Interview with John Hovis," *Multinational Monitor,* July–August 2001, p. 35.

EXHIBIT 2   **GE Business Segments, Sales, and Profits in 2000**   Source: *GE Annual Report: 2000.*

Business Segment	2000 sales (in billions)	2000 profits (in billions)
Aircraft Engines (commercial and military jet engines)	$10.8	$2.5
Appliances (refrigerators, washers, ranges, ovens, air conditioners)	5.9	0.7
Industrial Products and Systems (locomotives, lighting, electric motors, transformers)	11.9	2.2
NBC (television network with 220 affiliated stations)	6.8	1.8
Plastics (polymers, silicones, industrial diamonds)	7.8	1.9
Power Systems (power plants, gas and steam turbines)	14.9	2.8
Technical Products and Services (X-ray machines, MR and CT scanners)	7.9	1.7
GE Capital Services (credit cards, loans, insurance, aircraft leasing)	66.2	5.2
Corporate adjustments, elimination of businesses	(2.3)	
Totals	**$129.9**	**$5.2**

along with the company's shareholders. To reward his long-term leadership, in his last year the GE board awarded him a salary, bonus, special stock award, and options worth $174 million.[20] Welch had accumulated 22 million shares of stock and options in GE worth an estimated $917 million on the day he retired. This is astronomical compensation for one person, but $917 million is only two-thousandths of 1 percent of the $460 billion in equity value created during his tenure.

Not everyone, however, saw Welch's leadership as something to admire or emulate. Early in his career, Welch was compared with a speedboat going down a narrow canal, leaving considerable turbulence in its wake.[21] His detractors say that once Welch was at the master controls of GE he piloted the mammoth organization through global straits the same way. There is no denying that he created wealth. But what were the costs to people, communities, and society?

[20] General Electric Company, *Notice of 2001 Annual Meeting* and *Proxy Statement*, March 9, 2001, pp. 22 and 27.
[21] O'Boyle, *At Any Cost*, p. 59.

The flaws in the Welch performance, according to critics, include the following.

LOSS OF JOBS

Early on, Welch was caricatured as a ruthless job cutter. When he became CEO in 1981, the corporate culture reinforced loyalty. People went to work at GE directly out of college, stayed for 40 years, retired in communities of GE people, and attended GE alumni clubs until rigor mortis set in.

As Welch remodeled GE there were mass layoffs. Within a few years, one of every four employees was gone. Welch believed that the idea of loyalty in GE's culture retarded change, so he rooted it out. At meetings he told employees it was out of fashion. He instructed staff never to use the word *loyalty* in any company document, press release, or publication. He wanted all GE managers to prove their value every day and said people who knew they could be fired worked harder.

In the Welch years there was tumultuous change in the workforce. No total number exists for workers who lost jobs. When he took over there were 404,000 GE employees; when he left there were 313,000. In between, tens of thousands came and went. Union leaders estimate that in his last 15 years GE eliminated 150,000 jobs in the United States through layoffs, subcontracting, and outsourcing to foreign countries.[22] Welch expressed his feelings about these layoffs in his memoirs:

> Removing people will always be the hardest decision a leader faces. Anyone who "enjoys doing it" shouldn't be on the payroll and neither should anyone who "can't do it." I never underestimated the human cost of those layoffs or the hardship they might cause people and communities.[23]

Welch stressed globalization of production to lower costs. Many jobs still exist, but they have left the United States. In 1985 the electrical worker's union had 46,000 members working at GE, but by 2001 the number had declined to 16,000. Ed Fire, the union's president, estimates that two-thirds of the 30,000 lost jobs were simply transferred to low-wage countries.[24] GE has eliminated additional jobs in the United States by pressuring its suppliers to migrate along with it. After moving production to Mexico, for example, GE Aircraft Engines held a 1999 conference in Monterrey for supplier companies and told them to cut costs by moving their facilities (and jobs) to Mexico's low-wage labor market or face inevitable loss of their GE business.[25] Says Fire:

> GE is the quintessential American corporation that has engaged in what has been referred to as the "race to the bottom"—finding the lowest wages, the lowest benefit levels and most intolerant working conditions. . . . I don't think they have given enough consideration to the consequences, particularly the human consequences, of the decisions they make. In my opinion, the decisions are designed too much to increase the company's profitability at the expense of the employees.[26]

[22] "GE Fast Facts," GE Workers United, May 7, 2001, at www.geworkersunited.org/news/fast_facts.asp.

[23] Welch, *Jack*, p. 128.

[24] Ed Fire, president of the International Union of Electronic, Electrical, Salaried, Machine and Furniture Workers–Communications Workers of America, the Industrial Division of CWA, "Resisting the Goliath," *Multinational Monitor*, July–August 2001, p. 31.

[25] Robert Weissman, "Global Management by Stress," *Multinational Monitor*, July–August 2001, p. 20.

[26] Fire, "Resisting the Goliath," pp. 31 and 33.

A DEFECTIVE EVALUATION SYSTEM

The vitality curve rating method is flawed. Forced ranking hurts the morale of employees who are not placed on top. At first, GE ranked employees in five categories instead of three, but it was soon discovered that everyone who failed to land in the top category was demoralized. Hence, three categories were combined into one to create the "vital" 70 percent of Bs in the middle. Disheartening classifications as 2s, 3s, and 4s were abolished. The system also hurts teamwork by pitting people against each other. It may encourage back-stabbing behavior. Its inflexibility produces unfair results when high-performing and low-performing units must classify managers the same way. The bottom 10 percent in an outstanding business may be better than middle- or top-ranked managers on a weaker team. If the sublimated murder of the bottom 10 percent goes on for many years, people who were once in the middle range may find themselves lopped off. Of course, the curve calls the recruiting system into question if recent hires are lost. Finally, finding objective performance criteria for comparisons may be impossible if managers in the evaluation pool do not have identical jobs.

Forced ranking was just one source of pressure on GE managers, who were expected to meet high profit goals and knew that if there were too many mistakes or misjudgments Welch would get rid of them. His confrontational style reduced some to tears. He reportedly believed that overweight people were undisciplined. At GE businesses these people were hidden when he visited for fear they would catch Welch's eye and lose their jobs. One large manager trying to save his career had surgery to staple his colon.[27] Working at GE was also hard on marriages because of the long hours required to be a player. Welch himself divorced in 1987 and remarried in 1990.

Because of Welch's status as a management icon, his approach to forced ranking has spread widely, imposing the practice on many managers at other corporations. Sun Microsystems, for example, uses an identical 20-70-10 percent curve. Even small businesses have picked up the idea. The manager of a Fifth Avenue clothing store once took Welch aside and explained that he had 20 sales workers. "Mr. Welch," he asked, "do I really have to let two go?" "You

[27] O'Boyle, *At Any Cost*, p. 76.

probably do," replied Welch, "if you want the best sales staff on Fifth Avenue."[28]

Although the vitality curve created a high-performance management team, it failed to create diversity at GE. The year before Welch retired the *New York Times* reported that although women and minorities were 40 percent of its domestic workforce, white men dominated its top leadership. The paper ran a collage with faces of the top 31 executives, including heads of the 20 businesses that produced 90 percent of corporate earnings. All were male and all but one were white.[29] Diversity had not been a priority during Welch's tenure, so managers focused on their net income and market share goals. In the subhead for the story the *Times* raised a rhetorical question for Welch: "Can Only White Men Run a Model Company?"

POLLUTION IN THE HUDSON RIVERS

For 35 years several GE manufacturing plants in New York released polychlorinated biphenyls (PCBs) into the Hudson River. They followed permits that set release levels and stopped in 1977 when PCBs were outlawed because of evidence that they were toxic to humans and animals. There is widespread scientific agreement that PCBs cause cancer in test animals and probably cause cancer and a range of other illnesses in humans.

In 1983 the Environmental Protection Agency (EPA) made the Hudson River a Superfund site because more than 100,000 pounds of PCBs released by GE still lay on the river bed. Although the biggest deposits were covered by new sediments, slowing their release into the river, fish were unsafe to eat and the chemicals gradually spread downstream from hot spots of contamination. PCBs are stable molecules that persist in the environment, and because they are fat soluble, they accumulate in human tissue. The GE plants released more than a million pounds of PCBs, and most of this had already floated down 200 miles of river to the ocean, from there migrating around the planet.

The EPA and independent experts studied the river, concluding that dredging the bottom was necessary to remove the dangerous deposits. This would be extremely expensive, and GE was liable for the cost. GE objected. It sponsored studies showing that PCBs were not harmful to health, but these were rejected by the EPA and outside experts. It argued that removing the contaminated sediment would stir up embedded PCBs, doing more harm than good, but the EPA planned to monitor the dredging to prevent this. GE undertook an extensive public relations campaign in the Hudson River region to convince the public that dredging would be an ineffective nuisance. It succeeded in dividing the public to such an extent that people began to shop only at stores where the owners supported their position and classmates teased children over their parents' views.[30] GE hired 17 lobbyists, including a former senator and six former House members, to fight an extended political battle against the cleanup.[31] After many years of delay, the EPA finally ordered dredging in 2001. The cost to GE was estimated at $460 million.[32]

THE GE PENSION FUND

GE has a pension fund covering 485,000 people, including 195,000 who are now retired. As the stock market rose in the 1990s, the fund also rose, and by 2001 it totaled $50 billion. Its liabilities, the future payments it must make to retirees, were only $29 billion, leaving a surplus of $21 billion. GE's retirees and their unions requested increased benefits and cost-of-living increases for pensioners, but the company rejected their demands. By law, it did not have to meet more than the original obligations.

Welch understood that there were several benefits in leaving the pension plan overfunded. First, it generated bottom-line profits. Under current accounting rules, a company can put interest earned by the pension fund on the balance sheet as revenue, and during the Welch years these earnings increased GE's net by as much as 13.7 percent.[33] Second, these "vapor

[28] Welch, *Jack*, p. 434.

[29] Mary Williams Walsh, "Where G.E. Falls Short: Diversity at the Top," *New York Times*, September 3, 2000, sec. 3, pp. 1 and 13.

[30] John M. Glionna, "Dredging Up Ill Will on the Hudson," *Los Angeles Times*, October 1, 2001, p. A17.

[31] Charlie Cray, "Toxins on the Hudson," *Multinational Monitor*, July–August 2001, pp. 9–18.

[32] "Mrs. Whitman Stays the Course," *New York Times*, August 2, 2001, p. A20.

[33] Rob Walker, "Overvalued: Why Jack Welch Isn't God," *The New Republic*, June 18, 2001, p. 22. See *GE Annual Report 2000*, Notes to Consolidated Financial Statements, 6, "Pension Benefits."

profits" increased the salaries of top GE executives, whose bonuses were tied to corporate profits. And third, the excess funding made it easier for GE to acquire companies with underfunded pension plans. This eased deal making, but involved sharing funds set aside for GE workers and retirees with people who got a windfall coming in after careers in other companies.

After being pressured by unions and pensioners, GE announced increases of 15 to 35 percent in 2000. But since 1965 prices had risen by 60 percent, so retirees were still losing ground.[34] Helen Quirini, 81, was part of a group protesting GE's failure to be more generous. After working 39 years at a GE factory, one year less than Welch's 40-year tenure, she retired in 1980 and was receiving $737 a month, or $8,844 a year. She believed that GE management was "out all the time trying to figure out how to screw us" using "accounting gimmicks."[35]

Welch's GE pension is $357,128 a month. Court documents filed in proceedings when Welch divorced his second wife in 2002 revealed that he spent an average of $8,982 a month on food and beverages, slightly more than Helen Quirini's yearly pension income.[36] A 1996 retention agreement between Welch and the GE board also granted him nonmonetary perquisites in retirement. He got lifetime use of a spacious apartment owned by GE at the Trump International Hotel and Tower on Central Park West in New York, including a cook, a housekeeper, and a wait staff plus flowers, laundry and dry cleaning, newspaper and magazine subscriptions, and front-row seats at sporting and entertainment events.[37] He was allowed unlimited use of GE's corporate jets. Criticism of these arrangements arose when they were detailed during the divorce. Although he felt there was nothing improper with them, he elected to pay GE "between $2 and $2.5 million a year" for continued use of the apartment and planes.[38]

CRIMINALITY AT GE

Pressure for performance tempts employees to cut corners. Welch knew this.

> If there was one thing I preached every day at GE, it was integrity. It was our No. 1 value. Nothing came before it. We never had a corporate meeting where I didn't emphasize integrity in my closing remarks.[39]

Yet during his tenure, GE committed a long string of civil and criminal transgressions. The *Multinational Monitor* compiled a "GE Rap Sheet," listing 39 law violations, court-ordered remedies, and fines in the 1990s alone.[40] Many are for pollution hazards from GE facilities. Others are for consumer fraud, including a $165,000 fine for deceptive advertising of light bulbs and a $100 million fine on GE Capital for unfair debt-collection practices. Still others are for defense contracting fraud, including a $69 million fine for diverting fighter contract funds to other purposes and other fines for overcharging on defense contracts.

Since GE is such a large company, technical violations of complex regulations and incidents of wrongdoing by individual managers are inevitable. The *Multinational Monitor* sees "a consistent pattern of violating criminal and civil laws over many years."[41] The key question is whether GE's malfeasance increased because of relentless performance pressure on its managers.

ASSESSING THE SOCIAL RESPONSIBILITY OF GE

Corporate social responsibility is multidimensional. No company achieves the ideal. Profit pressures and other environmental forces dictate the need for compromise. Therefore, we must weigh overall achievement against what is possible, not against perfection.

General Electric in the Welch years fulfilled its primary economic responsibilities to society. It was remarkably profitable. It paid taxes—$5.7 billion in 2000. Shareholders, including pension and mutual funds, were enriched. Many of its managers became multimillionaires in GE stock. In the Welch system,

[34] "GE Pension Fund Story: Workers Pay, GE Benefits," GE Workers United, April 1, 2001, at www.geworkersunited.org/pensions/index.asp?ID+61.

[35] Vincent Lloyd, "Penny Pinching the Retirees at GE," *Multinational Monitor,* July–August 2001, p. 23.

[36] "Here's the Retirement Jack Welch Built: $1.4 Million a Month," *The Wall Street Journal,* October 31, 2002, p. A1.

[37] Geraldine Fabrikant, "G.E. Expenses for Ex-Chief Cited in Filing," *New York Times,* September 6, 2002, p. C1.

[38] Jack Welch, "My Dilemma and How I Resolved It," *New York Times,* September 16, 2002, p. A14.

[39] Welch, *Jack,* pp. 279–80.

[40] "GE: Decades of Misdeeds and Wrongdoing," *Multinational Monitor,* July–August 2001, p. 26.

[41] Ibid., p. 30.

however, there was a transfer of wealth from workers to shareholders. He insulated himself from the pain this caused by rationalizing that what he did was for the greater good.

> I believe social responsibility begins with a strong, competitive company. Only a healthy enterprise can improve and enrich the lives of people and their communities. . . . That's why a CEO's primary social responsibility is to assure the financial success of the company. Only a healthy, winning company has the resources and the capability to do the right thing.[42]

General Electric engages in a broad range of community activities. In 2000 its philanthropic foundation, the GE Fund, made $40 million in grants to colleges, universities, and nonprofit groups in the United States and in other countries. The Elfun Society, a global group of GE employees and retirees, undertook community projects, including tutoring, playground construction, repairing school equipment and recording machines for the blind, blood drives, and Special Olympics. In 2000 current and former GE employees volunteered 1 million hours of community service. Doing these things, GE clearly fulfilled a range of voluntary responsibilities. On the other hand, the company pressured cities, counties, and states to lower taxes by threatening to move

operations elsewhere, and this lowered budgets for schools and infrastructure.

General Electric obeys the law and complies with government regulations. However, critics believe that the company is too politically powerful and that it succeeds in having many laws and regulations written in favorable ways. Jack Welch emphasized integrity to managers. There were some lapses, and some of his actions related to employees will rise to the heavens for ultimate evaluation.

Questions

1. Corporate social responsibility is defined in Chapter 5 as the corporate duty to create wealth by using means that avoid harm to, protect, or enhance societal assets. Did GE in the Welch era fulfill this duty? Could it have done better? What should it have done?

2. Does GE under Welch illustrate a narrower view of corporate social responsibility closer to Friedman's view that the only social responsibility is to increase profits while obeying the law?

3. How well did GE comply with the "General Principles of Corporate Social Responsibility" set forth in the section of that title in the chapter?

4. What are the pros and cons of ranking shareholders over employees and other stakeholders? Is it wrong to see employees as costs of production? Should GE have rebalanced its priorities?

---

[42] Welch, *Jack*, pp. 381–82.

Chapter **Six**

Implementing Social Responsibility

The Chad-Cameroon Pipeline Project

In 1974 an exploratory Exxon well hit oil in a remote desert in Chad. It was in an inaccessible area and nothing further was done until the mid-1990s, when new geological data showed that the well sat on a billion-barrel pool of oil. Now Exxon wanted to develop the field. To get the oil it planned a 660-mile pipeline across Chad's scorching desert, through the Pygmy-inhabited rain forests of neighboring Cameroon, and out from the African coast to an offshore tanker facility in the Atlantic Ocean. Costing $3.7 billion, the pipeline would be the largest private project in Africa. To pay for it, Exxon formed a joint venture with two other energy giants, Petronas of Malaysia and ChevronTexaco.

This meant billions of dollars in oil revenue for Chad, one of the world's poorest countries, and ample pipeline-related revenues for Cameroon, a country only slightly more fortunate. Yet knowledgeable observers were alarmed. African oil bonanzas have a history of enriching foreign oil companies and dictators while aggravating local economic and social problems. The sudden wealth distorts national economies. Rising foreign earnings drive up local currencies, making domestic goods less competitive and causing manufacturing and agriculture to shrivel. People leave the land and relocate to cities where they cannot find work. Corruption rises as government officials take fees and payments from oil firms. Violence is common as autocratic politicians and rival tribes struggle to control oil royalties. The cumulative effect of all this is usually an increase in poverty, political repression, and environmental damage.

The cheerless story of black gold is repeated over and over in Africa. In Gabon and Equatorial Guinea dictatorial and single-party regimes sank into corruption and mismanaged their oil revenues. In Angola, the Congo, and Sudan civil war and ethnic strife were aggravated by sudden windfalls of oil riches. Nigeria has received $300 billion of oil revenue since 1979, yet average income is still under $1 a day.[1] What would happen in Chad and Cameroon?

According to an observer with an African antipoverty group: "Inserting massive oil revenues into countries with weak institutions, poor track records on democracy

---

[1] Gal Luft, "Africa Drowns in a Pool of Oil," *Los Angeles Times,* July 1, 2003, p. B13.

and governance, and few countervailing forces in society is generally a recipe for disaster."[2] Chad has a repressive government, an ongoing civil war, and a preindustrial economy that is 85 percent agriculture. According to Transparency International, Cameroon is the most corrupt nation in the world. Neither government has strong environmental laws.

When environmental and human rights groups learned about Exxon's plan, they drummed up a global campaign to stop it. However, they faced opposition from groups within Chad that abhorred the project but saw it as the nation's only chance for advancement. The estimated economic benefits for the 25- to 30-year life of the pipeline were enormous: $8.5 billion overall for Chad and $900 million for Cameroon.[3] Was there a way to build and operate it in a socially and environmentally responsible way?

Advocacy groups turned to the World Bank, pushing it to impose a novel scheme on Chad's government requiring oil revenue to be spent for the good of the nation's poor. Chad's legislature enacted a plan in which oil revenue will go into a special account in London controlled by an independent monitoring group. The group will then disburse money to banks in Chad for expenditures on social development. Under the plan, 72 percent of the revenues will go to health, education, agriculture, and environmental projects; 4.5 percent to development of towns near the oil fields; 10 percent to a fund for the benefit of future generations; and the remaining 13.5 percent to government expenses related to oil development.

Then the groups devised a way to impose social and environmental responsibility standards on the giant oil companies. They pressured them to submit their actions for approval by the World Bank, which required the companies to follow the strict guidelines it created for projects it sponsors in emerging economies. These guidelines support the Bank's primary goal of alleviating poverty. They also protect both the natural and sociocultural environments in less developed countries. Although World Bank loans to Chad are only a token 3 percent of project money, the oil companies understood that without the Bank's oversight they faced a prolonged battle against skilled and belligerent activists. They agreed to follow the guidelines.

To meet World Bank standards, ExxonMobil and the other companies went to extraordinary lengths. Among many actions taken, the companies

- Prepared a massive 19-volume social and environmental impact study.
- Agreed to fund two new national parks in Cameroon to compensate for rainforest wilderness lost to the pipeline.
- Sent trained facilitators to gatherings at more than 900 villages along the pipeline route, leading to numerous design and route adjustments.
- Undertook 165 consultations with Pygmy settlements in meetings attended by sociologists and representatives of human rights groups.
- Held 145 meetings to consult with 250 international and Chadian NGOs about the social and environmental assessment.

---

[2] Ian Gary, an advisor with Catholic Relief Services, quoted in Emily Wax, "Oil Wealth Trickles into Chad, but Little Trickles Down," *The Washington Post,* March 13, 2004, p. A16.

[3] Based on cost-benefit studies conducted by Esso Chad, "Cost/Benefit Analysis: Chad/Cameroon Development Project," at www.essochad.com.

- Set up a Web site, essochad.com, to publish voluminous documentation on the project, including quarterly and annual reports. This was done to ensure overall "transparency."

The Chad-Cameroon pipeline got off to a rocky start. In 2000, Chad's president, Idress Déby, received an initial $25 million payment from the oil companies. He used $4.5 million of it to buy weapons and another $478,000 to import new European cars for members of his regime. Subsequent construction was marred by the spread of HIV-AIDS along the pipeline route, rural migration to construction areas, inflation, and constant dust from unpaved roads around project sites.[4] But by mid-2003 the oil began to flow and late that year the oil companies deposited the first royalties of $6.5 million in a London bank.

Déby reacted to the opening of the pipeline by stifling dissent. When it was officially inaugurated in September 2003 with speeches and bands, some groups declared a national day of mourning for the future of Chad. Déby responded by closing a radio station that broadcast a critical report. Later in the month he held public executions after quick sham trials, an action interpreted as a message for human rights groups. Before the first flow of oil, he dismissed the head of the group charged with monitoring uses of oil revenue.

The Chad-Cameroon pipeline sets a precedent for social responsibilities of transnational energy corporations in the Third World. It imposes expansive, strict guidelines to carry them out. Unfortunately, much of the outcome depends on actions beyond the control of ExxonMobil, Petronas, and ChevronTexaco.

Few companies have guidelines for social programs that are as specific and extensive as those used by the pipeline consortium. And few stories of carrying out responsibilities are as dramatic and have such high stakes for millions of people. However, many firms attempt to define a social mission and then use a range of actions and management tools to carry it out. These efforts are the subject of this chapter.

KEY ELEMENTS OF MANAGING THE SOCIAL RESPONSE

Corporate social goals are like other business goals. Setting them does not assure achieving them. Lofty statements by leaders are common in this area. Less common is the managerial work required to embed social elements in the formal processes and cultural values that determine performance. In this chapter we discuss key elements of managing for social responsibility, including leadership; mission statements; issues management; alignment of structure, culture, and processes; and auditing and reporting. We conclude with a discussion of corporate philanthropy.

Leadership

Top management sets the tone for a company's social response. When founders or CEOs have a strong social responsibility philosophy, it is reflected throughout the organization. A few companies have been founded by progressive visionaries who

---

[4] Korinna Horta and Delphine Djiraibe, "Africa's Dangerous Treasure," *The Washington Post,* March 10, 2004, p. A29.

business model
The underlying idea or theory that explains how a business will create value by making and selling products in the market.

make social responsibility central to their business model. A *business model* is the underlying idea or theory of how a business will create value by making and selling something in the marketplace. The theory is correct if the business makes a profit. A socially responsible business model is one in which the central actions that create value are actions that would be considered voluntary corporate responsibilities for ordinary companies.

Anita Roddick, for example, conceived of The Body Shop as a beacon of ethical and social activism in a world darkened by capitalist greed. She saw cosmetics as "an industry dominated by men trying to create needs that don't exist," and she devoted herself to "harnessing commercial success to altruistic ideals."[5] Her business model predicted that women would buy from an honest company that used natural ingredients, made realistic product claims, and supported feminist and progressive causes. The company's ads encouraged women to accept their natural appearance. One read: "There are 3 billion women who don't look like supermodels and only 8 who do."

Progressive business models are rare; only a handful of companies are based on them. Other examples include Ben & Jerry's, the ice-cream company that has promoted progressive social causes; Patagonia, Inc., a clothing firm committed to enhancing the environment; Stonyfield Farm, an organic yogurt maker; Seventh Generation, which makes household products with nontoxic chemicals; and Working Assets, a long-distance phone company that supports progressive causes. The validity of a business model is determined by profit or loss. These businesses have succeeded, at least for an extended time, though each has faced major tensions between social missions and marketplace realities. Several have suffered financial difficulties and been absorbed by larger firms run on more traditional business models.

A second category of companies, more numerous, comprises those that, although based on traditional business models, have cultures emphasizing voluntary social responsibility in one or more dimensions because of the influence of founders. Bertelsmann AG, for example, was founded in 1835 to publish hymnals by Carl Bertelsmann, a Protestant inspired by the Great Awakening. He believed that the primary goal of his company should be to make society better. Bertelsmann shared half the firm's profits with employees and gave them pensions and other benefits long before other German companies. Bertelsmann AG has grown into the third-largest global media conglomerate owning, among other brands, BMG Music, Random House, CDNow, and RCA, but it is still controlled by descendants of the founder. The family recently fired its chief executive, in part because he bought Napster, a business that they believed was irresponsible.[6]

Companies in a third category, the most populous by far and including most of the largest transnational corporations, have no special founding impulse toward voluntary social responsibilities defined as actions that further a progressive social or environmental agenda. Their social performance is based on the response of their management teams to pressures in the business environment. Figure 6.1

---

[5] Anita Roddick, *Business as Unusual* (London: Thorsons, 2000), pp. 97 and 172.

[6] Matthew Karnitschnig and Neal E. Boudette, "History Lesson: Battle for the Soul of Bertelsmann Led to CEO Ouster," *The Wall Street Journal*, July 30, 2002, p. A1.

FIGURE 6.1
Sources of
Pressure for
Social
Responsibility

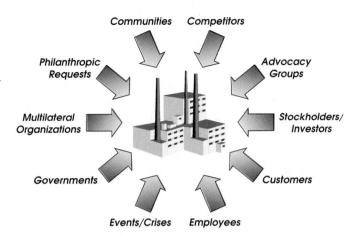

Communities Competitors

Philanthropic
Requests

Advocacy
Groups

Multilateral
Organizations

Stockholders/
Investors

Governments

Customers

Events/Crises Employees

shows multiple sources of these pressures for social actions on firms. Each source
may generate many separate demands, some contradictory. Figure 6.1 makes it
easy to visualize the huge number of potential demands on big corporations.

Corporations that lack a socially responsible business model or founder vary in
their reaction to these pressures across a spectrum of responses that run from reluctance to enthusiasm. At the left of this spectrum (see Figure 6.2), some companies focus on making a profit and resist demands to go beyond the minimum duty
of obeying the law. For them, the extent of corporate responsibility is determined
by the power of stakeholders over their behavior. In the middle, where perhaps
most are located, companies accept social obligations and may work to mitigate
adverse impacts on society before new laws and regulations are passed. And at the
right, a few companies seek to be proactive by anticipating demands and resolving
problems before they arise.

Executive leadership can shift the position of a company on the response spectrum. In the 1990s Royal Dutch/Shell was assaulted by activists. Among indications

FIGURE 6.2
A Spectrum
of Responses
to Social
Demands

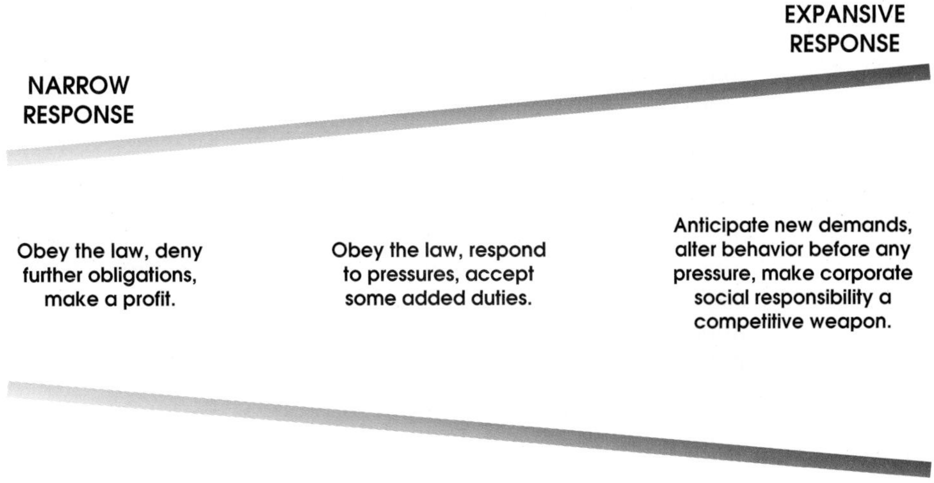

EXPANSIVE
RESPONSE

NARROW
RESPONSE

Obey the law, deny
further obligations,
make a profit.

Obey the law, respond
to pressures, accept
some added duties.

Anticipate new demands,
alter behavior before any
pressure, make corporate
social responsibility a
competitive weapon.

that it failed to anticipate social demands were accusations of aiding a brutal Nigerian government crackdown on native peoples opposed to oil drilling and a worldwide protest and boycott over its plan to sink a drilling platform in the North Sea. Royal Dutch/Shell was widely perceived as an arrogant firm, fixated on profits and disdainful of its social impacts. However, one top executive, Mark Moody-Stuart, emerged as a champion of change and led the company to set up management systems that built in greater social responsiveness. Moody-Stuart was heavily influenced by an encounter with an activist who convinced him that it was wrong to see the corporation at the center and all else revolving around it. Rather, he came to believe that the corporation was only one stakeholder of a broader society. Unfortunately, Moody-Stuart's successor as CEO was caught in 2003 exaggerating the company's reserves, thereby undoing much of the reputation building that had come from Moody-Stuart's work and underlining the importance of an example at the top.

Mission Statements

mission statement
A brief statement of the basic purpose of an organization and a useful tool for making corporate social responsibility an important part of corporate behavior.

A *mission statement* sets forth, with brevity, the basic purpose of an organization or company. The best ones define the business, differentiate it from competitors, explain relationships with stakeholders, and focus energy on critical activities and goals. The mission statement is a powerful tool for expressing priorities. If social responsibility is central to the company's mission, that should be reflected in its wording. The mission statement of The Body Shop starts by saying that [we] will "dedicate our business to the pursuit of social and environmental change" and will "creatively balance the financial and human needs of our stakeholders."

To be effective, the ideas in mission statements should be ones for which specific goals can be set and progress toward them measured. The Ben & Jerry's Ice Cream Co. mission statement sets forth its "social mission," which is "[t]o operate the company in a way that actively recognizes the central role that business plays in the structure of society by initiating innovative ways to improve the quality of life of a broad community." This idea of "initiating innovative ways" led over the years to specific actions. The company planted trees sufficient to replace the wood used in its popsicle sticks and it donated a percentage of the sales of its Peace Pops to fund research on world peace.

Most corporate mission statements emphasize product quality, markets served, and profitability. The mission of R. J. Reynolds Tobacco Company "is to strengthen the equity and performance of our key brands and thereby deliver strong financial results to our parent company." The mission of News Corporation is "the creation and distribution of top-quality news, sports and entertainment around the world." That of Hershey foods is "to consistently create shareholder value by achieving excellence in every aspect of our business." Often, however, companies state additional purposes, for instance, protecting the environment or improving society. Kellogg Co. says that

> Social responsibility is an integral part of our heritage. We are committed to be, and be recognized as, an economic, intellectual, and social asset in each community, region, and country in which we operate.

The Kellogg statement goes on to list actions that promote its values, such as encouraging employee volunteers. Unfortunately, many mission or value statements are filled with generalizations, platitudes, and motherhood-and-apple-pie statements. In a paragraph entitled "Our Vision," Bayer Corporation sets a lofty goal of "being good corporate citizens in the communities in which we work and live." However, in 14 subsequent sections the only elaboration on the meaning of community citizenship is a nonspecific admonition about "[t]aking an active role in the communities in which we work and live." Such general statements lack operational meaning and unless top management defines and implements them they are like the notes of national anthems that fade away when the ball game starts.

Ideally, mission statements should be based on an effort to discover or shape core values that can then be articulated in writing. One of the best examples comes from one of the oldest mission statements. In 1943 Robert Wood Johnson, the founder of Johnson & Johnson, wrote a one-page "Credo" setting forth in order the company's responsibilities toward, first, doctors, nurses, and patients; then employees; then communities; and last, stockholders. The Credo, which was far ahead of its time in its philosophy toward stakeholders, has been the firm's mission statement for more than 60 years. Although little changed, it is a living document that is modified from time to time on the basis of employee discussions and surveys.

Commitment to social responsibility is sometimes set forth in documents with other names, such as values or vision statements or charters. These may supplement or replace mission statements and they have the same potential to direct resources and enthusiasm toward social goals.

Managing Social Issues

Corporations, particularly large ones, are immersed in social issues. A relevant *social issue* is a matter of dispute arising from corporate behavior and its impact on social institutions or social problems. At any time one or a few of the many social issues swirling in the corporate environment may be poised to grow in importance. Often, such an issue seems to hit suddenly and create havoc, like a comet from the heavens. But signs and warnings have invariably preceded it. The earlier that such issues are detected, the easier it is to maneuver and adjust to them.

Managers have developed methods to detect, classify, analyze, track, and prioritize issues. The process of employing these methods is called *issues management.* The importance of issues management is clear. Some issues, if not addressed, may cause severe damage to the business. It therefore is important for a company to identify critical issues and decide what action, if any, to take.

The Life Cycles of Issues

Issues go through a life cycle, as shown in Figure 6.3. As they form (1) they have only a narrow following. At this point, some issues, such as those in the agendas of radical groups, are visible. Others, however, may be vague and unfocused and lack urgency. It is extremely difficult to predict if or when an issue will grow in

social issue
A matter of dispute growing out of corporate behavior and its impact on social institutions or social problems.

issues management
The use of methods to detect, classify, analyze, track, and prioritize social issues in the corporate environment.

FIGURE 6.3
The Issue Life Cycle

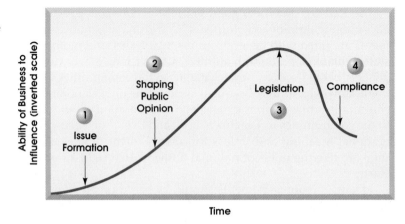

importance. Events or promotion by advocacy groups may, sometimes after many years, cause issues to emerge in the media and get wider attention (2). When they do, debate grows. It is in this part of the issue life cycle that corporations can most effectively intervene to shape public debate and opinion. This is the point at which corporations and industries propose voluntary codes of conduct and other forms of self-regulation. Over time, strong opinions on the issue form, the range of alternatives for its resolution narrows, and corporations have less ability to influence outcomes. Meanwhile, pressure on government to resolve the issue has grown and laws or regulations are likely to appear (3). During the legislative process or the rule-making process in agencies, corporations exert influence. However, when laws and rules appear, opportunities for influence narrow to interpretation of wording and methods of enforcement. Now, proposals for voluntary action are too late, options have evaporated, and the issue can no longer be "managed." The task is to comply with the new rules (4).

Today, a large company is faced with hundreds of issues that could influence its operations immediately or in the future. Some have issues management staffs and committees analyzing the field using methods such as the following.

intuitive search
Random, unsystematic, qualitative research on issues done by a manager.

- *Intuitive search.* This method is used when a manager does a random, unsystematic, qualitative search for issues in the company's environment. The selection of issues and their evaluation is based on experience, judgment, insight, and feel. When done by experienced managers this is an informative technique. Other techniques discussed here are more structured and systematic.

scenario
A plausible projection of the future based on assumptions about how current trends might evolve.

- *Scenarios.* A scenario is a plausible projection of the future based on assumptions about how current trends might evolve. Scenarios are written, disciplined, and structured narratives of what the world will be like if social, political, and economic trends proceed as assumed. Writing a single scenario is possible, but more frequently planners create several. As noted in Chapter 2, Royal Dutch/Shell is a leader in the use of scenarios based on social issues. Well-structured scenarios force managers to contemplate the impact of current trends and the possibility of unlikely events.

FIGURE 6.4
Probability/
Impact Matrix

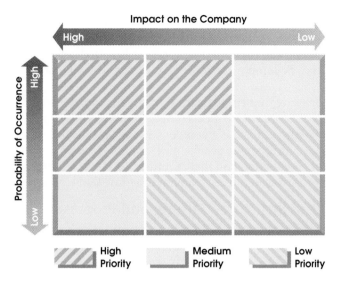

- *The probability/impact matrix.* In this technique, the likelihood of demands on the corporation is analyzed as to both their probability and their potential impact on the company. This is a powerful tool for ranking issues. If evaluation places a demand in the upper left of the matrix in Figure 6.4, attention to it should become a high priority for the firm. If, on the other hand, a demand falls into the lower right, it has low priority. Demands placed in medium-priority areas on the chart require continuing assessment.

- *Stakeholder engagement.* Powerful coalitions of stakeholders can form quickly to fight a corporation and mobilize public opinion against it. To avoid surprise and disruption corporations can contact stakeholders and converse with them before some unanticipated incident or action triggers contention. Formal methods for engaging stakeholders include surveys, private or public meetings, advisory panels, focus groups, workshops, and presentations.

   To begin, it is necessary to identify those stakeholders to be engaged, and the range can be narrow or broad. Shell–UK sought out consultation with stakeholders, including the activists in Greenpeace England, over the decision to sink the Brent Spar, its obsolete North Sea drilling platform. No alarm was raised. The company never contacted Greenpeace Germany. This group was irate over the issue and swiftly created a coalition to attack Shell, forcing abandonment of its plans.[7] If the company had extended its engagement, it might have avoided damage to its reputation.

   Advocates of engagement recommend seeking out stakeholders on different issues, in different countries and cultures, of different genders and races, and by different organizational types.[8] Engaging people who are hostile to

**probability/
impact matrix**
A method for
mapping
demands on a
company based
on the interac-
tion of two
factors: (1) the
probability that
they will arise
and (2) the
potential
importance of
their impact.

**stakeholder
engagement**
The process
of forming
relationships
and having
dialogue with
groups and
individuals who
can affect or are
affected by the
corporation.

---

[7] Stuart L. Hart and Sanjay Sharma, "Engaging Fringe Stakeholders for Competitive Imagination," *Academy of Management Executive,* February 2004, p. 11.

[8] Institute of Social and Ethical AccountAbility, *AccountAbility 1000 (AA1000) Framework* (London: ISEA, 1999), p. 107.

the corporation and uninterested in its welfare is difficult. Managers who meet with them sometimes receive training to suspend judgment so that open exchange can occur. If the process is handled correctly, unfriendly stakeholders may develop more understanding and even come to trust the corporation.

One company that emphasizes stakeholder engagement is Novo Nordisk, a large Denmark pharmaceutical company. An executive vice president of stakeholder relations heads a 27-member department that maintains contact with a spectrum of groups, politicians, and opinion leaders. When the department finds a stakeholder demand that requires a response, it is charged with changing business processes in the company to integrate that response.[9]

Alignment of Structure, Culture, and Processes

If the organization structure, culture, and processes of a company are misaligned with the social goals in its mission statement, those goals will be slighted. As with any business objective, a decision by management for action on corporate social responsibility is only an initial, tentative step. To be carried out, that decision must be translated into specific goals and performance objectives, embedded in policies and procedures, and supported by both the formal structure and the informal elements of the corporate culture.

Many companies create elements of formal structure to provide leadership for social responsibility. Examples of companies with social responsibility committees on their boards of directors are 3M, General Electric, Royal Dutch/Shell, Kellogg, Lockheed, and Target. Some corporations have other high-level committees that oversee social actions. Chugai Pharmaceutical of Korea recently formed a high-level Corporate Social Responsibility Committee composed of executives in charge of the company's departments. To signal the importance of an activity corporations set up departments or assign a manager to take responsibility for it. A few corporations, including Eddie Bauer, Starbucks, and Qwest Communications, have vice presidents of corporate social responsibility, but these are unique positions. More typically, separate departments are created for various elements of the social response, for example, environmental health and safety, diversity, ethics and legal compliance, community relations, and charitable foundations.

To create accountability for performance, the broad objectives and principles in mission and values statements must be translated into measurable objectives, goals, and targets. Pay, performance, and promotion can be linked to achieving them. Executive pay is linked to environmental performance at Alcoa, Dow Chemical, and Phillips Petroleum. At Coca-Cola and Texaco, which have suffered highly publicized discrimination suits, pay is linked to achieving diversity goals. At Eastman Kodak, up to one-third of a manager's compensation depends on employee satisfaction and responsibility to the public.[10]

---

[9] Don Tapscott and David Ticoll, *The Naked Corporation: How the Age of Transparency Will Revolutionize Business* (New York: Free Press, 2003), pp. 259 and 276.

[10] "Linking Manager Pay to Social Performance," *Business Ethics,* March–April 2001, p. 8.

Some companies formally recognize employees who undertake social projects. General Electric sponsors the Phillippe Awards, named after a former executive distinguished in public service. Each GE business nominates annually an employee with creative or heroic community service. Recent winners include a GE Lighting manager in Rio de Janeiro who organized support for 40 elderly people abandoned by their families and a GE Power systems employee in California who directs "GE Thursday Nights" on which GE volunteers cook and serve meals at a homeless shelter.

Corporate culture must be aligned with formal incentives. Where the culture contains deep-seated, informal values that conflict with official policies of social responsibility, those policies are likely to be ignored. If managers who are highly productive but ignore social duties are promoted, it indicates that formal policy is inconsistent with underlying beliefs about requirements for career advancement. And social policies must be aligned with business functions or, again, productivity requirements are likely to prevail.

At Timberland Co. executives promoted a program allowing employees to take one week a year at full pay to work at company-sponsored local charities. However, line managers felt pressured to meet production goals and resisted giving workers time off.[11] Finally, strong efforts at coordination are needed in very large corporations. In 2003 Pfizer created a Corporate Citizenship department after discovering that the principles in its mission statement were unevenly applied across functions and business units around the world. To force consistency it created a high-level cross-divisional team of 25 managers. The team elected to create a new citizenship policy to unify efforts.[12]

Corporate Social Reporting

corporate social reporting
The practice of assessing and publishing information about social performance.

Corporate social reporting is the practice of assessing and publishing information about social performance. In the last five years a wave of social reporting has risen, with many companies preparing what are commonly titled social responsibility, sustainability, or environmental reports. An initial wave of social reports, called social audits to differentiate them from traditional financial audits, came in the 1960s and 1970s. A *social audit* is an assessment of the social impacts of a corporation on society. At the time, a few large firms, including Bank of America, Chase Manhattan Bank, Exxon, and Philip Morris, did widely publicized social audits. Atlantic Richfield Company published an annual social balance sheet that candidly weighed the pluses and minuses of its social performance. A 1974 survey found that 76 percent of 284 large companies did some form of social auditing.[13]

social audit
An assessment of the social impacts of a corporation on society.

Early interest in social auditing waned after the massive increase in environmental and social regulation that hit business in the 1970s. New regulations contained strong reporting requirements that were, in effect, government-mandated

[11] Joseph Pereira, "Doing Good and Doing Well at Timberland," *The Wall Street Journal,* September 9, 2003, p. B1.

[12] Pfizer, Inc., "Aligning Corporate Citizenship in a Decentralized Company," January 15, 2004, at www.unglobalcompact.org.

[13] John J. Corson and George A. Steiner, *Measuring Business's Social Performance: The Corporate Social Audit* (New York: Committee for Economic Development, 1974), pp. 24–25.

GRI Indicators

Listed below are a few examples of triple bottom line indicators. The full list of indicators is longer and more detailed.

Economic Performance Indicators
- Net sales.
- Total payroll and benefits, by country.
- Taxes paid, by country.
- Subsidies received, by country.
- Donations to communities.

Environmental Performance Indicators
- Total materials use, by type.
- Percentage of materials used that are wastes.
- Energy use.
- Changes to natural habitats resulting from operations.
- Polluting emissions and effluents by type.
- Environmental impacts of principal products.

Social Performance Indicators
- Net employment creation.
- Percentage of unionized employees.
- Number of work-related injuries and fatalities.
- Evidence of consideration of human rights impacts.
- Composition of senior management using male/female ratio and other indicators of diversity.
- Number and types of breaches of advertising and marketing regulations.

Source: Global Reporting Initiative, *Sustainability Reporting Guidelines: 2002* (Boston: GRI Interim Secretariat, September 2002), part C.

triple bottom line
A standard that uses economic, environmental, and social indicators to define corporate performance.

social reports. But as time passed, rising expectations about corporate behavior exceeded the requirements in these regulations. The political climate was hostile to added regulation. This created an information gap between what stakeholders wanted to know and what regulations required firms to report. Therefore, in the late 1990s voluntary social reporting again emerged as a useful tool for companies to address stakeholders.

The leading effort to create a new auditing and reporting format is the Global Reporting Initiative (GRI), an international effort by accounting, investment, environmental, labor, and human rights groups to develop uniform standards for company reports. In the late 1990s, the GRI published guidelines for reporting on what it calls the *triple bottom line,* that is, a calculation of corporate economic, environmental, and social performance. (See the box above.) These guidelines, revised in 2002, were drafted after consulting with corporations, advocacy groups, universities, and accounting firms. They introduce a standard format and simplify comparisons between companies. The GRI standards are voluntary and large companies have begun to adopt them, including, for example, AT&T, British Airways, Ford, General Motors, Procter & Gamble, Sony, and Nokia. By 2005, more than 500 corporations had issued social reports conforming with the guidelines.

According to the GRI guidelines, a good social report meets certain criteria. Its content is useful to stakeholders, clear, timely, comparable to past reports, reliable, and verifiable. It should include a statement of management's vision and strategy; an extensive factual profile of the company; a description of its governance structure and management policies for matters such as executive pay and stakeholder engagement; reports on the core economic, environmental, and social indicators;

transparency
The requirement that social reports reveal "processes, procedures, and assumptions embodied in the reported information."

and an index. A transcending requirement is for *transparency*, which requires that readers be "fully informed of the processes, procedures, and assumptions embodied in the reported information."[14] The opposite of transparency is opacity, or the inability to see inside the company to know how it works and how it comes up with information. The GRI framework is intended to compliment rather than replace other reporting frameworks, such as those in international codes of conduct and industry certification programs.

The GRI, which is housed with the United Nations Development Programme and linked to the UN Global Compact, is a promising initiative to develop and standardize social reporting. Not only are more corporations following the guidelines, but the governments of the Netherlands, France, Australia, and Japan have legislated social reporting requirements that refer to the GRI as a means of compliance.[15]

Yet there are two major concerns as the quest moves forward. First, measuring social performance, and aspects of environmental performance, is far more difficult than measuring financial performance. There is strong ideological disagreement about what social performance should be. A leading environmentalist issued a scathing review of McDonald's 2001 corporate social responsibility report, a fairly standard example of the genre setting forth a range of laudable programs and efforts. The problem was that the report "presupposes that we can continue to have a global chain of restaurants that serves fried, sugary junk food that is produced by an agricultural system of monocultures, monopolies, standardization and destruction, and at the same time find a path to sustainability."[16] Second, stretching current boundaries on candor will be difficult because firms are reluctant to invite criticism. Does any chemical plant really want to estimate downwind mortality based on statistical risks of exposure to substances in its emissions? Should General Motors reveal the number of traffic fatalities involving its vehicles? However, neither constraints of definition nor candor stand in the way of expanded reporting and the evolution of harmonized standards.

CORPORATE PHILANTHROPY

philanthropy
Concern for the welfare of society expressed by gifts of money or property to the needy or to institutions that advance social welfare.

Philanthropy is concern for the welfare of society expressed by gifts of money or property to the needy or to institutions that advance social welfare. Large philanthropic contributions by American companies are a relatively recent phenomenon. Until about 50 years ago courts held that corporate funds belonged to shareholders; therefore, managers had no right to give money away, even for noble motives. This restrictive doctrine was strongest in the days when businesses were small and charity came mainly from their owners. But as businesses grew and professional managers took control from founding capitalists, the public started to expect giving from corporations as well.

---

[14] Global Reporting Initiative, *Sustainability Reporting Guidelines: 2002* (Boston: GRI Interim Secretariat, September 2002), p. 24.

[15] Glenn Cheney, "The Corporate Conscience and the Triple Bottom Line," *Accounting Today*, July 12, 2004, p. 12.

[16] Paul Hawken, "McDonald's and Corporate Social Responsibility?" at www.foodfirst.org.

A. P. Smith Manufacturing Company v. Barlow et al., 13 N.J. 145 (1953)

A. P. Smith was a New Jersey corporation set up in 1896. It made valves and hydrants. In 1951 the firm gave $1,500 to Princeton University's annual fund-raising drive. This was not its first charitable contribution. It gave to a local community chest fund and had donated to other nearby colleges.

These contributions were made in a legal environment clouded by inconsistency. On the one hand was the law of corporate charters. These charters were issued by states, and corporations were not allowed to act beyond the powers expressly granted in them. The assumption in the charters was that the corporation's duty was to maximize profits for shareholders. A. P. Smith's incorporation papers, like those of most firms at the time, did not grant specific authority to make charity gifts. On the other hand was a statute. New Jersey passed a law in 1930 giving its corporations the right to make such donations if they did not exceed 1 percent of capital.

Ruth Barlow and four other angry owners of common and preferred stock thought the company had no right to give away any amount of money, because it was rightfully theirs as shareholders.

They sued and in due course a trial was held. Luminaries from the business community appeared as witnesses for A. P. Smith to assert the merits of corporate charity. A Standard Oil of New Jersey executive argued that it was "good business" to show the kind of citizenship the public demanded. A U.S. Steel executive said that maintaining universities was essential to preserving capitalism. Nevertheless, the judge ruled against A. P. Smith, saying that the company had acted beyond its legitimate power.

A. P. Smith appealed. In 1953 the Supreme Court of New Jersey overturned the lower court, arguing that rigid interpretation of charters to restrict charitable giving was no longer fitting since, unlike the old days when corporations were small and had limited assets relative to individuals, they now had enormous assets and it was reasonable for the public to expect generosity from them.

The *Smith* case settled the legal question of whether corporations could give to charity. After it, the legal cloud of acting *ultra vires* dissipated, clearing the way for greater corporate giving.

The first major break from narrow legal restrictions on corporate giving was the Revenue Act of 1935, which allowed charitable contributions to be deducted from taxable earnings up to 5 percent of net profits before taxes (raised to 10 percent in 1981). Despite the Revenue Act, the legality of corporate giving remained doubtful, and managers were tight with charity dollars because they feared stockholder suits. Eventually, the *A. P. Smith* case in 1953 (see the box above) cleared away outdated rigidities in the law, freeing companies to be more generous.

Patterns and Magnitudes of Corporate Giving

Charitable giving is now a standard dimension of corporate social responsibility. Even so, most firms do not give a significant amount compared with their potential. Only about one-third of American companies set aside philanthropic funds; two-thirds do not engage in active giving.[17] Those that contribute do so in many

[17] Shirley Sagawa and Eli Segal, *Common Interest, Common Good* (Boston: Harvard Business School Press, 2000), p. 15.

FIGURE 6.5
Ten-Year Trend in Private Philanthropy: 1993–2003

Source: AAFRC Trust for Philanthropy in U.S. Census Bureau, *Statistical Abstract of the United States: 2003,* 123d ed. (Washington, DC, 2003), table 581; and Alison S. Welner et al., "Modest Signs of Rebound," *Chronicle of Philanthropy,* June 24, 2004, p. 27.

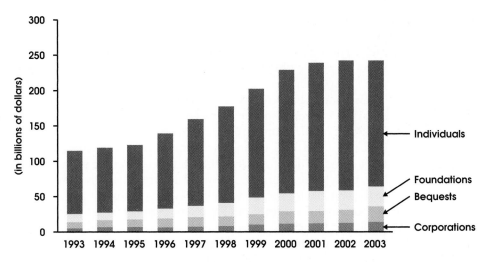

altruism
The desire to give to, help, or improve others and society with no expectation of self-gain in return.

ways, including cash, products, services, volunteered time, and use of facilities. Noncash giving is about one-quarter of total giving.[18] The largest portion of overall giving, about 35 percent, goes to education. Of the rest, 30 percent goes to health and human services, 14 percent to civic and community causes, 9 percent to culture and the arts, and the rest to a variety of other areas.[19] The basic motives for corporate giving are response to pressure, belief that it will bring monetary profit, desire for reputational gain, and *altruism,* or selfless concern for the welfare of others. Corporate giving often stems from a mixture of these. Although charitable actions are tax deductible, this is not a compelling motive, since many alternative uses of funds, for example advertising, are also tax deductible.

Corporations that give vary considerably in the amount and nature of their generosity. Few large companies ever give enough to approach 10 percent of pretax earnings, the level at which tax deductibility ceases. Eli Lilly and Company was the most generous company on lists of cash and in-kind gifts recently compiled by *BusinessWeek,* but its total of $273 million given away in 2003 was only 8.4 percent of its pretax earnings.[20] Still, this is generous by large corporation standards. Since the 1950s, overall corporate contributions have been remarkably consistent, hovering around 1 percent of pretax earnings, rarely deviating more than two-tenths of a percent and rising above 2 percent only once, in 1986 when a record of 2.38 percent was set.[21]

Corporate philanthropy is only a small part of overall private philanthropy in the United States. As shown in Figure 6.5, between 1993 and 2003 charitable giving

[18] Sophia A. Muirhead, *Corporate Contributions: The View From 50 Years* (New York: The Conference Board, 1999), p. 6.

[19] Audris D. Tillman, *Corporate Contributions in 1999* (New York: The Conference Board, 2000), p. 19.

[20] Jessi Hempel and Lauren Gard, "The Corporate Givers," *BusinessWeek,* November 29, 2004, p. 102; and Eli Lilly and Co., *Form 10K,* March 12, 2004, exhibit 13, p. 7.

[21] Paul Ostergard, "Should Corporations Be Praised for Their Philanthropic Efforts? Yes: A Golden Age," *Across the Board,* May–June 2001, p. 46.

rose from $117 billion to $248 billion. As the segments on the bars show, individuals gave by far the largest proportion, followed by foundations, charitable bequests, and, finally, corporations (including corporate foundations). Over these years corporate philanthropy rose from $8.5 billion to $13.5 billion, while maintaining a proportion of between 5 percent and 6 percent of total giving.

Corporate philanthropy is only a tiny portion of overall social welfare spending. Total private philanthropy in the United States since the mid-1990s has been about 1 percent of GDP compared with government social welfare spending of 18 percent of GDP.[22] This means that annual corporate contributions are only about three-hundredths of 1 percent of total social welfare spending. From this perspective, the welfare importance of what a corporation gives away pales in comparison to the benefits for society from its payrolls, taxes, dividends, and net earnings. Yet corporate philanthropy can have great impact where it is focused. When General Mills saw a formerly respectable Minneapolis neighborhood close to its headquarters declining into a criminal haunt it spent $2.5 million and its employees devoted time and expertise to revitalizing it. This made an enormous difference to the people living in the area.[23]

Fortunes in Action

Historically, wealthy entrepreneurs contributed large sums separately from their companies. The first prominent charitable bequest came with the death of the Philadelphia merchant and banker Stephen Girard in 1831. At the time, Girard's fortune, about $7.5 million, was the largest in the nation. In his will he left only small sums to his family and gave everything else for civic causes, notably education. This example cast the die. When John Jacob Astor died only 17 years later, his will provided for establishing a public library in New York City, but he left most of his money to family members, including a mentally ill son. New Yorkers were enraged by his perceived lack of civic charity and indignant opinions appeared in newspapers.[24] Public opinion already reflected wide belief that wealthy capitalists should be substantial philanthropists. Soon this belief evolved to an expectation that the wealthy should show magnanimity during their lifetimes.

In the next half-century John D. Rockefeller and Andrew Carnegie pioneered the art of living philanthropy and this example has endured. By the early 1990s Bill Gates, the founder of Microsoft, had built an extraordinary fortune, but he had given little to charity. Faced with mounting opinion that as the world's richest person he should do more, Gates carefully studied the actions of Rockefeller and Carnegie. In 1994 he set up a foundation, endowing it with cash from the sale of his Microsoft stock. By 2004, the Bill and Melinda Gates Foundation had an

[22] "Philanthropy: Doing Well and Doing Good," *The Economist,* July 31, 2004, p. 57, citing Lester M. Salamon et al., *Global Civil Society: Dimensions of the Nonprofit Sector,* vol. 2 (Bloomfield, CT: Kumarian Press, 2004).

[23] Michelle Conlin and Jessi Hempel, "The Corporate Donors," *BusinessWeek,* December 1, 2003, pp. 92–93.

[24] Peter Baida, *Poor Richard's Legacy: American Business Values from Benjamin Franklin to Donald Trump* (New York: William Morrow, 1990), pp. 56–58.

endowment of $27 billion and had already made grants of more than $7.2 billion.[25] Its projects are large and innovative but they continue the work of the great benefactors of yesteryear whom Gates looked to for inspiration. The foundation's primary mission is to develop and give out vaccines for the small number of diseases that are the leading causes of death in developing nations. Vaccinations paid for by the Gates Foundation have saved the lives of an estimated 100,000 children.[26] It funds research on vaccines for malaria and AIDS, the two top killers in Africa, trying to meet an ambitious goal of saving 1 million lives by 2010. This emphasis parallels the record of John D. Rockefeller's extraordinary support for medical research in his era. Like Rockefeller and Carnegie, Gates has also focused on support for education. The foundation's largest single gift is $1 billion for scholarships to the United Negro College Fund. And following Carnegie, who built public libraries in the age of books, the Gates foundation supports digitization in public libraries around the world.

No other American business leader approaches the $27 billion standard set by the Gates Foundation. In second place, Gordon Moore, cofounder of Intel, has more quietly given about $7 billion to education and environmental causes. After Moore, the next most generous American business philanthropist is George Soros, an investment fund manager best known for making $1 billion in one week in 1972 by currency speculation that undermined the English pound. His actions are estimated to have caused an average loss of £12 for every person in Great Britain.[27]

Soros was born in Budapest and lived through Nazi occupation as a child. This experience created in him a deep appreciation of liberty that is reflected in his actions as a philanthropist. He presides over a network of 33 foundations around the world that give to traditional educational, medical, and humanitarian causes. But their central focus is on promotion of free societies. In the 1980s they funded anticommunist groups in eastern Europe and the Soviet Union. Following breakup of the Soviet empire Soros poured more than $1 billion into the new Russia to promote stability. His foundations funded a range of efforts from fighting tuberculosis in Russian prisons to maintaining the Russian scientific community when government funding dried up. Soros foundations also played a central role in bringing down Yugoslavian president Slobodan Milosevic by supporting students who rebelled against him. So far, Soros has put more than $4.7 billion into his vision for what he calls an "open society."

While many who have earned fortunes in business are generous, there are a few relative skinflints. Lawrence J. Ellison, the founder of Oracle Corp. and the fourth-richest American, has donated only 0.4 percent of his net worth. He supports medical research, but argues that it is not worth giving more until new cures for diseases are found.[28]

[25] Figures are from www.gatesfoundation.org.

[26] Stephanie Strom, "Gates Aims Billions to Attack Illnesses of World's Neediest," *New York Times*, July 13, 2003, p. 15.

[27] David Rieff, "Can George Soros Save the World?" *Los Angeles Times Book Review*, September 1, 2002, p. 4.

[28] Julia Cosgrove et al., "The New Face of Philanthropy," *BusinessWeek*, December 2, 2002, p. 86.

The Secretive George Feeney

George F. Feeney, 73, is one of the greatest living philanthropists. In a style reminiscent of the old television program "The Millionaire," he has given away hundreds of millions of dollars using cashier's checks that do not reveal his name.

Feeney is an Irish-American who was raised in a working-class New Jersey neighborhood. With a partner he founded the Duty Free Shoppers stores found in airports around the world. In 1984 he experienced a revelation. "I simply decided I had enough money," he told a reporter. Without even informing his business partner, he set up a foundation in Bermuda so it would not be subject to U.S. laws requiring disclosure of contributions. Then he irrevocably transferred his ownership interest in Duty Free Shoppers to the foundation. At the time, this was worth about $500 million; over the years, the foundation has had assets as high as $4.8 billion, making it one of the world's largest.

Feeney could now be worth more than $5 billion, but his personal assets are only about $5 million. According to a friend, he does not own a house or a car. He wears a $15 watch and carries his papers in a plastic bag instead of a briefcase. He prefers casual clothes, doubts the need for more than one pair of shoes, and calls himself a "shabby dresser."

Most of the foundation's gifts go to hospitals, universities, and mainstream charities around the world.

His passion for secrecy stems from a desire to live life without constant importuning from suppliants and from his belief in the teachings of Maimonides, a twelfth-century philosopher who taught that the highest form of giving was anonymous and selfless. Feeney's staff painstakingly seeks out and probes individuals, groups, and causes to find worthy beneficiaries. Unsolicited requests for money are always disqualified. Feeney sometimes attends staff meetings with potential recipients, who are not told the identity of the quiet observer.

Feeney's reticence stands in contrast to the highly publicized donations of Bill Gates, George Soros, Ted Turner, and other billionaires. However, there is a tradition of anonymous contribution in American history. Chester F. Carlson, the inventor of xerography, gave away $300 million that way in the late 1960s (about $1 billion in today's dollars).

Most foundations give away only limited amounts each year, allowing them to maintain large endowments over time. In 2002, when Feeney was 70 years old, he instructed his foundation to exhaust its remaining $4 billion over the next 15 years. He believed that this would prevent it from becoming focused on its own perpetuation rather than on solving social problems.

Strategic Philanthropy

With historical roots in religious teachings, the act of philanthropy presumes a selfless motive of giving out of moral duty to benefit the needy or to advance society. Traditionally, corporate philanthropy conformed to such ideals of altruism and magnanimity. Companies, and their foundations, gave to help the destitute and deserving while funding social goods such as education and the arts. There was always a measure of self-interest in these donations. It was recognized that the elevating deed helped corporate reputations, created goodwill, and improved the economy by strengthening society.

As corporations gained experience with philanthropy, many concluded that the traditional approach of diffuse giving to myriad worthy causes was noble but flawed. Over time, the number of causes grew; and as charities became more numerous, the shrinking sums given to each had little impact on problems. Results were seldom measured. Top executives and their spouses diverted funds into pet artistic and cultural projects unimportant to the firm's main stakeholders. This passive approach to philanthropy lacked any underlying logic. In addition, by the 1980s it had become awkward for companies to give money away just when they were laying off groups of employees.

For these reasons, many firms decided to change their philosophy of giving from one of pure generosity to one that aligned charity with commercial objectives. This is known as *strategic philanthropy,* or the alignment of a corporation's business mission with its charitable mission. Today there is a strong trend toward strategic philanthropy and away from the old-style giving that is unconnected with a corporation's business interests.[29] Here are two examples.

strategic philanthropy
A philosophy of corporate giving in which charitable activities reinforce strategic business goals.

- The General Mills Foundation was set up in 1954 after the green light of the *A. P. Smith* decision. For many years, it emphasized giving to prestigious cultural and arts programs in the Minneapolis headquarters area. In 1997, however, it decided to target its support for projects helping families, children, and youth in more than 20 cities where it had facilities. This connected charity giving with the concerns of average grocery shoppers who buy Cheerios and Betty Crocker cake mixes.

- Mattel donated $25 million to put its name on the children's hospital at UCLA, now called Mattel Children's Hospital. The company has no role in running the hospital, although it gives toys to patients. Its large gift contributes to a compassionate corporate image among toy buyers. Adding the company name to the hospital increases brand recognition. These benefits reinforce the commercial goals of a toy company while also helping sick children. Hasbro, a Mattel competitor, made a similar donation to establish Hasbro Children's Hospital in Providence, Rhode Island.[30]

Not everyone approves of strategic philanthropy. The mixed motive of the corporation departs from the pure altruism depicted in religious parables about charity. One critic calls it "self-serving and self-interested," just "business by other means."[31] Defenders retort that looking behind good deeds to disparage the benefactor's motive is equally unworthy. In fact, it is unclear how far, if at all, corporate charity elevates reputations and profits. Surveys indicate that many consumers take charitable giving into consideration before they buy.[32] However, a recent study "found no evidence that corporate philanthropy enhances financial performance."[33]

[29] David H. Saiia, Archie B. Carroll, and Ann K. Buchholtz, "Philanthropy as Strategy," *Business & Society,* June 2003, pp. 181–85.
[30] Julie Edelson Halpert, "Dr. Pepper Hospital? Perhaps, for a Price," *New York Times,* February 18, 2001, sec. 3, p. 1.
[31] Benjamin R. Barber, "Should Corporations Be Praised for Their Philanthropic Efforts? No: Always an Angle," *Across the Board,* May–June 2001, p. 49.
[32] "Good Business," *Harvard Business Review,* January 2002, p. 22.
[33] Bruce Seifert, Sara A. Morris, and Barbara R. Bartkus, "Having, Giving, and Getting: Slack Resources, Corporate Philanthropy, and Firm Financial Performance," *Business & Society,* June 2004, p. 151.

Cause-Related Marketing

cause-related marketing
A marketing method linking a corporation or brand to a social cause so that both benefit.

Cause-related marketing is a marketing method linking a corporation or brand to a social cause so that both benefit. Marketers use branding to differentiate products, especially mass-produced products that consumers might see as interchangeable commodities if they lacked brand attributes. Companies spend heavily to endow brands with these attributes so they can charge a price premium. Traditional branding creates attributes in the consumer's mind in two dimensions. One is a description of products and their advantages directed to the logical mind. The other is image creation that allows consumers to fulfill emotional needs by using the product.

Consumer expectations of corporate social responsibility have expanded. Corporations realize that if their brand is connected to a social cause or charity a third attribute dimension is created, one that appeals to the conscience of a consumer. In cause-related marketing the corporation calculates that it will add this benevolent dimension to its brand while also doing a philanthropic good deed. Examples follow.

- In the early 1990s American Express encountered restaurant owners who felt its card fees were too high. Enough restaurants refused the cards when they were tendered that, rather than face rejection, many cardholders chose to use a competing card instead. To counteract this, the company started a cause-related marketing campaign called "Charge Against Hunger" in which it donated $.03 per transaction to nonprofit antihunger groups during the holiday months of November and December each year. The campaign created a clear link between using the card to pay for restaurant meals and fighting hunger. It raised $21 million in four years for donations to 600 antihunger groups. It also increased charge volume by 12 percent and raised the opinion of restaurant owners about the card.[34]

- In Australia, Kellogg's faces intense competition from two stronger cereal brands, Sanitarium and Uncle Toby's. To strengthen the value of its brand, it started a cause-related campaign to link Kellogg's cereals with social concern for young consumers. It entered a partnership with Kids' Help Line, a 24-hour telephone number that 5- to 18-year-olds can call to get free, confidential counseling. Kellogg's donates $.05 per package sold and advertises the service on cereal boxes. The help line has received more than $1 million, enabling it to hire more counselors and field more calls. Kellogg's cereal sales have had a strong increase.

- Avon Products is the world's largest seller of beauty products. Most of its revenues come from direct sales through 4 million part-time, predominantly female, sales representatives in 132 countries. The Avon brand is internationally known, but the company's reliance on direct selling carries an old-fashioned, downmarket connotation. Avon decided to use cause-related marketing to burnish its brand image. The vast majority of Avon's sales are to women.

[34] Sagawa and Segal, *Common Interest, Common Good*, p. 15.

Research showed that the cause of fighting breast cancer struck a responsive chord in them, so Avon began donating to breast cancer causes when customers bought its products. Since 1993 Avon has collected more than $300 million in this "crusade" and its brand increasingly benefits from a connotation of caring.

Cause-related marketing raises big sums of money for worthy causes but, like other forms of strategic philanthropy, its mixture of altruism and self-interest attracts criticism. Skeptics note that companies pick causes based on research into what consumers care about, instead of research to find the most desperate needs. Because the fight against breast cancer attracts the interest of female consumers over age 30, more than 300 companies now have marketing campaigns tied to it.[35] Other causes languish because of this convergence. There is plenty of cynicism about corporate motives. Lee Jeans started a Denim Day campaign in which it encourages workers nationwide to make a $5 breast cancer donation to buy the right to wear jeans to work on a Friday in October. One breast cancer survivor and activist resents this. "I'm not against them promoting their company or selling blue jeans, I'm just against them using breast cancer to do so."[36] Corporations, however, do not see commercial interest as an ethically inferior motive and believe that the concrete benefits of cause-related projects far outweigh any truth behind clever arguments about base motives.

CONCLUDING OBSERVATIONS

Good intentions are worth little if not reflected in actions. If a corporation announces aspirations to be socially responsible, it must follow up with the hard work of building those aspirations into its operations. To implement social strategies it must use the same managerial tools and levers that are required to implement business strategies. No social policy of any significance will be successfully carried out without coordinated use of most of these tools and levers.

Corporate philanthropy, while not a management method, is a long-standing way of implementing social responsibility. Public expectations of charitable giving have grown. Recently, corporations have shifted from a tradition of altruistic giving to a new style of philanthropy that aligns giving with business strategy. Some critics attack this new approach as too self-interested. However, strategic philanthropy may be a promising development because it injects thinking about corporate social responsibility into the strategic mainstream. Of course, in most companies business strategy will drive contributions to social needs rather than the other way around.

[35] Carol L. Cone, Mark A. Feldman, and Alison T. DaSilva, "Causes and Effects," *Harvard Business Review,* July 2003, p. 97.

[36] Suzanne S. Brown, "Rethinking Pink," *The Denver Post,* October 9, 2003, p. F1, quoting Barbara Brenner, executive director of Breast Cancer Action.

Marc Kasky versus Nike Inc.

Marc Kasky of San Francisco sees his world as a community and has a long history of caring about the others in it. He got his first lessons in business ethics from his father, who ran a car repair business.

> The customer would bring his car in and say there's something horribly wrong in my car: I think I need a new transmission. . . . My father would call them back an hour later and say, "Come get your car, there was a loose screw here and there; I fixed it. What does it cost? Nothing." I saw how that affected our family. It impressed me a great deal.[1]

After graduating from Yale University in 1969, he volunteered to work in poor Cleveland neighborhoods. Moving to San Francisco, he headed a nonprofit center for foundations that funded schools. He involved himself in civic and environmental causes. He also became an avid jogger and ran marathons.

Over the years Kasky wore many pairs of Nike shoes and considered them a "good product."[2] But he stopped buying them in the mid-1990s after reading stories about working conditions in overseas factories where they were made. By then Nike, Inc., had become the main focus of the antisweatshop cause, accused of exploiting low-wage workers who made its shoes and clothing. The more Kasky read about Nike, the more convinced he was that it was not only victimizing workers, but lying about it too. Kasky sought the help of an old friend, Alan Caplan, an attorney who had achieved fame in progressive circles by bringing the suit that forced R. J. Reynolds to stop using Joe Camel in its ads.

With Caplan's help, Kasky sued Nike in April 1998 for false advertising, alleging it had made untrue statements about its labor practices. This was not Kasky's first lawsuit. Previously, he had sued Perrier over its claim to be "spring water" and Pillsbury Co.

Marc Kasky. © AP Photo/Denis Poroy.

for labeling Mexican vegetables with the words "San Francisco style." Both suits were settled.[3] Nike sought dismissal of Kasky's suit, arguing that the statements he questioned were part of a public debate about sweatshops and protected by the First Amendment.

NIKE

Nike, Inc., is the world's largest producer of athletic shoes and sports apparel. It grew out of a handshake in 1962 between Bill Bowerman, the track coach at the University of Oregon, and Phil Knight, a runner he had coached in the 1950s. Knight had just received an MBA from Stanford University. In a term paper there he had written about competing against established athletic shoe companies by importing shoes made in low-wage Asian factories. Now he

---

[1] Quoted in Jim Edwards, "Taking It to the Big Guys," *Brandweek*, August 12, 2002, p. 1.

[2] Steve Rubenstein, "S. F. Man Changes from Customer to Nike Adversary," *San Francisco Chronicle*, May 3, 2002, p. A6. Kasky stated his ownership of Nike shoes in the interview for this article. However, his lawyer told the Supreme Court that he had "never bought any Nikes." *Nike v. Kasky*, No. 02-575, Oral Argument, April 23, 2003 (Washington, DC: Alderson Reporting Company, 2003), p. 30, lines 21 and 22. We give priority to Kasky's story, but this is a remarkable contradiction.

[3] Roger Parloff, "Can We Talk?" *Fortune*, September 2, 2002, p. 108.

was ready to try it. He and Bowerman each put up $550 and Knight flew to Japan, arranging to import 300 pairs of Onitsuka Tiger shoes. After seven years, Knight and Bowerman decided to stop selling the Japanese company's brand and create their own. So they designed a shoe and subcontracted its production to a factory in Japan. By now Bowerman and Knight had incorporated and an employee suggested naming the company Nike, for the Greek goddess of victory. Knight paid a design student at Portland State University $35 to create a logo. She drew a "swoosh," which the company adopted. The elements of future market conquest were now in place and the company grew rapidly.

Nike succeeded by following two basic strategies. Its product strategy is to design innovative, fashionable footwear and apparel for markets in developed nations, then have the items manufactured by contractors in low-wage economies. By outsourcing this way Nike avoids the cost of building and running its own factories. At first, most of its shoe production was done in Japanese factories (some shoes were made in the United States until 1980), but as wages rose in Japan it moved its contracts to plants in South Korea and Taiwan. When these countries took up higher value-added production in electronics and wages rose, Nike again shifted its production, this time to China, Indonesia, and Thailand, and later to Vietnam. Today 88 percent of its shoes are made in these four countries.[4]

Its marketing strategy is to create carefully calculated brand images. Nike spends heavily to accomplish this. Its annual advertising budget is about 10 percent of revenues, more than $1 billion in recent years. Advertising campaigns associate the Nike brand name with a range of ideas. Prominent among these is the idea of sport. Endorsements by professional athletes and college teams endow the swoosh with a high-performance image. Campaigns with the "just do it" slogan add connotations of competition, courage, strength, winning, and high performance. Other advertising associates the brand with urban hip-hop culture to make it "street cool." In this way Nike transforms shoes and T-shirts that would otherwise be low-cost commodities into high-priced, high fashion items that generate positive emotions when they are worn.

THE SWEATSHOP LABOR ISSUE

Nike grew rapidly. By 1980 when the company went public it had seized half the world athletic shoe market. Its growth would continue, but the outsourcing and advertising strategies that propelled it to the top put it on a collision course with a force in its social environment. This force, the sweatshop issue, would gain power and cause considerable damage when it emerged.

In 1988 an Indonesian union newspaper published a study of bad working conditions in a plant making Nike footwear.[5] Soon other critical articles appeared in the Indonesian press. Over the next few years a few stories about outsourcing first-world jobs to "sweatshops" in the third world appeared in the Western media. The AFL-CIO decided to investigate how workers were being treated in plants that manufactured for American firms and sent an investigator named Jeffrey Ballinger to Indonesia. Ballinger focused on Nike contractors, gathering detailed information.

In 1992 he published a clever indictment of Nike in *Harper's Magazine* by exhibiting the monthly pay stub of an Indonesian woman named Sadisah who made Nike running shoes and showing that Sadisah worked on an assembly line 10-and-a-half hours a day, six days a week, making $1.03 per day or about $0.14 an hour, less than the Indonesian minimum wage. She was paid only $0.02 an hour for 63 hours of overtime during the pay period. Her home was all she could afford, a rented shanty lacking electricity and plumbing. The Nikes that she made sold for $80 in the United States, yet the cost of her labor per shoe was only $0.12 cents. If anyone missed the point, Ballinger noted that the year before Nike had made a profit of $287 million and signed Michael Jordan to a $20 million advertising contract, a sum that Sadisah would have had to work 44,492 years to earn.[6]

Ballinger's article appeared with a flurry of other negative stories, but the issue did not immediately heat up. Nevertheless, Nike elected to show more responsibility for the welfare of foreign workers. In 1992 it adopted a "Code of Conduct" requiring its contractors to certify compliance with local minimum

---

[4] Figures in this paragraph are from Nike, Inc., Form 10-K, March 31, 2004, pp. 5, 6.

[5] Cited in Jeffrey Hollender and Stephen Fenichell, *What Matters Most* (New York: Basic Books, 2004), p. 190.

[6] Jeffrey Ballinger, "The New Free-Trade Heel," *Harper's*, August 1992, pp. 46–47.

wage, child labor, health, safety, workers' compensation, forced labor, environmental, and discrimination laws. In 1994, it hired the accounting firm Ernst & Young to audit code compliance by making spot checks at factories. These developments suggest that at some point CEO Philip Knight came to believe that even if Nike did not directly employ foreign workers it benefitted from their labor and so had an ethical duty toward their welfare. But Nike would not escape damage from the issue. Negative stories about its contract factories grew more numerous. According to Ballinger:

> I would describe the dramatic emergence of the sweatshop story as sort of a train wreck. Just as the big-name brands and department stores began outsourcing all of their production to contractors, the industry was moving to the most corrupt and repressive places in the world. . . . While business school case studies were heaping praise on corporations for shedding responsibility for manufacturing, the seeds were being sewn for a tremendous upheaval, once the contractors' brutal practices were exposed.[7]

If one event triggered the "train wreck," it may have been the April 1996 congressional testimony by the leader of a human rights group, who said that clothing for Wal-Mart's "Kathie Lee" apparel line was made at a Honduran factory where children worked 14 hours a day. Daytime television viewers saw talk show host Kathie Lee Gifford reduced to tears as she responded. "You can say I'm ugly, you can say I'm not talented, but when you say that I don't care about children . . . How dare you?"[8] Now the issue had emotional content for American consumers.

Soon after the Gifford spectacle antisweatshop activists decided to focus on Nike and attacks heated up. Nike was an industry leader. If it could be reformed, other clothing companies and retailers would fall into line. It was also vulnerable to a brand name attack. Progressive advocacy groups, including Global Exchange, the National Labor Committee, Press for Change, SweatshopWatch, and the Interfaith Center for Corporate Responsibility, joined forces to inform the public of what they saw as a gap

between the inspiring images in Nike's advertising and the grim reality of its labor practices. This alarmed Nike because bad publicity could rub away the image magic that made its brand cool.

NIKE AT WAR WITH ITS CRITICS

The war over Nike's image would be fought in the media. An early skirmish came when Bob Herbert at the *New York Times* wrote the first of what became a year-long series of columns berating Nike. After describing a climate of atrocities in Indonesia, including government-condoned killings and torture, he accused Nike of using "the magnificent image of Michael Jordan soaring, twisting, driving, flying" to divert attention from its exploitation of Indonesian workers. "Nike executives know exactly what is going on in Indonesia. They are not bothered by the cries of the oppressed. It suits them. Each cry is a signal that their investment is paying off."[9]

Nike CEO Philip Knight quickly responded with a letter to the editor, citing ways that Nike worked with contractors to benefit workers, and noting that Nike paid "double the minimum wage" and "had an oversight system that works." He accused Herbert of trying to "sacrifice enlightenment for hype."[10] Herbert's response was a second column rebuking Nike for running theme ads about women's empowerment while most of its shoes were produced "by grossly underpaid women stuck in utterly powerless and often abusive circumstances."[11]

Over the next two years, negative stories about Nike appeared with increasing frequency. An inspection report by the human rights group Vietnam Labor Watch reported that young women working in a Nike factory were paid subminimum wages. A supervisor had forced 56 women to run twice around the 1.2-mile factory boundary under a hot sun for failing to wear regulation shoes. Twelve of them fainted and required hospitalization.[12] Gary Trudeau

[7] Interview with Jeffrey Ballinger cited in Kevin Danaher and Jason Mark, *Insurrection: Citizen Challenges to Corporate Power* (New York: Routledge, 2003), p. 84.

[8] Rob Howe et al., "Labor Pains," *People Magazine*, June 10, 1996, p. 58.

[9] Bob Herbert, "Nike's Bad Neighborhood," *New York Times*, June 14, 1996, p. A29.

[10] "Nike Pays Good Wages to Foreign Workers," *New York Times*, June 21, 1996, p. A26.

[11] "From Sweatshops to Aerobics," *New York Times*, June 24, 1996, p. A15.

[12] Vietnam Labor Watch, "Nike Labor Practices in Vietnam," March 20, 1997, available at www.saigon.com/~nike/reports/report1.html#summary; and Ellen Neuborne, "Nike to Take a Hit in Labor Report," *USA Today*, March 27, 1997, p. 1A.

EXHIBIT 1
Rise of Negative News Stories about Nike's Labor Practices, 1988–1999

Source: S. Prakash Sethi, *Setting Global Standards* (New York: John Wiley & Sons, 2003), table 9.2.

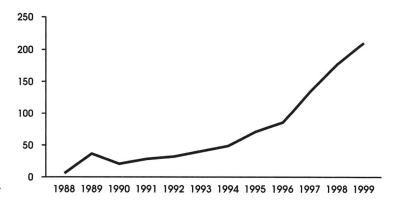

drew a series of *Doonesbury* cartoons based on the Vietnam Labor Watch allegations. A coalition of women's groups attacked Nike for running ads associating its brand with fit, healthy, and independent women while young Asian women in its factories endured sexual harassment, corporal punishment, and forced overtime.[13]

Activists urged people to return Nike sneakers during "shoe-ins" at Niketown outlets. A disgruntled Ernst & Young employee leaked a confidential spot inspection report on a Vietnamese shoe factory. It showed violations of Vietnamese working hours law and found that 77 percent of the employees suffered respiratory problems from breathing toxic vapors at levels that violated both Vietnamese and U.S. standards.[14] Another group, the Hong Kong Christian Industrial Committee, released a study of Nike factories in China documenting long work days, forced overtime, pay below minimum wages, and unsafe levels of airborne dust and toxic chemicals.[15] *The Oregonian,* the paper in Portland where Nike is headquartered, called Nike "an international human rights incident."[16]

Throughout 1996 and 1997, Nike found itself at the center of a worldwide debate over sweatshops. The company countered its critics by expanding

efforts to stop workplace abuses and by mounting a public relations campaign. At great expense it became the only shoe company in the world to eliminate the use of polyvinyl chloride in shoe construction, ending worker exposure to dangerous chlorine compounds. It revised its conduct code, expanding protections for workers. It set up a compliance department of more than 50 employees. Its staff members were assigned to specific Asian plants or to a region, where they trained local managers and did audits assessing code compliance.[17] Full compliance was elusive.

By the end of 1997 Nike, through its contractors, employed 450,000 workers worldwide. There were 150 factories in Asia alone. Foreign factory managers sometimes held values that condoned abusing workers. There were culture clashes. For example, tough Korean and Taiwanese managers, who brought in a demanding, authoritarian style of supervision, ran large factories in Vietnam. The Koreans are resented by many Vietnamese for sending troops to support the Americans during the Vietnam War. Nike oversight of these plants involves coming to grips with three languages and three sets of cultural values in tension. Nike also hired a senior vice president of social responsibility to oversee its efforts.

Working with Kathie Lee Gifford, other companies, and human rights groups, Nike helped to develop the Fair Labor Association code of conduct (see Chapter 5) and agreed to abide by its conditions. It hired Andrew Young, a former U.S. Ambassador to the United Nations, to visit Asian plants and write an

[13] Steven Greenhouse, "Nike Supports Women in Its Ads but Not Its Factories, Groups Say," *New York Times,* October 26, 1997, sec. 1, p. 30.

[14] Steven Greenhouse, "Nike Shoe Plant in Vietnam Is Called Unsafe for Workers," *New York Times,* November 8, 1997, p. A1.

[15] *Kasky v. Nike,* 93 Cal. Rptr. 2d 856.

[16] Jeff Manning, "Nike's Global Machine Goes on Trial," *The Oregonian,* November 9, 1997, p. A1.

[17] S. Prakash Sethi, *Setting Global Standards* (New York: John Wiley & Sons, 2003), p. 167.

EXHIBIT 2
The Nike Code of Conduct

Source: www.Nike.com.

The Code of Conduct has been revised and articulated since its introduction in 1992. Listed below are its seven "core standards." Another document, the Code Leadership Standards, elaborates 51 specific labor, safety, health, and environmental standards. The Code is translated into local languages and today is posted in more than 900 contract factories making Nike products.

1. **Forced Labor.** The contractor does not use forced labor in any form—prison, indentured, bonded or otherwise.

2. **Child Labor.** The contractor does not employ any person below the age of 18 to produce footwear. The contractor does not employ any person below the age of 16 to produce apparel, accessories or equipment. If at the time Nike production begins, the contractor employs people of the legal working age who are at least 15, that employment may continue, but the contractor will not hire any person going forward who is younger than the Nike or legal age limit, whichever is higher. To further ensure these age standards are complied with, the contractor does not use any form of homework for Nike production.

3. **Compensation.** The contractor provides each employee at least the minimum wage, or the prevailing industry wage, whichever is higher; provides each employee a clear, written accounting for every pay period; and does not deduct from employee pay for disciplinary infractions.

4. **Benefits.** The contractor provides each employee all legally mandated benefits.

5. **Hours of Work/Overtime.** The contractor complies with legally mandated work hours; uses overtime only when each employee is fully compensated according to local law; informs each employee at the time of hiring if mandatory overtime is a condition of employment; and on a regularly scheduled basis provides one day off in seven, and requires no more than 60 hours of work per week on a regularly scheduled basis, or complies with local limits if they are lower.

6. **Environment, Safety and Health (ES&H).** From suppliers to factories to distributors and to retailers, Nike considers every member of our supply chain as partners in our business. As such, we've worked with our Asian partners to achieve specific environmental, health and safety goals, beginning with a program called MESH (Management of Environment, Safety and Health).

7. **Documentation and Inspection.** The contractor maintains on file all documentation needed to demonstrate compliance with this Code of Conduct and required laws; agrees to make these documents available for Nike or its designated monitor; and agrees to submit to inspections with or without prior notice.

inspection report. Young toured 12 factories over 15 days and found that conditions "certainly did not appear to be what most Americans would call sweatshops."[18] Nike purchased full-page editorial advertisements in newspapers to broadcast his generally favorable findings, saying that the report showed it was "operating morally" and promising to act on his recommendations for improvement.

[18] Dana Canedy, "Nike's Asian Factories Pass Young's Muster," *New York Times,* June 25, 1997, p. D2.

Finally, Nike ran a public relations counteroffensive. Unlike some of rival firms that lay low, it chose to confront critics. It hired an experienced strategist to manage the campaign. Nike responded to every charge, no matter how small or what the source. Allegations were countered with press releases, letters to the editor, and letters to presidents and athletic directors of universities using Nike products. In these communications Nike sought to portray itself as a responsible employer creating opportunity for thousands of workers in emerging

At work in a Vietnam plant making Nike footwear.
Source: © Steve Rayner/Corbis.

economies. CEO Knight expressed the Nike philosophy, saying, "This is going to be a long fight, but I'm confident the truth will win in the end."[19]

THE KASKY LAWSUIT

While Knight thought he was fighting for truth, Marc Kasky perceived something less noble—a fraud conducted to sell shoes and T-shirts. He believed that Nike knowingly deceived consumers, who relied on the company's statements for reassurance that their purchases did not sustain sweatshops. Under an unusual state law, any California citizen can sue a corporation on behalf of the public for an unlawful business practice. Kasky took advantage of this provision, alleging that Nike had engaged in negligent misrepresentation, fraud and deceit, and misleading advertising in violation of the state's commercial code. The code prohibits "any unlawful, unfair, deceptive, untrue or misleading advertising."[20]

In his complaint, Kasky accused Nike of using a "promotional scheme," including its code of conduct, to create a "carefully cultured image" that was "intended . . . to entice consumers who do not want to purchase products made in sweatshop . . . conditions."[21] He set forth six classes of misleading claims.

- In its Code of Conduct and in a "Nike Production Primer" pamphlet given to the media, Nike stated that its contracts prevent corporal punishment and sexual harassment at factories making Nike products. But the Vietnam Labor Watch report told of workers forced to kneel in the hot sun and described frequent complaints by female employees against their supervisors.

- In a range of promotional materials Nike asserted that its products were manufactured in compliance with laws and regulations on wages and overtime. But evidence from a report by the Hong Kong Christian Industrial Committee and the leaked Ernst & Young audit showed that plants in China and Vietnam violated such laws.

[19] Quoted in Tony Emerson, "Swoosh Wars," *Newsweek*, March 12, 2001, p. 35.

[20] The law is California's Unfair Competition Law, which is codified as §17200 (source of the quotation) and §17500 of the California Business & Professions Code. Kasky also alleged violations of California Civil Code §1572 (which defines fraud) and §1709 and §1710 (which define deceit).

[21] First Amended Complaint of Milberg, Weiss et al., *Kasky v. Nike,* Superior Court, San Francisco County, No. 994446, July 2, 1998, pp. 5, 6, and 10.

- At the Nike Annual Shareholder Meeting in 1997 CEO Knight said that the air in Nike's newest Vietnam shoe factory was less polluted than the air in Los Angeles. But the Ernst & Young report documented exposures to excessive levels of hazardous air pollutants.
- In his letter to the editor of the *New York Times,* Knight stated that Nike paid, on average, double the minimum wage to workers worldwide. But this is contradicted by data from pay stubs in the Vietnam Labor Watch report. He also said that Nike gave workers free meals, but an article in the *Youth Newspaper* of Ho Chi Minh City reported that workers paid for lunches.
- In its paid editorial ads discussing Andrew Young's report on its factories, Nike made the claim that it was "doing a good job" and "operating morally." But the report was deficient because it failed to address central issues such as minimum wage violations.
- In a press release Nike made the claim that it guaranteed a "living wage for all workers." But the director of its own Labor Practices Department had written a letter defining a "living wage" as income sufficient to support a family of four, then stating that the company did not ask contractors to raise wages that high.[22]

California unfair competition law did not require Kasky to own a pair of Nike sneakers or to claim personal damages. He did not need to show that anyone else had relied on Nike's claims or been injured by them. He did not even have to prove that Nike had lied on purpose. Under the law it would be enough if a court judged the statements false. Kasky wanted the court to throw the book at Nike if lies were confirmed. He sought no monetary gain for himself. Instead, he asked for an injunction against further deception, a court-approved public information campaign forcing the company to correct misrepresentations, disgorgement of Nike profits from California sales, and payment of his legal expenses. Instead, Superior Court Judge David A. Garcia threw the case out. There was no trial to decide whether any of the statements made by Nike were misleading. The judge simply accepted Nike's claim that the statements in question were part of an ongoing public debate and, therefore, entitled to broad protection.

[22] Ibid., pp. 10–25.

COMMERCIAL SPEECH OR PROTECTED EXPRESSION?

Freedom of speech is a central value in American culture. It derives from a long philosophical tradition, exemplified in John Stuart Mill's classic essay *On Liberty.* Mill believed that freedom of opinion and expression were necessary to maintain a free society, the kind of society that could protect liberty and promote happiness. He wrote that a natural tendency existed to silence discomfiting, doubtful, or unorthodox views. But this is wrong, because no person is in possession of unerring truth.

Restricting debate deprives society of the opportunity to find new ideas that are more valid than prevailing ones. Even bizarre or incorrect comments should be valued. The former may contain partial truth and the latter make the truth more compelling because of its contrast to the falsehood. Censorship of any kind is wrong because no person, society, or generation is infallible. It is better to leave open many avenues for expression of views so that error and pretention can be opposed. Truth, said Mill, needs to be "fully, frequently, and fearlessly discussed."[23]

The First Amendment to the Constitution of the United States was intended to protect the kind of public debate that is critical to the functioning of a democracy.[24] A complicating factor is the legal distinction between commercial and noncommercial speech. Advertising is commercial speech, or "speech proposing a commercial transaction."[25] Commercial speech receives less protection than noncommercial speech. Noncommercial speech is speech in the broad marketplace of ideas, encompassing political, scientific, and artistic expression. Traditionally, it is entitled to expansive protection. For many years, advertising received no First Amendment protection,

[23] John Stuart Mill, *On Liberty,* ed. Currin V. Shields (Indianapolis: Bobbs-Merrill, 1956), p. 43. Originally published posthumously in 1907.

[24] The First Amendment reads, in part, "Congress shall make no law . . . abridging the freedom of speech, or of the press." The amendment originally applied to actions by the federal government, but the United States Supreme Court has held that through the due process clause of the Fourteenth Amendment it also limits state governments from infringing on speech.

[25] *Central Hudson Gas & Electric Corp. v. Public Service Commission,* 447 U.S. 562 (1980).

but beginning in the 1970s the Supreme Court began to give it some protection from restrictive laws. Many federal and state laws restrict advertising to prevent consumer fraud, but laws restricting comments about politics or public policy are regarded as invalid on their face and upheld only in unusual circumstances. Were Nike's comments commercial speech or non-commercial speech? The answer would determine how much protection from scrutiny about their accuracy they were entitled to receive.

At a Superior Court hearing in early 1999, Nike argued that the speech in question was noncommercial speech expressed in public debate on the sweatshop issue and protected by the First Amendment.[26] The judge agreed and dismissed the case.[27] That would have been the end of it, but Kasky appealed, arguing that Nike's statements were simply advertising. They fell into the category of commercial speech and were not entitled to broad protection. But in 2000 the appeals court rejected Kasky's argument. In a 3–0 decision it held that Nike's statements were properly classified as noncommercial speech and entitled to broad First Amendment protection.[28] Kasky appealed to the California Supreme Court.

In a 4–3 decision the California Supreme Court reversed the appellate court, holding that Nike's statements were commercial speech.[29] It sent the case back down to the appellate court for further proceedings preparatory to a trial on the accuracy of specific Nike statements.[30] Kasky had won. The majority created a three-pronged test of commercial speech and applied it to Nike's messages. For speech to be commercial it had to come from a business, be intended for an audience of consumers, and make representations of

facts related to products. Based on this test, the court found that Nike's statements were commercial speech. The majority acknowledged that commercial and noncommercial speech were intermingled in Nike's statements, but argued that "Nike may not 'immunize false or misleading product information from government regulation simply by including references to public issues.'"[31] In other words, what Nike was doing was the equivalent of a used car dealer falsely advertising that "none of our cars has ever been in an accident," but avoiding prosecution for fraud by adding, "and Congress should require tougher tests for driver's licenses."

Two dissenting opinions revealed serious disagreement among the justices. Justice Ming W. Chin, joined by his colleague, Justice Marvin R. Baxter, attacked the majority for unfairly tilting the playing field against Nike. "While Nike's critics have taken full advantage of their right to 'uninhibited, robust, and wide-open' debate," he wrote, "the same cannot be said of Nike, the object of their ire. When Nike tries to defend itself from these attacks, the majority denies it the same First Amendment protection Nike's critics enjoy."[32]

A second dissent came from Justice Janice R. Brown, who found Nike's commercial and noncommercial speech inseparable. In her view, "Nike's commercial statements about its labor practices cannot be separated from its noncommercial statements about a public issue, because its labor practices *are* the public issue."[33] She admonished the majority for creating a test of commercial speech that was unconstitutional because it made "the level of protection given to speech dependant on the identity of the speaker—and not just the speech's content."[34]

The consequences of the decision went far beyond Nike. Now any company doing business in California had to be careful about expressions of fact or opinion that reached consumers in the state. The sharpest and most ideological critics of a corporation could take issue with its statements, bring it to court, and force a trial about the accuracy of its claims. The decision was as unwelcome in the business community as it was unexpected. Nike would seek to overturn it.

[26] Nike also asserted speech protections under Article I, section 2(a), of the California Constitution which reads: "Every person may freely speak, write and publish his or her sentiments on all subjects, being responsible for the abuse of that right. A law may not restrain or abridge liberty of speech or press."

[27] *Kasky v. Nike,* Superior Court of the City and County of San Francisco, No. 994446 (1999). There is no written opinion.

[28] *Kasky v. Nike,* 79 Cal. App. 4th 165 (2000).

[29] *Kasky v. Nike,* 27 Cal. 4th 939 (2002).

[30] Nike's demurrer raised other objections to Kasky's allegations and the Appeals Court was instructed to consider these before remanding the case back to the Superior Court in San Francisco for a trial to determine if Nike's statements were fraudulent and misleading. A demurrer is a formal objection to a proceeding and request for dismissal on the basis that the opponent's allegations are in some way legally deficient.

[31] At 966, quoting *Bolger v. Youngs Drug Prods. Corp.,* 463 U.S. 68 (1983).

[32] At 970–971, quoting *Garrison v. Louisiana* 379 U.S. 75 (1964).

[33] At 980. Emphasis in the original.

[34] At 978.

IN THE UNITED STATES SUPREME COURT

Nike appealed to the United States Supreme Court, which accepted the case.[35] In its brief, Nike argued that the California Supreme Court decision should be reversed to remove its chilling effect on policy debate. Kasky maintained his argument that the First Amendment protected only expressions of ideas and points of view; it gave no shelter for false statements about how products are made. Oral argument before the nine justices took place on April 23, 2003. But, surprisingly, they never issued a decision.

On June 26, the Court abruptly dismissed the case as "improvidently granted."[36] In a brief concurring opinion Justice John Paul Stevens said the Court had erred in accepting the case before all California state court proceedings were exhausted. It would wait.

This view was not unanimous. Justices Anthony Kennedy, Stephen Breyer, and Sandra Day O'Connor dissented. They saw no reason to wait because of procedural issues. Justice Breyer hinted that these three would have struck down any restriction on Nike's speech.

> In my view . . . the questions presented directly concern the freedom of Americans to speak about public matters in public debate, no jurisdictional rule prevents us from deciding these questions now, and delay itself may inhibit the exercise of constitutionally protected rights of free speech without making the issue significantly easier to decide later on. . . . [A]n action to enforce California's laws—laws that discourage certain kinds of speech—amounts to more than just a genuine, future threat. It is a present reality—one that discourages Nike from engaging in speech. It thereby creates "injury in fact." Further, that injury is directly "traceable" to Kasky's pursuit of this lawsuit. And this Court's decision, if favorable to Nike, can "redress" that injury.[37]

[35] By now *Nike v. Kasky* had attracted considerable attention. The Court received 31 *amicus curiae*, or "friend of the court," briefs. Among these were briefs supporting Nike from the Chamber of Commerce, the Business Roundtable, several advertising associations, and large corporations, including ExxonMobil, Microsoft, and Pfizer. Kasky was supported by briefs from the attorneys general of 18 states, consumer groups, and advocacy groups such as the Sierra Club, Public Citizen, and Global Exchange.

[36] *Nike v. Kasky,* 539 U.S. 654 (2003), Per Curiam.

[37] At 667, 668.

SETTLEMENT

After the Supreme Court dismissal, lower courts in California could address Kasky's specific charges against Nike. The company might now be forced to defend the alleged misrepresentations about its labor practices in a trial. Its antagonists relished the prospect. Nike would need to produce internal documents related to its claims, perhaps opening it to further attack. However, on September 12, 2003, in another surprising development, Kasky and Nike announced an agreement to settle the case.

In settling, Nike agreed to pay $1.5 million to the industry-friendly Fair Labor Association to strengthen its factory monitoring programs. It may have paid Kasky's legal fees, but this has never been confirmed. Activists were disappointed that no grand show trial was forthcoming. The corporate community was disappointed that the California Supreme Court decision was allowed to stand. An *Advertising Age* editorial observed that "Nike would have had the respect, and support, of the larger business community if it had stuck it out and fought on."[38]

THE CONSEQUENCES

The settlement stopped further legal proceedings. Nonetheless, fear of expensive false advertising and fraud suits has led many companies to tighten their internal reviews before issuing ads or press releases and to restrict their communications on social issues. Nike is the best example. In 2001, Nike published a *Corporate Social Responsibility Report* about its environmental impacts, labor practices, and involvement with stakeholders. It prepared a second report for 2002, but after the California Supreme Court's decision it withheld it from publication. Its executives declined dozens of invitations to speak on social responsibility issues. Because it would have to release data about its social and environmental performance, it also declined to participate in the Dow Jones Sustainability Index, an indicator of socially responsible management that requires companies to report data.[39]

[38] "Nike May Settle but Fight Goes On," *Advertising Age,* September 22, 2003, p. 20.

[39] *Nike v. Kasky,* No. 02-575, Brief for the Petitioners, undated, p. 39.

Questions

1. What responsibility does Nike have for workers at the factories making its products? Has it carried out these responsibilities well? Should it do more?

2. Could Nike have better carried out its social programs to avoid or ease conflicts with advocacy groups? If so, what should it have done?

3. Should Nike be subject to false advertising lawsuits based on statements in editorial advertising, letters written by its executives, and press releases responding to issues raised by critics? Why or why not?

4. Did the California Supreme Court make the correct decision? Why or why not?

5. How should the line between commercial and noncommercial speech be drawn?

6. Should Nike have settled the case with Marc Kasky or should it have continued to fight?

Chapter **Seven**

Business Ethics

The Fall of Arthur Andersen

When a group of aggressive managers at Enron wanted to use dubious transactions for creating tax credits, they needed the approval of an auditor. They did not have to look far. Enron had outsourced its internal auditing to Arthur Andersen and 150 Andersen employees worked in Enron's Houston headquarters. A meeting was scheduled.

The managers wanted an opinion letter stating that the tax credits were legitimate. When the Andersen auditor entered the conference room one of them rocked the back of a chair under the doorknob and said, "Nobody leaves until I get that opinion letter."[1] For the next half hour they coaxed, implored, and intimidated the auditor, who, visibly upset, gave in, agreeing to write it. Afterward, no superior at Andersen would countermand the opinion.

This scene in June 2000 foreshadowed Arthur Andersen's collapse two years later when a federal jury would convict it of obstructing justice. How did a leading accounting firm, once a paragon of sound practice, fall to such faint integrity?

The story begins with founder Arthur Andersen. At the age of 16 he was orphaned when his parents, Norwegian immigrants, died. Working in a mail room he finished school and eventually became an accounting professor at Northwestern University. In 1913, when he was 28, he opened an accounting firm in Chicago with a partner. From the beginning, he insisted on principled work. Two stories of these early days entered company lore. In its first year, when the firm was struggling to survive, he refused to allow a railroad to defer major charges instead of registering them as current operating expenses. The president of the railroad released his wrath on Andersen, but Andersen stood firm. Within a year the railroad went bankrupt. Then, in 1915, a shipping company wanted the date on its financial results moved back so they would not reflect the loss of a vessel. Again Andersen refused and the shipper took its business away.

Andersen is described as "a stern, demanding man who set himself high standards for hard work and long hours."[2] He favored a slogan that his mother taught him— "think straight, talk straight"—and made it the firm's credo, putting it on memos and stationery. His commitment to integrity came to be called the "Andersen Way." As new offices opened, the Andersen Way stood for the idea that the same principles of

---

[1] Quoted in Robert Bryce, *Pipe Dreams: Greed, Ego, and the Death of Enron* (New York: Public Affairs, 2002), p. 232.

[2] Susan E. Squires, Cynthia J. Smith, Lorna McDougall, and William R. Yeack, *Inside Arthur Andersen: Shifting Values, Unexpected Consequences* (Upper Saddle River, NJ: FT Prentice Hall, 2003), p. 27.

independence, sense of duty, and absolute integrity should characterize every branch office. It defined a strong, unified corporate culture. New recruits were indoctrinated in its values at a campuslike training center. After Andersen died in 1947, artifacts of his vision were enshrined in lobby displays at offices around the world.

For years after his death, Andersen's firm maintained high standards. Yet the world was changing. In 1950 an employee planted one seed of change by building a primitive computer and experimenting with its business applications. When Andersen consultants began to help General Electric manage a computerized payroll, the company found a new source of revenue. Soon it set up a division offering a range of consulting services. It was this division that would challenge the Andersen Way.

Over time, the consulting division grew much faster than the basic accounting business. At first consultants had to have two years of accounting experience, but the requirement was dropped in the 1960s. By the mid-1970s consultants were bringing in more revenue than accountants and conflict arose between the two groups. Consultants resented reporting to auditors and disliked a compensation system that subsidized the accounting partners. Trying to resolve these growing tensions, the firm adopted a new structure in 1989 that split the consulting and auditing practices into separate businesses under a parent company called Andersen Worldwide.

Following the split, the accounting business started its own consulting operation in competition with the consulting business. This outraged the consultants and in 2000, after a long battle, they broke away completely to become an independent firm named Accenture. One effect of the protracted struggle was strain on the Andersen culture that caused it to change from a culture of unity to one of competitiveness, jealousy, and bitterness.

The consultants' breakaway left Arthur Andersen in an unattractive position. Its main audit and tax businesses faced heavy competition and showed little prospect for growth. Its still-small consulting business, however, could rapidly grow. One problem was that the Securities and Exchange Commission (SEC) viewed the growth of consulting in auditing firms with alarm, believing it would lead to conflicts of interest in which auditors took it easy on corporate clients who bought consulting services that were more lucrative than basic auditing.

Despite the SEC's preaching, Andersen set itself firmly on rapid expansion in consulting. In the old Arthur Andersen, auditors never sold services. But after the 1989 split between accounting and consulting, auditors were evaluated on the amount of additional services they sold to clients. Andersen began to move from an auditing culture to a sales culture. According to one former employee, "Somewhere along the way, Arthur Andersen's message—that you could make good money using good principles—got lost."[3] To cut costs, partners were forced to retire at age 56. This removed a layer of leadership experienced in the Andersen Way. As time passed, auditors faced growing revenue pressure and they became reluctant to alienate clients.

The result was a series of disgraceful audit performances that would have astounded the firm's founder. In 1993 Waste Management restated $1.7 billion in earnings. Although Andersen auditors had spotted the bad accounting, they signed off on it when the company's management refused to make changes. This cowardly act was

---

[3] Barbara Lay Toffler, *Final Accounting* (New York: Broadway Books, 2003), p. 232.

motivated by fear of losing Waste Management's fees. Andersen settled an SEC enforcement action against it for $7 million while denying any guilt.

Similar incidents followed. In 1998 falsified earnings of Boston Chicken and McKesson-HBOC had to be restated. In 2001 Sunbeam filed for bankruptcy after Andersen auditors failed to prevent earnings fraud. The collapse of Enron later that year sealed Andersen's fate. Although partners in the firm had held meetings about Enron's bizarre and suspicious balance sheet, they lacked the courage to confront their largest client. When Enron's earnings vaporized, the SEC began an investigation. The Andersen partner in Houston who ran the Enron account shredded documents, leading to an obstruction of justice indictment. The partner pled guilty, but because of Andersen's past behavior the government put the firm itself on trial and a jury found it guilty of obstruction of justice.

In late 2002 a federal judge sentenced Andersen to a $500,000 criminal fine and five years' probation.[4] But the firm was doomed. Two more of its clients, WorldCom and Qwest Communications, lit up in bankruptcy fireworks after earnings had to be restated. Andersen was a defendant in 90 civil lawsuits, most by stockholders of failed companies. One by one, its clients left. What company wanted an auditor whose name was synonymous with scandal? Since its conviction, Andersen has shrunk from an elite $9.3 billion firm with 85,000 employees to about 200 attorneys and staff working on one floor of its Chicago headquarters.[5]

Ethical behavior is never automatic. Managers must instill it and intervene to ensure its continuation. Arthur Andersen founded a culture of rectitude that warped because several generations of management allowed the Andersen Way to be undermined. They reduced training, eliminated experienced leaders, and introduced compensation and evaluation criteria that put pressure on the independence of auditors. These are classic danger signs. If they had been recognized, the outcome for Andersen, its clients, and their stakeholders might have been different.

In this chapter we will discuss ethical tools that managers at Andersen might have used. We begin by setting forth basic sources of ethical values. Then we look at the factors shaping ethical climates in organizations. Finally, we discuss how corporations manage ethics and try to elevate behavior.

WHAT ARE BUSINESS ETHICS?

ethics
The study of good and evil, right and wrong, and just and unjust.

business ethics
The study of good and evil, right and wrong, and just and unjust actions in business.

Ethics is the study of what is good and evil, right and wrong, and just and unjust. *Business ethics,* therefore, is the study of good and evil, right and wrong, and just and unjust actions in business. Ethical managers try to do good and avoid doing evil. A mass of principles, values, norms, and thoughts concerned with what conduct *ought* to be exists to guide them. Yet in this vaporous mass, the outlines of good and evil are at times shadowy. Usually they are distinct enough, but often not. So, using ethical ideas in business is an art, an art requiring judgment about both the motivations behind an act and the act's consequences.

Discussions of business ethics frequently emphasize refractory and unclear situations, perhaps to show drama and novelty. Although all managers face difficult ethical conflicts, applying clear guidelines resolves the vast majority of them. The

---

[4] *United States v. Arthur Andersen LLP,* Criminal Action No. H-020121, U.S.D.C. (S.D. Tex.), October 16, 2002.

[5] Jeffrey Zaslow, "Moving On," *The Wall Street Journal,* April 8, 2004, p. D1.

Eighth Commandment, for example, prohibits stealing and is plainly violated by taking tools home from work or theft of trade secrets. Lies in advertising violate a general rule of the Western business world that the seller of a product must not purposely deceive a buyer. This general understanding stems from the Mosaic law, the Code of Hammurabi, Roman law, and other sources and is part of a general ethic favoring truth going back at least 3,000 years.

Overall, ethical traditions that apply to business support truth telling, honesty, protection of life, respect for rights, fairness, and obedience to law. Some beliefs in this bundle of traditions go back thousands of years. Others, such as the idea that a corporation is responsible for the long-term health of its workers, have emerged more recently. In keeping with this long and growing ethical heritage, most business actions can be clearly judged ethical or unethical; eliminating unethical behavior such as bribery or embezzlement may be difficult, but knowing the rightness or wrongness of actions is usually easy.

This does not mean that ethical decisions are always clear. Some are troublesome because although basic ethical standards apply, conflicts between them defy resolution.

> Lockheed Aircraft Corp. made large campaign contributions to Japanese officials intended to influence the Japanese government to buy airplanes. This saved jobs for American workers. However, though such contributions were common in Japan and for the international aerospace industry overall, they violated U.S. business norms. Lockheed's actions are still debated.

Some ethical issues are hidden, at least initially, and hard to recognize.

> The A. H. Robins Co. began to market its Dalkon Shield intrauterine device through general practitioners while competitors continued to sell them only through obstetricians and gynecologists. This strategy was wildly successful in gaining market share for Robins and did not, initially, seem to raise ethical issues; but when dangerous health problems with the Shield started to appear, the general practitioners were slower to recognize them than the specialists. Robins's failure to make extra efforts in tracking the safety of the device then emerged as an ethical shortcoming.

And some ethical issues are very subtle, submerged in everyday workplace behavior. Managers must often work in a world of uncertainty and act or pass judgment without complete knowledge of facts. The following case involves a commitment, a promise.

> A regional manager tells a factory manager that replacement equipment for a factory with production problems due to breakdowns will be ordered from this year's budget. At year's end, however, the equipment has not been ordered because, as the regional manager explains, "there just wasn't enough money left to do it." Is the factory manager entitled to expect the budget to be managed so that the commitment could be kept? Why was the commitment not kept? Poor planning? Disguised withdrawal of cooperation? Another reason?

TWO THEORIES OF BUSINESS ETHICS

There is an ageless debate about whether ethics in business may be more permissive than general societal or personal ethics. There are two basic views.

Daniel Drew (1797–1879), speculator in railroad stocks and an exponent of the theory of amorality.
Courtesy of Picture History.

The first, the *theory of amorality*, is that business should be amoral, that is, conducted without reference to the full range of ethical standards, restraints, and ideals in society. Managers may use compromising ethics because competition distills their selfish actions into benefits for society. Adam Smith noted that the "invisible hand" of the market assures that "by pursuing his own interest [a merchant] frequently promotes that of the society more effectively than when he really intends to promote it."[6]

The apex of this view came during the latter half of the nineteenth century. It was widely believed that business and personal ethics existed in separate compartments, that business was a special sanctuary in which less idealistic ethics were permissible.[7] Daniel Drew, who made a fortune in the 1860s by manipulating railroad stocks without scruple, summed up the nineteenth-century compartmentalization of business decisions in these words:

theory of amorality
The belief that business should be conducted without reference to the full range of ethical standards, restraints, and ideals in society.

> Sentiment is all right up in the part of the city where your home is. But downtown, no. Down there the dog that snaps the quickest gets the bone. Friendship is very nice for a Sunday afternoon when you're sitting around the dinner table with your relations, talking about the sermon that morning. But nine o'clock Monday morning, notions should be brushed aside like cobwebs from a machine. I never took any stock in a man who mixed up business with anything else. He can go into other things outside of business hours, but when he's in the office, he ought not to have a relation in the world—and least of all a poor relation.[8]

The theory of amorality has far less public acceptance today, but it lives on quietly. Many managers still allow competitive pressures to justify acts that would

[6] *The Wealth of Nations*, ed. Edwin Cannan (New York: Modern Library, 1937), p. 423; originally published in 1776. Smith also believed that merchants must abide by prevailing societal ethics.

[7] This was the conviction of social Darwinist Herbert Spencer, who believed in two sets of ethics. *Family ethics* were based on the principle of charity and benefits were apportioned without relation to merit. *State ethics* were based on a competitive justice and benefits were apportioned on the basis of strict merit. Family ethics interjected into business or government by well-meaning people were an inappropriate interference with the laws of nature and would slowly corrupt the workings of Darwinian natural selection. See "The Sins of Legislators," in *The Man versus the State* (London: Watts, 1940); originally published in 1884. Dual ethical perspectives have developed in other cultures, such as Slavic cultures, that assert one set of ethical standards for personal relationships and a second set that justifies less perfection for business matters. See Sheila M. Puffer, "Understanding the Bear: A Portrait of Russian Business Leaders," *Academy of Management Executive*, February 1994, p. 47.

[8] Quoted in Robert Bartels, ed., *Ethics in Business* (Columbus: Bureau of Business Research, Ohio State University, 1963), p. 35.

James Cash Penney (1875–1971), son of a Baptist minister and an exemplar of the theory of moral unity.
© Oscar White/ CORBIS.

be wrong in private life. The theory of amorality releases them from feelings of guilt.

The second basic ethical view is the *theory of moral unity,* in which business actions are judged by the general ethical standards in society, not by a special set of more permissive standards. Only one basic ethical standard exists, so business actions are judged by the same principles as actions in other areas of life.

Many managers take this position today, and some did even in the nineteenth century. An example is James Cash Penney. We remember Penney for building a chain of department stores, but his first enterprise was a butcher shop. As a young man, Penney went to Denver, where, finding the shop for sale, he wired his mother for $3,000 (his life savings) to buy it. The departing butcher shop owner warned him that his success depended on orders from a nearby hotel. "To keep the hotel for a customer," the butcher explained, "all you have to do is buy the chef a bottle of whiskey a week." Penney regularly made the gift and business was good, but he soon had second thoughts. Resolving no longer to do business that way, he stopped the bribe, lost the hotel's business, and went broke when the shop failed. He was 23 years old. Penney later started the Golden Rule Department Store in Denver and always believed that principles of honesty led to its ultimate success. In contrast to the unsentimental lone wolf Daniel Drew, Penney reflects his focus on ethics in this little story.

theory of moral unity
Business actions are judged by the general ethical standards of society, not by a special set of more permissive standards.

> It seems that the manager of a chain store had run out of a certain line of goods and had appealed to the manager of another store in the chain for a share of the supply which this second man had on hand. This man consented—but sent some goods of poor quality which *he* had not been able to sell. He thought he was being very shrewd. But if I had the chance I would fire that man. He was not being square. He hadn't the instinct of fair dealing. You can't build a solid, substantial house with decayed planks, no matter what kind of a veneer is put over their rottenness. That man's action was rotten, even though it was veneered with temporary shrewdness.[9]

To J. C. Penney, and other exemplars of the theory of moral unity, desire to succeed is never an excuse to neglect principled behavior. Actions are not moral just because they make money. Ethical conflicts cannot be avoided simply because they arise in the course of business.

[9] J. C. Penney, "It Is One Thing to Desire—and Another to Determine," in Peter Krass, ed., *The Book of Business Wisdom* (New York: Wiley, 1997), p. 89. Reprinted from *American Magazine,* August 1919. Emphasis in the original.

ARISTOTLE'S THEORY OF RESPONSIBILITY

We turn now to a related question. Are there any factors that excuse or diminish ethical responsibility in business? The answer is yes. More than 2,000 years ago, Aristotle recognized that ethical behavior is based on voluntary choice. A person must be able to choose between alternatives to act ethically or unethically. If there is no choice, behavior is involuntary and the person is not culpable. In his *theory of moral responsibility,* Aristotle argued that two circumstances, *ignorance* and *involuntariness,* may restrict choice, thereby rendering behavior involuntary.

Aristotle's theory of moral responsibility
The theory that ethical behavior is based on voluntary choice. Ignorance and involuntariness diminish ethical responsibility for an action.

A person or corporation may be ignorant of facts or of the consequences of an act. The South African government once classified its citizens by race and used Polaroid film and cameras for pictures on racial identity papers. Black employees at Polaroid Corporation in the United States raised the issue of its complicity with racists, so it banned sales to the government while continuing sales to the South African public. For six years this policy held, but Polaroid's distributor secretly kept selling to the government. On the day that it learned about this deceit, Polaroid ended all sales in the country.[10]

Here Polaroid cannot be condemned; ignorance absolved management from any blame for condoning violation of its policy. Of course, in such situations, negligence in getting facts creates blame. A "willful blindness" doctrine exists in criminal law in recognition that intentional ignorance increases culpability. It applies in cases where a manager is suspicious of wrongdoing but fails to investigate.

Eric Pendergraft, a power plant manager, received a call from Rhonda Williams, a manager at Williams Energy Marketing & Trading Co. A California power plant that Pendergraft's company ran for Williams Energy was down for maintenance, creating a shortage of electricity and driving prices up so that electricity traders profited. On the phone, Williams said, "I don't wanna do something underhanded, but if there's work you can continue to do . . . " Pendergraft retreated from the implications of this remark. He replied: "I understand. You don't have to talk anymore."[11]

Involuntariness, according to Aristotle, arises when external factors limit or dictate behavior. First, an action may impose *unrealistically high costs*—for example, an automaker cannot be expected to prevent all traffic deaths since the costs of a completely safe vehicle in materials, design, and production would be staggering. Second, there may be *no power to influence* an outcome.

Amnesty International investigated a south Lebanon prison in which captors hung people from an electrical pylon, wet them, and administered shocks. The handcuffs used in this torture were marked "The Peerless Handcuff Co. Springfield, Mass. Made in USA."[12] Peerless is a family business started in 1914 that makes handcuffs,

[10] Tom L. Beauchamp, *Case Studies in Business, Society, and Ethics* (Upper Saddle River, NJ: Prentice Hall, 1998), pp. 275–81. Polaroid stayed out of South Africa for 17 years until apartheid, the official system of race segregation, ended.

[11] Quoted in Nancy Rivera Brooks, "New Evidence of Fraud in Power Crisis," *Los Angeles Times,* November 16, 2002, p. A1.

[12] Amnesty International, *Stopping the Torture Trade* (London: Amnesty International Publications, 2001), p. 3.

leg irons, and waist chains. It sells only to legitimate law enforcement agencies and refuses orders from some nations because it does not condone torture.[13] Although Peerless knows that its restraints could wind up in torture chambers, it lacks power to oversee the lifetime ownership and use of each device it makes.

Third, at times *no alternative exists.* In Nazi Germany, party officials allocated raw materials and controlled import-export licenses and other permissions necessary to do business. Companies were unable to function unless they paid the bribes these officials demanded. Fourth, *external forces may compel action.* For example, a company may pay excessive and unjust taxes in a country because a corrupt ruler imposes them.

Aristotle cautioned, however, that "[t]here are some things such that a man cannot be compelled to do them—that he must sooner die than do, though he suffer the most dreadful fate."[14] Unethical behavior involving coercion is voluntary if a manager can simply refuse to comply with the external force. Those who argue that market forces or an order from the boss are irresistible forces overriding individual choice give too little credit to the strength of human will.

MAJOR SOURCES OF ETHICAL VALUES IN BUSINESS

reciprocity
A form of social behavior in which people behave supportively in the expectation that this behavior will be given in return.

Four great repositories of ethical values influence managers. They are religion, philosophy, cultural experience, and law (Figure 7.1). A common theme, the idea of *reciprocity,* or mutual help, is found in each of these value systems. This idea reflects the central purpose of ethics, which is to bind individuals into a cooperative social whole. Ethical values are a mechanism that controls behavior in business and in other areas of life. Ethical restraint is more efficient with society's resources than are cruder controls such as police, lawsuits, or economic incentives. Ethical values channel individual energy into pursuits that are benign to others and beneficial to society.

Religion

The great religions, including the Judeo-Christian tradition prominent in American history, converge in the belief that a divine will reveals the nature of right and wrong behavior in all areas of life, including business. Despite doctrinal differences, major religions agree on ideas forming the basic building blocks of ethics in every society. For example, the principle of reciprocity is found, encapsulated in variations of the Golden Rule, in Buddhism, Confucianism, Hinduism, Islam, Judaism, and Christianity. These religions also converge in emphasizing traits such as promise keeping, honesty, fairness, charity, and responsibility to others.

Christian managers often seek guidance in the Bible. Like the source books and writings of other main religions, the Bible was written in a premodern, agricultural society, and many of its ethical teachings require interpretation before they can be applied to problems in the modern workplace. Much of the ethical teaching in the

[13] Robert Weissman, "The Torture Trade," *Multinational Monitor,* April 2001, p. 7.
[14] *Nichomachean Ethics,* trans. J. A. K. Thomson (New York: Penguin, 1953), p. 112; originally written c. 334–323 B.C.

FIGURE 7.1
**Major Sources
of Ethical
Values in
Business**

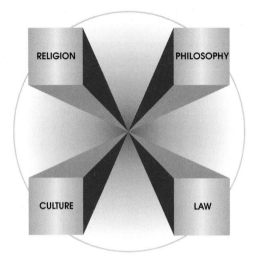

Bible comes from parables. The parable of the prodigal son (Luke 15:11–32) tells the story of an unconditionally merciful father—an image applicable to ethical conflicts in corporate superior–subordinate relationships. The story of the rich man and Lazarus (Luke 16:19–31) teaches concern for the poor and challenges Christian managers to consider the less privileged, a fitting admonition in a world where billions of people survive on less than $1 a day.[15]

In Islam the Koran is a source of ethical inspiration. The Prophet Muhammad says that "Every one of you is a shepherd and everyone is responsible for what he is shepherd of."[16] In a modern context, the Muslim manager is like a shepherd and the corporation is like a flock. The manager has a duty to rise above self-interest and protect the good of the organization.

In the Jewish tradition, managers can turn to rabbinic moral commentary in the Talmud and the books of Moses in the Torah. Here again, ancient teachings are regarded as analogies. For example, a Talmudic ruling holds that a person who sets a force in motion bears responsibility for any resulting harm, even if natural forces intervene (*Baba Qamma* 60a). This is discussed in the context of an agrarian society in which a person who starts a fire is responsible for damage from flying sparks, even if nature intervenes with high winds. In an industrial context, the ethics lesson is that polluting companies are responsible for problems caused by their waste.[17] Another passage comments on a situation in which laborers have been hired to dig in a field, but a nearby river has overflowed, preventing the work (*Bava Metzia* 76b–77a). The Talmud counsels that if the employer knew the river was likely to overflow then the workers should be paid, but if the flood was unpredictable then the workers should bear the loss. This teaching may inform

---

[15] See Oliver F. Williams and John W. Houck, *Full Value: Cases in Christian Business Ethics* (New York: Harper & Row, 1978), for discussion of these and other biblical sources of inspiration for managers.

[16] Quoted in Tanri Abeng, "Business Ethics in Islamic Context: Perspectives of a Muslim Business Leader," *Business Ethics Quarterly,* July 1997, p. 52.

[17] Moses L. Pava, *Business Ethics: A Jewish Perspective* (New York: Yeshiva University Press, 1997), pp. 72–73.

thinking about modern layoffs. In highly cyclical industries, workers can anticipate the risk of layoffs, but in more stable industries management may bear greater responsibility for job security.[18]

Parables and stories in the literature of ancient worlds can seem so innocent as to have little value for modern managers. However, as one rabbinic scholar notes, "Our world has undergone tremendous technological changes, but the issues stay the same—egotism, jealousy, greed, among others."[19] Thus, the central wisdom remains. When Confucius told Chinese merchants that "He who acts with a constant view to his own advantage (*li*) will be much murmured against," he planted a speck of truth visible in the atmosphere of any era.[20]

Philosophy

A Western manager can look back on more than 2,000 years of philosophical inquiry into ethics. This rich, complex tradition is the source of many notions about what is right or wrong in business. Every age has added new ideas, but it is a mistake to regard the history of ethical philosophy as a single debate that, over centuries, has matured to bear the fruit of growing wisdom and clear, precise standards of conduct. Even after two millennia, there remains considerable dispute among ethical thinkers about the nature of right action. If anything, standards of ethical behavior were arguably clearer in ancient Greek civilization than they are now.

In a brief circuit of milestones in ethical thinking, we turn first to the Greek philosophers. Greek ethics, from Homeric times onward, were embodied in the discharge of duties related to social roles such as shepherd, warrior, merchant, citizen, or king. Expectations of the occupants of these roles were clearer than in contemporary America, where social roles such as those of business manager or employee are more vague, overlapping, and marked by conflict.[21] Socrates (469–399 B.C.) asserted that virtue and ethical behavior were associated with wisdom and taught that insight into life would naturally lead to right conduct. He also introduced the idea of a moral law higher than human law, an idea that activists use to demand supralegal behavior from transnational corporations. Plato (428–348 B.C.), the gifted student of Socrates, carried this doctrine of virtue as knowledge further by elaborating the theory that absolute justice exists independently of individuals and that its nature can be discovered by intellectual effort. In the *Republic,* Plato set up a 50-year program for training rulers to rule in harmony with the ideal of justice.[22] Plato's most apt pupil, Aristotle, spelled out virtues of character in the *Nicomachean Ethics* and advocated a regimen of continuous learning to improve ethical behavior.[23]

---

[18] See Robert H. Carver, "If the River Stopped: A Talmudic Perspective on Downsizing," *Journal of Business Ethics* 50, 2004, pp. 144–45.

[19] Meir Tamari, quoted in Gail Lichtman, "Ethics Is Their Business," *The Jerusalem Post,* May 25, 2001, p. 13.

[20] *Analects,* book IV, chap. XII. Cited in Stephen B. Young, "The CRT *Principles for Business* as an Expression of Original Confucian Morality," *Caux Roundtable Newsletter,* Fall 2000, p. 9.

[21] Alasdair MacIntyre, *After Virtue: A Study in Moral Theory* (South Bend, IN: University of Notre Dame Press, 1981), p.115.

[22] Trans. F. M. Cornford (New York: Oxford University Press, 1945).

[23] *Nicomachean Ethics,* trans. Thomson, p. 51.

The Stoic school of ethics, spanning four centuries from the death of Alexander to the rise of Christianity in Rome, furthered the trend toward character development in Greek ethics. Epictetus (A.D. 50–100), for instance, taught that virtue was found solely within and should be valued for its own sake, arguing that this inner virtue was a higher reward than external riches or worldly success.

In business, the ethical legacy of the Greeks and Romans lives on in the conviction that virtues such as truth telling, charity, obeying the law, justice, courage, friendship, and the just use of power are important qualities. Today when a manager trades integrity for profit, we condemn this on the basis of the teachings of the ancient Mediterranean world.

Ethical thinking after the rise of Christianity was dominated by the great Catholic theologians St. Augustine (354–430) and St. Thomas Aquinas (1225–1274). Both believed that humanity should follow God's will; correct behavior in business and in all worldly activity was necessary to achieve salvation and life after death. Christianity was the source of many ethical teachings, including specific rules such as the Ten Commandments.

Christian theology created a lasting reservoir of ethical doctrine, but its command of ethical thought weakened during the historical period of intellectual and industrial expansion in Europe called the Enlightenment. Secular philosophers such as Baruch Spinoza (1632–1677) tried to demonstrate ethical principles with logical analysis rather than ordain them by reference to God's will. So also, Immanuel Kant (1724–1804) tried to find universal and objective ethical rules in logic. Kant and Spinoza, and others who followed, created a great estrangement with moral theology by believing that humanity could discover the nature of good behavior without reference to God. To this day, there is a deep divide between Christian managers who look to the Bible for divine guidance and other managers who look to worldly writing for ethical wisdom.

Other milestones of secular thinking followed. Jeremy Bentham (1748–1832) developed the idea of utilitarianism as a guide to ethics. Bentham observed that an ethical action was the one among all alternatives that brought pleasure to the largest number of persons and pain to the fewest. The worldly impact of this ethical philosophy is almost impossible to overestimate, because it validated two dominant ideologies, democracy and industrialism, allowing them first to arise and then to flourish. The legitimacy of majority rule in democratic governments rests in large part on Bentham's theory of utility as later refined by John Stuart Mill (1806–1873). Utilitarianism also sanctified industrial development by legitimizing the notion that economic growth benefits the majority; thus the pain and dislocation it brings to a few may be ethically permitted.

realist school
A school of thought that rejects ethical perfection, taking the position that human affairs will be characterized by flawed behavior and ought to be depicted as they are, not as we might wish them to be.

John Locke (1632–1704) developed and refined doctrines of human rights and left an ethical legacy supporting belief in the inalienable rights of human beings, including the right to pursue life, liberty, and happiness, and the right to freedom from tyranny. Our leaders, including business leaders, continue to be restrained by these beliefs.

A *realist school* of ethics also developed alongside the idealistic thinking of philosophers such as Spinoza, Kant, the utilitarians, and Locke. The realists believed that both good and evil were naturally present in human nature; human behavior inevitably would reflect this mixture. Since good and evil occurred naturally, it was futile to try to teach ideals. Ideals could never be realized because evil was a permanent human trait. The realist school, then, developed ethical theories that shrugged off the idea of perfect goodness. Niccolò Machiavelli (1469–1527) argued that important ends justified expedient means. Herbert Spencer (1820–1903) wrote prolifically of a harsh ethic that justified vicious competition among companies because it furthered evolution—a process in which humanity improved as the unfit fell down. Friedrich Nietzsche (1844–1900) rejected the ideals of earlier "nice" ethics, saying they were prescriptions of the timid, designed to fetter the actions of great men whose irresistible power and will were regarded as dangerous by the common herd of ordinary mortals.

Nietzsche believed in the existence of a "master morality" in which great men made their own ethical rules according to their convenience and without respect for the general good of average people. In reaction to this master morality, the mass of ordinary people developed a "slave morality" intended to shackle the great men. For example, according to Nietzsche, the mass of ordinary people celebrate the Christian virtue of turning the other cheek because they lack the power to revenge themselves on great men. He felt that prominent ethical ideals of his day were recipes for timidity and once said of utilitarianism that it made him want to vomit.[24] The influence of realists on managers has been strong. Spencer was wildly popular among the business class in the nineteenth century. Machiavelli is still read for inspiration. The lasting influence of realism is that many managers, deep down, do not believe that ideals can be achieved in business life.

Cultural Experience

Every culture transmits between generations a set of traditional values, rules, and standards that define acceptable behavior. In this way, individuals channel their conduct in socially approved directions. Civilization itself is a cumulative cultural experience consisting of three stages; in each, economic and social arrangements have dictated a distinct moral code.[25]

For millions of generations in the *hunting and gathering stage* of human development, ethics were adapted to conditions in which our ancestors had to be ready to fight, face brutal foes, and suffer hostile forces of nature. Under such circumstances, a premium was placed on pugnacity, appetite, greed, and sexual readiness, since it was often the strongest who survived. Trade ethics in early civilizations were probably deceitful and dishonest by our standards, and economic transactions were frequently conducted by brute force and violence.

Civilization passed into an *agricultural stage* approximately 10,000 years ago, beginning a time when industriousness was more important than ferocity, thrift paid greater dividends than violence, monogamy became the prevailing sexual custom because of the relatively equal numbers of the sexes, and peace came to be valued over wars, which destroyed crops and animals. These new values were codified

[24] His exact words were "the general welfare is no ideal, no goal, no remotely intelligible concept, but only an emetic." In *Beyond Good and Evil* (New York: Vintage Books, 1966), p. 157; originally published in 1886.
[25] Will Durant and Ariel Durant, *The Lessons of History* (New York: Simon & Schuster, 1968), pp. 37–42.

into ethical systems by philosophers and founders of religions. So the great ethical philosophies and theologies that guide managers today are largely products of the agricultural revolution.

Two centuries ago, society entered an *industrial stage* of cultural experience, and ethical systems began to reflect an evolving institutional, intellectual, and ecological environment. Powerful forces such as global corporations, population growth, the capitalist ideology, constitutional democracy, new technology, and ecological damage have appeared. Industrialism has not yet created a distinct ethic, but rising postmodern values put stress on ethical values that evolved in ancient, agriculture-based worlds. Postmodern values alter people's judgments about good and evil. For example, the copious outpouring of material goods from factories encourages materialism and consumption at the expense of older, scarcity-based virtues such as moderation and thrift. The old truism that nature exists for human exploitation is less compelling when reexamined in a cloud of industrial pollution.

Ethical Variation in Cultures

ethical universalism
The theory that because human nature is everywhere the same, basic ethical rules are applicable in all cultures. There is some room for variation in the way these rules are followed.

Ethical values differ among nations as historical experiences have interacted with philosophies and religions to create diverging cultural values and laws. Where differences exist, are some cultures correct about proper business ethics and others wrong? There are two ways to answer this question.

The school of *ethical universalism* holds that in terms of biological and psychological needs, human nature is everywhere the same. Ethical rules are transcultural because behavior that fulfills basic human needs should be the same everywhere—for example, basic rules of justice must be followed. Basic justice might be achieved, however, by emphasizing group ethics or by emphasizing individual ethics, leaving room for cultural variation.

ethical relativism
The theory that ethical values are created by cultural experience. Different cultures may create different values and there is no universal standard by which to judge which values are superior.

The school of *ethical relativism* holds that although human biology is everywhere similar, cultural experience creates widely diverging values, including ethical values. Ethical values are subjective. There is no objective way to prove them right or wrong as with scientific facts. A society cannot know that its ethics are superior, so it is wrong for one nation to impose standards on another.

We cannot settle this age-old philosophical debate. However, ethical variation is a practical and urgent issue. Because of globalization, corporations struggle with the question of how to apply conduct codes across cultures. If large multinationals vary behavior based on local customs, they open themselves to disturbing practices, for example, in countries that permit workplace discrimination against women. If, on the other hand, firms maintain absolute consistency of standards, they may offend local norms. Some flexibility seems appropriate.

hypernorms
Master ethical principles that underlie all other ethical principles. All variations of ethical principle must conform to them.

What guidelines exist for companies that want flexibility in their conduct codes? Some scholars argue that at a high level of abstraction, the ethical ideals of all cultures converge to basic sameness. Thomas Donaldson and Thomas W. Dunfee see a deep social contract underlying all human societies. This contract is based on what they call *hypernorms,* or principles at the root of all human ethics. Examples are basic rights, such as rights to life and to political participation. These hypernorms validate other ethical norms, which can differ from nation to nation but still be consistent with the hypernorms. For example, many U.S. corporations prohibit people from hiring their relatives. In India, however, tradition places a high value on supporting family and clan members, and some companies promise to hire workers' children when they grow up. Although these practices are inconsistent, neither violates any universal prohibition. They exist in what Donaldson and Dunfee call "moral free space" where inconsistent norms are permitted if they do not violate any hypernorms.[26]

Law

Laws codify, or formalize, ethical expectations. They proliferate over time as emerging regulations, statutes, and court rulings impose new conduct standards. For example, following a series of conspicuous business scandals in 2002, Congress responded to public anger by passing the Sarbanes-Oxley Act of 2002. This law created new duties for corporations and executives, increased criminal penalties for a range of financial crimes, and gave regulators more power.

Corporations and their managers face a range of mechanisms set up to deter illegal acts, punish offenses, and rehabilitate offenders. In particular, they face civil actions by regulatory agencies and private parties and criminal prosecution by governments. We will discuss these mechanisms to illustrate how legal controls and sanctions work.

Damages

compensatory damages
Payments awarded to redress concrete losses suffered by injured parties.

punitive damages
Payments in excess of a wronged party's actual losses. They are awarded to deter similar actions and punish a corporation that has exhibited malicious and willful misconduct.

In civil cases courts may assess damages, or payments for harm done to others by a corporation. *Compensatory damages* are payments awarded to redress concrete losses suffered by injured parties. *Punitive damages,* or payments in excess of a wronged party's actual losses, are awarded to deter similar actions and punish a corporation. In this way, they serve the same purposes as criminal penalties. Punitive damages may be awarded only if malicious and willful misconduct exists. For example, a regional manager for Browning-Ferris Industries ordered a district manager to drive a small competitor in Vermont out of business using predatory pricing. His instructions were: "Do whatever it takes. Squish him like a bug."[27] Subsequently, a jury awarded the competitor $51,146 in actual damages, then added $6 million in punitive damages.

Since the purpose of punitive damages is to punish and deter misconduct, they must be large enough to cause pain. Yet they raise many questions about fairness. There is no fixed standard for calculating their size and arbitrary sums may violate constitutional due process requirements. Given similar offenses, juries often assess higher damages against a big corporation than against a smaller one simply to make certain the penalty hurts. And sometimes the sums awarded are so large that they must be weighed against Eighth Amendment prohibitions against "excessive fines" and "cruel and unusual punishments."

The Supreme Court decided to rein in punitive damages in the case of an Alabama physician, Dr. Ira Gore, Jr., who bought a BMW automobile for $40,751 and drove it for nine months without noticing any problem. After an auto detailer

[26] Thomas Donaldson and Thomas W. Dunfee, "When Ethics Travel: The Promise and Peril of Global Business Ethics," *California Management Review,* Summer 1999, p. 61.

[27] *Browning-Ferris Industries v. Kelko Disposal,* 57 LW 4986 (1989).

told him that part of the car had been repainted, the owner found out that BMW North American was secretly repainting cars with shipping damage and selling them as new. Gore estimated his damages at $4,000 and sued, charging BMW with gross, oppressive, and malicious fraud. A jury awarded him $4 million in punitive damages—1,000 times his actual loss.

On appeal, the Supreme Court held that the award was unconstitutionally excessive.[28] (Subsequently, the Alabama Supreme Court reconsidered the case and awarded Gore only $50,000.)[29] However, the Court did not set up any formula for calculating punitive damages, so the definition of excessive is still imprecise. It continues to resist setting forth a mathematically precise ratio for permissible punitive damages, but in recent cases it has stated that few punitive awards of 10 times actual damages or greater are justified and that any punitive award of more than 4 times actual damages is suspect.[30] This guideline has greatly reduced punitive damage awards.

Criminal Prosecution of Managers and Corporations

Managers may be prosecuted for criminal actions undertaken in the course of their employment. Corporations are also subject to criminal prosecution. They are criminally liable for corrupt actions or omissions of managers if those actions are intended to benefit the corporation.[31] To establish guilty intent when criminal actions have occurred, the law assumes that the corporation has the aggregate knowledge of all its employees.

Criminal prosecution of corporations and their executives is exceptionally difficult. Unlike civil proceedings the defendants do not have to produce information, so pretrial investigations can be lengthy and expensive. Corporate defendants can far outspend government prosecutors with limited budgets. They hire experienced lawyers, including former prosecutors. When Royal Carribean Cruise Lines was indicted for criminal violation of the Clean Water Act, it put together an all-star defense team including two former federal prosecutors and two former United States attorneys general to defend itself.[32] Corporate crimes such as accounting frauds require prosecutors to educate lay juries about intricate financial transactions. Even experienced judges can be challenged in trying to understand them. Consequently prosecutors in some corporate scandal cases in 2002 and 2003 resorted to "sideshow charges," or indictments based on peripheral charges that are easier to understand and prove.[33]

---

[28] *BMW of North America, Inc. v. Gore,* 116 S.Ct. 1589 (1996).

[29] *BMW of North America, Inc. v. Gore,* 701 So. 2d 507 Ala. (1997).

[30] Most recently, the Court held a $145 million punitive damages award against State Farm Mutual Automobile Insurance Co. unconstitutional. This award was 145 times actual damages of $1 million awarded by a Utah jury. *State Farm Mutual Insurance Company v. Campbell,* 123 S. Ct. 1513 (2003).

[31] The Supreme Court established this precedent for liability in *New York Central & Hudson River Railroad Co. v. United States* 212 U.S. 481 (1909).

[32] However, the prosecution prevailed and the company finally paid $9 million in fines. See *United States v. Royal Caribbean,* No. 96-0333 (DPR), 1997.

[33] Dale A. Oesterle, "Early Observations on the Prosecutions of the Business Scandals of 2002–03," *The Ohio State Journal of Criminal Law,* Spring 2004, p. 446.

Frank Quattrone was an investment banker in California who presided over the initial public offerings of technology companies such as Amazon.com and Cisco Systems. A federal investigation revealed that he had designed a subtle scheme of handing out shares in these offerings to business executives who, in return, gave investment banking business to Quattrone's firm. Prosecutors feared indicting Quattrone on this kickback scheme, and then relying on a jury to agree on the crime after conflicting expert testimony by both sides. Therefore, they charged him with obstruction of justice for a single e-mail in which he advised his staff to destroy files and documents. Even so, Quattrone almost escaped when his trial ended with a hung jury. Prosecutors had to take the expensive course of trying him a second time. He was then found guilty and sentenced to 18 months in prison.[34]

In addition, at trial it is frequently difficult to assign individual fault to managers. Most corporate crimes result at least partly from group effort. Individual blame is clouded by committee decisions and by the fact that organization hierarchies may separate decisions from actions.

After Enron's fall Jeffrey Skilling, its former CEO, testified at a Congressional hearing that he had no knowledge of any financial manipulations. Skilling resigned as CEO of Enron in August 2001, saying that his decision was for personal reasons. He had been CEO for only six months. Just two months after he left, information about Enron's earnings fraud became public. In the two weeks leading up to his resignation he had started selling his stock and by the time its price was buckling he had sold $67 million worth of shares to unfortunate investors. At the hearing he stated his belief that all of Enron's financial statements were accurate and insisted he was "not aware of any financing arrangements designed to conceal liabilities or inflate profitability."[35]

This was too much even for his mother, Betty Skilling, who berated him, saying, "you can't get off the hook with me."[36] But in a criminal prosecution the government must prove beyond a reasonable doubt that an executive had specific knowledge of a fraud and acted to abet it. A provision in the Sarbanes-Oxley Act has eased the prosecutor's task by establishing a standard of culpability based on "conscious avoidance." That is, if an executive is aware that a probability of fraud exists, but not necessarily of the fraud itself, the failure to investigate is sufficient to establish criminal fault.[37] This enacts Aristotle's theory that moral responsibility is not excused by willful ignorance. Skilling has been indicted on 42 counts of fraud and insider trading, but so far the Department of Justice has not chosen to bring his case to trial.[38]

[34] Andrew Ross Sorkin, "Ex-Banking Star Given 18 Months for Obstruction," *New York Times,* September 9, 2004, p. A1.

[35] Carolyn Lochhead, "House Panel Skeptical of Ex-Enron CEO's Story," *San Francisco Chronicle,* February 8, 2002, p. A1.

[36] Quoted in "Ex-Enron Chief Is Told Off by His Mother," *The Herald* (Glasgow), February 12, 2002, p. 8.

[37] David Lowell and Kathryn C. Arnold, "Corporate Crime after 2000: A New Law Enforcement Challenge or Deja Vu?" *American Criminal Law Review,* Spring 2003, p. 229–30.

[38] *Superceding Indictment* in *U.S. v. Jeffrey K. Skilling and Richard A. Causey,* Cr. No. H-04-25, U.S.D.C. (S. Dist. Texas), February 18, 2004.

Sentencing, Fines, and Other Penalties

In 1991 the United States Sentencing Commission, a judicial agency that standard-izes penalties for federal crimes, released guidelines for sentencing both managers and corporations. When managers are convicted of a crime, prison sentences are imposed on the basis of a numerical point system. Calculations begin with a base score for the type of offense. Points are then added or subtracted on the basis of multiple factors. A sentence for fraud, for example, begins with a base score of 6, then factors such as the number of victims and the amounts lost are considered. If the loss to victims exceeds $1 million, 16 points are added. If there are 50 or more victims then 4 more points are added. The point total is then adjusted for factors such as criminal history or cooperating with authorities and, finally, translated into a prison sentence.[39] Managers may also be fined, put on probation, given commu-nity service, asked to make restitution to injured parties, or banned from working in their occupations.[40]

Corporations cannot be imprisoned, but they can be fined and their actions restricted. Fines are intended to punish, to deter future lawbreaking, to cause dis-gorgement of wrongful gains, and to remedy harms where possible. As with the prison sentences of managers, they are calculated using a point system. The calcu-lation begins with a fine range based on the seriousness of the offense, then adds or subtracts points on the basis of aggravating or mitigating factors such as the de-gree of top management involvement and cooperation during the investigation. If, for example, management "willfully obstructed" authorities, 3 points are added. Up to 5 points may be subtracted if top managers immediately reported the crime.[41]

A cynical public doubts that fines are large enough to deter corporate crime. Sometimes they are, indeed, too small to mar balance sheets. The Environmental Protection Agency once threatened to impose a $27,500 fine on General Electric each day it failed to clean up toxic waste at a factory. It was the equivalent of threatening a person making $1 million a year with a fine of three cents a day. When GE paid the government $1.84 million in fines to settle a billing fraud case, it was the same as a $25 parking ticket for a person making $50,000 a year. Yet fines can also be devastating. Although Arthur Andersen was fined only $500,000, the collateral effects of the criminal conviction drove it out of business. The largest fine ever levied was a $750 million civil penalty against WorldCom in 2003 by the Se-curities and Exchange Commission for accounting fraud.[42] The record criminal fine was a $500 million antitrust penalty imposed on F. Hoffmann-LaRoche Ltd. by the Department of Justice in 1999.[43] The company had led a decade-long conspir-acy between it and six other European and Japanese companies to cheat buyers of common vitamin supplements by allocating market shares and fixing prices.

[39] United States Sentencing Commission, *Guidelines Manual*, §2B1.1 (November 2002).

[40] Recently, the constitutionality of using these factors in sentencing was challenged. The Supreme Court, by a narrow 5–4 majority, allowed judges to continue using them if they were considered advisory, not mandatory. See *United States v. Booker,* 125 S. Ct. 738 (2005).

[41] Ibid., §8C2.1–§8C2.10.

[42] *SEC v. WorldCom Inc.,* Civil Action No. 02-CV-4963 (SDNY). See Litigation Release No. 18219, July 7, 2003.

[43] *U.S. v. F. Hoffmann-LaRoche Ltd.,* No. 3:99-CR-184-R (NDT), 1999.

Other methods for penalizing corporate crime exist. Courts have required advertisements and speeches to show contrition for wrongdoing. Some corporations have paid their fines to charities, and executives have done community service. Others have been made to adopt policies and procedures ensuring that they follow the law in the future. In a few cases a person outside the company is appointed to monitor its compliance.

Following a criminal conviction, both managers and corporations are subject to civil suits by parties such as shareholders who have been damaged. In these civil cases the burden of proof is lower than in criminal cases—a preponderance of the evidence—and the remedy sought is usually financial.

FACTORS THAT INFLUENCE MANAGERIAL ETHICS

Strong forces in organizations shape ethical behavior. Depending on how they are managed, these forces elevate or depress standards of conduct. We discuss here four prominent and interrelated forces that shape conduct: leadership, strategies and policies, organization culture, and individual characteristics (see Figure 7.2).

Leadership

The example of company leaders is perhaps the strongest influence on integrity. Not only do leaders set formal rules, but by their example they can reinforce or undermine right behavior. Subordinates are keen observers and quickly notice if standards are, in practice, upheld or evaded. Exemplary behavior is a powerful tool available to all managers. It was used wisely by this executive, who tells about taking over a financially troubled manufacturing operation.

> Most of our management was flying first class. . . . I did not want . . . my first act to be to tell everybody that they are not gonna fly first class anymore, so I just quit flying first class. And it wasn't long before people noticed it and pretty soon everybody was flying coach. . . . I never put out a directive, never said a word to anybody. . . . People look to the leader. If the leader cuts corners, they say it's okay to cut corners around here. If the leader doesn't cut corners, we must be expected not to do any of that around here."[44]

A common failing is for managers to show by their actions that ethical duties may be compromised. For example, when managers give themselves expensive perks, they display an irreverence for the stewardship of money that rightly belongs to investors as owners, not to management. An executive at one large corporation describes how arrogant behavior sends the wrong signals.

> Too often through my career I've been at management dinners—no customers—and I see $600 bottles of wine being ordered. Think about the message that sends out through the whole organization. And don't ever think such attitudes don't spread and infect the whole firm. Leadership, after all, is about communicating values. And deeds trump words any day.

[44] Interview quoted in Linda Klebe Treviño, Laura Pincus Hartman, and Michael Brown, "Moral Person and Moral Manager: How Executives Develop a Reputation for Ethical Leadership," *California Management Review,* Summer 2000, p. 134.

FIGURE 7.2
Four Internal
Forces
Shaping
Corporate
Ethics

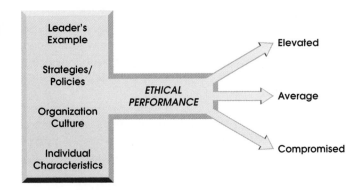

> The message in that bottle is this: Some sales representative and a couple of tech-
> nicians, supported by others, busted their butts to get that $600 to the bottom line.
> And their work, as evaluated by the guy who bought the wine, was worth a couple
> of tasty swallows.
> If money is the way we keep track of the good things our employees accomplish
> for our customers, then who do we think we are spilling it?[45]

Many employees are prone to cynicism. Diverting blame for mistakes, breaking small promises, showing favoritism, and diversion of even trivial company resources for personal use are ill-advised—because if the leader does it, an opportunistic employee can rationalize his or her entitlement to do it also. According to Sherron Watkins, who was *Time Magazine*'s Co-person of the Year in 2002 after blowing the whistle on accounting fraud at Enron, Andrew Fastow was such a person. Fastow was Enron's chief financial officer. He created a warren of complex and deceitful investments that not only contrived nonexistent revenue, but diverted corporate funds into his own pocket. This led to Enron's collapse and Fastow's incarceration. What inspired Fastow to act as he did? According to Watkins, it may have been the example set by Enron's CEO Ken Lay.

> Ken Lay had Enron as well as Arthur Andersen and Vinson & Elkins [Andersen's law
> firm in Houston] use his sister's travel agency. That gave millions of dollars to that
> agency and it was a wretched travel agency. The service wasn't even good and I can
> speak to that because I have some horror stories about their travel scheduling. This went
> on for years and years and years. Now, if you take someone like Andy Fastow who does
> not appear to have a good sense of right-and-wrong, that's telling him that "hey, my
> partnerships are helping Enron meet their financial statement targets so why shouldn't
> I carve some out for myself because Ken Lay has been carving some out for his sister?"[46]
> He also abused the corporate jet in really onerous ways. He moved a stepdaugh-
> ter back and forth to France—furniture, not her! . . . [O]nce again that sent a message
> to executives that when you get to the top, the company is there for you versus you
> being there to serve the company.[47]

[45] Betsy Bernard, President AT&T, "Seven Golden Rules of Leadership," *Vital Speeches of the Day,* December 15, 2002, p. 155.

[46] Sherron S. Watkins, "Ethical Conflicts at Enron: Moral Responsibility in Corporate Capitalism," *California Management Review,* Summer 2003, p. 17.

[47] Sherron Watkins, "Pristine Ethics," *Vital Speeches of the Day,* May 1, 2003, p. 435.

Strategies and Policies

A critical function of managers is to create strong competitive strategies that enable the company to meet financial goals without encouraging ethical compromise. In companies with deteriorating businesses, managers have great difficulty meeting performance targets and may feel pressure to compromise ethical standards. Even excellent overall strategies need to be carried out with policies that support honest achievement. Unrealistic performance goals can pressure those who must make them work.

> Chief Executive Richard McGinn of Lucent Technologies made the company's shares skyrocket by promising 20 percent yearly sales growth. When he twice missed quarterly targets, the stock plummeted. He could not miss again. Warned by subordinates that fourth quarter 2000 sales might fall short, he "went ballistic."[48] Under intense pressure to meet the revenue goal, the sales staff reacted. They offered legitimate discounts to customers, but these did not bring in enough to meet goals. Soon other methods popped up. Customers were given credits booked in the fourth quarter toward future purchases. Products were sold to distributors, not final customers, in a procedure called "channel stuffing." BellSouth signed a $95 million "software pooling" deal booked in the fourth quarter, though it had a year to decide how much software it would actually buy. Told again by the head of sales that the revenue target was hopeless, McGinn simply "didn't take no for an answer." Ultimately, the target was missed. McGinn was fired. Lucent notified government regulators that $679 million in fourth quarter revenue was unallowable. One sales agent lost his job for falsifying documents about when revenue was received. McGinn assured reporters that he "never asked anyone to do anything untoward."

Reward and compensation systems can also expose employees to ethical compromises.

> The Laser Vision Institute is a chain of 19 centers that does popular Lasik eye surgery to correct vision. The market for this surgery is extremely competitive. LVI's ads state a fee of $499 per eye, although an asterisk leads to small type stating "price may vary according to RX and astigmatism." When customers arrive they do not see physicians at first; instead, they meet with counselors who explain what type of surgery the person needs and collect a deposit. The deposit is not refundable unless the patient is later medically disqualified. There is no record of dissatisfaction with the outcome of LVI's laser treatments. What patients do not realize is that the counselors they see work on an incentive system. They make yearly base salaries of $40,000 but add to their income with bonuses paid when patients are upgraded to more expensive surgeries. For the $499 procedure they get a per-eye bonus of only $1. But the amount rises with the surgery's price—$2 for a $599 surgery, $6 for the $799 procedure, $16 for $999, and so forth, up to $40 for patients paying $1,599. To be eligible for these bonuses, however, the counselors must close on at least 75 percent of the people with whom they meet. It is no surprise, then, that prospects are subjected to aggressive tactics similar to those faced by car buyers and that, in the end, 88 percent of them pay more than $499.[49]

[48] Quotes in this paragraph are from Dennis K. Berman and Rebecca Blumstein,"Behind Lucent's Woes: All-Out Revenue Goal and Pressure to Meet It," *The Wall Street Journal,* March 29, 2001, pp. A1 and A8.
[49] Marc Borbely, "Lasik Surgery Sales Tactics Raise Eyebrows," *Washington Post,* September 4, 2001, p. A1.

When companies adopt policies that put employees under pressure, they should build in strong ethical rules too. Otherwise, the repetitive message to achieve profit goals drowns out the principles in the ethics code framed on the wall. When the tide of money runs high, shore up the ethical dikes.

Corporate Culture

corporate culture
A set of values, norms, rituals, formal rules, and physical artifacts that characterize a company.

Corporate culture refers to a set of values, norms, rituals, formal rules, and physical artifacts that characterize a company. Every corporate culture has an ethical dimension reinforced not primarily by formal policies but by daily habit and shared beliefs about which behaviors are rewarded and which are penalized.

Recent graduates of the Harvard MBA program who were interviewed about the ethical atmosphere in their organizations revealed the strong presence of four informal but powerful "commandments" conveyed to them early in their careers.

> First, performance is what really counts, so make your numbers. Second, be loyal and show us that you're a team player. Third, don't break the law. Fourth, don't overinvest in ethical behavior.[50]

The young managers believed, in the face of these informal norms, that if questionable behavior was accompanied by achievement, it advanced careers. They were in fear of taking ethical stands or blowing the whistle, and not without reason. When one manager persisted in challenging false figures that her superior used, she discovered that she was in trouble.

> He started treating other people better. He wasn't on my side anymore, and you needed him on your side to do things. He wasn't my buddy anymore . . . there were other cases of this. He did it by acting like you weren't that smart anymore. It made it really difficult to get the kind of support you needed to be a really top performer.[51]

moral muteness
The inability of managers to raise and discuss ethical issues.

A factor that contributes to lowered ethical climates in corporations is the inability to raise and discuss ethical issues between managers. At one oil company, an employee requested time to raise an ethical problem during a meeting of division presidents. They refused saying, "If he wants to talk ethics, let him talk to a priest or a psychiatrist."[52] This phenomenon, which was studied by Bird and Waters and labeled "moral muteness," is widespread. In their study, Bird and Waters found that "managers seldom discuss with their colleagues the ethical problems they routinely encounter."[53] Indeed, of 300 cases of ethical issues their interviews uncovered, only 12 percent were ever openly discussed. There are reasons for this restraint. Some managers think that verbalizing an ethical judgment is confrontational; it involves placing blame and creates anger or grudges. In organizations where formal standards are not followed and deceit is rewarded, ethical arguments lack legitimacy or force. In addition, many managers have a rich vocabulary and

[50] Joseph L. Badaracco Jr. and Allen P. Webb, "Business Ethics: A View from the Trenches," *California Management Review,* Winter 1995, p. 11.

[51] Ibid.

[52] Linda Klebe Treviño, Gary R. Weaver, David G. Gibson, and Barbara Ley Toffler, "Managing Ethics and Legal Compliance: What Works and What Hurts," *California Management Review,* Winter 1999, p. 143.

[53] Frederick B. Bird and James A. Waters, "The Moral Muteness of Managers," *California Management Review,* Fall 1989, p. 74.

logic for parsing business issues but lack these assets in the moral realm. Thus, they tend to reframe ethical issues as business matters. For example, if someone lays out a deceitful ad in a meeting, others will not accuse the person of dishonesty. Instead, they will discuss possible sales and revenue losses if the misrepresentation is discovered—even if their primary motive for opposing the ad is a desire to be honest. This tendency toward moral muteness is probably present to some degree in every company.

Individual Characteristics

Behavior is motivated by a mixture of internal disposition and situational incentives. In a corporation with a dreary ethical climate, corrupt leaders, and high pressure to achieve numbers, otherwise honest individuals may be pushed to compromise. However, all things being equal, having employees who are internally disposed to right action is best.

Researchers have tried to discover what personal qualities are associated with ethical behavior. However, strong relationships are elusive. There are indications that higher ethics come with advancing age and longer work experience.[54] Some studies show that women are more ethical than men, but results are mixed.[55] No studies find men to be more ethically sensitive than women, but some show no difference. A few studies suggest that people with more education are more ethical, but others do not. Similarly, some studies find that religious belief leads to more ethical attitudes, but many others fail to discover any relationship.[56] There is considerable evidence that the company environment influences conduct. Individuals seem to act less ethically as corporations increase in size, but they tend to be more ethical where companies have codes of conduct.[57]

HOW CORPORATIONS MANAGE ETHICS

In the past, it was assumed that right and wrong were matters of individual conscience. A few pioneers tried to elevate companywide ethics. In 1913 James Cash Penney introduced a conduct code in his department stores (one that is still used today, despite its archaic language). His effort was a lonely one. Until recently, most companies had more formal policies for managing petty cash than for elevating ethics. This has changed.

ethics program
A coordinated application of management methods to prevent law-breaking and promote more ethical behavior.

Now many companies set up *ethics programs,* or coordinated applications of management methods designed to prevent lawbreaking and promote more ethical behavior. Ethics programs grew from the soil of scandal. In response to a run of billing frauds and cost overruns in the 1980s, military contractors started the

[54] Terry W. Low, Linda Ferrell, and Phylis Mansfield, "A Review of Empirical Studies Assessing Ethical Decision Making in Business," *Journal of Business Ethics,* June 2000, p. 185.

[55] Donald Robin and Laurie Babin, "Making Sense of the Research on Gender and Ethics in Business: A Critical Analysis and Extension," *Journal of Business Ethics,* October 1997, pp. 79–81.

[56] Gary R. Weaver and Bradley R. Agle, "Religiosity and Ethical Behavior in Organizations: A Symbolic Interactionist Perspective," *Academy of Management Review,* January 2002, p. 79.

[57] See, for example, Marshall Schminke, "Considering the Business in Business Ethics: An Exploratory Study of the Influence of Organizational Size and Structure on Individual Ethical Predispositions," *Journal of Business Ethics,* April 2001.

U.S. Sentencing Commission
Guidelines   The 7 "Minimum Steps"

1. **Establish standards and procedures.**
2. **Create high-level oversight.**
3. **Screen out criminals.**
4. **Communicate standards to employees.**
5. **Monitor and set up an anonymous hotline.**

6. **Enforce standards, discipline violators.**
7. **Assess areas of risk, modify program.**

Source: *Guidelines Manual,* Chapter 8, as amended May 10, 2004.

Defense Industry Initiative, a project requiring firms to adopt ethics codes and train employees to obey laws. Today 50 of the largest defense firms have extensive ethics programs and even get together once a year at a conference to share best practices.

A second wave of scandal-spawned ethics programs came in the mid-1990s, when the federal government cracked down on hospitals and nursing homes for Medicare billing fraud. Corporations in the health care industry rushed to follow the defense industry model.

Meanwhile, the United States Sentencing Commission in 1991 established new sentencing guidelines. As previously explained, these guidelines set up systems of penalty and fine calculations for both managers and corporations. In addition, they allow major reductions in fines and penalties for companies with internal programs for preventing and reporting criminal behavior. These reductions provide an important incentive.

The need to manage ethics was driven home in the 1996 *Caremark* case. Caremark International, a health care company, was caught giving kickbacks to physicians who referred Medicare and Medicaid patients to its clinics. After being indicted, the company set up a compliance program, but it was too late to prevent a $250 million fine. Angry shareholders sued its directors for breach of duty because they had not set up an ethics program earlier, thereby exposing the firm to a big fine. Caremark's directors narrowly escaped paying damages from their own pockets after a settlement. However, the judge who approved the settlement made it plain that if directors fail to set up management systems promoting lawful behavior they can be held liable for fines.[58]

What should these systems be like? Chapter 8 of the U.S. Sentencing Commission's *Guidelines Manual* sets forth seven "minimum requirements" for an "effective" program that "encourages ethical conduct and a commitment to compliance with the law.[59] These requirements, shown in an abbreviated list in the box above, cover the range of management interventions used to promote ethics. The *Guidelines Manual* does not dictate how requirements must be met, but we elaborate on common methods used by companies.

[58] *In re Caremark International Inc. Derivative Litigation,* 698 A.2d 970 (1996).
[59] United States Sentencing Commission, *Guidelines Manual,* §8B2.1(a)(1), as amended May 10, 2004.

GE Code of Conduct

- Obey the applicable laws and regulations governing our business conduct worldwide.
- Be honest, fair and trustworthy in all your GE activities and relationships.
- Avoid all conflicts of interest between work and personal affairs.
- Foster an atmosphere in which fair employment practices extend to every member of the diverse GE community.

- Strive to create a safe workplace and to protect the environment.
- Through leadership at all levels, sustain a culture where ethical conduct is recognized, valued and exemplified by all employees.

Source: General Electric Company, *Integrity: The Spirit & the Letter of Our Commitment,* February 2004.

1. *Establish standards and procedures to prevent and detect criminal conduct.* Most companies meet this requirement with a variety of written documents. The centerpiece is often a list of basic values such as honesty, integrity, fairness, respect for others, obedience to the law, citizenship, and responsibility. Some codes of conduct, such as GE's (see the box), feature brief guidelines at a high level of abstraction. Beyond these statements, most code booklets set forth brief guidance in a range of problem areas, including conflict of interest, bribery, gifts, insider trading, antitrust violations, trade secrets, political contributions, and discrimination. While code booklets are typically 20 to 50 pages in length, their relatively brief treatments are backed by dozens of long and detailed corporate policy documents, so that the complete "ethics code" of a large company may run hundreds of pages.

Conduct codes contain other elements, including statements from top leaders, ways to report wrongdoing, tips for making ethical decisions, and disciplinary procedures. There is inexhaustible sameness in both the content and format of many corporate codes. They are saturated with similar principles, cover the same list of ethical issues, and contain virtually identical guides for reporting concerns. Creativity comes at the margins. Raytheon's colorful *Standards of Business Ethics and Conduct* booklet contains brief cases in question and answer format. This example comes from the page covering gifts, entertainment, and bribes.

Q: One of my suppliers regularly gives away box seats to our local professional baseball team. I know that the tickets cost more than the $20 maximum for gifts, but this supplier gives tickets away to all his customers, not just us, and he has never, ever, asked to swap a baseball ticket for a business favor. Why shouldn't I accept the tickets?

A: In our relationships with suppliers, even the appearance of favoritism can damage our reputation. Although the baseball tickets probably aren't intended to influence a specific business decision, this gift could be perceived as favoritism by customers or suppliers. It could also be used in the future to influence a business decision.[60]

[60] August 2001, p. 13.

Most American companies have a code of conduct.[61] They are usually distributed to all employees and recipients may be asked to sign a form in which they agree to comply with it. Some companies translate them into multiple languages. Statements in codes mean little without further steps to ensure fidelity to them. Enron had a typical "Code of Ethics" that was based on four principles—"respect, integrity, communication, and excellence"—but it was not enforced.

2. *Give oversight of the program to the board of directors and assign responsibility for it to a company executive who, in turn, will assign day-to-day operating responsibility to a high-level manager.* The *Guidelines Manual* requires that the board of directors exercise "reasonable oversight" over an ethics and compliance program, that one or more top executives take responsibility for it, and that specific managers be assigned the day-to-day work. In practice, the structures of programs vary with the operating structures of companies.

An example is the structure of the program at Abbott Laboratories, shown in Figure 7.3. After a federal investigation into Medicare fraud that led to $600 million in fines in 2003, Abbott revised its program. It set up an Office of Ethics and Compliance led by a vice president who is the chief ethics and compliance officer. This ethics chief reports directly to Abbott's top executive. The ethics chief gives an annual report to the full board, and periodically reports to the board's Public Policy Committee. In addition, the ethics chief chairs a 19-member Business Conduct Committee that includes the heads of Abbott's business divisions.

Each division has an ethics and compliance officer who reports to the divisional vice president of ethics and compliance, who in turn reports back to the corporate ethics chief.[62] In this way the program parallels Abbott's operating structure. Note that the reporting chain for the ethics staff remains separate from the line chain of command all the way up to the CEO. This provides an important check and balance. If ethics officers reported to division managers instead of an ethics leader, they would have less independence. Some companies have made this mistake.[63]

3. *Exclude individuals with a history of illegal or unethical conduct from positions of substantial authority.* Background checks for criminal records are inexpensive. Companies that fail to conduct them can be surprised, as was Smith & Wesson Holding Corp. when it discovered that its chairman was the notorious "Shotgun Bandit" who had terrorized his victims in a string of armed robberies years before.[64] The chairman resigned.

Companies also check for false claims about education and job experience on résumés. Is it possible to detect a corrupt disposition? Paper-and-pencil honesty tests are effective in screening out thieves among applicants for low-level

---

[61] A 2001 survey reported that 97 percent of responding companies had one. Sherrie McAvoy and Carole Basri, "Measuring Your Compliance Program," *New York Law Journal,* May 14, 2001, p. 56.

[62] Abbott Laboratories, *Touching Lives: 2003 Citizenship Report* (Abbott Park, IL, Abbott Laboratories, April 2004), p. 11.

[63] Notable is scandal-ridden Tyco International, which had general counsel charged with compliance oversight in business segments reporting to segment managers. See Eric M. Pillmore, "How We're Fixing Up Tyco," *Harvard Business Review,* December 2003, pp. 100–01.

[64] Vanessa O'Connell, "How Troubled Past Finally Caught Up with James Minder," *The Wall Street Journal,* March 8, 2001, p. A1.

FIGURE 7.3
Oversight
Structure of
Abbott
Laboratories
Ethics and
Compliance
Program

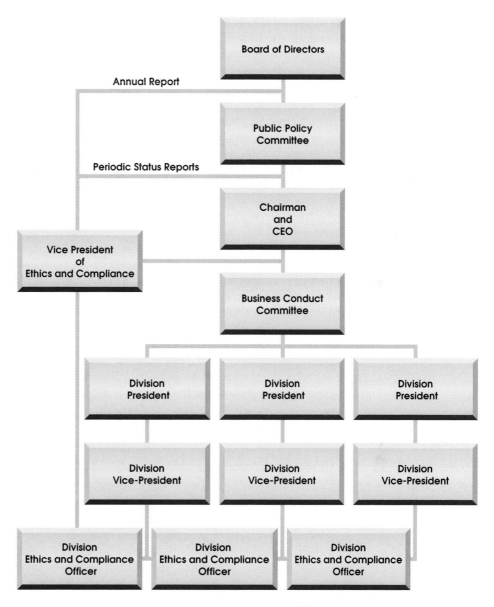

positions. But it is not clear exactly what aspect of personality they measure and they are inadequate to appraise the elements of inner character required for ethical leadership.

Some psychologists believe that integrity can be tested in interviews. One expert recommends building rapport with the subject, then eliciting comments on ethical issues late in an interview. He suggests statements and questions such as: "Give me an example of an ethical decision you have had to make on the job." "Have you ever had to bend the rules or exaggerate a little bit when trying to make a sale?" and "Tell me about an instance when you've had to go against company guidelines or procedures to get something done."[65] If the interviewer listens with a show of empathy to help the subject maintain self-esteem, responses can reveal ethical strengths and weaknesses.

4. *Take steps to communicate standards and procedures by giving out information and conducting training for all employees from the lowest up to the board of directors.* Companies emphasize ethics using everything from newsletters to T-shirts. At MCI every employee's security badge has printed on it the phrase "Do the right thing."

Training is a key element of any ethics program. Generally, ethics training is most effective when company managers do it, not outsiders, and when it steers away from abstract philosophy to focus on the work lives of attendees. A few companies offer in-depth seminars lasting one to three days with discussion of policies and case studies. Briefer sessions are more typical. One-to-three hour yearly sessions in which employees see a video and discuss cases are common. Also popular are interactive sessions on a company Web site or intranet in which employees take quizzes and respond to problem situations.

At Lockheed Martin employees attend two-hour training sessions where they watch a video, then divide into small groups to discuss ethical dilemmas. The groups are told to rate alternative solutions for each dilemma using an "Ethics Effect" meter with a five-point scale from "highly ethical" to "unethical." Here is an example.

> Bill, an acting manager, is asked to approve a travel expense report of Jim, a co-worker. Bill suspects that several expenses are fictitious.

What Bill Could Do:

1. Asked Jim for an explanation of the questioned expenses. *(Highly Ethical)*
2. Requested an audit. *(Ethically Sound)*
3. Sent Jim a copy of the travel policy. *(Gray Area)*
4. Waited for a permanent manager to be announced and let him or her deal with it. *(On Thin Ice)*
5. Approved it, but told Jim he expects a favor in return. *(Unethical)*

5. *Monitor and audit the organization to detect criminal conduct, and set up a system that allows anonymous reporting of suspicious conduct.* Monitoring entails collection of data related to illegal activity. For example, some companies require reports of unusual financial transactions. Ethical audits can also detect problems. HCA Healthcare Corp. conducts two-day ethical compliance audits to reveal strengths and weaknesses at its hospitals. Employees are interviewed randomly as auditors cover a 53-page checklist.

Most programs have 24-hour toll-free telephone and e-mail hotlines for anonymous reporting of problems. To protect users' identities, these hotlines are sometimes managed by outside parties. Many whistle-blowers are suspicious and fear revenge, so hotlines must be supported with strong policies against retaliation. On average, between 2 and 4 percent of employees use a hotline each year and these calls create an enormous amount of work for ethics offices. Many callers seek advice: "Would it be a conflict of interest for me to work in the evening?" Others have trivial complaints, such as "My supervisor came back an hour late from

---

[65] William C. Byham, "Can You Interview for Integrity?" *Across the Board*, March/April 2004, pp. 36–37.

lunch." Allegations must be investigated; for instance, "I think one of my team members is harassing a co-worker." Although few calls reveal criminal wrongdoing, hotlines open a critical channel of communication for those who might be intimidated by speaking to superiors.

6. *Enforce standards by using both incentives for ethical behavior and disciplinary measures to punish and deter criminal conduct.* It has been objected that doing the right thing should require no incentive. A few companies, for example, Tenet Healthcare and Boeing, have formally tied ethics to managers' performance reviews. However, what seems to be a powerful incentive is problematic in its execution. At Tenet Healthcare the top 800 managers receive increased bonuses on the basis of a numerical ethics score of between −5 and +5. Each point changes their bonus by 5 percent. Managers have felt humiliated, however, when they receive negative scores, called "dings" in company slang.[66]

At Boeing, compliance with the company's ethics code is part of every employee's evaluation. But according to a report on Boeing's ethics program, it almost never has any effect on the outcome.

> Managers perceive pressure (often self-imposed) not to rate any employee as below average in ethics. There is also resistance against rating any employee above average, as that implies that other employees are not doing as well in terms of ethical conduct. The strong tendency, therefore, is to award all employees an average score for this component, effectively rendering it meaningless.[67]

Written disciplinary policies, on the other hand, are widespread. Discipline is usually based on factors such as seriousness of the violation, the organizational level or leadership role of the violator, extent of cooperation with the investigation, prior misconduct, and willfulness of the action. A progressive range of disciplinary options—counseling, oral reprimand, written reprimand, probation, suspension, salary reduction, termination—can be used as fits the case.[68]

7. *If criminal conduct occurs, modify the program to prevent repeat offenses. Periodically assess the risks of criminal conduct and try to reduce them.* Unless lawbreaking is the isolated failure of one person, the program is not working. It should be modified by changing or adding elements, restructuring responsibilities, or reappraising the culture in which it operates.

Ethical risk assessment is an emerging art. The *Guidelines Manual* suggests that companies examine the nature of their business for risks, then take action to reduce them. GE's Aircraft Engines division monitors statistical indicators related to compliance. For example, it watches the number of sales representatives in foreign countries. When that number rises, it takes action to reduce the risk of violating antibribery laws, requiring more training and legal oversight.[69]

[66] Andrew W. Singer, "At Tenet Healthcare: Linking Ethics to Compensation," *Ethikos,* January–February 2001, pp. 4–5.

[67] Warren B. Rudman et al., *A Report to the Chairman and Board of Directors of the Boeing Company Concerning the Company's Ethics Program and Its Rules and Procedures for the Treatment of Competitors' Proprietary Information,* Paul, Weiss, Rifkind, Wharton & Garrison LLP, November 3, 2003, p. 36.

[68] John D. Copeland, "The Tyson Story: Building an Effective Ethics and Compliance Program," *Drake Journal of Agricultural Law,* Winter 2000.

[69] Andrew Singer, "GE Extends Its 'Quality' Effort to Compliance," *Ethikos,* January–February 2001, p. 6.

OGRAMS: A STRONG FUTURE

Ethics programs are a set of interrelated policies and methods. A firm estimate of the number of companies having them is elusive. Many companies have one or more of the central elements of an ethics program, such as a code of conduct; but only a small number, perhaps 100 to 200, have strong programs in which a broad range of methods is integrated into organizational structures and processes. Companies in this group include a fair number that engaged in criminal behavior and subsequently adopted their programs by court order or as part of a settlement.

Do the programs work? Tenet Healthcare and Boeing were exemplars of complete ethics and compliance efforts, but were engulfed by scandals nonetheless. These efforts are young and there is still much to be learned about teaching ethics to an organization. Despite trying for more than two millennia to overcome individual malfeasance there is little progress. We should not be too hasty in hoping for better results with organizations. But it is clear that collective behavior will deteriorate unless managers use the ethics and compliance tools at their disposal.

CONCLUDING OBSERVATIONS

The business environment is rich in sources of ethical values. Yet strong forces in both markets and corporations act to depress behavior. Managers can use a range of methods to discourage transgression and encourage high ethics. Likewise, individuals have a range of principles with which to enrich their ethical thinking and powerful methods with which to make ethical decisions. In the next chapter we take a closer look at individual decisions.

The Trial of Martha Stewart

From indictment to sentencing, the case of Martha Stewart was a matter of intense public interest. Some thought that her misdeeds, if any, were slight. Cynics believed that in the wake of corporate scandals the government was prosecuting a celebrity for a minor infraction to show it was tough on business crime. An indignant *Wall Street Journal* complained that innocent employees and shareholders of Martha Stewart Living Omnimedia were paying the price for the government's zeal.[1] Feminists argued that she was picked on for being a successful woman. "It's hard to imagine a male in precisely this spot," said Mary

Becker, a DePaul University law professor. "Targeting a successful woman is very consistent with dominant cultural values."[2]

Others believed that her prosecution was justified. "I don't buy any of it," wrote Scott Turow, a criminal defense lawyer and the author of best-selling legal fiction. "What the jury felt Martha Stewart did—lying about having received inside information before she traded—is wrong, really wrong."[3]

This is the story.

[1] "The Trials of Martha," *The Wall Street Journal*, February 13, 2004, p. A12.

[2] Quoted in Jonathan D. Glater, "Stewart's Celebrity Created Magnet for Scrutiny," *New York Times*, sec. 1, p. 1.

[3] Scott Turow, "Cry No Tears for Martha Stewart," *New York Times*, May 27, 2004, p. 29.

ETHICS PROGRAMS: A STRONG FUTURE

Ethics programs are a set of interrelated policies and methods. A firm estimate of the number of companies having them is elusive. Many companies have one or more of the central elements of an ethics program, such as a code of conduct; but only a small number, perhaps 100 to 200, have strong programs in which a broad range of methods is integrated into organizational structures and processes. Companies in this group include a fair number that engaged in criminal behavior and subsequently adopted their programs by court order or as part of a settlement.

Do the programs work? Tenet Healthcare and Boeing were exemplars of complete ethics and compliance efforts, but were engulfed by scandals nonetheless. These efforts are young and there is still much to be learned about teaching ethics to an organization. Despite trying for more than two millennia to overcome individual malfeasance there is little progress. We should not be too hasty in hoping for better results with organizations. But it is clear that collective behavior will deteriorate unless managers use the ethics and compliance tools at their disposal.

CONCLUDING OBSERVATIONS

The business environment is rich in sources of ethical values. Yet strong forces in both markets and corporations act to depress behavior. Managers can use a range of methods to discourage transgression and encourage high ethics. Likewise, individuals have a range of principles with which to enrich their ethical thinking and powerful methods with which to make ethical decisions. In the next chapter we take a closer look at individual decisions.

The Trial of Martha Stewart

From indictment to sentencing, the case of Martha Stewart was a matter of intense public interest. Some thought that her misdeeds, if any, were slight. Cynics believed that in the wake of corporate scandals the government was prosecuting a celebrity for a minor infraction to show it was tough on business crime. An indignant *Wall Street Journal* complained that innocent employees and shareholders of Martha Stewart Living Omnimedia were paying the price for the government's zeal.[1] Feminists argued that she was picked on for being a successful woman. "It's hard to imagine a male in precisely this spot," said Mary Becker, a DePaul University law professor. "Targeting a successful woman is very consistent with dominant cultural values."[2]

Others believed that her prosecution was justified. "I don't buy any of it," wrote Scott Turow, a criminal defense lawyer and the author of best-selling legal fiction. "What the jury felt Martha Stewart did—lying about having received inside information before she traded—is wrong, really wrong."[3]

This is the story.

[1] "The Trials of Martha," *The Wall Street Journal*, February 13, 2004, p. A12.

[2] Quoted in Jonathan D. Glater, "Stewart's Celebrity Created Magnet for Scrutiny," *New York Times*, sec. 1, p. 1.

[3] Scott Turow, "Cry No Tears for Martha Stewart," *New York Times*, May 27, 2004, p. 29.

lunch." Allegations must be investigated; for instance, "I think one of my team members is harassing a co-worker." Although few calls reveal criminal wrongdoing, hotlines open a critical channel of communication for those who might be intimidated by speaking to superiors.

6. *Enforce standards by using both incentives for ethical behavior and disciplinary measures to punish and deter criminal conduct.* It has been objected that doing the right thing should require no incentive. A few companies, for example, Tenet Healthcare and Boeing, have formally tied ethics to managers' performance reviews. However, what seems to be a powerful incentive is problematic in its execution. At Tenet Healthcare the top 800 managers receive increased bonuses on the basis of a numerical ethics score of between −5 and +5. Each point changes their bonus by 5 percent. Managers have felt humiliated, however, when they receive negative scores, called "dings" in company slang.[66]

At Boeing, compliance with the company's ethics code is part of every employee's evaluation. But according to a report on Boeing's ethics program, it almost never has any effect on the outcome.

> Managers perceive pressure (often self-imposed) not to rate any employee as below average in ethics. There is also resistance against rating any employee above average, as that implies that other employees are not doing as well in terms of ethical conduct. The strong tendency, therefore, is to award all employees an average score for this component, effectively rendering it meaningless.[67]

Written disciplinary policies, on the other hand, are widespread. Discipline is usually based on factors such as seriousness of the violation, the organizational level or leadership role of the violator, extent of cooperation with the investigation, prior misconduct, and willfulness of the action. A progressive range of disciplinary options—counseling, oral reprimand, written reprimand, probation, suspension, salary reduction, termination—can be used as fits the case.[68]

7. *If criminal conduct occurs, modify the program to prevent repeat offenses. Periodically assess the risks of criminal conduct and try to reduce them.* Unless lawbreaking is the isolated failure of one person, the program is not working. It should be modified by changing or adding elements, restructuring responsibilities, or reappraising the culture in which it operates.

Ethical risk assessment is an emerging art. The *Guidelines Manual* suggests that companies examine the nature of their business for risks, then take action to reduce them. GE's Aircraft Engines division monitors statistical indicators related to compliance. For example, it watches the number of sales representatives in foreign countries. When that number rises, it takes action to reduce the risk of violating antibribery laws, requiring more training and legal oversight.[69]

[66] Andrew W. Singer, "At Tenet Healthcare: Linking Ethics to Compensation," *Ethikos,* January–February 2001, pp. 4–5.

[67] Warren B. Rudman et al., *A Report to the Chairman and Board of Directors of the Boeing Company Concerning the Company's Ethics Program and Its Rules and Procedures for the Treatment of Competitors' Proprietary Information,* Paul, Weiss, Rifkind, Wharton & Garrison LLP, November 3, 2003, p. 36.

[68] John D. Copeland, "The Tyson Story: Building an Effective Ethics and Compliance Program," *Drake Journal of Agricultural Law,* Winter 2000.

[69] Andrew Singer, "GE Extends Its 'Quality' Effort to Compliance," *Ethikos,* January–February 2001, p. 6.

DECEMBER 27

On the morning of Thursday, December 27, 2001, Douglas Faneuil was on duty at the mid-Manhattan office of Merrill Lynch. Faneuil, 24, who had been in his job only six months, assisted a stockbroker named Peter Bacanovic. It was two days after Christmas and Bacanovic was on vacation. Staffing was thin and Faneuil expected a slow day with light trading activity.

Soon Faneuil took a call from Aliza Waksal. Aliza was the daughter of Samuel Waksal, cofounder of ImClone Systems, a biopharmaceutical company. She wanted to sell her ImClone shares. Faneuil executed the order and by 9:48 A.M. her 39,472 shares had been sold for $2,472,837. Then Faneuil had a call from Samuel Waksal's accountant requesting that another 79,797 shares held in his Merrill Lynch account be transferred to Aliza's account and then sold. The call was followed by a written direction saying that making the transfer and sale that morning was imperative.

Faneuil sought help on the transfer and called Peter Bacanovic in Florida. Bacanovic, 39, was an old friend of Waksal's. He had worked at ImClone for two years before coming to Merrill Lynch and he handled the personal accounts of Waksal and his daughter. When Bacanovic learned that the Waksals were selling, he instructed Faneuil immediately to call another of his clients, Martha Stewart, while he remained on the line.

Bacanovic, who was active in New York social life, first met Martha Stewart in the mid-1980s when they were introduced by her daughter Alexis. Stewart was one of his most important clients. He handled her pension and personal accounts. He also handled accounts for her company, Martha Stewart Living Omnimedia, Inc. Two years earlier, he had directed part of the firm's initial public offering and now he administered both its 401(k) and employee stock option accounts.

At 10:04 A.M. Faneuil dialed Stewart, but reached her administrative assistant Ann Armstrong, who said that Stewart was on an airplane. Bacanovic left a brief message, asking Stewart to call back when she became available. In her phone log, Armstrong wrote "Peter Bacanovic thinks ImClone is going to start trading downward." Bacanovic instructed Faneuil that when Stewart called back he should tell her that the Waksals were selling all their shares. At this time ImClone was priced at $61.53 a share.

This instruction from Bacanovic bothered Faneuil. Merrill Lynch had a written policy (see Exhibit 1) that required its employees to hold client information in strict confidence. But he was very busy and working under a sense of urgency, handling calls from the Waksals, and making calls to Merrill Lynch staff in several offices arranging the transfer of Sam Waksal's shares to his daughter.

Several hours later, Stewart's plane landed in San Antonio to refuel. She went into the airport and on her cell phone called Ann Armstrong to check for messages. At 1:39 P.M. she phoned Merrill Lynch, reaching Faneuil, who told her that Sam Waksal and his daughter had sold all of their shares. She asked for the current price of ImClone. Faneuil quoted approximately $58 a share. Stewart told him to sell all 3,928 shares she owned.

She hung up and immediately put in a call to Sam Waksal. The two were close friends who had been introduced by Stewart's daughter Alexis in the early 1990s. Unable to reach him, she left a message that his assistant took down as "Martha Stewart something is going on with ImClone and she wants to know what."[4] By 1:52 P.M. Stewart's ImClone shares had

[4] Complaint, *Securities and Exchange Commission v. Martha Stewart and Peter Bacanovic,* 03CV 4070 (NRB)(S.D.N.Y.), June 4, 2003, p. 7.

EXHIBIT 1
Client Information Privacy Policy

Merrill Lynch protects the confidentiality and security of client information. Employees must understand the need for careful handling of this information. Merrill Lynch's client information privacy policy provides that—

. . .

- Employees may not discuss the business affairs of any client with any other employee, except on a strict need-to-know basis.
- We do not release client information, except upon a client's authorization or when permitted or required by law.

been sold at an average price of $58.43, for a total of approximately $228,000.

THE PUZZLE OF THE WAKSAL TRADES

What *was* going on with ImClone? For almost 10 years Waksal had put ImClone's resources into the development of a promising new colon cancer drug named Erbitux. Two months earlier, in late October 2001, ImClone had submitted a licensing application for approval of Erbitux to the Food and Drug Administration (FDA). On December 26, Waksal learned from an ImClone executive that, according to a source within the FDA, on December 28 ImClone would receive a letter rejecting the Erbitux application. When the FDA's action was publicly announced ImClone's share price was sure to plummet.

Waksal was in possession of material insider information. It was material because any reasonable investor would find it important in deciding to buy or sell ImClone stock. It was insider information because it was not yet known to the public. Since the FDA application was so critical, ImClone's general counsel had declared a "blackout period" after December 21 when employees should not trade ImClone shares. The purpose of the "blackout" was to guard against illegal insider trading.

Despite being informed of the "blackout" and despite possessing knowledge of the law with respect to insider trading, Waksal elected to sell. This was exceptionally foolish. His motive was to escape the unpleasant consequences of debt. He had obligations of $75 million, most of which was margin debt secured by shares he owned in ImClone. Servicing this debt was costing him $800,000 a month. He knew that if ImClone's share price slipped very far many of his shares would be sold, dramatically lowering his net worth. He also tipped off members of his family, who sold along with him. Besides his daughter Aliza, his sister Patty sold 1,336 shares and another daughter, Elana, sold 4,000 shares on December 28. His father sold 110,000 shares on December 27 and 25,000 shares on December 28.

On Friday, December 28, the FDA faxed ImClone a "refusal to file" letter at 2:55 P.M. Later in the afternoon, after the market closed with ImClone trading at $55.25 a share, the company issued a press release disclosing the FDA's action. On December 31, the next trading day, ImClone opened at $45.39 a share. If Martha Stewart had waited until then to sell her shares, she would have gotten about $178,292 or $49,708 less than she received by selling on the afternoon of December 27. ImClone closed on December 31 at $46.46. It had dropped about 16 percent on the news of the FDA's action.

AN UNSETTLED AFTERMATH

Four days later a supervisor at Merrill Lynch contacted Faneuil to question him about the ImClone trades. Afterwards, Faneuil called Bacanovic, who was still vacationing in Florida. Bacanovic told him that Martha Stewart sold her shares because of a prearranged plan to reduce her taxes. He told Faneuil about a December 20 telephone call in which he and Stewart had gone down a list of the stock holdings in her account and decided which ones to sell at a loss to balance out capital gains from other sales during 2001. Soon, however, Faneuil had a call from Eileen DeLuca, Martha Stewart's business manager, who demanded to know why the ImClone shares had been sold, since the sale had resulted in a profit that disrupted her tax-loss selling plan. Again he called Bacanovic. This time, Bacanovic told him that Stewart had sold because they had a preexisting agreement to sell ImClone if the price fell below $60 a share.

Merrill Lynch had called the Securities and Exchange Commission (SEC) to report suspicions of insider trading in ImClone. On January 3, 2002, attorneys at the SEC called Faneuil to interview him about the events of December 27. Faneuil told them that Stewart had sold because the price of ImClone fell below $60 a share. He did not tell them that he had conveyed news about the Waksals' sales to her. On January 7, SEC attorneys interviewed Bacanovic on the telephone. He told them that he spoke to Martha Stewart on the day she traded and recommended that she sell based on their preexisting $60 sell agreement.

On January 16, Martha Stewart and Peter Bacanovic had a breakfast meeting. Their conversation is unrecorded. According to Faneuil, after the meeting Bacanovic told him, "I've spoken to Martha. I've met with her. And everyone's telling the same story. . . . This was a $60 stop-loss order. That was the reason for her sale. We're all on the same page, and it's the truth."[5] In at least five subsequent conversations Bacanovic reassured Faneuil of the need to stick to

[5] Brooke A. Masters, "Stewart Ordered Sale, Says Witness," *Washington Post,* February 5, 2004, p. E1.

this story. If he did, Bacanovic promised to give him extra compensation.

On January 30, in response to a request for documents by SEC investigators, Bacanovic turned over the worksheet that he said was used in his December 20 tax sale conversation with Martha Stewart. The worksheet was a single-page printout listing approximately 40 securities in her account and noting the number of shares and the purchase price. On the worksheet, near the entry for ImClone, the notation "@60" appeared.

On January 31, Martha Stewart had a lengthy conversation with a criminal attorney. Following the conversation she went to her assistant Ann Armstrong asking to see the telephone log. Sitting at Armstrong's computer, she changed Bacanovic's December 27 phone message from "Peter Bacanovic thinks ImClone is going to start trading downward," to "Peter Bacanovic re imclone."[6] Then, thinking better of it, she told Armstrong to restore the original wording and left.

INTERVIEWS

On February 2, Martha Stewart was interviewed in New York by attorneys from the SEC, the Federal Bureau of Investigation (FBI), and the U.S. Attorney's Office. Asked to explain her ImClone transaction, she said that she and Bacanovic had decided to sell if ImClone fell below $60 a share. On December 27 she had spoken to Bacanovic, who told her it had fallen below $60 and inquired if she wished to sell. She had assented, in part, because she was on vacation and did not want to worry about the stock market. She did not recall speaking to Faneuil on that day. She denied knowledge of the December 27 phone message from Bacanovic, even though only two days before she had gone to her assistant's computer to alter its wording. According to one attorney present, at the end of the interview Stewart asked in a "curt, annoyed" tone, "Can I go now? I have a business to run."[7]

On February 13, Bacanovic was subpoenaed by the SEC to testify under oath in New York. He reported a December 20 phone call with Stewart in which he recommended the sale of ImClone if it fell

below $60. The worksheet he turned over to the agency had notes of this conversation. He also stated that he had not discussed the matter of the ImClone stock sale with Stewart since December 27. Yet records of calls between Bacanovic's and Stewart's cell phones show that by this time they had spoken often, including once on the day of Stewart's interview in New York. The content of their conversations is unrecorded.

On March 7, Douglas Faneuil was interviewed by SEC attorneys and an FBI agent. Details of this session have not been made public, but his subsequent indictment alleges that he failed to fully and truthfully disclose all he knew about the events of December 27.[8] Following the interview, Bacanovic offered Faneuil an extra week of vacation and paid air fare for a trip as a reward for sticking to Bacanovic's script.[9]

On April 10, Stewart was interviewed again on the telephone by investigators from the SEC, FBI, and U.S. Attorney's Office. She told them that she had spoken with Bacanovic on December 27, but she could not remember if Bacanovic had mentioned the Waksals. She said again that the two had set up a $60 sell order on ImClone.

TURMOIL

After these interviews, government investigators continued with the painstaking work of gathering, verifying, and interpreting details. Meanwhile, the main actors in the ImClone trades struggled in the backwash from their actions. In late May, Samuel Waksal resigned as the CEO of ImClone. In early June, the Associated Press broke the story that Martha Stewart had sold ImClone the day before the FDA's decision on Erbitux, setting off a three-week decline in the share price of Martha Stewart Living Omnimedia from $19.01 to $11.47. Merrill Lynch suspended Peter Bacanovic without pay.

When Waksal was arrested and charged with criminal insider trading on June 12, shares in Stewart's company fell 5.6 percent. Waksal would eventually plead guilty to insider trading charges, receive a prison sentence of 87 months, and pay a fine of $4 million. Stewart issued a statement after the close of trading in which she said that she and her broker had agreed

---

[6] Matthew Rose and Kara Scannell, "Dramatic Flourishes at Stewart, Tyco Trials," *The Wall Street Journal*, February 11, 2004, p. C1.

[7] Thomas S. Mulligan, "Jurors Hear of Attempt by Stewart to Alter Phone Log," *Los Angeles Times*, February 11, 2004, p. C7.

[8] Misdemeanor Information, *United States v. Faneuil*, 02 Cr. 1287, S.D.N.Y. (2002), pp. 7–8.

[9] Ibid., p. 8.

on a $60 sell order in October 2001, that he had called her on December 27 and told her ImClone was trading under $60, and that she had told him to sell in line with their prior understanding. She denied having any nonpublic information at the time. Later in the month she repeated this story at a conference for securities analysts and investors. Her intent was to halt the decline in her company's shares. At this time she held 61,323,850 shares, so she suffered paper losses of more than $462 million in the three-week share price decline.

Douglas Faneuil's conscience bothered him. In late June he went to a manager at Merrill Lynch and volunteered what he believed was the complete and accurate story of December 27 and its aftermath. Subsequently, he spoke again to government investigators, who then subpoenaed both Stewart and Bacanovic to testify at an investigative hearing. This time, both declined, invoking their Fifth Amendment privilege against self-incrimination. Faneuil pled guilty to a misdemeanor charge of accepting money from Bacanovic in return for not informing federal investigators of illegal conduct. Merrill Lynch fired Bacanovic.

INDICTMENTS

It took the government a year and a half, but on June 4, 2003, in a "coordinated action," both the U.S. Attorney's Office and the SEC filed indictments against Martha Stewart and Peter Bacanovic.

The U.S. Attorney's Office filed a criminal complaint with multiple counts under the basic charges of, first, conspiracy, and second, obstruction of justice and making false statements.[10] The two were charged with conspiring to conceal evidence that Bacanovic had provided nonpublic information about ImClone to Stewart. And they were accused of lying to government attorneys to hamper their investigation. In addition, only Martha Stewart was charged with securities fraud. The charge was that she had made a series of false statements about her innocence to mislead investors and prop up her company's share price. Conviction on all counts could bring a maximum of 30 years in prison and a fine of $2 million. Bacanovic alone was additionally charged with perjury for altering the worksheet that listed Stewart's stocks by adding "@60" near ImClone to fool

investigators. He faced a maximum of 25 years in prison and a $1.25 million fine.

In its separate civil action, the SEC charged Stewart and Bacanovic with insider trading.[11] It sought disgorgement of illegal gains and the imposition of a fine. In addition, it sought to bar Stewart from acting as a director or officer of a public company.

Martha Stewart's lawyers immediately issued a statement challenging the government's case. "Martha Stewart has done nothing wrong," they said. They accused the government of making an "unprecedented" interpretation of the securities laws when it charged her with fraudulent manipulation simply because she spoke out publicly to maintain her innocence. And they questioned the government's motive for the other charges, raising themes that would course through the media during the subsequent trial.

> Is it for publicity purposes because Martha Stewart is a celebrity? Is it because she is a woman who has successfully competed in a man's business world by virtue of her talent, hard work and demanding standards? Is it because the government would like to be able to define securities fraud as whatever it wants it to be? Or is it because the Department of Justice is attempting to divert the public's attention from its failure to charge the politically connected managers of Enron and WorldCom who may have fleeced the public out of billions of dollars?[12]

A week later, Martha Stewart went to the FBI's Manhattan office for processing. She was given a mug shot, fingerprinted, and released without bail. She also resigned her positions as director and chief creative officer of Martha Stewart Living Omnimedia, taking on the nonofficer position of founding editorial director. She continued to receive her annual salary of $900,000 and in 2003 she was awarded an additional $500,000 bonus.

THE TRIAL OPENS

On January 20, 2004, Martha Stewart and Peter Bacanovic appeared in the Manhattan courtroom of the Hon. Miriam Goldman Cedarbaum, a federal district court judge with 18 years bench experience. They entered pleas of not guilty and jury selection for

[10] *United States v. Martha Stewart and Peter Bacanovic,* 03 Cr. 717 (MGC)(S.D.N.Y.), 2003.

[11] *Securities and Exchange Commission v. Martha Stewart and Peter Bacanovic,* 03 CV 4070 (NRB)(S.D.N.Y.), 2003.

[12] Robert G. Morvillo and John J. Tigue, "Press Statement," June 4, 2003, at www.marthatalks.com/trial.

a trial began. Potential jurors were given 35 pages of questions designed to detect biases. One question was, "Have you ever made a project or cooked a recipe from Martha Stewart?"[13] Then they were interviewed by attorneys for all sides in Judge Cedarbaum's office. Finally, a jury of eight women and four men was put together.

The trial began on January 27. The lead government prosecutor was Assistant U.S. Attorney Karen Patton Seymour. In her opening argument she told the jury that Martha Stewart sold ImClone after a "secret tip" from Bacanovic that the Waksals were selling. Then, she and Bacanovic tried to cover it up. Stewart's motive, she argued, was a desire to protect her "multimillion dollar business empire." Seymour pointed out that every $1 decline in the price of Martha Stewart's company decreased her net worth by $30 million. "Ladies and gentlemen," Seymour continued, "lying to federal agents, obstructing justice, committing perjury, fabricating evidence and cheating investors in the stock market—these are serious federal crimes."[14]

In his opening argument Stewart's attorney, Robert G. Morvillo, pronounced her "innocent of all charges" and tried to offer reasonable explanations for her actions. He pointed out that the ImClone shares she sold were less than 1 percent of her net worth. He told the jury that December was a busy month for her and she gets worn out. When she called Faneuil about the trade she was in a noisy airport on her cell phone and she thought she was talking to Bacanovic. She had no way of knowing that insider trading was taking place. "How," he asked, "was she supposed to figure out the broker, who has always been honorable, was asking her to commit a crime?" If, indeed, she had been told that Waksal and his daughter were selling, it meant that Merrill Lynch was making the sales, which it would not do if it believed them to be illegal.

Morvillo explained that Stewart and Bacanovic had established a $60 sell agreement the week before her trades. And he called Stewart's alteration of her assistant's entry in the phone log "much ado about nothing." He explained that she was changing it "to

be consistent with what she recalled," but then quickly realized that her change "might be misconstrued." He concluded his lengthy opening statement by asking the jury to "decide the case based upon what is correct and just."[15]

TESTIMONY

The government presented its case first. Its star witness was Douglas Faneuil. Under questioning by Seymour, Faneuil described his morning phone call to Bacanovic on December 27. On learning that the Waksals were selling Bacanovic said: "Oh my God, you've got to get Martha on the phone!" Faneuil said that he then asked Bacanovic, "Can I tell her about Sam? Am I allowed to?" "Of course," replied Bacanovic, "That's the whole point."[16] When Martha Stewart called in that afternoon, she asked, "What's going on with Sam?" Faneuil said that he told her, "We have no news about the company, but we thought you might like to act on the information that Sam is selling all his shares." He described her end of the conversation as a series of "clipped demands." Faneuil also recounted how Bacanovic had tried to pull him into a coverup. He described a scene at a coffee shop near their office in which he told Bacanovic, "I was on the phone. I know what happened." In response Bacanovic put an arm around him and said, "With all due respect, no, you don't."[17]

During cross-examination Bacanovic's attorney, David Apfel, tried to tarnish Faneuil as an unreliable witness. He called Faneuil an admitted liar who had changed his story seeking leniency from prosecutors. He brought out Faneuil's use of recreational drugs. And he introduced e-mail messages by Faneuil to show that he disliked Martha Stewart and might have held a grudge against her. One read: "I just spoke to MARTHA! I have never, ever been treated more rudely by a stranger on the telephone." Another was: "Martha yelled at me again today, but I snapped in her face and she actually backed down!

[13] Thomas S. Mulligan, "Stewart Case Poses Challenges for All Parties as Trial Begins Today," *Los Angeles Times,* January 20, 2004, p. C1.

[14] Kara Scannel and Matthew Rose, "Early Sparks at the Stewart Trial," *The Wall Street Journal,* January 28, 2004, p. C1.

[15] Quotations of Morvillo are from "Opening Argument on Behalf of Martha Stewart," January 27, 2004, at www.marthatalks.com/trial.

[16] Brooke A. Masters, "Broker's Aide Says He Was Told to Tip Off Stewart," *Washington Post,* February 3, 2004, p. E1.

[17] Testimony quoted in Constance L. Hays, "Witness Describes Stewart Cover-Up," *New York Times,* February 5, 2004, p. C4.

Baby put Ms. Martha in her place!!!"[18] Faneuil also testified about a time when he put Martha Stewart on hold. When he came back on the line she threatened to pull her account from Merrill Lynch unless the hold music was changed. This colorful testimony sometimes made the jurors laugh.

Faneuil's testimony took 13 hours over six days. On his last day he was cross-examined by Stewart's attorney Morvillo, who tried to depict him as overwhelmed by the rush of events on December 27. He pointed out that Faneuil had taken 75 phone calls on that day, and some e-mails. He questioned why his memory of Stewart's call was sharp, in contrast to some other calls about which he was less clear. He got Faneuil to admit that he suspected the Waksals of insider trading, but said nothing to Bacanovic.

Following Faneuil, several other prosecution witnesses gave notable testimony. Stewart's administrative assistant Ann Armstrong was called to testify about how Stewart altered the message of Bacanovic's call. Taking the stand, she began to sob. After getting a glass of water from the defense table she tried to resume, but could not. Judge Cedarbaum recessed the trial to the next day, when Armstrong recounted how Stewart first altered, then instructed her to restore, the wording of the phone message.

Maria Pasternak was a friend who had been traveling with Martha Stewart on December 27. Pasternak related conversations with Stewart at a resort in Los Cabos over the following days. She said Stewart told her that the Waksals were trying to sell all their shares in ImClone and that she had sold all her shares. She testified that Stewart remarked, "Isn't it nice to have brokers who tell you those things?" But under cross-examination she vacillated about the clarity of her recall. The judge instructed jurors to disregard the remark.

An expert ink analyst with the U.S. Secret Service was called for his analysis of Bacanovic's tax sale worksheet. Larry Stewart, who is not related to Martha Stewart, testified that tests he conducted showed two pens had been used on the worksheet. All the notations on it, except "@60," were made by a "cheap" Paper Mate pen. The "@60" was written with a second, unidentified pen. The second pen did not match any of 8,500 ink samples on record, so Stewart concluded that it was either foreign or very

rare.[19] This was important evidence for the prosecution, which argued that the "@60" had been added only after December 27, when the defendants constructed a coverup.

After the prosecution finished its case, Martha Stewart's lawyers elected to use a minimal defense. They called only one witness, a former Stewart lawyer and note-taker at the February 4 meeting with investigators, who testified for only 15 minutes. There was much speculation about whether Martha Stewart would take the stand in her own defense. If she did, prosecutors would push her, try to trap her in inconsistencies and provoke her temper. If she did not, the intense curiosity of the jurors to learn what she could say to them would be unfulfilled. In the end, she did not take the witness stand.

Late in the trial Judge Cedarbaum accepted a motion by Stewart's lawyers to dismiss the government's allegations of securities fraud. This charge had met with wide skepticism from the beginning. How could a defendant exercise her right to speak out in self-defense if doing so could be construed as criminal manipulation of share prices? In dismissing the charge Cedarbaum said that, given the evidence, no reasonable juror could find her guilty beyond a reasonable doubt.[20]

After the defense called its single witness, there had been 27 witnesses during 19 days of testimony. Closing arguments came on March 2. Prosecutor Michael Schachter told the jurors that Stewart and Bacanovic believed they would never be caught. But the mistakes they made trying to deceive left a trail of damning inconsistencies. He carefully listed the contradictions in their stories. Bacanovic's lawyer gave a closing argument trying once again to undermine the credibility of Douglas Faneuil's testimony.

In his closing argument for Martha Stewart, Morvillo began by ridiculing the conspiracy charge, saying that the events alleged by the government amounted to "a confederation of dunces."[21] Nobody," he argued, "could have done what Peter Bacanovic and Martha Stewart are alleged to have done and

[18] Brooke A. Masters, "Broker's Assistant, Stewart Clashed," *Washington Post*, February 5, 2004, p. E1.

[19] Matthew Rose and Kara Scannell, "Stewart Trial Gets Testimony of a Broker's Tip," *The Wall Street Journal*, February 20, 2004, p. C3.

[20] *United States v. Martha Stewart and Peter Bacanovic*, 305 F. Supp. 2d 368, February 27, 2004.

[21] "Closing Argument on Behalf of Martha Stewart," March 2, 2004, at www.marthatalks.com/trial, p. 1.

done it in a dumber fashion." He asked the jurors to consider that if the two had really conspired they would have been much more consistent in their stories. Their inconsistencies were a sign of innocence. This was a dangerous argument, because it conceded some contradictions in testimony.

Morvillo then made the case for Stewart's innocence. She had no evidence that anything was wrong with the trade. She had no reason to suspect that Waksal would behave so foolishly as to trade in front of the FDA announcement during a blackout period. She had a preexisting agreement with her broker to trade ImClone if it fell below $60. She could not hear well enough on the phone to know she was talking to Faneuil, not Bacanovic. The amount of the trade was too small to tempt jeopardizing her future. Her change in Ann Armstrong's telephone log was insignificant. Faneuil was an untrustworthy witness. Finally, he explained that she did not take the stand because she twice testified on the record at investigative hearings two years before and "her recollection [of the events] hasn't gotten any better." He concluded with this.

> This has been a two-year ordeal for this good woman. It's an ordeal based on the fact that she trusted her financial advisor not to put her in a compromising position. It's an ordeal based on the fact that she voluntarily submitted to a government interview. And it's an ordeal that is in the process of wiping out all the good that she has done, all her contributions, all her accomplishments. . . . [M]artha Stewart's life is in your hands. . . . I ask you to acquit Martha Stewart. I ask you to let her return to her life of improving the quality of life for all of us. If you do that, it's a good thing.[22]

THE VERDICT

The jury deliberated for 14 hours over three days. On March 5 one female juror wept as the verdicts were announced. Stewart and Bacanovic were each found guilty on four counts of lying and conspiring to lie to conceal the fact that she had been tipped with insider information. However, the jury could not agree that the government had proved beyond a reasonable doubt its allegation that Stewart and Bacanovic fabricated the $60 sale agreement and it acquitted them on those counts.

Jurors described their deliberations as calm. They had found Faneuil credible and gave much weight to

Martha Stewart outside the Manhattan courthouse after hearing the verdict. © AP Photo/Julie Jacobson.

his testimony. Ann Armstrong was also an important witness because she cried. "We feel that she knew that something was wrong," said the forewoman. Jurors were also suspicious of the January 16 breakfast meeting between Stewart and Bacanovic and they felt cynical about Stewart hiring a criminal defense lawyer even before she was contacted by government investigators. They put little stock in the "conspiracy of dunces" argument. "We felt that she was a smart lady who made a dumb mistake," said the forewoman.[23]

A juror named Chappell Hartridge characterized the verdict as "a victory for the little guys who lose money in the market because of these kinds of transactions."[24] After looking into Hartridge's background, Stewart's legal team believed he had not been completely honest on his jurors' questionnaire. When asked about contacts with law enforcement, he did not disclose an arrest for assaulting a former girlfriend, being sued, and several other problems. Arguing that they would have exercised a challenge to keep Chappell off the jury had they known, her

[22] Ibid., p. 10.

[23] Kara Scannell, Matthew Rose, and Laurie P. Cohen, "In Stewart Case, Reluctant Jurors Found Guilt after Skimpy Defense," *The Wall Street Journal,* March 8, 2004, p. A1.

[24] Constance L. Hays, "Martha Stewart Seeks New Trial, Saying a Juror Lied," *New York Times,* April 1, 2004, p. C3.

lawyers moved for a new trial. Judge Cedarbaum ruled that the allegations were little more than hearsay and there was no evidence that bias in Chappell had affected the verdict.[25]

Meanwhile, prosecutors had filed a criminal complaint against Larry Stewart, the ink expert who testified at the trial. Stewart was accused of perjury for saying that he had conducted the ink tests after a coworker came forward saying that, in fact, she had done them. Again Stewart's attorneys filed a motion for retrial. Again Cedarbaum denied the motion, because "there was no reasonable likelihood that this perjury could have affected the jury's verdict, and because overwhelming independent evidence supports the verdict . . ."[26] Subsequently, Larry Stewart was tried and acquitted of perjury based on evidence that his coworker had a history of harassment.[27]

SENTENCING

More than four months elapsed before sentencing. During this time Martha Stewart tried to mitigate her sentence in two ways. She appealed for leniency on the grounds that her imprisonment would risk layoffs at her company. She also hired a sentencing consultant who recommended that she offer to do public service instead of going to jail. She developed a plan to work 20 hours a week with a nonprofit organization in New York teaching low income women how to start businesses.

On July 16, 2004, Martha Stewart appeared before Judge Cedarbaum. Addressing the judge, she appealed for leniency, saying, "Today is a shameful day. I ask that in judging me, you remember all the good I've done and the contributions I've made." Prosecutor Seymour countered, arguing that Stewart was "asking for leniency far beyond" that justified for "a serious offense with broad implications" for the justice system. Judge Cedarbaum responded, "I believe that you have suffered, and will continue to suffer,

enough."[28] Her sentence was five months imprisonment followed by five months of home confinement. During home confinement she would be allowed to leave her house for 48 hours a week, but she could have only one land line telephone with no call forwarding or caller ID and could not go online with a computer. She was fined $30,000. This set of penalties was at the lenient end of what could have been imposed under federal sentencing guidelines and showed that Judge Cedarbaum was using what discretion she had to avoid a harsh sentence.

After the sentencing, Martha Stewart emerged from the courthouse to read another statement. "I'm just very, very sorry that it's come to this, that a small personal matter has been able to be blown out of all proportion, and with such venom and such gore—I mean, it's just terrible."[29]

At a separate hearing that day, Peter Bacanovic received a nearly identical sentence of five months in prison, five months of home confinement, and a $4,000 fine. A week later Daniel Faneuil appeared before Judge Cedarbaum. Tearfully, he apologized for his actions. His cooperation with federal prosecutors saved him from going to prison. His sentence was a $2,000 fine.

On October 8, Martha Stewart reported to a minimum-security prison camp in West Virginia to begin her incarceration. She had appealed her case, but the appeal was expected to take two years. Therefore, she elected to serve her sentence. Doing so would end much of the speculation and tumult affecting both her and her company. At the time of her decision Martha Stewart Living Omnimedia reported a second quarter net loss of $19.3 million. Its publishing revenue had fallen 44 percent for the year. Advertisers were holding back, uncertain of events related to Martha Stewart.[30]

Before going into prison, she renegotiated her contract with her company. For 2004 she continued to receive a salary of $900,000, was eligible for a bonus of between $495,000 and $1,350,000, and was to be paid $500,000 for use of her properties in television and

[25] *United States v. Martha Stewart and Peter Bacanovic,* 317 F. Supp. 2d 426, May 5, 2004.

[26] *United States v. Martha Stewart and Peter Bacanovic,* 323 F. Supp. 2d 606, July 8, 2004.

[27] "Jurors Acquit Stewart Witness," *Los Angeles Times,* October 6, 2004, p. C3.

[28] Thomas S. Mulligan, "Stewart Gets 5 Months in Prison, Then Delivers a Plug for Her Firm," *Los Angeles Times,* July 17, 2004, p. A4.

[29] Ibid., p. A1.

[30] "Martha Stewart Opts for Jail Now," *The Wall Street Journal,* September 16, 2004, p. 6.

magazine shoots. She would not receive any salary or bonus while in prison, but pay would resume during home confinement.[31]

Even when her sentence is served her legal difficulties will continue. The SEC has suspended its insider trading case pending the result of her appeal. If that case resumes, she could be barred permanently or for a period of years from acting as an officer or director of a public company, including Martha Stewart Living Omnimedia. In addition, she is a defendant in five shareholder suits. These civil suits charge her with breaching her fiduciary duties as an officer by engaging in insider trading and making false statements, by that injuring the company and its shareholders.[32]

[31] "Martha Stewart Living Renews Pay Pact of Founder for 5 Years," *The Wall Street Journal,* September 24, 2004, p. B4.

[32] See Martha Stewart Living Omnimedia, Form 10-K, March 12, 2004, pp. 12–13.

Questions

1. Did Martha Stewart commit the crime of insider trading when she sold her ImClone shares on December 27, 2001?

2. Did the U.S. Attorneys and the Securities and Exchange Commission use good judgment in indicting Martha Stewart? Do you believe that her indictment was based on evidence of a serious crime, or do you believe that prosecutors consciously or unconsciously had additional motives for pursuing the case?

3. Do you agree with the jury that she was guilty beyond a reasonable doubt of the conspiracy and obstruction of justice charges?

4. Was her sentence appropriate? Were the sentences of Peter Bacanovic and Douglas Faneuil appropriate?

Chapter **Eight**

Making Ethical Decisions in Business

Realtors in the Wilderness

In ancient times the Gunnison River flowed through what is now western Colorado, carrying abrasive particles and debris, scouring the hard rock as it went to form a deep canyon 50 miles long. This spectacular cut in the earth reaches depths of 2,900 feet and at one point is just 40 feet wide. It is so narrow that sunlight shines on the floor only an hour a day, hence its name—Black Canyon.

In 1999 this geologic marvel was upgraded from a national monument to a national park, entitling it to uncompromising protection from human intrusion. Just before the park was created, a limited partnership named TDX, L.P., bought 112 acres of private land on the south side of the canyon. Small, privately owned tracts such as this in national parks and monuments are called inholdings. Property rights to inholdings were acquired years ago, usually in the late 1800s or early 1900s, as homesteads or mining claims. By law, the government cannot take them or buy them back without the owner's consent. Nor can it restrict an owner's right to mine or develop their property.

Using a local realtor named Tom Chapman, TDX bought its Black Canyon holding for $240,000. Soon Chapman created a sales brochure advertising lots for the construction of luxury homes. Then a billboard rose on the site of the lots along the main road into the monument: "For Sale. Forty-acre building sites. Beautiful canyon views. World-class sunsets."[1] Chapman asked $4,500 an acre for the lots, an amount that would have returned a profit of 110 percent to TDX investors.

Environmentalists were enraged. Houses would be visible from canyon outlooks, blighting the atmosphere of wildness and natural splendor. The park superintendent was appalled and filed a lawsuit to stop the development, but the legal grounds for the suit were weak and a superior in the National Park Service ordered him to negotiate with Chapman instead. In the meantime, Chapman had acquired a building permit for a bed-and-breakfast on the site. The park service had the land appraised at $2,500 an acre, $2,000 below Chapman's original asking price. Chapman then listed the land on eBay's online auction at $11,000 to $13,000 an acre, indicating to

[1] Richard Miniter, "Real Estate Broker from Hell," *Reader's Digest,* February 2001, p. 114.

potential buyers that it could be used for a business such as a motel, RV park, or convenience store.[2]

Inholdings are a small but significant presence in the West, totaling 0.5 percent of park and wilderness acres. To protect the integrity of wilderness lands Congress years ago set up a fund to buy inholdings, but in the 1980s it was raided for money to lower the federal deficit. Now too little is left to buy much, and federal agencies generally offer inholders below-market amounts. This is where Thomas Chapman and TDX come in; they force the government to pay more.

In a prior foray into Black Canyon in 1984, Chapman represented a client who had been offered $200 an acre by the National Park Service for property in what was then the Gunnison National Monument. To raise the offer, he picked part of his client's land, a highly visible area on the rim of the striking canyon, and threatened to build a subdivision. After he brought in a bulldozer, the agency caved in and paid $510 an acre to buy the land and halt construction.

In 1992 Chapman had become an investor in TDX. He and the other partners bought 240 acres of inholdings in the West Elk Wilderness of Colorado for $4,000 per acre. They offered to sell the land to the U.S. Forest Service, but the agency said it could not afford it. So Chapman started to build a lodge. Since there was no road access into the island of property, work commenced with the roar of helicopters flying building materials over the surrounding forests. To stop the disruption, the Forest Service offered to swap the TDX inholding for 107 acres it owned near Telluride, Colorado. That parcel was near a ski resort, and after the swap TDX sold it for $4.2 million, giving the investors a sizable profit. Chapman's share was about $1 million.[3]

This coercive strategy has been repeated at least two other times. It works because once virgin areas are developed, the wilderness is gone. Property rights are fundamental in America, and long-standing federal law protects inholders from interference. Yet Chapman and TDX are criticized for extorting money that could be used for the welfare of pristine lands and their visitors. While the speculators profit, national parks and monuments are severely underfunded, rangers get low pay, and lands deteriorate. Their tactics have been called immoral, unethical, and outrageous. Chapman, however, defends them.

> I will never apologize for being a capitalist because capitalism is what created the cornucopia of goods and services that we enjoy in this country. Everybody, everybody wants to sell something for more than they paid. It's all American. Unless of course you own property in a wilderness area or in a national park or a national forest. Then all of a sudden you are a greedy capitalist, a profiteer. . . . Why should capitalism be removed from wilderness areas?[4]

The story of TDX reveals an ethically complex situation. Its investors exercise basic property rights, but rights are not absolute. Their methods resonate with free market values, but markets exhibit flaws. In a just world, laws and rules are fair. When inholders pay taxes on their property but cannot use it as they wish or sell it for current

[2] Nancy Lofholm, "Black Canyon Land Put on eBay for $1.2 Million," *Denver Post,* June 5, 2003, p. B5.
[3] Jason Blevins, "Real Estate Broker Defends Wilderness Tactics," *Denver Post,* August 13, 2000, p. M1.
[4] Ibid.

market value, that seems unfair. Arm-twisting land deals create lavish profits for a few, but they foreclose alternative uses of money that benefit many others.

In this chapter we set forth a wide range of principles and methods for making ethical decisions. These include principles great and small, character development, simple procedures that corporations suggest to their employees, and practical tips. Use of these devices makes ethical thinking more sophisticated. In themselves they do not resolve ethical issues. Judgment is still required. If you owned a pocket of land in a national park, would you threaten to build a subdivision of homes? If you decided to do that, would you feel comfortable explaining why on television? What are the rules when there is no definitive law? The material in this chapter can help to answer such questions.

PRINCIPLES OF ETHICAL CONDUCT

We begin with a compendium of ethical principles—some ancient, some modern. There are dozens, if not hundreds, of such principles in the philosophical and religious traditions of East and West.

From a larger universe, we set forth 14 principles that every manager should know and think about. (See the nearby box and discussion that follows.) The 14 principles here are fundamental guides or rules for behavior. Each of them has strengths and weaknesses. Some were created to be universal tests of conduct. Others have a more limited reach and apply only in certain spheres of human relations. Some are ideals. Others accommodate balancing of interests where perfection is impossible. A few invite compromise and can be used to rationalize flawed behavior. One principle, might equals right, is a justification for ignoble acts, but we include it here because it has been the subject of discussion since time immemorial.

These principles distill basic wisdom from 2,000 years of ethical thought. To the extent that they offer ideas for thinking about and resolving ethical dilemmas, they are not vague abstractions but useful, living guides to analysis and conduct. We present them alphabetically.

The Categorical Imperative

categorical imperative
Act only according to that maxim by which you can at the same time will that it should become a universal law.

The categorical imperative (meaning, literally, a command that admits no exception) is a guide for ethical behavior set forth by the German philosopher Immanuel Kant in his *Foundations of the Metaphysics of Morals*, a tract published in 1785. In Kant's words: "Act only according to that maxim by which you can at the same time will that it should become a universal law."[5]

In other words, one should not adopt principles of action unless they can, without inconsistency, be adopted by everyone. Lying, stealing, and breaking promises, for example, are ruled out because society would disintegrate if they replaced truth telling, property rights, and vow keeping. Using this guideline, a manager faced with a moral choice must act in a way that he or she believes is right and just for any person in a similar situation. Each action should be judged

[5] Immanuel Kant, *Foundations of the Metaphysics of Morals,* trans. Lewis White Beck (Indianapolis: Bobbs-Merrill, 1969), p. 44; written in 1785.

Fourteen Ethical Principles

The Categorical Imperative   Act only according to that maxim by which you can at the same time will that it should become a universal law.

The Conventionalist Ethic   Business is like a game with permissive ethics and any action that does not violate the law is permitted.

The Disclosure Rule   Test an ethical decision by asking how you would feel explaining it to a wider audience such as newspaper readers, television viewers, or your family.

The Doctrine of the Mean   Virtue is achieved through moderation. Avoid behavior that is excessive or deficient of a virtue.

The Ends–Means Ethic   The end justifies the means.

The Golden Rule   Do unto others what you would have them do unto you.

The Intuition Ethic   What is good or right is understood by an inner moral sense based on character development and felt as intuition.

Might-Equals-Right   Justice is the interest of the stronger.

The Organization Ethic   Be loyal to the organization.

The Principle of Equal Freedom   A person has the right to freedom of action unless such action deprives another person of a proper freedom.

The Proportionality Ethic   A set of rules for making decisions having both good and evil consequences.

The Rights Ethic   Each person has protections and entitlements that others have a duty to respect.

The Theory of Justice   Each person should act fairly toward others in order to maintain the bonds of community.

The Utilitarian Ethic   The greatest good for the greatest number.

test of universalizability
Could this act be turned into a universal code of behavior?

by asking: "Could this act be turned into a universal code of behavior?" This quick *test of universalizability* has achieved great popularity.

Kant was an extreme perfectionist. He walked the same route each day at the same time, appearing at places along the route so punctually that neighbors set their clocks by him. Before leaving his house he attached strings to the top of his socks and connected them to a spring apparatus held by his belt. As he walked, the contraption would pull the slack out of his socks. To no one's surprise, his ethical philosophies are perfectionist also, and that is their weakness. Kant's categorical imperative is dogmatic and inflexible. It is a general rule that must be applied in every specific situation; there are no exceptions. But real life challenges the simple, single ethical law. If a competitor asks whether your company is planning to sell shirts in Texas next year, must you answer the question with the truth?

conventionalist ethic
Business is like a game with permissive ethics and any action that does not violate the law is permitted.

The Conventionalist Ethic

This is the view that business is analogous to a game and special, lower ethics are permissible. In business, people may act to further their self-interest so long as they do not violate the law. The conventionalist ethic, which has a long history, was popularized some years ago by Albert Z. Carr in *Business as a Game*.[6] "If an

---

[6] Albert Z. Carr, *Business as a Game* (New York: New American Library, 1968).

executive allows himself to be torn between a decision based on business consid-erations and one based on his private ethical code," explained Carr, "he exposes himself to a grave psychological strain."[7]

Business may be regarded as a game, such as poker, in which the rules are different from those we adopt in personal life. Assuming game ethics, managers are allowed to bluff (a euphemism for lie) and to take advantage of all legal opportunities and widespread practices or customs. Carr used two examples of situations in which game ethics were permissible. In the first, an out-of-work sales agent with a good employment record feared discrimination because of his age—58. He dyed his hair and stated on his résumé that he was 45. In the second, a job applicant was asked to check off magazines he read, but decided not to check off *Playboy, The Nation,* or *The New Republic.* Even though he read them, he did not want to be labeled controversial. He checked tame magazines such as *Reader's Digest* instead.[8]

The conventionalist ethic is criticized by those who make no distinction between society's ethics and business ethics. They argue that commerce defines the life chances of millions and is not a game to be taken lightly. As a principle, the conventionalist ethic is a thin justification for deceptive behavior at the office.

The Disclosure Rule

disclosure rule
Test an ethical decision by asking how you would feel explaining it to a wider audi-ence such as newspaper readers, televi-sion viewers, or your family.

Using the disclosure rule, a manager faced with an ethical dilemma asks how it would feel to explain the decision to a wider audience. This simple idea appears in many company ethics codes. It is stated in Baxter International's *Global Business Practice Standards* in tests of ethics that are set forth in two questions.

- What will my manager, supervisor, co-workers, or family think about what I plan to do? (The "Others" Test)
- If what I do is reported in a newspaper, or on television, will I be proud of my actions? (The "Press" Test)[9]

This rule screens out base motives such as greed and jealousy, which are unacceptable if disclosed, but it does not always give clear guidance for ethical dilemmas in which strong arguments exist for several alternatives. Also, an action that sounds acceptable if disclosed may not, upon reflection, always be the most ethical.

The Doctrine of the Mean

doctrine of the mean
Virtue is achieved through mod-eration. Avoid behavior that is excessive or deficient of a virtue.

This ethic, set forth by Aristotle in the *Nicomachean Ethics* and sometimes called the *golden mean,* calls for virtue through moderation.[10] Right actions are found in the area between extreme behaviors, which are labeled excess on the one hand and deficiency on the other. Facing an ethical decision, a person first identifies the

---

[7] "Is Business Bluffing Ethical?" *Harvard Business Review,* January–February 1968, p. 149.

[8] Carr, *Business as a Game,* p. 142.

[9] Deerfield, IL: Baxter International Inc., 2000, p. 43.

[10] *Nicomachean Ethics,* trans. J. A. K. Thomson (New York: Penguin Books, 1982), book II, chap. 6.

ethical virtue at its core (such as truthfulness) and then seeks the mean or moderate course of action between an excess of that virtue (boastfulness) and a deficiency of it (understatement).

At ITT, Harold Geneen pushed managers to extraordinary personal sacrifices. Their time, energy, loyalty, and will were bent to corporate purposes. Obsessive work led to remarkable business successes but also to personal difficulties such as marital problems. While specific operations of ITT, taken one by one, were constructive and ethical, immoderation led some to sacrifice a balanced life.[11] To Aristotle, this would have been wrong.

The doctrine of the mean is today little recognized, but the underlying notion of moderation as a virtue lingers in Western societies. The doctrine itself is inexact. To observe it is simply to act conservatively, never in the extreme. The moderate course and specific virtues such as honesty, however, are defined as aspects existing between and defined in relation to polar extremes. What they are is open to wide interpretation.

The Ends–Means Ethic

ends–means ethic
The end justifies the means.

This principle is age-old, appearing as an ancient Roman proverb, *existus acta probat,* or "the result validates the deeds." It is often associated with the Italian philosopher Niccolò Machiavelli. In *The Prince* (1513), Machiavelli argued that worthwhile ends justify efficient means, that when ends are of overriding importance or virtue, unscrupulous means may be employed to reach them.[12] When confronted with a decision involving an ethically questionable act, a person should ask whether some overall good—such as the survival of a country or business—justifies cutting corners.

In the 1980s Oracle Corporation grew rapidly. To get this growth, founder and CEO Lawrence J. Ellison pressed his sales managers to double revenues every year. Methods used by the frenzied sales force were watched less closely than its ability to hit targets. In 1993 the Securities and Exchange Commission fined Oracle for overstating earnings by double-billing customers, invoicing companies for products never sold, and violating accounting standards by recording sales revenue before it was received.[13] However, by then Oracle had crushed its early competition in the relational database market. Today Oracle is a $10 billion corporation and Ellison is a billionaire. Oracle employs 41,600 people and has made many of them millionaires. Its software makes governments, businesses, and universities more productive. It pays taxes in 60 countries. It has a wide range of social responsibility programs. Does this end result justify the competitive tactics used to build the company?

Any manager using unscrupulous means concedes the highest virtue and accepts the necessity of ethical compromise. In solving ethical problems, means

[11] Manuel Velasquez and Neil Brady, "Catholic Natural Law and Business Ethics," *Business Ethics Quarterly,* March 1997, p. 95.

[12] Niccolò Machiavelli, *The Prince,* trans. T. G. Bergin, ed. (New York: Appleton-Century-Crofts, 1947); written in 1513 and first published in 1532.

[13] Mike Wilson, *The Difference between God and Larry Ellison* (New York: William Morrow, 1997), p. 239.

may be as important, or more so, than ends. In addition, the process of ethical character development can never be furthered by the use of expedient means.

The Golden Rule

Golden Rule
Do unto others as you would have them do unto you.

An ideal found in the great religions and in works of philosophy, the Golden Rule has been a popular guide for centuries. Simply put, it is: "Do unto others as you would have them do unto you." It includes not knowingly doing harm to others. A manager trying to solve an ethical problem places him- or herself in the position of another party affected by the decision and tries to figure out what action is most fair from that perspective.

practical imperative
Treat others as ends in themselves, not as means to other goals. This principle prohibits selfish manipulation of other people.

A related principle called the *practical imperative* was set forward by Immanuel Kant. It is: "Act so that you treat humanity, whether in your own person or in that of another, always as an end and never as a means only."[14] This principle admonishes a manager to treat employees as ends in themselves, not to manipulate them simply as factors of production for the self-interested ends of the company.

Around 1900, when E. H. Harriman owned the Southern Pacific railroad, train accidents killed between 5,000 and 6,000 people a year. One day on an inspection tour, his train hit a rough section of track and nearly derailed because a work crew had neglected to post a flagman. Instead of firing the crew chief, Harriman insisted on firing the whole crew. A top executive spoke up, arguing it was cruel to punish them all. "Perhaps," responded Harriman, "but it will probably save a lot of lives. I want every man connected with the operation to feel a sense of responsibility. Now, everybody knew that the man hadn't gone back with the flag."[15] Harriman used this crew of workers to send a message to all other crews. The workers were not treated as individuals; they were punished en masse to signal others in the company.

test of reversibility
Would you be willing to change places with the person or persons affected by your actions?

A manager may comply with both the practical imperative and the Golden Rule by using the *test of reversibility*, that is, by asking if he or she would change places with the person affected by the contemplated action. A problem with the Golden Rule is that people's ethical values differ, and they may mistakenly assume that their preferences are universal. In addition, it is primarily a perfectionist rule for interpersonal relations. So applying it in business life where the interests of individuals are subordinated to the needs of the firm is sometimes hard.

The Intuition Ethic

intuition ethic
What is good or right is understood by an inner moral sense based on character development and felt as intuition.

The intuition ethic, as defined by philosophers such as G. E. Moore in his *Principia Ethica* (1903), holds that what is good is simply understood.[16] That is, people are endowed with a moral sense by which they intuitively know the difference

[14] Kant, *Foundations of the Metaphysics of Morals*, p. 54.

[15] Quoted in Maury Klein, *The Life & Legend of E. H. Harriman* (Chapel Hill: University of North Carolina Press, 2000), p. 266.

[16] New York: Cambridge University Press, 1948; reprint.

between right and wrong. The solution to an ethical problem lies in what you sense or understand to be right.

Most people facing an ethical conflict have an emotional, gut reaction that occurs before reason illuminates the specific problem in logical terms. The situation just bothers them, even if they are not sure why. Something is wrong. This ethical intuition is not simply ungrounded self-judgment. A person's ethical instincts are the product of socialization, role expectations, and character development. Everyone carries a lifetime of moral lessons that can well up as strong emotions. Though fallible, intuition is usually accurate.

Some corporations recognize the intuition ethic in their conduct codes and offer it as a general guideline for employees. At Cummins Engine Company, Inc., for example, employees are told: "If . . . you are uncomfortable with a particular action . . . then DON'T DO IT."[17]

Drawbacks exist. The approach is subjective. Self-interest may be confused with ethical insight. No standard of validation outside the individual is used. It is unpersuasive to others for a manager to say, "It's wrong because I just think so." Also, intuition may fail to give clear answers.[18]

The Might-Equals-Right Ethic

might equals right
Justice is the interest of the stronger.

The classic statement of this ancient ethic is that of Thracymachus (thră-sĭm-ă-cŭs), an Athenian teacher of rhetoric who argued with Socrates that justice is "nothing but what is the interest of the stronger."[19] No era since has been without both its expression and its practice. In business this thinking is expressed in some competitive strategies and marketing tactics. What is ethical is what a stronger individual or company has the power to impose on a weaker one. When faced with an ethical decision, people should seize what advantage they are strong enough to take, without regard for lofty sentiments.

In the 1860s Ben Holladay, owner of the Overland Stage Line, perfected a competitive strategy based on overbearing power. He entered new routes with lowball coach fares, subsidizing this service with profits from monopoly routes, waiting until local competitors failed. In 1863 a small stage line between Denver and Central City in Colorado charged $6 per run. Holladay put an elegant new Concord Coach with a leather interior on the line and charged only $2. The competitor soon folded, then Holladay replaced the new stagecoach with a primitive vehicle resembling a freight wagon and raised the fare to $12.

The weakness of the might-equals-right ethic lies in its confusion of ethics with force. Exercising power is different than acting from ethical duty. An ethical principle that can be invalidated by its foundation (e.g., physical force) is not consistent, logical, or valid. Might equals right is not a legitimate approach in civilized settings. It invites retaliation and censure, and it is not conducive to long-term

[17] Patrick E. Murphy, *Eighty Exemplary Ethics Statements* (South Bend, IN: University of Notre Dame Press, 1997), p. 117; emphasis in original.

[18] For an excellent discussion of intuition in managers' decisions, see Joseph L. Badaracco Jr., *Defining Moments* (Boston: Harvard Business School Press, 1997), chap. 4.

[19] Francis MacDonald Cornford, *The Republic of Plato* (New York: Oxford University Press, 1966), p. 18.

advantage. Seizure by power violates the bedrock ethical duty of reciprocity on which all societies are based.

You are sailing to Rome (you tell me) to obtain the post of Governor of Cnossus. You are not content to stay at home with the honours you had before; you want something on a larger scale, and more conspicuous. But when did you ever undertake a voyage for the purpose of reviewing your own principles and getting rid of any of them that proved unsound?

Source: Epictetus, *The Discourses* (circa. A.D. 120).

The Organization Ethic

organization ethic
Be loyal to the organization.

Simply put, this principle is: "Be loyal to the organization." It implies that the wills and needs of individuals are subordinate to the overall welfare of the organization (be it a corporation, government, university, or army). A member should act consistent with the organization's goals. This ethic leads to cooperation and mutual trust.

Many employees have such deep loyalty to an organization that it transcends self-interest. Some Americans jeopardize their health and work excessively long hours without pay out of devotion to the employer. In Asian societies, which have strong collectivist values, identification with and commitment to companies is exceptionally strong. In Japan, workers are so afraid of letting down their work group or employer that they come to work despite broken limbs and serious ailments. This behavior is so common that a word for death from overwork, *karoshi*, has entered the Japanese language.

The ethical limits of obedience are reached when duty to the organization is used to rationalize wrongdoing. The Nuremberg trials, which convicted Nazis of war crimes, taught that Western society expects members of organizations to follow their conscience. Just as no war criminal argued successfully that taking orders in a military chain of command excused his behavior, so no business manager may claim to be the helpless prisoner of corporate loyalties that crush free will and justify wrongdoing.

The Principle of Equal Freedom

principle of equal freedom
A person has the right to freedom of action unless such action deprives another person of a proper freedom.

This principle was set forth by the philosopher Herbert Spencer in his 1850 book *Social Statics*. "Every man may claim the fullest liberty to exercise his faculties," said Spencer, "compatible with the possession of like liberty by every other man."[20] Thus, a person has the right to freedom of action unless such action deprives another person of a proper freedom. Spencer believed this was the first principle of ethical behavior in society because only when individual liberty was protected against infringement by others could human progress occur.

To use the principle, a person asks if an action will restrict others from actions that they have a legitimate right to undertake. Most people know the colloquial version: "Your right to swing your fist ends where my nose begins."

[20] New York: Robert Schalkenbach Foundation, 1970, p. 69; first published in 1850.

The principle of equal freedom lacks a tie breaker for situations in which two rights conflict. Such situations require invocation of some additional rule to decide which right or freedom has priority. Ethically permissible management decisions may abridge the rights of some parties for the benefit of others. For example, all employees have broad privacy rights, but management invades them when it hires undercover detectives to investigate theft.

The Proportionality Ethic

proportionality
A set of rules for making decisions having both good and evil consequences.

Proportionality, an idea incubated in medieval Catholic theology, applies to decisions having both good and evil consequences. For instance, a maker of small-caliber, short-barreled, handguns that are irreverently called Saturday Night Specials has a dual impact on society. It makes available cheap, easily concealable weapons for criminals. Yet it also creates a supply of affordable self-defense weapons for poor people in crime-ridden areas who cannot buy high-quality handguns costing as much as $500. In this and similar cases, where a manager's action has a good effect but also entails a harm, the idea of proportionality fits.

principle of proportionality
Managers can risk predictable, but unwilled, harms to people after weighing five factors: type of good and evil, probability, urgency, intensity of influence, and alternatives.

A classic formulation of proportionality into a specific principle is Thomas M. Garrett's *principle of proportionality.* It states that managers are responsible for the consequences when they create situations leading to both good and evil effects. The principle allows them to risk predictable, but unwilled, harms to people (for example, innocent victims being shot by handguns) if they correctly weigh five factors.

First, managers must assess the *type of good and evil* involved, distinguishing between major and minor forms. Second, they should calculate the *urgency* of the situation. For example, would the firm go out of business unless employees were laid off? Third, they must estimate the *probability* of both good and evil effects. If good effects are certain and risks of serious harm are remote, an action is more favorable. Fourth, the *intensity of influence* over effects must be considered. In considering handgun injuries, for instance, manufacturers might assume that criminal action was an intervening force over which they had no control. Fifth, the existence of *alternatives* must be considered. If, for instance, an advertisement subtly encourages product misuse, the most ethical action might be to change it. Garrett believed that taking these five factors into consideration would reveal fully the ethical dimension of a decision.[21]

principle of double effect
When both good and evil consequences result from a decision, a manager has acted ethically if the good outweighs the evil, if his or her intention is to achieve the good, and if there is no better alternative.

An alternative formulation of the idea of proportionality is the *principle of double effect,* which is that in a situation from which both good and evil consequences are bound to result, a manager will act ethically if (1) the good effects outweigh the evil, (2) the manager's intention is to achieve the good effects, and (3) there is no better alternative.[22]

These are intricate principles, requiring consideration of many factors. They force a manager to think about and weigh multiple factors in an organized way.

[21] Thomas M. Garrett, *Business Ethics* (New York: Appleton-Century-Crofts, 1966), p. 8.

[22] This is a simple version of the principle of double effect. For fuller treatment, see Lawrence Masek, "The Doctrine of Double Effect, Deadly Drugs, and Business Ethics," *Business Ethics Quarterly,* April 2000, pp. 484–87.

The Rights Ethic

rights ethic
Each person has protections and entitlements that others have a duty to respect.

natural rights
Protections and entitlements that can be inferred by reason from the study of human nature.

legal rights
Protections and entitlements conferred by law.

Rights protect people against abuses and entitle them to important liberties. A strong philosophical movement defining *natural rights*, or rights that can be inferred by reason from the study of human nature, grew in Western Europe during the Enlightenment as a reaction against medieval religious persecutions. Over time, many such rights were given legal status and became *legal rights.*

Basic rights that are now widely accepted and protected in Western nations include the right to life; personal liberties such as expression, conscience, religious worship, and privacy; freedom from arbitrary, unjust police actions or unequal application of laws; and political liberties such as voting and lobbying. In Eastern societies, especially those transfused by the collectivist values of ancient Chinese culture, there is far less recognition of individual rights.

Rights imply duties. Because individuals have rights, many protected by law, other people have clear duties to respect them. For example, management should not permit operation of a dangerous machine because this would deprive workers of the right to a safe workplace. This right is based on the natural right to protection from harm by negligent actions of others and is legally established in common law and the Occupational Safety and Health Act. If some risk in operating a machine is unavoidable, workers have the right to be given an accurate risk assessment.

Theories of rights have great importance in American ethical debates. A problem caused by our reverence for rights is that they are sometimes stretched into selfish demands or entitlements. Rights are not absolute and their limits may be hard to define. For example, every person has a right to life, but industry daily exposes people to risk of death by releasing carcinogens into the environment. An absolute right to life would require cessation of much manufacturing activity (for example, petroleum refining). Rights, such as the right to life, are commonly abridged for compelling reasons of benefit to the public.

The Theory of Justice

theory of justice
Each person should act fairly toward others in order to maintain the bonds of community.

A theory of justice defines what individuals must do for the common good of society. Maintaining the community is important because natural rights, such as the right to life, are reasonably protected only in a well-kept civil society. A basic principle of justice, then, is to act in such a way that the bonds of community are maintained. In broad terms, this means acting fairly toward others and establishing institutions in which people are subject to rules of fair treatment. In business life, justice requires fair relationships within the corporate community and establishment of policies that treat its members fairly.

In society, a person's chances for justice are determined by basic economic and political arrangements. The design of institutions such as business corporations and political constitutions has a profound effect on the welfare and life chances of individuals. A contemporary philosopher, John Rawls, has developed an influential set of principles for the design of a just society. Rawls speculates that rational persons situated behind a hypothetical "veil of ignorance" and not knowing their place in a society (i.e., their social status, class position, economic fortune, intelligence, appearance, or the like) but knowing general facts about human society (such as political, economic, sociological, and psychological theory) would

FIGURE 8.1
Three Spheres
of Justice

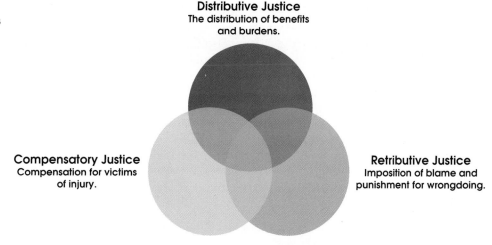

Distributive Justice
The distribution of benefits
and burdens.

Compensatory Justice
Compensation for victims
of injury.

Retributive Justice
Imposition of blame and
punishment for wrongdoing.

distributive justice
The benefits and burdens of company life should be distributed using impartial criteria.

retributive justice
Punishment should be evenhanded and proportionate to transgressions.

compensatory justice
Victims should receive fair compensation for damages.

utilitarian ethic
The greatest good for the greatest number.

deliberate and choose two rules to ensure fairness in any society they created. First, "each person is to have an equal right to the most extensive basic liberty compatible with a similar liberty for others," and second, "social and economic inequalities are to be arranged so that they are both (a) reasonably expected to be to everyone's advantage, and (b) attached to positions and offices open to all."[23] In general, inequality would only be allowed if it would make better the lot of the most disadvantaged members of the society.

The impartiality and equal treatment called for in Rawls's principles are resplendent in theory and may even inspire some business decisions, but they are best applied to an analysis of broad societal issues. Acting justly in daily business life, on the other hand, requires the application of maxims that more concretely define justice. Managers can find such guidelines in three basic spheres of justice, as shown in Figure 8.1.

Distributive justice requires that the benefits and burdens of company life be distributed using impartial criteria. Awarding pay raises based on friendship rather than performance criteria is unfair. All laws, rules, and procedures should apply equally to each employee. *Retributive justice* requires punishment to be evenhanded and proportionate to transgressions. A cashier should not be fired for stealing $5 if an executive who embezzled $10,000 is allowed to stay on the job and pay it back. And *compensatory justice* requires fair compensation to victims. A corporation that damages nearby property must restore it to its original state; one that hurts a customer must pay damages. The general idea of fairness in such maxims of justice supports orderly communities and organizations in which people secure human rights and meet human needs.

The Utilitarian Ethic

The utilitarian ethic was developed between the late eighteenth century and the mid-nineteenth century by a line of English philosophers, including Jeremy Bentham and John Stuart Mill. The principle of utility, on which this ethic is based,

[23] John Rawls, *A Theory of Justice* (Cambridge, MA: Harvard University Press, 1971), pp. 60–71.

Do Men and Women Reason Differently about Ethics?

Professor Lawrence J. Kohlberg of Harvard University became famous for research showing that from childhood on people pass through six stages of moral development.[24] These stages begin with utter selfishness and rise to the use of ethical principles. According to Kohlberg, not everyone gets to the highest, or principled-reasoning, stage—the moral development of most people is arrested at a middle stage.

To create and test his theory, Kohlberg measured changes over more than 20 years in the ethical thinking of 84 boys. Others who built on his work soon discovered that women, in particular, were unlikely to get to the higher stages. What was the reason? Were women less ethical than men? Professor Carol Gilligan, a colleague of Kohlberg's at Harvard, tried to answer these questions by studying the moral thinking of 144 men and women ranging in age from six to sixty.[25]

Gilligan learned that men and women approached ethical reasoning from different perspectives. The men in her studies grew to see themselves as autonomous, separate individuals in a competitive, hierarchical world of superior–subordinate relationships. As a result, male ethical thinking stressed protection of individual rights and enforcement of principled rules to channel and control aggression. The women, on the other hand, tended to see a world of relationships rather than

individuals, a world in which people were interconnected in webs rather than arrayed in dominance hierarchies. Women did not think using abstract rules and principles that set sharp boundaries on behavior; they focused on the importance of compassion, care, and responsibility in relations with others. They were not ethically stunted; they just thought differently than men.

Kohlberg built his stages on the way ethical reasoning developed in men. Gilligan's work, however, indicated the existence of an equally valid but different developmental process in women. Based on her research, a *care ethic* exists; that is, a person should have compassion for others, avoid hurt in relationships, alleviate suffering, and respect the dignity of others. The care ethic is violated in business by, for example, cruelty toward subordinates, exploitation of consumers, deceit in relationships, or focus on individual performance that is indifferent toward the welfare of co-workers.

If Gilligan is correct, men emphasize rules, individual rights, and duties that can be fixed impartially; women emphasize caring and accept an intuitive emotional instinct as a valid criterion for behavior. However, even if this marked contrast exists, it seems to disappear in business. Studies of managers, as opposed to studies of young adults and students, fail to show gender differences in ethical decision making.[26]

[24] See, for example, Lawrence Kohlberg, "The Cognitive-Development Approach to Moral Education," in Peter Scharf, ed., *Readings in Moral Education* (Minneapolis: Winston Press, 1978).

[25] Carol Gilligan, *In a Different Voice* (Cambridge, MA: Harvard University Press, 1982).

[26] See James Weber and David Wasieleski, "Investigating Influences on Managers' Moral Reasoning," *Business & Society*, March 2001; and Donald Robin and Laurie Babin, "Making Sense of the Research on Gender and Ethics in Business: A Critical Analysis and Extension," *Business Ethics Quarterly*, October 1997.

is that actions that promote happiness are right and actions that cause unhappiness are wrong. The utilitarians advocated choosing alternatives that led to the greatest sum of happiness or, as we express the thought today, the greatest good for the greatest number.

In making a decision using this principle, one must determine whether the harm in an action is outweighed by the good. If the action maximizes benefit, then it is the optimum choice over other alternatives that provide less benefit. Decision makers should try to maximize pleasure and reduce pain, not simply for themselves but for everyone affected by their decision. Utilitarianism facilitates the comparison of the ethical consequences of various alternatives in a decision. It is a popular principle. Cost-benefit studies embody its logic and its spirit.

The major problem with utilitarianism is that in practice it has led to self-interested reasoning. Its importance in rationalizing the social ills of capitalism can hardly be overestimated. Since the 1850s it has been used to argue that the overall benefits of manufacturing and commerce are greater than the social costs. Since the exact definition of the "greatest good" is subjective, its calculation has often been a matter of expediency. A related problem is that because decisions are to be made for the greatest good of all, utilitarian thinking has led to decisions that permit the abridgment of individual or minority group rights. Utilitarianism does not properly relate individual and community ends in a way that protects both.[27]

REASONING WITH PRINCIPLES

The use of ethical principles, as opposed to the intuitive use of ethical common sense, may improve reasoning, especially in complex situations. Say a bank teller pockets $20 at the end of the day. The person's supervisor strongly feels that stealing is wrong and fires the teller. Ethical common sense is all that is needed in this situation, but the following situation defies a simple solution.

> I was working as a manager in a division that was going to be closed. The secret clock was ticking away to the surprise mass layoff. Then a co-worker approached. He was thinking of buying a house. Did I think it was a good time to get into real estate?
>
> The man's job was doomed and I knew it. But spilling the secret, I believed, would violate my integrity as a corporate officer and doom the company to a firestorm of fear and rumor. There was no way to win and no way out.
>
> I considered it my fiduciary responsibility to the business to keep my mouth shut, and yet here was this person coming for advice as a friend and a business acquaintance and I had material information that would affect him. For someone with a sense of emphathy and sympathy, which I like to think I have some of, it was very, very hard.
>
> In the end I swallowed my anguish and kept silent. The man bought the house and lost his job. The secret held. But now 10 years later I have many times relived the story and second-guessed what I did that day.[28]

[27] See, for example, Mortimer Adler, *Desires: Right and Wrong* (New York: Macmillan, 1991), p. 61. John Stuart Mill's famous essay "Utilitarianism" deals directly and brilliantly with these and other criticisms. It is reprinted in Mary Warnock, ed., *Utilitarianism and Other Writings* (New York: New American Library, 1962), pp. 251–321.

[28] Paraphrased and quoted from Kirk Johnson, "In the Class of '70, Wounded Winners," *New York Times,* March 7, 1996, p. A12.

This is a vexing situation, and one created by the complexities of modern organizational life. The last paragraph finds the narrator alerted by the intuition ethic to the presence of an ethical conflict. Something in the situation causes anguish. In this predicament, however, simple moral homilies such as "tell the truth" or "be fair" are insufficient to resolve conflicts. Let us apply to this case three ethical principles, each of which offers a distinct perspective—utilitarianism, the rights ethic, and the theory of justice.

The *utilitarian* ethic requires the manager to calculate which course of action, among alternatives, will result in the greatest benefit for the company and all workers. A frank response here will disrupt operations. People would resign, take days off, work less efficiently, and engage in sabotage. Keeping the secret will cause hardship for a single employee about to buy a house and perhaps others in a similar situation. On balance, the manager must protect the broader welfare of customers, stockholders, and remaining employees.

From the standpoint of *rights,* the employee is entitled to the truth and the manager has a duty to speak honestly. On the other hand, rights are not absolute. The corporation has the competing right to protect its property, and this right must be balanced against the right of an employee to straight talk. In addition, the manager, in effect, promised to keep the layoff confidential and has a duty of promise keeping.

In *justice,* corporations are required to promote fair, evenhanded treatment of employees. Distributive justice demands the impartial distribution of benefits and burdens. It would be partial to signal the layoff to one worker and not others.

Based on the application of utility, rights, and justice, the manager's decision to remain silent is acceptable. Some judgment is required in balancing rights, but the combined weight of reasoning with all three principles supports the manager's decision. Yet the manager's intuition was not wrongly aroused. The situation required, by commission or omission, a lie, and it violated the practical imperative by treating the employee as expendable while achieving a corporate goal. So both good and evil result from the resolution of this situation. In such cases, application of the principle of double effect is apppropriate. Here the welfare of the company outweighs the welfare of one employee, the manager's intention is not to hurt the employee but to help the company, and no better alternative presents itself (it is possible that the manager could be wishy-washy and evasive; however, this raises suspicion in the employee and, in any case, avoids resolution of the ethical dilemma). So the principle of double effect reconfirms the manager's action.

CHARACTER DEVELOPMENT

virtue ethic
Ethical behavior stems from character virtues built up by habit.

Character development is a source of ethical behavior separate from the use of principled reasoning. The theory that character development is the wellspring of ethical behavior can be called the *virtue ethic*. It originated with the Greek philosophers. Aristotle wrote that moral virtue is the result of habit.[29] He believed that by their nature ethical decisions require choice, and we build

[29] *Nichomachean Ethics,* trans. Thomson, p. 91.

virtue, or ethical character, by habitually making the right choices. Just as we learn to play the piano through daily practice, so we acquire virtues by constant practice, and the more conscientious we are, the more accomplished we become. In a virtuous person ethical behavior comes from inner disposition, not from obeying external rules or applying abstract principles. Plato identified four fundamental traits—justice, temperance, courage, and wisdom—and these have come to be called the *cardinal virtues.* Numerous other virtues have been mentioned over the years, including prudence, reverence, charitableness, hopefulness, and integrity.[30]

cardinal virtues
The four most basic traits of an ethical character—justice, temperance, courage, and wisdom. They were identified by Aristotle.

Application of the virtue ethic requires conscious effort to develop a good disposition by making right decisions over time. Then acts are generated by inner traits ingrained from repetition and reflect the disposition of a virtuous character. When Sholom Menora, CEO of Tri-United Technologies, moved out of Chicago, he sent a check for $25 to the city, believing that over the years he had neglected to feed parking meters from time to time.[31] This act reveals a trait of obsessive integrity, not the application of an abstract, high-level ethical principle.

The idea of acting from virtue does not require rejection of the ethical principles explained earlier in the chapter. Virtuous individuals might be more sophisticated in their principled reasoning than less virtuous individuals.

PRACTICAL SUGGESTIONS FOR MAKING ETHICAL DECISIONS

There are practical steps to better define and resolve ethical problems in business. Here are some suggestions.

First, learn to think about ethics in rational terms using ideas such as universalizability, reversibility, utility, proportionality, or others. Such ideas enhance the ability to see ethical problems clearly and to create solutions.

Second, consider some simple decision-making tactics to illuminate alternatives. The philosopher Bertrand Russell advocated imaginary conversations with a hypothetical devil's advocate as an antidote for certitude. Write an essay in favor of a position and then a second opposed to it. Seek out a more experienced, ethically sensitive person in the company as an adviser. This person can be of great value in revealing the ethical climate of the firm or industry.

Use a two-column balance sheet to enter pros and cons for various alternatives, crossing out roughly equal considerations until a preponderance is left on one side or the other. Balance sheets organize information and discipline scattered, emotional thinking. Also, the process of entering all relevant factors sometimes brings new or unconscious considerations to light.

critical questions approach
A method of ethical reasoning in which insight comes from the answers to a preexisting, structured set of questions.

Another tactic is the *critical questions approach.* Ask yourself a series of questions about the ethical implications of an action. This approach is popular in corporations. If the questions are properly structured, answering them requires

[30] Dennis J. Moberg, "The Big Five and Organizational Virtue," *Business Ethics Quarterly,* April 1999, p. 246.
[31] "Chicago Businessman Does Right by Jewish Law," *Ha'aretz,* October 6, 2000.

employees to consider key policies, principles, and relationships. The Raytheon conduct manual, for example, sets forth a list of 24 critical questions to figure out "the right thing to do."[32] Here is a similar, but shorter, list used at Lockheed Martin.

Quick Quiz—When in Doubt, Ask Yourself

- Are my actions legal?
- Am I being fair and honest?
- Will my actions stand the test of time?
- How will I feel about myself afterward?
- How will it look in the newspaper?
- Will I sleep soundly tonight?
- What would I tell my child to do?
- How would I feel if my family, friends, and neighbors knew what I was doing?

If you are still not sure what to do, ask . . . and keep asking until you are certain you are doing the right thing.[33]

These critical questions are shorthand for a variety of approaches to ethical reasoning. Some invoke basic maxims such as "obey the law" and "tell the truth." Others summon up the disclosure ethic and the intuition ethic.

Third, sort out ethical priorities early. Serious ethical dilemmas can generate paralyzing stress. However, clear values reduce stress by reducing temptation and easing conscience as a source of anxiety. For example, when being honest means sacrificing a sale, it helps to clarify in advance that integrity is more important than money.

Fourth, be publicly committed on ethical issues. Examine the workplace and find sources of ethical conflict. Then tell co-workers about your opposition to padding expense accounts, stealing company supplies, price fixing, or other actions that might become issues. Colleagues will be disinclined to approach you with corrupt intentions, and public commitment forces you to maintain your standards or suffer shame.

Fifth, set an example. This is a basic managerial function. An ethical manager creates a morally uplifting workplace. An unethical manager can make money, but he or she (and the company) pay the price—and the price is the person's integrity. Employees who see unethical behavior by their supervisor always wonder when that behavior will be directed at them.

Sixth, thoughts must be translated into action, and ethical deeds often require courage. Reaching a judgment is easier than acting. Ethical stands sometimes provoke anger in others or cost a company business, and there are personal risks such as job loss.

---

[32] Raytheon Company, *Standards of Business Conduct: Guidelines for Action* (Concord, MA: Office of Business Ethics and Compliance, August 2001), p. 4.

[33] Lockheed Martin Corporation, *Setting the Standard: Code of Ethics and Business Conduct* (Bethesda, MD: Office of Ethics and Business Conduct, March 2003), p. 46.

Warning Signs

Lockheed Martin gives this list of phrases to all employees, telling them that when they hear one they are coming up on an ethical problem.

- "Well, maybe just this once."
- "No one will ever know."
- "It doesn't matter how it gets done as long as it gets done."
- "It sounds too good to be true."
- "Everyone does it."

- "Shred that document."
- "We can hide it."
- "No one will get hurt."
- "What's in it for me?"
- "This will destroy the competition."
- "We didn't have this conversation."

Source: Lockheed Martin, *Setting the Standard*, March 2003, p. 47.

Seventh, cultivate sympathy and charity toward others. The question "What is ethical?" is one on which well-intentioned people may differ. Marcus Aurelius wrote: "When thou art offended by any man's fault, forthwith turn to thyself and reflect in what like manner thou dost err thyself; for example, in thinking that money is a good thing, or pleasure, or a bit of reputation, and the like."[34] Reasonable managers differ with respect to such matters as the rightness of factory closings or genetic testing of workers.

Ethical perfection is illusory. We live in a morally complex civilization with endless rules, norms, obligations, and duties that are like road signs, usually pointing in the same direction but sometimes not. No decision ends conflicts, no principle penetrates unerringly to the Good, no manager achieves sainthood. There is an old story about the inauguration of James Canfield as president of Ohio State University. With him on the inaugural platform was Charles W. Eliot, president of Harvard University for 20 years. After receiving the mace of office, Canfield sat next to Eliot, who leaned over and whispered, "Now son, you are president, and your faculty will call you a liar." "Surely," said Canfield, "your faculty have not accused you of lying, Dr. Eliot." Replied Eliot, "Not only that, son, they've proved it!"

CONCLUDING OBSERVATIONS

There are many paths to ethical behavior. Not all managers appreciate the repertoire of principles and ideas that exist to resolve the ethical problems of business life. By studying ideas in this chapter, a person can become more sensitive to the presence of ethical issues and more resolute in correcting shortcomings. In addition, these principles and guidelines are applicable to ethical issues raised by the case studies throughout the book. We encourage referring to this chapter for conceptual tools.

[34] *The Meditations of Marcus Aurelius Antoninus,* trans. George Long (Danbury, CT: Grolier, 1980), p. 281; originally written circa A.D. 180.

Short Incidents for Ethical Reasoning

The following situations contain ethical conflicts. Try to define the ethical problems that exist. Then apply ideas, principles, and methods from the preceding two chapters to resolve them.

A CLOUDED PROMOTION

As chairman of an accounting firm in a large city, you were prepared to promote one of your vice chairmen to the position of managing partner. Your decision was based on a record of outstanding performance by this person over the eight years she has been with the firm. A new personnel director recently insisted on implementing a policy of résumé checks for hirees and current employees receiving promotions who had not been through such checks. Unfortunately, it was discovered that although the vice chairman claimed to have an MBA from the University of Michigan, she dropped out before completing her last 20 units of course work. Would you proceed with the promotion, retain the vice chairman but not promote her, or fire her?

THE ADMIRAL AND THE THIEVES

When Admiral Thomas Westfall took command of the Portsmouth Naval Shipyard, theft of supplies was endemic. It was a standing joke that homes in the area were painted gray with paint stolen from the Navy. Admiral Westfall issued an order that rules related to supply practices and forbidding theft would be strictly enforced. Within a few days, two career petty officers were appre-hended carrying a piece of Plexiglas worth $25 out of the base. Westfall immediately fired both of them and also a civilian storeroom clerk with 30 years' service, who lost both his job and his pension. According to Westfall, "the fact that I did it made a lot of honest citizens real quick." Did the admiral act ethically?

SAM, SALLY, AND HECTOR

Sam, Sally, and Hector have been laid off from middle-management positions. Sam and Hector are deeply upset by their misfortune. They are nervous, inarticulate, and docile at an exit meeting in the personnel department and accept the severance package offered by the company (two weeks' pay plus continuation of health benefits for two weeks) without questioning its provisions. Sally, on the other hand, manifests her anxiety about job loss by becoming angry. In the exit meeting, she complains about the inadequacy of the severance package, threatens a lawsuit, and tries to negotiate more compensation. She receives an extra week of pay that the others did not get. Has the company been fair in its treatment of these employees?

A PERSONALITY TEST

You are asked by a potential employer to take a psychological profile test. A sample segment includes the items shown in the table below.

Because you have read that it is best to fit into a "normal" range and pattern of behavior, and because it is your hunch that the personnel office will weed

	Yes	No	Can't Say
It is difficult to sleep at night.			
I worry about sexual matters.			
Sometimes my hands feel disjointed from my body.			
I sometimes smell strange odors.			
I enjoyed dancing classes in junior high school.			
Not all of my friends really like me.			
Work is often a source of stress.			

out unusual personalities, you try to guess which answers are most appropriate for a conservative or average response and write them in. Is this ethical?

AL

The CEO of a midwestern manufacturing company tells the following story.

> I was looking over recent performance reviews in the household products division and one thing that struck me was the review of a star sales rep named Al. I know Al because he handles our Wal-Mart account. Al had the highest annual sales for the past five years and last year nearly doubled the next highest rep's total. The sales manager's written evaluation was highly laudatory as expected, but cautioned Al to adhere strictly to discount policy, shipping protocol, and billing protocol. I got curious.
>
> A conversation with the division manager revealed that Al ingratiated himself with workers on the loading dock, socializing with them, sending them birthday cards, and giving them small gifts such as tickets to minor-league ball games. The loading dock supervisor complained that Al was requesting and sometimes getting priority loading of trucks for his customers despite the formal first-in, first-out rules for shipping orders. Second, Al had given several customers slightly deeper discounts than authorized, although the resulting orders were highly profitable for the company. And finally, late in December, Al had informally requested that one big account delay payment on an order by a week so that the commission would be counted in the next year. This would have gotten him off to a running start had not an accountant for the purchaser paid promptly and written to Al's manager in refusing the request.
>
> The division head stuck up for Al. I didn't press or request that any action be taken. Did I do the right thing?

How would you answer the CEO's question?

A TRIP TO SEA WORLD

A sales representative for a large manufacturer of consumer electronics equipment headquartered in Los Angeles, California, has courted a buyer from a nationwide chain of 319 retail stores for over a year. At company expense the buyer was flown to Los Angeles from Trenton, New Jersey, with his spouse, for a three-day sales presentation. The company is paying all expenses for this trip and for the couple to attend a Los Angeles Dodgers baseball game and dine at fine restaurants.

During the second day of meetings, the buyer discusses a one-year, $40 million order. The chain that the buyer represents has not sold the company's products before, but once it starts, reorders are likely. At dinner that evening, the buyer mentions that he and his wife have always wanted to visit Sea World in San Diego. While they are in southern California and so close, they would like to fly down. It is clear that he expects the company to pay for this trip and that he will delay making a commitment for the $40 million order until he gets a response.

The company has already spent $2,200 for the buyer's trip to Los Angeles. The San Diego excursion would cost about $500. The marketing manager estimates that the company can make a 9 percent gross profit on the sale. The sales representative stands to receive a .125 percent commission over base salary.

What should the sales representative do?

MARY AND TOM

Mary P., an aerospace engineer, tells about a difficult career experience in which her friend Tom plays a central role.

> My friend Tom and I are employed by Republic Systems Corporation. We started about the same time after graduating from engineering school five years ago. The company does a lot of defense work, mostly for the Air Force, and it's big. Tom and I worked on project teams doing tests to make sure that electonics shipped to customers met specifications. We have very similar backgrounds and job records, and there has always been a little competition between us. But neither one of us pulled ahead of the other on the corporate ladder. That is until last winter.
>
> At that time, we were assigned a special project to modify the testing protocol on certain radar components. The success of the projects was critical; it had to be done before Republic bid for two more years on its big radar systems contract. About 40 percent of our people work radar.
>
> We rolled up our sleeves and put in long hours. After a month, though, Tom volunteered to be on a companywide task force developing a new employee privacy policy. Privacy is a big deal to Al Manchester, our CEO.
>
> Tom continued to work with me, but he gradually put more and more of his energy into the privacy project. I had to start taking up some of the

slack. He enjoyed the task force meetings. They met in the dining room at the Kenthill Country Club and he could hobnob with Al and some of the other big shots. He worked overtime to impress them.

We finally finished the testing project and it was a success. But toward the end I did the lion's share of it. One day, Tom made me angry by ending a capacitor test at 94 hours instead of the 100 hours you really have to have for validity. He did it because he was late for a privacy task force meeting. Overall, I guess Tom helped a lot, but he didn't do his share all the way through.

Last month the assistant manager of the radar project left the company and Tom and I both applied for the position. It was a pay raise of several grades and meant getting a lot of recognition. They chose Tom. The announcement in the company newsletter said that he was a "strong team player" and mentioned both the testing project and the privacy task force as major accomplishments.

I don't think it was fair.

Was Tom fair to Mary? Was Tom's promotion fair to Mary? Was the company wrong to promote Tom?

THE HONDA AUCTION

Dave Conant co-owned and managed Norm Reeves Honda in Cerritos, California. Naturally, he worked closely with Honda marketing executives to get cars for his dealership. One day, one of these executives, Dennis Josleyn, the new zone sales manager, approached him, asking him to submit a bid on 64 company cars. These were near-new cars previously driven by corporate executives or used to train mechanics. Company policy called for periodic auctions in which Honda dealers submitted competitive bids, and the high bidder got the cars to sell on its lot. It was Josleyn's job to conduct the auction.

"I want you to submit bids on each car $2,000 below wholesale market value," Joselyn told Dave Conant.

Conant dutifully inspected the 64 cars and submitted the asked-for bids. Meanwhile, Josleyn busied himself creating fake auction papers showing that other Honda dealers bid less than Conant. Of course, others bid near the wholesale price, so their bids were higher. Completing the phony auction, Josleyn announced the winner—Conant's dealership. The next day he showed up there and handed Conant an envelope.

"I have a little invoice for you," he said.

Conant went to his office, opened it, and found a bill for $64,000 payable to an ad agency co-owned by

Josleyn and his brother. The message was clear. Josleyn wanted a 50–50 split with the dealer on the $2,000 windfall each car would bring, so he was billing Conant for half the extra $128,000 the entire batch of cars would bring in.

Conant faced a decision. If the invoice was paid, the dealership would make a $64,000 windfall. If he refused to pay, the cars would be rerouted to a dealer who was a "player" and future shipments of new Hondas might be slower. He decided to pay the invoice. In his own words: "I believed I had no choice. If I hadn't paid the amount, I would have incurred the wrath of Dennis Josleyn and possibly some of the other Honda gods, and I believe they would have taken our store down."[1]

Conant was not alone. Honda dealers around the country faced a dilemma. After investing large sums to build new showrooms and facilities and hire employees, they soon found themselves having to choose between two paths. If they gave bribes and kickbacks to Honda executives, they secured a copious flow of cars and made a fortune. On average, a favored dealer made almost $1,000,000 a year in personal income. However, if they stayed clean, no matter how modern their dealership and well trained its sales force, they received fewer cars and less profitable models. If they went bankrupt, and many did, the Honda executives arranged for less scrupulous owners to take over their dealerships. Many an honest dealer short on cars drove across town to see a rival's lot packed with fast-selling models in popular colors. Over time, it also became clear that the highest Japanese executives at Honda knew what was going on but chose to do nothing.

Did Conant make the right decision? What would you do in his position?

THE TOKYO BAY STEAMSHIP COMPANY

The Tokyo Bay Steamship Company operated a tourist ship between Tokyo and the volcanic island of Oshima 50 miles offshore. It also had a restaurant on the island. It was a modest business until February 1933, when Kiyoko Matsumoto, a 19-year-old college student, committed suicide by jumping into the crater of the volcano, which bubbled with molten

[1] Quoted in Steve Lynch, *Arrogance and Accords: The Inside Story of the Honda Scandal* (Dallas: Pecos Press, 1997), p. 106.

lava. Ms. Matsumoto left a poetic suicide note and, through newspaper stories, the Japanese public became obsessed with her story.

Soon other Japanese emulated Ms. Matsumoto. In the next 10 months, 143 people threw themselves into the crater. Many more came to watch. One Sunday in April, for example, 31 people tried to jump; 25 were restrained, but 6 succeeded. People crowded around the edge of the crater waiting for jumpers. Shouts of "Who's next?" and "Step right this way. Lots of room down in front" could be heard.[2]

The Tokyo Bay Steamship Company capitalized on the volcano's popularity. It increased its fleet to 30 ships and added 19 more restaurants. Meanwhile, the Oshima police chief met the boat and tried to weed out potential suicides using a crude behavioral profile (was someone too happy or too sad?). A police officer stood at the rim of the volcano. The Japanese government made purchase of a one-way ticket to Oshima a crime. Many suicides were prevented; others succeeded. Twenty-nine people who were stopped at the volcano killed themselves by jumping into the ocean on the return boat to Tokyo.

In the meantime, Tokyo Bay Steamship company prospered. Its shares rose on the Tokoyo exchange. But did it meet basic standards of ethics?

WOMEN AT IBM

In the spring of 1935 Thomas Watson, chairman of IBM, received a letter from Anne van Vechten, a 21-year-old college student at Bryn Mawr College who was friendly with his daughter. Watson agreed to meet her and discuss career opportunities in business. At the meeting she asked him why IBM did not hire women for professional careers.

Watson thought she had raised a good question. Soon van Vechten and 24 other young women were

[2] "Profits in Suicide," *Fortune*, May 1935, p. 116.

hired and enrolled for six weeks at the IBM school in Endicott, New York. This was a pleasant surprise to the 67 male sales and engineering candidates who arrived for the same training.

Watson was an intense autocrat who built IBM from a small calculating machine company, in part by creating a strong culture based on perfecting sales methods and absolute loyalty to the company. The six-week course would train these future IBM leaders in the IBM way. One way the culture was transmitted was through the songs employees sang. Watson composed many of them and hired a company band to play them. There was even one about women in the company.

"To Our IBM Girls"

(To the tune of "They're Style All the While")

They've made our IBM complete and worthwhile.
They work and they smile—so sweetly they smile.
Tall, short, thin, and stout girls—they win by a mile
With heavenly styles all the while.[3]

At the end of the six weeks, Watson threw a great dinner party for the students, where they mingled with IBM executives. Then, by tradition, the graduates went to IBM field offices where managers would assign them positions. But field managers refused to put the women in customarily male positions.

Watson had doted on these women. He was enraged and fired all 67 men in the class. If the men were not available, the field offices would have to accept the women or leave positions vacant. The men, many of whom had graduated from top colleges, were stunned at being thrown on the street while the nation was still in the grips of the Great Depression.

Did Watson make a good decision?

[3] From "Songs of the IBM," in Kevin Maney, *The Maverick and His Machine* (New York: John Wiley & Sons, 2003), p. 160. Copyright © 2003 John Wiley & Sons, Inc. This material is used by permission of John Wiley & Sons, Inc.

HCA—The Healthcare Company

Imagine injecting a shot of adrenaline into a lazy giant. This is what happened when one aggressive corporation brought business discipline to a health care system unaccustomed to the rigors of market competition. It ran hospitals for a profit—a big profit. Yet its success was also its undoing. As its star rose, jealous competitors, nervous regulators, and guardians of traditional values in medicine gave it a beating so severe that its management has grown timid and its methods lie dormant, awaiting resurrection.

HCA—The Healthcare Company is still the nation's largest hospital chain. It owns 191 hospitals and 79 outpatient centers. At its peak it owned 318 hospitals, but it remains a huge firm, taking in more annual revenues than companies such as Coca-Cola, Cisco Systems, and McDonald's.

RISING COSTS CHANGE AMERICA'S HEALTH CARE SYSTEM

The story is best begun by explaining long-term changes in the complex, chaotic network of entities and processes that is the U.S. health care system. The driving force behind these changes is rising costs. Health care in America is expensive. As a percentage of GDP it rose from 4.4 percent in 1950 to almost 15 percent in 2002, the highest of any nation.[1] Despite this expenditure, the system is characterized by tremendous inefficiency and poor service. And 44 million people who lack health insurance have only limited access to it.[2]

The origins of rising expenditures lie in the years after World War II when the federal government began to fund medical studies. This, along with research in companies, led to a steady stream of new machines, drugs, and treatments that increased the expense of medical intervention. As medical care began to cost more, demand for health insurance rose, and in the 1960s most Americans enrolled in health plans, most of which were paid for by employers. These plans usually allowed people unlimited access to doctors and hospitals if they met small annual deductibles and co-payments. Insurers paid claims one by one on a fee-for-service basis. Financial incentives to limit treatment costs that had existed when patients themselves paid vanished when insurance became widespread.

In 1965 the federal government set up Medicare to pay hospitalization and other expenses for people over 65 and, sharing expenses with the states, set up the Medicaid program to finance care for the poor. The two programs covered most people who were not in employer-sponsored plans. In effect, government gave every citizen access to medical treatment, and health care soon came to be seen as an entitlement. These government programs increased demand for medical services and, of course, expenditures climbed.

As costs rose, so did pressures to reduce them. By the early 1980s Medicare and Medicaid payments strained government budgets. Private employers and insurance companies complained loudly that paying for employee health care sapped productivity and held down wages. Hospital expenses were the primary reason; it was in hospitals that dazzling new machines and procedures escalated costs out of control.

MEDICARE CHANGES ITS BILLING PROCEDURE

To combat rising hospital costs, Medicare in 1983 changed its reimbursement method. Instead of paying one by one for each inpatient treatment and procedure, it now gave the hospital a lump sum based on one of 470 categories, or "codes," into which patients' illnesses were classified. The single payment that Medicare would make was based on the underlying costs of each hospital and the average severity of specific maladies. This coding system was intended to lower Medicare payouts by giving hospitals an incentive to cut the costs of treatment, and they did so.

When the 470 illness categories—or *diagnosis-related groups* (DRGs)—were introduced, the average length of hospitalizations shortened. There were cost savings in shortening patients' stays, but within two years Medicare payments began to creep up again. The incentive for hospitals was to spend less on patients and cut short their stays. However, shorter hospital stays led to a big rise in outpatient procedures and follow-up care, as many Medicare patients walked from hospital rooms to outpatient clinics for treatments.

The DRG system, which still functions, is terribly complex. The coding procedure is a labyrinth of rules covering more pages than the notoriously intricate Internal Revenue Code.[3] A small army of consultants exists to help hospitals digest it, and specialized software is used to ensure that Medicare is billed maximum rates. Despite their complexity, the rules

[1] "The Health of Nations: A Survey of Health-Care Finance," *The Economist,* July 17, 2004, p. 4.

[2] Michael E. Porter and Elizabeth Olmsted Teisberg, "Redefining Competition in Health Care," *Harvard Business Review,* June 2004, p. 65.

[3] Uwe E. Reinhardt, "Medicare Can Turn Anyone into a Crook," *The Wall Street Journal,* January 21, 2000, p. A18.

have never been clear and cannot be made so. This is because the diagnosis of an illness by a physician is somewhat subjective. Moreover, the maladies of patients and the treatments they need often defy standard definitions. So no set of codes can ever neatly classify all illnesses and the range of their severities.

This shortcoming leads to a cat and mouse game between hospitals and the federal government in which hospitals routinely engage in *upcoding,* or interpreting the illnesses of patients in such a way that they fall into higher-paying DRG codes. Upcoding is so common in the industry that for most of the 1980s and 1990s Medicare payments were adjusted downward in anticipation of inflated billings from hospitals. During this time, Medicare covered less than 90 percent of hospital costs, so hospitals made up the difference by raising charges to private patients.[4]

THE RISE OF MANAGED CARE

While the government struggled to hold down Medicare payments with its complicated billing code, insurance companies and employers tried to hold down their costs by implementing a philosophy of health care delivery that has come to be called *managed care.* Managed care reduces nonessential and marginally beneficial medical treatment by limiting reimbursement for it, causing it to be rationed.

Although managed care takes many forms, the primary form is the *health management organization,* or HMO. An HMO is an organization that includes an insurer and a network of physicians, hospitals, and services such as labs. Corporations enter contracts with HMOs under which they pay a fixed monthly or annual fee per employee in return for a full range of medical care. To compete for the business of employers, HMOs must control their costs, and they do so by limiting access to expensive specialists and treatments. The idea of managed care swiftly carried the day. As recently as the late 1980s, about 70 percent of insured employees were in older fee-for-service plans, but by the late 1990s, almost 85 percent of them were in some kind of managed care plan.[5]

The rise of managed care and the imposition of DRGs by Medicare made cost-cutting the hammer

of change. Both physicians and hospitals had to slash fees and discount services. This led to striking alterations in the medical industry. Physicians who had been solo practitioners were forced into HMOs to maintain full waiting rooms. Their traditional authority and the sanctity of the doctor–patient relationship were circumscribed in managed care where treatment decisions could be second-guessed by insurance bureaucrats who approved payments. Merger waves swept through all parts of the system, including insurers, managed care organizations such as HMOs, and hospitals. These mergers were attempts to lower per-unit costs by achieving economies of scale and to get power over pricing by controlling a larger share of the market.

Both the profit and the not-for-profit entities that provide health care feel competitive forces, and both are forced to respond. Even tax-exempt hospitals must reduce their costs or risk catastrophic loss of the paying patients who subsidize their charitable work. These competitive forces in the health care industry led to the predatory incarnation of HCA known as Columbia/HCA Healthcare Corporation, a name the company recently shed in the hope of restoring its reputation with the public.

THE RISE OF A PREDATOR

Columbia/HCA was the inspiration of a brilliant and hardworking entrepreneur named Richard L. Scott. In 1977 Scott graduated from law school and joined a Dallas law firm, where he worked on acquisitions and public offerings for health care corporations. After 10 years of this, Scott, who was no shrinking violet, decided that he wanted to run his own company. He soon startled the industry by lining up financing and offering $3.9 billion to buy Hospital Corporation of America, then the nation's largest hospital corporation. Its directors laughed at Scott. Here was a suitor, a relative unknown, whose only direct business experience was working at a donut shop in college, stepping up to take charge of a huge, complex company. Scott's bid failed.

Then, late in 1987 a Texas investor agreed to back Scott in starting a new hospital company. At the time, the hospital industry was ailing. Because of the introduction of DRGs by Medicare and the rise of managed care, both the number and length of hospital stays had declined. There was an oversupply of hospital beds. Many facilities could not cover costs and faced bankruptcy. Scott, however,

[4] Holman W. Jenkins, Jr., "A Hospital Chain's Lemonade Man," *The Wall Street Journal,* May 24, 2000, p. A27.

[5] Brian O'Reilly, "What Really Goes on in Your Doctor's Office?" *Fortune,* August 17, 1998, p. 166; and Mindy Charski, "A Healthy Trend Ends," *U.S. News & World Report,* September 28, 1998, p. 60.

had a penetrating vision of the industry in which he saw opportunity, not stagnation, and he got off to a running start. Setting up a Dallas office for the new company he named Columbia Hospital Corporation, he wrote 1,000 letters to hospitals around the country offering to buy them. Mostly, the answer was no, but eventually he bought two weak-performing El Paso hospitals.

With the two hospitals in hand, Scott began to inject the strategies that he would use to revolutionize the industry. First, he gave local physicians part ownership of the hospitals. Physicians are the source of patients for a hospital: no patient can be admitted without a doctor's signature. When physicians have an equity interest in a local hospital, they have a financial incentive to refer patients there. Second, he consolidated the El Paso market by buying a third hospital nearby and closing it. This reduced the number of beds available, raising demand for the remaining beds in Scott's hospitals. And third, he used the hospitals he owned as hubs to which he began attaching other health services, including a psychiatric hospital, diagnostic centers, and a cancer-treatment center. He planned to make money referring insured persons back and forth within a network of services owned by Columbia.[6]

Scott soon bought more hospitals. The pickings grew easier, because across the country, independent hospitals were floundering under the twin strains of an oversupply of beds and capped payments from insurers and Medicare. Scott promised the owners and trustees of stand-alone hospitals that he would take their struggling facilities and make them efficient cogs in his Columbia system.

While Scott rapidly bought individual hospitals, Columbia also expanded by acquiring other chains. In 1990 Columbia went public, and its successful offering and rising share price gave Scott more capital with which to finance acquisitions. Between 1990 and 1994 Columbia absorbed five competing hospital chains, bringing in 199 more hospitals and 96 surgical centers.[7] One of the chains was Hospital Corporation of America (HCA), whose directors had laughed off Scott's offer only three years before. After the HCA merger in 1994, the company's name became Columbia/HCA.

HOW COLUMBIA/HCA WORKED

As Scott took over hospitals, he wrung money from them by applying a hard-nosed business discipline exceeding anything ever seen in hospital management. He was a genius at coaxing efficiencies from a corporate system. Some of his methods were praiseworthy; others danced near ethical boundaries; all of them gamed the incentives in the industry environment to maximum advantage.

Because of Columbia/HCA's size and strong balance sheet, when it took over a hospital, it refinanced the facility's debt with cheaper capital. With the savings on debt service that this created, the corporation made the hospital more attractive by making cosmetic appearance changes, modernizing equipment, and installing a sophisticated information system. Rigorous cost cutting then took place.

Since the hospital was now in the large Columbia/HCA system, it could take advantage of the discounts and just-in-time deliveries that Scott demanded from suppliers. Columbia/HCA became the world's largest buyer of medical supplies, and Scott was an expert at squeezing vendors. Often, however, the staff had to use lower-quality items that cost less. At Good Samaritan Hospitals in Santa Clara County, California, nurses complained that the gloves the company bought were weaker and more likely to tear than those they had used previously and that the valves for chest tubes lacked open/shut indicators.[8]

Staff cuts also trimmed costs, and after Columbia/HCA takeovers there were fewer nurses and administrators and more part-time workers. This sometimes led to deteriorating patient care. At Columbia Sunrise Hospital in Las Vegas, the ratio of staff to patients fell 20 percent.[9] Nurses in critical-care units reported that it took more than six hours to get the results of urgent blood tests that should have been reported in minutes. In a poll of workers at the hospital, 44 percent believed that staffing cuts had increased medication errors and 4 percent attributed one or more patient deaths to understaffing.[10]

[6] Sandy Lutz and E. Preston Gee, *Columbia/HCA—Healthcare on Overdrive* (New York: McGraw-Hill, 1998) pp. 70–73.

[7] Robert Kuttner, "Columbia/HCA and the Resurgence of the For-Profit Hospital Business," *New England Journal of Medicine*, August 1, 1996, p. 362.

[8] Ibid.

[9] David R. Olmos, "Do Profits Come First at Vegas Hospital?" *Los Angeles Times*, September 26, 1997, p. A1.

[10] Diane Sosne, "The Truth about Hospitals That Exist to Make Money," *Seattle Times*, July 11, 1997, p. B5.

Scott moved in his own managers and pushed them to perform. Hospital administrators were focused on quarterly earnings and given ambitious targets, typically revenue growth of 15 percent to 40 percent per year. He used a system of "scorecards" that showed the performance of each hospital in multiple areas. For example, part of each scorecard had a "case-mix index" to track the relative proportion of patients with illnesses that were highly reimbursed under Medicare's coding system. Administrators were supposed to raise the index number.[11] Much of a hospital manager's pay was based on a salary bonus plan, and 90 percent of the bonus came from meeting short-term financial goals. In the mid-1990s a typical hospital manager had an annual salary of $150,000 but could earn up to $1 million with bonus and stock options.[12] This far exceeded the compensation of managers in not-for-profit hospitals.

The Columbia/HCA system included unsparing discipline—managers who missed their targets were abruptly replaced. Some hospitals had three or four new heads in a year. Many managers resigned when the pressure became too much or when they felt they were compromising their values. One chief administrator who left a Florida hospital had been asked to put a sign in the emergency room saying that patients' green cards would be inspected. Under federal law, no patient can be released from an emergency room until his or her condition is stabilized and so anyone who comes in must be seen. The sign was an effort to scare away to some competing hospital illegal immigrants with no health insurance or ability to pay.[13]

Columbia/HCA tried to increase revenues as well as cut costs. One way was by creating incentives for doctors. Giving them equity in the hospitals was a central tactic, and many Columbia/HCA hospitals were 15 to 20 percent physician-owned. A *New York Times* investigation examined referral patterns of 62 physicians in two Columbia/HCA hospitals in Florida and found that after investing in these facilities, the doctors as a group referred more patients to them

and fewer to competitors.[14] Sometimes Columbia/HCA also owned the physicians' practices. During its expansion, it purchased 1,400 practices and provider networks to funnel in patients. There were other incentives. On slow weekends at Sunrise Medical Center in Las Vegas, doctors who admitted the most patients won Caribbean cruises.[15]

Another method of raising revenues was aggressive Medicare billing. As it grew, Columbia/HCA got more than 30 percent of its revenues from Medicare and became Medicare's largest single claimant. A team of *New York Times* investigative reporters studied the results of zealous billing at Cedars Medical Center in Miami.[16] Because Medicare pays a fixed amount for any patient in a given disease category, a hospital gets more if patients are coded in high-reimbursement categories. For example, in DRG 79, which is the code for upper respiratory treatments, there are four categories of pneumonia. The highest-paid category is complex respiratory infection, for which Cedars would be reimbursed $6,800 per case. The lowest-paid category is simple pneumonia, which was reimbursed at $3,150 per case.

Studying records, the *Times* reporters learned that before being taken over by Columbia in 1992, Cedars billed 31 percent of pneumonia cases as complex respiratory infections. After the takeover, complex respiratory infections rose to 93 percent of cases. Meanwhile, a county hospital across the street billed only 28 percent of its cases as complex respiratory infection. Years later, when the company was accused of illegally upcoding, or increasing payments by billing in higher categories than justified, it would argue that the billing at Cedars and other hospitals was not fraudulent; it simply reflected greater mastery of Medicare's complex coding rules than competitors could develop.

Scott introduced bold marketing. Unique to the industry was a sales force that prospected for new business. He also started a national branding campaign with television and print ads designed to fix the Columbia/HCA name and logo in the public

[11] Lucette Lagnado, "Blowing the Whistle on Columbia/HCA: An Interview with Marc Gardner," *Multinational Monitor,* April 1998, p. 18.

[12] Michele Bitoun Blecher, "Rough Crossings," *Hospitals & Health Networks,* October 5, 1997, p. 40.

[13] Ibid.

[14] Martin Gottlieb and Kurt Eichenwald, "High Stakes Investments: Health-Care Giant Offers Its Doctors a Share of Hospitals," *Sun-Sentinel,* April 13, 1997, p. 1G.

[15] Olmos, "Do Profits Come First at Vegas Hospital?" p. 1G.

[16] Martin Gottlieb, Kurt Eichenwald, and Josh Barbanel, "Health Care's Giant: Powerhouse under Scrutiny," *New York Times,* March 28, 1997, p. A1.

mind so that when Americans needed a hospital they would seek out Columbia/HCA, just as when they wanted a hamburger, they looked for a McDonald's restaurant.

RESISTANCE AND CRISIS

As time went by, Scott's strategies became widely known and discussed. His methods abraded idealistic social values, built up over many generations, in which slighting treatment to save money is wrong. Competitors spoke against him. Labor unions resented his staff cutbacks and worked to undermine him. Soon resistance to new hospital acquisitions grew. In 1995 alone, Columbia/HCA had to back out of 30 pending deals when state regulators and civic groups that Scott's opponents had lobbied rose in opposition.

Nevertheless, the company prospered. Its growth showed in the rise of annual revenues from $4.9 billion in 1990 to $20 billion in 1996. Over this time, net profits averaged 7 percent a year, an excellent return that was 15 to 20 percent higher than at competing chains. By then, Columbia/HCA was not only the largest hospital chain in the country but the largest home care operation as well, with 590 facilities in 30 states. Home care was critical in Scott's strategy to develop a continuum of services. One attraction of it was that Medicare payments for home care were more generous than were payments for hospital stays. However, when Scott required hospital administrators to capture for Columbia/HCA facilities 85 percent of discharged patients needing home care, it angered Medicare bureaucrats, who had set a figure of 62 percent referrals as the maximum permitted.[17]

While Columbia/HCA grew, Scott became wealthy. He held 9.4 million shares and by 1996 had an annual salary exceeding $2 million. At this high point, however, the fall was near.

Entering 1997 Scott drove hard. He rose in the morning for 5:00 A.M. workouts and 6:00 A.M. strategy sessions. He worked frenetically and pushed those around him to do the same. Initiatives, policies, and directives spewed from him rapid-fire. Colleagues were fatigued by both his demands and the company's skyrocketing growth.

Then in March, federal authorities began a sweeping investigation into Medicare billing fraud at Columbia/HCA. Agents raided its hospitals in El Paso and removed billing documents. A federal grand jury in Florida indicted three executives for submitting false cost reports and claims. Soon federal agents served search warrants at 35 other facilities and issued subpoenas for all kinds of billing records.

These investigations punctured Columbia/HCA's stock price, stiffened resistance to acquisitions, foreshadowed friction with regulators, and threatened crippling fines. Yet Scott seemed unaware of the danger. On the day the FBI raided 35 facilities and the company's shares tumbled 12 percent, he appeared on CNN and assured listeners that "government investigations are matter-of-fact in health care."[18]

A media obsession grew. Investigative reports ran in newspapers and on television news programs, overwhelmingly built on horror stories about the effects of money incentives in Columbia/HCA hospitals. The company was strangely silent. Scott refused to respond; indeed, he seemed not to sense a crisis, but members of the Columbia/HCA board of directors did. In late July they summoned him to a meeting and forced his resignation. He got a $10 million severance package.

A NEW COURSE IN A SEA OF TROUBLES

Another board member, Thomas Frist, Jr., was picked to succeed Scott. Frist quickly backed away from Scott's more aggressive strategies. He ended annual bonuses for hospital administrators, undid the equity relationships of physicians in hospitals, sold the home health care business, stopped the national branding campaign, changed billing procedures, and increased audits and compliance reports on Medicare billings. He also created the post of senior vice president of corporate ethics, compliance, and corporate responsibility. Soon a new, warm "Mission and Values" statement was adopted (see the box). And eventually, he changed the firm's name. The new name, HCA—The Healthcare Company, dropped the word Columbia, disowning Scott's legacy.

---

[17] Lucette Lagnado, Anita Sharpe, and Greg Jaffe, "How Columbia/HCA Changed Health Care, for Better or Worse," *The Wall Street Journal*, August 1, 1997, p. A4.

[18] Lutz and Gee, *Columbia/HCA—Healthcare on Overdrive*, p. 135.

HCA—The Healthcare Company Mission & Vision

Above all else, we are committed to the care and improvement of human life.

In recognition of this commitment, we will strive to deliver high quality, cost-effective healthcare in the communities we serve.

In pursuit of our mission, we believe the following value statements are essential and timeless.

We recognize and affirm the unique and intrinsic worth of each individual.

We treat all those we serve with compassion and kindness.

We act with absolute honesty, integrity and fairness in the way we conduct our business and the way we live our lives.

We trust our colleagues as valuable members of our healthcare team and pledge to treat one another with loyalty, respect, and dignity.

Source: www.hcahealthcare.com

Downdrafts from the investigations hit hard. Patients were frightened away. With Frist's approval, 40 hospitals dropped Columbia/HCA from their names. Revenues and net income fell (see Exhibit 1). Share prices dived from a high of $45 in 1997 to a low of $17 in 1998. Acquisitions were typically financed with stock, but with share prices falling, the pending acquisition of another health care company was canceled. Hospital takeovers were shelved and construction of new hospitals stopped. Over the next several years, Frist sold more than 100 hospitals.

The assault by government was relentless. The Internal Revenue Service assessed $267 million in back taxes for wrongful deductions the company had made. Whistle-blowers emerged from within and filed lawsuits under the False Claims Act, which allows workers to bring fraud charges against employers on behalf of the U.S. government and receive part of any monetary settlements. In 2000, HCA pled guilty to criminal charges and agreed to pay $840 million in criminal fines, civil restitution, and other penalties to settle Medicare fraud charges. It agreed to $745 million in civil penalties while not admitting wrongdoing. In addition, it accepted a $95 million

criminal fine, pleading guilty to fraudulent pneumonia upcoding, false billing, and giving kickbacks to physicians for referring patients.[19] In 2003 the whistle-blower lawsuits were settled when HCA agreed to another $631 million in civil penalties and damages. Nine former employees received a total of $152 million as their share. In addition, the company paid a $250 million settlement to Medicare and Medicaid. Overall, it handed over more than $1.7 billion.[20]

These huge sums seemed to signal that HCA's management and culture were rife with fraud. Would executives go to jail? Remarkably, the government indicted only five mid-level managers on charges of criminal fraud. Of these, only two were convicted and their convictions were overturned in a unanimous U.S. appeals court ruling. The court found the Medicare

[19] "HCA—The Health Care Company & Subsidiaries to Pay $840 Million in Criminal Fines and Civil Damages and Penalties," U.S. Department of Justice press release, December 14, 2000.

[20] "Largest Health Care Fraud Case in U.S. History Settled: HCA Investigation Nets Record Total of $1.7 Billion," U.S. Department of Justice press release, June 26, 2003.

EXHIBIT 1 HCA Inc. Ten-Year Trend in Revenues and Net Profit
Revenues went into decline following charges of Medicare fraud in 1997.
Growth resumed in 2000.

Source: *Value Line,* 2004. Figures for 2004 are estimates.

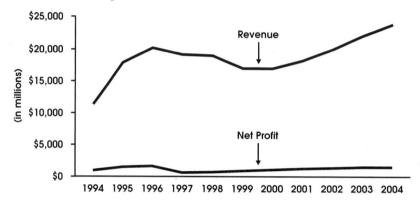

rules so unclear that the way the two managers had interpreted them seemed as reasonable as the way the government prosecutors did.[21] The dearth of successful prosecutions suggests that the government cannot find strong evidence of criminal intent.

The slow torture by investigation and prosecution of HCA petrified the health care industry. Companies pulled back from aggressive Medicare code interpretation. The sight of HCA twisting in the wind, in the words of one observer, "scared them into underbilling."[22] Instead of upcoding, the industry lobbied for higher payments, and in 2000 Congress responded by raising reimbursements in the DRG codes.[23] Whereas in the past Congress had squeezed payments in anticipation of upcoding, it now made them more generous to compensate for the wave of timidity sweeping industry billing practice.

As part of its 2000 criminal plea, HCA signed an agreement requiring it to set up an ethics and compliance program to be overseen by the Department of Justice until 2009.[24] The program includes training for all employees, a network of compliance managers throughout the company, hotlines, and ethical audits. Among other changes, HCA now requires employees in its billing offices to submit questions about coding to physicians on a written form. The forms are closely audited.

WHITHER CORPORATE HEALTH CARE?

Rick Scott's vision of corporate-delivered health care lies tattered. His company goes on, rendered submissive by government. The industry abides faintheartedly. Were Scott's strategies inherently bad ones for health care delivery, or were they appropriate but simply mismanaged?

Scott applied market solutions to intractable problems that had been growing in the health care system for half a century.[25] The central problem is that health care costs are rising prohibitively. Scott imposed the for-profit corporate form on health care delivery and worked it to every advantage, ruthlessly seeking cost savings and efficiencies wherever they could be found. Often the formula succeeded, elevating hospital performance to the advantage of a range of stakeholders beyond investors. For example, when the company took over Cape Fear Memorial Hospital in

[21] *United States v. Robert W. Whiteside and Jay A. Jarrell,* 285 F.3d 1352.

[22] Barbara Kirchheimer, "HCA Has Point to Prove," *Modern Healthcare,* December 18–25, 2000, p. 14.

[23] J. D. Kleinke, *Oxymorons: The Myth of a U.S. Health Care System* (San Francisco: Jossey-Bass, 2001), p. 19.

[24] Neil Weinberg, "Healing Thyself," *Forbes,* March 17, 2003, p. 66.

[25] J. D. Kleinke, "Deconstructing the Columbia/HCA Investigation," *Health Affairs,* March–April 1998.

Wilmington, North Carolina, in 1995, it made $1 million in improvements. A year later, admissions were up 6 percent, babies delivered up 40 percent, unpaid care to charity patients up 12 percent, and staffing up almost 25 percent.[26] Moreover, other hospitals in the area were forced to discipline their costs or Columbia/HCA would have underbid them for the business of local employers. This dampened medical cost inflation. Story lines such as this were less newsworthy than claims that Columbia/HCA was killing patients with its miserly ways, so the public mostly heard and read about scandal, not achievement.

Nurses' unions that stood to lose members in staff cuts opposed Scott. Federal and state regulators who stood to lose power if free market forces grew stronger opposed him. Many in the public opposed him, wanting to believe that unlimited, universal health care delivered by physicians in the mold of the old-fashioned, avuncular TV doctor Marcus Welby was a realistic, affordable option. And critics with traditional values opposed him, suspicious of business methods in the vicinity of life and death decisions. Not the least among these was Pope John Paul II, who, after the El Paso raids, issued a statement saying that "the centrality and dignity of the human person are ignored and trampled on . . . when healthcare is regarded in terms of profit and not as a generous service."[27]

The result of the HCA investigations has been to push corporate methods into the background. However, the market forces they thrive on remain. Costs keep rising. Payers resist price inflation. Government still distorts health care markets by setting prices for nearly $400 billion of health care each year, more than one-third of the total, supporting its invasion with a thicket of rules forming perhaps the single most confusing body of regulation existing in any nation. Scott fearlessly dove into the regulatory thickets and made himself at home in gray areas of the law. Although companies fear exploiting these ambiguities, they continue to exist. In any case, if these industry forces continue in health care markets, and they will, aggressive strategies based on efficiency at some point must again emerge. The alternatives are limited, but they include allowing the cost trajectory free upward movement until taxpayer revolt occurs and further restriction of access to health care beyond the 44 million Americans now uninsured—or both.

Questions

1. Is a market-driven approach valid for the health care industry? Do you support or oppose trade-offs between care quality and efficiency?

2. Is health care a basic right? Can it be limited if the cost of providing unlimited treatment is prohibitive? If so, should it be regarded as a commodity and limited by market mechanisms, or should it be rationed by government regulation? If not, how can the nation pay for it?

3. How should the strategies behind HCA's rise to prominence be assessed? Were they fundamentally flawed, ethically wrong, and unworkable? Or were they appropriate and workable in the industry environment but badly carried out?

4. On balance, did HCA use health care resources more efficiently than competitors, or did it compromise care by shifting costs to patients and staff and moving the savings to executive salaries, dividends, and acquisitions?

5. HCA experienced terrible difficulties. Could they have been prevented? If you could go back in time, replace Rick Scott, and run the company, at what point would you choose to arrive and what changes would you make to salvage the good and prevent the bad?

---

[26] Blecher, "Rough Crossings," p. 40.

[27] "News at Deadline," *Modern Healthcare*, July 7, 1997, p. 4.

Chapter **Nine**

Business in Politics

Public Law 108-357

On June 4, 2004, Rep. William M. Thomas (R-Calif.), chairman of the powerful House Ways and Means Committee through which tax legislation must pass, introduced a bill in the House of Representatives. So far in 2004 there had been 4,519 bills, so the Clerk of the House designated it H.R. 4520. Its working title was "To amend the Internal Revenue Code of 1986 to remove impediments in such Code and make our manufacturing, service, and high-technology businesses and workers more competitive and productive both at home and abroad."

The story behind H.R. 4520 begins in 1986, when Congress reduced the tax on products made in the United States for export by 8 percent. With lower taxes, American firms sold goods at lower prices and became stronger competitors in foreign markets. It worked so well that the European Union complained to the World Trade Organization (WTO), arguing that the tax break was, in effect, an illegal government subsidy. In early 2000 the WTO agreed, ruling that it violated international trade law.

Congress modified the tax rules, but again the European Union complained and in 2002 the WTO decided that the modification was also illegal. It would need to be eliminated. However, corporations were reluctant to see it go. About 1,800 American multinationals saved an estimated $5 billion a year in taxes. Lobbyists for the companies worked for new changes in the tax code, but while ideas fermented, the export tax reduction lingered.

When Congress failed to act quickly, the WTO allowed the European Union to impose punitive tariffs of $4 billion a year on American goods. In early 2004 the EU set a 5 percent tariff on U.S. steel, textiles, paper items, jewelry, and hundreds of other products. The tariff would automatically increase 1 percent a month until a 17 percent ceiling was reached. It was high enough to hurt, and congressional action became inevitable. It began when Rep. Thomas introduced H.R. 4520.

H.R. 4520 started as a straightforward measure to reform the tax code by eliminating the export tax break. As it went through the House and Senate it grew into a 633-page pile of tax breaks for scores of companies and industries. Lobbyists and legislators knew that, unlike most bills, this one would survive the congressional gauntlet to become law. They sought to amend it repeatedly, adding special provisions for their clients and home districts.

As passed by Congress on October 8, 2004, the bill ended the export tax break. It compensated by reducing the maximum tax rate for domestic manufacturers from 35 percent to 32 percent. Over the next decade, this reduction will save corporations

$25 billion more than they saved under the old subsidy regime. To spread the largesse, Congress expanded the definition of manufacturing to include more industries. Now, farmers, architects, civil engineers, construction firms, electric utilities, natural gas transporters, newspapers, loggers, roofers, and film companies qualify for lower taxes as manufacturers.

Another provision was a windfall for multinational corporations. For one year the tax on profits earned abroad and returned to the United States dropped from 35 percent to 5.25 percent. Small businesses were helped too. The limit for writing off business expenses was raised from $25,000 to $100,000 a year. Even the public gets a break. Nine states with no individual income tax rely heavily on sales taxes for revenue. Residents of these states were allowed to deduct state and local sales taxes from their federal taxes for two years.

Beyond these broad tax cuts, the bill contained special favors for dozens of companies and industries. ExxonMobil, Conoco Phillips, and British Petroleum received a $150 million tax reduction for a pipeline property in Alaska. A reduced excise tax on fishing-tackle boxes benefitted Plano Molding Co. in Illinois, which dominates in that industry. Oldsmobile dealers, who received substantial payments from General Motors at the end of the car's run in 2004, got extra time to invest the money in new franchises, avoiding a capital gains tax. Barge shipping and railroad companies no longer had to pay a 4.3-cent-per-gallon tax on diesel fuel. The railroads could also use track maintenance costs as tax credits. Up to $10,000 of annual expenses for operating Alaskan whaling vessels was allowed as a charitable deduction. Companies that build grandstands for NASCAR races got lower taxes. Import duties on ceiling fans from China were suspended, to benefit retailers such as Home Depot. Several corporations in Houston were allowed to continue using Bermuda reincorporation as a tax shelter although another tax bill passed by Congress prohibited it.

Overall, the bill replaced what would have been a $50 billion tax subsidy for multinationals with a series of tax cuts worth $146 billion, not counting a $10 billion federal buyout of tobacco quotas for growers in the South. Most of the tax breaks in the bill are temporary and will expire by 2014. But in the past, corporate tax breaks have rarely lapsed. The bill attempted to offset lost Treasury revenue by closing a few tax loopholes, including the practice of small business owners' expensing sport utility vehicles weighing more than 6,000 pounds. Few think that these offsets will equal the lost revenues.

Predictably, the bill was criticized. Among the milder reactions was a comment in *The Wall Street Journal* calling it "a treasure trove of tax breaks."[1] In Europe, *The Economist* thought it a "legislative monstrosity."[2] Democrats in Congress attacked the Republican majority that pushed it through. "I want this bill to reach the floor as fast as possible," said Rep. Charles Rangel (D-New York), "because it stinks to high heaven in terms of what we came here to do and the fertilizer [Mr. Thomas] has put on this."[3]

---

[1] Shailagh Murray and David Wessel, "Corporate Tax Bill Passes Senate, Goes to President," *The Wall Street Journal,* October 12, 2004, p. A1.

[2] "Veto One for the Gipper; Fiscal Outrages in America," *The Economist,* June 19, 2004, p. 27.

[3] Jeffrey Sparshott, "House Debates Expert Measure," *The Washington Times,* June 15, 2004, p. C6.

On October 22, 2004, President George W. Bush signed the tax bill into law. By then it had an attractive new title, the "American Jobs Creation Act of 2004." There was one more stop. The bill went to the National Archives & Records Administration where it was assigned a law number. It received the unglamourous designation of Public Law 108-357.

The tax bill was a bonanza for corporations and their lobbyists. Following the networks of influence that shaped it would be impossible. Campaign contributions and lobbying by corporations, business groups, trade associations, and Washington, DC, advocacy firms all played a role. In the end, the tax bill furthered both the public interest and selfish special interests. In this chapter we explain how corporations, now and in the past, have exercised political influence. In the process, we illuminate the mechanisms that lie behind passage of such a "legislative monstrosity." As a beginning, knowing how the Constitution shapes American politics is important. That is where we start.

THE OPEN STRUCTURE OF AMERICAN GOVERNMENT

federal system
A government in which powers are divided between a central government and subdivision governments. In American government, the specific division of powers between the national and state governments is set forth in the Constitution.

Business seeks and exercises political power in a government that is extraordinarily open to influence. Its power is exercised on constitutional terrain created by the Founding Fathers more than 200 years ago. The Constitution of the United States, as elaborated by judicial interpretation since its adoption in 1789, establishes the formal structure and broad rules of political activity. Its provisions create a system predisposed to a certain pragmatic, freewheeling political culture in daily political life.

Several basic features of the Constitution shape American politics. Each stands as a barrier to the concentrated power that the Founders feared would lead to tyranny. Each has consequences for corporate political activity.

First, the Constitution sets up a *federal system,* or a government in which powers are divided between a national government and 50 state governments. This structure has great significance for business, particularly for large corporations with national operations. These corporations are affected by political actions at different levels and in many places.

supremacy clause
A clause in the Constitution, Article VI, Section 2, setting forth the principle that when the federal government passes a law within its powers, the states are bound by that law.

The *supremacy clause* in the Constitution stipulates that when the federal government passes a law within its powers, that law preempts, or takes precedence over, state laws on the same subject. For example, a state agency in California devised a strict exhaust standard for trucking fleets that diesel engines could not pass. Engine manufacturers sued and the Supreme Court struck down the standard because it exceeded emission standards in the federal Clean Air Act.[4]

The federal system has many implications for the regulation of business. Sometimes business prefers federal regulation. It has to follow one law instead of as many as 50 different state laws. In the 1960s, for instance, several states tried to pass laws requiring health-warning labels on cigarette packs. If states had been allowed one by one to require labels, the tobacco companies would have had to print specially worded cigarette packs for sale in each state. Therefore, they

---

[4] *Engine Manufacturers Association v. South Coast Air Quality Management District,* 124 S. Ct. 1756 (2004).

separation of powers
The constitutional arrangement that separates the legislative, executive, and judicial functions of the national government into three branches, giving each considerable independence and the power to check and balance the others.

judicial review
The power of judges to review legislative and executive actions and strike down laws that are unconstitutional or acts of officials that exceed their authority.

First Amendment
An amendment to the Constitution added in 1891 as part of the Bill of Rights. It protects the rights of free speech, a free press, freedom to assemble or form groups, and freedom to contact and lobby government.

supported a bill in Congress that, when passed, preempted that area of regulation and required a uniform warning label across the country. The insurance industry, on the other hand, fights federal regulation, preferring instead oversight by state insurance commissions. Insurance companies are big employers and heavy campaign contributors in many states. They tend to receive gentle treatment from these commissions and fight all efforts to pass national regulations.

Second, the Constitution establishes a system of *separation of powers*, under which the basic functions of government—legislative, executive, and judicial—are set up in three branches of the federal government. Each branch has considerable independence and has the power to check and balance the others. The states mimic these power-sharing arrangements in their governments. For business, it is significant that the actions of one branch do not fully define policy. For example, if Congress passes a law despite business opposition, corporations can lobby regulatory agencies in the executive branch to get favorable application of its provisions or they can go to the judicial branch to challenge its constitutionality.

Third, the Constitution provides for *judicial review* by giving judges the power to review legislative and executive actions and to strike down laws that are unconstitutional or acts of officials that exceed their authority. A classic example of judicial review came in the spring of 1952 when a steelworkers' strike threatened to stop steel production while hard-pressed U.S. troops in Korea were desperate for supplies and equipment. To support the war effort, President Harry Truman issued an order for the government to take control of and run the steel industry. Steel companies sued to stop him and the Supreme Court held that Truman had exceeded his constitutional powers.[5]

The government structure created by the Constitution is open. It diffuses power, creates multiple points of access, and invites business and other interests to attempt influence. Because no single, central authority exists, government action often requires widespread cooperation between levels and branches of government that share power. This characteristic also makes the system particularly vulnerable to blockage and delay. Because important actions require the combined authority of several elements of government, special interests can block action by getting a favorable decision at only one juncture. To get action, on the other hand, an interest such as business must successfully pressure many actors in the political equation. Thus, there has developed a style in the American system, in which interests are willing to bargain, compromise, and form temporary alliances to achieve their goals rather than stand firm on rigid ideological positions.

The *First Amendment* is an additional element of the Constitution critical to business. It protects the right of business to organize and press its agenda on government. In its elegantly archaic language is stated the right "to petition the Government for a redress of grievances." The First Amendment also protects

---

[5] *Youngstown Sheet & Tube Co. v. Sawyer,* 343 U.S. 579. The basis for the Court's ruling was that Congress had once considered giving presidents the power to seize industries in similar circumstances but had not done so.

rights of free speech, freedom of the press, and freedom of assembly—all critical for pressuring government. Without these guarantees, the letter-writing campaigns, speeches, editorials, and ads that business orchestrates could be suppressed. Imagine how different the system would be if the public, agitated by a corporate scandal, could pressure Congress to restrict the lobbying rights of some industry. While corporate speech is expansive, it is restricted in one area. The Supreme Court years ago defined monetary campaign contributions as a form of speech and allowed them to be limited because of fears that corporate money corrupts elections.[6]

A HISTORY OF POLITICAL DOMINANCE BY BUSINESS

Though not ordained in the Constitution, the preeminence of business in politics is an enduring fact in America. The Revolutionary War of 1775–1783 that created the nation was, according to some historians, fought to free colonial business interests from smothering British mercantile policies.[7] The Founders who drafted the Constitution were an economic elite. John Jay and Robert Morris, for example, were among the wealthiest men in the colonies. It comes as no surprise that the government they designed was conducive to domination by business interests. The noted historian Charles Beard argued that the Constitution was an "economic document" drawn up and ratified by propertied interests, for their own benefit.[8] His thesis is controversial, in part because it trivializes the importance of philosophical, social, and cultural forces in the politics of constitutional adoption.[9] Yet the record since adoption of the Constitution in 1789 is one of virtually unbroken business ascendancy.

Laying the Groundwork

Business interests were important in the new nation but did not dominate to the extent that they soon would. There were few large companies. The economy was 90 percent agricultural, so farmers and planters were a major part of the political elite. Their interests balanced and checked those of infant industry. The fledgling government was a tiny presence. Economic regulation was virtually nonexistent. Nevertheless, under the leadership of Secretary of the Treasury Alexander Hamilton the new government was soon turned toward the promotion of industry. With the support of business leaders, Hamilton pursued his visionary policies, laying the groundwork for the unexampled industrial growth that roared through the next century. As the young nation's economy expanded, so also did the political power of business.

---

[6] *Buckley v. Valeo,* 424 U.S. 1 (1976).

[7] See, for example, Clarence L. Ver Steeg, "The American Revolution Considered as an Economic Movement," *Huntington Library Quarterly,* August 1957.

[8] Charles Beard, *An Economic Interpretation of the Constitution of the United States* (New York: Macmillan, 1913).

[9] See, for example, Robert E. Brown, *Charles Beard and the Constitution* (Princeton: Princeton University Press, 1956); and Forrest McDonald, *We the People: The Economic Origins of the Constitution* (Chicago: University of Chicago Press, 1963).

Economic development was rapid. Although Jefferson served as president from 1800 to 1808, it was already too late to reverse Hamilton's probusiness policies. As the young nation's economy expanded, so also did the political power of business.

Ascendance, Corruption, and Reform

During the nineteenth century, commercial interests grew in strength. When the Civil War between 1860 and 1865 decimated the power base of southern agriculture, a major counterweight to the power of northern industry vanished. In the period following the war, big business dominated state governments and the federal government in a way never seen before or since. It was a time of great imbalance, in which economic interests faced only frail obstacles.

Companies commonly manipulated the politics of whole states. West Virginia and Kentucky were dominated by coal companies. New York, a number of midwestern states, and California were controlled by railroads. Montana politics was engineered by the Anaconda Copper Mining Company. In Ohio, Texas, and Pennsylvania, oil companies predominated; the great critic of Standard Oil, Henry Demarest Lloyd, wrote that "the Standard has done everything with the Pennsylvania legislature, except refine it."[10]

Business was also predominant in Washington, DC. Through ascendancy in the Republican party, corporations had decisive influence over the nomination and election of a string of probusiness Republican presidents from Ulysses S. Grant in 1868 to William McKinley in 1900.[11] In the Congress, senators were suborned by business money; some even openly represented companies and industries. One observer noted that in 1889,

> a United States senator . . . represented something more than a state, more even than a region. He represented principalities and powers in business. One senator, for instance, represented the Union Pacific Railway System, another the New York Central, still another the insurance interests of New York and New Jersey. . . . Coal and iron owned a coterie from the Middle and Eastern seaport states. Cotton had half a dozen senators. And so it went.[12]

Under these circumstances, corruption was rampant. Grant's first term, for example, was stained by the famous "whiskey ring" scandals in which liquor companies cheated on their taxes and a member of Grant's cabinet solicited bribes in exchange for licenses to sell liquor to Indian tribes. In Grant's second term, the Crédit Mobilier Company gave members of Congress shares of its stock to avoid investigation of its fraudulent railroad construction work.

The soaring political fortunes of business in the post–Civil War era invited reaction. A counterbalancing of corporate power began that continues to this day. Late in the century, farmers tried to reassert agrarian values through the Populist party. They foundered, but not before wresting control of several

---

[10] "The Story of a Great Monopoly," *The Atlantic,* March 1881, p. 322.

[11] The exception was the election of the Democrat and reformer Grover Cleveland in 1884. But even Cleveland had strong business supporters, Andrew Carnegie and James J. Hill among them. His administration never threatened business interests.

[12] William Allen White, *Masks in a Pageant* (New York: Macmillan, 1928), p. 79.

PUCK.

THE BOSSES OF THE SENATE.

Nineteenth century political cartoonist Joseph Keppler (1838–1894) was a critic of big business who particularly resented the ascendancy of moneyed interests in politics. This cartoon appeared in the magazine *Puck* on January 23, 1889. Source: © CORBIS.

state legislatures from corporations and forcing through legislation to control the railroads, the biggest companies of that day. More important, the populist movement was the beginning of a long-lived democratic reform tradition opposed to big business power.

Two other formidable business adversaries emerged. One was organized labor, which was destined to be the strongest single element opposing industry over the following century. The other was the powerful Anti-Saloon League, which advocated prohibition of alcohol. Like labor, the Anti-Saloon League became a strong national adversary of business. Brewers and distillers were not its only adversaries. Big corporations in many industries worked against prohibition because they opposed the principle and onset of more government regulation.

After 1900, reforms of the progressive movement curtailed overweening corporate power. For example, the Seventeenth Amendment in 1913 instituted the direct election of senators by voters in each state. Corporations fought the amendment. Before, state legislatures had chosen senators, a practice that invited corrupting influence by big companies. For example, in 1884 representatives of Standard Oil called members of the Ohio legislature one by one into a back room where $65,000 in bribes was handed out to obtain the election of Henry B. Payne to the Senate.

One witness saw "canvas bags and coin bags and cases for greenbacks littered and scattered around the room and on the table and on the floor . . . with something green sticking out."[13]

Big business also fought suffrage for women. The battle was led by liquor companies that feared women would vote for prohibition. However, there was broader fear of women voters. It was widely believed by businessmen that women would vote for radical and socialist measures. The powerful Women's Christian Temperance Union, which had as many as 10,000 local chapters by 1890, frightened business by standing against liquor, child labor, and income inequality. Yet after adoption of the Nineteenth Amendment in 1920 giving women the vote, no strong shifts in voting patterns appeared.

The great political reforms of the progressive era were reactions to corruption in a political system dominated by business. It would be a mistake, however, to conclude that because of reforms and newly emerged opponents, the primacy of economic interests had been eclipsed. While business was more often checked after the turn of the century, it remained preeminent. Corruption continued. In 1920 Warren G. Harding, a backroom candidate picked by powerful business interests at a deadlocked Republican nominating convention, was elected president. His vice president was Calvin Coolidge, the rabidly antilabor ex-governor of Massachusetts. Harding's administration was so beset by scandals in which officials accepted money for granting favors to corporations that Congress was considering impeaching him when he died of a stroke in 1923. The worst scandal involved Secretary of the Interior Albert B. Fall, who accepted bribes from oil company executives in return for the right to pump oil from government reserves in Teapot Dome, Wyoming. The Teapot Dome affair came to light only after Harding's death, but so besmirched his reputation that it was eight years before his grand tomb in Marion, Ohio, could be dedicated.

Business Falls Back under the New Deal

By the time Harding was officially laid to rest, the stock market had crashed and catastrophic economic depression racked the country. Conservative business executives argued that the depression would correct itself without government action. After the election of Franklin D. Roosevelt in 1932, corporations fought his efforts to regulate banking and industry, strengthen labor unions, and enact social security. Against social security, for example, business lobbyists argued that children would no longer support aging parents, that the required payroll tax would discourage workers and they would quit their jobs, and that its protection would remove the "romance of life." Leaders of DuPont, General Motors, Standard Oil, U.S. Steel, J. C. Penney, Heinz, and other firms formed the anti-Roosevelt American Liberty League to campaign against "unconstitutional" and "socialistic" New Deal measures.

Many executives hated Roosevelt. They said that he was bringing communism to the United States and called him names such as "Stalin Delano Roosevelt."[14] But business had lost its way. Corporate opposition to New Deal measures ran counter to public sentiment. It became ineffective and was sometimes disgraceful. In 1935,

---

[13] Quoted in Henry Demarest Lloyd, *Wealth Against Commonwealth* (New York: Harper, 1898), pp. 377–78.

[14] William Manchester, *The Glory and the Dream,* vol. 1 (Boston: Little, Brown, 1973), p. 126.

for example, utility lobbyists sent Congress 250,000 fake letters and telegrams in a losing effort to stop a bill. Subsequently they ran a whispering campaign saying Roosevelt was insane.

Much New Deal legislation was profoundly egalitarian and humanitarian and reasserted the tradition of agrarian idealism. Because business lacked a positive philosophy for change, its political power was greatly diminished. According to Edwin M. Epstein, "corporate political influence reached its nadir during the New Deal."[15] Roosevelt was hurt by all the hate and felt that through his major New Deal programs, he had saved capitalism in spite of the capitalists.

The New Deal was a political sea change born out of the Great Depression. One lasting legacy of the era was the philosophy that government should be used to correct the flaws of capitalism and control the economy so that prosperity would no longer depend solely on unbridled market forces.[16] Government would also be used to create a "welfare state" to protect citizens from want. Whereas, in the past, government had kept its hands off corporations, now it would actively use interest rates, regulation, taxes, subsidies, and other policy instruments to control them. Whereas, in the past, most domestic spending had been for infrastructure programs that promoted business, spending would increasingly focus on social programs such as social security. These changes laid the groundwork for an increasingly large, powerful, and activist federal government.

Postwar Politics and Winds of Change

In the 1940s, industry's patriotic World War II production record and subsequent postwar prosperity quieted lingering public restiveness about corporate political activity. During the 1950s, corporations once again predominated in a very hospitable political environment. In the years between 1952 and 1960, Dwight D. Eisenhower was a probusiness president with a cabinet dominated by political appointees from business. A probusiness conservative coalition of southern Democrats and Republicans in Congress ensured legislative support. Corporations could promote their policy agendas by influencing a small number of leaders. Charls E. Walker, an official in the Eisenhower administration and later a business lobbyist, recalls how only four men shaped economic policy.

> These four officials were President Eisenhower, Treasury Secretary Robert Anderson, Speaker of the House Sam Rayburn, and Senate majority leader Lyndon B. Johnson. These four men would get together every week over a drink at the White House and the President would say, "I think we ought to do this or that." Then Mr. Sam or LBJ might say, "Well, that's a real good idea; send it up and we'll get it through." And they would. They could deliver because at that time they had great influence in Congress, partly because of the seniority system.[17]

However, changing political trends soon led business into more sophisticated methods of political intervention. During the 1960s and 1970s, national politics

[15] *The Corporation in American Politics* (Englewood Cliffs, NJ: Prentice Hall, 1969), p. 31.

[16] For the story of how this philosophy developed during the New Deal years, see Alan Brinkley, *The End of Reform: New Deal Liberalism in Recession and War* (New York: Knopf, 1995).

[17] Quoted in Gene E. Bradley, "How to Work in Washington: Building Understanding for Your Business," *Columbia Journal of World Business,* Spring 1994, p. 53.

became dominated by a liberal reform agenda. New groups rose to defy corporations, internal reforms made Congress more openly democratic and responsive to business's foes, business was bridled with massive new regulatory schemes, and government swelled with new tiers of authority.[18] Business suffered unaccustomed defeats at the hands of public interest groups and agency staffs in government, defeats that encouraged more aggression from companies.

THE RISE OF ANTAGONISTIC GROUPS

During the late 1960s, the climate of pressure politics changed with the rise of new groups focused on consumer, environmental, taxpayer, civil rights, and other issues. Some, including Ralph Nader's Public Citizen, the Natural Resources Defense Council, and the Consumer Federation of America, grew to have many members and enough power to push an agenda of corporate regulation.

The presence of these groups changed the political arena for business. A decade earlier, corporations had dominated Washington politics with quiet, behind-the-scenes influence over key leaders. Now they faced hostile groups that used a favorable climate of public opinion to wrest control of the policy agenda away from business. The result was a remarkable period, lasting roughly from the late 1960s to the late 1970s, during which the antagonists of business pressured Congress to enact one massive regulatory program after another.

The rise of groups hostile to business is part of a broader trend in which new groups of all kinds, including business groups, have been stimulated by growth of government. Government growth is reflected by fast-rising federal spending. In 1960 the federal budget was $92 billion. By 1980 it reached $591 billion, an increase of more than 600 percent, and by 2003 it was $1.8 trillion.[19] As government grows, interest groups proliferate around policy areas. One estimate is that there are about 23,000 organized interest groups, roughly 400 percent more than in the 1950s.[20]

The heyday of the public interest movement was short-lived. By the late 1970s, business interests had mobilized to fight the public interest movement in more sophisticated ways, and never again would the movement win great victories, although it remains as an institutionalized foe of business.

DIFFUSION OF POWER IN GOVERNMENT

A second change in the climate of politics, besides new groups, has been the diffusion and decentralization of power in Washington, DC. Three major reasons for this are (1) reforms in Congress, (2) the decline of political parties, and (3) increased complexity of government.

[18] These factors are analyzed by David Vogel in *Fluctuating Fortunes: The Political Power of Business in America* (New York: Basic Books, 1989), chaps. 3–6.

[19] Bureau of the Census, *Statistical Abstract of the United States: 2003,* 123d ed. (Washington, DC: U.S. Government Printing Office, 2003), table 475. This figure is a rounding of the $1.836 trillion estimate.

[20] Burdett A. Loomis and Allan J. Cigler, "Introduction: The Changing Nature of Interest Group Politics," in Cigler and Loomis, *Interest Group Politics,* 5th ed. (Washington, DC: Congressional Quarterly Press, 1998), p. 11.

Traditionally, the House and Senate were run autocratically by a few party leaders and powerful committee chairs. But the stubborn resistance of southern Democrats to civil rights legislation in the 1960s eventually led in 1974 to an uprising of junior legislators, who passed procedural reforms that democratized Congress by taking power from the party leaders and spreading it widely. After 1974, subcommittees could hold hearings on any subject they wished; they developed large staffs and often became small fiefdoms of independent action. Instead of an institution dominated by a few leaders, Congress was described by one observer as "like a log floating down a river with 535 giant ants aboard, and each one thinks he or she is steering."[21]

After the reforms, business lobbyists had to contact nearly every member of a committee or subcommittee to get support for a measure, rather than just the chair. Veteran lobbyist Charls E. Walker muses about the old days. "On a tax issue if you had the agreement of the chairman of Ways and Means, you could go out and play golf," but "these days you can't rest easy unless you've worked all the members."[22]

Changes outside Congress further undermined party leaders. One change was the rise of political action committees (PACs) formed by interest groups and corporations to contribute campaign money. Previously, Senate and House members who were loyal to party leaders could count on substantial campaign funds from the Republican and Democratic parties. After 1974, however, special-interest PACs began contributing such large amounts that legislators could act more independently of party leaders and still raise enough money to be reelected.

Other factors also eroded party authority. The media, particularly television, have replaced to some extent the parties as a source of information about candidates. Using television, politicians can bypass their parties and speak directly to voters. Also, the electorate is more highly educated and independent than it was in past eras and many voters identify only weakly with parties. Increasingly, they split their ballots and use decision cues other than party labels.

An additional cause of power diffusion is the growth in size and complexity of the federal government. Washington today is a maze of competing power centers, including elected officials, congressional committees, cabinet departments, regulatory agencies, political parties, courts, and interest groups. Relations among these power centers continuously shift as partisan tides, personal ambitions, power struggles, and emerging issues glide across the political landscape.

The sum total of government activity has a much greater impact on business than in the past, and because of this, corporations are far more politically active than in past eras. The expanded size and scope of government mean that its actions can be critical to company operations. Many bills passed by Congress directly affect earnings. Legislation affects taxes, interest rates, import/export rules, antitrust policy, defense spending, regulatory compliance costs, health care costs, the dollar exchange rate, uses of information, and much more.

---

[21] Bradley, "How to Work in Washington," p. 55.

[22] Quoted in Jill Abramson, "The Business of Persuasion Thrives in Nation's Capital," *New York Times,* September 29, 1998, p. A23.

THE UNIVERSE OF ORGANIZED BUSINESS INTERESTS

Literally thousands of groups represent business. What follows is a summary of this universe.

peak association
A group that represents the political interests of many companies in multiple industries.

The most prominent groups are *peak associations* that represent many different companies and industries. Their strength lies in representing a wide expanse of the business community. Their weakness is that many political issues divide their members and they can lobby aggressively only on the broad issues that unite diverse company interests.

The largest peak association is the U.S. Chamber of Commerce, which was founded in 1912. The Chamber is a federation of 3,000 local and state chapters, 830 trade associations, and 3 million businesses, 96 percent of which have fewer than 100 employees. The next largest is the National Association of Manufacturers (NAM), founded in 1895, which, as the name suggests, represents manufacturers. It has a membership of 12,000 companies and trade associations.

Both the Chamber and the NAM carry a conservative business agenda to Congress and the public. They work on issues that unite their members, such as reducing regulation and lowering health care costs for employers. Narrower issues are often divisive. Within the NAM, for example, large manufacturing companies benefit by sourcing cheap components from China, but many small American firms that make components are struggling to survive the Chinese competition. This split prevents the NAM from taking a forceful position on trade policy with China.

Two other peak associations have more unified memberships. The National Federation of Independent Businesses (NFIB), founded in 1943, represents 600,000 small businesses, most with 5 or fewer employees and less than $500,000 a year in sales. It is the most conservative and least bipartisan of the business associations. It pursues a lobbying agenda of easing compliance with government rules, reducing taxes, and keeping a lid on the minimum wage. Most of its campaign contributions go to Republican candidates. The president of the Chamber once said, "I love the NFIB, the way they get out there on the edge, like when they said, 'Get rid of the IRS.' They make us sound reasonable."[23] The Business Roundtable is the organization that speaks for big business. It was founded in 1972 and consists of about 150 CEOs whose companies pay membership dues to support it. Each year it confines its advocacy to a few issues critical to the largest multinational corporations. The great strength of the Roundtable is that its member CEOs are its lobbyists. They go to Washington carrying its message directly to lawmakers.

trade association
A group formed to advocate the interests of an industry or industry segment.

Besides these peak associations, more than 6,000 *trade associations* represent companies grouped by industry. Virtually every industry has one or more such associations. Illustrative are the American Boiler Manufacturers Association, the Compressed Gas Association, the Oxygenated Fuels Association, the National Turkey Federation, and the Institute of Makers of Explosives. Beyond lobbying for the industries they represent, trade groups also act as early warning systems in Washington for companies, hold training conferences, and publish data. Trade associations such as the American Petroleum Institute have large staffs

[23] Quoted in Jeffrey H. Birnbaum, "Power Player," *Fortune Small Business*, October 2001, p. 56.

and deep financial resources and are among the most powerful players in Washington. Corporations with diversified business lines often belong to many trade associations.

Washington office
An office in Washington, DC, set up by a corporation and staffed with experts in advocating the firm's point of view to lawmakers and regulators.

More than 700 corporations have staffs of government relations experts in Washington. These *Washington offices* are set up mainly by big companies. General Electric, for example, has a staff organized into teams that specialize in lobbying for the needs of GE's business segments. Some specialize in contacting Republicans; others work more with Democrats. The office also gives GE managers information about how events in Washington affect their operations. Most firms supplement their Washington offices by hiring lobbyists from independent lobbying firms. To influence a 2004 corporate tax bill, GE hired lobbyists from three firms that specialize in tax lobbying.[24] Few small firms can afford to have Washington outposts, so they work through trade associations or hired lobbyists. There are dozens of independent lobbying firms in Washington, DC. The most prominent ones employ former top officials, ex-legislators, and ex-congressional staff members from both political parties to offer a potent mix of access, influence, and advice.

coalition
A combination of business interests—including corporations, trade associations, and peak associations—united to pursue a political goal.

Business interests also form *coalitions* to create broader support. There are dozens of business coalitions in Washington at any given time. These groupings of instant allies can be ephemeral. Most form around a single issue and break up when that issue loses urgency. The advantage of membership in a coalition is that lobbying by a range of diverse allies can get support from more legislators and officials than would the efforts of any single entity. Frequently, coalition allies on one issue find themselves opposing each other on another issue.

Business gains strength when it is united, but there is chronic disunity. Longstanding tensions exist between domestic and foreign firms, truckers and railroads, manufacturers and retailers, and raw material producers and end-product manufacturers. To illustrate, for many years the American Sugar Alliance, which represents sugar growers and refiners, has fought to preserve federal price supports on raw cane and beet sugar. It is opposed by big corporations such as RJR Nabisco and Coca-Cola, because higher sugar prices raise the cost of manufacturing cookies, candy, and soft drinks. More recently a schism has developed between the film and recording industries, which want to stop file sharing services that violate copyright law, and the manufacturers of the computers and software that facilitate file sharing.

LOBBYING

There are two broad areas of business involvement in politics. The first is government relations, or lobbying, in which business influences policy by contacting government officials. The second is the electoral process, in which business influence is exercised to elect or defeat candidates, primarily by contributing money. Naturally, the two areas are closely related.

[24] Jeffrey H. Birnbaum and Jonathan Weisman, "GE Lobbyists Mold Tax Bill," *Washington Post*, July 13, 2004, p. A1.

lobbying
Advocating a viewpoint to government.

Lobbying is advocating a viewpoint to government. A lobbyist presents the position of a corporation, interest group, or trade association to a government official. The word "lobbyist" entered the language in the early 1800s to describe people who stood in the lobbies of legislatures trying to intercept lawmakers on their way in and out. The word carries negative connotations, and business lobbyists are often caricatured as pleading selfish interests, ignoring the public interest, and corrupting officials. Although sainthood escapes the profession, its craft is political art, the exercise of which makes the system work.

In general, lobbyists channel and articulate the voices of many interests in the sea of American pluralism. In particular, they perform two specific functions. First, they give lawmakers and officials useful technical information. Legislators, for example, cannot possibly investigate each issue and provision in roughly 12,000 bills before Congress each year, some of them hundreds of pages long. Second, they give them crucial political information about how constituents and interests stand. Every industry has quirks and problems about which its lobbyists have special knowledge.

Lobbyists can mislead a lawmaker with bias and falsehood, but this is counterproductive. A former member of Congress explains the consequences.

> There is a proper term for a lobbyist who lies or misleads or distorts, and that proper term is *former lobbyist.* When you are dealing with each other . . . the truth is your . . . real capital. Once you mislead, once you exaggerate, once you fail to give an accurate picture, you'll never be allowed in the office again.[25]

A lobbyist who lacks integrity loses access to the very people he or she earns a living from influencing. In addition, effective business lobbyists must defend their proposals based on public benefit, since legislators and regulators, as a rule, cannot justify acting simply to promote corporate self-interest.

In Washington today, legislators are receptive to lobbyists. In Congress, both parties have set up regular meetings with groups of corporate lobbyists. On Tuesdays and Wednesdays top Republican lobbyists meet with Republican Senators. On Mondays and Fridays top Democratic lobbyists meet with high-ranking staff of Senators and Representatives. In these meetings, lobbyists and legislators exchange information. The congressional leaders seek advice on how to get their legislation passed and ask lobbyists for tactical help. The lobbyists learn about the progress of bills and cultivate close relationships. By unwritten rule there is no direct pleading for clients at these strategy sessions, but it is understood that later they can ask for the legislator's help.[26] Lawmakers often form coalitions of lobbyists around specific pieces of legislation and meet regularly with them while these bills are pending.

Lobbyists are loosely regulated. Restraints on them are suspect because the First Amendment protects both the right of speech and the right of citizens to contact

---

[25] Quoted in Michael Watkins, Mickey Edwards, and Usha Thakrar, *Winning the Influence Game: What Every Business Leader Should Know About Government* (New York: Wiley, 2001), p. 173; emphasis in original.

[26] Jeffrey H. Birnbaum, "Lawmakers, Lobbyists Keep in Constant Contact," *Washington Post,* June 28, 2004, p. E1.

government officials. Beyond antibribery laws and limits on the value of gifts, there are few legal restrictions on lobbying. In 1995 Congress adopted the gift-giving rules to prevent the appearance of impropriety. The House prohibits lobbyists from giving gifts of any size to members, including meals. The Senate prohibits any gift over $50 or any series of gifts over $10 that add up to $100 a year.[27] Inevitably, gaping loopholes have opened. Although lobbyists cannot take a legislator to a restaurant, every evening in House office buildings lobbyists and trade associations sponsor lavish receptions overflowing with food. These are permitted if there are no forks! According to rule interpretations of the House Ethics Committee, if forks were present, the receptions would be meals.

Lobbying Methods

The art of persuasion admits of many approaches. In-person contact with officials is the gold standard. Presenting the client's case in a face-to-face meeting is often the most effective way to get action. Access to decision makers is a precious commodity. Members of Congress, for example, typically have appointments booked at 5- to 10-minute intervals. An unwritten rule is that campaign contributions entitle the corporations or lobbyists who make them to access. Often lobbyists meet with a legislator's assistants or committee staff members. They also attend committee meetings in the House and Senate, and it is common practice for them to catch a representative's eye and give a thumbs-up or thumbs-down signal as various provisions come to a vote. Unless they are former senators or representatives, they are not allowed on the floor of either chamber, but they may stand in hallways and confer with passing lawmakers. And sometimes the hallways are crowded. Former Senator David L. Boren (D-Oklahoma) writes about the press of supplicants.

> On several occasions when we were debating important tax bills, I needed a police escort to get into the Finance Committee hearing room because so many lobbyists were crowding the halls, trying to get one last chance to make their pitch to each Senator. Senators generally knew which lobbyist represented the interests of which large donor.[28]

Most advocacy work is done away from legislative chambers and direct contacts. Public relations skills are applied to get favorable media coverage of issues. Lobbyists generate research and policy analysis to give their positions a patina of scientific or scholarly validity. Business lobbyists may try to influence decisions by having their customers, employees, or other constituents, including the public, pressure government officials for action. These efforts are called *grassroots lobbying*.

grassroots lobbying
The technique of generating an expression of public, or "grassroots," support for the position of a company or lobbyist.

[27] The Lobbying Disclosure Act of 1995 requires lobbyists to register with Congress and both they and their clients must fill out disclosure forms that report their fees (rounded to the nearest $20,000) and expenditures. The disclosures far underreport activity because (1) only lobbyists who spend more than 20 percent of their time lobbying Congress or executive branch officials must register and (2) the definition of lobbying in the act is very narrow, covering only personal or written contact with officials and excluding an important range of other influence activities.

[28] Quoted in *McConnell v. FEC*, 124 S. Ct. 751.

FIGURE 9.1
Paths of
Pressure
A corporation
can directly
lobby for its
interests or it
may lobby
indirectly with
a grassroots
campaign
aimed at the
public or
certain groups
and interests
within the
public. It may
be assisted in
both efforts by
independent
lobbying firms.

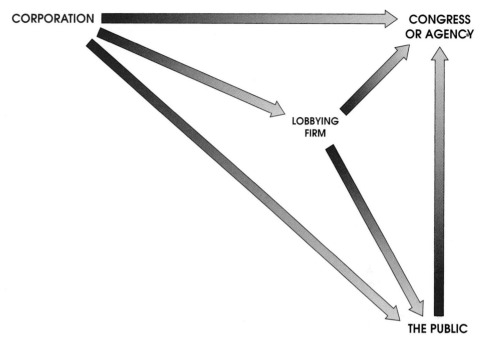

Showing this support assures a lawmaker that the corporation is not simply asking for special treatment. Grassroots efforts require an additional set of activities. Opinion polls are used to measure public attitudes. Advertising campaigns are launched to shape opinion. Special efforts are made to cultivate mass mail, phone calls, faxes, e-mail, or visits to lawmakers. For example, telemarketers call and request that people contact their representatives if they agree with the company's position. There are many versions of the grassroots strategy.

> A group of HMOs hired Fierce & Isakowitz, a Washington firm that represents corporations and trade associations. The HMOs sought to defeat a bill called the Patients' Bill of Rights that would make it easier for patients to sue them. Partner Mark Isakowitz learned that key Republican Senators up for reelection disliked the bill but feared voting against it because voters were angry at HMOs. Isakowitz created an ad campaign that framed Senators who supported HMOs as working for the public. Then, he planted pro-HMO speakers in the town hall meetings the Senators held back in their home states. It worked. The Senators came to believe that they could support HMOs and still be reelected. The Patients' Bill of Rights failed to pass in the Senate.[29]

Major lobbying efforts now resemble political campaigns in the way they combine a broad range of methods, including direct contact, public relations, legal support, polling, policy analysis, and grassroots work (see Figure 9.1). The need for

[29] Jeffrey H. Birnbaum, "The Persuaders," *Fortune*, August 11, 2003, p. 124.

this spectrum of skills has led to a merger wave in which large Washington lobby firms absorb smaller firms that specialize in one aspect of lobbying. The larger firm can then offer one-stop "full service" to client corporations.

THE CORPORATE ROLE IN ELECTIONS

In the first presidential campaign, George Washington did little campaigning and spent only £39 on "treats" for the voters.[30] Since then, the length and cost of campaigns for federal offices—president, vice president, senator, and representative—have soared. In the 1999–2000 election cycle, total campaign spending for federal races was $3 billion, a large sum, but one that should be kept in perspective. It was less than the cost of an aircraft carrier and less than the nation spent on video games.

Efforts to Limit Corporate Influence

Throughout the nineteenth century, companies gave money directly to candidates. As companies grew and large trusts emerged the amounts given grew also. Eventually, excess invited reaction. After the Civil War, business money went disproportionately to the Republican party, which promoted the doctrine of conservative, laissez-faire economics. Corporate giving peaked in the presidential campaigns of William McKinley. The election of 1896 matched the probusiness Republican McKinley against the radical populist William Jennings Bryan, who ran as the Democratic candidate. Bryan, a spellbinder on the stump, terrified eastern bankers by advocating an end to the gold standard, a radical change that they opposed.

McKinley's campaign manager, Marcus Hanna, capitalized on their fright by establishing recommended levels of dollar contributions to the McKinley campaign. He assessed .25 percent of the assets of each bank from the trembling financiers and, overall, raised about $3.5 million.[31] This inflated McKinley's campaign funding to double that of any prior election and he was victorious.

In 1900 Bryan again ran against McKinley, this time on a platform of breaking up trusts. So Hanna assessed big trusts such as Standard Oil and U.S. Steel amounts based on their assets. He raised a new record sum, estimated as high as $7 million, an astronomical amount for that day. If the estimate is correct, it was not exceeded until the election of 1960 when both John F. Kennedy and Richard Nixon raised approximately $10 million each. McKinley won again, by an even larger margin.

Hanna believed his assessment scheme elevated the ethics of fundraising above the borderline bribery and petty extortion that had long characterized it. Companies did not give wanting special favors in return; instead, each put in a fair amount and in return would share in the general economic prosperity of a McKinley administration. In fact, the success of Hanna's formula created public hostility toward corporate money as the greatest threat of corruption in American elections. An effort at reform was inevitable and it came after the election of 1904, when

[30] James V. DeLong, "Free Money," *Reason,* August–September 2000, p. 42.
[31] See Herbert Croly, *Marcus Alonzo Hanna: His Life and Work* (New York: Macmillan, 1912), p. 220. A grateful McKinley engineered Hanna's appointment to the U.S. Senate.

Republican Theodore Roosevelt, who campaigned as a reformer, was embarrassed by his opponent, Democrat Alton B. Parker, for taking large cash contributions from corporations.

Progressive reformers sought to derail the business juggernaut. In 1907 they passed the Tillman Act, making it a crime for banks and corporations to directly contribute to candidates in *federal elections,* and this is still the law today.[32] The law was sponsored by Senator Benjamin R. "Pitchfork Ben" Tillman (D-S. Carolina). Tillman was not an idealist seeking fair elections. His purpose was to stop the gusher of corporate money flowing to the Republican party, breaking its dominance. He was a racist with a vicious hatred of the Republicans who had freed the slaves and given them the right to vote in his state. He bragged on the Senate floor about riding with vigilantes and shooting blacks at polling places. Tillman simply capitalized on the sentiment of the day to pursue his darker motive.

Tillman's venom is now a historical artifact. What endures from the era is fear of corporate money in politics. American political culture is shaped by egalitarian ideals. Large campaign contributions from business strained popular belief in a rough equality among interests. The Tillman Act was the first of many efforts to protect the electoral system from lopsided corporate influence. But money, especially corporate money, plays an essential role in funding elections. It is a resource that can be converted to power. Candidates use it to persuade voters. Contributors use it to buy access, influence, and favors. Because money is elemental, new sources and methods of giving arise when old ways are foreclosed.

After 1907 the spirit of the Tillman Act was quickly and continuously violated. Forbidden from giving directly, companies found clever, indirect ways to funnel dollars into campaigns. They loaned money to candidates and later forgave the debts, paid lavish sums for small ads in political party booklets, assigned employees to work for campaigns, and provided free services such as rental cars and air travel. Since the Tillman Act did not limit individual contributions, wealthy donors stepped in. These "fat cats," who included corporate executives, legally gave unlimited sums. And many companies gave salary bonuses to managers for use as campaign contributions. The history of election law after the Tillman Act has been one of trying to limit corporate influence by shutting off the range of these indirect methods for giving. But, as we will see, as each channel is blocked a new one quickly appears.

federal elections
Elections for president, vice president, senator, and representative. The 435 representatives are elected every two years, the president and vice president every four years, and the 100 senators every six years (with one-third of the senators up for election biennially). Elections are held on the first Tuesday after the first Monday of November in even-numbered years.

The Federal Election Campaign Act

In the years following the Tillman Act, Congress added to the body of election law from time to time, requiring candidates to disclose contributions, prohibiting elected officials from using federal employees in their campaigns, and barring direct contributions from labor unions to candidates.[33] Besides being riddled with loopholes, none of these measures limited the influence of what continued to be the main source of campaign funding—corporations.

[32] Its formal title is Act of January 26, 1907, 2 U.S. Code §441b.

[33] The laws were, respectively, the Publicity Act of 1910, the Federal Corrupt Practices Act of 1925, the Hatch Act of 1939, and the War Disputes Act of 1943 (a temporary measure made permanent by the Taft-Hartley Act in 1947).

In 1968, Republican Richard Nixon outspent his Democratic opponent Hubert Humphrey largely because of contributions from wealthy business magnates. One was W. Clement Stone, an insurance company executive, who set a record by giving $2.2 million to Nixon through a maze of committees. Angry Democrats passed the Federal Election Campaign Act (FECA) of 1971 to stiffen disclosure requirements on campaign contributions and expenditures. Immediately after its passage, the election of 1972 again made corporate money in politics a major reform issue. Investigations related to the Watergate scandals found that 21 corporations had violated the Tillman Act by giving direct contributions totaling $842,000 to the Nixon campaign.

In reaction to this illegality, Congress extensively amended the FECA in 1974 (the first of five amending acts over a decade). As revised, the FECA curbed wealthy donors by placing ceilings on both campaign contributions and expenditures. Instead of giving as much as they wanted, individuals could contribute only $1,000 per election to a candidate and only $25,000 a year in total to any combination of candidates or political committees. The Tillman Act's prohibition on direct corporate contributions continued. In an attempt to put more enforcement power behind election law, the amendments created a new regulatory agency, the Federal Election Commission. The intent of the amendments was to limit corporate influence. However, over the 30 years that the legal framework remained in force it failed to do so. There were three reasons.

First, in 1976 the Supreme Court severely compromised the FECA's design for controlling campaign money. In *Buckley v. Valeo,* the Court held that giving and spending money in political campaigns are forms of expression protected by the guarantee of free speech in the First Amendment.[34] The Court upheld the FECA's *contribution* limits, saying that the government had a legitimate interest in avoiding corruption and the appearance of corruption that unlimited contributions invited. But it struck down *expenditure* limits as too great a restraint on political speech. This badly compromised the law's ability to limit campaign spending.

Second, the proliferation of interest groups caused by the growth of government created more organized interests to fund campaigns. Because the FECA—even after the *Buckley* decision—limited individual contributions, the era of fat cats seemed to be over, though as we will see, only temporarily. So corporations raced to set up devices called political action committees (PACs), which could legally contribute to candidates in their name. The number of PACs grew rapidly, and with them the sums of money entering politics.

Third, corporations and lobbyists adapted to the new FECA regime by learning how to exploit, avoid, and live with its regulations. Their machinations over 30 years paralleled those that followed the Tillman Act in 1907 and showed again that political money is like water in a stream; dammed up in one place, it flows around and over in another. The two most important maneuvers around the spirit of the law were (1) the use of political action committees and (2) the rise of soft money used for issue advertising.

[34] 421 U.S. 1.

FIGURE 9.2
Contributions to Candidates by Corporate and Labor Political Action Committees, 1986–2002

Source: Federal Election Commission.

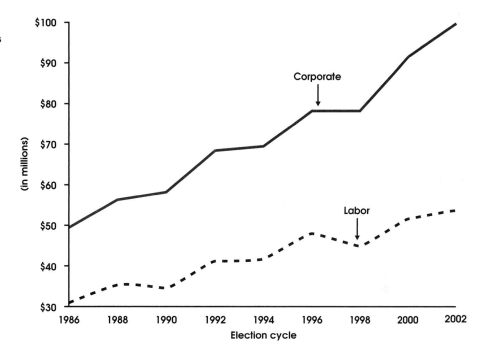

Political Action Committees

political action committee
A political committee carrying a company's name formed to make campaign contributions. The money it gives to candidates comes from individual employees, not from the corporate treasury.

When Congress limited individual contributions, it left open a loophole permitting corporations to set up *political action committees*, or political committees carrying a company's name. These committees make campaign contributions, not with corporate money, but with money put in by employees. Although corporations previously had not formed PACs, unions had used them since the 1940s to support prolabor candidates and already had more than 200. When the new FECA contribution limits went into effect in 1974, corporations started forming PACs too. The number rose steadily, peaking at 1,816 PACs in 1988, then slowly declining to 1,508 in 2001 as some corporations found other avenues for contributing money. However, as we will explain, when new reforms cut off these other avenues the number went back up, rising to 1,712 in 2004.[35]

Other interests also use PACs and in 2004 there were 4,713 in all, including 326 labor union PACs and 967 trade association and other membership-group PACs.[36] As Figure 9.2 shows, despite fluctuations in number, contributions by corporate PACs have risen over the long term, and business PACs far outspend union PACs.

How PACs Work

To start a PAC, a corporation must set up an account for contributions, a "separate segregated fund," to which it cannot legally donate 1 cent (because of the prohibition since 1907 of direct corporate giving). Corporate PACs get their funds primarily

[35] Federal Election Commission Press Release, "PAC Activity Increases at 18 Month Point in 2004," September 1, 2004. FEC data cited in this chapter can be found on the FEC Web site at www.fec.gov.
[36] Ibid.

from contributions by employees. Executives and managers can be solicited in person or by mail. Many corporations suggest giving amounts based on a percentage of salary, usually .25 to 1 percent of annual salary. Some corporations encourage enrollment in monthly paycheck deduction plans. Hourly employees can be solicited only twice a year, and then only by mail to their homes. It is illegal for companies to apply pressure for PAC contributions. However, many employees feel subtle pressure to contribute and resent the solicitations.

The money in a PAC is disbursed to candidates based on decisions made by PAC officers, who must be corporate employees. Their decisions are aligned with corporate political goals. Under the FECA, PACs are allowed to give up to $5,000 per election to candidates, but most contributions are smaller ones of only $500 to $2,000. In 2004 a $2,000 contribution was less than one-hundredth of 1 percent of the cost of an average Senate race and less than one-tenth of 1 percent of the cost of an average House race. Company lobbyists know that even these minor contributions create an expectation of access, or a hearing of the corporation's position, after the candidate is elected. There are no dollar limits on the overall amounts that PACs may raise and spend. Most corporate PACs contribute less than $50,000 during a two-year *election cycle,* although in 2004 a handful had contributed more than $1 million to candidates and about two dozen gave more than $500,000.[37]

election cycle
The two-year period between federal elections.

Soft Money and Issue Advertising

Just as the amount of corporate PAC money was rising, a new way of avoiding the law's strict contribution limits for wealthy executives and PACs appeared. In 1979 Congress amended the FECA to encourage support for state and local political parties by suspending limits and prohibitions on contributions to them. These contributions came to be called *soft money,* or money given to political parties that is unregulated as to source or amount under federal law. Soft money is contrasted to *hard money,* which is money raised under the strict contribution limits and rules in federal election law. Soft money could be given directly to the parties. It was anticipated that it would be used for such things as yard signs, posters, brochures, newsletters, and mailings. Soon, however, the national parties began to collect large sums of soft money and transfer them to state parties, which used the money in inventive ways, not to buy lawn signs, but to further the election of federal candidates.

soft money
Money contributed to political parties that is unregulated as to source or amount under federal election law.

hard money
Money raised under the strict contribution limits and rules in federal election law.

Although corporations are barred from contributing to federal campaigns, a series of advisory opinions by the Federal Election Commission opened the door for them to give unlimited soft-money contributions to national party committees.[38] The national party committees then disbursed it to state and local parties. Corporations and executives began to give large and rising sums. In the 1992 election cycle the two parties raised $87 million and by the 2000 election cycle corporations were virtually unrestrained in their giving and the amount ballooned to $495 million (see Figure 9.3). AT&T, the largest soft-money donor in that period,

---

[37] Ibid., attachment "Top 50 Corporate PACs by Contributions to Candidates."

[38] The national party committees are the Democratic National Committee, the Democratic Senatorial Campaign Committee, the Democratic Congressional Campaign Committee, the Republican National Committee, the National Republican Senatorial Committee, and the National Republican Congressional Committee.

FIGURE 9.3 Soft Money Receipts by Democratic and Republican National Party Committees—
1992–2002 Election Cycles

Source: Federal Election Commission.

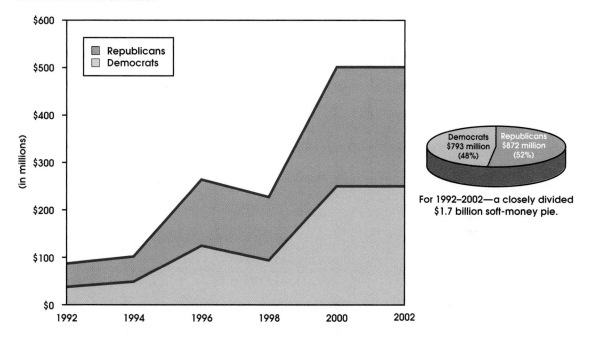

For 1992–2002—a closely divided
$1.7 billion soft-money pie.

contributed totals of $2.3 million to the Republican party and $1.5 million to the
Democratic party in payments from subsidiaries and executives.[39]

In 1996 the Supreme Court held that soft money could be used to pay for political
ads.[40] The Court made a distinction between "issue advocacy," which presents a
political view or comment on an electoral race, and "express advocacy," which
specifically suggests the election or defeat of a candidate using words such as "vote
for," "defeat," or "support." Soft money could be used for issue advertising that tip-
toed around direct electioneering by avoiding the use of these words, although the
intent to support or oppose a candidate for federal office was clear. Within a few
years most soft money was buying television ads, not lawn signs and bumper stickers for local candidates. Corporations wrote big checks to the Democratic and
Republican parties, which forwarded the money to state and local parties, which
used it to pay for thinly disguised ads for and against federal candidates.

Reform Legislation in 2002

By the election of 2000, the spectacle of big companies and wealthy executives
giving soft money in unlimited amounts mocked the spirit of election law. As
Americans grew increasingly cynical of a political system fueled by millionaires
and big corporations, Senators John McCain (R-Arizona) and Russell Feingold
(D-Wisconsin) waged an uphill, seven-year battle in Congress to pass reform

[39] Common Cause, "Top Soft Money Donors," www.commoncause.org.
[40] *Colorado Republican Federal Campaign Committee v. FEC,* 116 S. Ct. 2390 (1996).

legislation. Finally, after strong public reaction to news that Enron Corporation had manipulated government officials with big campaign contributions, McCain's bill was enacted as the Bipartisan Campaign Reform Act of 2002 (BCRA).

The new law amended the Federal Election Campaign Act. The ban on direct corporate contributions to candidates remains in effect. Corporations may still contribute through PACs. But the BCRA attempts to close off the soft money loophole, further limiting the indirect means that corporations have used to influence elections. The most important changes are these.

- National parties are prohibited from raising or spending soft money. Corporations and individuals may give up to $10,000 a year to state and local parties, but only in states that permit soft money. Even then, the funds can be used only for voter registration and get-out-the-vote drives, not for issue ads.

- Corporations can give unlimited amounts of soft money to advocacy groups for electioneering activity, but during blackout periods beginning 30 days before primary elections and 60 days before general elections these groups are prohibited from using corporate funds for issue ads on television or radio if the ads refer to a federal candidate (newspaper, magazine, and Internet ads are permitted). Soft money from individuals can still be used for these issue ads. And any ad funded by hard dollars (that is, dollars contributed under the limits in federal law set forth in Figure 9.4) is legal during the blackout periods.

FIGURE 9.4
Contribution and Expenditure Rules under Current Federal Campaign Law

Source	Prohibitions, Limits, and Unregulated Areas
 Corporations	• Prohibited from contributing to federal candidates using corporate accounts • $10,000 to state political party committees where permitted by state law for registering and turning out voters • May set up and contribute through a "separate, segregated fund" or political action committee (PAC) • Unlimited direct contributions to 501c and 527 organizations
Individuals	• $2,000* per election[†] to candidates • $5,000 per year to political action committees • $10,000 per year combined limit to state and local party committees • $25,000* per year to national party committees • $95,000* per two-year election cycle as follows: $37,500 per cycle to candidates and $57,500 per cycle to national parties and PACs (of which no more than $37,500 per cycle can go to PACs) • Unlimited contributions to 501c and 527 organizations • Unlimited expenditures to own campaign if running for office • Unlimited independent expenditures on behalf of or against candidates or causes
Political Action Committees	• $5,000 per election[†] to candidates and their committees • $5,000 per year combined limit to state and local parties • $15,000 per year to national party committees • $5,000 per year to other political action committees • Unlimited independent expenditures

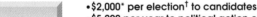

*These limits are indexed for inflation.
[†]Primary elections, general elections, special elections, and nominating conventions or caucuses are all separate elections, and individuals or committees may contribute up to the legal limit in each.

- Contribution limits for individuals are raised. Under the previous limits, which had been set in 1974, individuals could give just $1,000 per election to candidates and could not give more than $25,000 per year to any combination of candidates and political committees. The new limits, shown in more detail in Figure 9.4, allow individuals to give $2,000 per year to candidates and up to $95,000 to all recipients per two-year election cycle.
- New disclosure requirements for contributions and expenditures are introduced and penalties for violating the law are increased. An additional provision raises contribution limits for Senate and House candidates who are opposed by wealthy individuals spending large amounts of their own money.

The main purpose of the new law is to end the use of corporate soft money for issue ads run just before elections. National parties can no longer receive it and state and local parties can receive only limited amounts that cannot be spent on issue ads. The ban on its use by advocacy groups, for example, the Chamber of Commerce or the Sierra Club, before elections is intended to prevent corporations from turning to electioneering through these groups as a substitute for soft money gifts to the parties. The higher individual contribution limits are intended to make it easier for parties and candidates to raise hard money from a larger number of less affluent sources, thereby compensating for the loss of soft money.

The 2004 election cycle was the first under BCRA rules. The new law did not stop the rise in overall spending. Spending in the 2004 elections was estimated at $3.9 billion, considerably higher than the $3 billion estimated for the 2000 presidential election cycle.[41] Shifts in contribution patterns more than compensated for the loss of almost $500 million in soft money contributions denied to the national parties.

PAC contributions climbed from $288 million to $384 million. In addition, corporations gave more to fund the national party presidential nominating conventions. Corporations are allowed to give unlimited funds to the conventions because an indulgent interpretation of the law by the Federal Election Commission defines this as a civic contribution, not as a prohibited campaign contribution. Corporate support for conventions rose from $56 million in 2000 to $104 million in 2004.[42] More dramatic increases in giving came elsewhere, however.

First, hard money contributions went way up. With individual contribution limits raised, contributions to candidates and parties jumped from $1.5 billion to $2.5 billion.[43] The higher limits brought into prominence a fundraising technique known as *bundling*. Bundling occurs when an individual solicits contributions for a candidate, then "bundles" them together and passes them on. For example, in 2004 the Bush campaign turned wealthy individuals who could no longer write large soft money checks into bundlers. There were three named categories of these

bundling
Fundraising by an individual who solicits contributions for a candidate, then "bundles" the checks and passes them on.

---

[41] opensecrets.org, "'04 Elections Expected to Cost Nearly $4 Billion," Press Release, October 21, 2004, p. 4.
[42] Jeanne Cummings, "Political Contributors Step Up to the Plate," *The Wall Street Journal,* July 29, 2004, p. A4.
[43] opensecrets.org, "'04 Elections Expected to Cost Nearly $4 Billion," p. 4.

fundraisers. Pioneers pledged to raise $100,000 by getting 100 others to write a $1,000 check to Bush for President. Rangers raised $200,000 and Super Rangers, $300,000. An estimated 385 bundlers, most of them heads of companies and lobbyists, raised more than $200 million for President Bush.[44] The bundlers met their targets by calling friends and, often, by writing fundraising letters to subordinates in their homes. This networking technique was copied by Sen. John Kerry's campaign.

Second, new advocacy groups formed to take in the soft money that corporations, unions, and individuals could no longer give to parties. These groups are set up under the tax codes and popularly called *501c and 527 groups,* after the sections of the Internal Revenue Code under which they incorporate. They are then regulated as tax exempt organizations by the IRS. Both 501c and 527 groups take in soft money contributions. The 501c groups cannot have political activity as their primary purpose or engage in explicit electioneering to elect or defeat individual candidates. But they can run issue ads if "magic words" such as "vote for" and "vote against" are avoided.[45] New 527 groups arose after passage of the BCRA claiming to be exempt from federal election law if they avoided expressly advocating the election or defeat of candidates. They collected soft money contributions from corporations, unions, and individuals to run issue ads before blackout periods and to conduct get-out-the-vote efforts. Much of the spending by 527 groups is unreported, but one estimate of the total in 2004 is $386 million.[46]

Third, *independent expenditures* for and against candidates increased. Individuals and PACs can spend unlimited amounts to elect or defeat candidates in addition to direct contributions. An independent expenditure is money spent for or against a candidate, buying a television ad or billboard, for example, that is not coordinated in any way with the candidate. So while it is illegal for an individual to give more than $2,000 or a corporate PAC to give more than $5,000 to Jones, a candidate for Congress, either can spend an unlimited amount buying media ads to "elect Jones" if the Jones campaign is not informed or consulted. Independent expenditures are legal because the courts define them as free speech that cannot be limited. Before the BCRA, exploitation of this loophole was limited, but independent expenditures exceeded $104 million in the 2004 elections.[47]

So far, the new restrictions of the Bipartisan Campaign Reform Act have worked to cut the flow of unregulated soft money into federal elections. But overall growth of campaign giving and spending has not been slowed. There are signs that money is flowing around the new legal barriers in ways that challenge the spirit of the law. As Figure 9.5 suggests, this fits the historical pattern of failed electoral reforms.

501c and 527 groups
Groups organized under Sections 501c and 527 of the Internal Revenue Code to undertake electioneering and advocacy.

independent expenditure
Expenditures made by individuals, political action committees, or party committees to advocate the election or defeat of a federal candidate. Such expenditures are unlimited in amount provided there is no coordination with the candidate's campaign. PACs and party committees may use only hard money for such expenditures.

---

[44] Thomas B. Edsall, Sarah Cohen, and James V. Grimaldi, "Big Wheels in Bush's Money Machine," *Washington Post National Weekly Edition,* May 24–30, 2004, p. 8.

[45] George J. Terwilliger III and John C. Wells, "'527' Organizations," *National Law Journal,* September 13, 2004, p. 16.

[46] opensecrets.org, "'04 Elections Expected to Cost Nearly $4 Billion," p. 4.

[47] Federal Election Commission Press Release, "September Independent Expenditure Disclosure Summarized," October 5, 2004, p. 1.

FIGURE 9.5
The Flow of Money into Federal Elections
When the flow of political money into elections is blocked by reform, the money flows around the barrier through loopholes in the regulations. In the long run, each milestone effort to stem the tide has failed.

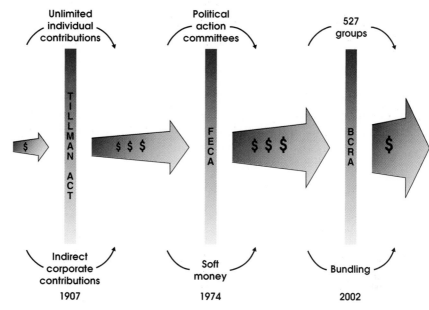

However, the new reforms disarmed corporations in the 2004 election cycle. They could no longer give soft money to parties or fund partisan issue ads just before elections. Although 527 groups were set up to receive soft money contributions, corporations gave them very little for two reasons. Their legality was challenged, raising fear of lawsuits. Also, when companies gave soft money directly to political parties it created obligations in the parties and their candidates, but when money went to 527s the impact on elections was indirect and less obligation resulted. Though corporations gave more to the conventions and more through PACs, their overall giving declined. If history is any guide, this corporate reticence is temporary. The BCRA regulations will be probed and tested in future elections. Inevitably, new openings will be created for corporate money.

The 527 groups were more useful to individuals. Ideologically motivated big spenders, such as billionaire George Soros, put millions of dollars into groups such as America Coming Together, which conducted voter registration, and The Media Fund, which did issue advertising. Soros set a record for an individual in an election cycle, giving $23.7 million, much of it to 527s. A total of 45 individuals and couples gave $167 million to 527s in 2004, with Republicans outgiving Democrats by almost 2-to-1.[48]

[48] See Lisa Getter, "With 527s, New Power Players Take Position," *Los Angeles Times,* November 1, 2004, p. A16; and James V. Grimaldi and Thomas B. Edsall, "The Big Spenders of Election 2004," *Washington Post National Weekly Edition,* October 25–31, 2004, p. 6.

THE INFLUENCE PROCESS

In America, there is a historic fear that business money will corrupt officeholders. Critics believe that corporate money creates unwholesome obligations to special interests. Business contributions are seen as blatant efforts to buy action; they are investments from which donors expect a return. Bribery is illegal. If lawmakers or regulators accept money as a condition for official action, they commit a crime. This does not mean that contributions associated with lobbying are given for ideological reasons with no expectation of a return. According to Robert Rozen, a partner at Ernst & Young,

> You are doing a favor for somebody by making a large . . . donation and they appreciate it. Ordinarily, people feel inclined to reciprocate favors. Do a bigger favor for someone—that is, write a larger check—and they feel even more compelled to reciprocate. In my experience, overt words are rarely exchanged about contributions, but people do have understandings.[49]

Proof or measurement of business influence in politics is elusive. Often there is a correlation between contribution and action, that is, one occurs followed by the other. Did the contribution cause the lawmaker to vote a certain way? Or did the contribution reward earlier support by a like-thinking representative? There are other strong influences on representatives apart from money, including party loyalty, ideological disposition, and the opinions of voters back home. What, then, caused the vote or action to occur?

Sometimes the influence of business money is barely visible to researchers. A lobbyist is alleged to have said that figuring out political influence is like finding a black cat in the coal bin at midnight. Former U.S. Senator William Proxmire (D-Wisconsin), who throughout his career declined to accept campaign contributions, once said this:

> The payoff may be as obvious and overt as a floor vote in favor of a contributor's desired tax loophole or appropriation. Or it may be subtle . . . a floor speech not delivered . . . a bill pigeonholed in subcommittee . . . an amendment not offered. . . . Or the payoff can come in a private conversation with four or five key colleagues in the privacy of the cloakroom.[50]

Tension over Corporate Political Expression

Debate is perennial over whether too much corporate money enters politics. Beginning with the 1907 Tillman Act, efforts to eliminate it have been unsuccessful. More than a century after the McKinley elections radiated corporate financial power, the nation has made only limited progress in controlling the spectacle. Why not more? The answer lies in the tension between two strong values in the American political system, freedom of speech and political equality.

[49] Quoted in *McConnell v. FEC*, 124 S. Ct. 662–63.

[50] Quoted in Center for Responsive Politics, "Ten Myths about Money in Politics," in Anthony Corrado et al., *Campaign Finance Reform: A Sourcebook* (Washington, DC: Brookings Institution Press, 1997), p. 155.

FIGURE 9.6   The Fundamental Vision of Election Law

The challenge to the courts and to Congress with respect to election law is to balance the guarantee of free speech in the First Amendment against an implied duty to maintain elections free of corruption and the appearance of corruption.

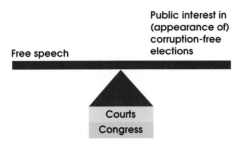

Government regulation to silence speech, including corporate speech, goes against the grain of the First Amendment, which gives expansive protection to free expression and debate. In *Buckley,* the Supreme Court held that a money contribution is a form of speech entitled to First Amendment protection. Therefore, restrictions of campaign donations by any group or interest, including corporations, are constitutionally suspect. Yet since 1907, legal restraints on corporate giving have been permitted to ensure political equality in elections. The Supreme Court has held that these speech restrictions on corporations are permitted for two reasons.

First, the corporate form, which allows the accumulation of immense wealth based on success in economic markets, is an unfair advantage in the political arena.

> [T]he resources in the treasury of a business corporation . . . are not an indication of popular support for the corporation's political ideas. They reflect instead the economically motivated decisions of investors and customers. The availability of these resources may make a corporation a formidable political presence, even though the power of the corporation may be no reflection on the power of its ideas.[51]

Second, the Court recognizes a "compelling governmental interest" in preventing corruption or the appearance of corruption in elections."[52] The presence of unlimited corporate cash, even if there is no overt corruption, undermines perceptions of integrity on which democratic elections depend for their legitimacy. So the Court finds it permissible to balance the right of free speech against the importance of maintaining elections free of both the appearance and reality of corruption. Figure 9.6 illustrates this fundamental vision of election law.

However, not everyone agrees. Conservative dissenters on the court refuse to accept this balancing. In 2003 corporations and free speech advocates challenged the constitutionality of the Bipartisan Campaign Reform Act, arguing that its soft

---

[51] *Federal Election Commission v. Massachusetts Citizens for Life,* 479 U.S. 257 (1986), from the opinion by Justice William J. Brennan, Jr.

[52] *Austin v. Michigan Chamber of Commerce,* 58 LW 4373 (1990).

money and advertising bans violated the First Amendment. By a slim, 5 to 4 majority, the Court upheld the new restrictions in the law, saying they were justified by "reams of disquieting evidence" that the parties had sold favors in return for big corporate contributions.[53] But the dissents were strong. Justice Antonin Scalia argued that it was "a sad day for freedom of speech" when the government could muzzle corporations, "the voices that best represent the most significant segments of the economy and the most passionately held social and political views."[54] Justice Clarence Thomas, also dissenting, accused the Court majority of allowing "what can only be described as the most significant abridgment of the freedoms of speech and association since the Civil War."[55] And a slightly more restrained Justice Kennedy faulted the Court for permitting "a new and serious intrusion on speech."[56]

The dissenters have repeatedly argued that corporations have the right to unlimited speech, that they should be able to make campaign contributions and spend as much money as they wish. Prohibiting corporate funds in elections is, in the words of Justice Scalia, "incompatible with the absolutely central truth of the First Amendment: that government cannot be trusted to assure, through censorship, the 'fairness' of political debate."[57] He and the others trust the ability of the public to judge the validity of corporate arguments and to withdraw support from politicians who succumb to corporate influence and sell out the public interest. If the composition of the Supreme Court were to shift, allowing this position to prevail, the central purpose of federal election law—to limit corporate influence—would be rejected.

CONCLUDING OBSERVATIONS

Clearly, business retains its historically dominant position among interests. There is a significant imbalance of resources between corporate interests and other interests such as poor people, environmentalists, and consumer advocates. Labor can sometimes match the political muscle of business, but often not. However, an equal or greater imbalance has existed since the end of the colonial era, and business is today forced to deal with more, and stronger, opposing interests than in the past.

The rise of soft money and refinements in lobbying methods create a perception that corporate money is undermining the independence of officials. However, specific evidence of deep corruption, as opposed to periodic and healthy exposures of lawbreaking, is not forthcoming. In part because of disclosure rules, American politics is cleaner than the politics of most other nations and cleaner than in past eras.

[53] *McConnell v. FEC,* 124 S. Ct. 666.
[54] Ibid., at 720, 726.
[55] Ibid., at 730.
[56] Ibid., at 762. The fourth dissenter was Chief Justice William Rhenquist.
[57] Dissenting in *Austin,* 58 LW 4379.

The challenge for American society is to balance the First Amendment right of corporations to free political expression against the societal interest of maintaining corruption-free elections and government decisions. So far, our society has successfully maintained a rough, if not perfect, balance.

Westar Goes to Washington

How does politics really work? For outsiders, the process is mostly opaque. Its hidden action and overwhelming complexity invite cynicism and simplistic judgments. The Westar story is a rare opportunity to look inside Washington and focus on a single instance of corporate influence. It is not clear if the story is typical. Its lessons for a working democracy are uncertain.

METAMORPHOSIS OF A COMPANY

Until the mid-1990s, Western Resources, Inc., was a staid public utility providing retail electric service to about 640,000 people in Kansas. As a utility with a monopoly over its service area it was overseen by the Kansas Corporation Commission, which regulated the rates it could charge. The Federal Energy Regulatory Commission had jurisdiction over its wholesale electricity transactions and its transmission lines. It was a tight web of constraint.

Given their regulatory environments, energy utilities often have had conservative, plodding strategies. But when a climate of deregulation arose in the 1980s and early 1990s, arguments for allowing them greater strategic freedom gained strength. In this environment, John Hayes, the chairman and CEO of Western Resources, adopted an adventurous diversification strategy. He wanted to expand out from the regulated utility business into nonregulated businesses with potentially higher profits.

Looking for assistance, he hired a Wall Street merger wizard named David Wittig. He might as well have brought in Willie Sutton, but that is getting ahead of the story. Wittig seemed ideal for the job. He grew up in a small town on the wheat-covered Kansas plains, graduated with honors from the University of Kansas, and went on to become a star investment banker in New York. At Salomon Smith Barney he headed mergers and acquisitions during the era of takeover wars in the 1980s. His picture once appeared on the cover of *Fortune* magazine.[1]

At Hayes's invitation, Wittig returned to Kansas to head corporate strategy at the utility. His job was to acquire other companies, taking Western Resources down the path of growth and diversification. Wittig soon bought an equity interest in an Oklahoma natural gas company. Then, for tax reasons, he created a new holding company named Westar Capitol that was owned by Western Resources. Its purpose was to acquire and hold interests in nonutility businesses. Working through Westar, he took on equity interests in the Wing Group, an overseas power plant builder; ADT, Inc., and Protection One, home burglar alarm companies; and several paging companies. When Hayes retired in 1999, Wittig was appointed president, passing over several of Western's senior managers.

Wittig used debt financing for these investments and the borrowing was approved by the Kansas Corporation Commission. The Commission did not regulate the holding company and its diverse businesses. But it had the authority to approve or restrict actions of any kind that affected Western Resource's electricity ratepayers.

SPLITTING THE COMPANY

Adversity soon strained Wittig's strategy. The stock market fell, halting a planned merger between Western Resources and another utility. Protection One had losses and restated its earnings. The paging company investments declined in value. Western Resources had $3.2 billion in debt and its investments were foundering. Its share price fell and its debt rating sank. The Kansas Corporation Commission was alarmed. It imposed close supervision and disallowed more borrowing for further acquisitions.

[1] The cover story was "Wall Street's Overpaid Young Stars," *Fortune*, November 24, 1986.

Wittig seethed under the restrictions. He wanted to wheel and deal. Relations with regulators grew hostile. Rethinking the strategy, he hatched a plan to separate Western Resources, which he renamed Westar Energy, from the holding company Westar Capitol, which he had renamed Westar Industries. Each would become a separate, publicly traded company. In theory, this could maximize the market value of both new companies. The utility's shares would no longer be depressed by poorly performing investments in the holding company. And when the nonregulated businesses were unchained from oversight by the Kansas Corporation Commission their shares would be more attractive.

Since the borrowing needed to finance Wittig's acquisitions was secured by the utility company's cash flow and assets, the utility would be left with most of the debt. When the holding company broke away, its balance sheet would be clean. At the time of the split, Wittig planned to jump from the utility and take charge of the other company, where he could escape the bonds of utility regulation. The utility's ratepayers would be left to face the debt he had run up.

There was one obstacle. The holding company held equity shares of its businesses, much like a mutual fund. If it became an independent, publicly traded company, it would be subject to regulation under the Investment Company Act of 1940, a depression-era law regulating mutual funds and other public companies that bought and held securities. To protect consumers from investment fraud, the law severely limits debt financing, transactions with subsidiaries, and even incentive compensation for managers. Its requirements are incompatible with the needs of operating companies. They would block the execution of an aggressive strategy.

There was a way to avoid Investment Company Act regulation. That was to apply for classification of Westar as an exempt holding company under the Public Utility Holding Company Act of 1935 (PUHCA). Its Section 3 allowed companies structured like Westar to qualify for such an exemption. There was one problem, however, Congress was about ready to do away with this statute. An energy bill, H.R. 4, which had recently been introduced in the House of Representatives, would repeal it in order to further deregulate the public utility industry. If H.R. 4 was enacted, Westar would no longer have a legal basis to exempt itself from inconvenient and undesirable Investment Company Act regulation.

Wittig decided to make sure that even if the PUHCA was taken off the books, a Westar Industries spinoff would still be spared this oppression.

CALLING ON CONGRESS

Aside from occasional contact with the Kansas congressional delegation, Westar had no political strategy. So early in 2001, it hired a small Washington, DC, lobbying firm named Governmental Strategies Inc. (GSI). GSI represents energy companies. It advertises itself as helping clients to "extract real dollar value from . . . [the] legislative and regulatory process," and promises that a client's "expectations for investment in federal advocacy should match those for any other business investment. There must be a real return."[2] It has four lobbyists, all former congressional staff members having extensive contacts with lawmakers and regulators.

Richard H. Bornemann was the GSI lobbyist who took the lead for Westar. In June he met with Rep. Joe Barton (R-Texas). Years before, Bornemann had worked with Barton as a young staff member on a House committee. Now Barton was in a key position to help Bornemann's client Westar. Barton was an expert in energy law who chaired the subcommittee that was considering H.R. 4, a massive energy bill. Barton worked closely with his friend and House colleague Rep. W. J. "Billy" Tauzin (pronounced TOE-zan) (R-Louisiana), the chairman of the House Committee on Energy and Commerce through which H.R. 4 had to move.

A provision to repeal the PUHCA was debated but not included as H.R. 4 passed in the House and went over to the Senate for consideration. But Barton, who had a conservative ideology and favored deregulation, was writing another energy bill, H.R. 3406, that would repeal the PUHCA. In the fall of 2001 he circulated a discussion draft of this bill to members of his subcommittee. In it, as Section 125, was a provision to exempt Westar from the Investment Company Act if the PUHCA was repealed (see Exhibit 1). If the bill passed, an independent Westar Industries would be free of Investment Company Act shackles.

Section 125 was soon noticed. Democrats on Barton's subcommittee read it and became uneasy when they found out that the Securities and Exchange Commission (SEC) had granted a similar

2 "About GSI," at www.govstrat.com/public/about/about_main.php.

EXHIBIT 1   The Westar Energy Provision

This is the initial wording inserted in a discussion draft of H.R. 3406, the Electric Supply and Transmission Act, by Rep. Barton on September 21, 2001. Note that the name Westar nowhere appears in the text. Wording in paragraph (a) refers to "a person," in keeping with the legal standing of a corporation as a person under the law. Because of objections that the exemption created by this section could apply to many corporations, later versions were reworded to narrow down the type of "person" it applied to until only Westar Industries was covered. The word "grandfather," in paragraph (a), is used in legislation to signify an exemption granted to parties based on their situation before passage of a statute. Parties meeting the criteria are "grandfathered out" of having to comply with new rules.

SEC. 125. EFFECT ON INVESTMENT COMPANY ACT REGULATION

   (a) GRANDFATHER OF EXISTING HOLDINGS.—A person that, on December 31, 2001—

   (1) was an affiliate of a holding company, and

   (2) held investment securities in one or more companies engaged directly or indirectly in the electric or gas utility business, or other permitted business activities for a registered holding company and its subsidiaries,

shall not be treated as being an investment company under section 3(a)(1)(C) of the Investment Company Act of 1940 (15 U.S.C. 80a–3(a)(1)(C)) on the basis of investment securities issued by companies in which such person held such investment securities as of such date.

---

exemption to Enron, allowing it to avoid scrutiny of deals implicated in its astonishing bankruptcy.

Early in 2001, Reps. John D. Dingell (D-Michigan) and Edward J. Markey (D-Massachusetts) wrote a letter to the SEC asking it to explain the consequences of the Westar provision if it became law.[3] The SEC responded that the loophole it created might be a big one. Hundreds of companies could transform themselves into unregulated mutual funds—a potential disaster for consumers.[4]

At the next subcommittee hearing on the bill, Rep. Markey confronted a surprised utility executive who was testifying by asking him whether he intended to start a mutual fund if the bill passed. The puzzled executive said no, that was not his business. "And that's good," Markey said, adding that others in the industry might be more inclined to take advantage of the exemption. ". . . [W]e know that Mr. Lay and Mr. Skilling would have taken advantage of it."

Rep. Barton responded to Markey's provocation with surprisingly little commitment to the provision he had inserted. It was put in "for a company or companies in the midwest," he said, and "if it is controversial, we will take it out in its entirety."[5] Barton did not seem ready to fight for Westar.

"A SEAT AT THE TABLE"

For Westar the action in Washington was heating up. The House was working a bill that contained its special exemption. The Senate was now moving to pass a version of H.R. 4 that repealed the PUHCA. It was a situation with possibilities, but Westar was only a minor player in a grand legislative game. If it wanted to shape events, it needed more influence. Its hired lobbyist, Richard Bornemann, had a plan to get it.

On April 22, Bornemann sent a confidential plan to Westar entitled "Federal Elections Participation," with "recommendations for beginning to develop a significant and positive profile for the Company's federal presence." Westar, he wrote, needed "a committee and leadership-based approach to Capitol

---

[3] Letter from John D. Dingell and Edward J. Markey to Harvey L. Pitt, January 30, 2002.

[4] Letter from Harvey L. Pitt (with attached memorandum from Paul F. Roye) to John D. Dingell and Edward J. Markey, February 13, 2002.

[5] Quotations in this paragraph are from a Hearing before the Subcommittee on Energy and Air Quality of the Committee on Energy and Commerce, *The Effect of the Bankruptcy of Enron on the Functioning of Energy Markets,* 107th Congress, 2nd Session, February 13, 2002, pp. 140–41.

PROGRESS

Late in June, the House-Senate conferees met. The group met only once more over the summer. The versions of the bill to be reconciled were both hundreds of pages long and discussion did not reach the subject of PUHCA repeal. In August, Bornemann attended two more Tex-Cajun fundraisers. Westar also hired another lobbyist, Marianne K. Smythe, a former SEC lawyer. As required by law, she registered in the Senate Office of Public Records as a Westar lobbyist, putting down that she was hired to advocate "an exemption from [the] Investment Company Act for [a] Single Company." Her job was to reword the Westar provision so that it indisputably applied only to Westar. This was an effort to counter the argument that it would unleash hundreds of unregulated mutual funds.

With the conferences under way, Westar was ready to continue its investment in the political process. Rep. Tauzin planned a fundraiser in Louisiana and the contributions schedule called for a $5,000 contribution. Wittig again set out a formula for contributions from his management team (in Exhibit 4).

An accompanying memo from Lawrence reaffirmed the need for everyone's participation and explained Rep. Tauzin's importance.

Right now we have made significant progress with . . . Tom DeLay. . . . The contributions made in the first round were successful in opening the appropriate dialogue. Now, as the conference committee begins meeting, Representative Tauzin will play a key role. Beyond serving on the conference committee, Representative Tauzin as chairman of the full committee is extremely influential in the decision to maintain the House position on our provision.[14]

Bornemann attended Tauzin's fundraiser. Tauzin recognized him and had his staff throw him out. Tauzin felt that Bornemann had deceived him years before about a railroad bill and since then had banned him from his office.[15] It is unclear whether anyone at Westar ever learned what happened, but Bornemann was still working for Westar when he arranged a July meeting with Rep. Barton. At the meeting, Marianne Smythe gave a PowerPoint presentation about the reworded grandfather clause. Soon Barton circulated the draft of a House offer to the Senate conference committee on H.R. 4, and it contained the Westar provision. The new wording, now more lengthy, narrowed the Investment Company Act exemption by restricting it to companies with ownership and incorporation characteristics matched only by Westar.[16]

On September 19, the House conferees met to discuss H.R. 4. and Rep. Markey introduced an amendment to strike the Westar provision. He was supported by his Democratic colleague Rep. John Dingell. Debate ensued.

MARKEY: Now, we are told that this is only a special interest provision that is aimed at benefitting a single company. . . . This company reportedly claims that they need an exemption from the Investment Company Act because of their holdings, but I see no reason why we should give it to them. . . . They should not be wasting our time with a legislative fix. The fact that they are doing so raises some alarm bells to me as to what their real motivation might be. . . . Please support the Markey amendment to block this attempt at circumventing the legitimate oversight responsibilities of the Securities and Exchange Commission.

BARTON: The chair would recognize himself in mild opposition to the Markey amendment. We have been round and round on this. . . . The reason I put it in is because this company is in a unique situation. . . . [A]t the appropriate time I think that this would be a subject that we could work [on] together with our colleagues in the Senate.

DINGELL: But it is interesting to note that any company which could structure itself to be roughly the same as Western Resources could come in under that loophole and then could function . . . as a mutual fund . . . totally without any scrutiny, totally without any protection for the investors. . . . [W]e have no assurances that this splendid loophole is not going to be available to any number of smart rascals, MBAs and others on Wall Street so that they can skin the American investors in the most scandalous and outrageous ways.

BARTON: . . . [I]t does just deal with just one company. It does not deal with potentially hundreds of companies . . .

---

[14] Douglas Lawrence, "Re: Campaign Contributions," memorandum of June 25, 2002, p. 1.

[15] Juliet Eilperin, "Westar Lobbyist's Role Detailed," *Washington Post*, June 10, 2003, p. A4.

[16] "Proposed House Offer," H.R. 4, Subtitle A, Section 156, July 19, 2004, pp. 45–47.

EXHIBIT 4
Contribution
Amounts for
Tauzin
Fundraiser

Name	Amount
David Wittig	$1,500.00
Doug Lake	$1,000.00
Doug Sterbenz	$500.00
Paul Geist	$425.00
Dick Dixon	$300.00
Jo Hunt	$225.00
Doug Lawrence	$150.00
Lee Wages	$150.00
Bruce Akin	$150.00
Larry Irick	$150.00
Peggy Loyd	$150.00
Caroline Williams	$150.00
Kelly Harrison	$150.00

MARKEY: All in all, a really, really nice exemption from the laws which you would think somebody would be requesting in 1928, right before the 1929 crash, not in year 2002. . . . I think it's a terrible, terrible thing for us to be doing.[17]

A vote was taken. The committee divided along party lines, with its six Democrats voting "aye" and its eight Republicans voting "nay." Markey's amendment failed. The grandfather clause stayed in the bill.

The next week, on September 25, Bornemann arranged a meeting for Wittig and Lawrence in DeLay's Capitol Hill office. It lasted only 10 to 15 minutes. Wittig presented DeLay with another briefing book on the grandfather clause.

"THINGS ARE GRIM"

The stars were aligned for Westar, but then came a sudden reversal of fortune. On September 27, John Wine, chair of the Kansas Corporation Commission, wrote Rep. Markey opposing the Westar provision. Wine informed Markey that the Commission had prohibited Westar Energy from splitting itself into two companies because the plan misallocated more than a billion dollars of debt to its electric utility operations.[18] Westar was fighting this ruling. The

Westar provision, he wrote, "would have the effect of removing an important obstacle to Westar splitting its companies and leaving non-utility debt with the utility companies."[19]

On the same day, Westar filed a form 8-K with the Securities and Exchange Commission. Companies must file 8-K reports to announce important changes and events. The filing announced that Westar had been subpoenaed by the United States Attorney in Topeka, Kansas, for information about improper use of company airplanes.[20] Eventually, the federal grand jury investigation behind this subpoena would reveal that Wittig was using his position to loot Westar. But only a hint of the scandal to come existed at this time.

Still, Rep. Markey had enough to kill Westar's legislative hopes. He wrote to the co-chairs of the energy bill conference committee, Rep. Tauzin and Sen. Jeff Bingaman (D-New Mexico), urging that the Westar provision be excised from H.R. 4.

It is not too late for my Republican colleagues to reverse . . . [their] earlier decision to grant Westar a new, ill-advised legal loophole. This company is under federal investigation and the state commission with regulatory authority over this company has come out strongly in opposition to the provision, as well as the underlying business transaction it is aimed at advancing. Accordingly, I strongly urge the House Republican conferees to reconsider

---

[17] Condensed from stenographic minutes, "House-Senate Joint Conference on H.R. 4, Securing America's Future Energy Act of 2001," September 12, 2002, pp. 107–19.

[18] State Corporation Commission of the State of Kansas, "Order for Western Resources to Permanently Halt Restructuring," Docket No. 01-WSRE-949-GIE, July 20, 2001.

[19] Letter from John Wine to Edward J. Markey, September 27, 2002, p. 1.

[20] Westar Energy, Inc., Form 8-K, September 27, 2002.

their support for this ill-considered loophole and I urge the Senate conferees to resist adoption of this Enron-like loophole.[21]

That afternoon, Doug Lawrence sent a pessimistic e-mail to Wittig. It implied contact with Rep. DeLay's office and reveals his impression that a deal to support Westar had existed.

Things are grim in DC. The DeLay staff has asked us to release people from their commitment to support our provision. The Wine letter has killed us, it has been circulated along with last week's 8K. . . . At this point my recommendation is to release them . . .[22]

Nothing more was ever heard of the Westar provision.

KANSAS POSTSCRIPT

Wittig was in deep trouble. A federal grand jury indictment revealed that he was engaged in a fraudulent scheme with a local bank president. Wittig had made a personal $1.5 million loan to the banker, who had then arranged for a $20 million line of credit from the bank to buy stock in the company to be split from Westar.[23] In late November, he resigned as CEO. He and the banker would eventually be convicted of conspiracy, false bank entries, and money laundering. In 2004 he was sentenced to 51 months in prison and fined $1 million.

Meanwhile, another investigation revealed that Wittig had defrauded Westar. A report from the company's board of directors concluded that Wittig (sometimes conspiring with Douglas Lake, his second in command) had exploited his position for personal gain.[24] His use of company airplanes revealed extreme arrogance. After joining Westar he purchased two corporate jets, set up a "flight department," and hired six pilots. Then he used the airplanes for personal trips. He took his children to summer camp, his friends to sporting events, and his family on vacation. The corporate jet could not fly across the Atlantic without refueling in Iceland. So on European business trips he had it take him to New York, where he took commercial flights to Paris. The corporate jet flew separately. When it got to France, it was used to fly Wittig around Europe. Wittig then returned to the United States on a commercial airline and Westar was billed for first-class fare both ways. He also charged the company for a $6 million remodeling of his home.

Twice Wittig tricked the board of directors into approving acquisitions in which he had an undisclosed financial interest. And because of stock compensation awards he had cajoled the board into approving, he stood to make as much as $65 million from the split of Westar into two companies, even as he left the utility business saddled with $3 billion in debt.

Wittig's avarice caused some internal opposition on the board and in senior management. When dissent surfaced in Westar's six-member executive council, he removed three members and another retired. From then on, only he and Douglas Lake reviewed major decisions. When outside directors opposed him he forced them out and reduced the size of the board. He traced employees' calls to find out who was speaking with state regulators or journalists. And he had private investigators check the backgrounds of regulators and senior managers.

Wittig and Lake were eventually indicted on 51 counts related to a conspiracy to defraud Westar.[25] Their trial began in late 2004.

WASHINGTON, DC: POSTSCRIPT

Tom DeLay had political enemies. One was Rep. Tom Bell (D-Texas), who would be defeated for reelection because the Texas State Legislature had redrawn congressional district lines based on a plan masterminded by DeLay. Boundaries were shifted to pack Democratic voters into as few districts as possible, thereby increasing the number of districts with Republican majorities. Bell's redrawn district became nearly all black and Bell was white. He was defeated in the Democratic primary by a black candidate.

When Bell learned of Westar's political contributions strategy, he filed a complaint against DeLay with the House Committee on Standards of Official

---

[21] Letter from Edward J. Markey to Billy Tauzin and Jeff Bingaman, September 30, 2002, p. 4.

[22] E-mail from Douglas Lawrence to David Wittig, "Subject: Washington DC," September 30, 2002, 2:45 P.M.

[23] *United States v. Clinton Odell Weidner II and David C. Wittig*, No. 02-40140-01/02-SAC (U.S.D.C., Kansas), 2004.

[24] Westar Energy, Inc., *Report of the Special Committee to the Board of Directors*, pp. 3–4.

[25] Superceding Indictment, *United States v. David C. Wittig and Douglas T. Lake* (U.S.D.C., Kansas), July 14, 2004. The original indictment was December 4, 2003.

EXHIBIT 5
United States
Code, Title 18,
§201(b)(1)(2)

Bribery of public officials
(b) Whoever—
  (1) directly or indirectly, corruptly gives, offers or promises anything of value to any
      public official, or offers or promises any public official or any person who has been
      selected to be a public official to give anything of value to any other person or
      entity, with intent—
      (A) to influence any official act; or
  (2) being a public official . . . , directly or indirectly, corruptly demands, seeks, receives,
      accepts, or agrees to receive or accept anything of value personally or for any other
      person or entity, in return for:
      (A) being influenced in the performance of any official act;
      . . . shall be fined under this title or not more than three times the monetary equiva-
      lent of the thing of value, whichever is greater, or imprisoned for not more than
      fifteen years, or both, and may be disqualified from holding any office of honor,
      trust, or profit under the United States.

Conduct. He accused DeLay of "illegal solicitation of political contributions from corporations such as Westar Energy in return for official action benefitting such corporations." He demanded an investigation into whether DeLay had violated criminal bribery laws in Title 18 of the United States Code (in Exhibit 5).[26]

Rep. DeLay denied that any exchange of favors for money took place, saying "It never ceases to amaze me that people are so cynical they want to tie money to issues, money to bills, money to amendments."[27] Bell also charged that DeLay had used his political action committee to funnel illegal corporate contributions, including Westar's $25,000 soft money contribution, to state legislators in Texas, violating Texas election law. DeLay denied this, saying that the soft money was legally expended on administrative expenses, not on campaign contributions.

The Standards and Official Conduct Committee never made a formal investigation. Instead, Rep. Joel Hefley (R-Colorado), its chairman, and Rep. Alan B. Mollohan (D-West Virginia), its ranking minority member, looked into the charges and recommended that the committee send DeLay a "letter of admonition." The two senior members accepted DeLay's denial of trading favors for contributions. But they were suspicious about the July 2002 energy company

fundraiser attended by Westar. Since it was held just when a major energy bill was coming to conference and DeLay had just gotten himself appointed to the conference committee, it created an improper appearance. The letter from the committee admonished him on this point.

> . . . [A] member may not make any solicitation that may create even an appearance that, because of a contribution, a contributor will receive or is entitled to either special treatment or special access to the Member in his or her official capacity. . . . In the same vein, a Member should not participate in a fundraising event that gives even an appearance that donors will receive or are entitled to either special treatment or special access. . . . [T]he energy company fundraiser . . . created such an appearance. [28]

The Committee postponed consideration of Bell's charges against DeLay's political action committee because Westar and other corporate contributors had been indicted for violation of Texas election laws.[29] It decided to let the legal proceedings run their course.

After the Committee on Standards of Official Conduct rebuked DeLay, there were calls for his resignation as Majority Leader. Minority Leader Nancy Pelosi (D-California) called him "unfit to

[26] Chris Bell, M.C., Complainant; Tom DeLay, M.C., Respondent, *Complaint,* U.S. House of Representatives, Committee on Standards of Official Conduct, 108th Congress, 1st Session, June 15, 2004, p. 2.

[27] Eilperin, "Westar Lobbyist's Role Detailed," p. A4.

[28] Letter from Joel Hefley and Alan B. Mollohan to Tom DeLay, October 6, 2004, p. 1.

[29] *Texas v. Westar Energy, Inc.,* Criminal Action No. 9-04-0579, D.C. Travis County, Tex. (2004).

lead the party."[30] But House Speaker Dennis Hastert (R-Illinois) came to his defense, saying "Tom DeLay is a good man."[31] DeLay declared himself absolved of wrongdoing, since the committee had chosen not to formally sanction him.

Questions

1. Examine again in Exhibit 5 the wording of §201(b)(2) in Title 18 of the United States Code. Did Reps. DeLay, Barton, or Tauzin engage in criminal bribery? Reexamine the wording of §201(b)(1). Did Wittig, Lawrence, or Bornemann commit criminal acts of bribery? If not, were there errors of judgment?

[30] "Tom DeLay Reprimanded for Violating House Rules," *Foster Electric Report,* October 13, 2004, p. 1.

[31] Ibid.

2. Is there any difference between what these contributors and lawmakers did and daily practice in Washington, DC? Where should the line be drawn?

3. Should the House Standards and Official Conduct Committee have imposed a stronger sanction on Rep. DeLay? If so, what penalty was deserved?

4. Was Westar's strategy for political action appropriate? If not, what would be a better strategy?

5. Is a strategy of political influence based on the exchange of favors inherently corrupt? Or is it a constructive way to make the complicated trade-offs necessary in a democracy?

6. Did Westar or any of its officers violate the letter or spirit of federal campaign finance laws as they existed at the time (before the new rules of the Bipartisan Campaign Reform Act took hold)? If so, what was the violation?

Chapter **Ten**

Federal Regulation of Business

Lockheed Martin Skunk Works

One of the most secretive production facilities in the United States, the "Skunk Works," produced some of the most spectacular airplanes ever built. The Skunk Works was a nondescript-looking facility located at the Lockheed Airport in Burbank, California. Among the major aircraft built there were the highly respected P-38 fighter of World War II (10,000 of these planes were built); the P-80, the first U.S. jet fighter; the F-104, the first supersonic jet fighter; the unequaled, high-flying U-2 and SR-71 reconnaissance planes; and the F-117A, the stealth tactical fighter that performed so spectacularly in Desert Storm.

Skunk Works is the name attached to Lockheed Martin's Advanced Development Project. The name dates to the beginning of World War II. It was derived from the "Skunk Works" in a comic strip called *Li'l Abner* created by Al Capp in the 1930s. The term was applied to a place used by Lonesome Polecat and Hairless Joe to brew an illicit drink called Kickapoo Joy Juice, a concoction made from dead skunks, old shoes, and other strange ingredients. For Lockheed (later merged with Martin) *Skunk Works* meant a facility having virtual freedom to produce airplanes without close supervision by the Department of Defense or Lockheed management. It was expected that this unusual arrangement would facilitate the production of new technically advanced aircraft in less time and at lower cost than traditionally. The expectation became reality.

Clarence "Kelly" Johnson was the founder of the Skunk Works and was given a good bit of leeway from federal regulations until he turned over the management of the organization in 1975 to Ben R. Rich. Rich faced management frustrations that Johnson avoided because of new social, in contrast to military, regulations. Many of the problems he faced are chronicled in the book *Skunk Works,*[1] by Rich and Leo Janos. For instance, he was forced by law to purchase 2 percent of his materials from minority or disadvantaged businesses, but many of them, he complained, could not meet his high-security requirements. He also was required by the Equal Employment Opportunity Commission (EEOC) to demonstrate a policy of nondiscrimination.

[1] Ben R. Rich and Leo Janos, *Skunk Works* (Boston: Little, Brown, 1994).

The SR-71 Blackbird, first flown in 1964, broke all speed and altitude records, setting marks that still stand. The plane flies at more than 2,000 mph (Mach 3 +, or more than three times the speed of sound) at altitudes of over 85,000 feet. At its top speed, the plane traveled about 35 miles per minute. It flew from New York to London in less than two hours. It was called the Blackbird because of a special black finish designed to withstand high heat generated on the surface of the plane by high speed. Although retired from the U.S. Air Force, several are still used today by the National Aeronautics and Space Administration. Source: © Bettman/Corbis.

"I was challenged," he said, "as to why I didn't employ any Latino engineers. 'Because they didn't go to engineering school' was my reply. If I didn't comply I could lose my contract, its high priority notwithstanding. And it did no good to argue that I needed highly skilled people to do very specialized work, regardless of race, creed, or color. I tried to get a waiver on our stealth production, but it was almost impossible."[2]

Rich said that on the later airplanes, especially the F-117A, he had to work with exotic materials on the plane's outer skin. "The radar-absorbing ferrite sheeting and paints required special precautions for workers. The Occupational Safety and Health Administration (OSHA) demanded 65 different masks and dozens of types of work shoes on stealth alone. I was told by OSHA that no worker with a beard was allowed to use a mask while spraying coating. Imagine if I told a union rep that the Skunk Works would not hire bearded employees—they'd have hung me in effigy."[3]

OSHA created other problems for Rich. He tells how an OSHA inspector visited the old facilities of the Skunk Works, many of them dating to World War II days. Ladders were everywhere, lots of wires, a few oil slicks, inadequate ventilation, and other disarray characteristic of a highly talented organization that knew how to avoid

[2] Ibid., p. 78.
[3] Ibid., pp. 75–76.

hazards and produce high quality under pressure. An inspector from OSHA came, at the invitation of Rich, and fined the company $2 million for no fewer than 7,000 violations. "He socked it to me," Rich said, "for doors blocked, improper ventilation, no backup emergency lighting in a workspace, no OSHA warning label on a bottle of commercial alcohol. That latter violation cost me three grand. I felt half a victim, half a slumlord."[4]

The story of the Skunk Works illustrates a serious problem with intrusive regulations that complicate business activity. Ask any business manager what his or her major concern is and the answer will generally be government regulations. A 2003 survey of 1,394 chief executive officers (CEOs) around the world, made by Price Waterhouse Coopers, showed that among a list of 11 major threats to business the one that was the greatest was "overregulation."[5]

regulation
A simple definition of this word, as applied to business, is the control by government of specified activities. Actually, as indicated throughout this and other chapters, this word has many meanings.

Regulation (federal, state, and local) is ubiquitous. "Regulation is today the dominant form of domestic policy," say the editors of the *Congressional Quarterly,* "and the regulatory process is the chosen method of policy making."[6] This subject is of high importance to any serious business student.

The regulatory relationship between government and business is frequently fiercely adversarial. Government sets the rules for business operations and business provides the dynamism of the free enterprise system, but business managers do not like regulations. As Murray Weidenbaum, a prominent economist, wrote: "The continuing challenge is how to constructively harness the innovative power and motivating incentive of the business enterprise so that it meets society's needs without weakening business's unique characteristics that [are] at the heart of a free society."[7]

Because of the massive volume of federal regulations today, government officials are active managerial partners with business executives. Government has always been a partner with business, but it has never before been so directly active in management. It is involved in decisions made by the highest corporate managers, from specific ways in which products are made and distributed, to what takes place between producer and customer after products are sold. But as shown in the box on page 291, government is also frequently very helpful to business. And managers today often act as unofficial agents of government.

In this chapter we discuss the reasons for government regulation of business, the historical and current patterns of federal regulation, the scope of federal regulations, attempts by many presidents to stem the tide of advancing regulation, the legal basis for regulations, how regulations are made, the overall costs and benefits of regulations, what governments around the world are doing in regulating business, and the likelihood that regulation will continue to expand.

---

[4] Ibid., p. 78.

[5] Reported by Mac Champion, "CEO's Worst Nightmares," *The Wall Street Journal,*" January 1, 2004, p. A13. The second was "increased competition" and the third was "currency fluctuations."

[6] *Federal Regulatory Directory* (Washington, DC: CQ Press, 2003), p. 2.

[7] Murray Weidenbaum and Carol Tucker, *Regulation: Benefit or Bane* (Center for the Study of American Business, Washington University in St. Louis, July 1999), p. 2.

UNDERLYING REASONS FOR GOVERNMENT REGULATION OF THE PRIVATE SECTOR

Government regulation of the private sector is justified under two circumstances: when flaws appear in the marketplace that produce undesirable consequences; and when adequate social, political, and other reasons for government regulation exist. For the first century and a half of U.S. history, regulations were introduced mostly in response to flaws in the market mechanism; thereafter, regulations were increasingly introduced for broad social reasons.

Flaws in the Market

When functioning perfectly, the competitive market mechanism determines which of society's resources can be used most efficiently in producing the goods and services that people want. It yields the "best" answer to the questions of what should be produced and when and how the product will be distributed. The market mechanism has great appeal in democratic societies because, through it, social welfare can be advanced without central government control. Although highly efficient, the free market competitive model is not flawless. Some of the more important market failures that have justified government action are as follows.

Natural Monopoly

When a firm can supply the entire market for a good or service more cheaply than any combination of smaller firms, it is said to have a natural monopoly. Under such circumstances, without government regulation, it can restrict output and raise prices without fear of competition. The typical example of a natural monopoly is local public utilities, and state commissions have long regulated them.

Destructive Competition

When companies dominate an industry, they may engage in unfair or destructive competition. For example, they may cut prices enough to force competitors from the market and then raise prices. Several large firms may conspire to fix prices. This is illegal, and the Department of Justice consistently prosecutes companies that engage in such practices.

Externalities

externalities
Costs of production that are borne not by the enterprise that causes them but by society.

Externalities are costs of production that are borne not by the enterprise that causes them but by society. For example, a factory that dumps toxic waste into a river may pollute it. It costs the factory nothing, but the community may have to pay dearly to clean up the mess. Why does the factory not invest in equipment to avoid the waste? Competition inhibits it. Suppose one steel mill tries to eliminate water pollution, but competing mills avoid the expense. Costs of the first mill will rise and, if high enough, could bankrupt the company. So society either pays for cleanup or forces all factories to bear the costs. The principle applies to industrial safety practices, health hazards, and jet noise, to give just a few examples.

Inadequate Information

Competitive markets operate more efficiently when everyone associated with them has enough information to make informed choices. To the extent that such information is not available, government finds justification for regulating the knowledge in question. This category covers a very wide range of information, including information for consumers about product quality, warranty, content, and so on; information to workers about work hazards; and disclosure of financial information for investors.

Social, Political, and Other Reasons for Regulation

Socially Desirable Goods and Services

Many socially beneficial goods and services will not be produced under free market conditions, and governments act to supply them. In this category are highways, clean air, clean water, and toxic-waste disposal. Other goods and services might be exploited in free market conditions, and if they are important, the government regulates their use. Examples are grazing lands, groundwater, rivers, ocean fishing grounds, and scarce water resources.

Protecting Individual Rights and Privacy

This concern has always been a cause of federal regulation. The first Congress passed legislation to help poor and indigent sailors. Help to individuals has expanded to include programs for safe working conditions, better and safer products for consumers, elimination of discrimination in employment, provision for improved health care, and investor protection from misinformation and fraud. The Internet has stimulated strong demands for government regulations to secure privacy for individuals.

Resolution of National and Global Problems

As the nation has grown, the federal government has taken on more and more responsibilities to resolve national problems not effectively resolvable by state and local governments or individuals. Examples are regulation of railroads, banks, pollution, discrimination, safe foods, and so on. In the global economy are fierce and competent competitors for U.S. goods and services. The federal government helps American firms compete more effectively in that market. Actions to protect American farmers and steelworkers from foreign companies selling products under cost in U.S. markets have been continuous for many years. The government has acted to correct unfair trade practices in foreign countries that restrict U.S. exports.

Regulation to Benefit Special Groups

It is possible for regulations to be passed largely as a result of legislative pressures by individuals or groups to pass measures for their own benefit. The expressed justification for such legislation, however, is not based on that objective but on more lofty goals. Nevertheless, much regulation does protect the interests of special groups, such as manufacturers of steel and producers of peanuts.

Conservation of Resources

Federal regulations seek to conserve our natural resources, such as agricultural land, pristine forests, lakes, clean air, and endangered species.

HISTORICAL PATTERNS OF FEDERAL REGULATION OF BUSINESS

The volume of government regulations historically has moved in a wavelike pattern, as shown in Figure 10.1. Each wave has been triggered by the rise of popular demand for government to solve particular problems. After each burst of activity, the rate of new regulation has leveled off or declined. Except after wartime, the declines have been minimal. Most of the controls imposed during wartime have been lifted following the end of hostilities.

The "scale" to the left of Figure 10.1 is our estimate of relative volume and impact of federal regulation of business. Though it is only an estimate with all the limitations of such a measure, we offer it to sharpen the reader's perspective on regulatory growth. Following are highlights of a few major events in each wave.

The First Wave

During this period, regulations were predominantly promotional for business. The government gave vast financial subsidies and huge grants of land (to be sold) to private interests for the building of turnpikes, canals, and railroads. Through these actions, the federal government facilitated the building of a much-needed infrastructure. There were also tariffs to protect "infant" industries.

FIGURE 10.1   **Historical Waves of Government Regulation of Business**

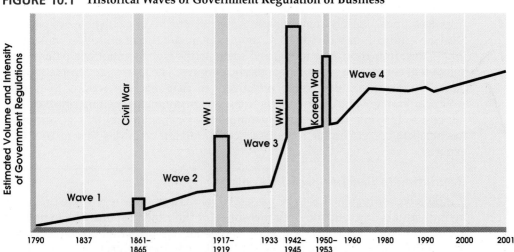

The Scope of Government Relations with Business

Following, briefly, are the many ways in which the federal government is involved with business.

Government prescribes rules of the game. Government sets broad rules of business behavior within which individuals are comparatively free to act in conformity with their self-interest. The regulations vary in the extent to which they restrain an individual business, but they serve to establish the "rules of the game."

Government is a major purchaser of the output of business. Out of a gross domestic product (GDP) of $11.6 trillion in 2004, the federal government is expected to spend $793 billion. State and local governments are expected to spend $1.3 billion.[8] Few companies do not benefit directly or indirectly from such procurement.

Government uses its contracting power to get business to do things the government wants. Businesses that want government contracts must subcontract to minority businesses, pay prevailing minimum wages, comply with safety and sanitary work regulations, refrain from discrimination in hiring, and meet pollution standards. It is a case of "no compliance, no contract."

Government promotes and subsidizes business. The government has a complex and powerful network of programs to aid business. Promotion ranges from tariff protections to loans, loan guarantees, maintenance of high levels of economic activity, and direct subsidies.

Government owns vast quantities of productive equipment and wealth. The government is an important producer of goods and services, such as ammunition, guns, ships, atomic energy, postal services,

weather-reporting services, and dams. The federal government owns vast stockpiles of raw materials and most of the land in many western states.

Government is an architect of economic growth. It has assumed responsibility for achieving an acceptable rate of stable economic growth, as set forth in the Employment Act of 1946.

Government protects interests in society against business exploitation. For instance, many laws protect the interests of investors, customers, employees, and the competitors of a business.

Government directly manages large areas of private business. "Manages" here means that government dictates certain decisions through regulation and joint decision making.

Government is the repository of the social conscience and redistributes resources to meet social ends. Government increasingly redirects resources by transfer payments, research and development expenditures, tax incentives, and subsidies. In mind here, among other things, are Social Security, Medicare, and Medicaid. The government also exerts moral pressure on business to conform with generally accepted social goals.

Government is our national security protector. This includes, of course, maintenance of our national military forces.

Government is the arbiter of disputes. This function cuts across a number of those noted above. In mind, for example, are laws governing labor disputes in which the government can step in to either decide an issue or determine how it can be resolved. Many laws enacted by Congress grow out of disputes among interest groups. Pending legislation on health management organizations (HMOs) is directly related to disputes among patients, administrators, and insurers.

[8] *The UCLA Business Forecast for the Nation and California* (Los Angeles: The Anderson School, UCLA, March 2004).

The Second Wave

This era of regulation was dominated by public demands for government to regulate big business, and the Supreme Court gave the federal government new power to act. Prominent in this wave were railroad regulations and antitrust laws.

The Third Wave

The burst of activity in this wave was the result of the many New Deal laws designed to deal with the ravages of the Great Depression of the 1930s.

The Fourth Wave

A groundswell of interest in improving the quality of life in the 1960s and 1970s led to the fourth wave of government regulation. The result was the development of new controls that involved government more deeply in managerial decisions, enormously increased the volume of regulation, and expanded government's control over business. As a result, government regulatory agencies today are involved in decisions in major functional and operational areas of a typical large firm.

War Blips

As Figure 10.1 shows, wars have brought sudden increases in government controls. During the Civil War, there was little control over production and prices, but the North created the National Banking System to help finance the war, and this had lasting impact on the financial system. World War I witnessed the introduction of substantial controls over industry, but the war ended before the controls began to bite. The federal government exercised complete control over the economic system during World War II and to a lesser but still substantial extent during the Korean War. After both wars, the wartime controls were completely abandoned. There was no comparable increase in regulation during the Vietnam War or the wars in the Middle East.

Attempts to Stem the Tide

For more than 50 years, major efforts have been made to restrain the growth of federal regulation, reverse the trend, and reform the system. The first was the Hoover Commission, chaired by former President Herbert Hoover and completed in 1949. Since then, each president has campaigned against excessive regulation (some established commissions like the Hoover Commission) and, like King Canute, has tried in vain to stem the tidal wave. Each succeeded in creating some reforms, but expansion continued.

The federal government has struggled to exercise sufficient strength to control an exuberant economy while at the same time restraining the growth of regulation over the economy. The sculpture in the photograph on page 293 in which a strong man and a spirited horse tug at each other illustrates the point. It is one of two at the main entrances to the Federal Trade Commission building in Washington, DC. Following are a few highlights of the efforts of recent presidents to govern an expanding business sector while at the same time allowing it sufficient freedom to remain healthy.

The Carter administration (1976–1980) was noteworthy for deregulating a number of industries. The most extensive and widely known effort was airline industry deregulation. Other industries, including natural gas, railroads, and trucking, also were partly deregulated.

"Man Control-
ling Trade" was
completed in
1942 by New
York sculptor
Machael Lanz.
Source: © Elliot
Teel.

President Reagan (1980–1988), upon taking office, named Vice President George H. W. Bush to head a new Task Force on Regulatory Relief, and issued Executive Order No. 12291 to give the Office of Management and Budget (OMB) strong powers to establish a new agency, the Office of Information and Regulatory Affairs (OIRA). OIRA was given the authority to review newly proposed regulations. The executive order mandated that agencies make cost-benefit analyses of their proposed rules and gave the OMB and the OIRA power to ensure before issuance that benefits were greater than costs. Thus, cost-benefit screening became a new and important strategy in federal regulation. There was a sharp decline in the imposition of new regulations in the early Reagan years. However, by the end of Reagan's second term, the trend of regulatory growth resumed.

The record of the George H. W. Bush administration (1988–1992) was mixed. On the one hand, the administration tried to limit the imposition of new regulations. For example, President Bush appointed Vice President Dan Quayle to head a new Council on Competitiveness. This group had overall authority to review proposed regulations and was successful in stopping many that business believed were "unfair" or too costly. On the other hand, two new statutes were passed by the Congress that have led to many new and costly regulations. They were the Clean Air Act Amendments of 1990 and the Americans with Disabilities Act of 1990.

President Clinton in September 1993 issued Executive Order 12866, "Regulatory Planning and Review." This order reinforced President Reagan's order for cost and benefit analysis, as noted above. It also established a new planning process that required agencies to prepare plans each year for the most important actions they anticipate. These are then reviewed by OIRA, circulated among affected agencies, and returned to the originating agency for revision or action.[9]

President Clinton also asked Vice President Gore to head a commission called the National Performance Review. The commission set out "to make government *work better* and *cost less*." The final report made hundreds of specific suggestions for cutting red tape and costs, many of which were implemented.[10]

Immediately on taking office in 2001, President George W. Bush rescinded many orders that President Clinton had signed and set about naming heads of regulatory agencies who sympathized with his intention to reduce regulatory burdens. For example, one of the first laws signed by the new president was a measure revoking OSHA rules concerning the prevention of carpal tunnel syndrome, tendinitis, and other maladies suffered by people engaged in repetitive

[9] For details of this Executive Order, see Susan E. Dudley and Angela Antonelli, "Congress and the Clinton OMB," *Regulation,* Fall 1997.

[10] Al Gore, *Creating a Government That Works Better & Costs Less,* Report of the National Performance Review (Washington, DC: U.S. Government Printing Office, 1993).

motions. He cited excessive costs by industry to comply with the new regulations. The president issued an ambitious and detailed document called "The President's Management Agenda" that set forth an agenda for widespread actions to improve governmental performance.[11]

The new administration worked closely with federal agencies to modify proposed rules in the interests of industry.[12] It sent new guidelines to the agencies intended to improve the procedures they used in preparing new regulations. For example, detailed guidelines for the analysis of new regulations sent to the OMB for review were sent to the agencies in 2004.[13] Their purpose was to encourage better regulatory impact analysis and to standardize the way cost-benefit calculations were developed and measured.

The OIRA announced that during the first three years of the Bush administration more regulatory proposals were rejected than in a comparable period of the Clinton Administration. This conclusion was confirmed in testimony before Congress from James L. Gattuso, a Research Fellow in Regulatory Policy at the Heritage Foundation. But he concluded that ". . . while regulatory growth has been curbed during the Bush Administration—it has not been stopped. Regulation is still expanding, not shrinking."[14] Other critics of regulation have also expressed disappointment in the administration's limited ability to cut the flow of federal regulations. Brian Mannix, an analyst at the Mercatus Center, a conservative think tank, lamented that ". . . after two years, Bush's appointees have made few major changes to the regulatory initiatives begun in the final months of the Clinton administration, nor have they successfully changed the terms of the debate."[15]

THE LEGAL BASIS OF GOVERNMENT REGULATION OF BUSINESS

commerce clause
Article I, Section 8, of the U.S. Constitution gives Congress the power "To regulate Commerce with foreign Nations, and among the several States, and with the Indian Tribes." It has been interpreted to give the federal government wide powers to regulate business activity.

The fundamental authority for federal regulation of business is the Constitution of the United States. In the Constitution, most of the economic powers exercised by the federal government are contained in Article I, Section 8. This section gives Congress wide powers. Included is the power "to regulate commerce." This is the *commerce clause,* and upon its authority the federal government has extended its reach widely over business. There are, however, other powers in Article 1, Section 8, that also provide a base for the exercise of federal power over business. Included, for example, is the power to provide for "the general welfare of the United States," to levy and collect taxes, to provide for the common defense, to borrow money, to establish bankruptcy laws, to promote science and useful arts by granting patents

---

[11] *The President's Management Agenda* (Washington, DC: Executive Office of the President, Office of Management and Budget, 2002).

[12] Stephen Power and Jacob M. Schlesinger, "Bush's Rules Czar Brings Long Knife to New Regulations," *New York Times,* June 12, 2002, p. A1.

[13] John D. Graham, *OMB's Circular No. A-4, New Guidelines for the Conduct of Regulatory Analysis,* (Washington, DC: Executive Office of the President, Office of Management and Budget, March 2, 2004).

[14] James L. Gattuso, "Testimony before the Subcommittee on Regulatory Reform and Oversight, Committee on Small Business, House of Representatives," Washington, DC, May 21, 2004.

[15] Brian Mannix, "A Mid-Term Grade for the Bush Administration," *Regulation,* Fall 2003, p. 1.

and exclusive rights over writings and discoveries, and "[t]o make all Laws which shall be necessary and proper for carrying into Execution the foregoing Powers, and all other Powers vested by this Constitution in the Government of the United States, or in any Department or Officer thereof."

The federal government's ability to exercise these powers to regulate business depends on the interpretation of them by the Supreme Court. As a result of liberal interpretations by the Court, the federal government today is able to impose on business just about any regulation that can be passed through the congressional law-making machinery.

SUPREME COURT INTERPRETATIONS OF CONSTITUTIONAL POWER

Chief Justice Charles Evans Hughes is reported to have said when the governor of New York that "we are under a Constitution, but the Constitution is what the judges say it is." This is true. To understand regulation in the United States it is important to observe the evolution of Supreme Court decisions concerning Constitutional regulatory powers.

Early History

For a century and a half, the Court took two major paths so far as legal authority over business is concerned. On the one hand, it protected business from government regulation, both federal and state. On the other hand, it opened the door to new regulations. We briefly look at landmarks in these paths.

For example, in 1819 the Supreme Court gave business a strong protective shield against arbitrary state power in the *Dartmouth College* case. The New Hampshire legislature amended the charter of Dartmouth College, a private institution, to make it a public institution. The Supreme Court ruled that state legislatures could not impair a contract, and that the charter "is a contract, the obligation of which cannot be impaired without violating the Constitution of the United States."[16]

In other cases, the Supreme Court firmly established the legal foundation for the supremacy of federal law over state law. In *McCulloch v. Maryland*, also in 1819, the Court outlawed a tax levied by Maryland on the Bank of the United States, a federally chartered bank.[17] In another famous case in this period, the Court expanded federal power to control interstate commerce. The state of New York sought to regulate steamboats on the Hudson River. In *Gibbons v. Ogden*, the Court struck down such laws on the grounds that they interfered with federal powers over commerce granted in the Constitution.[18]

But then, in 1837, the Supreme Court entered the second path in the *Charles River Bridge* case. The Charles River Bridge Corporation was chartered by the Massachusetts legislature in 1785 to build and operate for 75 years a bridge aross the Charles River between Charleston and Boston. In 1828 the legislature authorized another company to build a bridge a few yards from the first span. The

---

[16] *Dartmouth College v. Woodward,* 4 Wheaton 519 (1819).

[17] *McCulloch v. Maryland,* 4 Wheaton 316 (1819).

[18] *Gibbons v. Ogden,* 9 Wheaton 316 (1819).

property was to be surrendered to the state and be free of tolls after a period of time not exceeding six years. The Charles River Bridge Corporation sued, charging it had been granted exclusive rights for 75 years. The Supreme Court ruled that the state had a right to exercise its power over private property unless it said in "plain words" that it intended to surrender its power.[19]

Milestone Decisions: Post–Civil War to 1911

The populist movement, described in Chapter 4, led to state laws regulating railroads after the Civil War. The Supreme Court said these laws were constitutional in *Munn v. Illinois* (1877) and declared that "When private property is devoted to a public use, it is subject to public regulation.[20] It becomes "affected with a public interest." This case provided a new foundation for broad regulation of industry. It supported the creation of the Interstate Commerce Commission in 1887 to control railroads, the Sherman Antitrust Act in 1890, the Food and Drug Act of 1906, the Meat Inspection Act of 1906, and other major pieces of legislation. The thrust of these new laws was to curb the abuses of an ebullient, aggressive, and often irresponsible business world.

There were, however, some positive developments for business. The Supreme Court said in the *Santa Clara* case in 1886 that corporations are cloaked in the mantle of the Fourteenth Amendment to the Constitution.[21] This amendment had been adopted in 1868 to protect freed slaves and forbade states to abridge the "privileges and immunities" of citizens; to "deprive any person of life, liberty, or property without due process of law"; or to "deny to any person within its jurisdiction the equal protection of the laws." The Court accepted the idea that a corporation is a person and that therefore the benefits of the amendment extend to it. In effect, states could regulate corporations, but the regulations had to be developed through accepted legal procedures and be nondiscriminatory. This armor proved to be highly protective to business in the legal jungles of regulation.

Efforts by federal, state, and local governments to introduce social reforms, such as permitting workers to strike and improving working conditions, met with repeated rebuffs by the Supreme Court. For example, the state of New York attempted to reduce the hours of work in bakeries to 10 a day. But this attempt, said the Court in *Lochner v. New York* in 1905, was an unreasonable, unnecessary, arbitrary, illegal, and "meddlesome interference with the rights of the individual" and contrary to the Fourteenth Amendment.[22]

On the other hand, the Court did permit state and local regulations over business for certain purposes falling within state powers. Generally, the Court permitted state regulations where they were believed to promote the morals, peace and good order, or health and safety of the public. For example, a Minnesota law prohibiting the sale of habit-forming drugs was permitted in *Hodge v. Muscatine Co.* (1905).[23]

---

[19] *Charles River Bridge v. Warren Bridge*, 11 Peters 420 (1837).

[20] *Munn v. Illinois*, 94 U.S. 113 (1976).

[21] *Santa Clara County v. Southern Pac. RR.*, 118 U.S. 394 (1886).

[22] *Lochner v. New York*, 198 U.S. 45 (1905).

[23] *Hodge v. Muscatine Co.*, 221 U.S. 1 (1911).

The ruling of the Supreme Court in the first antitrust case brought by the federal government under the Sherman Antitrust Act of 1890 was not promising for those interested in breaking up monopolies. In *U.S. v. Knight* (1895),[24] the Court decided that a sugar-refining company that controlled 98 percent of the market had not violated the act. In a series of later cases, the Court reversed itself. Illustrative were *U.S. v. Standard Oil* (1911)[25] and *U.S. v. American Tobacco* (1911).[26] Both companies controlled about 95 percent of their respective markets, and the Court declared this percentage contrary to the law.

The Court Invalidates New Deal Laws

When President Franklin Roosevelt was elected in 1932, he faced the most devastating economic depression the country had ever suffered. A few statistics reveal the extraordinary tragedy. For instance, the gross national product dropped (in current dollars) from $103.1 billion in 1929 to $58 billion in 1932. Industrial production was almost halved between these two dates. Durable goods production in 1932 was one-third the 1929 level. Steel production in 1932 was at 20 percent capacity. The unemployment rate rose in 1933 to 25 percent of the labor force and stayed at that level for months. Thousands of businesses and farmers went bankrupt, and millions of investors lost their life savings.

To deal with this economic catastrophe, President Roosevelt's New Deal broke new federal regulatory ground. The federal government for the first time assumed responsibility for stimulating business activity out of an economic depression. It undertook to correct a wide range of abuses in the economic machinery of the nation, particularly business, and amassed more far-reaching laws to this end in a shorter period of time than ever before or since. It assumed responsibility on a large scale for relieving the distress of businesses, farmers, workers, homeowners, consumers, investors, and others.

The new laws were quickly challenged and received harsh treatment. In one day, May 27, 1935, the Supreme Court declared three laws to be unconstitutional! The most celebrated was the *Schechter* case, which struck down the National Industrial Recovery Act (NIRA). The NIRA was a major enactment that established "codes of fair competition" for all industries. The codes included minimum wage scales, maximum hours of work, collective bargaining by labor unions, prohibitions against employing child labor, fair prices, and boycotts for nonsigners of each code. The codes were agreements hammered out by trade associations and organized labor. When federal officials approved the codes, they became law.

The Schechter Poultry Corporation was a New York City firm that slaughtered chickens and resold them to local retail dealers. The government said the company violated several provisions of the Live Poultry Code, including a ban on the sale of sick chickens. The government argued that the chickens sold in New York City were from out of state and substantially affected the stream of interstate commerce.

---

[24] *U.S. v. Knight Co.*, 156 U.S. 1 (1895).

[25] *U.S. v. Standard Oil Co.*, 221 U.S. 1 (1911).

[26] *U.S. v. American Tobacco Co.*, 211 U.S. 106 (1911).

The Burden of Complying with Regulations

We can measure or characterize the burden of regulation in many ways. One important measure is total dollar costs. Two scholars made a detailed study of regulatory costs and concluded that total federal regulatory cost was $843 billion in the year 2000 (in 2000 dollars).[30] This figure is 8.6 percent of the total GNP of $9.8 trillion for the American economy in 2000. Not included in the cost figure is the cost of running federal agencies to administer the regulatory process. This figure, therefore, understates total costs by that amount. It includes only estimates of the spending by business to install abatement equipment, hire engineers, and so on. It does not include indirect costs such as impact on a company's employment or productivity. Nor does it include indirect costs borne by other firms or the community. Estimates for these costs do not exist but the total given above significantly underestimates the total costs of regulations.

One major finding of the report was that small businesses bear a disproportionately large share of the federal regulatory burden. The cost per employee of firms employing fewer than 20 people was about $6,975. This contrasts with $4,463 per employee for firms with more than 500 employees.[31]

Another measure of burden is the cost of administering the regulatory process in the federal government. The growth of this cost since 1960 is shown in Figure 10.3. The assumption, of course, is that the more spent on administering the regulatory process the more regulations are produced and the heavier is the burden borne by business. Expenditures on administration have shown a continuous upward movement from $533 million in 1960 to a little over $39 billion estimated for 2005.[32] Two trends are obvious in Figure 10.3. One is the continuous upward trend in total expenditures. The other is that expenditures for social regulation are far greater than those for economic regulation.[33]

Federal Register
A journal issued every working day by the United States Government Printing Office. It publishes rules, proposed rules, meeting notices, and other information that federal regulatory agencies are required by law to make public.

Some analysts count the number of pages in the *Federal Register* as a measure of burden. As pages add up, so presumably do the costs and burdens of regulations. This is so because the publication includes all the currently proposed and final versions of regulations. The journal is formidable. It is a fine-print, three-column-per-page, mind-numbing read. It is published every working day. The total number of pages has grown each year. At the end of 2002, for example, it had accumulated 80,332 pages in contrast to 67,702 the previous year.

Some observers justifiably conclude that the present mass of regulations is so huge that no corporation can faithfully comply with all the laws and rules to which it is subject. This generalization is supported by the results of a General Accounting Office study in which the agency sought to learn the costs of regulations borne by individual companies. Not one of the 15 companies studied could

[30] W. Mark Crain and Tomas D. Hopkins, "The Impact of Regulatory Costs on Small Firms," A Report for The Office of Advocacy, U.S. Small Business Administration, REP No. SBAHQ-00-R-0027, Washington, DC, 2000.

[31] Ibid., p. 3.

[32] Susan Dudley and Melinda Warren, *Regulators' Budget Continues to Rise* (Mercatus Center, George Mason University, Arlington, Virginia; and Weidenbaum Center on the Economy, Government, and Public Policy, Washington University in St. Louis, July 2004).

[33] Ibid.

FIGURE 10.3   Administrative Costs of Regulation

Source: Susan Dudley and Melinda Warren, Regulators' Budget Continues to Rise: An Analysis of the U.S. Budget for Fiscal Years 2004 and 2005. Reprinted with permission of the authors. Note: Social regulations include those for consumer safety and health, working conditions, environment, and energy. The economic regulations include those for finance and banking, industry-specific regulations, and general business.

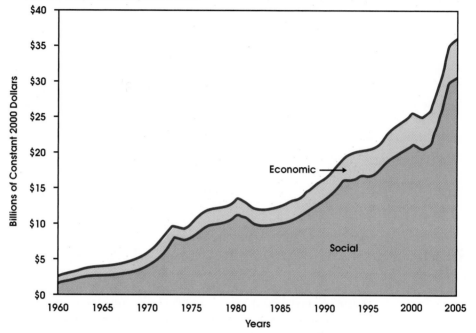

provide total cost data or identify all the regulations with which it was supposed to comply.[34]

Benefits of Government Regulations

Measuring the benefits of government regulations is far more difficult than calculating costs. At an aggregate level, business could not operate and society could not prosper without certain types of regulation. Regulation has helped to improve the position of minorities, clean the environment, prevent monopoly, reinforce free competition, prevent corruption, strengthen the banking system, reduce industrial accidents, provide resources for the elderly, control communicable diseases, and so on. These benefits are enormous and incalculable.

When new regulatory proposals are made to the OMB they must be accompanied with estimates of benefits, as well as costs. For some regulations, calculation of the benefits to a particular firm or individual can often be reasonably made. Examples are loans to small businesses, subsidies to farmers, and financial aid to companies in making international sales. Estimates of the aggregate benefits to society, however, have little credibility given the mushiness of the available data.

[34] General Accounting Office, *Regulatory Burden: Measurement Challenges and Concerns Raised by Selected Companies* (Washington, DC: General Accounting Office, November 1966) p. 52.

Major Regulatory Agencies

Consumer Product Safety Commission (CPSC)—1972

Environmental Protection Agency (EPA)—1970

Equal Employment Opportunity Commission (EEOC)—1964

Federal Aviation Administration (FAA)—1958

Federal Communications Commission (FCC)—1934

Federal Deposit Insurance Corporation (FDIC)—1933

Federal Energy Regulatory Commission (FERC)—1977

Federal Reserve System (FRS)—1913

Federal Trade Commission (FTC)—1913

Food and Drug Administration (FDA)—1931

National Highway Traffic Safety Administration (NHTSA)—1970

National Labor Relations Board (NLRB)—1935

Occupational Safety and Health Administration (OSHA)—1971

Securities and Exchange Commission (SEC)—1934

Transportation Safety Administration (TSA)—2001

GROWING DEMANDS FOR NEW REGULATIONS

Pressures for new regulations are strong, numerous, and likely to continue in the future. For example, uncertainties about global warming, disposal of nuclear and other toxic wastes, new demands for increased internal security, and the introduction of genetically engineered plants and animals are today raising demands for federal regulation from the public and sometimes from business managers.

Business interests will exert great pressure for federal help in reducing costs of regulation. But individual businesses will pressure the federal government to throw hand grenades at their competitors, both domestic and foreign. For example, for years butter producers lobbied the Congress to tax oleomargarine, a competitive product to butter. Congress eventually passed a law taxing margarine in response to these pressures, but it was repealed. Businesses have petitioned the federal government to set uniform standards in some areas, such as insurance, banking, and advertising, to avoid having to deal with 50 individual state regulatory laws. One business executive explained it this way: "I would rather deal with one 800-pound gorilla than 50 state monkeys."

The Mixed Economy

Regulation has evolved to the point that virtually no aspect of economic activity is closed to government action. Despite this comparative open door to intervention, the remarkable fact about the American economy is not how much of economic life the government controls but how much it does not. Although the federal government directly controls or indirectly influences economic activity to a significant degree, the economy is in no way centrally administered or controlled. People are rather free to pursue their economic interests as they see fit. Ours is a mixed economy in which individuals enjoy much economic freedom and the free market mechanism is still a powerful allocator of resources, but governments, especially the federal government, exercise pervasive and strong controls.

REGULATION IN FOREIGN COUNTRIES

Teuku, an entrepreneur in Jakarta, wants to open a textile factory. To do so he must apply to the government for permission. He has customers and the machinery needed to operate the plant. His permission to do so involves completing a variety of forms and paying fees for such items as stamps to register. It takes him 168 days to complete the process and legally start operations. In this length of time he complains he has lost valuable customers.

Ina, an entrepreneur in Panama, gets started with her construction company in 19 days. Her business is booming and she wants to hire someone for only two years. She encounters a law that will allow her to hire someone only for a term of one year and to perform a specific task. In the meantime one of her current workers, who makes costly mistakes, has left. Naturally she wants to replace him and has found a more qualified worker to fill the job. To do so requires her to notify and get approval from the workers' union and to give five months severance pay to the departed worker. Faced with such barriers Ina feels obliged to reject the more qualified worker and keep the underperforming worker.

Avik, a businessman in India, is losing money and goes out of business. To go through bankruptcy will take 10 years so Avik absconds. He abandons his workers, leaves the bank with his unpaid loans, and evades the tax agency.[35]

Wide Variation in Regulation and Its Impact

As the above three cases illustrate, there is great diversity of government regulations among countries and their impact differs widely. This is the major conclusion of a comprehensive study made by The World Bank.[36] This study classifies business regulations in 130 countries into the following categories: starting a business, hiring and firing workers, enforcing contracts, getting credit, and closing a business. Here are a few other conclusions:

Poorer countries generally have many regulations on business. Regulations there tend to be badly enforced and subject to corruption. The result is that people in business choose to operate underground. In Bolivia, for example, 82 percent of business activity takes place in the underground. Workers have no paid vacations or maternity leave. Businesses have difficulty getting credit, and it is hard to resolve disputes. The infrastructure deteriorates because underground businesses pay no taxes and, as a result, government has less revenue to undertake needed

[35] *Doing Business in 2004* (Washington, DC: World Bank and Oxford University Press, 2004), p. xi.
[36] Ibid.

programs that could help business. Businesses remain small in the hope of avoiding government inspectors. In such situations, investment and productivity are low and unemployment is high.

Another conclusion is that the regulatory burden tends to be heavy in poor countries and light in rich countries. Belarus, Algeria, and Chad have the greatest number of steps to follow in starting a business. The longest delays in starting a business occur in the Democratic Republic of Congo, Honduras, and Haiti. Among the least regulated countries are the wealthy ones, such as the United States, Canada, Denmark, Singapore, and the United Kingdom.

Principles of Good Regulation

The World Bank study found that if countries wish their economies to perform well, they should take five major steps.

1. Simplify and deregulate in competitive markets.
2. Focus on enhancing property rights.
3. Expand the use of technology.
4. Reduce court involvement in business matters.
5. Make reform a continuous process.[37]

CONCLUDING OBSERVATIONS

In this chapter we have described how federal regulation of business has expanded over time. There have been ups and downs in the trend of regulations, but the basic direction has been up, with respect to both total volume and complexity. Successive efforts of presidents during the past 50 years have not succeeded in slowing the expansion despite the fact that some of them ran their campaigns on the promise that, if elected, they would reduce the size of government. J. M. Clark, one of the great economists of the twentieth century, astutely observed in 1932:

> The frontiers of control . . . are expanding . . . they are expanding in the range of things covered and the minuteness of regulation. . . . Whether one believes government control to be desirable or undesirable, it appears fairly obvious that the increasing interdependence of all parts of the economic system . . . will force more control in the future than has been attempted in normal times in the past.[38]

As we have seen, the cost of federal regulations is huge, but the cost is offset in significant degree by the many benefits of regulation to society as a whole, individuals, companies, and industries. Analysis of both costs and benefits suggests that costs can be reduced and benefits increased by reforms in the regulatory system. That is the subject of the next chapter.

---

[37] Ibid., p. 92.

[38] J. M. Clark, "Government Regulation of Industry," *Encyclopedia of the Social Sciences*, vol. 3 (New York: The Macmillan Company, 1932), p. 129.

The FDA and Tobacco Regulation

On August 10, 1995, President Bill Clinton held a White House media event to announce a new regulatory initiative. As was his custom, he exercised a little showmanship by walking in through a red carpeted hallway that ran behind the podium in the East Room. He then spoke to the press corps and to a group of children assembled for the occasion.

> Today I am announcing broad executive action to protect the young people of the United States from the awful dangers of tobacco. Today, and every day this year, 3,000 young people will begin to smoke; 1,000 of them ultimately will die of cancer, emphysema, heart disease and other diseases caused by smoking. That's more than a million vulnerable young people a year being hooked on nicotine that ultimately could kill them.
>
> Therefore, by executive authority, I will restrict sharply the advertising, promotion, distribution and marketing of cigarettes to teen-agers. . . . We need to act, and we must act now, before another generation of Americans is condemned to fight a difficult and grueling personal battle.[1]

The president's announcement came because the Food and Drug Administration (FDA), reversing a long-held position, had decided to regulate nicotine as a drug. This is the story of that reversal and of the subsequent effort to get the regulations implemented.

THE FOOD AND DRUG ADMINISTRATION

The Food and Drug Administration is a federal regulatory agency with headquarters in Washington, DC, and field offices around the country. Its origins lie in the progressive era of the early 1900s when reformers agitated to protect the public from adulterated foods and unsafe drugs.

In 1906 Congress passed the Pure Food and Drug Act to ban adulterated or misbranded foods, drinks, and drugs from interstate commerce. The new law went to a small agency within the Department of

Agriculture which grew into the present-day FDA. After more than 100 people died from a patent medicine called elixir of sulfanilamide in 1937, Congress passed the Food, Drug, and Cosmetics Act of 1938, greatly extending the FDA's authority. It received the power to regulate medical devices and the safety of new drugs and to inspect production facilities of regulated products. Since then, more than 30 additional laws and amendments have broadened its powers.

THE QUESTION OF AUTHORITY TO REGULATE TOBACCO

In early America, smoking was mostly confined to southern states, but during the Civil War, Union troops occupying the South picked up the habit and brought it home with them, creating national demand for smoking tobacco. In the century following the Civil War, smoking became widely accepted, and by the 1950s, the majority of men and about one-third of women smoked.

From the beginning, however, suspicion of adverse health effects hung over cigarettes. Suspicion turned into realization in 1964, when the Surgeon General of the United States published a report on accumulated medical research. The report warned of a strong association between smoking and lung cancer.[2] It stated, for example, that death rates for male smokers were 170 percent those of male nonsmokers, and that mortality increased with the number of cigarettes smoked. There was no longer any question that smoking was deadly.

Following the surgeon general's landmark report, damning medical evidence continued to accumulate. As it did, pressure was put on the FDA to regulate tobacco. Many people wondered why an agency set up to protect public health from dangerous products failed to ban a product that killed 400,000 Americans a year. Because of the Delaney Amendment of 1953, the FDA was required to ban any food containing a

---

[1] Reuters, "Teen-agers and Tobacco: Excerpts from Clinton News Conference on His Tobacco Order," *New York Times*, August 11, 1995, p. A18.

[2] Department of Health, Education, and Welfare, *Smoking and Health: Report of the Advisory Committee to the Surgeon General of the Public Health Service* (Washington, DC: Government Printing Office, 1964).

substance that caused cancer in humans or animals, no matter how small the amount or danger. As a result, the agency at one time banned saccharine, though the substance posed only a slight theoretical risk with ingestion of massive amounts requiring superhuman gluttony. Yet it never outlawed cigarettes filled with strong carcinogens.

In 1977 a coalition of groups led by Action on Smoking and Health filed a citizens' petition with the FDA requesting the agency to assert jurisdiction over tobacco. The petition was based on the statutory authority given to the FDA by the Food, Drug, and Cosmetics Act of 1938. Nowhere does the act mention tobacco. Instead, it sets forth general definitions of "drug" and "device" and empowers the agency to decide which substances and objects fall into those categories. In the statute, the term "drug" means:

> (A) articles recognized in the official United States Pharmacopoeia, official Homoeopathic Pharmacopoeia of the United States, or official National Formulary, or any supplement to any of them; and (B) articles intended for use in the diagnosis, cure, mitigation, treatment, or prevention of disease in man or other animals; and (C) articles (other than food) intended to affect the structure or any function of the body of man or other animals; and (D) articles intended for use as a component of any article specified in clause (A), (B), or (C).[3]

The statute defines a "device" as:

> [A]n instrument, apparatus, implement, machine, contrivance, implant, in vitro reagent, or other similar or related article, including any component, part, or accessory, which is . . . intended to affect the structure or any function of the body of man or other animals, and which does not achieve its primary intended purposes through chemical action within or on the body of man or other animals and which is not dependent upon being metabolized for the achievement of its primary intended purposes.[4]

Action on Smoking and Health requested that the FDA define cigarettes as a "device" containing the "drug" nicotine, thereby giving it the authority to restrict their sale. It also requested that cigarettes be sold only through pharmacies. The FDA rejected the petition. It argued that the law allowed classifying a substance as a drug only when the manufacturer made a health claim for the product or intended it to be used as a drug. Since the tobacco companies did not make health claims for cigarettes or state an intent that nicotine be used for its pharmacological effects in the body, the agency had no statutory authority.

In addition, it argued that Congress had known for many years that the FDA did not classify tobacco as a drug. If Congress had wanted to, it could have amended the law to clarify that tobacco fell under the agency's jurisdiction. However, it never did so, although it had regulated tobacco in other ways, for example, by requiring warning labels on cigarette packs.

Action on Smoking and Health was disappointed. The group strongly believed that nicotine was a drug under any literal or common sense reading of the 1938 law. It appealed the rejection of its petition but lost when a federal court agreed with the FDA, holding that a regulatory agency was entitled to "substantial deference" in the reading of those laws it is in charge of administering.[5] There matters stood for many years.

NEW LEADERSHIP UNDER DAVID KESSLER

The FDA, bred of nineteenth-century progressive outrage, is a reformist creation that thrives in an atmosphere of correction. While the consumer movement rode high in the 1960s and 1970s, the agency's powers steadily expanded. Then, following the election of President Ronald Reagan in 1980, the political atmosphere changed. Like other federal agencies, the FDA found its budget squeezed and its staff cut as the Reagan administration tried to reduce regulation of business. With fewer resources, it grew less aggressive, and its staff felt deflated. Business criticized it as a sluggish bureaucracy. Consumer advocates were disappointed by its loss of zeal. Its reputation hit a low in 1989 when, to speed drug approvals, a department head accepted gifts of fur coats and video equipment from a manufacturer.

---

[3] 21 U.S.C. 321(g)(1). This citation references Title 21 of the *Code of Federal Regulations*, where all statutes that give the FDA its authority are codified along with the rules and regulations the agency has adopted. Section 321 is found in Chapter 9, Subchapter II.

[4] 21 U.S.C. 321(h)(3).

[5] *Action on Smoking and Health v. Harris*, 655 F.2d 237 (1980).

However, in 1990 a new era dawned when President George Bush appointed David Kessler as commissioner. Kessler, then 39, was a Republican with a JD from the University of Chicago Law School and an MD from Harvard Medical School. He was dynamic, and he intended a new regime of vigorous enforcement. Immediately, he set to the task by confiscating 24,000 cartons of Procter & Gamble's Citrus Hill orange juice, which the company had labeled as "fresh" even though it was made from concentrate. The business community soon learned that it once again faced an energetic watchdog.

One day Jeff Nesbit, associate commissioner for public relations, approached Kessler to suggest that the time was right for regulating tobacco. Although Kessler did not know it then, Nesbit's father, a smoker, was in the hospital dying of cancer. Kessler was noncommittal, but he called a staff meeting to discuss the idea. Intense debate broke out. Some staffers thought that taking on the tobacco industry was a losing game. It invited reprisals from Congress and from conservative elements in the Bush White House. Others saw tobacco regulation as a righteous cause. How could anyone say with a straight face that the agency upheld its mission to protect public health when it pounced on mislabeled orange juice and ignored cigarettes? One attorney said that cigarette regulation was so important she was willing to devote the rest of her career to the cause if necessary.[6]

STUDY AND RESEARCH

The meeting revealed that the agency was divided, and Kessler remained noncommittal. A small interdepartmental group was formed to give the idea more study. Eventually, a member of this group, an attorney named David Adams, approached Kessler with an idea. Adams pointed out that tobacco companies could vary nicotine levels in cigarettes. Their manipulation of nicotine might be evidence that cigarettes were a product intended to have a druglike effect on the body. If so, the agency could satisfy legal criteria for regulating the nicotine in tobacco as a drug.

Kessler now saw a way to bring cigarettes within the agency's jurisdiction. Under the definition of a drug in the 1938 law, a manufacturer had to intend

David A. Kessler (1951–), commissioner of the Food and Drug Administration from October 1990 to February 1997. Source: © AP Photo/ Gene J. Puskar.

that its product "affect the structure or any function of the body." The FDA had always rejected cigarette regulation because the tobacco companies made no health claims in their ads. However, if the agency could prove that the companies knew nicotine was addictive and supplied it to satisfy smokers' cravings, then the criteria of intent in the 1938 act's definition of a drug could be met.

The immediate problem for Kessler was that no one in the agency knew much about cigarettes. Did the tobacco industry intentionally manipulate nicotine levels? The manufacturing processes of many industries are well known, but the tobacco industry had a history of secrecy about its methods. Lawsuits by smokers had made companies wary. Departing employees were asked to sign confidentiality agreements subjecting them to adverse consequences if they revealed information about research or production. Cleverly, the companies put lawyers in charge of operations, then claimed that information and documents were protected by the attorney-client privilege. Furthermore, since the FDA had no jurisdiction over tobacco, it had no legal authority to inspect cigarette factories or to require disclosure of data about tobacco products.

By this time, the tobacco companies were aware that the FDA intended to pursue tobacco regulation.

---

[6] This was Catherine Lorraine of the general counsel's office. David Kessler, *A Question of Intent* (New York: Public Affairs, 2001), p. 34.

They were not about to help. Therefore, the agency started an investigation on its own to prove that nicotine levels were being manipulated, first to addict smokers, then to satisfy their cravings.

One avenue of inquiry was library research. Kessler and staff members immersed themselves in literature about smoking and tobacco. When the agency tried to get articles from a tobacco collection at North Carolina State University, it ran into resistance from a librarian who felt that the FDA was going to hurt the southern economy. Kessler sent a young intern to the campus with instructions to carry a backpack and look like a student. The intern subsequently found valuable material.

Informants were critical sources of information. The agency's Office of Criminal Investigations was soon in touch with "Deep Cough," a former R. J. Reynolds manager who described how the company created a slurry from old tobacco scraps, added nicotine, and then put this reconstituted tobacco into cigarettes. There were many informants. "Philip," a former research director at Philip Morris, told FDA investigators that a process to remove all nicotine from tobacco existed. "Cigarette" had done lab research with rats at Philip Morris, once writing a paper about how the animals became addicted to nicotine and pushed levers in their cages to get more. "Saint," a chemical engineer at Philip Morris, described a technique she had developed that removed carcinogens from tobacco. The company had abruptly and without explanation stopped her research.

The identities of these informants were concealed to protect them from reprisals by their former employers for violating confidentiality agreements. Contacts with them were often bizarre and frequently involved clandestine meetings. Once Kessler even borrowed a voice synthesizer from the Central Intelligence Agency to disguise his identity in phone conversations with informants, but it sounded so strange that he elected not to use it.

Information from informants had to be verified before it could be taken as factual. For example, "Macon," an employee of Brown & Williamson, revealed that the company had genetically engineered a high-nicotine tobacco plant known as Y–I. FDA investigators searched for a patent on the plant but could not find one. "Macon" remembered that Y–I had been field tested by a "Farmer Jones" in North Carolina. Investigators laughed at the name "Farmer Jones," but they eventually found a small farm owned by an L. V. Jones and verified its use for an experimental tobacco crop. "Macon" also believed that large quantities of Y–I were growing in Brazil. An investigator was assigned to examine customs forms stored in large warehouses and after considerable searching came upon an invoice showing that Brown & Williamson had imported almost 500,000 pounds of Y–I from Brazil.

A team from the FDA also visited cigarette plants owned by Philip Morris, R. J. Reynolds, and Brown & Williamson. It received carefully scripted briefings and facility tours. The visit to Brown & Williamson's manufacturing plant in Macon, Georgia, was particularly frosty. The team's hosts had received information about its two prior visits to the other companies, including information that one team member was a "bully," another was "aggressive" and "underhanded," and a third a "zealot."[7] As the team questioned Brown & Williamson representatives during the morning, the atmosphere became hostile. A lengthy lunch break was called during which the FDA team was separated from its hosts for lunch. After lunch, the team was rushed through the cigarette factory and in the end had little to show for the day.

However, after more than three years, the investigative, legal, and scientific research done by the tobacco working group had uncovered extensive evidence of intent by manufacturers to manipulate nicotine as a drug. They now knew that tobacco firms had conducted research into the addictive qualities of nicotine, that they blended tobacco to manipulate nicotine content in cigarettes, and that cigarette paper and filter material was engineered to control nicotine doses to the smoker. Moreover, informants and documents from tobacco companies made publicly available by disgruntled employees suggested that tobacco advertising had been designed to attract new smokers. Kessler felt that the time had come to compose tobacco regulations.

WRITING REGULATIONS

Although the tobacco investigation had produced enough data to justify writing new regulations, the consequences of such regulations were disturbing. In Kessler's words: "Once the FDA classified nicotine as a drug, the tobacco companies would be required to

---

[7] Ibid., p. 180.

file an application that showed cigarettes to be safe and effective; since they would be unable to do so, we would have to ban them."[8] However, with 50 million addicted smokers, a ban was politically untenable. The cigarette companies would tell smokers that government prohibition had robbed them of their freedom. A black market for cigarettes was inevitable. The agency would put itself on a collision course with elected officials and a powerful, vindictive tobacco lobby.

To escape the dilemma, Kessler decided to classify cigarettes as medical devices. The FDA had the authority to regulate a wide range of medical products such as tongue depressors, breast implants, and X-ray equipment. It could put restrictions on the sale and advertising of cigarettes if they were classified as devices made with the intention of delivering the drug nicotine to users. Kessler believed that this way the agency could regulate cigarettes without banning them, as it did with medical devices that posed risks. It could start with limited restrictions and tighten them in the future.

Kessler also believed that nicotine addiction began as a pediatric disease. Children and teenagers who experimented with tobacco got hooked. They continued smoking over many years, often a lifetime. Adults who smoked did so not because of measured decisions they made—what the industry called free choice—but because of unthinking, impulsive decisions made by a teenager years before. Therefore, he elected to design regulations to reduce the incidence of this pediatric disease. Adult smoking would not be affected. The FDA would only restrict the industry's ability to target youth in its advertising and marketing.

In the summer of 1995, Kessler set up a rule-making team to draft text for publication as a proposed rule in the *Federal Register*. After four months of hard work, a draft regulation was ready.

PLAYING POLITICS

Since the FDA is housed in the Department of Health and Human Services, Kessler needed the approval of Secretary Donna Shalala before going further. At a meeting in late November 1994, he outlined key provisions in the draft to Shalala and her staff.

[8] Ibid., p. 266.

- Advertising in publications with more than 15 percent or more than 2 million under-18 readers would be limited to black-and-white text only and include warnings such as: "ABOUT 1 OUT OF 3 KIDS WHO BECOME SMOKERS WILL DIE FROM THEIR SMOKING." Pictures and cartoon figures would be prohibited.
- Outdoor advertising within 1,000 feet of a school would be banned.
- The use of cigarette brand names on nontobacco items such as T-shirts and hats would be prohibited.
- Cigarette brand names could no longer be used to sponsor sports events.
- Vending machines would be banned. Tobacco could be sold only in face-to-face transactions.
- Tobacco companies would be made to conduct FDA-approved public education campaigns to counteract their image from advertising among those under 18.
- If underage smoking had not declined by 50 percent five years after the rules went into effect, additional restrictions would be invoked.

Shalala was favorably impressed with the general content and told Kessler to work with her staff on a final draft. But Kessler soon discovered that her staff thought the regulations were a political blunder. Believing that he had Shalala's support, he decided to circumvent the staff and take the next step, which was getting White House approval.

Even though he was a Republican, Kessler had been reappointed as FDA head in 1992 by President Bill Clinton, a Democrat. This was probably political expediency on Clinton's part, since Kessler's activist approach was popular with the American public. Yet Kessler was barely acquainted with Clinton, having talked to him only once at a White House dinner. He did not have enough weight to call and schedule a meeting on his own. In fact, Clinton was worried about tobacco regulation. He believed that the two issues of tobacco and gun control had cost the Democrats control of the House of Representatives in the 1994 midterm elections. He and powerful members of his staff thought that reaction against tobacco regulation in key southern states might cost him a second term in the upcoming 1996 election.

Kessler approached Abner Mikva, an old law school acquaintance, who was an attorney on Clinton's staff.

He asked Mikva to discuss with Clinton the potential public health benefits of restricting tobacco advertising and marketing. From Mikva he learned that the tobacco companies were also lobbying the White House to forestall FDA regulation. Next, working through another acquaintance, he got an appointment with Vice President Al Gore, who was widely known to support tobacco regulation. Kessler's meeting with Gore lasted only five minutes, but the vice president made a strong appeal to Clinton on behalf of the FDA.

Ultimately, the breakthrough in the battle for Clinton's support came because of Dick Morris, a shadowy figure who gave Clinton political advice based on public opinion polls. It was because of the presence and influence of Morris that Clinton had gotten the reputation of taking policy positions based on polling rather than principle. With tobacco, that reputation would prove accurate. Morris took polls in five southern states that were key to Clinton's reelection. The results showed large majorities were enthusiastic about regulations to reduce youth smoking. Morris advised the president that support of the FDA regulation was a winning position.

Soon Clinton met with Secretary Shalala and Kessler to discuss the proposed regulations. Kessler found the president supportive but unwilling to give the FDA a green light just yet. However, a month later, Kessler was back in the East Room listening to Clinton announce that tobacco regulation would go forward.

The next day, Friday, August 11, 1995, the FDA published its proposed rule in the *Federal Register.* It was a massive entry in number 155 starting on page 44,314 and ending 473 pages later on page 44,787. The proposed rule, entitled "Regulations Restricting the Sale and Distribution of Cigarettes and Smokeless Tobacco Products to Protect Children and Adolescents," covered 139 typical pages of small type in triple columns. The rest of the entry was a reproduction of the document the FDA had written to justify regulating cigarettes as a device containing the drug nicotine.[9] This part covered the remaining 334 pages.

In the proposed rule, the FDA estimated that its regulations would prevent more than 60,000 deaths and produce monetary benefits of $28 to $43 billion in lower medical costs, productivity gains, and hedonic values. It estimated an annual record-keeping burden on the industry of 1.2 million hours, increased annual costs of $227 million per year, and a revenue decline of 4 percent in 10 years.

After a proposed rule is published in the *Federal Register,* there is by law a comment period during which the agency must consider and respond to substantive comments from the public. The tobacco industry chose to take advantage of this requirement by swamping the FDA with more than 710,000 comments, a number far exceeding the previous record of 45,000. The tobacco companies submitted a 2,000-page comment with 45,000 pages of supporting documents. Many of the other comments were generated by form letters sent out by the industry.[10] Working from a rented warehouse, the FDA staff painstakingly answered each one.

It took 12 months, but on August 28, 1996, the final rule appeared in the *Federal Register.* Although no major changes were made in the regulations, the agency responded to various written comments, swelling the entry to 922 pages.[11] More than four years had passed since Kessler first convened a staff meeting to discuss the prospects of regulating tobacco.

TO THE COURTS

Immediately the tobacco industry, joined by advertisers and tobacco retailers, filed suit in a federal district court in North Carolina to stop implementation of the rule. It challenged the FDA with three main arguments. The first was that the agency lacked jurisdiction over tobacco products because Congress had never given it a specific grant of authority. FDA attorneys responded that as a point of law it was wrong to claim a product was excluded because it had not been named in the Food, Drug, and Cosmetics Act of 1938. Congress had defined drugs and devices, leaving it up to the agency to determine what products fit these definitions. Under the *Chevron* doctrine, the agency was entitled to deference in its reading of the statute.[12] The second argument by the industry was that cigarettes did not fit the definition of a drug or device because manufacturers made no health claims about them. The FDA responded that its research on

[9] The title of this document is *Nicotine in Cigarettes and Smokeless Tobacco Products Is a Drug and These Products Are Nicotine Delivery Devices under the Federal Food, Drug, and Cosmetics Act.*

[10] Kessler, *A Question of Intent,* pp. 336–37.

[11] 61 FR 44396–45318 (1996).

[12] *Chevron U.S.A. Inc. v. Natural Resources Defense Council,* 467 U.S. 837 (1984).

nicotine manipulation confirmed the classification was appropriate. The third argument was that the proposed restraints on advertising violated the industry's First Amendment guarantee of free speech. The FDA argued that the restrictions met legal guidelines for advertising restrictions as set forth previously by the U.S. Supreme Court.[13]

In its decision, the district court rejected the industry's first two arguments, upholding the restrictions on sales in the FDA rule. However, it concluded that the advertising restrictions were unconstitutional.[14] This was a win for the FDA. It left intact the agency's power to regulate tobacco.

Both sides appealed the decision, hoping for a complete victory. The appeals court reversed the district court, and the tobacco industry emerged triumphant. In a 2–1 decision, the court ruled that Congress had never intended to give the FDA jurisdiction over tobacco. Therefore, the agency had exceeded its powers.[15] The FDA appealed to the U.S. Supreme Court.

ENDGAME IN THE SUPREME COURT

On March 21, 2000, the Supreme Court, in a 5–4 decision, invalidated the FDA's tobacco rule. The justices divided into the conservative and liberal groups that have characterized many of the Court's decisions related to government regulation of business.[16] Associate Justice Sandra Day O'Connor, often regarded as a swing vote because she sometimes joins with the Court's liberals, joined with conservatives William Rehnquist, Antonin Scalia, Clarence Thomas, and Anthony Kennedy to build a five-member majority. She also wrote for the majority.

In her opinion, Justice O'Connor stated that although tobacco was one of the nation's most troubling public health problems, the FDA had no jurisdiction over it. She argued that if the FDA held that nicotine was a drug and cigarettes were a device to deliver that drug to the body, it would have to ban them. The Food, Drug, and Cosmetics Act of 1938 required that any drug or device regulated by the FDA had to be, in the language of the law, "safe" and "effective." Since the FDA had shown cigarettes to be an extremely dangerous health risk in its final rule, it would be required by law to prohibit tobacco companies from marketing them. However, said O'Connor, a cigarette ban would violate the clear intent of Congress. She pointed out that in 1929 and in 1963 bills were introduced in Congress to give the FDA authority over tobacco. They were not passed. Instead, the lawmakers had passed six statutes regulating tobacco since 1965.[17] Collectively, these laws established a framework of regulation and showed that Congress rejected prohibition in favor of more limited regulation. O'Connor summed up the majority opinion this way.

> By no means do we question the seriousness of the problem that the FDA has sought to address. The agency has amply demonstrated that tobacco use, particularly among children and adolescents, poses perhaps the single most significant threat to public health in the United States. Nonetheless, no matter how "important, conspicuous, and controversial" the issue . . . an administrative agency's power to regulate in the public interest must always be grounded in a valid grant of authority from Congress.[18]

The dissenting opinion was written by Justice Stephen G. Breyer, who was joined by Justices John Paul Stevens, David Souter, and Ruth Bader Ginsburg. Justice Breyer began the dissent by pointing out that the purpose of the Food, Drug, and Cosmetics Act of 1938 was to protect public health. Since cigarettes

---

[13] The definitive test of the constitutionality of commercial speech restraints imposed by government is set forth in *Central Hudson Gas & Electric Corp. v. Public Service Commission,* 447 U.S. 557 (1980).

[14] *Coyne Beahm, Inc. v. Food and Drug Administration,* 966 F.Supp. 1374 (1997).

[15] *Brown & Williamson v. Food and Drug Administration,* 153 F.3d 155 (1998).

[16] See, for example, *Adarand v. Pena,* the case study in Chapter 18.

[17] These are the Federal Cigarette Labeling and Advertising Act of 1965, the Public Health Cigarette Smoking Act of 1969, the Alcohol and Drug Abuse Amendments of 1983, the Comprehensive Smoking Education Act of 1984, the Comprehensive Smokeless Tobacco Health Education Act of 1986, and the Alcohol, Drug Abuse, and Mental Health Administration Reorganization Act of 1992.

[18] *Food and Drug Administration v. Brown & Williamson,* 529 U.S. 120, at 152.

posed a clear danger to public health, the statute had to be interpreted in a way that was "consistent with [this] overriding purpose."[19] Breyer thought the literal wording of the law gave the FDA authority to classify cigarettes as "devices" that delivered the "drug" nicotine and then to regulate their sale and use.

Rejecting the reasoning of the majority that Congress had chosen not to ban tobacco, he pointed out that nowhere in any law was there specific language denying the FDA authority over tobacco or denying the agency a right to ban tobacco products. "[O]ne can just as easily infer," he wrote, "that Congress did not intend to affect the FDA's tobacco-related authority at all."[20] Breyer believed that the FDA had made a reasonable interpretation of the 1938 law in light of its "overall health-protecting purpose" and that, under the *Chevron* doctrine, the agency was entitled to broad deference. He concluded by observing that since a policy of tobacco regulation was of great import to the nation, the public could, and would, hold the president and elected representatives in Congress accountable for it. Therefore, implicitly, the Court should defer to the public rather than surmise the intent of Congress in the absence of any direct statement.

POSTSCRIPT

Early in 1997 David Kessler resigned as FDA administrator to become dean of the Yale University School of Medicine. Even after leaving, he still had an obsessive interest in tobacco regulation. He often sat late at night poring over tobacco company documents in his garage, still working out the issues. The Court's holding pained him. In his own words: "The decision that could have saved hundreds of thousands of lives had been lost by a single vote."[21]

Although the tobacco industry staved off FDA regulation, it did not escape restrictions. In 1998 tobacco companies agreed to pay $246 billion over 25 years to settle suits by state attorneys general seeking to recover billions of Medicaid dollars paid out to treat smokers' illnesses. As a condition of settlement, they also agreed to many advertising restrictions, most notably bans on billboards, cartoon figures, event sponsorships, and the use of logos on promotional items. In addition, the industry must pay for $25 million of antismoking ads each year for 10 years.

Since the settlement, the industry environment has further deteriorated. Profits are eroding for many reasons. The number of smokers is declining. States are raising excise taxes on tobacco. The $246 billion Medicaid settlement adds about $0.50 to the cost of each cigarette pack sold by the big tobacco companies that participated. Since the settlement new competitors have sprung up marketing new brands at lower cost. They can undercut big company prices because they are not required to participate in the settlement. As a result, discounters now have 10 percent of the American market. Finally, legal costs keep rising. Major tobacco companies now must defend 1,500 to 2,000 lawsuits at a time. The biggest case is a civil racketeering lawsuit brought by the Department of Justice against the six largest tobacco firms.[22] The government accuses these defendants of having participated in a conspiracy since 1953 to mislead smokers about health risks and it seeks disgorgement of $280 billion, their combined profits over five decades.

In this environment, Philip Morris recently changed course and negotiated with supporters of tobacco regulation in Congress on proposed legislation to finally give the FDA regulatory powers.[23] But the proposal, which failed to pass, was not the kind of police power envisioned by Kessler. It would have allowed the FDA to restrict advertising to children, require new and larger warning notices, and prevent vending machine sales. These provisions would have helped Philip Morris cement its dominant market position. It sells half of all cigarettes and its most popular brand, Marlboro, has a 40 percent market share. R. J. Reynolds Tobacco,

---

[19] 529 U.S. 162.

[20] 529 U.S. 163.

[21] Kessler, *A Question of Intent*, p. 384.

[22] *United States v. Philip Morris Incorporated et al.*, Civil No. 99-CV-02496 (GK).

[23] The proposal, "A Bill to Protect the Public Health by Providing the Food and Drug Administration with Certain Authority to Regulate Tobacco Products," was introduced as identical bills (the DeWine–Kennedy Bill, 2. 2461, and the Davis–Waxman Bill, H.R. 4433) in both the Senate and the House of Representatives in the 108th Congress, second session (2004). By the end of the session the proposal advanced to a House–Senate conference committee as part of a corporate tax bill, but it was deleted.

the second largest in the industry, opposed the new legislation along with smaller companies because these restrictions on marketing would make it far more difficult to steal market share from Philip Morris.

The proposed new regulations prohibited the FDA from ever eliminating nicotine in cigarettes or banning their sale to adults. They even required the FDA to work for the tobacco makers by acting to stop the sale of counterfeit and illegal tobacco products. Foreign manufacturers would have had to register with the FDA and conform their products to its standards. And any new cigarettes or tobacco products would have required a "new product" approval by the FDA. Supporters of tobacco regulation, who felt that the proposed measure was better than no regulation at all, hope to reintroduce it.

Questions

1. Do you agree with the Food and Drug Administration that nicotine can be classified as a drug and that cigarettes can be classified as devices under the definitions in the Food, Drug, and Cosmetics Act?

2. Did the FDA make any legal or political errors that defeated its efforts to regulate tobacco?

3. Do you agree with the decision of the U.S. Supreme Court? Why or why not?

4. Do you believe that the story reveals flaws in American government and the regulatory process, or do you believe that the story reveals a system that, despite faults, is ultimately responsive and just?

5. Should Congress enact FDA regulation of tobacco products even if it adds to the competitive advantage of Philip Morris?

Chapter **Eleven**

Reforming Regulation

Ted Turner Attacks Media Giants

Ted Turner, the largest shareholder of Time-Warner, is unlikely in the role of a "pit bull" attacking large concentrations in the telecommunications industry. (Time-Warner had revenues in 2003 of more than $40 billion.) He founded Turner Broadcasting System in 1970, which today has the second-largest cable system in the United States, a large film studio, and several cable-TV networks and is a prominent magazine publisher. Turner is an independent director of Time-Warner and has served as vice chairman. He is the founder of CNN. He owns the Atlanta Braves. He won the prestigious America's Cup and has been a generous philanthropist.

In 1997 he pledged $1 billion to the United Nations for humanitarian projects and he still has billions left. He created a charitable foundation in 1990 to advance environmental causes. He is an independent thinker and a daring entrepreneur, flamboyant and controversial. Today he is involved in a controversy over new rules set forth by the FCC concerning mergers and acquisitions in the telecommunications industry. What is Turner's attack on big media giants all about?

In June 2003 the FCC approved sweeping revisions of its regulations concerning the allowable structure of the media marketplace. The FCC rules liberalized the ability of a single company to acquire TV stations, cable companies, newspapers, and other media in a single market. A company can now own TV stations that cover 45 percent of households in their areas. The FCC also ended a ban on ownership of newspapers and broadcast stations in the same city. However, it continued to ban mergers of the four major networks: ABC, CBS, NBC, and Fox.[1]

Michael K. Powell, chairman of the FCC, presented the case for the new rules in these words. "The days of free television may be numbered. We are in the midst of change that is having a dramatic effect on how we watch television. . . . It used to be that the 'big three' networks, ABC, CBS, and NBC, were just about the only game in town."[2] That is no longer true, he said. Viewers now have access to many channels for sports, news, children's programs, minority programming, documentaries, history, and other entertainment. These are programs for which an increasing number of viewers are willing to pay.

---

[1] For a more detailed description of the new rules, see Manatt, "FCC Adopts New Media Ownership Rules," undated, http://www.rclpc.com/showarticle.asp?id=733&Cat=Articles+By+Us, accessed 11/20/2004.

[2] Michael K. Powell, "And That's the Way It Is," *The Wall Street Journal,* September 11, 2003.

FCC commissioners who voted for the change (it was a 3–2 decision) have added to these justifications for their vote. Kathleen Q. Abernathy, for example, told a Congressional committee: "We have preserved core values by maintaining safeguards to protect against undue concentration, we have altered rules as necessary to respond to dramatic changes that have occurred in the marketplace since the adoption of our media ownership rules many years ago, and we have provided a rigorous justification with an exhaustive study based on the record."[3]

Ted Turner, along with many politicians and advocacy groups, blasted the new rules. Turner is concerned that " . . . media companies are more concentrated than [at] any time in the past 40 years, thanks to a continual loosening of ownership rules by Washington." He says: " . . . without the proper rules, healthy capitalist markets turn into sluggish oligopolies, and that is what's happening in media today. . . . Unless we have a climate that will allow more independent media companies to survive, a dangerously high percentage of what we see—and what we don't see—will be shaped by the profit motives and political interests of large, publicly traded conglomerates. . . . When the independent businesses are gone, where will the new ideas come from? We have to do more than keep media giants from growing larger; they're already too big. We need a new set of rules that will break these huge companies to pieces."[4]

Turner believes that when large companies dominate a market not only do they choke innovation but they focus more on profits than on public interests. Furthermore, "If the only media companies are major corporations, controversial and dissenting views may not be aired at all. . . . Consolidation gives them more power to tilt the news and cut important ideas out of the public debate. And it's precisely that power that the rules should prevent."[5]

Turner suggests the need for drastic action. "At this late stage," he says, "media companies have grown so large and powerful, and their dominance has become so detrimental to the survival of small, emerging companies, that there remains only one alternative: bust up the big conglomerates."[6] If the current rules had existed in 1970, he notes, he could not have created Turner Broadcasting or, 10 years later, created CNN.[7]

WHY REGULATORY REFORM?

Although measures to calculate regulatory costs are imperfect, they suggest that the burdens on business and the economy are heavy and growing. For many regulations the benefits achieved clearly exceed the costs, but the costs of some cannot be justified by their benefits.

Demands for reform and/or a showing of justification arise from many regulatory shortcomings, for example, poorly drafted basic legislation and the influence

[3] Kathleen Q. Abernathy, "Written Statement on the 2002 Broadcast Ownership Biennial Regulatory Review, Before the Committee on Commerce, Science, and Transportation, United States Senate," June 4, 2003.

[4] Ted Turner, "My Beef with Big Media," *Washington Monthly,* July/August 2004, pp. 2–3.

[5] Ibid.

[6] Ibid.

[7] Ted Turner, "Monopoly or Democracy?" *Washington Post,* May 30, 2003, p. A23.

of special interests in the drafting of statutes and the preparation of agency rules. Regulations costly enough to lead business managers to go out of business should be examined carefully for proof they are necessary in their present form. Some regulations conflict with others, some are poorly implemented, some impose directives better developed by private enterprises, and some fail to achieve the objective for which they were originally created. The environment (e.g., technology, competition, consumer interests, products on the market, changes in public policy goals) may have changed over the life of a regulation, making revision necessary. When reforms are introduced to correct situations such as these, substantial benefits can accrue to producers, consumers, investors, and society generally. Regulatory reform that enhances free competition by altering taxes or tariffs is an example. Reforms can provide incentives for businesses to improve the quality of products and services, increase productivity, reduce prices, and hire more employees.

RECOMMENDATIONS FOR REGULATORY REFORM

The remainder of this chapter elaborates some main reform recommendations for improving federal regulation. (They are equally applicable to state and local regulations but space does not permit extending the discussion to that area.) Before presenting some reform proposals it is appropriate to note that in the gigantic

Source: © Chicago Sun-Times: Cartoon by John Fischetti. Reprinted with permission.

federal bureaucracy efforts at reforming the regulatory system and specific regulations are extremely difficult, time consuming, and not at all sure to succeed. The cartoon on page 318 illustrates the point.

Statutory Reform

statutory reform
Reform accomplished by revising the statutes that underlie a regulatory authority.

The most fundamental type of regulatory reform is *statutory reform* by Congress, because it is Congress that grants authority to regulatory agencies. "The underlying statutes," editorializes the *Washington Post*, "are not a coherent body of law but a kind of archeological pile, each layer a reflection of the headlines and political impulses of the day."[8] Congress passes statutes with admirable goals and broad grants of authority, then denounces agencies for aggressive and costly regulations to carry them out. Some statutes mandate or forbid specific actions by regulatory agencies. For example, Congress directed the Consumer Product Safety Commission in the Child Safety Protection Act of 1994 to require certain labeling on toys intended for children aged three to six. And the Occupational Safety and Health Act prohibited the use of cost-benefit analysis in developing workplace regulations, said the Supreme Court in a decision made when the agency wanted to use the cost-benefit tool.[9] Such mandates led critic Murray Weidenbaum, a well-known scholar of regulation, to observe, "Experience over the years confirms that the fundamental shortcoming of government regulation results more from statutory than from executive deficiencies."[10]

Congress likes to make new laws rather than revise old ones. A classic illustration is the Mining Act of 1872. Under the provisions of this act, it is possible to buy public lands for $2.50 to $5.00 an acre when ore is discovered. Secretary of the Interior Bruce Babbitt in September 1995 signed over title to federal land containing more than $1 billion in minerals to a Danish mining company for $275 under the terms of the law. He called the signing a "tawdry process" and a "flagrant abuse of the public interest," but the law mandated his action. In 1994 he signed title to land containing about $10 billion in gold to a Canadian firm for about $10,000 and called it "the biggest gold heist since the days of Butch Cassidy."[11] Table 11.1 shows other mining rights issued under the law since then.

President Clinton tried to persuade Congress to revise this law to prevent such lavish gifts, but without success. However, he found a way to modify the law. He authorized the Bureau of Land Management to place a moratorium on new mining rights over millions of acres of federal lands because mining would damage the environment. The moratorium has remained in force. For decades critics have clamored for changes in the Mining Act, but until President Clinton's action western political interests in Congress had prevented change.

---

[8] "Good Move on Regulation," *Washington Post,* March 26, 1995, p. C6.

[9] *American Textile Manufacturers Institute v. Donovan,* 452 U.S. 490 (1981).

[10] Murray L. Weidenbaum, *Business and Government in the Global Marketplace,* 7th ed. (Upper Saddle River, NJ: Pearson Prentice Hall, 2004), p. 176.

[11] See Mark Zepezauer and Arthur Naiman, *Take the Rich Off Welfare,* excerpt at www.thirdworldtravelere.com/Corporate-Welfare/Mining_Subsidies.html.

TABLE 11.1
Examples of Mining Patents Issued Since 1994

Source: Department of the Interior; and *Economic Report of the President* (Washington, DC: U.S. Government Printing Office, 1997), p. 218.

Location of Patent	Date	Mineral	Mineral Value	Paid to United States
Eureka and Elko Counties, Nevada	5/1994	Gold	$10,000,000,000	$9,765
Clark County, Idaho	9/1995	Travertine limestone	1,000,000,000	275
Humboldt County, Nevada:				
Imperial County, California	3–6/1995	Gold	1,200,000,000	3,585
Pima County, Arizona	12/1995	Copper and silver	2,900,000,000	1,745
Eureka County, Nevada	9/1995	Gold	68,000,000	540
Mohave County, Arizona	4/1996	Gypsum	85,000,000	100
Seward Peninsula, Alaska	9/1996	Gold	38,600,000	2,680
Pinal County, Arizona	9/1996	Copper	56,000,000	500
Total			$15,348,000,000	$19,190

The following are a few other important recommendations made by knowledgeable critics.

- Congress should review major past legislation and change the laws where appropriate.
- Congress should create a congressional office of regulatory analysis to independently assess old legislation and new proposals from agencies.[12]
- All regulatory agencies should be required to pass rules through the Office of Management and Budget. Presently, some major agencies (e.g., the Federal Reserve System, the Securities and Exchange Commission) need not do this. In addition, the information sent to the OMB should be available on the Internet.
- Congress should require all agencies to prepare cost-benefit analyses for major rules. Some laws, such as the Clean Air Act, sometimes preclude consideration of costs.

Privatization

privatization
A method of reducing regulation by shifting authority or assets from government to the private sector, which will perform the same function.

In recent years, there has been a worldwide movement for governments to rely more on market forces and less on regulation to achieve desired benefits to society. *Privatization* has many dimensions, ranging from almost complete deregulation of industries to fostering competition through application of the antitrust laws. Here we discuss briefly privatization, deregulation, and substitution of command regulations with incentives. There is no clear demarcation among the three, for each has aspects of the others.

[12] Robert W. Hahn, Director of AEI-Brookings Joint Center for Regulatory Studies, "Capitol Hill Hearing Testimony," Federal Document Clearing House Congressional Testimony, March 11, 2003.

"Privatization is commonly defined as any process aimed at shifting functions and responsibilities, in whole or in part, from the government to the private sector."[13] Privatization can take the form of shifting functions from the public to the private sector. Here are a few examples. The Transportation Safety Administration has shifted some functions concerning baggage and passenger screening all or in part to private companies. The private United Space Alliance is a joint venture between Boeing, Lockheed Martin, and the National Aeronautics and Space Administration (NASA) to prepare space shuttles for flight, conduct astronaut training, aid in mission control operations, maintain bases, and launch satellites. In some cases, such as the disposal of unnecessary military bases, the asset is sold. The Elk Hills Naval Petroleum Reserve and a small Helium Reserve have been sold to private companies. Congress has appropriated billions of dollars to hire private contractors, such as Haliburton, to build the infrastructure in Iraq.

Business and government often work together to blend the unique characteristics of each. For example, government has been a partner with business in the production of goods and services for national defense. Government has used its regulatory powers to help business. For example, if the government wants to protect a company or industry from foreign competition it can do so by raising a tariff. If it wishes to speed the development of automobile engine emissions free of pollution, it can subsidize research by automobile companies.

A widespread policy of state and local governments to contract out public services should be noted. State governments, for example, have contracted with private firms to manage prisons and build roads. They have sold public utilities to private corporations. Municipal governments have long used private firms to perform such functions as vehicle towing, legal services, streetlight operations, solid-waste disposal, street repair, hospital operations, data processing, zoo management, fire fighting, and many others.

The claim is made that private enterprise can do these things more cheaply and efficiently than state and local governments. That is not always true. Studies have shown that sometimes both cost and efficiency are about the same. Occasionally government costs and efficiency may be superior to private companies.[14]

Privatization is not unique to the United States. Many foreign countries have tried this program with success. For instance, Japan, France, and Germany have sold all or major parts of their telecommunications systems. Russia in recent years has conducted the world's largest privatization program by transferring huge government-owned assets to private entrepreneurs.

Deregulation

deregulation
The removal or substantial reduction of the body of regulation covering an industry.

Deregulation refers generally to the removal or substantial reduction of government regulations of entire industries. Beginning in the 1970s, the United States deregulated one major industry after another. Examples are trucking, banking,

[13] General Accounting Office, *Privatization: Lessons Learned by State and Local Governments,* GAO/GGD-97-48, March 1997, p. 1.

[14] "Privatization a Roll," *The American Enterprise,* November–December 1997; and David Field, "Scrambled Screening," *Airline Business,* June 1, 2004.

airlines, railroads, shipping, telecommunications, and electricity. In each case, this development reversed a century of growing government control in the industry. Proponents of deregulation claim it brings competition, lowers prices, stimulates innovation, and stops abuses engendered by government control. Sometimes there are negative consequences such as higher prices, poorer service, and lower productivity. Some deregulation has led to significant benefits for society, but some has not. Following are several examples of flawed deregulation.

The Airline Deregulation Act of 1978 removed federal regulation of routes and fares (while retaining safety regulation by the Federal Aviation Administration). The intent was to create more competition among the airlines, make service more efficient, and reduce fares. There was, indeed, a rapid drop in fares and travelers saved billions of dollars a year. But the major airlines developed strategies such as frequent flyer programs and route hubs to drive new, low-cost competitors out of business. Even so, they suffered from high labor costs imposed by union contracts and found it difficult to make money. As leading carriers were weakened financially by high labor costs, rising fuel prices, and inability to raise fares, there followed a wave of mergers leading to an oligopolistic industry structure dominated by six major airlines.

This was not at all what the reformers who had backed deregulation had in mind, but the industry was still unstable and changing. Eventually changes in its environment allowed low-cost new entrants and regional carriers to take business from the bigger airlines. A key change was the rise of the Internet. After travelers could get instant prices and find bargains online, the big airlines were unable to continue charging higher rates, especially to business travelers.[15] Low-cost carriers were not saddled with the high-wage labor agreements of the majors and underpriced them on route after route. Now several of the largest airlines are in bankruptcy or teetering on the brink of it. Are consumers better off? They pay less to travel, but face the loss of service to some smaller cities and towns, reduced amenities on board the planes, congested terminals, and flight delays. Declining service is not what the deregulators had envisioned, but at least the competition they hoped to see has arrived. The deregulated airline industry will continue to evolve, perhaps in unanticipated ways.

During the 1980s and 1990s the nation suffered a terrible financial disaster in the savings and loan industry. The causes were many and spread over a long time but one major catalyst was flawed deregulation. S&Ls had made mortgage loans at low rates, interest rates rose sharply, and many firms found profits diminishing. In part because of large political contributions from the industry and in part because of a pervasive ideological climate of deregulation, federal regulators had loosened restraints on the S&Ls. Their net worth requirements were lowered, new and more lax accounting rules were introduced, and oversight from the Federal Home Loan Bank Board was reduced. This led to more risk taking in S&L lending and, in some instances, opened the door to corrupt managers to engage in fraud. The consequence of loosening regulation was a string of bankruptcies that forced the federal government to bail out the industry at a cost of more than $100 billion.

---

[15] Susan Carey and Scott McCartney, "How Airlines Resisted Change for 25 Years, and Finally Lost," *The Wall Street Journal,* October 5, 2004, p. A3.

Another example of flawed deregulation has been California's deregulation of its electric utility industry. The plan worked reasonably well to benefit consumers until 2000. Then disaster struck with a series of blackouts, the bankruptcy of one utility, and financial distress at others. There were some serious mistakes in the deregulation. For example, the utilities were to sell their power plants and get their power at low prices from competition among electricity producers. But the electric power producers did not add capacity to meet growing demand and soon they could engineer shortages. The result, of course, was rising prices. Since the deregulating legislation fixed the price that utilities could charge customers, they could not raise revenue to cover higher payments to suppliers. Extortionist managers at Enron and other electric trading companies manipulated spot prices of electricity. In the end, California was forced to sign long-range contracts at exorbitant rates to assure future supplies of electricity. The net result was that California had to float a $12 billion loan and incur a $43 billion bill for long-term contracts. Fortunately for California consumers, these contracts are now being renegotiated under the supervision of the Federal Energy Regulatory Commission (FERC).

Reduce Command Controls in Favor of Incentive Controls

command controls
Regulations that require firms and individuals to meet specific standards or perform certain behaviors.

A significant route to harnessing the benefits of the free market is to replace command controls with incentive controls. *Command controls* require firms and individuals to meet specific standards or perform certain behaviors. *Incentive controls* seek to achieve desired regulatory ends by permitting affected firms or individuals flexibility in choosing methods to meet goals. If this is done, the presumption is that innovation will be inspired in technology, service, pricing, management, and/or organization. In turn this will lead to more efficiency, government standards will be met, and compliance costs will be lowered.

incentive controls
Regulations that allow individuals and firms flexibility in the means of achieving regulatory goals.

Government agencies increasingly are looking for ways to replace command-and-control regulations with those that harness the power of private economic motives. OSHA, for example, has had for years a program to encourage and expand voluntary compliance with the agency's regulations. OSHA is responsible for work safety in thousands of establishments but has only a limited staff to do the job. So it has introduced several types of voluntary programs to reduce the need for compliance inspections. As shown in Figure 11.1 at the end of 2003 the agency had approved voluntary programs in more than 1,000 worksites. In another example, the government has exempted automobile companies from the antitrust laws so they can form a consortium to develop new engines. The EPA, the Department of Agriculture, and other federal agencies have also developed incentive programs.

Incentives to stimulate individual initiative in free markets can be an effective way to replace command controls and achieve social goals more effectively. Charles Schultze, former chair of the President's Council of Economic Advisers, evaluated this force as follows: "Harnessing the base motive of material self-interest to promote the common good is perhaps the most important social invention mankind has yet achieved."[16]

---

[16] Charles L. Schultze, *The Public Use of Private Interest* (Washington, DC: The Brookings Institution, 1977) p. 18.

FIGURE 11.1
Growth in
Voluntary
Compliance
Programs,
1993 to 2003

Source: OSHA.

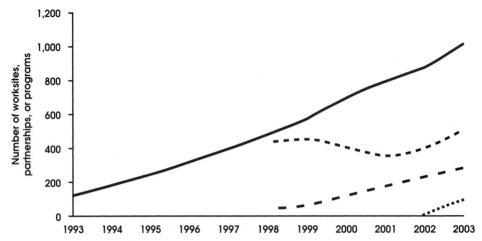

— **Worksites with exemplary safety and health programs in Voluntary Protection Programs**

- - - **Small business worksites recognized by state programs for having exemplary safety and health programs (Data only available for states under federal OSHA authority from 1998 on)**

— — **Strategic partnership agreements addressing specific industry problems at multiple worksites**

•••••• **Alliance agreements primarily with trade or professional organizations to conduct training and outreach-related activities**

Reduce Paperwork

Congress passed the Paperwork Reduction Act in 1995 to reduce the burden for businesses and individuals in spending hours completing forms mandated by the federal government. As shown in Figure 11.2 the result was disappointing. Since the passage of the law the hours of work spent on paperwork have steadily grown to about 8.2 billion hours in 2002. In 2003 there was a slight reduction of 1.5 percent.[17]

Remove Flapdoodle and Conflicting Standards and Specifications

Among the massive volumes of federal regulations there exist some that are absurd, trivial, or nonsensical. Classic examples are found in early OSHA regulations, many of which now have been expunged. They are, however, amusing. For instance, "Jacks which are out of order shall be tagged accordingly, and shall not be used until repairs are made." In 2001 Congress required U.S. military installations in Kaiserslautern, Germany, to use U.S. coal as their energy source for heat.[18] The Department of Agriculture defined standards for making pickles in eight mind-numbing pages of fine print in the *Federal Register*. Among the standards was this

---

[17] Office of Management and Budget, "Bush Administration Slashes Paperwork and Regulatory Burdens," Press Release, April 20, 2004.

[18] *The President's Management Agenda, Fiscal Year 2002* (Washington, DC: Executive Office of the President, Office of Management and Budget, August 2001), p. 6.

FIGURE 11.2
Government-wide Paperwork Burden-Hour Estimate Continues to Grow

Source: OMB and agencies' ICB submissions.

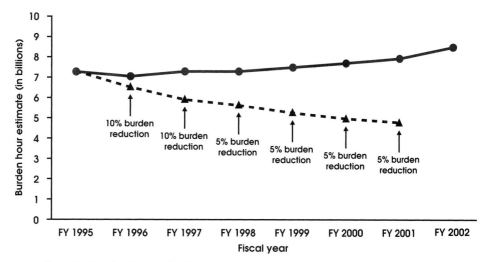

Agencies' burden-hour estimates

- ▲ - Burden-reduction goals envisioned in PRA

Note: Date are as of the end of each fiscal year. The governmentwide burden-hour estimate as of September 30, 2002, was about 8.2 billion hours.

definition: "The diameter in whole style means the shortest diameter measured transversely to the longitudinal axis at the greatest circumference of the pickle."[19] Given the huge mass of federal regulations foolish directives are inevitable. Some critics believe there are so many that removing them would be a significant reform.

Regulatory Analysis

President Reagan's Executive Order 12291 and President Clinton's Executive Order 12866 require federal agencies to write a *regulatory impact analysis* (RIA) for major new rules. A "major" rule is one predicted to have an annual impact on the economy of $100 million or more. The presumption is that new rules that impose this much of a burden on the economy should be examined carefully to ensure that they are badly needed or that their benefits exceed the cost burdens they impose. The RIA is then sent to the OMB for review. The OMB may request revisions in the rule or approve it.

In a recent report, the OMB explained that in each RIA it requires " . . . three basic elements: (1) a statement of the need for the proposed action, (2) an examination of alternative approaches, and (3) an evaluation of the benefits and costs— quantitative and qualitative—of the proposed action and the main alternatives identified by the analysis."[20] The report then explained in 48 pages of detail how the RIA should be prepared.

regulatory impact analysis
An analytical report that agencies submit to the Office of Management and Budget when they seek approval of "significant" rules predicted to have an annual impact on the economy of $100 million or more.

[19] Bridget O'Brian, "Government Sets New Standards for Ways to Get Properly Pickled," *The Wall Street Journal,* September 25,1991, p. B1.

[20] OMB, *Circular A-4 to the Heads of Executive Agencies and Establishments* (Washington, DC: OMB, September 17, 2003), p. 2.

While the quality of these RIAs has improved over the years, the submissions to the OMB are a jumble of procedures. Some complain that the reports need to be strengthened. A mandate from Congress now requires the OMB to issue guidelines to agencies to make their RIAs available for public review.

Sunset Laws

sunset laws
Laws that limit the life of a specific regulation or require legislative review at a specific time.

There have been repeated recommendations for Congress to pass *sunset laws*. A sunset law is one that limits the life of a regulatory program at the time it is authorized. A persistent problem with rules, authorities, and agencies is that they sometimes continue in force long after the world has changed and they are no longer needed. Over time, special interests and bureaucratic entrenchment combine to make regulatory programs nearly impossible to eliminate. Sunset laws would combat this tendency.

There are proposals for different types of sunset legislation. For example, one form would require major regulations to include a provision for automatic review by Congress on a certain date, say 10 years after passage. Another would require the OMB or the president to recommend to Congress possible agencies or programs for elimination. A few states have sunset laws but the experience has been mixed. One reason is that at the time of review by the legislative body special interests that have benefitted from a regulation lobby to maintain their selfish advantages. Another proposal would require Congress to approve new regulations that place heavy burdens on the private sector.

Regulatory Reform in Foreign Countries

In the last decade regulatory reform has been continuous and substantial in most developed countries. It has been less aggressive in most underdeveloped countries, but where undertaken, the results have for the most part been positive. Figure 11.3 shows the satisfactory results of efforts to reduce the regulatory impediment to starting a business in Russia. Major privatization reforms have recently been undertaken or are in progress in Japan. For example, Japan has privatized Nippon Telegraph & Telephone Public Corporation (NIT). Sweeping reforms have been made in financial markets and the country is now privatizing its postal system. A significant reform in Japan permits hundreds of local public entities to seek and get exemptions to regulations over agriculture, industry, and social welfare.[21]

Regulatory reform is actively pursued in all of the economically advanced member nations of the Organisation for Economic Co-operation and Development. France has significantly reduced state ownership of companies. Germany has taken important steps in reducing business regulation. Australia has adopted "sunset" provisions in new legislation. Denmark has adopted a regulation to have cost-benefit analyses made for proposed regulations. Sweden has eliminated many regulations following a government requirement for regulatory agencies to register all essential regulations.[22]

[21] Nakajo Yoshiro, "Taking Exception to Regulations," *Look Japan,* September 2003; and Moishita Kazunoi, "A Good Job for Deregulation," *Look Japan,* February 2001.

[22] World Bank and Oxford University Press, *Doing Business 2004: Understanding Regulation* (Washington, DC: The World Bank, 2004).

**FIGURE 11.3
Starting a
Business in
Russia, before
and after
Reforms**

Source: World Bank,
*Doing Business in
2004:* Understanding
Regulation.
Copyright © 2003
by World Bank.
Reproduced with
permission of World
Bank via Copyright
Clearance Center.

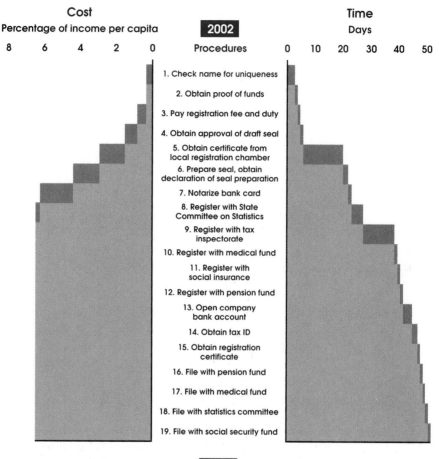

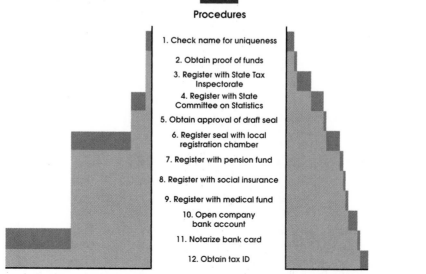

We now turn to a great body of reform regulation in the United States, namely the antitrust laws. These laws have been the basis for carrying forth the government's commitment to improving and maintaining a competitive business environment.

THE BASIC ANTITRUST LAWS

trust
A form of business organization in which the owners of stock in competing organizations transfer legal title to a group of trustees and receive certificates in return. The trustees then can control the group of companies as a single company. This form of incorporation is now illegal.

Fundamental to the effective operation of the individual enterprise system is the idea of competing economic units that perform to benefit consumers. From the beginning of the American nation, this idea was written into law. Throughout its history, these laws have been redefined and reformulated by the Supreme Court and the antitrust regulatory agencies. The antitrust laws were so named because of the method of corporate consolidation in the late nineteenth century called the *trust*. Briefly, owners of stock of competing organizations transferred legal title to a group of trustees and received certificates in return. The trustees then exercised control of the firms as a single company. There are four major antitrust laws, and we briefly explain each one.

The Sherman Antitrust Act (1890)

During the nineteenth century, the states regulated local monopolistic practices but ran into difficulty in exercising control over the giant trusts that were being formed. For example, the Standard Oil Trust formed by John D. Rockefeller and many of its imitators in the 1880s provoked formidable opposition among small-business owners, farmers, and the public. So widespread and strong was the opposition to the trust movement that the Sherman Act of 1890, designed to curb the trusts, passed the Senate with but one dissenting vote and passed the House without opposition. This law is still the foundation of antitrust enforcement today.

The two most significant sections of the Sherman Act are 1 and 2. Section 1 reads: "Every contract, combination in the form of trust or otherwise, or conspiracy in restraint of trade or commerce . . . is hereby declared to be illegal." Section 2 says: "Every person who shall monopolize, or attempt to monopolize . . . trade or commerce . . . shall be deemed guilty."

The Supreme Court refused to use the Sherman Act until 1911. Demands arose for more precise definitions of illegal monopolistic practices, and Congress responded in 1914 by passing the Clayton Act and the Federal Trade Commission Act.

price discrimination
The pricing of products and services based not on cost but on desire to limit competition or to exploit a monopoly position.

The Clayton Act (1914)

The Clayton Act named and outlawed specific practices when, in the words of the act, "the effect . . . may be to substantially lessen competition or tend to create a monopoly." For example, the act outlaws *price discrimination* when it substantially lessens competition or tends to create a monopoly. To sell a product at a low cost with the purpose of driving a competitor out of business is illegal. If several companies had the same directors who conspired to control a market,

director interlock
Occurs when the same individuals sit on the boards of directors of two or more companies. It is illegal when the companies are in direct competition.

tying contracts
Contracts that require the buyer of a good or service to purchase additional goods or services from the seller, whether needed or not, as a condition of the sale. This is illegal when competing goods or services are available.

that would be *director interlock* and would be illegal. Another practice the act specified as illegal was the use of *tying contracts*. If a supplier company sold one product to a customer only if the customer also bought other products sold by the supplier, that would be illegal tying. Many other anticompetitive practices were defined in this act.

The Federal Trade Commission Act (1914)

This act established an agency, the Federal Trade Commission, to continuously supervise and administer the antitrust laws, to stop "unfair methods of competition in commerce, and unfair or deceptive acts or practices in commerce." The act was amended in 1938 by the Wheeler-Lea Act, which gave the FTC power to regulate deceptive advertising.

The Department of Justice has authority to enforce the Sherman Act and shares jurisdiction with the FTC in Clayton Act cases. The Supreme Court, of course, has the final word in interpreting both laws and various statutes reinforcing them.

Through the years, exceptions to the antitrust laws have been granted. For example, excepted are labor unions, agricultural cooperatives, the insurance industry, baseball, certain joint export trading activities, and certain joint research efforts in some industries.

The Hart-Scott-Rodino Antitrust Improvement Act (1976)

This law requires companies to notify the FTC and DOJ of an intention to merge if their valuations exceed specified amounts. The act provides for a 30-day waiting period after the information is submitted. It also expands the powers of state attorneys general to institute triple damage suits on behalf of those injured by any violations of the Sherman Act. Some observers consider this act of equal importance to the Sherman Act.

Theories of Antitrust Enforcement

Much has been written about the purpose of the antitrust laws. One of the best statements is that given in a Supreme Court opinion made in a Sherman Act case:

> The Sherman Act was designed to be a comprehensive charter of economic liberty aimed at preserving free and unfettered competition as the rule of trade. It rests on the premise that the unrestrained interaction of competitive forces will yield the best allocation of our economic resources, the lowest prices, the highest quality, and the greatest material progress, while at the same time providing an environment conducive to the preservation of our democratic political and social institutions. But even were that premise open to question, the policy unequivocally laid down by the Act is competition.[23]

Antitrust policy is not solely an economic policy. It has social as well as political implications. Socially it means greater welfare for individuals. Politically it supports democracy by preventing concentrated economic power able to distort popular impulses.

[23] *U.S. v. Northern Pacific R.R. Co.*, 356 U.S. 1 (1958).

In seeking to achieve this fundamental objective, two major theories of enforcement have developed, namely the *structure* and the *performance* theories. Until recently, the Supreme Court, as well as government regulators and academic economists, leaned toward the structure theory in deciding antitrust cases. In the late 1960s, however, a body of impressive evidence emerged that contradicted this view and supported the performance theory.

The Structure Theory

structure theory
The theory that a firm will violate the antitrust laws if it controls an excessive concentration of assets or sales in a single market. Both the DOJ and the FTC have formulas for calculating concentration.

Until recently, the main view of the Court was that corporate size and large market share are a reliable index of monopoly power. The typical measure of power is concentration of assets or sales of one or a few companies in an industry. (Concentration is calculated as the ratio of sales and/or assets of one or a few companies in an industry to total sales and/or assets of the entire industry.) The structure theory argues that excessive concentration of market power gives corporate managers discretionary power to fix prices, determine which products come to market and in what volume, and make huge profits. Extraordinary market power produces price inflation, inefficiencies in production, and, of course, a decline in competition. Adherents of this theory argue that the way to ensure competitive markets is to break up concentrations of economic power or prevent them from developing. This is the essence of the structure theory. It was supported for decades by economists and expounded in scholarly research.[24]

The Performance Theory

performance theory
The theory that it is the marketplace performance of a firm, not its concentration of assets or sales, that determines if it has monopoly power.

This theory argues that public policy should seek efficient business performance as well as appropriate market structures. Efficient performance ensures product and process innovation, reduced costs that benefit consumers with lower prices, productive capacity in balance with product demand, profits not out of line with other industries, and emphasis on service to consumers. Furthermore, any assertion that concentration inhibits competition is seriously challenged when world markets are considered. American industry is faced with powerful global competitors. The concentration numbers tend to shrink substantially when foreign competition is considered. For example, there is high concentration in the United States in jet engine production, but when sales of foreign producers are considered, the ratio drops significantly.[25]

Research Findings

These assertions have been supported by economists and scholarly research. For example, studies show a lack of correlation between measures of concentration and excessive profits.[26] Research concludes that substantial price flexibility exists in

[24] For example, see John M. Blair, *Concentration, Structure, Behavior and Public Policy* (New York: Harcourt Brace, 1973).

[25] J. Fred Weston, *Concentration and Efficiency: The Other Side of the Monopoly Issue* (Croton-on-Hudson, NY: Hudson Institute, 1978).

[26] Ibid.

concentrated industries and that price increases during inflationary periods have been lower in industries dominated by "super concentrations" than in those less concentrated. Productivity also has risen faster in industries that are concentrated than in other industries. If high profits are found in large firms, say performance theorists, this may be due more to efficiency than to any market power they possess.[27]

Such research does not refute completely every assertion by structural theorists. Some concentrations at some times and places may result in excessive profits, price inflexibility, inhibitions to innovation, and so forth. They do show, however, that for most cases of concentration, structure theory describes the opposite of reality.

The Theories in Practice

Up to the 1970s, decisions of the Supreme Court and Department of Justice concerning monopolistic practices were based largely on the structure theory. In 1974 the Supreme Court held that the calculation of the effects of a merger should not rely exclusively on structural tests but should take into account a much broader range of economic information.[28] In 1986 a decision of a lower court based strictly on the structure theory was rejected by the Supreme Court in a decision reflecting the performance theory.[29]

The Supreme Court and the Department of Justice have not abandoned the structure theory. Rather, there has been a noticeable shift in theory and policy toward favoring efficiencies in markets over formal criteria of structure. Antitrust decisions, therefore, face a major challenge in balancing the two theories.

MERGERS

As Figure 11.4 shows, total value of mergers and acquisitions increased rapidly from 1995 to 2000. Then there was a precipitous drop. Declining stock valuations and weakness in the global economy led to a significant decline in corporate investment.[30] This reduced the number of mergers and their dollar value. In evaluating proposed mergers and deciding which ones to challenge, enforcement agencies face difficult choices. For example, a merger may yield significant cost savings by eliminating duplications and creating other efficiencies. However, it may also leave fewer companies in the industry, which increases concentration and could lead to price increases from collusion among the remaining companies.

[27] Ibid.

[28] *U.S. v. General Dynamics Corp.*, 415 U.S. 486 (1974).

[29] *Cargill, Inc., and Excell Corporation v. Montford of Colorado Inc.*, 551 L. W. 4027 (1986).

[30] United Nations Conference on Trade and Development, *World Investment Report 2003* (New York: United Nations, July 2003), p. xiii.

FIGURE 11.4
**Announced
World M&A
Activity
($ Billions)**

Source: J. Fred
Weston, "Notes
for Mergers and
Acquisitions
Programs,"
University of
California, Los
Angeles, September
19–20, 2004.
Reprinted with
permission.

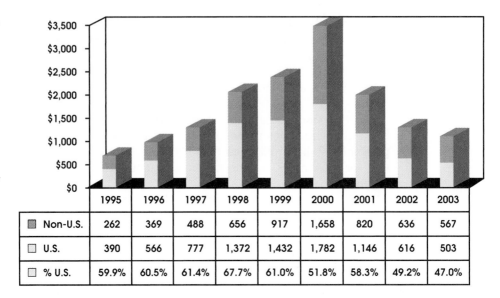

	1995	1996	1997	1998	1999	2000	2001	2002	2003
▨ Non-U.S.	262	369	488	656	917	1,658	820	636	567
☐ U.S.	390	566	777	1,372	1,432	1,782	1,146	616	503
☐ % U.S.	59.9%	60.5%	61.4%	67.7%	61.0%	51.8%	58.3%	49.2%	47.0%

Guidelines for Antitrust Action

To facilitate evaluation of mergers, in 1992 the Department of Justice jointly with the FTC established "Horizontal Merger Guidelines." The guidelines have been modified periodically since then. The most important are as follows:

- Define the relevant market, and calculate its concentration before and after the merger.
- Assess whether the merger raises concerns about adverse competitive effects.
- Determine whether entry by other firms into the market would counteract those effects.
- Consider any expected efficiency gains.[31]

Market Definition

The first step is to define the market where the merger is to take place. Then the impact on concentration is evaluated. The relevant market is generally specific products and geographic areas where a merger is likely to raise prices significantly. For example, the FTC challenged the proposed merger of Staples, Inc. and Office Depot Inc. in 1997 on these grounds. It said the relevant market was "the sale of consumable office supplies through office superstores," and these were the largest firms in that market. Staples countered that the combined firms would account for less than 6 percent of the broad market for office products, including sales by discount stores, drug stores, and wholesale clubs. The FTC said the products of the two stores were much less inclusive of products in these other stores and, in the relevant market of the two stores, the merger would significantly increase concentration and be anticompetitive.[32]

[31] *Economic Report of the President* (Washington, DC: Government Printing Office, 1998), p. 98.
[32] *FTC v. Staples, Inc.* 970 F. Supp. 1066 (1997).

high-technology industries
unications, computer chips,
servers wonder whether the
they create. Companies such
ositions in the markets they
perties. A question arises for
tellectual monopoly power
clearly is squashed if com-
new entries. Antitrust laws
that adversely affects con-
ts and services that clearly
-quality products. Antitrust
nore on innovation than on
e Microsoft case at the end

sharply from 2000 to 2001
Antitrust Division and the
This compared with 80 in
that of Microsoft, which
ubject of the case study at

ding to the National Asso-
engaged in prosecuting
y pharmaceuticals, health
d on price-fixing contrary

essively pursued foreign
American consumers. For
nufacturers and their U.S.
thermal fax paper. In the
d BASF of Germany paid
onspiracy to fix the price
aid fines for their part in

so concentrate an industry
r anticompetitive practices.
on. Sometimes the antitrust
merged companies agree to
ther arrangement to prevent
ger of Time Warner Inc. and
reed to the merger only if the

icult for merged companies to
say entry must be timely and
practices. For example, the
entry of competitors.

ficiencies to be gained through
sed on to consumers in lower
nay be verifiable, a remaining
sumers. The Staples and Office
s that while there undoubtedly
the minds of the regulators as to
mers in lower prices.

t combine the businesses of com-
e combination of two steel mills.
ergers occur when a company ac-
nain toward raw materials, or for-
rvices. For example, the merger of
forms with one mining iron ore or
er. A *conglomerate merger* combines
ple, a software company and a coal
ers may share common activities,
in different product markets.
competitive problems than other
n among sellers in a market. The
cable to all types of mergers, but
l mergers. For example, the FTC
f a small company with a large one
ould be a "deep pocket" or a "rich
r the small company to undersell or
n."[33]

he Heart of the New
w Journal, Spring 2001.
tock: Recent Trends in U.S.

nt filed in the U.S. District
eneral, No. 98CV012333.
ement," *Loyola Consumer*

High-Technology Industries

Many of the fastest-growing companies are found
such as computer software and hardware, telecom
biotechnology, and wireless communications. Some (
antitrust laws are capable of dealing with the issues
as Microsoft, Cisco, Dell, and Intel have dominant
serve. Their products and services are intellectual pr
antitrust regulators about how to deal with such
while at the same time assuring innovation. Innovat
panies that dominate a segment of an industry can st
traditionally have been concerned with competitic
sumers. But these companies have produced prod
have benefited consumers with lower-priced and high
regulators in dealing with such issues tend to focus
competition.[34] More will be said about this subject in
of this chapter.

Recent Trends in U.S. Merger Enforcemer

Federal antitrust challenges to proposed mergers f
and increased slightly in 2003. The Justice Departme
FTC challenged 34 mergers in 2002 and 36 in 200
2000.[35] In recent years the highest profile case has
started in 1998 and concluded in 2004. This case is t
the end of the chapter.[36]

State attorneys general have been more active. Ac
ciation of Attorneys General they have been prim
abuses of the antitrust laws in certain industries, prir
care, and telecommunications. Their attention has fo
to state laws and injury to consumers.[37]

In the past few years the Antitrust Division has
companies for price-fixing arrangements that goug
example, in 1999 the DOJ fined some Japanese paper
importers $6.5 million for conspiring to fix the pric
same year, F. Hoffman-La Roche, Ltd., of Switzerlan
fines of $500 million and $250 million, respectively, f
of vitamins. Several executives of these companies a

---

[34] Robert Pitofsky, "Antitrust and Intellectual Property: Unsolved Iss
Economy," keynote address, Symposium Beyond Microsoft, *Techno*

[35] William J. Baer, Deborah L. Feinstein, and Randal M. Shaheen, "T
Merger Enforcement," *Antitrust,* Spring 2004, p. 16.

[36] *United States v. Microsoft Corporation,* Civil Action No. 98-132, (
Court for the District of Columbia, May 18, 1998; and 20 state atto

[37] Patricia A. Conners, "Current Trends and Issues in State Antitrust
Law Review, vol. 16 (2003), p. 37.

the conspiracy. Mitsubishi Corp. of Tokyo agreed to pay a fine of $134 million for its involvement in a cartel composed of seven companies to fix the price of graphite electrodes used in steel production. Total fines levied in this case added up to $437 million.[38]

Foreign Merger Laws and Activity

Around the world, nations are adopting antitrust laws, but many have little experience in enforcing them. The rise of antitrust laws is caused by economic globalization and trade liberalization. In order to become or remain competitive the governments of emerging economies have deregulated and privatized in the shift from centrally regulated or state-run economies to free market ones. Many have opened their economies to cross-border mergers. And they have enacted or enhanced antitrust laws. Antitrust regulation—like a banking system, a free press, an independent judiciary, and supportive cultural values—is a fundamental institutional underpinning of a market economy. It ensures healthy competition. Introducing an effective antitrust policy and enforcing it is challenging, however. The transition to a strong competition policy is so widespread that the American Antitrust Institute seeks to establish an International Academy of Competition Policy to train enforcement officials.[39]

Recently, the European Union (EU) Competition Commissioner, Mario Monti, has been the most active foreign antitrust regulator in the world. (Monti was replaced as Competition Commissioner in September 2004.) He aggressively pressured European countries, particularly France and Germany, to reduce subsidies to weaker companies. He also gained worldwide recognition when he blocked the $45 billion merger of General Electric Co. and Honeywell International Inc. even though the U.S. Department of Justice (DOJ) had approved it. This was the first time the EU had rejected a merger of two U.S. companies that was cleared by the DOJ. Why?

The official EU statement blocking the merger said it would give GE a dominant position in Europe in the supply of avionics, nonavionics, and corporate jet engines. The EU concluded that individual European companies could not compete against such "portfolio power." This decision reflected a different philosophy of mergers than in the United States. In Europe the emphasis is on protecting competitors. In the United States it is on protecting consumers. Consequently, European antitrust law makes it easier for competitors to sue to stop mergers than does U.S. law.

The EU has forced some U.S. companies proposing mergers with European firms to make important concessions before approval. This was the case with Microsoft's proposed acquisition of Telewest, a British firm. In another case, Mario

---

[38] Steven L. Katz, Jerrold E. Fink, and Yoshiaki Tsuchitani, "Extraterritorial Enforcement of the United States Antitrust Laws," Masuda Funai, undated, www.lmasudafunai.com/English//articles/sales/salels1.asp.

[39] "Request for Funding to Complete a Preliminary Study for the Establishment of an International Academy of Competition Policy, Submitted by the American Antitrust Institute," March 19, 2001, http://antitrustinstitute.org/recent/.

Monti fined Microsoft more than $600 million for trying to extend its dominance in computer operating systems to other sectors of the software industry.

China has been developing antitrust laws. These laws are now applied more to foreign companies than to its huge state-owned companies that control industries such as oil, rail transportation, and tobacco. A recent government report on market competition identified for criticism Microsoft Corp., Eastman Kodak Co., and Tetra Pak AB (a Swedish packaging company). The report said some large foreign companies were restricting competition in China by using predatory pricing and acquiring local competitors.[40]

CONCLUDING OBSERVATIONS

Reform of government regulations is clearly needed. In undertaking regulatory reforms, two important considerations must not be neglected. First, care should be taken to avoid eliminating needed regulations. Second, we probably should not expect too much.

The Tolchins remind us in the following words that no right-minded person wants to get rid of *all* regulations.

> Regulation is the connective tissue, the price we pay for an industrialized society. It is our major protection against the excesses of technology, whose rapid advances threaten man's genes, privacy, air, water, bloodstream, lifestyle, and virtual existence. It is a guard against the callous entrepreneur, who would have his workers breathe coal dust and cotton dust, who would send children into the mines and factories, who would offer jobs in exchange for health and safety, and leave the victims as public charges in hospitals and on welfare lines. . . . Regulations provide protection against the avarice of the marketplace, against shoddy products and unscrupulous marketing practices from Wall Street to Main Street.[41]

In the future we can expect some regulatory reform. But how much? The answer is not too much because reform has a weak political base. One reason for this is that the public is not excited about it. Aside from business, the ultimate beneficiaries are generally unaware of their stake in reform. Because the benefits of reform to one person are very small in relation to the costs involved in bringing it about, there is a lack of initiative by individuals, except those in business. The result is a coalition of congressional committees, bureaucrats who administer the laws, and interest groups, constituting political power that resists quick and substantial regulatory reform. There is no comparable opposing political coalition.[42]

[40] Rebecca Buckman, "China Hurries Antitrust Law," *The Wall Street Journal*, June 11, 2004, p. A7.

[41] Susan J. Tolchin and Martin Tolchin, *Dismantling America. The Risk to Deregulation* (New York: Oxford University Press, 1983), pp. 22–23.

[42] James Q. Wilson, ed., *The Politics of Regulation* (New York: Basic Books, 1980).

Microsoft Corporation and Antitrust

The rapid growth and dominance of Microsoft in the computer industry is one of the most, if not the most, spectacular success stories in the history of American business. From a two-man shoestring operation in 1975, revenues of the small firm leaped to over $25 billion in 2001. The dominance of Microsoft in PC operating systems attracted the attention of the Antitrust Division of the Department of Justice, which sued Microsoft for antitrust violations. Microsoft denied the allegations. This case focuses on that issue.

JOEL KLEIN AND BILL GATES JOIN IN COMBAT

On October 20, 1998, Joel I. Klein, assistant attorney general in charge of the Department of Justice (DOJ) Antitrust Division; 20 state attorneys general; and William Gates, chairman and chief executive officer of the Microsoft Corporation, joined in an epic struggle before Judge Thomas Penfield Jackson in the U.S. District Court for the District of Columbia. The issues before the court were serious charges against the Microsoft Corporation set forth in briefs presented to the court. Attorney General of the United States Janet Reno, in a press release announcing the action, said:

> The Justice Department today charged Microsoft with engaging in anticompetitive and exclusionary practices designed to maintain its monopoly in personal computer operating systems and to extend that monopoly to internet browsing software.

Microsoft denied the charges.

The following discussion sets forth briefly the main arguments of the government and Microsoft and raises the question: Who is right? Is Microsoft a monopolistic predator that uses illegal means to stifle competition? Or is Microsoft acting legally in the context of a market driven by rapid technological change?

DOJ AND STATE ATTORNEYS GENERAL CHARGES

The complaints of the DOJ and attorneys general are similar and, except as noted, will be attributed to the DOJ.[1]

Microsoft Has Monopoly Powers

Microsoft has a monopoly in its PC Windows operating system, which enjoys 90 percent of the market. It uses that monopoly power to engage in unfair competitive practices. The exercise of this power inhibits innovation, restricts consumer and manufacturer's choices, and restrains new entry into the market. The attorneys general add that the anticompetitive practices of Microsoft threaten loss or damage to the general welfare and economies of the states.

To protect its Windows monopoly against potential competitive threats, the company has engaged in a pattern of anticompetitive activities. Included are

> agreements tying other Microsoft software products to Microsoft's Windows operating system; exclusionary agreements precluding companies from distributing, promoting, buying or using products of Microsoft's software competitors or potential competitors; and exclusionary agreements restricting the right of companies to provide services or resources to Microsoft's software competitors or potential competitors.

The prosecution says that attempting to maintain its monopoly in the market, unreasonably restraining

---

[1] *United States of America v. Microsoft Corporation*, Civil Action No. 98–1232, complaint filed in the United States District Court for the District of Columbia, May 18, 1998; and *Attorneys General, States of New York, California, Connecticut, District of Columbia, Florida, Illinois, Iowa, Kansas, Kentucky, Louisiana, Maryland, Massachusetts, Michigan, Minnesota, New Mexico, North Carolina, Ohio, South Carolina, Utah, West Virginia, Wisconsin v. Microsoft Corporation*, No. 1:98CVO12333, complaint filed in the United States District Court for the District of Columbia, May 18, 1998. The Department of Justice press release and complaint can be found at www.usdoj.gov/atr.

trade, and unfairly competing are all in violation of Sections 1 and 2 of the Sherman Antitrust Act.

Franklin M. Fisher, an MIT economist, both in his written and oral testimony at the trial, strongly supported the DOJ's allegations that Microsoft had monopoly power and used it.[2] A number of executives from firms such as Intel, IBM, and Sun Microsystems portrayed Microsoft in their testimony as a bullying monopolist.[3]

Microsoft and Netscape Communications Corporation

Both the DOJ and attorneys general said that Microsoft's response to Internet browsers is a prominent and immediate example of the pattern of anticompetitive behavior taken to maintain and extend its monopoly. In May 1995 Gates said the Internet was "the most important single development to come along since the IBM PC was introduced in 1981." At that time, Netscape had developed an Internet browser that had 70 percent of the market. Gates saw in the Internet browser, and specifically Netscape's browser, a significant competitive threat to his Windows operating system. On January 5, 1996, he said: "Winning Internet browser share is a very, very important goal for us." On August 20, 1996, he directed: "Internet Explorer (IE) [the Microsoft browser] will be distributed every way we can . . . Bundled with Windows 95 upgrade and included by OEMs [original equipment manufacturers]."

What is the threat of Netscape's browser? The browser is software for viewing and navigating the Internet. It has the potential of offering consumers an alternative platform for software applications in competition with Windows. Java (described later) is a program language used in developing software applications. When connected with an Internet browser such as Netscape's, the two can be a serious threat to the Windows monopoly.

In May 1995, not long before Microsoft introduced its first version of IE, the company's executives visited with Netscape executives. The government's charge is

that at this meeting Microsoft attempted to persuade Netscape not to compete with Microsoft but to divide the browser market, with Microsoft the sole supplier of the browser for use with Windows 95 operating systems. This proposition, said the DOJ, "was a blatant and illegal attempt to monopolize the Internet browser market." Netscape declined the offer.

The Netscape browser continued to serve all computer users who worked on Windows 95 as well as other operating systems. It continued to have potential to become an alternative platform to Windows and, of course, a major threat to Microsoft. So Microsoft embarked on a series of moves aimed at eliminating the threat. The company developed and introduced its own browser, the IE, and used its monopoly power to drive competing Internet browsers from the market. Here are some of the actions Microsoft took that the government said were illegal and anticompetitive practices.

Bundling

This is a marketing strategy by which a weaker product is attached to a more popular one. Microsoft bundled its IE in its Windows operating system and said it was free to consumers, as a strategy to induce consumers to use it in favor of any other browser. Once incorporated in Windows, it could not easily be separated. This was confirmed by Professor David Farber of the University of Pennsylvania, a longtime expert in Internet technology, in testimony at the trial.[4] This was an attempt, said the DOJ, to exclude Netscape in favor of IE.

Exclusionary Agreements with Internet Service Providers (ISPs) and Online Services (OLSs)

Microsoft entered into anticompetitive agreements with virtually all the major and most popular ISPs and OLSs. These firms (such as AT&T Worldnet, MCI, and Earthlink) provide communications links between PC users and the Internet. They are sometimes called Internet access providers. The agreements with these firms commit them to offer Microsoft's IE primarily or exclusively through all the channels they employ to distribute their services. They cannot promote or mention to their subscribers the existence of competing browsers. They must eliminate links on

[2] Declaration of Franklin M. Fisher, in the United States District Court for the District of Columbia, *United States of America, Plaintiff, v. Microsoft Corporation, Defendant,* Civil Action No. 98–1232, filed May 18, 1998.

[3] Steve Lohr, "The Prosecution Almost Rests: Government Paints Microsoft as Monopolist and Bully," *New York Times,* January 8, 1999.

[4] "Software Expert Criticizes Microsoft," *Los Angeles Times,* December 9, 1998, p. C3.

their websites by means of which subscribers can download a competing browser. They are to use the Internet sites in such a way as to ensure that Microsoft's browser is more effective than any competing system when using the service.

Why did these companies agree to do this? Microsoft agreed to place icons (notices of services) on the Windows desktop (the computer screen first seen when the computer is turned on) in a prominent place. This is an important advantage. Once the desktop position is established, it will remain because original equipment manufacturers are obliged to use the screen designed by Microsoft and not modify it without permission. As a result, these service providers are assured a position in the location where users first look when they make a decision about which service to use. If the agreements are not met, the contracts permit Microsoft to delete the mention of the service on the desktop.

Exclusionary Agreements with Internet Content Providers (ICPs)

Firms such as Disney, Hollywood Online, and CBS Sportsline are ICPs that provide news, entertainment, and other information from sites on the Web. Microsoft also made exclusionary agreements with them similar to but not the same as those noted.

Restrictions on Original Equipment Manufacturers

Around August 1996, Microsoft imposed restrictions on OEMs that were anticompetitive and illegal. They were enjoined from modifying or obscuring the sequence of any desktop screen displays unless the user initiated action to change the sequence. They cannot include any display, sound, or welcome screens until after the Windows desktop screen first appears.

With such restrictions, Microsoft, among other things, can reward firms with which it has agreements with preferred positions on the desktop screen. The restrictions provide Microsoft leverage to ensure that Microsoft-designed applications or other software reaches Windows users. For example, it ensures a preferred position on the desktop screen for its IE and a more obscure placement for competitors.

OEMs have objected to these restrictions, but Microsoft has refused to change them and threatened to deny Windows licenses to those who violate the agreement.

America Online Inc. (AOL)

Stephen M. Case, chairman of AOL, testified that he was approached in the spring of 1996 to make Microsoft's IE the main browser for his subscribers, which at the time were in the millions. For this, Microsoft agreed to give AOL a prominent position on the Windows desktop. However, Case complained to the DOJ that Microsoft planned to introduce its own online server in August 1996 and place it in a prominent position on the desktop of Windows. He argued that this bundling of Microsoft's online service to its operating system gave the company an unfair competitive advantage over AOL.

Java

Java is a programming language developed by Sun Microsystems Inc. that produces programs capable of running on almost any computer or operating system. Functioning through browsers, it can link on the Internet many computers at the same time. For example, it permits a person to play a game of poker with others on separate computers, or collect sales figures from many sources simultaneously.

The government charges that Microsoft executives saw in Java a serious threat to its operating system and took action to "neutralize" it. At the trial, the government presented e-mail and other documents purportedly showing how concerned Microsoft was. For example, in September 1996, Gates wrote an e-mail saying: "This scares the hell out of me," and called on Microsoft staff to make it a top priority to stop Java.

Sun made an agreement in March 1997 whereby it would license Java technology to Microsoft in exchange for Microsoft's ability to distribute the technology. In October 1997 Sun filed a lawsuit against Microsoft for breach of contract. Sun alleged that Microsoft was "polluting" the technology to weaken Java's use and developing its own technology to replace it. In March 1998 Judge Whyte of the U.S. District Court in San Jose, California, granted Sun an injunction enforcing the provision of the agreement that prevented Microsoft from altering Java.

Browser Market Shares

Netscape's Navigator browser was introduced in December 1994. Within two months, it captured 60 percent of the market and reached 90 percent in early 1996. Then it began to decline and reached less than 50 percent by mid-1998. In the meantime, Microsoft's IE share rose from 5 percent after its introduction to almost 50 percent in mid-1998. There were many practitioners who asserted that Netscape's browser was superior to Microsoft's. Why, therefore, did these market shares move as they did? The primary cause, said the government, was Microsoft's anticompetitive behavior.

MICROSOFT'S RESPONSE

Microsoft replied point by point to the charges of both the DOJ and the state attorneys general.[5] The company denied it was a monopoly and had engaged in uncompetitive practices. It said, "computer software is one of the fastest moving, most innovative and most competitive businesses in history." At the trial, Microsoft's lead attorney, John Warden, said, "everything Microsoft has done is standard competitive behavior; its actions don't even come close to violating antitrust law."[6]

Warden caustically assailed the government's case. He said the case was "not really an antitrust case, but a return of the Luddites, the nineteenth century reactionaries who . . . went around smashing machines with sledgehammers." Admittedly, Microsoft is a tough competitor, he said, but such behavior is legal: "the antitrust laws are not a code of civility."[7]

Competition in the Computer Industry

In a comprehensive white paper, Microsoft described in detail why it was not a monopoly and why it was not in violation of the antitrust laws. "Antitrust policy," said the company, "seeks to promote low prices, high output, and rapid innovation. On all three measures, the personal computer software industry generally—and Microsoft in particular—is a model of competitiveness."[8] The high market share of Microsoft in operating systems today may easily be gone tomorrow.

Microsoft claims that personal computer hardware and software prices are constantly falling and that, in important degree, is due to Microsoft's development of its standard operating system. Furthermore, Microsoft has substantially reduced prices on its own products.

Innovation in the computer industry has been dazzling. Product life cycles are very short, typically 12 to 18 months. Microsoft and other software producers are shipping products that were nonexistent a few years ago. Microsoft has been a major catalyst in innovation, and this will continue. Its research budget for 1998 amounts to $2.6 billion. The rapidity of innovation, of course, contributes to the intense competition in the industry. There is always the threat of new technology rendering existing products completely obsolete.

Relations with Netscape

Unless otherwise specified, the following is from Microsoft's response to the government's charges.

One of the reasons Netscape lost market share is because consumers believed Microsoft's IE was a superior product. At the beginning, Microsoft admits Netscape's Navigator was a better product than IE. When IE was developed, however, many reviewers said that it was the superior product. Actually, it was only after IE began beating Navigator on its merits that it started gaining users. Microsoft admits, however, that Netscape continues as a vigorous competitor to Microsoft with new successful versions of its Navigator.

Bundling

Microsoft has often used free software as a competitive strategy. Wrapping IE into Windows is just another application of that strategy. Not only is Microsoft giving consumers what they want, but it benefits them in terms of price. If consumers do not want to use IE, they can delete it from the operating system. Furthermore, consumers can use Netscape if

[5] *Defendant Microsoft Corporation's Answer to the Complaint Filed by the U.S. Department of Justice, United States of America v. Microsoft Corporation,* United States District Court for the District of Columbia, No. 98–1232 (TPJ), July 28, 1998; and *Defendant Microsoft Corporation's Answer to Plaintiff States' First Amended Complaint and Counterclaim, State of New York, ex. rel. v. Microsoft Corporation,* United States District Court for the District of Columbia, No. 98–1232 (TPJ), July 18, 1998.

[6] Quoted in Joseph Nocera, "High Noon," *Fortune,* November 23, 1998, p. 166.

[7] Quoted in John R. Wilke, "Microsoft Blasts Prosecution as 'Return of the Luddites,'" *The Wall Street Journal,* October 21, 1998.

[8] Microsoft PressPass, "Competition in the Software Industry," January 1998, www.microsoft.com/presspass/doj/1-98whitepaper.htm, p. 5.

they choose because it can be introduced into Windows. So they have a choice. "It takes no more than a few mouse-clicks or keystrokes to install, say, Netscape's browser and display it prominently on the PC desktop. Given that Netscape's share of browser usage remains at more than 50 percent, many Windows users clearly do just that."[9]

The government wants Microsoft to include Netscape's browser with Windows. Microsoft says that Netscape has consistently said it planned to use its browser technology as a basis for a new computing platform to make Windows obsolete. The DOJ, therefore, is asking Microsoft to incorporate a competitor's product that is intended to undermine and destroy Windows. That is unprecedented and unreasonable. Microsoft should not be asked to distribute its competitor's products along with its own. In response to allegations that Microsoft bundled its browser into Windows to thwart competition, James E. Allchin, a senior vice president of Microsoft, testified that the decision to give away free the IE "was a straightforward product-design decision that benefits consumers."[10]

Contracts with OEMs

The licensing agreements Microsoft has made with OEMs have been standard in the industry. It is common practice that these contracts contain a provision not to modify or delete any part of Microsoft's copyrighted Windows software without license from the company to do so. Microsoft rightfully insists that the first time an end user turns on the computer, the system is permitted to go through the sequence as designed. OEMs, as well as users, can add icons on the Windows desktop. Such agreements are widespread in industry and are both legal and pro-competitive.

Contracts with ISPs and ICPs

Microsoft responded as follows to the government's charges that these contracts included unfair competitive practices:

> In attacking Microsoft's cross-marketing agreements with other firms, the Complaint seeks to deny to Microsoft the use of ordinary competitive arrangements. The challenged contracts (i) foreclose no one

from full and complete access to the many available channels for the distribution of software providing web browsing functionality and (ii) are contracts for the promotion of commerce.

These contracts are commonplace in the industry and work to the mutual benefit of both parties. Microsoft helps to promote and distribute its products and the providers help to promote and distribute Microsoft's. There is nothing wrong with that. It is legal and pro-competitive.

Java

Microsoft claimed its "tweaking" of Java was within the contractual agreement. At the trial, Microsoft's lawyers said many consumers were frustrated with Java's shortcomings and Microsoft was trying to improve the language. In the meantime, the company said, it had developed its own technology that was much faster than Java and better designed.

WHO WAS HARMED?

A reporter at the trial observed that Microsoft's defense "boils down to one question: Where's the harm?"[11] While Warden never used these words, the question was put in hundreds of ways to the witnesses. As noted above, the DOJ and some of its witnesses claim that Microsoft's monopoly and behavior have harmed consumers. Franklin Fisher, in his written testimony said: "There is substantial probability that these anti-competitive actions will permit MS to retain its power over price in operating systems and will inhibit development of MS-independent innovations. Both would harm consumer welfare."[12]

Microsoft has repeatedly taken the position that consumers have benefited. Richard Schmalensee in his written testimony concluded: "Consumers have benefited from lower prices, greater output, better software and higher rates of innovation as a result of the actions taken by Microsoft that Plaintiffs seek to enjoin."[13]

---

[9] Microsoft PressPass, "Fact vs. Fiction," www.microsoft.com/presspass/fvsf.htm, December 18, 1998, p. 3.

[10] Steve Lohr and Amy Harmon, "Microsoft Executive Defends Folding Browser into Windows," *New York Times*, January 18, 1999, p. C1.

[11] Steve Lohr, "Microsoft Refrain: Who Was Harmed?" *New York Times*, October 26, 1998, p. 4.

[12] Franklin M. Fisher, Direct Testimony in the United States District Court for the District of Columbia, *United States of America, Plaintiff, v. Microsoft Corporation, Defendant*, Civil Action No. 98–1232, filed May 18, 1998, p. 11.

[13] Richard L. Schmalensee, Direct Testimony in the United States District Court for the District of Columbia, *United States of America, Plaintiff, v. Microsoft Corporation, Defendant*, Civil Action No. 98–1232 (TPJ), January 13, 1999, p. E–2.

FINDINGS OF FACT

At the end of the year-long trial in early 1999, each side had an opportunity to present its case in writing to Judge Jackson. Each did so in book-size documents, fundamentally summarizing the positions taken in court testimony. Following Judge Jackson's review of these documents, he issued his conclusions in a document called *Findings of Fact* on November 5, 1999. It contains his evaluation of which side presented the most believable and compelling case. Here are a few highlights of this 206-page document.[14]

First, Microsoft's share of the market for Intel-compatible PC operating systems is extremely large and stable. Second, Microsoft's dominant market share is protected by a high barrier to entry. Third, and largely as a result of that barrier, Microsoft's customers lack a commercially viable alternative to Windows. Microsoft possesses a dominant, persistent, and increasing share of the worldwide market for Intel-compatible PC operating systems. Every year for the last decade, Microsoft's share of the market for Intel-compatible PC operating systems has stood above 90 percent.

Microsoft's dominant market share is protected by barriers that prevent an aspiring entrant into the relevant market from drawing a significant number of customers away from Microsoft, even if Microsoft priced its products substantially above competitive levels for a significant period of time. "Because Microsoft's market share is so dominant, the barrier has a similar effect within the market: It prevents Intel-compatible PC operating systems other than Windows from attracting significant consumer demand, and it would continue to do so even if Microsoft held its prices substantially above the competitive level."

Judge Jackson proceeded to specify exactly how he saw Microsoft exercising its monopoly power. For example, "Microsoft attaches to a Windows license conditions that restrict the ability of OEMs to promote software that Microsoft believes could weaken the applications barrier to entry." In great detail Judge Jackson explained how he saw Microsoft's success in advancing its Internet Explorer at the expense of Netscape's Navigator until the latter was no longer

a viable threat. He mentioned how Microsoft pressured OEMs not to install Navigator; how Microsoft spent $100 million a year to upgrade its IE to the point where it enjoyed, in the minds of many observers, technical superiority over Navigator; how Microsoft bundled its IE into Windows to entice customers; and how Microsoft gave valuable inducements at no cost to Internet access providers (IAPs) to exclude Navigator from their distribution channels. The net result is that Navigator's share of the browser market fell drastically after early 1996 while IE's share significantly increased in the same period. "These interactions," said the judge, "demonstrate that it is Microsoft's corporate practice to pressure other firms to halt software development that either shows the potential to weaken the applications barrier to entry or competes directly with Microsoft's most cherished software products."

Judge Jackson's key decision was that Microsoft was a monopoly and used its monopoly power aggressively. He said:

> Microsoft has demonstrated that it will use its prodigious market power and immense profits to harm any firm that insists on pursuing initiatives that could intensify competition against one of Microsoft's core products. Microsoft's past success in hurting such companies and stifling innovation deters investment in technologies and businesses that exhibit the potential to threaten Microsoft.

Judge Jackson apparently was determined to establish without question the facts in the case so that when he issued his final recommendations, the appellate court, where the case would go if Microsoft appealed, would not overturn them. His findings could be overturned only if they were clearly in error or if he had abused his discretion.

RESPONSES TO JUDGE JACKSON'S *FINDINGS OF FACT*

Representatives of Microsoft looked at the same information as Judge Jackson and came to opposite conclusions. In a 70-page document issued on January 18, 2000, Microsoft gave its response to Judge Jackson's *Findings of Fact*. Here are a few excerpts from this document.[15]

---

[14] *United States of America v. Microsoft Corporation; State of New York, et al., v. Microsoft Corporation, Findings of Fact,* Civil Action No. 98–1232 (TPJ), undated but issued November 5, 1999.

[15] *United States of America v. Microsoft Corporation, Defendant Microsoft Corporation's Proposed Conclusions of Law,* Civil Action No. 98–1232 (TPJ), January 18, 2000.

"Plaintiffs" (throughout these excerpts Microsoft referred to the Department of Justice and the state attorneys general as plaintiffs and did not refer specifically to Judge Jackson) "failed to prove that Microsoft unlawfully maintained a monopoly in 'Intel-compatible PC operating systems' in violation of Section 2 of the Sherman Act." Microsoft contended that the offense of unlawful monopolization had two elements. One was the possession of monopoly power in the relevant market, and the second was "the willful acquisition or maintenance of that power as distinguished from growth or development as a consequence of a superior product, business acumen, or historical accident."

Although the Court concluded in its findings of fact that Microsoft possesses monopoly power in the market for "Intel-compatible PC operating systems . . . the individual *facts* found by the Court do not establish monopoly power in a relevant antitrust market: (i) under the governing legal principles, the arena of competition relevant to decision of this case extends beyond "Intel-compatible PC operating systems" to encompass all platforms competing for the attention of software developers and users, and (ii) Microsoft does not have monopoly power within the meaning of Section 2 in the market defined by the Court or any other market at issue.

On the demand side, consumers looking for computing solutions have an increasing array of alternatives, including, among other options, an Apple Macintosh running the Mac 05 or a workstation running some variant of the UNIX operating system.

In the future, said Microsoft, consumers who have simplified computers will have many more choices. "On the supply side . . . developers of mainframe and server operating systems such as IBM, Hewlett-Packard and Sun have the technical resources to develop operating systems for a variety of hardware platforms and to supply the entire market for such operating systems."

"Microsoft does not have durable monopoly power in any relevant antitrust market because it cannot control prices or exclude competition for a substantial period of time." Microsoft noted that the plaintiffs had argued that it had monopoly power because it had a large share of the market for operating systems. That was a specious argument, said Microsoft. To begin with, "today's sales do not always indicate power over sales and price tomorrow." Innovation is sure to change Microsoft's share tomorrow.

Also, market share indicates monopoly power "only when sales reflect control of the productive assets (i.e., capacity to supply) in the business. . . . There is no finding, nor could there be, that Microsoft controls a significant percentage of the productive assets in the software business or any part thereof."

On the price issue, Microsoft contended that according to a court decision, monopoly power "comes from the ability to cut back the market's total output and so raise price."

There is no finding that Microsoft could restrict the total market output of operating systems and thereby raise prices. In fact, existing operating system competitors . . . could readily expand their "output" to meet the entire demand for operating systems without acquiring new productive assets. It is simply a matter of signing new license agreements.

On the ability of Microsoft to establish "applications barriers to entry," Microsoft described the rapid technological advances in the industry. It then quoted from another court decision that "it would be difficult to design a market less susceptible to monopolization."

"Having an extremely popular product does not make a company a monopolist," said Microsoft.

Microsoft has successfully competed with vigorous companies like IBM and Sun and maintained the popularity of its operating systems by improving its own products to the greater satisfaction of consumers. . . . Microsoft also has kept the price of its operating systems low—in fact, lower than the price of competing operating systems such as IBM's OS/2 Warp and Apple's Mac OS.

Microsoft then quoted a court decision as follows:

When a producer deters competitors by supplying a better product at a lower price, when he eschews monopoly profits, when he operates his business so as to meet consumer demand and increase consumer satisfaction, the goals of competition are served, even if no actual competitors see fit to enter the market at a particular time. . . . If a dominant supplier acts consistent with a competitive market—out of fear perhaps that potential competitors are ready and able to step in—the purpose of the antitrust laws is amply served.[16]

Microsoft denied wrongdoing with respect to every conclusion of Judge Jackson. Here are a few

[16] *United States v. Syufy Enters.*, 903 F.2d 976 (2d Cir. 1984) at 668–69.

examples other than the monopoly charge. Both the Department of Justice and Judge Jackson portrayed the bundling of the IE with Windows as part of a scheme to thwart Netscape's Navigator. Microsoft saw the practice as making its products user-friendly and not a violation of the Sherman Act. The Department of Justice and Judge Jackson cited Microsoft for unlawful exclusive agreements with various Internet servers, but Microsoft said they failed to prove the charge. In another area, Microsoft said there was no proof it had license agreements with OEMs to restrain others from Windows desktop displays. What this amounts to is revisiting the arguments pro and con made in the trial.

JUDGE JACKSON'S FINAL DECISION

Following the *Findings of Fact,* the next step in the legal process was the decision, which was given by Judge Jackson on November 5, 1999. In a 12-page statement the judge ordered divestiture. He said that not later than four months after the *Final Judgment* is issued, "Microsoft shall submit to the Court and the Plaintiffs a proposed plan of divestiture. The Plaintiffs shall submit any objections to the proposed plan of divestiture to the Court within 60 days of receipt of the plan, and Microsoft shall submit its response within 30 days of receipt of the plaintiffs' objections."[17] Following approval of a final plan, and after any delays pending appeals, "Microsoft shall implement such Plan."

The *Final Judgment* prescribes a number of actions to implement the plan and prohibits certain actions. For example, within 12 months Microsoft will complete the separation of the Operating Systems Business from the Applications Business and the transfer of assets and personnel, distribution of intellectual property used in product development, and transfer of ownership of stock. After implementing the plan, the Operating Systems Business and the Applications Business are prohibited from merging or entering into agreements with one another, or other enterprises, on terms more favorable than available to third parties. Threats, exclusive agreements, or restrictions with OEMs are prohibited. Microsoft is ordered to disclose technical information and communications

interfaces used in its software operating systems. Within 90 days after the effective date of the *Final Judgment,* Microsoft is ordered to establish a Compliance Committee of its corporate board of directors of no fewer than three members who are not present or former employees of Microsoft. The Compliance Committee is ordered to hire a chief compliance officer who will report to the Compliance Committee and the CEO of Microsoft. It will be this officer's responsibility to supervise Microsoft's internal programs to ensure compliance with antitrust laws and the *Final Judgment.*

RESPONSES TO THE *FINAL JUDGMENT*

Microsoft said that

> the government's requested relief is extreme and unprecedented. . . . Draconian measures like breaking Microsoft into two companies, confiscating Microsoft's intellectual property (by forcing Microsoft to disclose proprietary information about its operating systems to competitors) and interfering with the design of Microsoft's products far exceed any reasonable remedy for the antitrust violations found by the Court, and are punitive in concept and effect.[18]

Microsoft then explained in detail the harm that the proposed remedy would cause the company and consumers. The company then petitioned the District of Columbia Circuit Court of Appeals for a review of the case. The Court took the case, and here are some highlights of its June 2001 opinion.

THE COURT OF APPEALS DECISION

The Appeals Court concluded that "Microsoft possesses monopoly power in a relevant market."[19] Defining the market as Intel-compatible PC operating systems, the District Court had found that Microsoft has a greater than 95 percent share. It also found the company's market position protected by a substantial

---

[17] *United States of America v. Microsoft Corporation, Final Judgment,* Civil Action No. 98–1232 (TPJ), undated.

[18] *United States of America v. Microsoft Corporation, Defendant Microsoft Corporation's Summary Response to Plaintiffs' Proposed Final Judgment,* Civil Action No. 98–1232 (TPJ), May 10, 2000.

[19] *United States of America v. Microsoft Corporation,* No. 00–5212, June 28, 2001.

entry barrier. "We uphold the District Court's finding of monopoly power in its entirety," said the Appeals Court. However, it added, the District Court "failed to provide an adequate explanation for the relief it ordered." The Court then sent the case back to the District Court to decide whether the remedy of divestiture was appropriate. "The District Court also should consider whether plaintiffs have established a sufficient causal connection between Microsoft's anticompetitive conduct and its dominant position in the OS market." On the charge that Microsoft illegally tied its browser to its operating system, the Court said the government must prove, in a new trial, that the anticompetitive effect outweighed its improved efficiency. Again, this issue should be settled in a new trial.

The Court considered other allegations of anticompetitive behaviors. For example, it concluded that license restrictions Microsoft imposed on OEMs are anticompetitive. Microsoft's conduct that destroyed incipient threats to its operating system from Netscape, Navigator, and Java is exclusionary, said the Court, and in violation of the Sherman Act.

Microsoft wanted to have the Court reject the District Court's decision on the grounds that Judge Jackson violated the code of conduct for United States judges and showed a bias against the defendant. Judge Jackson out of court had made a number of injudicious remarks about William Gates and Microsoft. For example, he said that Gates's "testimony is inherently without credibility." Gates, he said, "has a Napoleonic concept of himself and his company, an arrogance that derives from power and unalloyed success, with no leavening hard experiences, no reverses."[20] The Court sharply rebuked Judge Jackson for such remarks but also said it could find no bias in the judge's documents and that such remarks, therefore, had no bearing on the case at hand.

THE DEPARTMENT OF JUSTICE AND MICROSOFT REACH AGREEMENT

The attorney general of the United States on November 2, 2001, said, "Today we are announcing a strong, historic settlement reached by the Department of Justice and the Microsoft Corporation that will put an end to Microsoft's unlawful conduct, bring effective relief to the marketplace, and ensure that consumers will have more choices in meeting their needs of computing and working with their computers."[21] On the same day, Microsoft signed a consent decree with the government. Here are highlights of the agreement:

- Microsoft must disclose technical information such as licenses, patents, copyrights, and other intellectual property to permit systems of software competitors to operate smoothly on Microsoft's operating system.

- OEMs will have flexibility to contract freely with competing software developers. They can place on Microsoft's operating system their middleware products such as browsers, instant messaging software, and media players.

- Microsoft is prohibited from retaliating against PC makers and competing software developers for producing computers with competing software.

- Microsoft will be prohibited from making certain types of exclusive contracts supporting Microsoft's products.

- A full-time, on-site enforcement team of independent computer experts will be created and have broad powers and complete access to Microsoft source codes, records, facilities, and personnel. The team, composed of one member chosen by DOJ, a second by Microsoft, and a third by the first two team members will serve for 30 months and have offices at Microsoft headquarters. It will monitor compliance and have power to resolve disputes.

- The agreement will be in force for five years when the District Court judge approves it.

ARE MICROSOFT'S ANTITRUST PROBLEMS OVER?

Microsoft faced a new trial in the U.S. District Court as prescribed by the Appellate Court. The trial was scheduled for March 2002. Nine state attorneys general considered the agreement too liberal and said it would not change significantly the behavior of Microsoft. So they prepared a remedy plan that Microsoft said was far too harsh but would be considered at the trial. In addition, individuals who believe they have been injured by Microsoft can bring

[20] Reported by John Schwartz, "A Judge Overturned by an Appearance of Bias," *New York Times*, June 29, 2001.

[21] Attorney General John Ashcroft, transcript of news conference, November 2, 2001.

civil suits. Corporations also can sue. Top executives of Sun Microsystems, AOL, and Netscape, for example, voiced strong dissatisfaction with the agreement. If they file suits, their cases will be strengthened by the Appellate Court decision, especially its determination that Microsoft has a monopoly.

The agreement received bipartisan criticism in Congress. Senator Patrick J. Leahy, a Democrat and chair of the Senate Judiciary Committee, said he would schedule hearings on the agreement. Senator Orrin G. Hatch, a Republican, voiced concern. Finally, European Union regulators are investigating Microsoft's behavior and could impose fines or restrictions or both on the company's activities. In sum, Microsoft is likely to continue to be confronted with potentially serious legal challenges.

UPDATE

The U.S. Court of Appeals for the District of Columbia returned Microsoft's controversial case to the U.S. District Court in Washington, DC. The court chose Judge Colleen Kollar-Kotely to hear the case. The Court charged her with the responsibility for determining what remedies should be imposed on Microsoft to deal with abuse of its monopoly power which the Appeals Court, as noted above, determined existed. Her decision was made on November 1, 2002.

She approved most of the provisions of the settlement with the Department of Justice and freed Microsoft from the threat of crippling sanctions. She rejected proposals from nine state attorneys general for harsh remedies. The states, for example, wanted Microsoft to disclose more of Windows's code for the Internet Explorer browser. She ruled that computer makers would be permitted to install any applications for Windows that they wanted and Microsoft was prohibited from intimidating or threatening them in any way for doing so. A major new remedy was surveillance of compliance with the decisions. She created a committee composed of members of the Microsoft board of directors to advise her on the compliance of the company with all remedies imposed by the government. The committee was also charged with hiring a compliance officer to report to the committee and to Microsoft's CEO. In sum, Judge Kollar-Kotely's decisions had but a minor impact on Microsoft's operations.

The ruling of Judge Colleen Kollar-Kotely was unanimously accepted by a six-judge panel of the U.S. Court of Appeals for the District of Columbia in response to an appeal by the state of Massachusetts. These two decisions effectively put to rest the antitrust suits in the United States. But Microsoft ran into a severe challenge in Europe.

TROUBLES WITH THE EUROPEAN UNION'S ANTITRUST REGULATORS

After five years of investigation and settlement talks with Microsoft, EU Competition Commissioner Mario Monti announced the decision of the European Commission on March 24, 2004, that Microsoft was guilty of violating EU antitrust rules. The Commission ordered Microsoft:

- To offer computer makers a version of Windows without its Media Player multimedia software.
- To provide enough information to permit other software companies such as Sun Microsystems, Inc., to make software that could work on Windows.
- To pay a fine of $613 million for past violations of the EU antitrust laws.

These sanctions elicited a sharp rejoinder from Microsoft, which was echoed by many supporters of the company. For example, Microsoft argued that sharing its computer code would seriously reduce its ability to innovate new products. It would actually reduce consumer choice. It would importantly affect the way the company does business. The removal of the Windows Media Player (WMP) would encourage more attacks on Microsoft's software. This decision would have a chilling impact on legal protections of private intellectual property.[22]

Competition Commissioner Mario Monti responded that the Commission was simply trying to assure that anyone who develops new software has a fair opportunity to compete. He also said the purpose of the remedies was to alter Microsoft's past illegal behavior.[23] Commission Council Per Hellstrom said, "The fact that consumers want a media player on

[22] "Software: EU Competition Law on Trial in EU-Microsoft Court," *Europe Information Service European Report*, October 2, 2004; Kevin O'Brien, "Microsoft Asks for Delay in Sanctions," *International Herald Tribune*, October 1, 2004.
[23] "EU Orders Microsoft to Pay $613 Million," *MSNBC News*, March 24, 2004.

their computer does not imply that it must be included in the operating system." The Commission said, "If ever there was a case for regulatory intervention, this is it."[24]

On Microsoft's appeal the case moved to the European Court of First Instance in October 2004 with Judge Bo Vesterdorf presiding. The judge promised a decision on the application of the sanctions within two months.

Questions

1. Do you believe Microsoft has a monopoly?

2. Should Microsoft be split into two companies?

3. Do you believe Microsoft used its power in the market to prevent potential competitors from challenging its dominant market position in operating systems?

4. Do you believe Judge Jackson's *Final Judgment* contained appropriate remedies for violations of law he found in his *Findings of Fact*?

5. Many observers believe the Department of Justice was not severe enough in its final agreement with Microsoft. Argue the issue pro and con.

6. Do you believe that it is fair for the European courts to reject practices of Microsoft that were accepted by U.S. courts?

7. Do you agree with the decision of Mario Monti in the Microsoft case?

[24] "European Service Report," March 2004, p. 3.

Chapter **Twelve**

Multinational Corporations and Trade

The Coca-Cola Company

Coca-Cola was invented in 1886 by a pharmacist named John S. Pemberton. After failing with a drug store, he experimented with soft-drink formulas until he found one that pleased him. At the suggestion of a friend he named it Coca-Cola, based on two ingredients, namely, "coca," the dried leaf of a South American shrub, and "cola," an extract of the kola nut. Pemberton persuaded an owner of soda fountains in Atlanta to try selling the drink. He did, and it was immediately popular. On Pemberton's death in 1888 the ownership of and all rights to the formula were acquired by Asa G. Candler for $2,300. Candler eventually formed the Coca-Cola Company in 1882 to produce the drink that the public had begun to call "Coke."[1]

The Coca-Cola Company today is the world's largest manufacturer, distributor, and marketer of soft-drink concentrates and syrups. Its products are sold in nearly 200 countries, and its brands are the leading soft drinks in most of them. The company also sells juice and juice-drink products. Sales in 2003 were $21 billion, of which 62 percent came from outside the United States. Its net profit for the year was $4.4 billion. It had 49,000 employees; only 9,200 of them worked in the United States.[2]

The company has relationships with three types of bottlers to which it sells its proprietary concentrates and syrups. First are independent bottlers in which the company has no ownership interest. Second are bottlers in which the company has a minority equity position. Third are bottlers in which the company holds a controlling interest. In 2003 the first group sold 24 percent of the worldwide case volume; the second, 58 percent; and the third, the remaining percentage.

The company has transformed itself from a single-product firm into a producer and marketer of beverages favored by local consumers. The result is 230 different products designed to accommodate consumer preferences in foreign markets. Besides carbonated drinks, Coca-Cola is selling more bottled water, tea, and other noncarbonated beverages. For example, in the Asia Pacific area, the company developed 35 new brands to satisfy different consumer tastes. Its brands also change taste. In Japan,

---

[1] Hannah Campbell, *Why Did They Name It?* (New York: Ace Books, 1954), pp. 63–64.
[2] The Coca-Cola Company, Form 10-K, 2004.

its Georgia Coffee is drunk by traditional tea drinkers. In Africa and the Middle East, brands from the United States such as Fanta Strawberry, Fanta Apple, lemon-flavored Limca, and Hi-C juices are big sellers.

Although the company has millions of satisfied customers in foreign lands it sometimes is confronted with violent critics. Coca-Cola is a dominant worldwide brand, and its commercial activity cannot be separated from foreign political attitudes toward the power and presence of the United States. Like other American companies such as Nike, McDonald's, and Kentucky Fried Chicken, Coca-Cola is a target for critics who resent American influence.

Here are a few illustrations. Hours after the U.S. bombing raids in Afghanistan, demonstrators targeted high-profile American companies, including Coca-Cola. Activist groups complained about "Coca-Colonization" of the planet. In India, the Peoples' War Group blew up the Hindustan Coca-Cola bottling plant and trucks in the Gunthur district.[3] In 2003 Hindu nationalists smashed pop bottles and burned cola ads. A civic organization in India, the Center for Science and Environment, said its research found carcinogens in concentrations above standards set by the European Union. Coca-Cola replied that these results were not correct. Nevertheless the accusations caused a serious decline in Coke sales. The Indian parliament banned the sale of Coke in its cafeteria following test results that showed it contained traces of pesticides.

In the United Kingdom in 2004 Coca-Cola withdrew from the market all of its Dasani bottled water, about 500,000 bottles. Tests of the product showed excessive levels of bromate, a chemical that can increase the risks of cancer. This action prompted the English tabloids to hyperbolize the event. One headline read "Coke Tap Water Is Cancer Warning." The English do not like the idea of having their bottled water from a tap rather than the spring water that Europeans expect. Coca-Cola uses tap water and treats it to surpass applicable standards.[4]

The company has faced difficult challenges in other countries. For example, it was accused of complicity in the murder of a union leader at a bottling plant in Colombia. However, the case was dismissed for lack of evidence that the company had any knowledge of or control over events at the independently owned and run facility.[5] It has battled charges of monopoly, tax avoidance, bribery, and human rights violations.

We should not conclude this discussion without reference to a few of the activities of the company which benefit the communities in which it does business. In 2001 Coca-Cola signed a three-year partnership with UNAIDS, the United Nations agency coordinating activities fighting HIV and AIDS. Coca-Cola will provide multiple services throughout Africa to support AIDS education; distribute preventive measures, such as AIDS testing kits and condoms; and publicize treatment programs. The company's distribution system will extend these services to the far corners of the

[3] Amit Srivastava, "Coke with Yet Another New Twist: Toxic Cola," January 20, 2004, http://www.guerrillanews.com/corporate_crime/doc3764.html.

[4] "Dasani Recall Hurts Coke's Bid to Boost Water Sales in the EU," *The Wall Street Journal,* March 22, 2004, p. B1.

[5] *Sinaltrainal v. Coca-Cola Co.,* 256 F.Supp 2d 1345 (2003).

continent.[6] Natalie Rule, a representative of the company, said: "We want to use our infrastructure, our presence in local communities. We want to help in providing our marketing expertise to develop public awareness and information campaigns. And we're looking more internally at our human resources policies in Africa."[7]

The Coca-Cola story illustrates the development, strategy, and unique problems of a large multinational corporation. In this chapter we first define the multinational corporation (MNC), then we examine the power of large MNCs and their critics. This is followed by analysis of relationships between governments and MNCs. Trade protectionism creates problems for MNCs, and that is discussed next. Finally, the chapter closes with a discussion of corruption in business and government transactions.

THE MULTINATIONAL CORPORATION DEFINED

The River Rouge plant of the Ford Motor Company was renowned throughout the world for decades after it was built in the 1920s in Dearborn, Michigan. In one huge complex, the company produced virtually everything needed to manufacture its Model A. Iron ore entered the factory at one end, and a shiny new black Ford car drove out the other end.

A new model of production has replaced this one. It is epitomized in this label attached to an electronic device sold by a U.S. company: "Made in one or more of the following countries: Korea, Hong Kong, Malaysia, Singapore, Taiwan, Thailand, Indonesia, or the Philippines. The exact country of origin is unknown."[8] This is a bit dramatic but makes the point that today's multinational corporation is a far different enterprise from the typical company of the past.

The MNC is an organization engaged in doing business in foreign countries. It is not always incorporated or private. It can be a cooperative, a private company, or a state-owned entity. Almost every large business today has some direct or indirect involvement with foreign countries, but only when it performs one or more of the functions of designing, producing, marketing, staffing, or financing its products or services for foreign operations does it become truly multinational. Many MNCs progress through the following stages:

1. Exports products to foreign countries.
2. Establishes sales organizations abroad.
3. Licenses use of patents and technology to foreign firms that make and sell the MNC's products.
4. Establishes foreign manufacturing facilities, but important decisions about such matters as product design, marketing, and finance are made at the home office.

---

[6] John Donnelly, "Activists Hope Firms' Involvement Boosts Battle against AIDS in Africa," *Boston Globe*, September 4, 2001, p. D1.

[7] Ibid.

[8] For a fuller discussion of this point, see Gail Dutton, "Building a Global Brain," *Management Review*, May 1999.

5. Gives foreign production facilities substantial autonomy but still reserves some important decisions for the home office.
6. Decentralizes authority throughout the company so that functions at home and abroad are done by executives from different countries.

There are, of course, many models for the operation of companies as they move through these steps. Some companies give foreign subsidiaries substantial authority to make their own decisions. Others prefer to retain important decision making at home. The mix varies considerably. Companies in the later stages noted above have been given different names, such as transnational, global, international, multinational, and worldwide. There is no consensus on the meaning of any of these names, although some observers do distinguish different characteristics among them. For simplicity, we choose to use MNC interchangeably with the others.

Some MNCs are said to be stateless or borderless, meaning that if they choose, they can with impunity, move their world headquarters anywhere. This distinction, however, is more theoretical than operational. They are national firms with international operations. Even a company such as Canada's Thomson Corporation, although 98 percent of its sales and 98 percent of its assets are outside the home country, is not likely to move its headquarters for many reasons. The common stock ownership and control of the typical MNC remains national rather than international. Most employees at company headquarters are nationals of the home nation. The company keeps its records in the home currency and is subject to its tax and other laws. These ties are part of the culture of the company, which is not easily modified. Finally, each U.S. company must get a charter from a state. The charter grants a company the right to do specific things in defined ways. The authority given can be modified or withdrawn by the state. The state, therefore, has legal authority over the actions of the MNC.[9]

Becoming a mature multinational corporation involves much more than rearranging the functions of a business. Managers and staffs who think in global dimensions are found throughout the enterprise. They are sensitive to and comfortable with the thinking of those from different cultures. They search for and accept best practices wherever they are found. Status is determined by merit rather than nationality. These are a few characteristics of what might be called a global mind-set. Today there are not many companies that illustrate this idea, but they are growing in number.

THE SIGNIFICANCE AND POWER OF MNCs

The United Nations calculates there are 61,900 MNCs in the world and they have 900,000 affiliates.[10] Figure 12.1 shows that the concentration and dominance of the largest 100 transnational corporations is formidable (the UN prefers the word transnational to identify large global corporations). Most of the

[9] Yao-Su Ha, "Global Corporations Are National Firms with International Operations," *California Management Review*, Winter 1992.

[10] United Nations, *World Investment Report 2004* (New York: United Nations, 2004), p. 8.

FIGURE 12.1   **The Dominance of the Largest Transnational Corporations**
According to the United Nations, there are now 61,900 transnational corporations.
Of these, the largest 100 nonfinancial corporations are less than two-tenths of
1 percent of the total number but have a disproportionately great impact on the
global economy. All but 13 are from the United States, Europe, and Japan.

Source: United Nations Conference on Trade and Development, *World Investment Report 2004* (New York: United
Nations, 2004), pp. 11, 21, and annex table A.1.4. Reprinted with permission.

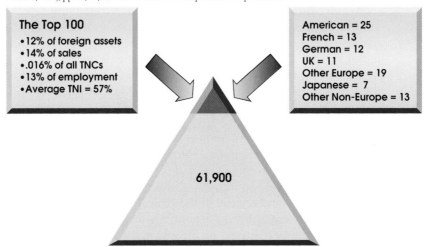

parent firms of the largest MNCs are based in the developed economies of the
United States, Europe, and Japan. *Forbes* magazine calculates that if we consider
the 50 largest MNCs in the world, their sales collectively reach $4.9 trillion. The
collective assets of the top 50 amount to $29 trillion, and their collective profits
equal $342 billion. This is 45 percent of the total profits of the 2,000 largest
MNCs in the world! These are truly eye-popping numbers.[11] In Table 12.1 the
world's largest MNCs are ranked by sales, assets, and transnationality. The sales
of the top five MNCs in the middle column of Table 12.1 exceed the GDPs of all
but seven nations.

The international operations of these corporations have grown dramatically
in recent years. For example, between 1989 and 1995 world *foreign direct investment* (FDI) averaged about $200 billion a year. But by 1999 it had jumped to
$800 billion. Thereafter it declined to $560 billion in 2003.[12] Cross-border mergers and acquisitions accounted for most of the FDI, most of which flowed between developed countries. The greatest amounts moved between the United
States, the European Union, and Japan. The 49 least developed countries (LDCs)
got only a fraction of the FDI inflows. Despite this comparatively low level of
investment in the LDCs, it did, according to the UN, strongly promote their
economic growth.

**foreign direct
investment**
Funds invested
by multina-
tional corpora-
tions for
starting, acquir-
ing, or expand-
ing foreign
affiliates. They
may derive
from new
equity offerings,
debt financing,
or reinvestment
of foreign
affiliate
earnings.

[11] *Forbes*, May 24, 2004, centerfold.
[12] *World Investment Report 2004*, p. xvii.

TABLE 12.1
Sales, Assets, and Profits of the 10 Largest Global MNCs in 2003

Source: From Forbes 2000, April 12, 2004. Reprinted by permission of Forbes Magazine © 2004 Forbes Inc.

Rank	Company	Assets ($MIL)	Country
1	Citigroup	1,264,032	US
2	Mizuho Financial	1,115,895	JA
3	Fannie Mae	1,019,171	US
4	Sumitomo Mitsui Finl	868,424	JA
5	UBS	853,232	SZ
6	Allianz Worldwide	851,237	GE
7	Mitsubishi Tokyo Finl	827,481	JA
8	JP Morgan Chase	792,700	US
9	Deutsche Bank Group	792,495	GE
10	Barclays	791,537	UK

Rank	Company	Sales ($MIL)	Country
1	Wal-Mart Stores	256,329	US
2	BP	232,571	UK
3	ExxonMobil	222,883	US
4	General Motors	185,524	US
5	Ford Motor	164,196	US
6	DaimlerChrysler	157,125	GE
7	Toyota Motor	135,819	JA
8	General Electric	134,187	US
9	Royal Dutch/Shell	133,499	NE/UK
10	Total	131,638	FR

Rank	Company	Profits ($MIL)	Country
1	ExxonMobil	20,960	US
2	Citigroup	17,853	US
3	General Electric	15,589	US
4	Bank of America	10,810	US
5	BP	10,267	UK
6	Freddie Mac	10,090	US
7	Altria Group	9,204	US
8	Wal-Mart Stores	9,054	US
9	Microsoft	8,878	US
10	Total	8,836	FR

How Multinational Is a Corporation?

Another way of gauging the largest MNCs is by measuring the degree to which they have extended critical elements of their operations into foreign countries. Corporations vary in a range of international dimensions. These include the ratio of domestic to foreign operations; the number of foreign countries entered; the extent of foreign direct investment; the geographic span of operations; the extent of cross-country integration of steps in the production chain; and the nationality of

TABLE 12.2
TNI for GE and Philips

Source: UNCTAD, *World Investment Report 2004*, ch. 1 annex, annex table A.1.3. Reprinted with permission.

General Electric		Ratio	Philips Electronics		Ratio
Foreign assets	229,001		Foreign assets	27,880	
Total assets	575,244	39.8%	Total assets	33,849	82.4%
Foreign sales	45,405		Foreign sales	28,673	
Total sales	131,698	34.5%	Total sales	30,099	95.3%
Foreign employees	150,000		Foreign employees	140,827	
Total employees	315,000	47.6%	Total employees	170,087	82.8%
Average TNI		40.6%	Average TNI		86.8%

shareholders, employees, managers, and directors. Since MNCs differ greatly in these dimensions, no single measure can capture the definitive meaning of "multinational."

transnationality index (TI)
The average of three ratios: foreign assets to total assets, foreign sales to total sales, and foreign employment to total employment.

Yet measures have been created. The most widely used one is the *transnationality index*, or TNI, used by the United Nations to rank corporations based on the relative importance of their domestic and foreign operations. The TNI is the average of three ratios: (1) foreign assets to total assets, (2) foreign sales to total sales, and (3) foreign employment to total employment.

In Table 12.2 we look at the TNI index for two of the largest 100 multinational corporations: General Electric, a diversified conglomerate headquartered in the United States; and Philips Electronics of the Netherlands, a global manufacturer of electrical and electronic equipment.

Although General Electric ranks first in assets among the largest 100 nonfinancial MNCs, it ranks near the bottom at 83 of 100 in its transnationality index score. Philips Electronics, on the other hand, ranks 37th in assets, but is 7th in its TNI score, making it one of the most internationalized of the largest MNCs. Although GE has more foreign assets, sales, and employees than Philips, they are a much smaller proportion of GE's operations than are the foreign elements of Philips's operations. One reason is that Philips has a much smaller domestic market in the Netherlands than does GE in the United States. It must move its business into other nations to grow. Table 12.3 shows the five most and least transnational firms among the 100 largest nonfinancial corporations.

The economic and political clout of MNCs is not defined solely by numbers on any dimension. They have other powers. For example, they can move their foreign assets around to favor some countries at the expense of others. They can "persuade" a country's leaders to adopt policies favorable to them by increasing or decreasing their investments, employees, and use of technology in the country. Professor Thomas Donaldson of Georgetown University observes that "with the exception of a handful of nation-states, multinationals are alone in possessing the size, technology, and economic reach necessary to influence human affairs on a global basis."[13]

[13] Thomas Donaldson, *The Ethics of International Business* (New York: Oxford University Press, 1989), p. 31.

TABLE 12.3 **Most and Least Transnational of the Top 100 Nonfinancial Corporations in 2002**

Source: UNCTAD, *World Investment Report 2004*, annex table A.1.3, based on company annual reports. Reprinted with permission.

Most Transnational				
Rank	**Corporation**	**Home Country**	**Industry**	**TNI**
1	NTL Inc.	U.S.	Telecommunications	99.1
2	Thomson Corp.	Canada	Media	97.9
3	Matsushita Electric Industrial Corp.	Japan	Electrical equipment	95.5
4	CRH Pl	Ireland	Lumber, building products	94.7
5	ABB	Switzerland	Machinery, equipment	94.5
Least Transnational				
Rank	**Corporation**	**Home Country**	**Industry**	**TNI**
1	Verizon Communications	U.S.	Telecommunications	7.3
2	Deutsche	Germany	Telecommunications	15.9
3	Duke Energy Corp.	U.S.	Electricity, gas, water	20.3
4	Telecom Italia	Italy	Telecommunications	20.3
5	Mitsubishi Corp.	Japan	Wholesale trade	21.9

CRITICS OF MNC POWER

The harshest critics of multinational corporations are leftists, who see them as the dominant force in a process of economic globalization that violates their vision of a better world. On the far left, Marxists attack them as the instruments of capitalist imperialism. The progressive left attacks them as too powerful. As they see it, MNCs exert the power that comes from their size and wealth to further a set of built-in values, or an institutional imperative, including hypergrowth, exploitation, cultural manipulation, materialism, consumerism, efficiency, and concentration of power. These values move the world away from the progressive vision of communal, democratic societies focused on local production and nonmaterial lifestyles.

To progressives, MNCs are like economic missionaries, converting emerging nations to the ideology of Western economic development and subjugating their peoples to the evils of congested cities, growing inequality, environmental pollution, and low wages. There are two schools of thought in the community of critics—abolition and reform.

Abolitionists seek to end the global dominance of MNCs by changing the corporate form to eliminate legal characteristics that allow what they see as pathological behavior. For example, MNCs should no longer be allowed to commit crimes and continue to exist. Their charters should provide for a death penalty or asset breakup. Regulations and tax policies can be used to discourage growth in size and concentration of power. The scale of many MNCs is not necessary. According to one group of critics, "there is no reason why giant transnational corporations are needed to run hamburger stands, produce clothing and toys, publish books and magazines, grow and process and distribute food, make the goods we need, or provide most of the things that contribute to a satisfying existence."[14] "We must," they conclude, "dramatically change the publicly traded, limited liability global corporation just as previous generations set out to eliminate or control the monarchy."[15]

Reformists accept the existence of MNCs as inevitable and seek to mitigate disagreeable tendencies. The primary tool at their disposal is the call for corporate social responsibility. Organized activists have been effective in getting MNCs to meet many of their demands. For example, they pressured corporations to get out of South Africa when the nation was practicing apartheid and to get out of Myanmar because of the human rights abuses in that country. Activist campaigns have forced changes and reversals in the policies of MNCs including Monsanto, Nike, Polaroid, and Royal Dutch/Shell.

The reformist method is to create a tension between the social values of corporate stakeholders and the values in the corporation's policy. Coca-Cola's defiance of activist critics who wanted it to leave South Africa crumpled as blacks in its huge American market emptied cans of Coke into gutters in protest. Besides successful advocacy campaigns, reform-oriented activists have affected MNCs through their leadership role in developing codes of ethics and social responsibility, as described in Chapter 5.

CONFLICTS BETWEEN GOVERNMENT AND MNC OBJECTIVES

The fundamental motive of going abroad is, of course, profit. Besides making a satisfactory profit, the typical large MNC has many additional goals. Governments in host countries also have multiple goals. Seven major goals of each are shown in the accompanying summaries.

It is clear from a cursory glance at these goals that conflict between them is inevitable. In recent years, however, host countries, especially those with emerging economies, recognize more the benefits that MNCs can bring. The proof is in the generous advantages offered to MNCs as inducements to do business in these countries. Included are tax holidays, exemptions from import duties, construction of infrastructure, low-interest loans, guarantees of cheap labor, and relaxation of environmental protections. Rubens Ricupero, the Secretary-General, United Nations Conference on Trade and Development, said, "All countries in the world, with no exceptions that I know of, are trying to attract foreign direct investment, which is an important condition for development."[16]

[14] The International Forum on Globalization, *Alternatives to Economic Globalization* (San Francisco: Berrett-Koehler, 2002), p. 145.

[15] Ibid., pp. 123–24.

[16] Transcript of press conference by Kofi Annan and leadership of the International Chamber of Commerce, July 7, 1999, M2 Communications, Ltd.

Seven Major Goals of MNCs

- Buy and sell anywhere in the world to take advantage of the most favorable price and product quality available.
- Obtain a high and rising return on invested capital.
- Increase sales revenues.

- Hold risks within reasonable limits in relation to profits.
- Maintain and improve technological and other company strengths.
- Maintain control of important decisions.
- Reduce production costs.

Seven Major Goals of LDCs

- Achieve full employment and economic growth.
- Increase exports and develop a favorable balance of trade.
- Retain a fair share of profits made by MNCs in their country.

- Create technological development.
- Retain control over the economy.
- Maintain social and political stability.
- Protect the natural environment.

MNCs AND LESS DEVELOPED COUNTRIES (LDCs)

Relationships between MNCs and LDCs have changed dramatically during the past two decades. Former resentments and deep suspicion have given way to the welcome mat as the LDCs have seen the benefits that infusion of MNC capital and technology bring to their and other countries. Indeed, LDCs offer generous inducements to MNCs to place plants in their countries. For example, Ford was offered a package of free land, lower taxes, and infrastructure worth about $300 million to build a plant outside Salvador, Brazil. In return, Ford was expected to provide 5,000 jobs and to jump-start industrialization of the area.[17] Indonesia exempts exporters from its value-added tax to encourage local affiliates of foreign-owned MNCs. Some countries have established official agencies to help MNCs in their development of affiliates. Examples are the Economic Development Board of Singapore, the Welsh Development Agency of Wales, and the National Linkage Programme of Ireland. The latter was established in 1998 to help foreign MNCs match their sourcing requirements with local companies. Many LDCs today

[17] Chris Kraul, "Brazil Debates High Cost of Car Plant in Poor State," *Los Angeles Times,* December 5, 1999, p. C1.

Concerns about Negative Effects of MNCs in Developing Countries

- Anticompetitive practices by foreign affiliates.
- Volatile flows of investment and related payments deleterious for the balance of payments.
- Tax avoidance and abusive transfer pricing by foreign affiliates.
- Transfers of polluting activities or technologies.
- Crowding out local firms and suppressing domestic entrepreneurial development.
- Crowding out local products, technologies, and business practices with harmful sociocultural effects.

- Concessions to TNCs, especially in export processing zones, allowing them to skirt labour and environmental regulations.
- Excessive influence on economic affairs, with possible effects on industrial development and national security.

Source: UNCTAD, *World Investment Report 2003* (New York: United Nations, 2003), p. 88. Reprinted with permission.

10 Benefits MNCs Say They Can Bring to a Country

- Provide employment.
- Improve the skills of workers and managers.
- Introduce new product and production technologies.
- Provide products and services that raise the standard of living.
- Introduce and develop new technologies.

- Improve national productivity.
- Provide greater access to international markets.
- Raise the gross domestic product.
- Help build foreign exchange reserves.
- Encourage the development of new industries.

have similar government organizations that work in partnership with private enterprises at home and abroad to facilitate FDI.[18]

The LDCs have many complaints, which they have not been modest in bringing to the attention of developed nations and MNCs. The first box above lists some of them. On the other hand, managers of MNCs claim there are many benefits they can bring and have brought to host countries. The second box presents 10 of them.

MNC managers have their own litany of complaints about doing business in the LDCs. There are, of course, many variations, but several complaints stand out. The dominant obstacles they find are poor infrastructure, corruption, crime and theft, inflation, taxes, conflicts with political authorities, poor local managers, lack of skilled employees, and burdensome regulations.

[18] United Nations, *World Investment Report 1999* (New York: United Nations, 1999), pp. 141–52.

MNCs AND INDUSTRIALIZED NATIONS

LDCs are not alone in seeking advantages offered by MNCs. For example, California, Tennessee, and other states brought in Japanese automobile plants with various inducements. European countries have offered inducements to semiconductor companies to locate there. This has existed for years in the developed countries. Indeed, it was the inducement of capital from England in the 1800s that helped build the railroad system in the United States.

Industrialized countries may impose barriers of various types that disgruntle foreign investors. For example, foreign company investments in the United States are restricted in many areas: national defense, nuclear energy, coastal shipping, and broadcasting. Industrial countries also impose barriers to protect some industries from foreign competition. Examples are automobile companies in the 1980s, peanuts, and steel. Foreign managers, like those in the United States, chafe at government rules they must obey. All business managers have a long litany of complaints about government regulations.

U.S. MNC–Government Relations

A policy of the United States for many decades has been, and still is, to foster worldwide economic progress. The government has always viewed the MNC as an instrument of this global development effort. Sometimes, however, the goals of MNCs and U.S. foreign policy conflict. In addition, as noted in Chapters 10 and 11, corporations based in the United States have strong complaints about regulatory restrictions.

While the basic business–government relationship can be adversarial, there is still plenty of cooperation between MNCs and government agencies. Remember, too, there are thousands of lobbyists in Washington and state capitals who successfully pressure government to favor the interests of the companies and industries they represent.

Examples of specific aids to the MNCs provided by governments abound. Substantial subsidies are made to encourage agricultural exports, and special measures help companies that explore for scarce resources, such as oil. The government provides abundant information without cost about foreign business opportunities. The Export-Import Bank, created in 1934, is a government-owned corporation that promotes U.S. foreign trade in the form of direct and guaranteed loans to foreign buyers of U.S. export products. The U.S. Trade Representative stands ready to negotiate with foreign countries for agreements that benefit U.S. exporters.

The federal government, on the other hand, also restrains MNCs. For instance, the Clinton administration, because of tensions with China over human rights, told the Export-Import Bank it should not help American MNCs participate in China's mammoth $30 billion Three Gorges dam project. For national security reasons, U.S. manufacturers of sophisticated electronics equipment are forbidden to sell these products abroad. The United States has invoked economic sanctions for many countries that, of course, limit U.S. export business with them.

Raymond Vernon, a prominent scholar of the MNC and professor at Harvard University, sees increasing conflict in the future between MNCs and their home governments. He writes: "My concern . . . is that some of the most important political struggles which multinational enterprises face in the future will originate within the home countries of the multinationals."[19] He predicts heightened conflict between those who advocate free markets and those who feel disadvantaged by the MNCs. That is happening now. For instance, labor unions attack the MNCs for exporting jobs. Activist critics, such as Ralph Nader, denounce MNCs, alleging that in foreign operations they abuse human rights, exploit workers, pollute, and in general fail to act responsibly. These groups are becoming more vocal and organized in their attacks. On the other side are groups that believe the world will benefit from free markets left to operate comparatively unfettered.

MNC–Government Relations in Other Industrialized Countries

The United States is not the only country encouraging or inhibiting home-based MNCs. A good illustration is Europe's Airbus Industries four-nation consortium. Since 1970 this group has received billions of dollars in government aid to finance the development of commercial airliners. The consortium was formed and supported by France, Great Britain, Germany, and Spain as a direct challenge to American dominance in the civilian jet airliner business. It has worked. At the time Airbus was started, three U.S. companies (Boeing, Lockheed, and McDonnell Douglas) dominated the world's commercial jet market. Airbus today has captured a large piece of the market and is a strong challenger to Boeing, the only current U.S. producer of these airplanes.

The relationships between business and government in European countries are much more cooperative than in the United States, except Great Britain, where the link is similar to that in the United States. The French government owns a number of large companies. In countries such as the Netherlands, Sweden, Norway, and Denmark, there are close relationships between government and large companies. There are intimate relationships between large companies and the Japanese government. The government there is deeply involved in helping Japanese companies penetrate foreign markets and protect their turf at home from foreign competition. In China, South Korea, and in many countries in Southeast Asia, the relationship is very close, with companies owned and operated by officers in the military (as in China) or by family members (as in Indonesia).

FREE TRADE VERSUS PROTECTIONISM

free trade
The elimination of all barriers to international trade.

Free trade has been the policy throughout most of the history of the United States. However, there have been significant deviations from that policy. In recent years, the United States has taken the lead in creating international agencies to advance free trade throughout the world. At the same time, protectionist pressures have increased in the United States and in most other nations. Why free trade? Why *protectionism?*

[19] Raymond Vernon, *In the Hurricane's Eye* (Cambridge, MA: Harvard University Press, 1998), p. 109.

Why Free Trade?

The case for free trade is comparatively simple. By virtue of climate, labor conditions, raw materials, capital, management, or other considerations, some nations have an advantage over others in the production of particular goods. For example, Brazil can produce coffee beans at a much lower cost than the United States. Coffee beans could be grown in hothouses in the United States, but not at a price equal to that which Brazilians can charge and make a profit. But the United States has a distinct advantage over Brazil in producing computers. Resources will be used most efficiently when each country produces that for which it enjoys a cost advantage. Gain will be maximized when each nation specializes in producing those products for which it has the greatest economic edge. This is what economists call the *law of comparative advantage*. It follows that maximum gain on a worldwide basis will be realized if there are no impediments to trade, if there is free competition in pricing, and if capital flows are unrestricted.

law of comparative advantage
Efficiency and the general economic welfare are optimized when each country produces that for which it enjoys a cost advantage.

It is not always easy, however, to see just where a nation has a comparative advantage. At the extremes the case is clear, but not in the middle range. Differences in monetary units, rates of productivity of capital and labor, changes in markets, or elasticities of demand, for instance, obscure the degree of advantage one nation may have over another at any time. Nevertheless, it is argued that free trade will stimulate competition, reward individual initiative, increase productivity, and improve national well-being. It will enlarge job opportunities and produce for consumers a wider variety of goods and services at minimum prices and with higher quality.

This is the theory. In practice, all countries have erected restraints on imports to protect their industries. We now discuss pressures for and against free trade around the world.

The United States Moves toward Free Trade

Because of international trade negotiations, global trade is far freer, more open, and more efficient than in years past, leading to an extraordinary leap in world trade, as shown in Figure 12.2. A milestone in world trade was the ratification of the General Agreement on Tariffs and Trade (GATT) in 1947. In a series of meetings among representatives of participating nations (called rounds) GATT was successful in slashing tariff walls. At its last meeting in 1994, for example, tariffs were reduced 30 percent overall and by a higher percentage in industrialized nations. At that meeting representatives concluded a faster method to settle trade disputes was needed and they created the World Trade Organization (WTO) (see the case on the WTO at the end of Chapter 13).

Since the WTO's formation in 1994, the United States and other nations have used the WTO dispute settlement procedure to resolve trade questions. The United States has formulated and carried out with other nations many treaties, tariff eliminations, and tariff reductions. For example, a milestone was reached in U.S. trade policy with the creation of the Canada–United States Free Trade agreement signed in 1987. Another significant step in free trade was made in 1992 when the United States, Canada, and Mexico signed the North American Free Trade

FIGURE 12.2
World
Merchandise
Trade by
Major Product
Group

Source: *World Trade Statistics*, WTO, 2004.

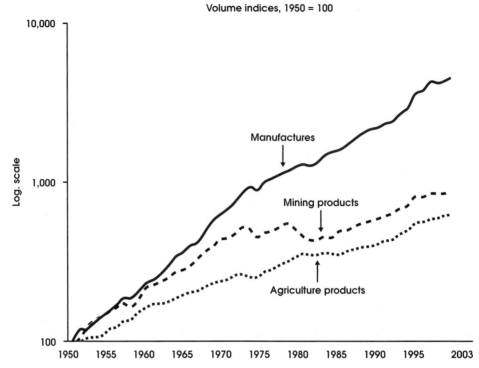

Pressures for Protectionism

protectionism
An action taken by governments to shelter, or protect, industry by tariffs or other trade barriers.

Agreement (NAFTA). Area free trade agreements are being formed around the world. The most important one, in terms of scope, is the European Union (EU). These treaties will be discussed in detail in the next chapter.

Most domestic businesses, whether engaged in foreign trade or not, feel pressures from foreign competitors with better products and lower prices. Many seek and get protection from the government. This is protectionism, and it exists in the trade history of all nations.

In the early history of the United States, the motivation for protectionism was to protect infant industries. Recently, there have been powerful pressures on government to protect some mature industries (e.g., automobiles, steel, textiles) from foreign competition. Three justifications are often given for protectionist measures.

First, the United States has large trade deficits that must be reduced. In 1975 the United States enjoyed a small trade surplus (the difference between total exports and total imports of goods and services). Each year since there have been large deficits. In August 2004, exports were $95.9 billion and imports were $150 billion, leaving a deficit of $54.2 billion. Protectionists are concerned about the persistence and size of these deficits, believing they are detrimental and should be eliminated. One way, they assert, is to discourage excessive imports and encourage exports.

Second, protectionists want to shield industries from foreign competition. For example, foreign competitors have penetrated the U.S. market with products such as textiles, steel, shoes, motorcycles, dolls, luggage, automobiles, and television sets. A significant result, say protectionists, is loss of jobs.

Third, trade barriers in foreign countries (discussed later in the chapter) restrict American imports to them. These barriers cost Americans jobs. If nations refuse to remove them then the United States should retaliate.

The Politics of Protectionism

Protectionism is not solely an economic issue. There is a significant political dimension. For example, President Bush has said often that expanding free trade is one of his highest priorities. In a speech before the Council of the Americas, he said: "When we negotiate for open markets we are providing new hope for the world's poor . . . and when we promote open trade we are promoting political freedom."[20]

Why then did he support substantial restrictions on imports of steel in his first major trade initiative? His staff explained that the decision followed a thorough examination of the problems of the steel industry and help was justified. For example, the industry today employs one-fifth the number of steelworkers it did in 1980, production has slumped, steel mills have closed, and the financial strength of the industry has weakened. This is a result, the industry claims, of lower-priced imports from many different countries. Another reason for the president's decision is that the industry and its unions have political strength. They are major financial contributors to political campaigns, and their workers' votes can spell the difference between winning or losing electoral votes in several critical states, such as Pennsylvania, Ohio, and West Virginia.

Free Trader Responses to Protectionists

Free traders advance many arguments against protectionism. One main argument is the logic for free trade. Another is that the cause of the exceptional rise in world trade, as shown in Figure 12.2, say anti-protectionists, has been in no small measure the world's reduction in tariff barriers. Former Senator Phil Gramm argued that impediments or hindrances to free trade are "immoral." "They limit my freedom," he said. "If I want to buy a shirt in China, who has the right to tell me as a free person that I can't do it?"[21] Protectionists claim that tariffs will save jobs. That is true, but they also may cost jobs. For example, when President Bush imposed tariffs to protect United States steelworkers the price increase in steel resulting from the tariffs cost jobs in companies using the steel. Protectionists are creative in developing new arguments to protect against foreign competitors.[22] Anti-protectionists are fond of quoting John Stuart Mill, a famous nineteenth century economist and philosopher: "Trade barriers are chiefly injurious to the countries imposing them."

[20] Reported by Joseph Kahn, "Bush Moves against Steel Imports; Trade Tensions Are Likely to Rise," *New York Times,* June 6, 2001, p. 1.

[21] Reported by Gerald F. Seib and John Harwood, "Disparate Groups on Right Join Forces to Make Opposition to China's Trade Status a Key Issue," *The Wall Street Journal,* June 10, 1997, p. A20.

[22] Jagdish Bhagwati, "Protectionism," *The Concise Encyclopedia of Economics,* http:www.econlib.org/library/Enc/Protectionism.html, accessed 12/13/2004.

U.S. Deviation from Free Trade Policy

Despite strong free trade rhetoric and the steady lowering of tariff and other trade barriers, the United States protects industries from foreign competition. Over the years, it has raised tariffs, imposed quotas, and prohibited the import of various products. There are hundreds of examples of deviation from free trade theory and policy that have added to the crazy quilt of world trade impediments. Here are some examples.

"buy American" laws
Laws that require or seek to influence governments and agencies to purchase U.S.-made goods and services rather than foreign-made goods and services.

Trade records are marbled with *"buy American" laws.* The Federal Buy American Act of 1933, still in force, requires federal agencies to pay up to a 6 percent differential for domestically produced goods. Many states have similar laws covering a wide range of products. The Merchant Marine Act prohibits foreign vessels from plying domestic waterways. The Passenger Vessel Services Act requires ships going from one U.S. port to another to be U.S. flagged, U.S. built, and U.S. crewed.

U.S. tariffs have declined significantly in recent years, but there are many exceptions. For example, we have high tariffs on imports of sugar, peanuts, certain types of glassware, textiles, motorcycles, and steel. At the same time, we have given duty-free status to hundreds of products under a Generalized System of Preferences (GSP). The purpose of this system is to foster economic development for many LDCs by increasing their trade with the United States. While the total value of products involved is not great in terms of total U.S. trade, it can be very important to developing countries.[23]

Tariff Barriers in Other Countries

Despite the benefits of free trade, all nations have some trade barriers. There is no doubt that tariffs levied on imported products have generally been cut, especially in the developed countries, but nontariff barriers have increased. Examples of nontariff barriers are excessive delays in inspections of imported products; unreasonable technical standards for product characteristics, such as size, quality, health, and safety; practices that inhibit consumer purchases of foreign goods and services; and quotas. Such barriers are illustrated by the following.

China has cleaned up its trade practices to meet the standards of the WTO, which it has joined, but it still imposes substantial barriers. It has quotas on imports of more than 40 products including watches, automobiles, steel, textiles, wheat, corn, rice, cotton, and vegetable oils. Ineffective enforcement of intellectual property rights is a major trade problem in China. The U.S. government is also concerned about unscientific bans on U.S. beef from livestock treated with hormones and U.S. poultry treated to minimize bacteria risks. Japanese tariffs range from 10 percent to 40 percent for products such as beef, oranges, apples, ice cream, citrus fruit juices, and tomatoes. Rice imports are virtually completely restricted. When even a small amount of rice is imported it must be mixed with domestic rice. Various restrictions among European Union countries are applied to genetically engineered commodities. Taiwan restricts imports of rice. Brazil has reduced many tariffs but still retains high tariffs on technology products that double the

---

[23] General Accounting Office, *International Trade, Comparison of U.S. and European Union Preference Programs* (Washington, DC: General Accounting Office, June 2001).

cost of computers. Brazil also prohibits importation of products such as machinery, automobiles, and clothing. India has a wide variety of trade restrictions, which have prevented growth in U.S. exports to India for more than five years. The U.S. government is concerned about Korean subsidies to semiconductor production and exports. While the NAFTA treaty has led to a doubling of U.S. exports to Mexico, that country still retains substantial trade restrictions on products such as meat, poultry, vegetables, and fruits. Accession to the WTO has led Russia to undertake reforms in its trading system, but Russian tariff restrictions on imports remain, such as quotas on meat imports. Nontariff barriers include import licensing, standards and certification procedures, and service and investment restrictions. And so it goes around the world.[24]

Classical Free Trade Theory versus Reality

The reality is that the global economy is a mixture of free trade and protectionism. It always has been. Furthermore, classical free trade theory based on comparative advantage, explained above, has lost much validity for a large part of world trade. Many of the assumptions of the seventeenth and eighteenth centuries, upon which the theory is based, no longer are valid in today's world.

competitive advantage of nations
A phrase coined by Professor Michael Porter identifying a nation as having a cluster of similar producers which gives the nation a special advantage over other countries.

Professor Michael Porter of the Harvard Business School has formulated a major modification to classical theory to fit the modern world. He calls it *competitive advantage of nations.* Porter asks: Why does a nation achieve global superiority in one industry? He answers that it is because "industrial clusters" are formed in the nation. These clusters are composed of firms and industries that are mutually supporting, innovative, competitive, low-cost producers, and committed to meeting demanding consumer tastes.

Why is it, he asks, that Switzerland, a landlocked country with few natural resources, is a world leader in the production of chocolates? Why is it that Italy is a world leader in producing quality shoes? Why is it that Japan, a country whose economy was in shambles after World War II, is a global leader in making low-cost, mass-produced, good quality high-technology products?

Porter's answer lies in a congeries of factors that go beyond natural resources. Among the factors are a sizable demand from sophisticated consumers, an educated and skilled workforce, intense competition in the industry, and the existence of related and supporting suppliers. Government plays a part, but not a major one. Porter's theory is convincingly and amply illustrated in a major research project on the subject.[25] Classical theory is still valid for many products. Porter's work modernizes it to better fit the current reality of trade among nations in a vast range of products.

Classical economic doctrine postulates that when industries are granted relief from foreign competition, they fail to make needed capital investments, grow lazy, forget product quality, lose incentives, fail to innovate, raise prices, and

[24] These illustrations were taken principally from *U.S.T.R. Releases 2003 Inventory of Trade Barriers* (Washington, DC: U.S. Trade Representative, April 1, 2003). The U.S. Trade Representative also publishes detailed reports of many nations.
[25] Michael E. Porter, *The Comparative Advantage of Nations* (New York: Free Press, 1990).

enjoy excess profits from captive markets. Recent experiences in five protected industries in the United States contradict this theory. Indeed, relief from predatory foreign trade practices in the automobile, steel, textile, semiconductor, and machine tool industries has produced just the reverse results. In each of these industries, foreign competitive practices have had serious adverse impacts. But in each case, federal protective measures from foreign imports have had remarkably beneficial results.[26]

The experience in these industries does not mean, of course, that protectionism is a good policy. It means, rather, that a government can help an industry recover from predatory foreign trade when it chooses the appropriate means, on a limited scale, for a limited period of time, for a few industries, and for the right reasons. Free trade should be the policy, but with some exceptions.

CORRUPTION IN BUSINESS AND GOVERNMENT TRANSACTIONS

Cultural differences, practices, and laws among the many countries where MNCs do business create extremely difficult moral, ethical, and legal problems for MNCs. The way in which business is conducted around the world sometimes entangles U.S. companies in a complex web of influence, politics, customs, and subtle business arrangements. Companies have found in many LDCs, and even in some highly industrialized countries, that to do business it is necessary to make a variety of payments. This is not new. It has been going on for centuries. What is new is the widespread and often intense publicity given to instances of corruption involving high government officials. In today's age of instantaneous communications and investigative journalism, it is much more difficult to keep corruption out of the limelight.

corruption
The debasement of integrity for money, position, privilege, or other self-benefit. It ranges over a spectrum with petty lubricating bribes at one end and outright extortion at the other. It undermines markets by substituting bribery for honest competition based on price, quality, and service.

What Is Corruption?

There is no consensus about a definition of *corruption;* there is more agreement about types of corruption. At one end of a possible spectrum is what might be called petty corruption or "grease" payments. These are bribes involving small amounts of money made to facilitate action by a low-level employee. They range from tips for services rendered to "requests" for money to get someone to do their regular duties, such as unloading articles off ships or clearing incoming products through customs. These small bribes are often called "lubrication bribes," "honest graft," "tokens of appreciation," "contributions," and so on. The practice is accepted around the world as legitimate for services rendered. These payments are often justified as offsets to low salaries in foreign countries. At the other end of the spectrum are extortion and outrageous bribery.

Between the extremes the lines of demarcation that may distinguish the probably acceptable and legitimate from the clearly unethical are not always clear. Suppose, for example, the normal practice in a country is for an import expediter to charge a

[26] Alan Tonelson, "Beating Back Predatory Trade," *Foreign Affairs,* July–August 1994.

The High Costs of Pilgrimages

" . . . One of our clients, a charter airline, had a $20 million contract with the Indonesian government to fly Moslem pilgrims from Jakarta to Jeddah. Shortly before the contract signing, the management team was told that a key provision had not been discussed. As it was explained to them, preference for the flight was given to elderly Moslems who had not yet made the pilgrimage.

"As many of the pilgrims were in their 70s and 80s, it seemed likely that some would die and no arrangements had been made to deal with that contingency. The governmental officials who were organizing the trip asked for $250,000 to cover the costs of any situations that might arise. Given the amount of the contract, the airline negotiators thought that $250,000 in incidental costs was not excessive.

"Of course, once the contract was performed, no money was left in the $250,000 fund. The SEC investigated the payment as a possible violation of the Foreign Corrupt Practices Act (1977), but they eventually dropped the case because there was no way to prove that the payment was a bribe."

Stephen Potts
Director
Office of Government Ethics

Source: Ronald E. Berenbeim, Company Programs for Resisting Corrupt Practices (NY: The Conference Board, October 2000), p. 14.

moderate commission for services. However, the person involved not only charges a somewhat higher than customary fee, but also has close ties to a government agency buying the imported item. When is the payment "normal," and when does it become tainted with bribery? Paying a tax collector to reduce a company's tax load would be a clear example of bribery. Expensive jewelry given to an official's spouse would be considered bribery if the official could grant important favors to the giver. Paid vacations and free air travel, lavish entertainment, and, of course, cash given to a high political official would be forms of bribery. These types of corruption, depending partly on their size, have different degrees of importance. See the box above for another example.

offsets
Actions taken by a foreign corporation, at the recommendation of the government purchaser, to spend substantial sums of money to produce a good or service in exchange for the purchase.

A different problem in identification of bribery is *offsets,* which have become popular in the international arms trade. For example, in exchange for purchasing military hardware from Boeing, Northrop Grumman, and Lockheed Martin, the United Arab Emirates pressed the contractors to spend millions of dollars on a variety of activities to create jobs and improve the well-being of its population. These companies financed medical centers, built a shipyard, helped to clean up oil-spills, and started a laser-printer recycling business. U.S. arms makers have helped the Dutch to export yarn and missile parts. Offsets can be part of an agreement to bring investment to a country. Contractors dislike offsets but they are an essential part of doing business in many countries.[27]

Costs and Consequences of Corruption

The World Bank concludes that worldwide bribes total $1 trillion each year. This number, calculated using 2001–2002 economic data, compares with the size of the world economy at that time of about $30 trillion. The phenomenon is present in

[27] Leslie Wayne, "A Well-Kept Military Secret," *New York Times,* February 16, 2003, sec. 3, p. 1.

TABLE 12.4
Highest and Lowest Scoring Nations on the TI Corruption Perceptions Index

Source: Transparency International. Reprinted with permission.

Highest		Lowest	
Finland	9.7	Indonesia	2.0
New Zealand	9.6	Tajikistan	2.0
Denmark	9.5	Turkmenistan	2.0
Iceland	9.5	Azerbaijan	1.9
Singapore	9.3	Paraguay	1.9
Sweden	9.2	Chad	1.7
Switzerland	9.1	Myanmar	1.7
Norway	8.9	Nigeria	1.6
Australia	8.8	Bangladesh	1.5
Netherlands	8.7	Haiti	1.5

both highly industrialized as well as developing countries.[28] Kimberly Ann Elliott points out in her book *Corruption* that "widespread corruption threatens the very basis of an open, multilateral world economy."[29] Corruption raises the costs of doing business; it distorts government allocation of expenditures; it can, as with present-day Russia, slow the development of a free market; it can have a corrosive impact on both government service and business efficiency; it distorts competition; and it can undermine political legitimacy.

The degree of corruption varies significantly among countries. Every year Transparency International (TI) publishes an index of corruption that ranks nations. Table 12.4 shows the 10 highest scores and the 10 lowest scores in its survey of 146 countries. TI says that a total of 106 countries out of the 146 scored less than 5 against a top score of 10. In 60 countries the scores were less than 3 out of 10, indicating rampant corruption. The United States ranked 17th in a three-way tie with Belgium and Ireland, all having a score of 7.5. An examination of the scores reveals that there is less corruption in developed countries than in underdeveloped ones, a conclusion that corroborates the point that corruption inhibits economic growth. The index is compiled from polls, surveys of business people, interviews, and country analysts.[30]

Laws and Codes to Control Corruption

Following the Watergate scandals in the Nixon administration, the Securities and Exchange Commission began investigations in 1974 to find to what extent corruption was involved in U.S. corporate foreign operations. The agency "invited" corporations to make voluntary disclosures of this activity. More than 400 responded and disclosed they had made almost $1 billion in questionable

---

[28] The World Group, "The Costs of Corruption," DevNews Media Center, April 8, 2004.

[29] Kimberly Ann Elliott, *Corruption and the Global Economy* (Washington, DC: Institute for International Economics, June 1997), p. 13.

[30] Transparency International, *Corruption Perceptions Index 2004* (London, October 20, 2004), http://www.transparency.org/cpi/2004/cpi2004.en.html.

payments, mostly foreign. The need for new regulations became obvious and Congress passed the Foreign Corrupt Practices Act (FCPA) in 1977.

This act makes it a criminal offense to offer a bribe to a foreign government official. For unlawful acts, companies may be fined $2 million and individual managers may face fines of up to $1 million and five years in jail. The law does not apply to facilitating or "grease" payments intended only to expedite normal business affairs. The law prohibits offering money or anything of value to any person (foreign or domestic) if it is known that any or all of the money or value offered will be used to influence a foreign official, politician, or political party. This means, of course, that a corporation or an individual manager may run afoul of the law if it is known that commission payments are used to induce government officials to do something for the company. The law also requires companies to keep accounting records that accurately and fairly reflect transactions.

In response to complaints from business, Congress amended the FCPA in 1988 to clarify some ambiguities in the original version. Congress also urged the president to initiate discussions about prohibitions of bribery with the Organization for Economic Co-operation and Development (OECD). Eventually the OECD countries in 1997 approved the Convention Combating Bribery of Foreign Public Officials in International Business Transactions. This was a major step in the battle over corruption and for the first time committed the OECD's 40 members to outlaw the most significant forms of it.

These commitments were paralleled by initiatives in the United Nations, nongovernmental organizations, and transnational corporations. In 2003, the United Nations approved the UN Convention Against Corruption. Today there are few large corporations in the United States that do not have strict policies about their managers' involvement in foreign bribery of one type or another.[31]

CONCLUDING OBSERVATIONS

MNCs are extremely powerful institutions roaming the globe. They have major impacts on markets, social systems, and political institutions. Consequently, they are obliged to act responsibly to society as well as to their shareholders. Most of the large MNCs appear to have discharged their power reasonably well, but not well enough to meet and help resolve some major problems of today and tomorrow. On their behalf, we observe that complexities of doing global business raise serious economic, ethical, political, social, and moral issues for their managements. We believe more top managers of U.S. corporations, with help and prodding from government and strong activist critics, are exercising power responsibly. We continue this discussion of MNCs in the next chapter.

---

[31] A good example is *FCPA Guidelines*, prepared by Raytheon Company's Office of Business & Compliance for all employees. This is a clear, reasonably short, but thorough analysis of what every employee should know and do.

Union Carbide Corporation and Bhopal

On December 3, 1984, tragedy unfolded at the Union Carbide pesticide plant in Bhopal, India. Water entered a large tank where a volatile chemical was stored, starting a violent reaction. Rapidly, a sequence of safety procedures and devices failed. Fugitive vapors sailed over plant boundaries, forming a lethal cloud that moved with the south wind, enveloping slum dwellings, searing lungs and eyes, asphyxiating fated souls, scarring the unlucky.

Bhopal is the worst sudden industrial accident ever in terms of human life lost. Death and injury estimates vary widely. The official death toll set forth by the Indian government for that night is 4,037, with an additional 60,000 serious injuries. Greenpeace has put the death toll at 16,000, with an estimated 500,000 injured.[1]

The incredible event galvanized industry critics. "Like Auschwitz and Hiroshima," wrote one, "the catastrophe at Bhopal is a manifestation of something fundamentally wrong in our stewardship of the earth."[2] Union Carbide was debilitated and slowly declined as a company after the incident. The government of India earned mixed reviews for its response. The chemical industry changed, but according to some, not enough. And the gas victims endure a continuing struggle to get compensation and medical care.[3]

UNION CARBIDE IN INDIA

Union Carbide established an Indian subsidiary named Union Carbide India Ltd. (UCIL) in 1934. At first the company owned a 60 percent majority interest, but over the years this was reduced to 50.9 percent. Shares in the ownership of the other 49.1 percent traded on the Bombay Stock Exchange. This ownership scheme was significant because although UCIL operated with a great deal of autonomy, it gave the appearance that Union Carbide was in control of its operations. By itself, UCIL was one of India's

largest firms. In 1984, the year of the incident, it had 14 plants and 9,000 employees, including 500 at Bhopal. Most of its revenues came from selling Eveready batteries.

Union Carbide decided to build a pesticide plant at Bhopal in 1969. The plant formulated pesticides from chemical ingredients imported to the site. At that time, there was a growing demand in India and throughout Asia for pesticides because of the "green revolution," a type of planned agriculture that requires intensive use of pesticides and fertilizers on special strains of food crops such as wheat, rice, and corn. Although pesticides may be misused and pose some risk, they also have great social value. Without pesticides, damage to crops, losses in food storage, and toxic mold growth in food supplies would cause much loss of life from starvation and food poisoning, especially in countries such as India. Exhibit 1 shows a Union Carbide advertisement from the 1960s that describes the company's activities in India.

The Bhopal plant would supply these pesticides and serve a market anticipated to expand rapidly. The plant's location in Bhopal was encouraged by tax incentives from the city and the surrounding state of Madhya Pradesh. After a few years, however, the Indian government pressured UCIL to stop importing chemical ingredients. The company then proposed to manufacture methyl isocyanate (MIC) at the plant rather than ship it in from Carbide facilities outside the country. This was a fateful decision.

Methyl isocyanate, CH_3NCO, is a colorless, odorless liquid. Its presence can be detected by tearing and the burning sensation it causes in the eyes and noses of exposed individuals. At the Bhopal plant it was used as an intermediate chemical in pesticide manufacture. It was not the final product; rather, MIC molecules were created, then pumped into a vessel where they reacted with other chemicals. The reaction created unique molecules with qualities that disrupted insect nervous systems, causing convulsions and death. The plant turned out two similar pesticides marketed under the names Sevin and Temik.

In 1975 UCIL received a permit from the Ministry of Industry in New Delhi to build an MIC production unit at the Bhopal plant. Two months before the issuance of this permit, the city of Bhopal had enacted a development plan requiring dangerous industries to

[1] "Has the World Forgotten Bhopal?" *The Lancet,* December 2, 2000, p. 1863.

[2] David Weir, *The Bhopal Syndrome* (San Francisco: Sierra Club Books, 1987), p. xii.

[3] Kim Fortun, *Advocacy After Bhopal* (Chicago: University of Chicago Press, 2001).

EXHIBIT 1
Union Carbide Advertisement
This ad appeared in *Fortune* magazine in April 1962.

Source: Photo courtesy of Union Carbide Corporation.

Science helps build a new India

Oxen working the fields . . . the eternal river Ganges . . . jeweled elephants on parade. Today these symbols of ancient India exist side by side with a new sight—modern industry. India has developed bold new plans to build its economy and bring the promise of a bright future to its more than 400,000,000 people. ▷ But India needs the technical knowledge of the western world. For example, working with Indian engineers and technicians, Union Carbide recently made available its vast scientific resources to help build a major chemicals and plastics plant near Bombay. ▷ Throughout the free world, Union Carbide has been actively engaged in building plants for the manufacture of chemicals, plastics, carbons, gases, and metals. The people of Union Carbide welcome the opportunity to use their knowledge and skills in partnership with the citizens of so many great countries.

A HAND IN THINGS TO COME   UNION CARBIDE

WRITE *for booklet B-3 "The Exciting Universe of Union Carbide", which tells how research in the fields of carbons, chemicals, gases, metals, plastics and nuclear energy keeps bringing new wonders into your life.*
Union Carbide Corporation, 270 Park Avenue, New York 17, N.Y.

relocate in an industrial zone 15 miles away. Pursuant to the plan, M. N. Buch, the Bhopal city administrator, tried to move the UCIL pesticide plant and convert the site to housing and light commercial use. For reasons that are unclear, his effort failed, and Buch was soon transferred to forestry duties elsewhere.

The MIC unit was based on a process design provided by Union Carbide's engineers in the United States and elaborated by engineers in India. The design required storage of MIC in big tanks. An alternative used at most other pesticide plants would have been to produce small amounts of MIC only as they were consumed in pesticide production. The decision to use large storage tanks was based on an optimistic projection that pesticide sales would grow dramatically. Since an Indian law, the Foreign Exchange Regulation Act of 1973, requires foreign multinationals to share technology and use Indian resources, detailed design work was done by an Indian subsidiary of a British firm. Local labor using Indian equipment and materials built the unit.

In 1980 the MIC unit began operation under UCIL's management. During the five years of design and construction, densely populated shantytowns sprang up nearby, inhabited mainly by impoverished, unemployed people who had left rural areas seeking their fortunes in the city. A childlike faith that the facility was a benevolent presence turning out miraculous substances to make plants grow was widespread among them.

In fact, when the MIC unit came on line the plant began to pose higher risk to its neighbors; it now made the basic chemicals used in pesticides rather than using shipped-in ingredients. One step in the manufacture of MIC, for example, creates phosgene, the lethal "mustard gas" used in World War I. The benighted crowd by the plant abided unaware.

In 1981 a phosgene leak killed one worker, and a crusading Indian journalist wrote articles about dangers to the population. No one acted. A year later, a second phosgene leak forced temporary evacuation of some surrounding neighborhoods. Worker safety and environmental inspections of the plant were done by the state Department of Labor, an agency with only 15 factory inspectors to cover 8,000 plants and a record of lax enforcement.[4] Oversight was not vigorous.

[4] Sheila Jasanoff, "Managing India's Environment," *Environment*, October 1986, p. 33.

Meanwhile, the Indian economy had turned down, and stiff competition from other pesticide firms marketing new, less expensive products reduced demand for Sevin and Temik. As revenues fell, so did the plant's budget, and it was necessary to defer some maintenance, lessen the rigor of training, and lay off workers. By the time of the incident, the MIC unit operated with six workers per shift, half the number anticipated by its designers.

UNION CARBIDE'S RELATIONSHIP WITH THE BHOPAL PLANT

What was the organizational relationship of Union Carbide Corporation in the United States to its subsidiary, Union Carbide India Ltd., and ultimately to the Bhopal plant? How much direction and control did the corporate parent half a world away in Danbury, Connecticut, exercise over the facility?

The Bhopal plant fit into the Union Carbide management hierarchy as shown in the chart in Exhibit 2. Although Carbide employees from the United States managed the plant in its early years, in 1982, under pressure from the government, it was turned over to Indian managers. The experience of colonial rule in India created a strong political need for leaders to put on shows of strength with foreign investors. Indians felt a burning desire to avoid any appearance of subjugation and demanded self-sufficiency. This is what had led to passage of the law requiring foreign investors to use Indian firms and workers in certain ways—and to put pressure on Union Carbide to turn the plant completely over to its Indian subsidiary.

The Bhopal plant was but one of 500 facilities in 34 countries in the Union Carbide Corporation universe. There was no regular or direct reporting relationship between it and Union Carbide's headquarters in Danbury, Connecticut. At the request of UCIL, employees of Union Carbide had gone to India twice to perform safety inspections on the plant. Other than those occasions, managers in the United States had received information or reporting about the plant only infrequently and irregularly when major changes or capital expenditures were requested. Thus, the Bhopal plant was run with near total independence from the American corporation. In litigation to determine where victims' lawsuits should be

EXHIBIT 2
Union
Carbide's
Organization
Structure as
Related to the
Bhopal Plant

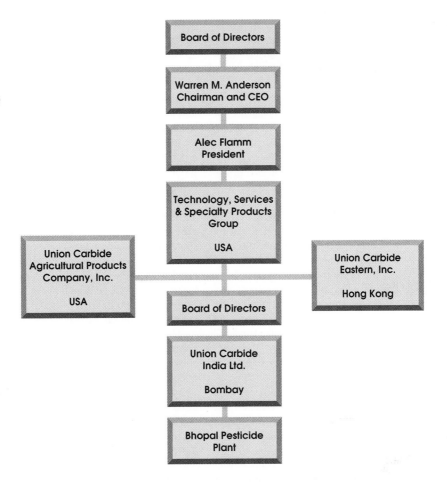

tried, a U.S. court described its autonomy in these words:

> . . . [Union Carbide Corporation's] participation [in the design and construction of the plant] was limited and its involvement in plant operations terminated long before the accident . . . [It] was constructed and managed by Indians in India. No Americans were employed at the plant at the time of the accident. In the five years from 1980 to 1984, although more than 1,000 Indians were employed at the plant, only one American was employed there and he left in 1982. No Americans visited the plant for more than one year prior to the accident, and during the 5-year period before the accident the communications between the plant and the United States were almost nonexistent.[5]

[5] *In re Union Carbide Corporation Gas Plant Disaster at Bhopal*, 809 F.2d 195 (1987), at 200.

Thus, the Bhopal plant was run by UCIL with near total independence from the American corporation. Despite this, shortly after the gas leak Chairman Warren M. Anderson said that Carbide accepted "moral responsibility" for the tragedy.

THE GAS LEAK

On the eve of the disaster, tank 610, one of three storage tanks in the MIC unit, sat filled with 11,290 gallons of MIC. The tank, having a capacity of 15,000 gallons, was a partly buried, stainless steel, pressurized vessel. Its purpose was to take in MIC made elsewhere in the plant and hold it for some time until it was sent to the pesticide production area through a transfer pipe, there to be converted into Sevin or Temik.

At about 9:30 P.M. a supervisor ordered an operator, R. Khan, to unclog four filter valves near the MIC production area by washing them out with water. Khan connected a water hose to the piping above the clogged valves but neglected to insert a slip blind, a device that seals lines to prevent water leaks into adjacent pipes. Khan's omission, if it occurred, would have violated established procedure.

Because of either this careless washing method or the introduction of water elsewhere, 120 to 240 gallons of water entered tank 610, starting a powerful exothermic (heat building) reaction. At first, operators were unaware of the danger, and for two hours pressure in the tank rose unnoticed. At 10:20 P.M. they logged tank pressure at 2 pounds per square inch (ppsi). At 11:30 P.M. a new operator in the MIC control room noticed that the pressure was 10 ppsi, but he was unconcerned because this was within tolerable limits, gauges were often wrong, and he had not read the log to learn that the pressure was now five times what it had been an hour earlier.

Unfortunately, refrigeration units that cooled the tanks had been shut down for five months to save electricity costs. Had they been running, as the MIC processing manual required, the heat from the reaction with the water might have taken place over days instead of hours.

As pressure built, leaks developed. Soon workers sensed the presence of MIC. Their eyes watered. At 11:45 someone spotted a small, yellowish drip from overhead piping. The supervisor suggested fixing the leak after the regular 12:15 A.M. tea break. At 12:40 the tea break ended. By now the control room gauge showed the pressure in tank 610 was 40 ppsi. In a short time it rose to 55 ppsi, the top of the scale. A glance at the tank temperature gauge brought more bad news: The MIC was 77°F, 36° higher than the specified safety limit and hot enough to vaporize. Startled by readings on the gauges, the control room operator ran out to tank 610. He felt radiating heat and heard the concrete over it cracking. Within seconds, a pressure-release valve opened and a white cloud of deadly MIC vapor shot into the atmosphere with a high-decibel screech.

Back in the control room, operators turned a switch to activate the vent gas scrubber, a safety device designed to neutralize escaping toxic gases by circulating them through caustic soda. It was down for maintenance and inoperable. Even if it had been on line, it was too small to handle the explosive volume of MIC shooting from the tank. A flare tower designed to burn off toxic gases before they reached the

atmosphere was also off line; it had been dismantled for maintenance and an elbow joint was missing. Another emergency measure, transferring MIC from tank 610 to one of the other storage tanks, was foreclosed because both were too full. This situation also violated the processing manual, which called for leaving one tank empty as a safeguard.

At about 1:00 A.M. an operator triggered an alarm to warn workers of danger. The plant superintendent, entering the control room, ordered a water spraying device be directed on the venting gas, but this last-resort measure had little effect. Now most workers ran in panic, ignoring four emergency buses they were supposed to drive through the surrounding area to evacuate residents. Two intrepid operators stayed at the control panel, sharing the only available oxygen mask when the room filled with MIC vapor. Finally, at 2:30, the pressure in tank 610 dropped, the leaking safety valve resealed, and the venting ceased. Roughly 10,000 gallons of MIC, about 90 percent of the tank's contents, was now settling over the city.

That night the wind was calm, the temperature about 60°, and the dense chemical mist lingered just above the ground. Animals died. The gas attacked people in the streets and seeped into their bedrooms. Those who panicked and ran into the night air suffered higher exposures.

As the poisonous cloud enveloped victims, MIC reacted with water in their eyes. This reaction, like the reaction in tank 610, created heat that burned corneal cells, rendering them opaque. Residents with cloudy, burning eyes staggered about. Many suffered shortness of breath, coughing fits, inflammation of the respiratory tract, and chemical pneumonia. In the lungs, MIC molecules reacted with moisture, causing chemical burns. Fluid oozed from seared tissue and pooled, a condition called pulmonary edema, and its victims literally drowned in their own secretions. Burned lung tissue eventually healed, creating scarred areas that diminished breathing capacity. Because MIC is so reactive with water, simply breathing through a wet cloth would have saved many lives. However, people lacked this simple knowledge.

UNION CARBIDE REACTS

Awakened early in the morning, CEO Warren M. Anderson rushed to Carbide's Danbury, Connecticut, headquarters and learned of the rising death toll. When the extent of the disaster was evident, a senior management committee held an emergency meeting. They decided to send emergency medical supplies, respirators, oxygen (all Carbide products), and an American doctor with knowledge of MIC to Bhopal.

The next day, Tuesday, December 5, Carbide dispatched a team of technical experts to examine the plant. On Thursday, Anderson himself left for India. However, after arriving in Bhopal, he was charged with criminal negligence, placed under house arrest, and then asked to leave the country.

With worldwide attention focused on Bhopal, Carbide held daily press conferences. Christmas parties were canceled. Flags at Carbide facilities flew at half-mast. All of its nearly 100,000 employees observed a moment of silence for the victims. It gave $1 million to an emergency relief fund and offered to turn its guest house in Bhopal into an orphanage. Months later, the company offered another $5 million, but the money was refused because Indian politicians trembled in fear that they would be seen cooperating with the company. The Indian public reviled anything associated with Carbide. Later, when the state government learned that Carbide had set up a training school for the unemployed in Bhopal, it flattened the facility with bulldozers.

CARBIDE FIGHTS LAWSUITS AND A TAKEOVER BID

No sooner had the mists cleared than American attorneys arrived in Bhopal seeking litigants for damage claims. They walked the streets signing up plaintiffs. Just four days after the gas leak, the first suit was filed in a U.S. court; soon cases seeking $40 billion in damages for 200,000 Indians were filed against Carbide.

However, the Indian Parliament passed a law giving the Indian government exclusive right to represent victims. Then India sued in the United States. Union Carbide offered $350 million to settle existing claims (an offer rejected by the Indian government) and brought a motion to have the cases heard in India. Both Indian and American lawyers claiming to represent victims opposed the motion, knowing that wrongful death awards in India were small compared with those in the United States. However, in 1986 a federal court ruled that the cases should be heard in India, noting that "to retain the litigation in [the United States] . . . would be yet another example

of imperialism, another situation in which an established sovereign inflicted its rules, its standards and values on a developing nation."[6] This was a victory for Carbide and a defeat for American lawyers, who could not carry their cases to India in defiance of the government.

In late 1986 the Indian government filed a $3.3 billion civil suit against Carbide in an Indian court.[7] The suit alleged that Union Carbide Corporation, in addition to being majority shareholder in Union Carbide India Ltd., had exercised policy control over the establishment and design of the Bhopal plant. The Bhopal plant was defective in design because its safety standards were lower than similar Carbide plants in the United States. Carbide had consciously permitted inadequate safety standards to exist. The suit also alleged that Carbide was conducting an "ultrahazardous activity" at the Bhopal plant and had strict and absolute liability for compensating victims regardless of whether the plant was operating carefully or not.

Carbide countered with the defense that it had a holding company relationship with UCIL and never exercised direct control over the Bhopal plant; it was prohibited from doing so by Indian laws that required management by Indian nationals. In addition to the civil suit, Carbide's chairman, Warren Anderson, and several UCIL executives were charged with homicide in a Bhopal court. This apparently was a pressure tactic, since no attempt to arrest them was made.

On top of its legal battle, Carbide had to fight for its independence. In December 1985, GAF Corporation, which had been accumulating Carbide's shares, made a takeover bid. After a suspenseful month-long battle, Carbide fought off GAF, but only at the cost of taking on enormous new debt to buy back 55 percent of its outstanding shares. This huge debt had to be reduced because interest payments were crippling. So in 1986 Carbide sold $3.5 billion of assets, including its most popular consumer brands—Eveready batteries, Glad bags, and Prestone antifreeze. It had sacrificed stable sources of revenue and was now a smaller, weaker company more exposed to cyclical economic trends.

[6] *In re Union Carbide Corporation Gas Plant Disaster,* 634 F.Supp. 867 (S.D.N.Y. 1986).

[7] *Union of India v. Union Carbide Corp. and Union Carbide India Ltd.,* Bhopal District Court, No. 1113 (1986).

INVESTIGATING THE CAUSE OF THE MIC LEAK

In the days following the gas leak, there was worldwide interest in pinning down its precise cause. A team of reporters from the *New York Times* interviewed plant workers in Bhopal. Their six-week investigation concluded that a large volume of water entered tank 610, causing the accident.[8] The *Times* reporters thought that water had entered when R. Khan failed to use a slip blind as he washed out piping. Water from his hose simply backed up and eventually flowed about 400 feet into the tank. Their account was widely circulated and this theory, called the "water washing theory," gained currency. However, it was not to be the only theory of the accident's cause.

Immediately after the disaster, Union Carbide also rushed a team of investigators to Bhopal. But the team got little cooperation from Indian authorities operating in a climate of anti-Carbide popular protest. It was denied access to plant records and workers. Yet the investigators got to look at tank 610 and took core samples from the bottom residue. These samples went back to the United States, where more than 500 experimental chemical reactions were undertaken to explain their chemical composition. In March 1985 Carbide finally released its first report on the accident. It stated that entry of water into the tank caused the accident, but it rejected the water washing theory.

Instead, Carbide scientists felt the only way that an amount of water sufficient to cause the observed reaction could have entered the tank was through accidental or deliberate connection of a water hose to piping that led directly into the tank. This was possible, because outlets for compressed air, nitrogen, steam, and water were stationed throughout the plant. The investigators rejected the water washing hypothesis for several reasons. The piping system

was designed to prevent water contamination even without a slip blind. Valves between the piping being washed and tank 610 were found closed after the accident. And the volume of water required to create the reaction—1,000 to 2,000 pounds—was far too much to be explained by valve leakage.

The Carbide report gave a plausible alternative to the water washing theory, but within months an investigation by the Indian government rejected it. This study, made by Indian scientists and engineers, confirmed that the entry of water into the MIC tank caused the reaction but concluded that the improper washing procedure was to blame (see Exhibit 3).

There matters stood until late 1985, when the Indian government allowed Carbide more access to plant records and employees. Carbide investigators sought out the plant's employees. More than 70 interviews, and careful examination of plant records and physical evidence, led them to conclude that the cause of the gas leak was sabotage by a disgruntled employee who intentionally hooked a water hose to the tank.

Here is the sequence of events on the night of December 2–3 that Carbide set forth. At 10:20 P.M. the pressure gauge on tank 610 read 2 ppsi. This meant that no water had yet entered the tank and no reaction had begun. At 10:45 the regular shift change occurred. Shift changes take half an hour, and the MIC storage area would have been deserted. At this time, an operator who had been angry for days about his failure to get a promotion stole into the area. He unscrewed the local pressure indicator gauge on tank 610, hooked up a rubber water hose, and turned the water on. Five minutes would have sufficed to do this.

Carbide claimed to know the name of this person, but it has never been made public. Its investigative team speculated that his intention was simply to ruin the MIC batch in the tank; it is doubtful that this worker realized all that might happen. The interviews revealed that the workers thought of MIC chiefly as a lacrimator, a chemical that causes tearing; they did not regard it as a lethal hazard.

Now the plot thickens. A few minutes after midnight, MIC operators noted the fast pressure rise in tank 610. Walking to the tank, they found the water hose connected and removed it, then informed their supervisors. The supervisors tried to prevent a catastrophic pressure rise by draining

[8] The team wrote a series of articles. See Stuart Diamond, "The Bhopal Disaster: How It Happened," *New York Times,* January 28, 1985; Thomas J. Lueck, "Carbide Says Inquiry Showed Errors but Is Incomplete," *New York Times,* January 28, 1985; Stuart Diamond, "The Disaster in Bhopal: Workers Recall Horror," *New York Times,* January 30, 1985; and Robert Reinhold, "Disaster in Bhopal: Where Does Blame Lie?" *New York Times,* January 31, 1985.

EXHIBIT 3   Two Theories Clash on Water Entry into MIC Tank

According to the water washing theory of the Indian government, water was introduced through a hose into bleeder A at filter pressure safety valve lines. As the hose kept running, water proceeded through the leaking valve in that area and rose up into the relief valve vent header line (RVVH). It took a turn at the jumper line, B, and moved into the process vent header line (PVH), filling it in the reverse direction all the way to the slip blind, C. When PVH was completely filled, water rose at line D and proceeded into MIC storage tank 610.

On February 8, 1985, two months after the leak, India's Central Bureau of Investigation drilled a hole in the PVH line at point E to drain any water left in the line. No water emerged. Carbide says this fact alone disproves the water washing theory. The fact that various valves in the pathway to the tank were closed also disproves the theory, according to Carbide.

Carbide espouses an alternative theory: The company says it has proof that water was introduced by a "disgruntled employee" who removed pressure gauge F, attached a hose to the open piping, and ran water into the MIC tank. Gas then escaped through a rupture disk and proceeded through the RVVH and out the vent gas scrubber.

Source: Courtesy of Union Carbide.

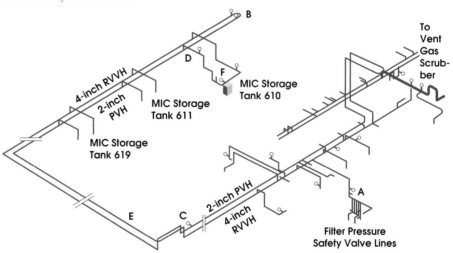

water from tank 610. Between 12:15 and 12:30 A.M., just minutes before the explosive release, they transferred about 1 metric ton of the contents from tank 610 to a holding tank. Water is heavier than MIC, and the transfer was made through a drain in the tank's bottom; thus, the supervisors hoped to remove the water. They failed, and within 15 minutes the relief valve blew.

The investigators had physical evidence to support this scenario. After the accident, the local pressure gauge hole on tank 610 was still open and no plug had been inserted, as would have been normal for routine maintenance. When the MIC unit was examined, a crude drawing of the hose connection was found on the back of one page from that night's log book. Also, operators outside the MIC unit told the investigation team that MIC operators had told them about the hose connection that night. In addition, log entries had been falsified, revealing a crude cover-up effort. The major falsification was an attempt to hide the transfer of contents from tank 610.

EXHIBIT 4   A Breakdown of the $470 Million Settlement
The settlement was based on calculations about the number and size of payments in a range of categories.

Source: Kim Fortun, *Advocacy after Bhopal* (Chicago: University of Chicago Press, 2001), p. 38.

Amount	Medical Categorization
$ 43,500,000	$14,500 payments for 3,000 deaths
$ 50,000	$25,000 payments for up to 2,000 victims with injuries of "utmost severity"
$156,000,000	$5,200 payments to 30,000 permanently disabled
$ 64,300,000	$3,215 payments to 20,000 temporarily disabled
$140,600,000	Amount to cover 150,000 minor injuries, future injuries, property damage, commercial loss, and other claims
$ 15,600,000	Medical treatment and rehabilitation of victims
$470,000,000	Total settlement

Why did the supervisors and operators attempt a cover-up? The Carbide investigators gave this explanation.

> Not knowing if the attempted transfer had exacerbated the incident, or whether they could have otherwise prevented it, or whether they would be blamed for not having notified plant management earlier, those involved decided on a cover-up. They altered logs that morning to disguise their involvement. As is common in many such incidents, the reflexive tendency to cover up simply took over.[9]

A SETTLEMENT IS REACHED

The theory of deliberate sabotage became the centerpiece of Carbide's legal defense. However, the case never came to trial. In 1989 a settlement was reached in which Carbide agreed to pay $470 million to the Indian government, which would distribute the money to victims (see Exhibit 4). In return, India agreed to stop all legal action against Carbide, UCIL, and their executives. India agreed to this settlement, which was far less than the $3.3 billion it was asking for, because a trial and subsequent appeals in the Indian court system would likely have taken 20 years.

Carbide paid the settlement using $200 million in insurance and taking a charge of $.43 per share against 1988 net earnings of $5.31 per share. Victims'

groups were upset because they thought the settlement too small, and they challenged it. In 1991 the Indian Supreme Court rejected these appeals but permitted reinstatement of criminal proceedings against Warren Anderson and top managers at UCIL.[10] An arrest warrant for Anderson on manslaughter charges was issued in India in 1992, but it has never been served. A criminal trial of several UCIL managers began in 1989 and has now dragged on in India for more than 15 years with no end in sight. Only half of several hundred scheduled witnesses have been called.

The Indian government was slow and inefficient in distributing settlement funds to gas victims. In 1993, 40 special courts began processing claims, but the activity was riddled with corruption. Healthy people bribed physicians for false medical records with which they could get compensation. Twelve court officials were fired for soliciting bribes from gas victims who sought payments. More than 569,000 claims have been paid, including 14,824 death claims, with average compensation about $1,300. Ninety percent of all claims were settled for $550, the minimum allowed.[11] Because the claims process moved at a glacial pace for years, the settlement money accrued interest and after all claims were paid $325 million remained. The government wanted to use the interest to clean up soil contamination at the plant. But in 2004 the Indian Supreme Court ordered it distributed to the victims and

[9] Ashok S. Kalelkar, "Investigation of Large-Magnitude Incidents: Bhopal as a Case Study," paper presented at the Instititution of Chemical Engineers conference on Preventing Major Chemical Accidents, London, England, May 1988, p. 27.

[10] *Union Carbide Corp. v. Union of India*, AIR 1992 (S.C.) 248.

[11] Paul Watson, "Cloud of Despair in Bhopal," *Los Angeles Times*, August 30, 2001, p. A6; and Government of Madhya Pradesh, "Claim and Compensation," http://www.mp.nic.in/bgtrrdmp/facts.htm.

families of the dead in amounts proportioned on the basis of claims already paid.[12]

POSTSCRIPT

In 1994 Union Carbide sold for $90 million its 50.9 percent equity in UCIL to the Indian subsidiary of a British company. Much of the money from the sale funded a hospital in Bhopal. In 1991, at the request of the Indian Supreme Court, Union Carbide and UCIL had agreed to provide up to $17 million for a hospital to be built by the Indian government in fulfillment of an offer made in 1986. Meanwhile, this commitment had increased to $20 million. An additional $54 million from the sale of Union Carbide's shares of UCIL went to the hospital and local clinics. This ended Carbide's involvement in India.

After Bhopal, Union Carbide became a smaller, less resilient company. It was forced to sell or spin-off its most lucrative businesses. In 1984, the year of the gas leak, Carbide had 98,400 employees and sales of $9.5 billion; by 2000 it had only $5.9 billion in sales and 11,000 employees. The end for Union Carbide came in 2001 when it merged with a much larger Dow Chemical Co. and its workforce suffered the bulk of cost-reduction layoffs.[13]

The Bhopal plant never reopened. It was dismantled and some of its equipment sold. Each year on the anniversary of the gas leak, people return to repaint graffiti on plant walls that still stand. "HANG ANDERSON" is an example.[14]

Activists among the gas victims, motivated by anger or vengeance, keep demanding further justice. Survivors complain of chronic medical conditions including headaches, joint pain, shortness of breath, and psychiatric problems. In 1999 victims' groups sought more compensation by filing a new lawsuit in the United States accusing Union Carbide of human rights violations. The suit was dismissed.[15] They then amended the complaint seeking monetary damages for illness caused by groundwater contamination from the abandoned plant. In 2004 an appeals court decided that their claims must be considered, so litigation continues.[16]

In 2002 an Indian court ordered the government to begin extradition proceedings for return of Warren Anderson to face charges of "culpable homicide not amounting to murder." The U.S. Department of Justice denied the request in 2004 on a technicality. Anderson is now in his mid-80s. He travels between homes in Florida and New York and plays golf daily. If extradited, he would face a lengthy trial and a sentence of up to 20 years in an Indian prison.

In 2003, two prominent activists, Rahida Bee and Champa Devi Shukla, staged a hunger strike near the statue of the giant bull on Wall Street to embarrass Dow Chemical into helping gas survivors with medical problems. The next year they returned to the United States to receive the Goldman Prize, an environmental award set up by a member of the Levi-Strauss family. They toured 24 cities and protested outside the Dow Chemical shareholders meeting in Midland, Michigan. Inside, the shareholders were voting on a resolution sponsored by the Church of the Brethren asking management to prepare a report on what it was doing "to address the health, environmental, and social concerns of the survivors." The company responded that all "legal liabilities to the victims have been settled" and the measure got only 6 percent of the vote.[17] Dow's position continues to be that there is no basis, legal or otherwise, for further action on its part.

In the wake of Bhopal, Congress passed legislation requiring chemical companies to disclose the presence of dangerous chemicals to surrounding populations and create emergency evacuation plans. It also gave federal regulators more authority over chemical plants. The industry adopted the Responsible Care initiative to improve both its safety and its public image. Are chemical plants now safer? A recent assessment finds significant progress, but notes that dangers still exist. "No one can say for sure," is how it answers the question.[18]

[12] "Compensation for Bhopal Victims," *New York Times,* July 20, 2004, p. A6.

[13] Susan Warren, "Cost-Cutting Effort at Dow Chemical to Take 4,500 Jobs," *The Wall Street Journal,* May 2, 2001, p. A6.

[14] Daniel Pearl, "An Indian City Poisoned by Union Carbide Gas Forgets the Past," *The Wall Street Journal,* February 12, 2001, p. A17.

[15] *Bano v. Union Carbide Corp. and Warren Anderson,* 99 Civ. 11329 (S.D.N.Y. 2000).

[16] *Bano v. Union Carbide Corp. and Warren Anderson,* 361 F.3d 696 (2004).

[17] Dow Chemical Company, *Notice of the Annual Meeting and Proxy Statement,* March 29, 2004, pp. 14–15.

[18] Ernie Hood, "Lessons Learned: Chemical Plant Safety since Bhopal," *Environmental Health Perspectives,* May 2004, p. A359.

Despite the passage of time, Bhopal does not fade away. It has been the subject of at least four documentary films, and in 2000 a dramatized feature film, *Bhopal Express,* was a box office hit in India. Told as a tragedy, the story seems to touch basic emotions. A Canadian play on Bhopal was recently reviewed as badly written and acted, but nevertheless "a touching tale of human suffering" raising "such imposing themes as the relative worth of a human life and the intersection of greed and development in the Third World."[19] In 2002 a tendentious piece of reality fiction by noted French author Dominique Lapierre and a coauthor climbed bestseller lists in France and Spain.[20] According to Lapierre, film director Oliver Stone is negotiating for movie rights. So Bhopal may come to a theater near you.

[19] Kamal Al-Solaylee, "Bhopal: A Chemical and Theatrical Disaster," *The Globe and Mail,* October 25, 2003, p. R17.

[20] Dominique Lapierre and Javier Moro, *Five Past Midnight in Bhopal* (New York: Warner Books, 2002).

Questions

1. Who is responsible for the Bhopal accident? How should blame be apportioned among parties involved, including Union Carbide Corporation, UCIL, plant workers, governments in India, or others?

2. What principles of corporate social responsibility and business ethics are applicable to the actions of the parties in question?

3. How well did the legal system work? Do you agree with the decision to try the lawsuits in India? Were victims fairly compensated? Was Carbide sufficiently punished?

4. Did Union Carbide handle the crisis well? How would you grade its performance in facing uniquely difficult circumstances?

5. Does Dow Chemical Company have any remaining legal liability, social responsibility, or ethical duty to address unresolved health and environmental claims of Bhopal victims?

6. What lessons can other corporations and countries learn from this story?

Chapter **Thirteen**

Globalization

McDonald's Corporation

Imagine a machine so colossal that it casts a shadow over much of the earth. At the back moves a stream of farmers pouring potatoes and lettuce through an opening, while beside them a line of cows, pigs, and chickens glides in and disappears. Inside, a uniformed crew of 418,000 people works levers and buttons. And out the front, to a waiting crowd, flow 544 meals a second, 24 hours a day. A side door regularly opens and bags of money drop out. A vent releases bursts of paper, polystyrene, and other waste. On top, the stars and stripes snap and weave against the sky. As you watch, the machine slowly expands and quickens.

McDonald's Corporation is such a machine. It all started in 1948 when brothers Richard and Maurice "Mac" McDonald built several hamburger stands with golden arches in southern California. One day a traveling salesman named Ray Kroc came by selling milkshake mixers. The popularity of their $0.15 hamburgers impressed him, so he bought the world franchise rights and spread the golden arches around the globe.

McDonald's is still spreading. In 2003 it had 31,129 restaurants, a 120 percent increase in a decade. More than half of the restaurants are outside the United States, and these bring in 64 percent of company revenues. The percentage of foreign earnings is rising because most of the 1,000 to 2,000 new restaurants opened every year are in one of more than 119 foreign countries where McDonald's does business.[1] A British magazine, *The Economist,* has noted the company's global spread and publishes a "Big Mac Index" that uses the price of a Big Mac in foreign currencies to assess exchange-rate distortions.[2]

McDonald's is not one of the transnational titans in revenues. Its systemwide sales are only about one-fifth those of ExxonMobil or Wal-Mart Stores. However, it is a brand titan. According to *BusinessWeek,* it has the world's seventh most valuable brand.[3] The golden arches are familiar to more people than the Christian cross.[4] After Santa Claus, the company's clown, Ronald McDonald, is the second-most-recognized person by children of the world.[5]

---

[1] McDonald's Corporation, Form 10-K, March 5, 2004.

[2] See, for example, "Big Mac Index," *The Economist,* December 18, 2004, p. 162.

[3] Diane Brady, "Cult Brands," *BusinessWeek,* August 2, 2004, p. 64.

[4] Eric Schlosser, *Fast Food Nation* (Boston: Houghton Mifflin, 2001), p. 4.

[5] "Big Mac's Makeover," *The Economist,* October 16, 2004, p. 64.

As a prominent global brand McDonald's symbolizes perceived evils of globalization that agitate a range of ideologues, including leftists, anarchists, nationalists, farmers, labor unions, environmentalists, consumer advocates, religious orders, intellectuals, and protectors of animal rights. Its restaurants have been bombed or burned in 11 countries. When President George W. Bush attended a summit of Asia-Pacific leaders in Santiago, Chile, antiglobalization protesters attacked a local McDonald's and outside a Buenos Aires restaurant police detonated a bomb left by a group opposed to the International Monetary Fund. For others, it symbolizes an evil America. Within hours after U.S. bombers began to pound Afghanistan in 2001, angry Pakistanis damaged McDonald's restaurants in Islamabad and an Indonesian mob burned an American flag outside another.[6]

Worldwide, the company is a lightning rod for the discharges of critics angry about Americanization, capitalism, fast food, meat eating, commercialism, and environmental degradation. "Its profits continue to rely on the mass exploitation of workers, immeasurable animal suffering, the promotion of processed food wrapped in wasteful packaging and the mass manipulation of children," goes one tirade.[7] Activists in Great Britain organize an International Anti-McDonald's Day each year on October 16 and maintain a Web site, mcspotlight.org, that meshes anti-McDonald's campaigns.

According to former McDonald's CEO Jack Greenberg, protesters "are more interested in using McDonald's as a convenient symbol than in understanding the facts of our business."[8] In developing nations, the arrival of a McDonald's is regarded as a sign of modernization. The company is often one of the first foreign corporations to enter, and one commentator regards it as "the canary in the coal mine of economic success" because it arrives when disposable income rises and there is promise of more growth and progress.[9] For many consumers in emerging economies McDonald's signifies a connection with world culture, "an imagined global identity that they share with like-minded people."[10]

In fact, McDonald's does transfer cultural values and practices. A group of anthropologists documented its influence on east Asian cultures. They found that in Hong Kong and Taiwan the company's clean rest rooms and kitchens set a new standard that elevated expectations throughout the country. In Hong Kong, children's birthdays had traditionally gone unrecognized, but McDonald's introduced the practice of birthday parties in its restaurants, and now birthday celebrations are widespread in the population.[11] A journalist recently set forth a "Golden Arches Theory of Conflict Prevention" based on the notion that countries with McDonald's restaurants do not go to war with each other.[12] And a professor writes that the significance of the company

[6] David Barboza, "When Golden Arches Are Too Red, White and Blue," *New York Times,* October 14, 2001, p. C1.

[7] Lee Hall, "Friends of Animals," *The Nation,* October 6, 2003, p. 19.

[8] Quoted in Moises Naim, "McAtlas Shrugged," *Foreign Policy,* May 2001, p. 26.

[9] Jonah Goldberg, "The Specter of McDonald's," *National Review,* June 5, 2000, p. 30.

[10] Douglas B. Holt, John A. Quelch, and Earl L. Taylor, "How Global Brands Compete," *Harvard Business Review,* September 2004, p. 71.

[11] James L. Watson, ed., *Golden Arches East: McDonald's in East Asia* (Stanford, CA: Stanford University Press, 1997), pp. 103 and 134.

[12] Thomas L. Friedman, *The Lexis and the Olive Tree* (New York: Farrar Straus Giroux, 1999), chapter 10.

At a shopping mall in Riyadh, Saudi Arabia, women line up at the "ladies" sign and men at the "gentlemen's" sign. The mall is patrolled by Saudi religious police who enforce segregation of the sexes. Source: © AP Photo/Hasan Jamali.

lies in its spread of "McDonaldization," a powerful force of global change based on principles of "efficiency, calculability, predictability, and control."[13]

On the other hand, many foreign customs seem resistant to broad change based on what people eat for lunch. Most of McDonald's international restaurants are franchises, run as local businesses. The entrepreneurs who run these businesses adapt them to local custom. In France, where there are 1,040 McDonald's, the restaurants adapt their food and decor to French tastes, selling the French soft drink Orangina, offering fruit yogurts for children, and lining walls with art posters.[14] In Saudi Arabia, McDonald's restaurants close five times each day for prayers. Eating zones for men and women are segregated and women who arrive without their husbands are not admitted.[15] One franchise ran a promotion in which for every Big Mac sold it gave $0.30 to treat Palestinian casualties in Gaza.[16] The world's largest McDonald's is in Beijing, where managers fly the flag of China outside and work with the People's

[13] George Ritzer of the University of Maryland, in *The Globalization of Nothing* (Thousand Oaks, CA: Pine Forge Press, 2004), pp. 82–83.

[14] "Burger and Fries à la Française," *The Economist,* April 17, 2004, p. 60.

[15] In the United States, the National Organization of Women has attacked McDonald's for creating "McPartheid" as it chooses "to ignore universal human rights laws in favor of the laws of profit." Nicole Manning, "U.S. Companies Support Gender Segregation in Saudi Arabia," *National NOW Times,* Summer 2002.

[16] Philip F. Zeidman, "The Global Brand: Asset or Liability?" *Franchising World,* May 2003, p. 52.

Liberation Army to arrange patriotic events. Almost half of the city's children under age 12 believe that McDonald's is a Chinese company.[17]

The story of McDonald's illustrates the complexity of globalization. A small, local, typically American business swelled into a far-reaching transnational corporation with a radiant brand. It spread American business and cultural values, shaping both national cultures and an amorphous world culture. Yet its restaurants everywhere adapt to local tastes and customs.

In this chapter we explain globalization in more depth. Besides discussing its impacts on culture, we also discuss the growth of trade agreements, the importance of the international financial system, global varieties of capitalism, and the erosion of nation-state sovereignty.

WHAT IS GLOBALIZATION?

globalization
Growth in networks of economic, political, social, military, scientific, or environmental interdependence to span worldwide distances.

Globalization occurs when networks of economic, political, social, military, scientific, or environmental interdependence grow to span worldwide distances. Economic globalization refers to the development of an increasingly integrated commercial system based on free markets in which nations are open to foreign trade and investment. Globalization is a multifaceted phenomenon and observers see different elements in it. Some economists define it as the integration of economic systems. Political scientists may see it as a process that creates diffusion of national political authority through large trade blocks and the power of MNCs. Sociologists may see it as a process that erodes national cultures. Globalization is a controversial term because of such differences in perspective.

Some observers see today's globalization as nothing new. It has its roots, they point out, in the growth of huge trading companies in the sixteenth century. Other observers say today's globalization is far different from anything in the past. Bosworth and Gordon observe that global integration in recent years far exceeds that of the past "in degree, intensity, speed, volume, and geographic reach."[18] So rapid has been the change that some analysts speak of it as a revolution.

Major Forces in Expanding Globalization

There have been many forces behind the extraordinary growth of globalization in recent decades. The following are major ones.

- Technological advances have significantly increased the speed and reduced the costs of communications. In 1930, for example, the cost of a one-minute telephone call to London from New York was about $244.65. In 1990 it was $3.32. Today a comparable communication over the Internet via e-mail is virtually instantaneous and costless not only to London but around the world.

- World trade has risen spectacularly over the past several decades, as shown in Figure 12.2, and foreign trade has become a larger proportion of GDP for many

[17] Randall E. Stross, "The McPeace Dividend," *U.S. News & World Report,* April 1, 2002, p. 36.
[18] Barry Bosworth and Philip H. Gordon, "Managing a Globalizing World," *Brookings Review,* Fall 2001, p. 3.

nations. In the United States, for example, trade has increased from about 5 percent of GDP in the 1930s to 28 percent today.

- MNCs, as noted in the last chapter, have grown significantly in numbers, foreign investments, sales, employees, and worldwide influence.
- There has been an explosive growth in the amount of money floating around the world to finance trade and acquire foreign assets. Speculative money has also become abundant.
- Many countries have been receptive to free market ideas and have implemented them.
- Transportation costs and delivery schedules of goods have been substantially reduced.
- Standardized products of similar quality, such as cameras, soft drinks, watches, computers, chemicals, and drugs, have become popular around the world with but minor modifications to fit local situations.
- Relative peace has prevailed in the world. However, the impact on globalization of the current battle with terrorism remains to be determined.
- A number of multilateral organizations have facilitated globalization, including the World Trade Organization (WTO), the United Nations, the World Bank, and the International Monetary Fund (IMF).
- It should be mentioned that many nongovernment organizations (NGOs) have pressured MNCs to be more concerned with environmental issues, human rights, and social responsibilities.

A broad perspective on the forces of globalization is shown in Figure 13.1. This chart makes clear that globalization is more than an economic phenomenon. Unfortunately, there is no way to show the relative impact of these forces. They vary from time to time, country to country, person to person, industry to industry, and organization to organization. Some of these forces are benign and others may be malign. In this chapter we can only touch lightly on some of the forces shown in the figure.

Pros and Cons of Globalization: An Overview

The primary benefits of globalization as seen by its supporters are the following.

- It has lifted millions of people out of poverty into middle-class status.
- Consumers have benefited with more variety, lower costs, and higher quality of products.
- Working conditions have improved for millions of workers.
- Human rights, especially in developing countries, have improved.
- Per capita income has grown for millions of people, especially in developing countries.
- Globalization has spurred the spread of capitalism.
- Globalization has stimulated more nations to adopt democratic governance.

Globalization, however, has attracted many critics with a multitude of complaints. Here are a few of the more significant ones.

FIGURE 13.1   Main Forces in Globalization

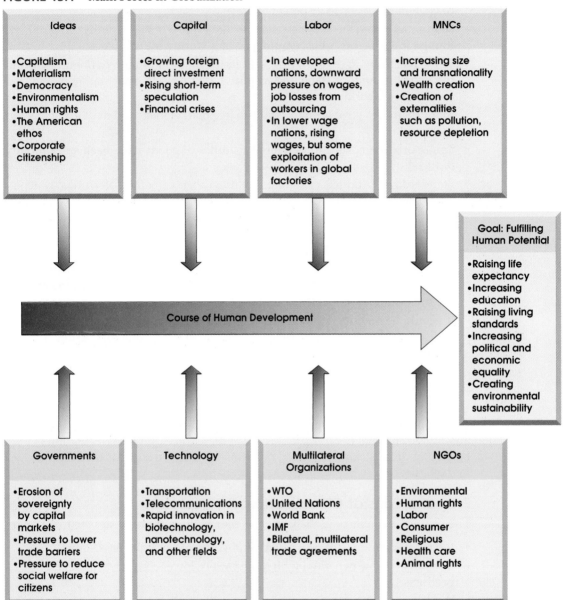

- Workers in developed countries are displaced as companies employ more workers paid lower-wages in developing countries.
- Millions of people in the developing countries remain in poverty.
- The gap between per capita incomes of developed and developing countries has widened.

- Globalization has resulted in growing environmental degradation.
- Globalization has contaminated the cultures of both developed and undeveloped countries.
- Globalization has undermined the sovereignty of developing countries.
- Globalization has produced world financial instability.

Much has been written on the benefits and the drawbacks of globalization. *In Defense of Globalization* by Jagdish Bhagwati, a professor at Columbia University, is an excellent example of the former.[19] This book responds to the critics of globalization and rejects their arguments. While the main focus of the book is on economic globalization, it does not neglect globalization's social dimensions. The book concludes that globalization may need a few changes to smooth out some of its rough edges but it is the most powerful force in the world today for social good. Among well-known critics of globalization is Ralph Nader, who said, "The essence of globalization is a subordination of human rights, of labor rights, consumer, environmental rights, [and] democracy rights to the imperatives of global trade and investment."[20]

One opinion poll revealed that 56 percent of Americans believe globalization is good for the United States but are concerned about its impact on them personally. Only 36 percent believe a global economy will help their financial situation and 29 percent say it will probably hurt them. Many people are concerned and rightly so that the forces of globalization will influence the security of their jobs.[21]

INCREASING FOREIGN COMPETITION

The pace and intensity of economic competition have increased with globalization. Before the 1980s, foreign trade was such a small part of total U.S. output (about 5 percent) that it received little attention. Then, more and more, foreign producers successfully challenged American corporations both at home and abroad. In some major industries and important products, foreign companies were able to penetrate the U.S. market with higher quality and lower prices than comparable American products. This awakened the United States and its corporations to the comparatively weak competitive position of some industries. For example, consumer electronics virtually disappeared in the United States. Radios and television sets were clear examples. By the end of the 1980s, only one company, Zenith, was making TV sets in the United States, and that company stopped production in 1995. Semiconductors, invented in the United States, were dominated by Japanese companies. In steel, automobiles, machine tools, and other industries, statistics of

[19] Jagdish Bhagwati, *In Defense of Globalization* (New York: Oxford University Press, 2004).

[20] Ralph Nader, from a transcript of "Globalization and Human Rights," a PBS program, www.pbs.org/globalization/prologue.html.

[21] Harris Interactive for the Chicago Council on Foreign Relations and the German Marshal Fund, June 2002, in "Opinion Pulse," ed. Karlyn Bowman, *The American Enterprise,* June 2004.

FIGURE 13.2
Number of Regional Trade Agreements Reported to GATT and WTO

Source: WTO Secretariat.

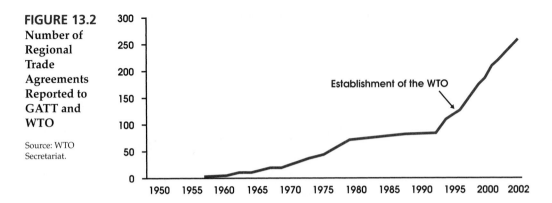

decline were compelling. The United States once was the world leader in robotics, structural ceramics, and flexible manufacturing, but it lost those positions to foreign businesses.

American managers got the message and the U.S. economy strengthened to the point where in recent years not only has it met the foreign competitive challenges but it is the strongest economy in the world. For over two decades the World Economic Council has prepared a Business Competitiveness Index each year for over 100 countries. In 2003 the United States was first in the world.[22] The highest ranked countries below the United States were, in order of ranking, Finland, Germany, Sweden, Switzerland, the United Kingdom, Denmark, and Japan. The index is based on a detailed evaluation of two specific areas, the sophistication of operating practices and strategies, and the quality of the business environment.

U.S. corporations responded to global competitive threats in many ways. They significantly improved corporate governance, and they employed more superior foreign managers. They cut costs by coordinating departments, improving inventory controls, employing low-wage foreign workers, expanding capital expenditures in countries with lower production costs, merging and forming alliances with foreign companies, and increasing productivity.

EXPANDING REGIONAL TRADING AGREEMENTS

Rapid increase in the number of trade agreements has been a major force in globalization. Figure 13.2 shows the growth of regional trade agreements as reported to GATT and the WTO. Virtually all countries in the world, with few exceptions, are partners in at least one trading club. These agreements range from groupings of many countries to bilateral agreements with only one other nation. Trade agreements have helped to increase global competition and have accelerated world trade. The largest of these in terms of population are the European Union (EU), the North Atlantic Free Trade Agreement (NAFTA), and the Asia-Pacific Economic Cooperation (APEC) forum.

[22] World Economic Forum, *The Global Competitiveness Report 2003–2004*, October 14, 2004.

FIGURE 13.3
The European Union

Source: *The Economist,* September 25, 2004, p. 5.

The European Union (EU)

On January 1, 1993, the EU became a unified regional market. On that date, a long list of customs, tariffs, and nontariff barriers were removed between the 12 European nations of the Union at that time. Many national laws and policies affecting trade were annulled. They were replaced with hundreds of new rules and regulations concerning such matters as health, environment, and quality standards. A few years later three more nations joined the European Union, and on May 1, 2004, a major milestone was reached when 10 additional nations, mostly eastern European countries, were added. The result was the largest trading agreement in the world with 454 million people and a GDP of $11.1 trillion, rivaling that of the United States. Figure 13.3 shows the current and prospective members of the EU as of May 1, 2004.

The fundamental objective of the EU is to form a union of member nations that will assure political and economic stability among the dominant nations of

Europe. A milestone step in this direction took place on January 1, 1999, when the EU adopted a uniform currency, the euro. The European Central Bank (ECB), established in 1998, arranged the conversion of the currencies of the members of the European Monetary Union (EMU), which took place on January 1, 2002.[23] Jeffrey Garten, dean of the Yale School of Management, predicts that the euro "will be the most important change in the global economy well into the next century."[24]

Another milestone in EU history was reached when leaders of the 25 European nations signed the 50-article EU constitution in Rome, in the meeting hall where the forerunner of the EU was formed 47 years before. The document must now be ratified by every country in the EU before it becomes operational. Critics complain that the document is "toothless," with watered-down provisions necessitated to accommodate the differing interests of 25 nations.[25] There is truth to this statement. But there is general agreement that major problems remain before the 25 countries will function in harmony. There is, for example, no agreement on a uniform shape of electrical plugs. Accounting standards differ among countries. In 2001 Germany scuttled a proposal for a common law about mergers and acquisitions.[26] Member countries are concerned about laws which allow movement of workers throughout the Union, so they are adopting measures to restrain unwanted immigration. For instance, Germany intends to prevent immigration of workers by barring them for seven years. Denmark will permit entry of new workers only if they have jobs. In retaliation, some new member countries in Eastern Europe threaten to erect barriers to products from the Western countries.[27]

Many individuals in the newly joined nations face serious problems in complying with EU statutes found in some 80,000 pages of EU laws. Hygiene, safety, and quality standards may force some farmers out of business. Krysztof Siediecki, for instance, a farmer in Poland, has followed the centuries-old farming custom of keeping his 12 pigs and 7 cows in the same building. He has always arranged for the waste of these animals to seep into the land behind his barn. Under the new EU regulations he is obliged to build a separate septic tank for the animal waste but there is insufficient land for it. Mr. Siediecki expects to stop farming within a year.[28]

Some futurists see great promise for the EU in stabilizing Europe to achieve economic growth and a political stability that prevents wars that in the past periodically devastated the continent. There are skeptics, however, who see serious internal problems. They predict that individual countries will become frustrated by the loss of financial sovereignty that comes with the creation of the ECB.

[23] At the time of conversion, three countries had declined to join the EMU, namely, Great Britain, Denmark, and Sweden.

[24] Jeffrey Garten, "The Euro Will Turn Europe into a Superpower," *BusinessWeek,* May 4, 1998.

[25] Maria De Cristofaro and Tracy Wilkinson, "Nations of EU Sign Its First Constitution," *New York Times,* October 30, 2004, p. A3.

[26] David Fairlamb and Christine Tierney, "One Currency—But 15 Economies," *BusinessWeek,* December 1, 2001.

[27] Christopher Rhoads and Marc Champion, "As Europe Expands, New Union Faces Problems of Scale," *The Wall Street Journal,* April 29, 2004, p. A1.

[28] Ibid.

Some think countries will be so pressured by business to change policies concerning working conditions, hours of work, and social contributions that the result will be political turmoil. Some observers believe the EMU can exist in the long term only with complete political union, and they are skeptical that European nationalists will accept the necessary loss of sovereignty such a union entails.

The North American Free Trade Agreement (NAFTA)

free trade block
Two or more nations that have signed an agreement to engage in free trade.

This agreement created a *free trade block* consisting of the United States, Canada, and Mexico. The first step in its formation was taken in 1987 when the United States and Canada signed the Canada–United States Free Trade Agreement (CFTA). In 1994 the agreement was extended to Mexico. By linking the United States, Canada, and Mexico, NAFTA created the largest trading block in the world at that time with more than 400 million people in countries with a combined annual gross domestic product in 2001 of more than $12 trillion.

Labor unions in the United States opposed NAFTA from its beginning. They are concerned about the movement of American industry to Mexico to take advantage of the lower wages paid Mexican workers. Particularly hard hit has been the textile industry in the United States. It is very difficult to trace the jobs created or lost in both the United States and Mexico. Some analysts have concluded that while jobs have been lost to Mexico, a roughly equal number of jobs have been created in the United States in the production of exports to Mexico. Others conclude that the net balance is more jobs lost than gained. E. Anthony Wayne, Assistant Secretary of State for Economic and Business Affairs, in testimony before Congress, concluded: "As this transition has progressed . . . positive economic growth has been generated, efficiencies have been improved and costs have been lowered for both consumers and industries, helping to raise average incomes."[29]

However, for workers on both sides of the border there have been individual losses and gains. Clearly, as U.S. companies have relocated in Mexico, workers in the United States have suffered. When Green Giant and other food processing plants closed their doors in Watsonville, California, the town lost about 4,000 jobs, a serious problem for the community.[30] Hundreds of Mexican farmers were devastated when imports of U.S. subsidized crops such as corn depressed agricultural prices in Mexico. On the other hand, new jobs were created in other economic sectors in both countries. Expanding trade between the United States and Mexico, as shown in Figure 13.4, has opened new opportunities in both countries.

Important problems have arisen in the operation of NAFTA. One concerns trucking. The treaty specifies that Mexican trucks will have free access to American markets, but from the beginning there have been restrictions put on this provision. The restrictions are largely because too many Mexican trucks do not meet U.S. domestic trucking standards and their costs are far below those of U.S. truckers.

---

[29] E. Anthony Wayne, "NAFTA: Ten Years After," testimony before the Senate Foreign Relations Committee, Subcommittee on International Economic Policy, Export, and Trade Promotion, U.S. Congress, April 20, 2004.

[30] Evelyn Iritani, "U.S. Reaps Bittersweet Fruit of Merger," *Los Angeles Times*, January 19, 2004, p. A1.

FIGURE 13.4
U.S. Trade with Mexico 1985–2004

Source: Bureau of the Census.

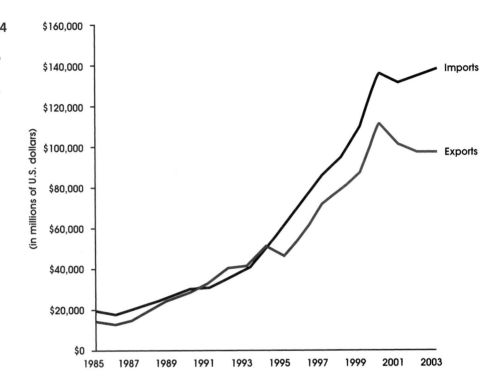

The Teamsters Union has been especially strident in opposing the treaty provision. In 2004 the U.S. Supreme Court overturned a ruling that had prevented Mexican trucks and buses from delivering goods and passengers in this country.[31] The Department of Transportation now must establish standards and an inspection system. The door will be opened for as many as 34,000 Mexican trucks that qualify to operate on American highways. This can be devastating competition for many U.S. truckers. Roger Hogeland, for example, the owner of a big rig, said he is used to netting from 32 to 34 cents a mile. He cannot compete, he says, with Mexican drivers who are used to netting about 13 cents a mile.[32]

Important issues have arisen about the environment. Employment has increased rapidly along the border in a zone of manufacturing populated by many *maquiladoras*. These are Mexican companies that set up factories to produce for export under a Mexican government program that allows them special advantages. They can be financed with foreign capital and run by foreign managers. Their production inputs, for example machinery and raw materials, are allowed into Mexico duty free. The maquila program, begun by a 1989 government decree, allows foreign corporations to enter Mexico and take advantage of free trade arrangements with the United States. Maquila factories can be located anywhere, but they are most often found near the Mexico–United States border.

maquiladora
A Mexican corporation set up under a program of the Mexican government to operate factories that make goods for export. These companies may have up to 100 percent foreign capital and foreign management, and manufacturing inputs such as machinery and materials are allowed into Mexico duty free.

[31] *Department of Transportation v. Public Citizen*, 124 S. Ct. 2204 (2004).
[32] Ronald D. White, "Truckers See More Traffic Up Ahead," *Los Angeles Times*, June 14, 2004.

The largest number are in the heavily populated region near the Tijuana–San Diego border crossing. After NAFTA, employment rose there because of a provision that permitted American companies to ship in components duty free and to get back finished products duty free. In 1994 there were approximately 600,000 people in the area and by 2001 about 1.6 million. Thereafter, there was a sharp decline as jobs moved to China. A consequence, however, is serious environmental degradation. According to an assessment completed in 1999, 12 percent of the population did not have access to potable water, 30 percent lacked wastewater treatment facilities, and 25 percent needed access to solid-waste disposal facilities.[33] Both countries have spent billions to clean up the mess but it persists.

These are not the only important problems arising with NAFTA, but examination of all of them is beyond the scope of our discussion. We conclude with two broad evaluations of NAFTA.

Public Citizen, a progressive reform group, prepared a "Report Card" to assess the performance of NAFTA in a number of areas, such as job creation, agriculture, environment, public health, wage levels, and others. The report stated "on each of the issues examined, the only fair grade for NAFTA is a failing one."[34] This assessment of failure made in 1998 was repeated by Public Citizen in evaluations on the 10th anniversary of the implementation of NAFTA in 2004.

Assistant Secretary of State Wayne has a different view. Overall, he reported to Congress, NAFTA has been a "resounding success" for all three countries in the trade pact. NAFTA has generated "clear growth" in trade, reduced costs across the board for consumers and businesses, improved the quality of life for citizens of the three signatory countries by providing consumers more and better choices at competitive prices, and "helped foster the democratic and civil society reforms that have transformed Mexico, while serving as a beacon of hope for other developing countries with whom the United States is negotiating FTA's around the world."[35]

Other Trade Agreements

The world is honeycombed with special trade agreements ranging from the largest, such as the EU, to arrangements between only two countries, such as between Mexico and Israel and between Chile and Korea. There are none as large and structured as the EU and NAFTA. There are a few of note and some of promise. Mercado Comun del Sur (Mercosur), for example, is an agreement negotiated in 1991 among Argentina, Brazil, Paraguay, and Uruguay. It was later joined by Chile and Bolivia. It has been more active as a forum for political dialogue than for trade. The Asia-Pacific Economic Cooperation (APEC) forum was established in 1989. Today it includes 211 countries, including the United States, China, and Japan. The organization is primarily a forum for the discussion of many different problems in the area, apart from trade. The Association of South East Asian Nations (ASEAN)

[33] General Accounting Office, *U.S.–Mexico Border* (Washington, DC: General Accounting Office, March 2000), p. 4.

[34] Public Citizen Global Trade Watch, *Report Card,* December 1998, www.citizen.org/pctrade/nafta/reports/5years.htm. See, for example, Public Citizen, "The Ten Year Track Record of the North American Free Trade Agreement: U.S. Workers' Jobs, Wages, and Economic Security," www.citizen.org/trade/nafta/.

[35] Wayne, testimony.

was established in 1967 with five countries. It has expanded to 34 countries today. Improving trade relations is one of its objectives. But it has more expansive objectives to bind the nations together in friendship and to advance the well-being of the more than 50 million people in its region. The United States has been active in creating new trade agreements. In 2003 it entered into agreements with a few South American countries, including Chile. President George W. Bush has been interested in creating the Free Trade Area of the Americas (FTAA). This is an ambitious agreement to be forged among 34 democracies and 800 million people in the Western Hemisphere. If it is consummated it will be the world's largest free-trade area.[36]

NONGOVERNMENTAL ORGANIZATIONS

nongovern-mental organizations Voluntary organizations formed for collective action to meet shared needs and goals; sometimes called civil society groups.

Nongovernmental organizations, or NGOs, are a new major force in the way government and business operate. Many of them are influential in the formulation of government policy and business strategy. They are nonprofit associations that are formed to influence government and private enterprise policy and action. They can be permanent groups or temporary associations. Their objectives and actions cover a wide spectrum. Some are welcomed by governments and businesses. Some are irritants to these organizations.

NGOs differ in focus, size, organization, membership, life cycle, methods of operation, relations with other NGOs, and along other dimensions. At one end of the spectrum are well-established NGOs such as the American Red Cross, Amnesty International, and the Carnegie Endowment for International Peace. At the other end are groups that adopt violent methods for making their demands. In between is an unparalleled diversity of organizations. Collectively they are powerful stakeholders for business and important constituents of governments. Jonathan P. Doh and Hildy Teegen, editors of the excellent book *Globalization and NGOs: Transforming Business, Government, and Society,* observe: "The emergence of NGOs has had a direct impact on public policy, corporate strategy and operations, and the interactions between business and government."[37]

How Many NGOs Are There?

According to the United Nations, the first international NGO was formed by the Anti-Slavery Society in 1839. By 1874 there were 32. The UN reported 37,000 international NGOs in 2000.[38] These are modest numbers in light of the estimate that the United States is home to more than 1.2 million NGOs of all types.[39] The classification of international NGOs is shown in Table 13.1.

---

[36] Robert B. Zoellick, "A Free Trade Area of the Americas (FAA), *The Wall Street Journal,* November 17, 2003, p. A20.

[37] Jonathan P. Doh and Hildy Teegen, eds., *Globalization and NGOs: Transforming Business, Government, and Society* (Westport, CT: Praeger, 2003) p. xix.

[38] *Human Development Report 2000: Deepening Democracy in a Fragmented World* (New York: Oxford University Press, 2002), p. 102.

[39] Doh and Teegen, *Globalization and NGOs,* p. xix.

TABLE 13.1
Classification
of Inter-
national
NGOs
International
NGOs grew
quickly in the
1990s.

Source: Anheier,
Glasius and Kaldor,
2001. *UN Human
Development Report*
(New York: Oxford
University Press,
2002), p. 103.

Purpose	1990	2000	Growth (percent)
Culture and recreation	2,169	2,733	26.0
Education	1,485	1,839	23.8
Research	7,675	8,467	10.3
Health	1,357	2,036	50.0
Social services	2,361	4,215	78.5
Environment	979	1,170	19.5
Economic development, infrastructure	9,582	9,614	0.3
Law, policy and advocacy	2,712	3,864	42.5
Religion	1,407	1,869	32.8
Defence	244	234	−4.1
Politics	1,275	1,240	−2.7
Total	**31,246**	**37,281**	**19.3**

How NGOs Influence Government and Business

NGOs have been influential in the formulation of many government and business policies and operations. They have employed a wide variety of methods to do this, including lobbying government officials, publicizing their positions on issues, confronting company officials, participating in high-profile protests, and maintaining Web sites. Some have worked closely with both governments and businesses, supplying research and other support. Others have confronted policy makers with their demands. Many publicize issues to inform the public or to threaten publicity-shy administrators. For example, Doctors Without Borders has successfully pressed pharmaceutical companies to reduce costs of drugs to help AIDs victims. The Sierra Club has been influential in the conservation of natural resources through direct dialogue with corporations as well as by publicizing issues. Starbucks Coffee has helped Conservation International, an NGO, to improve the quality of coffee grown by small farmers. When Greenpeace pressured Gerber to remove genetically modified ingredients from its baby foods the company complied because it did not want publicity about it.[40]

GLOBALIZATION AND INTERNATIONAL FINANCIAL STABILITY

Today the forces of globalization have produced a large and rapid movement of trillions of dollars across national boundaries. These funds have been immensely important in the world's prosperity of the last decade. At the same time, they have been a dominant force in financial crises of many countries. The most serious manifestation of negative results was the crisis in Southeast Asia beginning in 1997. Starting in Thailand, the crisis spread almost immediately to Indonesia, Malaysia, the Philippines, and South Korea. In 1998 the Russian financial system collapsed and countries in Latin America also came under intense pressure. For a decade, the Southeast Asian countries had been increasing

[40] Ibid., pp. 144–145.

their GDP at 6 percent or more a year. Millions of people rose from poverty to middle-income levels. Then a financial crisis reversed these trends. What happened?

Forces at play in these crises differed among the nations. But there is general agreement on the most important factors. Of great significance were huge inflows of money into these countries. One estimate is that $1.5 trillion was involved in daily foreign exchange transactions. In addition, foreign banks loaned generously to these countries, and domestic banks freely used the money to make loans. Billions if not trillions of dollars generated by speculators in foreign currencies and securities added to the volume. Hundreds of billions of dollars of this money could be transferred instantly by the touch of a computer key.

The banking systems of many countries lagged the expansion of financial transactions. There was insufficient bank regulation and weak supervision. Banks borrowed money with short-term maturities and loaned it with long maturities to borrowers with political connections who often employed it unwisely. Important information about banks and private corporations was not available to investors, so they could not make appropriate risk assessments. Such practices led to excessive construction of factories and office buildings, a real estate boom with accompanying inflated prices, and soaring stock markets. Laws, ideas, and institutions needed to accompany vibrant capitalism were weak or absent.

Eventually, borrowers were unable to repay loans, export markets weakened, and a few banks and companies became insolvent. Foreign investors and speculators lost confidence and withdrew their funds. The result, of course, was financial disaster. This was a pattern that started in Thailand and then developed in other South Asian countries. The same pattern appeared in Russia, Mexico, and Brazil. Thailand asked the International Monetary Fund (IMF) for help, and the agency responded with $17.2 billion. Rescue packages amounting to billions of dollars were also sent to other nations.

The International Monetary Fund was created in 1945 when 29 countries at a conference in Bretton Woods, New Hampshire, agreed to its mission and responsibilities. Currently, 182 member-countries contribute to its reserve, which amounts to about $300 billion. The statutory purposes of the IMF are fundamentally to promote international monetary cooperation among its members, promote financial stability, and extend credits and loans to members who are experiencing problems in meeting their financial obligations. The IMF has no authority over its members but provides financial aid when needed. When making loans, it can and does prescribe various measures and policies that should be taken to resolve the financial problems of the borrower. The IMF works closely with the World Bank, a sister institution concerned with the economic development of poorer nations and their efforts to resolve financial problems and create economic growth.

Bitter controversy has developed over the prescriptions made by the IMF when it extends financial aid. Specifically, reputable economists—such as Martin Feldstein, former chairman of the President's Council of Economic Advisers and professor of economics at Harvard, and Joseph Stiglitz, winner of the Nobel prize in economics and former chief economist of the World Bank—have been extremely critical of the medicine the IMF prescribed for Thailand and other nations in the Southeast Asia financial crisis. In Thailand, the IMF prescribed a balanced budget, higher interest rates, closing insolvent banks, closer supervision of financial institutions, and support of the exchange value of the baht (the local currency). Feldstein and Stiglitz said such austerity measures were mostly the reverse of what should have been done in these countries.[41]

Lawrence Summers, then deputy secretary of the treasury and now president of Harvard University, and Stanley Fischer, the IMF first deputy managing director and former professor at the Massachusetts Institute of Technology, came to the defense of the IMF. Secretary Summers said the IMF has bailed out and strengthened many countries, such as Russia and Poland, and has advanced trade liberalization around the world. It has not had a major default in 50 years. He added that the agency is indispensable.

Before and after the Southeast Asia crisis the IMF has bailed out many countries. Fortunately there have been none of the dimensions of the Southeast Asia crisis. Leal Brainard, who served as deputy national economic adviser during the Clinton administration, reminds us "it is only a matter of time before we again confront a financial crisis of potentially worldwide proportions."[42] Will the IMF and other international agencies have learned from the Southeast Asia crisis how to deal with such a new crisis?

SPREADING CAPITALISM

The global spread of capitalism is one of the most significant trends in recent history. This development resulted from many forces. Highly important was the defeat of authoritarian governments in World War II and the imposition by the victorious powers of democratic free market principles and institutions. The model was American capitalism. Following the war, a major foreign policy of the United States was to foster democracy and free market economies throughout the world. The rapid economic growth of the United States after the war also attracted admirers. The exhilarating burst of economic activity around the world confirmed the notion that the American model of capitalism was the best approach to wealth and national power.

Deviations from the American Capitalistic Model

The classical capitalism model has been the foundation of the free market economy of the United States. As amply illustrated throughout this book, however, there have been substantial deviations from this model in the United States. There is no country today with the same democratic free market structure as the United States. The most economically advanced countries, however, display most of the basic features of its economy. But there are significant differences.

To oversimplify, for example, while the Japanese economy fundamentally is free market, it is dominated by an interlacing of companies in massive aggregations

---

[41] See Joseph Stiglitz, *Globalization and Its Discontents* (New York: W. W. Norton, 2002); and Martin Feldstein, "Focus on Crisis Management," *The Wall Street Journal,* October 6, 1998.

[42] Leal Brainard, "Capitalism Unhinged: The IMF and the Lessons of the Last Financial Crisis," *Foreign Affairs,* January/February 2002.

keiretsu

In Japan, a group of informally linked companies centered around a large bank that coordinates business activities among its members (pronounced CARE-et-sue). Similar groups in South Korea are called *chaebol* (pronounced *CHA-bull,* rhymes with rabble).

crony capitalism

A name given to a system in which state-owned enterprises are controlled by friends of a country's leader or ruling elite.

called *keiretsu.* So dominant a feature is this system that one author calls it *alliance capitalism.*[43] South Korea has adopted the Japanese model of gigantic alliances of companies in comparatively few conglomerates, called *chaebol.* In some Southeast Asian countries, popular leaders give close friends and family members control of state enterprises. This has been called *crony capitalism.* The Chinese model features government by the Communist Party and much central planning and control over the economy. However, it has established free market zones, loosened the reins over banking, and ended the control of military leaders over state enterprises. It is toe deep into capitalism and slowly moving deeper. Most countries have embraced free markets and other forms of capitalism, but each has adopted variations in political controls, state ownership of productive enterprises, government relationships with corporate enterprises (both public, and private), protectionism, and financial structures. There are obviously many different brands of capitalism around the world, but the central point is that globalization and capitalism have expanded together in recent years.

Critics of Global Capitalism

Jeffrey E. Garten wrote an article entitled, "Can the World Survive the Triumph of Capitalism?"[44] This was a review of a book by William Greider, a thoughtful and incisive critic of global capitalism. Garten answers his question in the affirmative, but, he says, we must take the critics seriously. Greider points out in his book that the global economy has made possible the accumulation of great wealth but at the same time has serious flaws.[45] Among them, first, is that global capitalism is repeating some of the shortcomings of capitalism experienced 100 years ago in the United States, for example, exploitation of workers, including children, and inequality of income distribution. Second, uncontrolled investments lead to excessive productive capacity and overproduction of many products. Third, the exuberant growth of global capitalism leads to degradation of the environment. Fourth, the extraordinary growth of money and its free flow inevitably will result in destabilizing the world's financial systems. Greider wrote his book before the 1997–1998 world financial crisis. He was, therefore, prescient.

Greider, and many other critics, see fallacies in some fundamental assumptions of capitalism. For example, rising incomes created by vigorous global capitalism will raise all boats. That demonstrably has not happened. In fact, while the income gap between rich and poor nations has been rising since the early 1800s, the percentage of people living in poverty has declined.

Another assumption is that if left alone from government interference the free market system will function efficiently and effectively to resolve a nation's economic problems. This assumption is flawed, say critics, because history shows that

[43] Michael I. Gerlach, *Alliance Capitalism: The Social Organization of Japanese Business* (Berkeley: University of California Press, 1992).

[44] Jeffrey E. Garten, "Can the World Survive the Triumph of Capitalism?" *Harvard Business Review,* January–February 1997.

[45] William Greider, *One World, Ready or Not: The Manic Logic of Global Capitalism* (New York: Simon & Schuster, 1997).

if left to its own forces, the free market system can lead to serious social and also economic problems.

Another assumption is that free markets and political democracy go together. Without democracy, free markets will wither and fade away. That is demonstrably not true say critics. They point to many nations where this has not happened. In the fascist societies of Italy, Germany, and Spain in the 1940s, for example, there were free markets but no democracy. Today in China, as noted above, there are a few free market areas, and they are growing, but there is no political democracy. Indeed, the Chinese government has been diligent in stifling praise for democracy. The free market has thrived under authoritarian rule in Singapore.

Most of the critics of capitalism do not wish to abolish it but only to reform it. They accept the view that there has never been an invention in the history of the world as capable of improving the general welfare of society as capitalism. But it does exhibit defects that in the political democracies are gradually being corrected to meet the needs of the times.

Institutions and Ideas of Capitalism

There is also growing realization that for capitalism to produce its potential advantages there must be certain fundamental structural arrangements. Toward the end of the twentieth century, conventional wisdom among many observers was that if a nation embraced the free market philosophy it would reap the same benefits as the advanced democracies with strong capitalistic systems. When this did not work too well, in Russia, for example, more observers saw that for capitalism to work there had to be many fundamental institutional arrangements in place. What they had in mind, for example, was a trustworthy financial system with general transparency, bankruptcy courts, antitrust laws, a minimum social security net, limited government regulation, an efficient tax system, an acceptance of the idea of private property and a legal system to protect it, an understanding and acceptance of the profit motive in private enterprise, and an assumption of private enterprise responsibilities to workers and communities.

These institutions and ideas cannot be installed overnight. Most are either absent or slowly evolving in many developing countries. The failure of global capitalism to benefit and transform many less developed countries is the result of the absence of some of these requirements. For example, most of the less developed countries know that they must have capital to grow. Sources of capital do not exist in their countries, so they must depend upon foreign investment. But foreign investors will not deploy their capital in the absence of institutions to protect it.

Jeffrey Sachs, director of the Institute for International Development at Harvard, says that even when these institutions are developing in a nation, other factors may be decisive. For example, difficult geography, poor public health, and skewed demographics can inhibit economic development. Disease in the tropics, illiteracy, and internal wars have also kept countries from prosperity.[46]

[46] Peter Passell, "Capitalism Doesn't Always Take; Location Is Destiny," *New York Times*, June 12, 1997.

GLOBALIZATION ERODES NATION-STATE SOVEREIGNTY

sovereignty
The power of
every nation to
govern its
affairs free
of outside
interference.

Market forces have eroded the *sovereignty* of nations, and yet the nation-state still retains unlimited authority within its own borders. How is this paradox explained?

As demonstrated in the prior discussion of the financial crisis in Southeast Asia, governments felt helpless to prevent the wreckage created by abrupt and voluminous capital withdrawals. To make their industries competitive in global markets, governments must attract capital and technology. This cannot be done, they know, if too much restraint is placed on the free flow of money. The competitiveness imperative amounts to an infringement on state authority.

Another type of erosion on sovereignty flows from agreements that governments make with international institutions that supplant decisions heretofore made by governments—such as decisions of the WTO about trade rules that bind members. Similarly, NAFTA ties Canada, the United States, and Mexico to its provisions. The European Commission has issued hundreds of economic rules that bind its members. We explained how the IMF imposes decisions on countries receiving its financial aid. The ECB makes important monetary decisions formerly made by central banks of individual countries of Europe.

At a different level, governments in both industrialized and developing countries are held hostage to the power of large multinational corporations. A case in point is DaimlerChrysler. This third-largest car maker in the world in sales, and the biggest industrial company in Europe after Royal Dutch Shell PLC, has exceptional clout. The German government will be receptive to its pressures for tax and social reforms that improve the firm's competitive position. If costs of production in Germany are prohibitively high, the company can move its headquarters to the United States, close plants in Germany, and build assembly plants elsewhere. LDCs can be expected to respond faster to pressures of giant MNCs than large industrial states.

Many analysts expect such erosion of sovereignty to continue as globalization expands. For example, Kenichi Ohmae, a well-known Japanese management consultant, believes we are witnessing the end of the nation-state.[47] This view, or slight modifications of it, has been expressed by many other observers.[48] The argument is that the market is becoming much more powerful than the nation-states in determining economic, political, cultural, and social affairs. This is inevitable as globalization expands.[49] It is not a bad thing, this side argues. Free and open markets, integrated in a world economy, will secure the greatest prosperity for all.

Opposed to this view are those who acknowledge that some powers of government have been yielded to the market. But, they argue, free markets have not been

[47] Kenichi Ohmae, *The End of the Nation State* (New York: Free Press, 1995).

[48] See, for example, Walter B. Wriston, *The Twilight of Sovereignty: How the Information Revolution Is Transforming Our World* (New York: Scribners, 1992); and Susan Strange, *The Retreat of the State: The Diffusion of Power in the World Economy* (New York: Cambridge University Press, 1996).

[49] Thomas L. Friedman, *The Lexus and the Olive Tree: Understanding Globalization* (New York: Farrar, Straus, Giroux, 1999).

particularly effective in providing a social net for people, environmental quality, or human rights. Government remains the solution of last resort to meet these needs. Sometimes, in France and Germany, for example, market forces have forced moderate retrenchment in social programs. However, worldwide the trend is toward more rather than less concern about social demands. Robert Gilpin, emeritus professor from Princeton University, points out that "despite the significance of globalization, it has not replaced the state, national differences, and politics as the really important determinants of domestic and international affairs."[50]

Peter Drucker, an eminent professor at Claremont College, looks at this issue with a historian's perspective:

> Since the early Industrial Revolution, it has been argued that economic interdependence would prove stronger than nationalist passions. Kant was the first to say so. The "moderates" of 1860 believed it until the first shots were fired at Fort Sumter. The Liberals of Austria-Hungary believed to the very end that their economy was far too integrated to be split into separate countries. So, quite clearly, did Mikhail Gorbachev. But whenever in the last 200 years political passions and nation-state politics have collided with economic rationality, political passions and the nation-state have won.[51]

EROSION OF CULTURES

Officials from 19 countries met in Ottawa, Canada, in 1998 to discuss the growing impact throughout the world of U.S.-produced movies, television shows, music, and other entertainment. Their purpose was to decide what to do to protect their cultures from this infusion of American values. In Canada, for instance, the vast majority of movies, CDs, books, and magazines are American and the bulk of Internet content is U.S. generated. Regulatory proposals were made to the Canadian government to limit television time devoted to U.S.-made programs. "Market forces, left to their own devices," said Sheila Copps, the minister of Canadian heritage, "would have made the entire Canadian broadcasting system a U.S. subsidiary."[52] This raises a question, of course: Is the issue the alteration of *culture* or commercial self-interest?

culture
A system of shared knowledge, values, norms, customs, and rituals acquired by social learning.

The rapid and explosive spread of American culture throughout the world is one significant trend within globalization. Coca-Cola is consumed worldwide. American movies are shown even in remote corners of the world in preference to other films. Baseball caps of American teams and American blue jeans are worn by teenagers everywhere. Kentucky Fried Chicken and McDonald's can be found the world over. American Internet content is available wherever a computer can be found. All this is conveyed in English, a language used universally.

[50] Robert Gilpin, *The Challenge of Global Capitalism* (Princeton, NJ: Princeton University Press, 2000), p. 312.

[51] Peter Drucker, "The Global Economy and the Nation-State," *Foreign Affairs,* September–October 1997, p. 172.

[52] Roge Ricklefs, "Canada Fights to Fend off American Tastes and Tunes," *The Wall Street Journal,* September 24, 1998, p. B1.

	"Spread of Ideas"		Music/TV/Movies		Science/Tech	
	Good	**Bad**	**Good**	**Bad**	**Good**	**Bad**
Europe						
France	25%	71%	66%	32%	65%	33%
Germany	28	67	66	29	64	34
Great Britain	39	50	76	19	77	17
Italy	29	58	63	29	79	12
Mideast						
Egypt	6%	84%	33%	57%	51%	36%
Jordan	13	82	30	67	59	39
Pakistan	2	81	4	79	42	22
Turkey	11	78	44	46	67	24

TABLE 13.2 Opinion Poll of Attitudes about the United States

Source: Reported by Justin Ewers–USN& WR. Robert Kunzig, "French Kiss-Off," *U.S. News & World Report,* December 16, 2002, p. 43.

Throughout the world there is resentment about the transmission of certain Western cultural values. The French for years have sought to reject entry of English words and phrases into their language. Members of the French Académie Française cringe at the use by the general population of such expressions as *le hotdog*. The French government identified 3,000 English words that should be expunged from their language. It did not happen. A poll taken by the U.S. State Department in the fall of 2000 asked people in Europe and the United States, "How much of a threat do you think American popular culture such as music, television and films is to the cultures of other countries in the world?" The most responses of "threats" came from France, where 8 percent said "very serious threat" and 30 percent said "serious threat." In the United States, the corresponding figures were 7 and 17 percent. But a more favorable response was given to this question: "In general, what is your opinion of American popular culture, such as music, television and films?" Nine percent of the French said "very favorable" and 43 percent said "somewhat favorable." Corresponding figures for Great Britain were 20 and 47 percent. People in Germany and Italy responded about the same as the British. Americans did not see their culture as a threat to foreign cultures.[53]

Majorities of people in Europe like American music, television, and films and technology but dislike the spread of American ideas, according to the survey results shown in Table 13.2. Middle-Eastern populations seem to dislike American ideas, music, and television, but do favor American technology.[54]

There is much ambivalence about the impact of the U.S. exports on other cultures. Around the world, shrill rhetoric from activists and intellectuals damns the United States, while ordinary people flock to see the violence and sexuality in American-made films. French critics blast McDonald's for the pernicious impact of its fast-food philosophy on the country's traditional leisurely way of eating, while they watch French citizens, indifferent to the menace, fill its restaurants.

[53] Reported by Steven Kull, "Culture Wars? How Americans and Europeans View Globalization," *Brookings Review,* Fall 2001, p. 20.

[54] Robert Kunzig, "French Kiss-Off," *U.S. News & World Report,* December 16, 2002.

Communications and the sale of American products are not the only forces spreading new cultural values around the world. Economic forces of globalization have encouraged massive migrations of peoples. In Germany, for example, the demand for workers brought a large influx of Turkish workers who, of course, brought with them their cultures, some aspects of which infiltrated into German society. In the United States, recent Latin American and Asian immigrants have influenced American language and music. Throughout the world, globalization has stirred migrations of workers, leading to the diffusion of many different ethnic, religious, and commercial values.

A major question, of course, is: How much of the spread of cultures around the world really changes the core values of peoples? This was addressed by Samuel P. Huntington in his seminal book on civilizations.[55] He points out that much of the cultural diffusion may be faddish and does not alter underlying values. There are core cultural values in societies that are not easily changed. For example, he says, use of the English language in the world is more a convenient means of intercultural communication than a force to change core values.

There seems little doubt that globalization has significantly influenced the flow of values. Some forces, such as types of entertainment, may have temporary impact. Other forces, such as technological innovations (e.g., computers, biotechnology, pharmaceuticals, motor vehicles), may have more lasting impact. However, it is difficult to reject the thesis of Huntington and others that the core cultures of peoples are not easily and significantly changed.

CONCLUDING OBSERVATIONS

Globalization is a revolutionary phenomenon. It has created enormous wealth for people all over the world. At the same time, it has led to exploitation, dislocation, and suffering for some who have yet to experience its benefits. It has changed business–government–society relationships in profound and fundamental ways. On balance, there seems to be little question that the forces of globalization are beneficial to the peoples of the world and promise even greater benefits in the future. To achieve this promise, however, important reforms are necessary.

[55] Samuel P. Huntington, *The Clash of Civilizations and the Remaking of World Order* (New York: Simon & Schuster, 1996).

The World Trade Organization and Its Critics

The WTO was relatively unknown to the world's public until a meeting of the organization's ministers in Seattle in 1999 scheduled for November 30–December 3. At that meeting, the WTO dramatically gained worldwide recognition as a result of the tens of thousands of activists who demonstrated against the organization and forcefully advanced their demands. Activist groups are not the only critics of the WTO. Responsible voices in countries around the world, members of the U.S. Congress, academics, lawyers, and others have voiced specific criticisms of the organization. This case presents important criticisms leveled at the WTO and responses of supporters of the organization. Before examining these complaints, we describe briefly the origin, organization, and functions of the WTO.

WHAT IS THE WTO?

The WTO was established in 1994 at the last meeting of GATT (General Agreement on Tariff and Trade). GATT was created in 1947 by 23 nations to stabilize and advance free trade around the world. World trade had been devastated by high tariffs in the 1930s and World War II. GATT was successful in achieving its objectives after eight rounds of meetings extending over five decades. Tariffs were dramatically reduced and world trade exploded sixteenfold. As noted in the chapter, trade has been one significant driving force in the expansion of globalization. However, GATT was narrowly focused on tariffs, and national representatives believed its reach should be expanded. In addition, they believed that further trade liberalization was needed and new rules were necessary to stiffen the spines of politicians to thwart special interest drives for tariff protections.[1] For these reasons, delegates decided to create a new agency, which they did on January 1, 1995. There were 90 member-nations at the birth of the WTO. Today there are 144 nations, which, together, generate most of the world's trade.

The most important function of the WTO is to administer the implementation of several trade agreements and trade rules built over a 50-year period under the operation of GATT. In addition to administering the GATT agreements, which focus principally on trade, the WTO administers other agreements. Different agreements, for example, have been negotiated concerned with food safety laws, product standards, telecommunications, finance, and intellectual properties.

Aside from administering these agreements, there are other functions of the WTO, including being a forum for trade negotiations, adjudicating trade disputes, monitoring national trade policies, providing technical assistance to developing countries, and cooperating with other international organizations. The WTO says a major function is to assure that "trading conditions are stable, predictable, and transparent."[2]

Exhibit 1 is the organization chart of the WTO. The highest decision-making body, as shown in the chart, is the *Ministerial Conference*. It is composed of representatives from all WTO members and meets at least once every two years. This body tries to decide

---

[1] "Who Needs the WTO," *The Economist*, December 4, 1999.
[2] WTO, "10 Common Misunderstandings about the WTO," www.wto.gov, undated.

important policy by consensus. Each member-country has one vote. At the next level is the *General Council,* which normally is composed of ambassadors and heads of delegations in Geneva, the home of the WTO. Representatives of countries may on occasion join the Council. It meets several times a year in Geneva. This Council also meets as the Trade Policy Review Body, which, as the name implies, reviews trade policies. It also meets as a Dispute Settlement Body, which examines and generally approves panel decisions concerning trade disputes. Under the General Council are special committees and working groups that deal with individual agreements and general operating problems. The range of activities of the WTO is identified in the chart.

Exhibit 2 is a flow chart of the dispute settlement process called the *Dispute Settlement Understanding (DSU).* This process is a core function of the WTO in settling member disputes. It is a more formal process than that of GATT but is still based upon principles of negotiation, conciliation, mediation, and arbitration laid down by GATT. The first step in the dispute process is the *consultation stage,* in which members are given 60 days to seek a resolution of their dispute through discussions among themselves. If the parties in the dispute cannot resolve their differences, an impartial panel of experts meets to adjudicate the dispute. Deliberations of the panel are confidential, and minutes of its meetings are not made public. Panels are composed of three people, or more if the parties so desire. Panel members vary depending on the issue to be adjudicated. They may be government or nongovernment personnel, but they are to be experts in the substantive fields relevant to the issue at hand.

Panel members are chosen by agreement among the parties, and once chosen, they act as individuals in their deliberations and not as government officials. There are rules concerning these panelists. For example, they are charged with avoiding conflicts of interest and must notify the WTO of any question concerning their independence and impartiality. If the panel concludes that a nation has violated a WTO agreement, it can recommend that the nation should withdraw the offending measure.

Countries involved in a dispute can appeal a panel decision to a seven-member *Standing Appellate Body (SAB).* Members of this body are appointed by the WTO for four-year terms and each person may be reappointed once. Members of the SAB must not be affiliated with any government but be "broadly

EXHIBIT 1 WTO Structure

All WTO members may participate in all councils, committees, and so forth, except the Appellate Body, Dispute Settlement panels, Textiles Monitoring Body, and plurilateral committees.

Source: World Trade Organization.

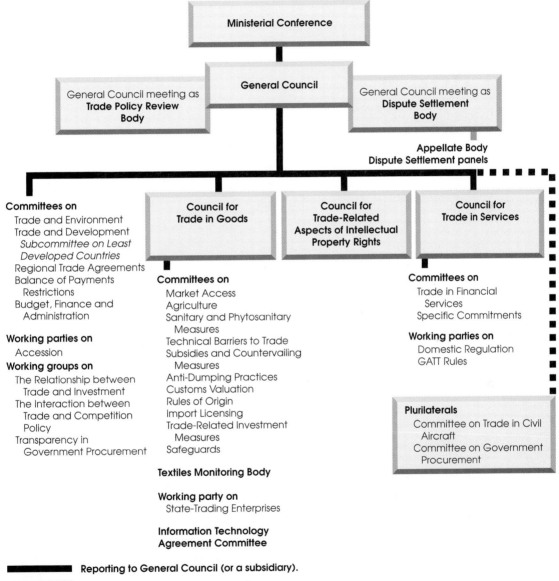

Reporting to General Council (or a subsidiary).

Reporting to Dispute Settlement Body.

Plurilateral committees inform the General Council of their activities although these agreements are not signed by all WTO members.

The General Council also meets as the Trade Policy Review Body and Dispute Settlement Body.

For the current negotiations, the Services Council and Agriculture Committee meet in "special sessions" and report directly to the General Council.

EXHIBIT 2
Flow Chart of WTO's Dispute Settlement Process

Source: General Accounting Office.

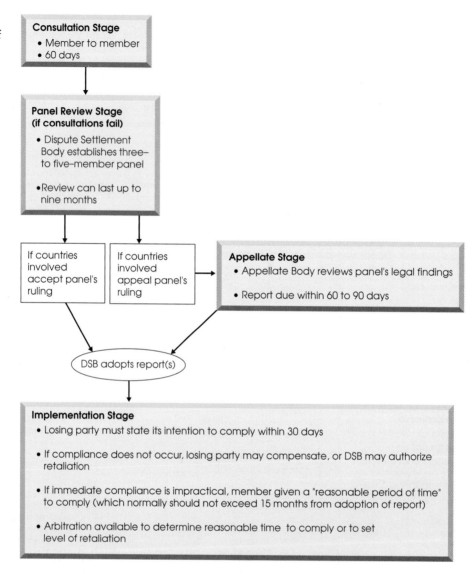

Consultation Stage
- Member to member
- 60 days

Panel Review Stage (if consultations fail)
- Dispute Settlement Body establishes three- to five–member panel
- Review can last up to nine months

If countries involved accept panel's ruling

If countries involved appeal panel's ruling

Appellate Stage
- Appellate Body reviews panel's legal findings
- Report due within 60 to 90 days

DSB adopts report(s)

Implementation Stage
- Losing party must state its intention to comply within 30 days
- If compliance does not occur, losing party may compensate, or DSB may authorize retaliation
- If immediate compliance is impractical, member given a "reasonable period of time" to comply (which normally should not exceed 15 months from adoption of report)
- Arbitration available to determine reasonable time to comply or to set level of retaliation

representative" of the WTO membership. The SAB reviews the panel findings, which are binding according to a "reverse consensus" rule. This rule binds the parties unless a consensus (a unanimous vote) develops *against* the report among the WTO membership. This will not happen because the winning party is not likely to vote against a ruling in its favor.[3]

[3] John O. McGinnis and Mark L. Movsesian, "The World Trade Constitution," *Harvard Law Review,* December 2000, pp. 530–36.

If the losing party does not accept the SAB decision, it may accept retaliation or offer compensation to the aggrieved party. If implementation of the ruling is immediately impractical, an extension of a reasonable period of time, not to exceed 15 months, may be accepted. If the losing party does not conform to the ruling within the implementation period, the complaining party may ask the WTO for permission to retaliate. Retaliation can take the form of raising a tariff on the noncomplying country's goods, or taking trade actions equivalent to the amount of harm suffered by the complaining country.[4] For example, the United States took this kind of action in the case of banana restrictions imposed by the European Union in 1995. In that case, the EU granted duty-free quotas for bananas grown in former colonies of some EU members while imports from Latin America were restricted. The United States and Latin American countries complained that this violated WTO rules. The claim was upheld in the DSU, and the EU modified its restrictions, but this too was ruled as violating rules. The United States was then permitted by the WTO rules to retaliate by imposing import restrictions on specified products from the EU amounting each year to $191.4 million, an amount calculated as equaling the harm done to U.S. economic interests.[5]

CRITICS OF THE WTO: PRO AND CON

Critics of the WTO cover a wide spectrum of ideologies and complaints. At one extreme are those who are strong supporters of the WTO but see flaws in the organization and want them corrected. At the other extreme are those who want the WTO abolished. At this end of the spectrum are an ill-defined group of environmentalists, human rights activists, anarchists, and an assortment of malcontents who loathe the current economic order and object to about everything in it.

For the first time, these groups came together at the WTO meeting in Seattle in a more organized way and in greater numbers than in past demonstrations. Their targets included not only the WTO but the World Bank, the International Monetary Fund, capitalism and globalism, and the world economic, social, and political systems. The complaints ranged from reasoned positions to simple slogans. Exhibit 3 lists a sampling of criticisms of different activist groups. Many of the complaints expressed in Seattle have been reflected in corporate, government, and nongovernment policy-making bodies. *The Economist* editorialized, "This new kind of protest is more than a mere nuisance: It is getting its way."[6] Following are pros and cons of more important criticisms of the WTO.

---

[4] General Accounting Office, *World Trade Organization: Issues in Dispute Settlement* (Washington, DC: GAO/NSIAD–00–210, August 2000), p. 8.

[5] Ibid., pp. 41–42.

[6] "Anti-Capitalist Protests," *The Economist,* September 23, 2000, p. 85.

NATIONAL SOVEREIGNTY

The WTO has been accused of intruding on national sovereignty because of the binding nature of the organization's decision-making authority in trade disputes. Developing countries are particularly concerned because they fear that the WTO will formulate rules impinging on their authority over the environment, working conditions, and other national prerogatives. National sovereignty has three important facets: economic, social, and political. It is important to note that the WTO has limited power over governments if they do not choose to abide by WTO decisions. The major decisions of the Ministerial Conference may require ratification of each nation's legislative body before they can be implemented.

The WTO has no enforcement powers. It cannot overturn national laws or levy fines on violators. Judge Robert H. Bork, a well-known constitutional authority, said the sovereignty issue "is merely a scarecrow."[7] The WTO cannot bind any nation if it does not wish to be bound. However, the WTO can strengthen sovereignty by developing a world trading system that lessens the ability of special interest groups to force protectionism in a nation.

The WTO can impinge on sovereignty but only if a nation accepts it. As noted in this chapter, nations are willing to accept this intrusion for various gains. Nations are less willing to accept impingement on social and political elements of national sovereignty than on economic elements. This explains in part why some developing nations may warmly embrace free trade engendered by WTO rules but at the same time strongly oppose them because of impacts on their social and political sovereignty.

THE WTO IS UNDEMOCRATIC

The WTO lacks the checks and balances of democracy and as a result is arbitrary and biased in favor of the rich and powerful countries, claim the critics. There is no place where representatives of workers, farmers, consumers, communities, environmentalists, and human rights groups can be heard. Furthermore, the most important policies made at the

---

[7] McGinnis and Movsesian, "The World Trade Constitution," pp. 373–74.

EXHIBIT 3   Who They Are, What They Want

A look at some of the groups protesting the World Trade Organization in Seattle.

This was compiled from interviews, news releases, and Web sites.
Source: Lynn Marshall, *Los Angeles Times,* December 3, 1999, p. A22.

Group/Description	Position on the WTO
Alliance for Sustainable Jobs & the Environment Alliance formed between locked-out Kaiser Steel workers and environmental groups in Northern California.	Believes that the WTO subverts the labor and environmental laws of this country.
American Federation of Labor and Congress of Industrial Organizations AFL-CIO is a federation of 68 unions—13 million members.	Persuade the WTO to incorporate rules to enforce worker rights and environmental and consumer protections.
Direct Action Network Coalition of grassroots and street theater groups from the western United States and Canada.	Persuade public that WTO represents the next step in multinational corporate control.
Global Exchange International human rights group based in San Francisco.	Charges that among other things the WTO serves only the interests of multinational corporations, tramples over labor and human rights, and is destroying the environment.
Humane Society of the United States Promotes the protection of all animals.	Wants the WTO to become animal-friendly. Some members of these groups dressed as sea turtles in the protest to highlight the importance of turtle-exclusion devices.
Institute for Agriculture and Trade Policy Research and advocacy group working for change in agriculture and natural resources.	Seeks to educate people about the implications of the WTO's actions on issues of agriculture, food safety, food security, dumping, and so on.
International Forum on Globalization U.S.-based think tank of intellectuals and activists from 20 countries.	Seeks to provide as much information as possible to the public and activists so they are aware of the issues that drive the WTO.
People's Assembly International group representing 13 nations; came together specifically to protest the WTO.	Educate people about the impact of the WTO and expand the linkages among anti-imperialist groups.
Rainforest Action Network Works to protect the Earth's rainforests.	Contends the WTO is fundamentally flawed, because trade provisions come before the laws of nations and power is shifted away from local communities and governments and given to corporations.

Ministerial Conference are decided by each member-country having but one vote. The result is a powerful organization that can establish international trade standards, operate in a nondemocratic manner, and be biased toward trade that overrides other values, such as environmental damage and human rights.

Defenders of the WTO point out that the agency's decisions are based upon an established body of laws (which fill 700 pages) developed over a period of 50 years. Decisions of the WTO are generally by consensus. This means that every country accepts the decision. Basic trade rules negotiated by governments are ratified by parliaments or other legislative bodies of member-nations. In negotiations among countries, issues other than tariffs can be addressed under various agreements administered by the WTO. There are, however, rules governing such inclusions. For example, some agreements provide that "technical regulations shall not be more trade-restrictive than necessary to fulfil a legitimate objective, taking account of the risks nonfulfillment would create."[8] Precisely what this means depends upon decisions of the Appellate Body concerned with specific cases.

ENVIRONMENTAL IMPERIALISM

Some activist groups accuse developed countries of environmental imperialism, which is using economic power to ignore or downgrade environmental factors in trade decisions. The World Wildlife Fund (WWF), for example, is seeking levies on imported goods produced by methods it does not approve. The failure of the WTO to protect turtles in one of its decisions was criticized by some Seattle activists not only in words but by costumes that made them look like turtles. In the case, the United States placed an embargo on the import of certain shrimp and shrimp products from countries that did not adopt fishing regulations to protect endangered sea turtles from drowning in shrimp nets. Countries affected by the embargo took the issue to the WTO. Both the WTO panel and the Appellate Body ruled against the United States on grounds such as the United States did not engage seriously in negotiations with the countries affected, the U.S. decision was applied in an arbitrary and discriminatory manner, and the United States did not have a right to take unilateral measures to protect a resource not in its territory.[9] The WTO rulings were based strictly on legal grounds.

The environment, working conditions, food safety, and human rights, for example, are factors critics say the WTO neglects and should do more about. Fundamentally, they want the WTO to impose sanctions on countries that do not meet their standards. While the WTO should study these factors, says William H. Lash III, a recognized expert in these matters, the goal of the WTO should be to remove barriers to trade, not add new ones. He says, "Those who advocate linking trade and labor or the environment at the WTO are not interested in promoting world trade. They are interested in the leverage of trade to promote their often statist views. They seek not the spirit of the WTO but its perceived power and prestige."[10]

LACK OF TRANSPARENCY

Critics complain that the proceedings of the panels and the Appellate Body are confidential. The public cannot attend and proceedings are not made public. However, parties may disclose their own submissions to these groups but must not make public the submissions of the other party. Opinions of individual panelists remain anonymous.

Some agreements endorse transparency. For example, "The Sanitary and Phytosanitary Standards and the Technical Barriers to Trade agreements require members to publish measures 'promptly' and in a manner accessible to interested members."[11]

Activities of the WTO, aside from panel and Appellate Body decisions, are made public. McGinnis and Movsesian recommend that greater transparency rules be adopted in dispute settlements. They say "if the decisions of the WTO adjudicative system are to enjoy public confidence, the process must be as transparent to the public as possible."[12]

[9] General Accounting Office, *World Trade Organization,* p. 70; and McGinnis and Movsesian, "The World Trade Constitution," pp. 591–94.

[10] William H. Lash III, "The Limited but Important Role of the WTO," *The Cato Journal,* Winter 2000, p. 372.

[11] McGinnis and Movsesian, "The World Trade Constitution," p. 597.

[12] Ibid., p. 603.

[8] Ibid., pp. 598–99.

410 Chapter 13 *Globalization*

COMPLAINTS OF LESS DEVELOPED NATIONS

Unresolved complaints of the less developed nations (LDCs) were the basic reason for the failure of the last three world meetings of the WTO. (These were the meetings in Seattle, 1999; Doha, Qatar, 2001; and Cancun, Mexico, 2003.) The chief grievance of the LDCs concerns the agricultural subsidies and tariffs employed by the rich countries.

Annual agricultural subsidies worldwide are about $300 billion. Tariffs vary considerably among developed nations, but the overall effect is that of restricting imports such as textiles. A major complaint of the LDCs is that agricultural subsidies permit farmers in rich countries to produce and export products such as corn, rice, and cotton to LDCs at costs far below those of farmers in LDCs. The result, say the LDCs, is that subsidies undermine the livelihoods of millions of poor farmers around the world.[13]

The LDCs have diverse interests, but there is fundamental unity on agricultural issues. West African farmers say they cannot compete with subsidized cotton grown by U.S. cotton farmers. Some countries, such as South Korea, feel the pinch of rice subsidies. Mexican farmers are hurt by corn subsidies. Soybean farmers in Argentina are pushed out of world soybean markets by subsidies.

The gravity of agricultural issues was brought to the attention of the world when Kyng-hae Lee, a South Korean rice farmer, plunged a knife into his chest and killed himself at the Cancun meeting. He wore a sign that read "The WTO kills farmers" and passed around a handout that said imports were cheaper than domestic goods and his income was less than his costs. Korean farmers, he said, were forced to go to work in the urban slums.[14]

Proposals for reducing subsidies and tariffs were made at Cancun by the richer nations' representatives. Robert Zoellick, the U.S. Trade Representative, proposed "to slash subsidies and tariffs on farm goods and eliminate tariffs and non-tariff barriers on manufactured goods."[15] Other proposals were made, but the LDCs considered them all insufficient to deal with the issue. In the end, representatives of the LDCs walked out of the meeting.

EU Trade Minister Pascal Lamy said, "The WTO is a medieval organization. The procedures and rules of this organization have not supported the weight of the task. There is no way to structure and steer discussions among 146 members in a manner conducive to a consensus. The decision-making needs to be revamped." Zoellick, however, commented, "It would not be very fruitful to try to move to other voting structures."[16] He noted that the WTO members were able to come to an agreement in a dispute over the access of medicines a few weeks before the Cancun meeting.

In defense of the LDC criticisms that offers of reductions in subsidies and tariffs were insufficient, Zoellick noted that there were strong protectionist pressures in the United States. He undoubtedly had in mind that manufacturers of steel, textiles, agricultural, and chemical interests had pressed the U.S. government for relief from foreign competition. These and other groups want protection from importing that they perceive as dumping products below the costs of foreign producers. Politically strong unions want to protect jobs in industries unable to compete with foreign producers.

Former U.S. Trade Representative Charlene Barshefsky said that she realized there were many trade problems of poorer countries. "The least developed countries, the poorest, are of greatest concern because they are falling behind," she told reporters. Helping such nations, she said, "is very important, in and of itself—no strings attached." She also noted that those countries that were most open to the global economy had been benefited by it.[17]

---

[13] Elizabeth Becker, "Delegates from Poorer Nations Walk Out of World Trade Talks," *New York Times,* September 15, 2003, p. A1.

[14] Elizabeth Becker and Ginger Thompson, "Poorer Nations Plead Farmers' Case at Trade Talks," *New York Times International,* September 11, 2003, p. 3.

[15] Robert Zoellick, "Committed in Cancun," *The Wall Street Journal,* September 8, 2003, p. A16.

[16] Quoted in Bruce Stokes, "The Culture Clash at Cancun," *National Journal,* September 20, 2003, p. 2891.

[17] Quotes and observations from Jonathan Peterson and Evelyn Iritani, "Rich-Poor Tensions Divide WTO," *Los Angeles Times,* November 30, 1999, p. C1.

ABOLISH THE WTO?

Many critics want to abolish the WTO. One powerful voice is that of Ralph Nader's Public Citizen. In an editorial, the organization based its recommendation to abolish the organization on three grounds:

> First, the WTO's trade rules intentionally prioritize trade and commercial considerations over all other values. Never does the WTO say, "Trade should be undertaken in such a way as to promote values that the international community has agreed are important in their own right such as protection of human rights, the environment or labor rights." WTO rules generally require domestic laws, rules and regulations designed to further worker, consumer, environmental, health, safety, human rights, animal protection or other non-commercial interests to be undertaken in the "least trade restrictive" fashion possible.
>
> Second the WTO intentionally overrides domestic decisions about how economies should be organized and corporations controlled. Its rules drastically shrink the choices available to democratically controlled governments, with violations potentially punished with harsh penalties.
>
> Third, the WTO does not just regulate, it actively promotes, global trade. Its rules are biased to facilitate global commerce at the expense of efforts to promote local economic development and policies that move communities, countries and regions in the direction of greater self-reliance—a direction necessary to move towards a world of ecological sustainability and democratic governments.[18]

These quotes are not the full text of the recommendation, which can be found in a special issue of Ralph Nader's *Multinational Monitor.* Placards were present at the Seattle WTO summit meeting supporting this recommendation. On the other hand, many supporters of the WTO see it, and its predecessor organizations, as an important force behind a broad increase in the world's general welfare in the past 50 years. It must be maintained and strengthened, they say.

THE WTO RESPONDS

The WTO set forth arguments of its value in a document entitled "10 Benefits of the WTO Trading System."[19] Here are a few quotes from this document.

The System Helps Promote Peace

Peace is partly an outcome of two of the most fundamental principles of the trading system: *helping trade to flow smoothly,* and providing countries with a constructive and fair outlet for *dealing with disputes over trade issues.* It is also an outcome of the *international confidence and cooperation* that the system creates and reinforces.

. . . [I]f trade flows smoothly and both sides enjoy a healthy commercial relationship, political conflict is less likely. What's more, smoothly flowing trade also helps people all over the world become better off. People who are more prosperous and contented are also less likely to fight.

Smaller Countries Are Helped with WTO

Without a multilateral regime such as the WTO system, the more powerful countries would be freer to impose their will unilaterally on their smaller trading partners. Smaller countries would have to deal with each of the major economic powers individually, and would be much less able to resist unwanted pressure.

Freer Trade Cuts Costs of Living

Protectionism is expensive: it raises prices. The WTO's global system lowers trade barriers through negotiation and applies the principle of non-discrimination. The result is reduced costs of production (because imports used in production are cheaper) and reduced prices of finished goods and services, and ultimately a lower cost of living.

Trade Stimulates Economic Growth, Including Jobs

Trade clearly has the potential to create jobs. In practice there is often factual evidence that lower trade barriers have been good for employment. But the picture is complicated by a number of factors. Nevertheless, the alternative—protectionism—is not the way to tackle employment problems.

---

[18] "Dismantle the WTO," *Multinational Monitor,* October–November 1999, p. 5.

[19] "10 Benefits of the WTO Trading System," www.wto.gov, 1999.

Governments Are Shielded from Lobbying

One of the lessons of the protectionism that dominated the early decades of the twentieth century was the damage that can be caused if narrow sectoral interests gain an unbalanced share of political influence. The result was increasingly restrictive policy which turned into a trade war that no one won and everyone lost.

Protectionism can also escalate as other countries retaliate. . . . That's exactly what happened in the 1920s and 30s with disastrous effects. Even the sectors demanding protection ended up losing.

Governments need to be armed against pressure from narrow interest groups, and the WTO system can help.

CONCLUDING OBSERVATIONS

An organization such as the WTO, dealing with world trade, seeking to harmonize trade relations among the many nations of the world, and making decisions that affect nations and people, is bound to be highly controversial. In this case study, after presenting the nature and operations of the WTO, we succinctly presented the more important criticisms of the WTO and responses in its support.

Questions

1. What is the WTO and how is it organized?
2. Describe the WTO decision-making process for trade disputes. Do you think it is an effective system?
3. Who are the dominant critics of the WTO? What do they complain about?
4. What major positive responses to these criticisms are made on the WTO's behalf?
5. Should the WTO be abolished, as suggested by some critics?

Chapter **Fourteen**

Industrial Pollution and Environmental Policy

The Indian Health Service Solves a Mystery

Daniel Schultz, a surgeon at the Santa Fe Indian Hospital in New Mexico, was puzzled and alarmed when, in an 18-month period in 1984 and 1985, he diagnosed three cases of malignant mesothelioma in Indians from a nearby pueblo. An investigation of a state tumor registry revealed two more cases from this pueblo in 1970 and 1982, for a total of five cases over 15 years. On average, the victims were 65 years old and lived only 3.8 months after diagnosis.[1]

Malignant mesothelioma is an incurable tumor in the lining of the chest cavity that is virtually always caused by exposure to asbestos. It has a latency period of 40 to 50 years. Five cases of this unusual cancer in a pueblo of 2,000 Indians was roughly 1,000 times the number predicted over 15 years by standard mortality tables. Normally, five cases could be expected in a city of two million. Samples of lung tissue from the three cases in the Indian Hospital revealed the presence of all three types of asbestos used in commerce—chrysotile, amosite, and crocidolite. The Indians had been exposed to air-borne asbestos fibers. But how? Schultz called in Richard J. Driscoll, an environmental health officer with the Indian Health Service (IHS), a small agency in the Department of Health and Human Services. Driscoll, along with colleagues from the IHS, set out to do some detective work to learn how asbestos exposure was occurring.

Immediately, the investigators ran into a problem. The Indians were reluctant subjects. They had a superstitious belief that fatal illness was explained by the presence of evil in its victims. They believed that people who discussed disease were wishing it on others and inviting additional sickness. The Indians also disliked attention and interference from outsiders because they wanted to keep their native culture and ways intact. Tribal elders finally agreed to discuss possible causes of asbestos exposure. Here is the story that emerged.

In the 1930s, a brick-manufacturing plant was built in the vicinity of the pueblo. A small private railroad was started to shuttle between the plant and a nearby main line of the Santa Fe Railroad, and a steam locomotive operated on it. When the boiler and

---

[1] Richard J. Driscoll, Wallace J. Mulligan, Daniel Schultz, and Anthony Candelaria, "Malignant Mesothelioma: A Cluster in a Native American Pueblo," *The New England Journal of Medicine*, June 2, 1988, p. 1437.

pipe insulation on the locomotive needed replacement, workers discarded the old asbestos insulation near the tracks, where it was found by members of the tribe and brought back to the pueblo. It was put to many uses. Asbestos pads were used for worktable insulation by silversmiths making Indian jewelry. Dancers at religious festivals scraped and pounded their deer-hide leggings with crumbling wads of pipe insulation to whiten them, releasing clouds of floating asbestos fibers. Gradually the Indians found more and more uses for asbestos, and the trackside scrap was supplemented by tribe members in construction work who scavenged at their job sites for more.

The investigators discovered that four of the five mesothelioma victims had been silversmiths and that all five had been active participants in ceremonial dances. The Indians were reluctant to give up their asbestos; selling it had become a cottage industry in the pueblo. When the investigators went door to door, they found that Indian families were hoarding asbestos in bags, pots, and jars. It was hard to get them to part with it, but they found that by emphasizing the harm it could cause to children, most of it could be removed.

The story of what happened to the Indians in the pueblo is analogous to what has happened to large populations in industrial societies. In both cases, dangerous substances with useful qualities promised better living. In both cases, elevated exposure to these substances predated adequate knowledge of their harmful effects. And in both cases, it was only after substantial exposures had occurred and sickness began to appear that government agencies mobilized to protect public health.

In this chapter we discuss the nature of industrial pollutants and the practices and social philosophies that allowed them to darken skies, poison waters, and despoil land. We then discuss how, in the United States beginning in the 1970s, massive regulatory programs developed to control industrial pollution. We explain the current operation of these programs, how they affect corporations, and how well they work.

POLLUTION

pollution
A substance released into the environment that endangers human welfare.

Pollution refers to release of substances into the environment that inconvenience or endanger humans. Much of it comes from natural sources. Forest fires release particles and toxic metals such as mercury into the atmosphere. Water picks up asbestos as it flows over rocks, gravel, and sand. Natural background radiation in North America is about 300 millirem a year, the equivalent of 50 chest X rays. Tons of oil seep from fissures in the ocean floor.

Human activity adds more contaminants. For millions of years, hunter-gatherer bands generated little pollution. However, a gradual revolution in agricultural methods beginning about 10,000 years ago led to more settled societies in which populations grew and people gathered in cities. Wherever they lived, the primary pollution problem people faced was gases and particles from indoor fuel combustion for cooking and heating. Significant death and disease rates are associated with exposure to the smoke of animal dung, wood, and charcoal, although this was unknown in those days.[2]

---

[2] Nigel Bruce et al., "Indoor Air Pollution in Developing Countries: A Major Environmental and Public Health Challenge," *Bulletin of the World Health Organization,* September 2000.

Eventually, cities filled with workers showing up as a result of the industrial revolution, and population densities increased markedly. The pollution problem this created, on top of haze from the smoke of many indoor fires, was the concentration of huge amounts of human and animal waste. Few homes had lavatories. Primitive sewers were not flushed with water. Dead animals, dung from beasts of burden, and entrails from butcher shops littered streets.[3]

Water plant technology, widely introduced only in the late 1800s, eventually ensured sanitary water supplies, but not soon enough to prevent a high death toll from waterborne disease. By this time, contaminants from fossil-fuel combustion and manufacturing activity were a serious, added problem.

Most industrial pollution simply adds to background levels of naturally occurring substances, so that human exposures to metals, carbon compounds, radiation, and other substances reach artificially high levels. It is estimated, for example, that because of environmental exposure, the average American carries a tissue concentration of lead at least 1,000 times greater than prehistoric people.[4] Some industrial pollutants, however, are not found in nature. The rise of synthetic chemical production since the 1940s has led to the creation and dispersal of persistent, complex artificial molecules used in plastics, fumigants, and pesticides. The average person carries many of these substances in his or her tissues. One study detected 150 industrial chemicals, most of which did not exist 75 years ago, in the tissues of nine people. Their exposures came from some of the 11,700 products made by 164 manufacturers that contain these chemicals.[5]

Industrial activity both harms human health and disturbs natural ecology. We will briefly discuss its impact in each area.

Human Health

Disease caused by industrial pollution is significant, but it is far less significant than disease caused by older, nonindustrial forms of pollution. Table 14.1 shows the estimated burden of disease caused by air, water, and land pollution. The total burden of disease caused by pollution is calculated in *disability-adjusted life years*, or DALYs. DALYs combine in a single measure years of life lost because of premature death and years of life lived with disabilities.[6]

As the table shows, exposure to pollution is estimated to produce 18 percent of the disease burden in less developed nations but only 4.5 percent in developed ones. Most of the burden in developing nations is attributable to the age-old risks

disability-adjusted life year
A year of healthy life as measured by a statistic that combines years of life lost because of premature death and years of life lived with disability.

[3] Clive Ponting, *A Green History of the World* (New York: St. Martin's Press, 1992), p. 354.

[4] Joel Schwartz and Ronnie Levin, "Lead: Example of the Job Ahead," *EPA Journal,* March–April 1992, p. 42.

[5] Joseph W. Thornton et al., "Biomonitoring of Industrial Pollutants: Health and Policy Implications of the Chemical Body Burden," *Public Health Journal,* July–August 2002, p. 315. See also Centers for Disease Control and Prevention, *Second National Report on Human Exposure to Environmental Chemicals* (Atlanta, GA: National Center for Environmental Health, March 2003), which reports on body burdens of 116 industrial chemicals in the general population.

[6] Calculation of DALYs is based on estimates of life expectancy, subjective quantification of disability weights by expert panels, and age-based discounting techniques in which years of life in the most productive years have higher value.

TABLE 14.1   Health Risks Posed by Major Sources of Environmental Pollution

Source: Kseniya Lvovsky, "Health and Environment," World Bank, draft working paper, Washington, DC, April 2000, p. 4.

	Percent of DALYs	
Environmental Health Risk	**Less Developed Countries**	**Developed Countries**
Water supply and sanitation	7%	1%
Indoor air pollution	4	0
Urban air pollution	2	1
Agricultural chemicals and industrial waste	1	2.5
All pollution-related causes	**18**	**4.5**

of unsanitary water and indoor combustion of wood and coal.[7] Urban air pollution from factories and vehicles plus pesticides and toxic waste—the by-products of modern industry—is responsible for only 3 percent of DALYs in developing nations and 3.5 percent in developed ones. Clearly, when nations industrialize, far from creating a deadly blizzard of pollution, they instead greatly reduce the overall burden of disease by reducing exposures to lethal nonindustrial pollutants. The main advances are access to water unpolluted by feces and the transition from dirty fuels to cleaner ones such as gasoline, electricity, and nuclear energy.

The Biosphere

Beyond harming human health, industrial activity also impinges on the biosphere, the slender margin atop the earth's surface that supports life, a space "so thin it cannot be seen edgewise from an orbiting spacecraft."[8] Among the unintended effects of global economic growth within this delicate space are these:

- *Disruption of natural chemistry.* The carbon cycle is overwhelmed by carbon released in fossil fuel combustion and from soil and vegetation as land is cleared. Unabsorbed carbon dioxide is building up in the atmosphere, raising concerns about climate change. The nitrogen cycle is overwhelmed by nitrogen releases during fossil fuel combustion, tilling of soil, and application of fertilizers. Airborne nitrogen oxides create acid rain. Waterborne nitrogen causes eutrophication in water bodies. The fresh-water cycle is strained by diversion of large quantities of water for agricultural and industrial uses that returns to water bodies polluted by chemicals and fertilizers.

- *Land conversion.* Humans have converted 25 percent of land area to agriculture and another 4 percent to cities.[9] This adds up to 29 percent of the world's land surface that has been changed from its pristine state. Biodiversity in

[7] Susmita Dasgupta et al., *Who Suffers from Indoor Air Pollution? Evidence from Bangladesh* (Washington, DC: World Bank Policy Research Working Paper No. 3428, October 2004).

[8] E. O. Wilson, "Hotspots: Preserving Pieces of a Fragile Biosphere," *National Geographic,* January 2002, p. 86.

[9] United Nations Development Programme et al., *World Resources 2000–2001* (Washington, DC: World Resources Institute, 2000), p. 24.

converted areas has been reduced. Reflectivity of incoming solar radiation is altered.

- *Degradation of broad ecosystems.* Over the past 10,000 years, global forests have been reduced by 20 to 50 percent. Although temperate forests are stable, 0.52 percent of tropical forest area is lost each year, an area the size of Indiana.[10] Grasslands are shrinking. Polar systems show signs of climate warming. Coastal ecosystems are overfished, and more than a quarter of the world's coral reefs are damaged from human activity. The number of plant and animal species is declining, though the rate of species decline is unclear because statistics are highly speculative estimates. Ozone in the upper atmosphere is besieged by a murderous gang of molecules having no counterpart in nature.

Full consequences of these disruptions within the biosphere are unknown. However, they raise serious concerns and imply broad ethical duties for businesses and industrial societies.

INDUSTRIAL ACTIVITY, POLLUTION, AND THE ENVIRONMENT

There is no question that economic activity, broadly defined, is the source of enduring pollution problems. And world economic activity is greater than in the past. As noted in Chapter 2, global output of goods and services since 1950 exceeds that for all preceding human history. The world economy continues to become more integrated and to accelerate.

Today there are nations on every continent with ambitious development plans that put industry before environmental protection. Poor nations house the vast majority of the 2.8 billion people with purchasing power of less than two U.S. dollars per day.[11] Their leaders see industrial growth as the only practical way of raising living standards and building national power. If these populous, underdeveloped nations take the path of the environmentally destructive eighteenth and nineteenth century industrial revolution in Europe, the United States, and Japan, the resulting pollution and resource depletion could lead to ecological disaster.

sustainable development
Nonpolluting economic growth that raises standards of living without depleting the net resources of the earth.

Much interest today is focused on the notion of *sustainable development*, that is, nonpolluting economic growth that raises standards of living without depleting the net resources of the earth. However, the modern industrial revolution, as it is currently unfolding in developing nations, bears little resemblance to this ideal. In fact, at least in its early stages, it promises to exceed the old-time industrial revolutions in generating pollution and depleting resources. The new industrialization is faster. Economic growth rates in countries such as Korea, Thailand, and China have compressed the transformation into less than two decades rather than the 100 years and more it took England and the United States. As growth skyrockets, a range of modern industries quickly appears,

[10] World Bank, *World Development Report 2003* (Washington, DC: World Bank, 2002), p. 3.

[11] United Nations Development Programme, *Human Development Report 2003* (New York: Oxford University Press, 2003), p. 41.

FIGURE 14.1
The Environmental Kuznets Curve

Source: Adapted from Håkan Nordström and Scott Vaughan, *Trade and Environment* (Geneva: WTO Publications, 1999), p. 48.

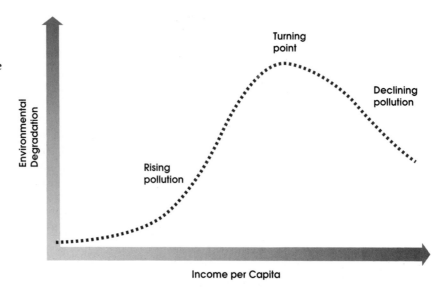

creating more varied and dangerous pollutants than were typical of eighteenth and nineteenth century factories.

However, there is evidence that environmental quality in growing economies does not follow a path of long-term deterioration as in the old industrial revolution model. Studies suggest that developing economies now follow a sequence in which pollution rises in the early stages of growth when incomes are low. As per capita gross domestic product continues to rise, pollution reaches a peak and eventually decreases, even as GDP continues to rise. This phenomenon can be represented as an inverted U-shaped curve, known as an *environmental Kuznets curve*,[12] illustrated in Figure 14.1.

environmental Kuznets curve
An inverted U-shaped curve illustrating that as gross domestic product rises in emerging economies pollution goes through stages of rapid increase, leveling off, and decline.

Researchers studying more than 50 countries found, for example, that there was a rapid rise of sulfur dioxide emissions in the cities of countries undergoing economic development. Sulfur dioxide, a by-product of coal and oil combustion, is closely associated with industrialization. But this rise slowed and eventually leveled off when per capita GDP, measured as purchasing power parity with U.S. dollars, reached about $4,000. After that, emissions began to decline even as incomes continued to rise. Particle emissions leveled off somewhat later, at a per capita GDP of around $8,000, and three measures of water quality based on oxygen demand caused by organic pollutants leveled off at a per capita GDP of $7,500. Waterborne concentrations of the heavy metal arsenic stabilized at $4,900 and began to decline at $10,000.[13]

[12] Simon Kuznets won the 1971 Nobel prize in economics for his studies of economic growth. He also said that, in addition to environmental quality, income inequality followed an inverted U-shaped relationship during development, first worsening, then leveling off, then declining.

[13] Gene M. Grossman and Alan B. Krueger, "Economic Growth and the Environment," *Quarterly Journal of Economics,* May 1995 p. 353. Data are from the Global Environmental Monitoring System, a joint project of the World Health Organization and the United Nations Environmental Programme.

These findings support the existence of an inverted U pattern for these pollutants. Although not all studies have arrived at the same figures and not all pollutants studied trace an inverted U pattern, there is general support for the theory.[14]

A number of factors explain the environmental Kuznets curve. To begin, as countries industrialize, their economies change in composition. During the early stages, less capital-intensive agricultural and food processing sectors are dominant. Pollution from these industries is quantitatively less and less toxic than from industries that come later. In the middle stages of industrialization, enough capital has accumulated to bring on more heavily polluting industries such as cement making, chemicals, and rubber. Later stages characteristically see the growth of industries that require both capital and technical skill, including basic metals, paper and printing, and machinery.[15] Then, in the last structural shifts, much cleaner technology and service industries rise.

While the advent of heavily polluting industries increases degradation, growth brings other changes. With greater affluence there is more education. Changes in values occur as the population ascends from poverty. Preserving environmental quality and protecting public health assume more importance. Corporations, particularly highly visible MNCs, may be pressured to use cleaner technologies. Governments grow stronger and may become more responsive to citizen demands for pollution reduction. Regulatory agencies strengthen with an influx of technically skilled personnel. These factors all underlie the observed pollution reductions coming with continued GDP growth.

If the environmental Kuznets curve predicts the future, economic growth does not necessarily lead to steadily increasing levels of pollution. The view that development inevitably brings ruinous degradation is rooted in the historical experience of the West. Modern growth may be much cleaner. In fact, long-term growth may mitigate environmental problems. However, as rising foreign direct investment extends production chains into emerging economies more pollution will result in the short run. The World Bank estimates that relative to high-income nations, manufacturers in the poorest nations "have an approximately tenfold differential in pollution intensity" (the ratio of polluting emissions to a given quantity of output).[16] As poorer nations increase their share of global production, average pollution intensity will increase.

Although sustainable development is a useful philosophy, and as we will see, some nations and corporations attempt to approach it in practice, the broad global reality bears little resemblance to the sustainable ideal. Still, current fascination with sustainability suggests a shift in thinking about the relationship between industry and ecology. In the next section we discuss ideas that arose to support industrialization and then explain how they are now being challenged.

[14] Bruce Yandle, "Environmental Turning Points, Institutions, and the Rise to the Top," *The Independent Review,* Fall 2004.

[15] Richard M. Auty, "Pollution Patterns during the Industrial Transition," *The Geographic Journal,* July 1997, p. 206.

[16] David Wheeler, *Racing to the Bottom? Foreign Investment and Air Pollution in Developing Countries* (Washington, DC: World Bank Research Group, January 2001), p. 12.

IDEAS SHAPE ATTITUDES TOWARD THE ENVIRONMENT

What is the proper relationship between business and nature? In the past, and to some extent still, Western values that regard nature as an adversary to be conquered have legitimized industrial activity. These values were incubated in ancient Mediterranean society. Eventually they appeared in biblical text, giving them religious sanction and magnifying their influence. In the story of creation in Genesis, God creates first nature and then man and afterward instructs man on how to relate to nature.

dualism
The theory that humans are separate from nature because they have the power of reason and, unlike plants and animals, souls.

> Be fruitful and multiply, and replenish the earth and subdue it; and have dominion over the fish of the sea, and over the fowl of the air, and over every living thing that moveth upon the earth. (1:28)

This Judeo-Christian view laid the foundation for the conviction in Western civilization that humans were both separate from and superior to the natural world. It also incorporated the idea that humans must exercise wise stewardship over their dominion, but until recently the stewardship idea languished as a minor theme.

When Church dogma began to lose its primacy during the Renaissance in Europe, secular philosophers did not reject the biblical doctrine of human superiority to nature but reinforced it with their own worldly thinking. Within the comparatively short span of 150 years, four new ideas appeared that, combined, determined how nature would be regarded and treated during the coming industrial revolution.

progress
The belief that history is a narrative of improvement in which humanity moves from lower to higher levels of perfection.

The theory of *dualism* held that humans were separate from nature. The French philosopher René Descartes (1596–1650) believed that nature operated like a machine, according to fixed laws that humans could study and understand. Humans were separate from nature and other living organisms because they alone had the power of reason and, unlike plants and animals, had souls. Descartes's perspective laid the foundation for modern experimental science but also established a dualism reinforcing the Judeo-Christian idea that humans were superior to and apart from nature.

The Renaissance brought improved living conditions, growth of cities, inventions, and the birth of industries. Such events kindled great optimism in European intellectuals who wrote about the idea of *progress,* or the belief that history was a narrative of improvement in which humanity moved from lower to higher levels on an inevitable march to perfection. This idea rejected the pessimism of previous civilizations that had looked back on past golden eras. Charles Darwin's theory of evolution supported the idea of progress in the popular mind. As industry expanded, the exploitation of nature for human welfare was soon entwined with the notion of progress.

capitalism
An economy in which private individuals and corporations own the means of production and, motivated by the desire for profit, compete in free markets under conditions of limited restraint by government. In this economy, nature is valued primarily as an input into the production process.

Then, during the early years of the industrial revolution in England, powerful doctrines of economics and ethics arose, which in additional ways justified the exploitation of nature. The theory of *capitalism,* based on principles set forth by Adam Smith in 1776, valued nature primarily as a commodity to be used in wealth-creating activity that increased the vigor, welfare, and comfort of society.

As a practical matter, early capitalism in action largely ignored environmental damage. This tendency still exists. For example, the gross domestic product, the accounting system of capitalism, rises when goods and services are produced but does not fall when pollution damage occurs. Thus, the GDP rose because of the *Exxon Valdez* oil spill, adding the millions of dollars spent by Exxon on the cleanup but not subtracting the costs of dead animals and degraded shoreline.

utilitarianism
The ethical philosophy of the greatest good for the greatest number.

Finally, the doctrine of *utilitarianism,* or "the greatest good for the greatest number," arrived in England simultaneously with the rise of capitalism. It also was used to justify economic activity that assaulted nature. Industry made the utilitarian argument that, although pollution was noxious, the economic benefits of jobs, products, taxes, and growth outweighed environmental costs and were the "greatest good." Utilitarianism was an ethical worldview that rationalized the destructive side effects of commerce. It blinded Western societies to alternative, but less exploitive, views of nature.

In Eastern civilization, the values of Buddhism, Confucianism, and Taoism placed stronger emphasis on the interconnection of people and nature. They supported a more humble, less domineering role for humanity. However, their main impact was on interpersonal relations. Industrialization in Asia has been as destructive of the environment as in the West.

land ethic
An ethical theory that humans are part of a community that includes not only other human beings but all elements of the natural environment as well. It implies an ethical duty to nature as well as to humanity.

New Ideas Challenge the Old

In the second half of the twentieth century, an alternative, nonexploitive environmental ethic emerged. Naturalist Aldo Leopold pioneered the revised worldview. His seminal statement of a new *land ethic* in a 1949 book, *A Sand County Almanac,* inspired others to rethink traditional ideas about the man–nature relationship. He wrote:

> All ethics so far evolved rest upon a single premise: that the individual is a member of a community of interdependent parts. . . . The land ethic simply enlarges the boundaries of the community to include soils, waters, plants, and animals, or collectively: the land. . . . In short, a land ethic changes the role of *Homo sapiens* from conqueror of the land-community to plain member and citizen of it. It implies respect for his fellow members and also respect for the community as such.[17]

For Leopold, the conventional boundaries of ethical duty were too narrow. Expansion was merited to include not only duties toward fellow humans but also duties to nonhuman entities in nature, both living and nonliving.

deep ecology
A theory that rejects human domination of nature and holds that humans have only equal rights with other species, not superior rights. Human interference with nature is now excessive and must be drastically reduced.

In the early 1970s, a more radical form of this land ethic came from Norwegian philosopher Arne Naess. Naess argued that Leopold and mainstream environmentalists were too shallow in their thinking because they were conciliatory with the industrial-age worldview. Naess said there were "deeper concerns" than how to compromise the protection of nature with ongoing economic activity. His position came to be called *deep ecology*. Naess argued that human domination of nature should cease. Philosophies of domination should be replaced by a "biospheric egalitarianism" in which all species had equal rights to live and flourish. Nature should no longer be valued only as inputs for factories as in capitalist economics

---

[17] Aldo Leopold, *A Sand County Almanac* (New York: Ballantine, 1970), pp. 239–40.

because it has an intrinsic value that must not be compromised. In short, Naess rejected the four traditional ideas about the man–nature relationship that support industrial activity. He concluded that the present level of human interference in nature was excessive and detrimental and that drastic changes were needed.[18]

The views of Naess and other philosophers who share his thinking inspired anti-corporate environmental groups. Some, such as Earth First! and the Environmental Liberation Front, believe that extreme measures, including disregard for the law, are warranted by the moral obligation to end destruction of nature.

Other new philosophies justify the expansion of rights to nonhuman entities. For example, philosopher Peter Singer popularized the idea of *speciesism,* or "a prejudice or attitude of bias toward the members of one's own species and against those of members of other species," that is analogous to racism or sexism.[19] The racist and sexist believe that skin color and sex determine people's worth; the speciesist believes that the number of one's legs or whether one lives in trees, the sea, or a condominium determines one's rights. Traditionally, when *Homo sapiens* compete for rights with plants and animals, the latter have lost. Singer argues that humans, though superior in important ways, are simply one species among many. And the others have intrinsic value independent of any economic usefulness to *Homo sapiens.*

speciesism
Bias by humans toward members of their own species and prejudice against members of other species.

Singer's arguments, like those of Naess, challenge the age-old view of human dominance and undermine the human-centered morality of industrial development—unless such development occurs in a way that respects nature. Recently, Singer has argued that because of modern scientific insights, traditional ethical values about the environment no longer conform to basic tenets of fairness. New ethical rules are needed. Our values evolved when the atmosphere, the forests, and the oceans seemed to be unlimited resources. Now, he writes, we know that "[b]y driving your car you could be releasing carbon dioxide that is part of a causal chain leading to lethal floods in Bangladesh."[20] Traditional values—for example, the sanctity of private property in capitalism—fail to impose adequate duties to protect assets that belong to all humanity.

ENVIRONMENTAL REGULATION IN THE UNITED STATES

The dominant approach to industrial pollution control in the United States has been to pass laws that strictly regulate emissions, effluents, and wastes. Before the 1970s there was little environmental regulation; but by the 1960s the public had become frightened of pollution, and a strong popular mandate for controlling it emerged. As a result, during what came to be called the "environmental decade" of the 1970s, Congress passed a remarkable string of new laws, creating a broad statutory base for regulating industry.

---

[18] Naess's basic arguments are in "The Shallow and the Deep, Long-Range Ecology Movement: A Summary," *Inquiry,* Spring 1973; and "A Defense of the Deep Ecology Movement," *Environmental Economics,* Fall 1984.

[19] Peter Singer, *Animal Liberation* (New York: Avon, 1975), p. 7.

[20] Peter Singer, *One World: The Ethics of Globalization* (New Haven, CT: Yale University Press, 2002), pp. 19–20.

Although additional laws have been passed since the 1970s, the ones from that decade still form the basic regulatory framework. Most have been reauthorized and amended, some several times, and some of these revisions, such as the Clean Air Act Amendments of 1990, were so extensive that they fundamentally altered the statute, always by making it more complex and requiring more expensive regulation. To illustrate, the Clean Air Act passed in 1970 was 50 pages long, but when Congress amended it in 1990 it ballooned to 800 pages. These 800 pages rolled out 538 specific requirements for new rules, standards, and reports, imposing rigid deadlines on 361 of them.[21]

The Environmental Protection Agency

The Environmental Protection Agency (EPA) is the nation's largest regulatory agency. Its mission is to protect human health and to preserve the natural environment. Although many agencies administer environmental laws, the EPA enforces more than 30 statutes making up the overwhelming bulk of regulation in this area. In 2005 it had almost 18,000 employees and a budget of $7.6 billion, making it larger and better funded than the Department of State.

When Congress passes an environmental law, EPA employees write detailed, specific rules to carry out its general directives. According to one study, between 1981 and 1999 the agency issued more than 2,700 regulations, 115 of which had an impact on the economy of $100 million or more.[22] The EPA can enforce these rules directly on corporations, but laws permit delegating enforcement to the states. State regulators, acting with federal funding and following EPA guidelines, now do most of the enforcement of the nation's environmental laws.

Although the EPA remains an aggressive agency, it suffers from work overload. Moreover, since the early 1990s its budget has been under constant pressure from Republicans in Congress wanting to reduce the regulatory burden it imposes on corporations.

PRINCIPAL AREAS OF ENVIRONMENTAL POLICY

There are three media for pollution: air, water, and land. Here we give a brief overview of regulations that protect them from degradation. In each area, we describe laws, basic problems, central concerns for business, and progress.

Air

Air pollution is best described as a set of complex interrelated problems, each requiring different control measures. The Clean Air Act, most recently amended in 1990, is the primary air quality statute. Although this law permits the use of some market incentives, these provisions depart from its core philosophy, which is to impose inflexible, draconian, command controls. We now discuss regulation of different air pollution problems.

---

[21] General Accounting Office, *Air Pollution: Status of Implementation and Issues of the Clean Air Act Amendments of 1990,* GAO/RCED–00–72, April 2000, p. 3.

[22] General Accounting Office, *Environmental Protection: Assessing the Impacts of EPA's Regulations through Retrospective Studies,* GAO/RCED–99–250, September 1999, p. 3 and fn. 4.

National Air Quality

The Clean Air Act requires the EPA to set national standards that limit pollution from substances harmful to public health and the environment. These standards are supposed to be set without regard for cost and must provide an "adequate margin of safety" that protects even the most sensitive people. To do this, the EPA has set standards to curb emissions of six substances, called *criteria pollutants*, that are the primary threat to air quality because they are emitted in large quantities:

criteria pollutants
Six natural substances released in large quantities that cause substandard air quality—carbon monoxide, nitrogen dioxide, sulfur dioxide, ozone, particulates, and lead.

- *Carbon monoxide* (CO) is a gas produced from incomplete combustion of carbon in fuels such as gasoline. Its largest source is vehicle emissions. High concentrations of CO reduce the oxygen carrying capacity of the blood and may aggravate cardiovascular disease.

- *Nitrogen dioxide* (NO_2) is a gas resulting from oxidation in the atmosphere of nitrogen oxide (NO), a pollutant formed during high temperature combustion. It comes mainly from vehicle exhaust and fuel combustion in industry. It is a lung irritant and aggravates respiratory disease.

- *Sulfur dioxide* (SO_2) is a colorless gas that comes primarily from the burning of fossil fuels, which releases trapped sulfur compounds. Two-thirds of SO_2 is emitted by electric utilities burning coal and oil. SO_2 contributes to acid rain and fine particle pollution. It is a lung irritant that triggers asthma attacks and is associated with heart attacks and cancer.

- *Ozone* (O_3) molecules are not directly emitted from vehicles or industrial processes. Instead, they form in the air by chemical reactions between nitrogen dioxide and molecules known as *volatile organic compounds* (VOCs), which are essentially vapors from substances such as gasoline, paint, floor waxes, and similar petroleum-based compounds. These airborne reactions are promoted by the energy in sunlight, which is why urban smog is often worse on sunny days. Industry accounts for about half of all VOC emissions and vehicles for the other half. Ozone is a bluish gas that irritates the lungs, and high concentrations damage lung tissue. Near ground level, ozone is considered a pollutant. High in the atmosphere, ozone absorbs solar radiation, making life possible on earth.

- *Particulates* (PM, or particulate matter) are dust particles raised primarily by industrial activity and vehicles traveling over roads. Coal-burning power plants, for example, emit massive numbers of particles because fly ash is not completely removed from stack gases by existing control methods. The EPA regulates particles that are 10 micrometers in size, about one-seventh the diameter of a human hair, or smaller. Industry releases only about 9 percent of the particulate emissions. Most particles come from dust raised by the wind. Particulates pose the greatest health risk of all the criteria pollutants. They are associated with respiratory and cardiovascular disease and heavy exposures raise near-term death rates for infants, the elderly, and the infirm.[23] Recently the agency introduced standards for very small particles of 2.5 micrometers or

---

[23] See, for example, C. A. Pope et al., "Lung Cancer, Cardiopulmonary Mortality and Long-Term Exposure to Fine Particulate Air Pollution," *Journal of the American Medical Association*, March 6, 2002.

TABLE 14.2
Estimated
Emissions by
Source of
Criteria
Pollutants,
2000 (in
thousands of
tons)

Source: EPA,
*National Air Quality
and Emissions Trends
Report, 2003,*
Tables A-2 to A-9.

Substance	Industry[a]	Vehicles[b]	Other[c]	Total
Carbon monoxide	9,585	76,426	23,332	109,343
Nitrogen oxides	10,326	13,251	1,322	24,899
Sulfur dioxide	16,250	1,805	146	18,201
Volatile organic compounds	8,190	8,396	3,759	20,345
Particulates (PM_{10})	1,681	662	22,530	24,873
Particulates ($PM_{2.5}$)[d]	1,137	608	6,000	7,746
Lead	4	1	0	5
Totals	46,036	100,541	51,089	197,666
Percentages	**23%**	**49%**	**28%**	**100%**

[a]Includes industrial fuel combustion and industrial processes.
[b]Includes aircraft.
[c]Includes, *inter alia*, residential wood burning, agricultural burning, forest wildfires, structural fires, and (for particulates) fugitive dust.
[d]$PM_{2.5}$ is included in PM_{10} and not added into totals.

less, which are especially dangerous to human health because they go more deeply into the lungs.

- *Lead* (Pb) is a metal that causes seizures and mental retardation. With the elimination of leaded gasoline, the problem of lead in urban air has ended. Airborne lead is now a danger only in areas around lead processing sources such as lead smelters and battery plants.

With each criteria pollutant, the EPA sets standards for maximum concentrations. The CO standard, for example, is 9 parts per million (ppm) averaged over eight hours, or 35 ppm in one hour. As shown in Table 14.2, industrial activity is the source of less than one-quarter of aggregate criteria pollutant emissions. Note, however, that industry is the major source of both SO_2 and Pb. By far the largest industrial sources of criteria pollutants are coal-fired power plants.

To suppress criteria pollutants, the Clean Air Act mandates a range of expensive actions including, most importantly, emission controls on power plants, factories, smelters, and vehicles. Since controls began in 1970, emissions have dropped nearly one-fourth. Figure 14.2 shows how remarkable this reduction is, since it was achieved in an uphill battle against a growing economy.

Hazardous Air Pollutants

hazardous air pollutants
Chemicals that pose a health risk of serious illness such as cancer or birth defects even in small exposures.

Besides controlling the six criteria pollutants, the Clean Air Act mandates control of *hazardous air pollutants*. Hazardous air pollutants, sometimes called air toxics, cause or pose the risk of cancer and other serious health effects such as birth defects. The EPA has identified 329 air toxics and estimates overall annual releases at 4.7 million tons, only a fraction of 1 percent of the amount of criteria pollutants.[24] Examples are arsenic, benzine, chromium, radionuclides, and methyl chloride.

[24] Environmental Protection Agency, *National Air Quality and Emissions Trends Report* (Washington, DC: EPA, 2003), p. 64.

FIGURE 14.2
Declining
Emissions of
Six Criteria
Pollutants
(1970–2003)

Source: Adapted
from EPA, *FY 2003
Annual Report*, p. 29,
and "Air Emissions
Trends—Continued
Progress through
2003," www.epa.
gov/airtrends/
econ-emissions.html.

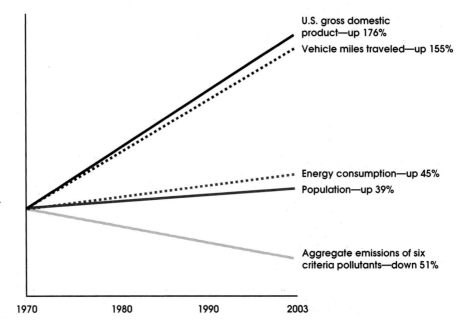

U.S. gross domestic
product—up 176%

Vehicle miles traveled—up 155%

Energy consumption—up 45%

Population—up 39%

Aggregate emissions of six
criteria pollutants—down 51%

1970   1980   1990   2003

Large industrial sources such as electric utilities, oil refineries, paper mills, and chemical plants are responsible for about 25 percent of air toxic releases. The remainder comes from smaller sources, such as dry cleaners and gas stations, and from mobile sources—for example, the organic gases and particulate matter in diesel exhaust are classified as air toxics.

The Clean Air Act requires the EPA to set emission standards for 188 air toxics at levels that prevent disease and requires industry to use the "maximum achievable control technology" to comply. In practice, *maximum achievable control technology* is emissions control equal to the control achieved by the best-performing 12 percent of sources in the industry. The agency has begun to set standards and monitor air toxic releases, but even before standard setting was completed and enforcement begun, air toxic releases declined significantly—about 60 percent between 1990 and 2000. Corporations are required to publicly reveal the amount of these chemicals they release, motivating them to reduce emissions. And other EPA actions reduced toxic emissions. For example, required reformulation of gasoline, intended to reduce criteria pollutants, has cut levels of the carcinogen benzene in urban air by almost 50 percent.[25] The EPA reports a broad, downward trend for the air toxics it monitors.

**maximum
achievable
control
technology**
A performance
standard used
by the EPA to
control emissions of hazardous air
pollutants. It
requires control
of toxic emissions equal to
(or better than)
that achieved
by the top
12 percent of
sources in the
industry.

Acid Precipitation

Acid precipitation is caused primarily by releases of two criteria pollutants, sulfur dioxide and nitrogen oxides. In the atmosphere, these gases undergo chemical

[25] Ibid.

TABLE 14.3 Annual Nationwide Emissions of Acid Rain Pollutants and Acid Rain Program Reduction Goals

Source: General Accounting Office, *Acid Rain*, GAO/RCED–00–47, March 2000, p. 5; and Environmental Protection Agency, *National Air Quality and Emissions Trends Report, 2003*, Tables A-4 and A-9.

	Annual Emissions (in millions of tons per year)			
	1980	**1990**	**2002**	**2010 Goal**
SO_2	25.9	23.7	18.2	15.9
NO_x	24.8	24.0	24.9	22.8

acid precipitation Deposition of acids formed when sulfur and nitrogen compounds undergo chemical reactions in the atmosphere. The phenomenon is often called acid rain, but it also occurs in other forms of deposition including snow, fog, and dry fallout of acidic particles.

reactions and return to earth as acids that alter the pH of water, degrading lakes and forests and causing deterioration of human structures. When Congress amended the Clean Air Act in 1990, it responded to public alarm about acid rain by requiring the EPA to reduce emissions of the two key precursor substances that cause it.

When the amendments were passed in 1990, annual nationwide SO_2 emissions totaled 23.7 million tons and NO_x emissions 24 million tons. Profligate amounts of these substances coming from coal-fired electric utility boilers in the Northeast and Midwest were blamed for degrading sensitive eastern lakes and forests located downwind of emission plumes. Coal combustion releases large amounts of SO_2 and NO_x. About two-thirds of the SO_2 in the United States comes from electric utilities and there are effective, though extremely expensive, methods for removing it from boiler exhaust streams. Electric utilities are responsible for only about one-fifth of the nation's NO_x, but control equipment is less effective.

So far, the acid rain program has had promising results. It has reduced utility pollution. Power plant emissions of SO_2 are down 38 percent and emissions of NO_x are down 37 percent from their levels in 1990 at the program's inception.[26] The Office of Management and Budget found that acid rain regulation had the largest monetized human health benefits of any federal regulatory program— $80 billion over 10 years—and a 40 to 1 ratio of annual benefits over costs.[27] However, ecosystem recovery is elusive. The EPA estimates that utility emissions need to be cut by another two-thirds to revive sensitive lakes and forest soils in the Northeast and Upper Midwest. And, as Table 14.3 shows, although nationwide emissions of SO_2 from all sources are dropping, there is no overall reduction of NO_x. More reduction is needed. The United States is far behind Japan, the world leader in reducing acid rain emissions. Japanese SO_2 and NO_x emissions, measured in grams per kilowatt hour of electricity generated, are only 5 percent and 12 percent, respectively, of U.S. emissions.[28]

[26] Environmental Protection Agency, *EPA Acid Rain Program: 2003 Progress Report* (Washington, DC: EPA Office of Air and Radiation, September 2004), pp. 1 and 7.

[27] Office of Management and Budget, *Informing Regulatory Decisions: 2003 Report to Congress on the Costs and Benefits of Federal Regulations* (Washington, DC: OMB Office of Information and Regulatory Affairs, 2003), pp. 7–8.

[28] Osmu Sawaji, "Clear Skies over Tokyo," *Look Japan*, January 2004, p. 7.

Indoor Air Pollution

Indoor air in developed nations is contaminated by a mixture of harmful substances. These include asbestos, radon, tobacco smoke, combustion by-products from cooking, chlorine gas released from chlorinated water, biological contaminants such as mite dust, and vapors from household insecticides, glues, and paints. They pose serious health problems because Americans spend 80 to 90 percent of their lives indoors, where concentrations of air pollutants can be two- to five-times greater than in outdoor air. *Radon,* for example, is a colorless, odorless, radioactive gas commonly found in soils. It seeps up from the ground into homes, building up to dangerous concentrations in still air. Radon causes an estimated 15,400 to 21,800 lung cancer deaths yearly.[29] This is more than 10 times the estimated number of cancer deaths from all toxic chemical emissions by industry.

In 1987 the EPA ranked indoor air as one of the top five human health risks, but the agency has done little about the problem. Congress is reluctant to let EPA inspectors invade homes and offices with air sampling equipment, forms, and ticket books. Beyond spending on research that is very modest in relation to the risks posed, the agency has a voluntary radon measurement program and publishes information to educate the public. Meanwhile, the health problem grows worse as more tightly sealed, energy-efficient buildings trap pollutants. It is estimated that indoor air annually causes 85,000 to 150,000 deaths, compared to between 65,000 and 200,000 deaths from outdoor air pollution.[30]

Ozone-Destroying Chemicals

While ozone in tropospheric smog is regarded as a pollutant, ozone in the stratosphere screens out ultraviolet energy harmful to living tissue. Emissions of long-lived molecules such as *chlorofluorocarbons* (CFCs), halons in fire extinguishers, the solvent carbon tetrachloride, and other chemicals pose a threat to the ozone layer. CFCs, used primarily as refrigerants, are a family of large, tough molecules that persist until they reach the upper atmosphere, where the energy in ultraviolet radiation breaks them apart. They have extreme longevity, typically 50 to 100 years, and in one case up to 1,700 years. When a CFC molecule migrates into the upper atmosphere, its breakdown releases chlorine atoms, starting a chain reaction that consumes thousands of ozone molecules. Other ozone-destroying substances create similar chain reactions.

In high latitudes, the ozone layer has thinned as much as 30 percent as a consequence of the action of these industrial chemicals. This exposes planetary life and ecosystems to higher ultraviolet radiation, causing skin cancers, eye cataracts, weakened immune systems, lowered crop yields, and other ill effects. Even the highest levels of ozone in urban smog are inadequate to protect humans from radiation damage. Ninety percent of ozone resides in the stratosphere.

radon
An inert, colorless, odorless, radioactive gas found in soil and rock formations. It is a naturally occurring decay product of radium.

chlorofluorocarbons
Compounds of chlorine, fluorine, and carbon created by industry for use as refrigerants, aerosol propellants, foams, and solvents. They are inert and exceptionally stable, but break down in the upper atmosphere in ozone-consuming reactions.

[29] Jonathan M. Samet, "Risk Assessment and Child Health," *Pediatrics,* April 2004, p. 952. See also, R. W. Field et al., "Residential Radon Gas Exposure and Lung Cancer," *American Journal of Epidemiology,* June 2000.

[30] Bjørn Lomborg, *The Skeptical Environmentalist* (Cambridge: Cambridge University Press, 2001), p. 184, citing Centers for Disease Control figures.

In 1987 a treaty called the Montreal Protocol set timetables to phase out worldwide use of 96 ozone-depleting chemicals. To meet treaty obligations, the United States and other developed nations ceased production of CFCs in 1996. Production of other ozone-depleting chemicals will end in 2010. Developing nations, however, have not met even the more extended timetables given them for ceasing production and consumption in the treaty. Compliance is difficult for several reasons. Substitutes for CFCs, the primary ozone-depleting chemicals, are more expensive and many businesses in poor and transitional countries cannot afford the cost of conversion. Economic turmoil in the Russian Federation slowed phase-out there. Economic growth in Asia has led to increased use of CFCs. Around the world, a thriving black market in CFCs exists to avoid taxes and penalties imposed by governments.

Despite such problems, progress is substantial. The United Nations recently estimated that without the Montreal Protocol, by 2050 only 30 percent of the ozone layer would be left in higher latitudes. Increased radiation would cause more than 20 million additional skin cancers and 130 million more eye cataracts.[31] However, if the treaty is carried out, scientists estimated that by 2050 the ozone layer will return to 1980 levels.

Greenhouse Gases

greenhouse gases
Atmospheric gases that absorb energy radiated from the earth, preventing it from being released into space.

The industrial revolution led to rising emissions of a group of gases, called *greenhouse gases,* that trap heat in the atmosphere instead of allowing it to radiate into space. Electrons in the atoms of greenhouse gas molecules are excited by the energy in infrared wavelengths of outgoing terrestrial radiation, causing atmospheric heating. The most important of the greenhouse gases is carbon dioxide (CO_2), which makes up about 60 percent of greenhouse gas emissions. Between 1850 and 2004, CO_2 resident in the earth's atmosphere rose from about 280 to 380 parts per million by volume. Wood and fossil fuel combustion have released such huge amounts of carbon that natural processes of carbon absorption by forests and oceans are overwhelmed. So more carbon remains in the atmosphere as CO_2.

Over the last century, the global mean surface air temperature warmed an estimated 0.6° Celsius. A scientific consensus has grown that this warming is caused by greenhouse gas emissions and added warming of 1.4° to 5.8° Celsius (2.5° to 10.4° Farenheit) will follow by 2100.[32] This warming is expected to cause disruptive climate change.

The major effort to slow global warming is an international treaty, the Kyoto Protocol, which went into effect in 2005. It requires industrial nations to cut emissions of six primary greenhouse gases an average of 5.2 percent below 1990 levels by 2012.[33] The United States is not a party to the Kyoto Protocol because it has never been submitted to the Senate for ratification. Tremendous political opposition exists because it calls on the United States, which emits 36 percent of global

[31] United Nations Environment Programme, *Backgrounder: Basic Facts and Data on the Science and Politics of Ozone Protection* (Nairobe, Kenya: UNEP, October 5, 2001), p. 5.

[32] See the third report of the Intergovernmental Panel on Climate Change: J. T. Houghton et al., eds., *Climate Change 2001: The Scientific Basis* (Cambridge: Cambridge University Press, 2001), pp. 2 and 13.

[33] The six main greenhouse gases are carbon dioxide (CO_2), methane ($C4_4$), nitrous oxide (N_2O), hydrofluorocarbons (HFCs), perfluorocarbons (PFCs), and sulphur hexaflouride (SF_6).

warming gases, to undertake the greatest percentage reductions of any nation—7 percent below 1990 emission levels. U.S. CO_2 emissions have risen by as much as 3 percent a year since 1990, so this 7 percent reduction actually requires a 30 percent reduction of the emissions that are predicted in 2012 absent reduction measures. Opponents say that American consumers would bear a heavy cost to meet this target and that more American jobs would move overseas.

Developing nations, including China, India, Mexico, Brazil, and Nigeria, are not committed to reductions under the treaty because of their fear that greenhouse gas emission cuts would slow economic growth. Since they are not making cuts, global emissions will continue to rise even as the treaty is enforced. Scientists estimate that treaty reductions will have little effect on climate change. One projection is that temperature increases and sea level rises predicted for 2100 will be delayed only six years, until 2106.[34] However, signatory nations have agreed to negotiate added rounds of emission cuts to come after 2012.

The EPA has only voluntary programs to reduce greenhouse emissions. An example is Green Lights, a project that encourages companies to install low-energy lighting. Such programs produce only infinitesimal CO_2 emissions reductions.[35] Recently, the agency rejected a petition by environmentalists to regulate CO_2 under the Clean Air Act, saying that because CO_2 is not classified as a pollutant this would exceed its authority.[36] In 2002 President Bush announced a voluntary initiative to reduce the *emissions intensity* of greenhouse gases by 18 percent by 2012. Emissions intensity is the amount of greenhouse gases emitted per unit of economic output, measured as tons of emissions per million dollars of GDP.

emissions intensity
The amount of greenhouse gases emitted per unit of economic output, measured as tons of emissions per million dollars of the gross domestic product.

Because of growing energy efficiency, emissions intensity will decline about 14 percent by 2012 anyway, so the 18 percent goal is modest.[37] The Bush administration plan allows total emissions to rise even as their proportion to economic output falls. Overall, no regulatory authority exists to limit greenhouse emissions significantly. However, some large U.S. corporations are making voluntary emissions cuts, because (1) they operate in the European Union where Kyoto measures are being enforced, (2) they often can lower operating costs by reducing energy use, and (3) they anticipate stricter regulation.

Water

The basic statute for fighting water pollution is the Federal Water Pollution Control Act Amendments of 1972, usually called the Clean Water Act. Congress intended it to be a powerful measure that would stop the deterioration of the nation's lakes, rivers, streams, and estuaries. The act set a goal of eliminating *all* polluting discharges into these waters by 1985. However, the goal was not met and will not soon be met.

[34] Lomborg, *The Skeptical Environmentalist,* p. 304.

[35] Guy Gugliotta and Eric Pianin, "Bush Plans on Global Warming Alter Little; Voluntary Programs Attract Few Firms," *Washington Post,* January 1, 2004, p. A1.

[36] *International Center for Technology Assessment v. Browner,* Docket No. A–2000–04, denied August 28, 2003 (68 FR 52922, September 8, 2003).

[37] General Accounting Office, *Climate Change: Preliminary Observations on the Administration's February 2002 Climate Initiative,* GAO–04–131T, October 1, 2003, p. 1.

The Clean Water Act is effective in reducing, but not eliminating, polluted factory outflows, or effluents. Every industrial plant uses water, and sources of pollution are numerous. In production processes, water is used as a washing, scrubbing, cooling, or mixing medium. It becomes contaminated with a variety of particles and dissolved chemicals. The Clean Water Act prohibits the release of any polluted factory discharge without a permit.

The EPA regulates industrial effluents from "point sources," that is, sites that discharge from a single location, using a permit system called the National Pollution Discharge Elimination System (NPDES). Under the NPDES, each industrial facility must get a permit specifying the volume of one or more substances it can pour into a water body. Effluent limits are based on scientific estimates of how much of a substance the water body can absorb before deteriorating unacceptably and on the ability of available equipment to remove a particular pollutant. The EPA sets water quality criteria for pollutants. Usually there are two standards, one for protecting human health and the other for aquatic life. To give examples, the chloroform standard prohibits chronic exposure of aquatic life to concentrations of more than 1,240 µg/l (micrograms per cubic liter) and exposure of humans to more than 470 µg/l. As noted, permit limits are also based on how much pollution the best control devices can remove from wastewater. These devices range from simple screens for large particles to intricate chemical and biological treatment systems.

For example, plants that make paperboard out of wastepaper have small amounts of the wood preservative pentachlorophenol (C_6HCl_5O) in their wastewater streams. C_6HCl_5O is so poisonous that swallowing one-tenth of an ounce, about a teaspoon, can be lethal. However, for this substance the EPA has defined the best control technology standard as effluent containing no more than 0.87 pound of C_6HCl_5O for each 1 million pounds of paperboard produced because the best control technology cannot remove more of it. In other words, a paperboard factory can drain almost 14 ounces of C_6HCl_5O into a river or stream every time it makes a million pounds of paperboard. Currently, about 96,000 facilities operate under an NPDES permit.

While the EPA has limited factory discharges, "nonpoint" effluent, or runoff that enters surface waters from diffuse sources, is largely uncontrolled. Runoff from agriculture—animal wastes, pesticides, and fertilizers—is now the primary cause of impaired water bodies. Although general language in the Clean Water Act permits the EPA to act against any source of water pollution, the law avoided specific language aimed at farmers because of their political power. However, growing pollution from big animal feedlots and poultry farms led the EPA to place several thousand factory farms under permits.

Urban runoff is another major contributor to poor water quality. As urban areas increase in size, more water flows over their streets, collecting pollutants and carrying them to water bodies. The Clean Water Act empowers the EPA to require control measures by cities, including detention ponds, street sweeping, and public education programs. Nonpoint sources are now the biggest contributors to water pollution and efforts to control them are just beginning.

Overall, the quality of surface waters is much improved from 1972 when the Clean Water Act was passed. Then, it was estimated that only 30 to 40 percent of the nation's waters met the law's water quality goals.[38] Today, 60 to 90 percent do.[39] However, progress from now on will be difficult. The current Clean Water Act emphasizes control of point source pollution by industry using end-of-the-pipe equipment. Yet the biggest source of pollution now is copious and little-controlled runoff from farms and cities. Adequate regulation of runoff requires a revision of the law to give the EPA new tools and powers. The existing permit system is ill-suited to control nonpoint pollution.

Land

After Congress passed air and water pollution control laws early in the 1970s, it became apparent that poor handling and disposal of solid hazardous wastes was a major problem. Also, devices that removed air- and waterborne poisons from industrial processes under the new laws produced tons of poisoned sludge, slime, and dust that ended up in poorly contained landfills. Authority over the handling of hazardous waste was inadequate to prevent mismanagement. Responding to the menace, Congress passed two laws.

The Resource Conservation and Recovery Act (RCRA) of 1976 gave the EPA authority to manage hazardous waste "from cradle to grave," that is, from the moment it is created to the moment it is finally destroyed or interred. Firms must label, handle, store, treat, and discard hazardous waste under strict guidelines, keeping meticulous records all the while.

The RCRA is a difficult statute to administer and with which to comply. It demands that regulators keep track of literally all hazardous waste produced anywhere in the country—an exhausting job. It relies on smothering command-and-control regulation and prohibits balancing costs against benefits. One indication of the regulatory burden it imposes is that when it was first implemented, nearly 80 percent of the nation's waste disposal facilities elected to close rather than comply with it. Figure 14.3 illustrates a typical installation of wells required to monitor groundwater quality under a solid-waste disposal site.

The RCRA is, in the words of one observer, "an amazingly inflexible law with extraordinarily detailed regulations, demanding controls, and a glacially slow permitting system [that] entails almost astronomically high costs."[40] One steel company had to wait seven months simply for a permit to put a fence around its waste pit and use propane-powered cannons to scare animals away.[41] Because the law contains no requirement that the benefits of regulation exceed its costs, it has invited many lawsuits by industry. The chemical industry sued the EPA for trying to regulate residue from the treatment of hazardous waste without taking into account whether the residue was hazardous or not. It lost the case.[42] General Motors

[38] Kevin Kane, *How's the Water? The State of the Nation's Water Quality,* Working Paper 171 (St. Louis: Center for the Study of American Business, January 2000), p. 3.

[39] U.S. Census Bureau, *Statistical Abstract of the United States, 2003,* 123rd ed. (Washington, DC, 2003), Table 369.

[40] Robert J. Smith, "RCRA Lives, Alas," *Regulation,* Summer 1991, p. 14.

[41] General Accounting Office, *Hazardous Waste: Progress under the Corrective Action Program Is Limited,* GAO/RCED–98–3, October 1997, p. 9.

[42] *American Chemistry Council v. EPA,* 337 F.3d 1060 (2003).

FIGURE 14.3 RCRA Landfill Groundwater Monitoring Requirements
The EPA grants permits to all operators of hazardous waste dumps that comply with standards for physical layout, groundwater monitoring, and emergency planning. The drawing is a cross section of ground below a landfill illustrating minimal RCRA monitoring requirements. Water samples drawn from downgradient wells can detect chemical contamination seeping into the groundwater (saturated zone) from the landfill above.

Source: Environmental Protection Agency.

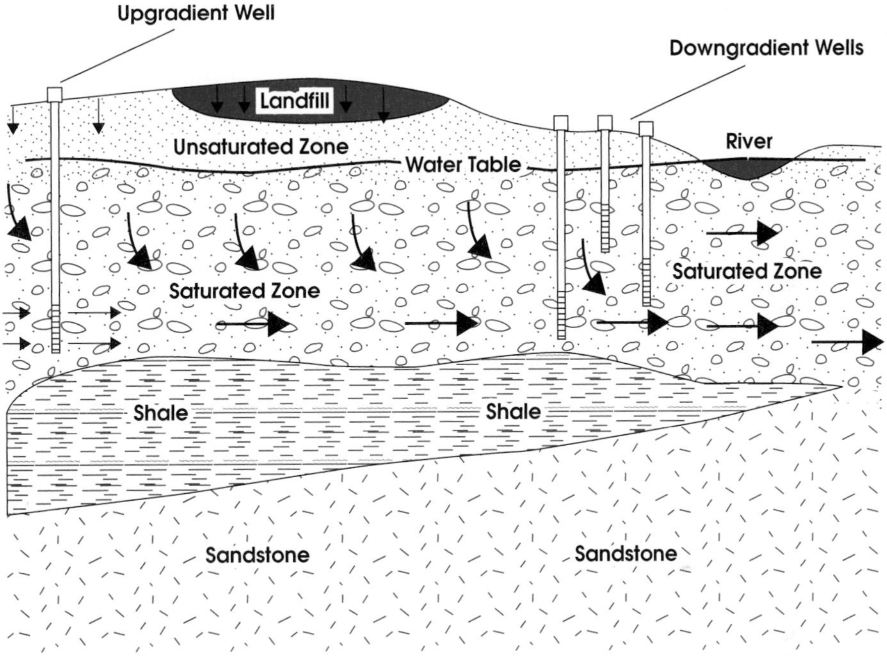

Superfund
The program to clean up abandoned toxic waste sites set up by the Comprehensive Environmental Response, Compensation, and Liability Act of 1980. It takes its name from the trust fund in which the program's money for cleanup projects is held.

uses solvents to clean automobile spray painting guns when it changes colors, then recirculates them until, after repeated uses, they go to a waste tank. GM sued when the EPA tried to impose hazardous waste regulations on the recirculation piping. It argued that the solvents were not a waste while still in use during an industrial process. GM lost when the case was dismissed.[43] Strict enforcement invites litigation over such pinhead technicalities, but there is no question that hazardous waste is much better handled than before the RCRA.

While the RCRA ensured that existing facilities would operate at a high standard, it did nothing about thousands of abandoned toxic waste sites around the country. So Congress passed another law to clean them up. This law is the Comprehensive Environmental Response, Compensation, and Liability Act of 1980, better known as *Superfund,* so-named after the large trust fund it set up to pay for cleanups. This trust fund was generated from special taxes on oil and chemical companies and a small—0.12 percent—addition to the general corporate income

[43] *General Motors v. EPA,* 363 F.3d 442 (2003).

tax. However, the taxes expired in 1995 and Congress, under pressure from industry, has refused to reinstate them. About 80 percent of Superfund money now comes from Congressional appropriations, which have declined by 21 percent since the taxes expired.[44] Most of the rest comes from payments by companies responsible for contaminating sites.

Congress intended Superfund to be a temporary measure that would be phased out when existing hazardous sites were cleaned. However, the number of sites is higher than predicted and the cleaning process more difficult and expensive than envisioned in 1980. After passage of the law, the EPA set up a priority list of sites posing the greatest risk to human health and the environment, usually because of groundwater or drinking water contamination. Since then, 1,523 sites have been on this priority list. Only 274 have been removed with cleanup work completed.[45] Cleanup is in progress at another 360.[46] As completed sites depart the list, new ones rotate on from a waiting list of another 2,500 eligible sites. The priority list still contains about 1,240 heavily contaminated sites.

Superfund sites are complicated and expensive to restore. A major project takes a decade and costs $20 to $30 million. Methods of decontamination and containment differ from site to site. In San Bernardino, California, two plumes of groundwater contaminated by chemicals used in metal plating have moved as far as eight miles under the city. At a cost of more than $100 million so far, the EPA dug seven wells that extract water from the leading edge of the underground stream. The wells pump 14,000 gallons per minute through four miles of large water mains laid under city streets for the project. The water goes to a treatment plant, where toxic chemicals are removed using activated charcoal. In Midvale, Utah, a milling plant that extracted lead, zinc, and copper from ore closed in 1971, leaving mounds of tailings up to 50 feet high. High winds blew particles of lead, cadmium, and arsenic from the piles into the surrounding community, where they contaminated soils.[47] The EPA is building a cap made of soil mixed with a stabilizing chemical to prevent wind erosion.

Sometimes, for example, when dirt is contaminated by dioxins from herbicide manufacturing, EPA rules require that it be dug up and incinerated at high temperatures. Figure 14.4 shows a diagram of an incinerator. At a rate of 20 tons per hour and a cost of about $1,200 per ton, excavated soil is trucked to a giant revolving kiln, where it is heated to 1,800° F to break down the hazardous organic compounds into simple molecules of CO_2 and H_2O. The dirt is then backfilled.

Superfund cleanups must conform to strict RCRA standards. In incineration, for example, the standard for dioxins requires 99.9999 percent destruction efficiency, that is, for every 1 million molecules entering the incinerator, only 1 can emerge. Waste

[44] General Accounting Office, *Superfund Program: Breakdown of Appropriations Data,* GAO–04–787R, May 14, 2004, p. 3.

[45] Katherine N. Probst and Diane Sherman, *Success for Superfund: A New Approach for Keeping Score* (Washington, DC: Resources for the Future, April 2004), p. 1. Figures are for 2003.

[46] Figure is for 2004. For current figures see www.epa.gov/superfund/.

[47] These examples are in General Accounting Office, *Superfund: Analysis of Costs at Five Superfund Sites,* GAO/RCED–00–22, January 2000, apps. I and IV.

FIGURE 14.4 Typical Rotary Kiln Incinerator at a Superfund Site

Source: EPA. From: General Accounting Office, *Superfund: EPA Could Further Ensure the Safe Operation of On-Site Incinerators*, GAO/RCED–97–43, March 1997, p. 4.

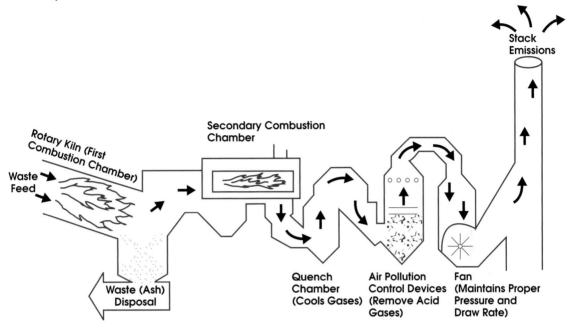

ash is treated and disposed of as hazardous waste. Incinerators are surrounded by air pollution monitors that set off alarms if stack emissions fail to meet standards.

Who pays for all this? The law establishes harsh rules of liability for any company that has ever dumped hazardous waste in a Superfund site. In legal terminology, this liability is strict, retroactive, and joint and several. In practical terms, this means that any company that ever dumped hazardous waste on a site can be responsible for the full cleanup cost even if it obeyed the law of years past, was not negligent, and dumped only a small part of the total waste. So far, the EPA has spent about $27 billion fixing contaminated sites, but it has recovered $21 billion. The job is far from over. It is estimated that the program will cost the EPA another $15 billion by 2009.[48]

ASSESSING THE NATION'S ENVIRONMENTAL LAWS

How well do the laws work? A fair overall assessment is that while they have forced industry to cut emissions and have reduced hazards to public health and the environment, they are flawed in important ways. Basic statutes were passed in the 1970s, before the nation had much experience with the complex task of environmental regulation. The laws of the 1970s are now called "first generation" laws

[48] General Accounting Office, *Superfund Program: Current Status and Future Fiscal Challenges*, GAO–03–850, July 2003, p. 27.

in anticipation of a second generation of laws in which Congress incorporates lessons of experience. The great strength of these early laws is that they set very high standards, enforcement of which is strict. Their weaknesses, however, are multiple and include the following.

- *Inconsistent philosophy.* The costs of environmental protection are high, yet major statutes differ in allowing money to be taken into consideration. The Toxic Substances Control Act permits balancing public health benefits against pollution control costs. The Clean Air Act, however, forbids considering costs and mandates air quality standards that protect against "any adverse health effects," presumably at any cost. A central lesson from more than three decades of environmental enforcement is that the costs of absolute purity and total risk elimination are usually prohibitive.

- *Rigidity.* The laws most often rely on a command-and-control philosophy of regulation that allows little leeway in compliance. In enforcing the Clean Water Act, for example, the EPA specifies the procedures for testing water samples down to the capacity of laboratory glassware. If a test requires a 100-milliliter beaker, the lab cannot deviate from this size without submitting a formal application for modification.

- *Bureaucratic sluggishness.* The EPA is a massive, complex bureaucracy under constant budget constraints and its mechanisms grind slowly. While the agency tries to improve its administrative efficiency, its actions are delayed by bureaucratic tendencies such as the need for multiple approvals, a predilection for undertaking lengthy reviews, and fear of deviation from procedures.

- *Complexity.* Air emissions at large industrial plants such as petroleum refineries, chemical plants, and electric power stations are often controlled under multiple laws and regulatory programs. Chemical plants, for example, are subject to as many as 16 different emission-control programs. These programs can have different goals, timetables, permits, rules, and paperwork, imposing a confusing burden of duties on management.

- *Adversarial approach.* The EPA's inflexible manner of regulation lends itself to a combative style in which there is heavy emphasis on penalizing violators.

transmedia pollution
The phenomenon of pollutants moving from one environmental medium—air, land, or water—to another after being trapped in pollution control devices and being disposed of.

- *Transmedia pollution.* The basic laws are inadequate to deal with pollution that moves between water, air, and/or land. When pollutants are caught in control devices, they are not destroyed but merely trapped and eventually transferred elsewhere in the environment (one exception is high-temperature incineration that breaks down dangerous molecules into harmless water vapor, oxygen, and simple organic compounds). For example, devices that remove small particles from coal boiler exhaust create a sludge containing impurities found in coal, including mercury, arsenic, and radioactive particles. The sludge is dumped in landfills that then become hazardous waste sites. At these landfills, aromatic compounds from the sludge can evaporate back into the atmosphere, and other pollutants can bind with soil particles or seep into groundwater. Typically, older statutes direct that a pollutant be controlled in one medium without full consideration of its migration to another, reflecting the more limited scientific understanding of the 1970s.

For many years, business has advocated changes in environmental laws. Industrial companies facing heavy compliance requirements would like to see much more flexibility. Industry has suggested setting targets, then letting corporations achieve emission cuts in innovative and cost-effective ways. It wants more market-oriented enforcement such as the emissions trading regime set up to reduce pollutants that cause acid rain. And it wants more flexibility in compliance rules for corporations that set up voluntary pollution-reduction programs. These proposals have a wide following, even in the EPA, and the agency runs a series of pilot and experimental programs incorporating such ideas. However, until environmental statutes are rewritten based on a changed regulatory philosophy, the future application of such experiments is limited.

CONCLUDING OBSERVATIONS

Industrial processes damage the environment and cause serious local and global deterioration. A first wave of environmental statutes in the United States has reduced pollution and deterioration, primarily through rigid and expensive regulations. Now that experience has been gained with these laws, their high cost, inflexibility, and adversarial nature are seen as shortcomings. There are many suggestions for more cost-effective and flexible regulation. In the next chapter we discuss methods for determining how regulatory programs can become more efficient and effective and also what corporations are doing to reduce pollution and protect the environment.

Owls, Loggers, and Old-Growth Forests

On May 25, 2001, John Shelk, the great grandson of the founder of the Ochoco Lumber Co., reluctantly closed the company's Prineville, Oregon, sawmill after 63 years of operation. It was a bad day, but the people of Oregon are used to such news. In the previous 10 years, 89 sawmills had closed in the state.

For the small logging community of Prineville, it was a disaster. One-hundred and eighty jobs and a payroll of nearly $5 million a year evaporated. Another $8 to $10 million a year paid to contract loggers and truck drivers disappeared. The $15 million or so a year that the company paid into the United States Treasury for timber purchases on federal lands vanished.[1] Under current revenue sharing policy, 25 percent of money generated on federal lands is shared with local government to support local schools and road construction—a loss to Prineville of about $3.75 million a year.

Beyond the economic toll, Prineville lost a socially responsible citizen. The Ochoco Lumbermill gave scholarships to 50 college students. Along with other firms, it had helped build the high school stadium and a local museum. Dislocated mill workers lacked opportunities. The Viles family, for instance, lost two salaries. Dan Viles, 51, a skilled lumber grader, was out of a job after 19 years at the mill. His wife Teena, a planer lead person, had worked there for 15 years. The Vileses are eligible for federally funded retraining. Dan took some aptitude tests that showed he would be a good short-order cook or brewmaster. However, there is little prospect of finding such jobs in Prineville now.

The Prineville sawmill took felled trees from surrounding forests, mostly ponderosa pine, and turned them into boards and molding. Its output was in high

[1] Statement of Bruce Daucsavage, prepared for the Subcommittee on Public Lands and Forests, Energy and Natural Resources Committee, U.S. Senate, October 2, 2001, p. 4.

demand. Consumption of lumber in the United States is rising. Prineville is also home to several manufacturing companies that took the high-quality pine lumber and turned it into products such as doors, windows, and cabinets. Thus, lack of demand did not shutter the mill.

Lack of raw timber did. Until the late 1970s the sawmill used large logs from the surrounding forests of central and eastern Oregon. The U.S. Forest Service conducted frequent timber sales. Ochoco Lumber Co. bid on stands of trees, and if the bid was accepted, the company sent a check to the agency, hired loggers to cut the trees, and engaged independent truck drivers to bring the raw logs to the mill's pond.

Then, growing national debate about the uses of wilderness areas caused the Forest Service to impose restrictive new rules. Some ancient forests were closed to timber sales. Clear-cutting, the common practice of felling every tree in an area, was forbidden. Many timber sales allowed only the thinning of stands in younger forests, resulting in harvests of smaller diameter logs.

The Ochoco Lumbermill adjusted to these changes. It bought 60,000 acres of forests to supply part of its sawtimber needs, about 20 percent. By the late 1980s it had spent more than $15 million on new machinery that was more efficient for small-log milling. However, almost as soon as this capital investment was made, the Forest Service again cut back on timber sales, this time because of lawsuits by environmental groups to protect the northern spotted owl. Lacking the needed flow of sawtimber, the mill closed.

The northern spotted owl (*Strix occidentalis caurina*) is a reclusive, nocturnal bird that lives deep in the forests of Washington, Oregon, and northern California. Since the 1800s timber cutting and land development have reduced the owl's habitat by as much as 80 percent, threatening its extinction. Congress passed the Endangered Species Act in 1973 to prevent the demise of such creatures, and in 1990 the owl was added to the list of species entitled to special protection.

Unfortunately for the wood products industry, the owls live in the most productive timber lands of the Pacific Northwest. Their predicament has caused federal timber harvests to decline more than 90 percent. It is this decline that starved the saws in Prineville—and in many other small mill towns in the forested regions of the West coast. An industry and a way of life are moribund. This is the story.

THE NORTHERN SPOTTED OWL

The northern spotted owl is a perch-and-dive predator with a wingspan of 2 feet and a weight of about 1½ pounds. Its body is mottled brown with patches of white. Its habitat ranges from British Columbia in the north to the redwood stands above San Francisco in the south.

Like other owls, the northern spotted owl is anatomically adapted to nighttime activity. It has a large head and a large brain, compared with other birds, and big round eyes. "Indeed," notes one biologist, "the heads of owls are basically little more than brains with raptorial beaks and the largest possible eyes and ears attached."[2] Spotted owls' eyes have rod-rich retinas, endowing them with exceptionally acute black-and-white vision in low-light conditions. They can locate and dive on scampering mice in illuminations as much as 30 times below the lowest reported human visual threshold.

Their hearing is similarly acute. Without benefit of vision, they can locate tree squirrels or mice that make small rustling noises in frequency ranges inaudible to humans. Their brains calculate time lags of microseconds in the arrival of sounds at each ear, enabling them to fly unerringly through darkness to a sound source. The spotted owl, despite its sedentary daytime roosting, has a high metabolism and hunts actively through the night. Its prey is mainly small mammals such as flying squirrels, wood rats, rabbits, mice, and tree voles, but it also kills reptiles and small birds.

Northern spotted owls exhibit a wide range of social behavior. They have courtship rituals, and pairs bond for extended periods. They communicate with postural signals, displays of aggression, and a variety of hoots and calls. They are territorial and announce their presence with a series of four hoots (described phonetically as "hooo hoo hoo hooo").[3] These low hoots have long wavelengths especially suited for penetrating dense foliage. The territory of a mated spotted owl pair is huge; observation with radiotelemetry reveals foraging

[2] Paul A. Johnsgard, *North American Owls: Biology and Natural History* (Washington, DC: Smithsonian Institution Press, 1988), p. 42.

[3] This is what ornithologists refer to as its "four-note location call." It has other vocalizations as well, including "barks" and whistles. U.S. Department of the Interior, *Recovery Plan for the Northern Spotted Owl—Draft* (Washington, DC: U.S. Government Printing Office, April 1992), p. 15.

The northern spotted owl. Source: U.S. Fish and Wildlife Service.

ranges from 1,000 to 27,000 acres.[4] Reproduction occurs in spring and summer, when females lay an average of two eggs. After hatching, the young owls are cared for by the parents for only a month before flying away to establish their own territories.

OLD GROWTH

Spotted owls prefer old-growth forests. Forests develop in stages, during which they undergo changes in composition. Although the definition of an old-growth forest is not precise, it is generally held to be a forest that is 200 or more years old. Such ancient forests are more structurally and biologically complex than younger forests.

Old-growth forests achieve great natural beauty and inspire comparisons with cathedrals. They have much richer biotic communities than younger forests and are repositories for species that have adapted to ecological niches created under old-growth conditions.

[4] Ibid., p. 23.

The spotted owl is one such species. The dense vegetation protects them from predators such as the red-tailed hawk. A thick, multilayered forest canopy also provides thermal cover, insulating them from extremes of heat and cold. Owls nest in the cavities of standing snags, and fallen snags create conditions that support abundant prey to satisfy their voracious appetites. The spotted owl plays a role in the old-growth ecosystem by culling small mammal and bird populations.

Early studies of northern spotted owls suggested that they lived only in old-growth stands.[5] Biologists believed that the owl was like a canary in a coal mine. If the owl at the top of the forest food chain was in danger of extinction, this was a warning that other species and the old-growth habitat itself were also endangered. Subsequent studies have shown that some northern spotted owls live and breed in younger forests and forests that have been logged.

Some owls do try to nest, roost, and forage in early-succession forests, but ornithologists believe that these are juvenile owls dispersing from old-growth stands. Spotted owls are territorial, live up to 18 years, and maintain large domains in remaining stands of old growth. This makes it difficult for juvenile owls to stake out territories in the limited stands of high structural complexity. Therefore, some young owls leaving nests after breeding season are pushed into younger forests. They forage and breed there, but scientists believe that their reproduction and survival rates are lowered.

LOSS OF OLD GROWTH IMPERILS THE SPOTTED OWL

The expansion of America came at the expense of wilderness. When pilgrims landed at Plymouth Rock, the landmass destined to become the continental United States had 850 million acres of forest. By the 1920s only 138 million acres of virgin forest remained, roughly 16 percent of what had existed.[6] The rest had been burned, grazed, cut, radically

[5] A study in Washington, for example, found that 97 percent of spotted owls lived in old growth, with no known reproductive pairs in second-growth areas. "Proposed Threatened Status for the Northern Spotted Owl," 54 FR 26668, June 23, 1989.

[6] Figures for forest size are from Michael Williams, *Americans and Their Forests: A Historical Geography* (New York: Cambridge University Press, 1989), pp. 3–4.

disturbed, or converted to other uses. Reduction of forest area stopped in the 1870s, and, on balance, regrowth now exceeds losses.

The northwest coastal forest inhabited by spotted owls covered about 94 million acres in the 1860s when settlers and loggers first arrived. Today only about 30 million acres of this coastal forest remain, including just 7.7 million acres of old growth. Much of this old growth is not contiguous; rather, it is a checkerboard of old stands mixed with bare timber-harvest areas, young growth, and tree farms. Of these 7.7 million acres, 2.8 million acres are in national parks or wilderness areas closed forever to logging. By the late 1980s about 2 percent of the remaining 4.9 million acres of old growth was being cut each year, largely for timber sales on federal lands. At this rate, nearly all old-growth habitat outside national parks would have been gone in 50 years.

Little remaining old growth is on private land; most is on federal land managed by the Forest Service and the Bureau of Land Management. These agencies are required by law to open forests for "multiple use" activities such as logging, mining, and recreation. So they hold timber auctions in which logging companies bid for the right to fell selected stands of timber. Once the winning bids are picked, timber harvesting proceeds based on precise regulations describing boundaries, logging techniques, and the restoration and replanting that is necessary. In 60 years a replanted forest can be reharvested; a high-density replanting will yield more timber than the original old growth.

In 1989 government biologists estimated that there were only 1,550 breeding pairs of the owls in the Pacific Northwest.[7] This low count worried scientists who believed that the owl was on the margin of survival as a species.[8] When species decline to very low numbers, there is danger that even if human impacts are reduced or removed, events in nature, such as random fluctuations of climate or food supply, cannot be overcome. When numbers fall, the reproductive pattern of the species is critical. Unfortunately, the spotted owl has a very low reproductive efficiency. A mated pair produces an average of .50 young per year. Then juvenile owls suffer an 88 percent morality rate in their first year.[9]

ENVIRONMENTALIST CAMPAIGN TO PROTECT THE OWL

In the 1980s environmental groups took up the cause of the northern spotted owl. They believed that the owl had intrinsic, unlimited value as a species; its extinction would be an irrevocable mistake. Equally important, they knew that the owl's use of old growth as habitat made saving owls a convenient pretext for saving ancient forests from the logger's ax. Using the owl, they could invoke the Endangered Species Act and elevate the goal of forest preservation above the economic interests of timber companies, lumber mills, and loggers.

The Endangered Species Act is an exceptionally strong statute. Passed in 1973, it set forth procedures for designating, or "listing," such species. The act defines an *endangered* species as one that is "in danger of extinction throughout all or a significant portion of its range." It also permits listing of a *threatened* species that is "likely to become an endangered species in the future throughout all or a significant portion of its range." Once a species is listed in either category, it is entitled to a great deal of protection. Under threat of civil or criminal penalties, it is illegal to "take"—that is, "to harass, harm, pursue, hunt, shoot, wound, kill, trap, capture, or collect"—any individual of the listed species on public or private lands.

The law also protects geographically defined "critical habitat" of listed species. And it requires that listings be based solely on scientific evidence about species' survival needs; consideration of economic and political consequences is generally

---

[7] "Protected Status Proposed for the Northern Spotted Owl," *Endangered Species Technical Bulletin,* July 1989, p. 1.

[8] Two subspecies of spotted owl, the northern spotted owl *(Strix occidentalis caurina)* and the California spotted owl *(Strix occidentalis occidentalis)* mix together at the extremes of their ranges in northern California. Although the California spotted owl is more plentiful, environmental groups have sued the U.S. Fish and Wildlife Service demanding that it also be listed as threatened or endangered. A third subspecies, the Mexican spotted owl *(Strix occidentalis lucida),* lives in the forests of Arizona, Utah, Colorado, Texas, and Mexico. It was listed as threatened in 1993; see "Final Rule to List the Mexican Spotted Owl as a Threatened Species," 58 FR 14248, March 16, 1993.

[9] Daniel Simberloff, "The Spotted Owl Fracas: Mixing Academic, Applied, and Political Ecology," *Ecology,* August 1987, p. 768.

prohibited.[10] The law is enforced by two agencies. The Fish and Wildlife Service within the Department of the Interior is responsible for plants and animals found on land and in freshwater environments and for migratory birds. The National Marine Fisheries Service within the Department of Commerce enforces the law with respect to marine species.

In 2004 there were 1,264 species listed as threatened or endangered—518 animals and 746 plants. Another 308 were being studied for listing. Since its inception more than 30 years ago, only 41 species have been delisted and of these only 16 were removed because of recovery. Another 9 became extinct, and the rest were taken off for a variety of reasons, but mainly because they had been misclassified as a separate species.[11]

At first, the Fish and Wildlife Service declined to list the northern spotted owl as endangered. Its biologists believed that evidence of a long-term threat to its survival was insufficient. Angry environmentalists sued the agency. In 1990, bowing to the pressure, it listed the spotted owl as a "threatened" species.[12] This set the powerful devices of the Endangered Species Act in motion, and soon an entire region of the country felt the consequences.

The Fish and Wildlife Service adopted protective rules that remain in force today. Logging is banned near known spotted owl nests. Even when a nest is found empty, there is a three-year moratorium on logging to ensure that it is abandoned. Before activities such as forestry or road maintenance and construction can take place in owl habitat, the agency must issue a clearance, called a "biological opinion."

In 1991 a federal district court in Seattle issued an injunction virtually halting timber sales in the government-owned old-growth forests of the Pacific Northwest until the Fish and Wildlife Service developed a species recovery plan for the owl. The Endangered Species Act requires a written plan to serve as a road map for the eventual recovery and delisting of a species. This was a boon for the owls, which could sleep during the day without the annoying buzz of chainsaws, but it was a disaster for the forest products industry, which depended on timber harvests. In 1990, the year before the injunction, 10.6 billion board feet of timber were cut on federal lands. (A board foot is a measure of timber volume. One board foot equals a volume of $12 \times 12 \times 1$ inches.) In 1991 only 4.4 billion board feet were harvested before the injunction took hold. And the next year only 0.7 billion board feet were sold.[13]

HARD TIMES IN THE PACIFIC NORTHWEST

Halted timber sales brought hardship. Hundreds of small-town economies built on jobs created by logging, milling, and related trucking and shipping spiraled downward. The owl injunction came on the heels of a prolonged recession in the Pacific Northwest. Thousands of loggers and mill workers had already lost jobs because of adverse market forces and technological modernization of mills that reduced employment. Now, because of the spotted owl, more would be jobless.

Despair and anger permeated logging towns. In Forks, Washington, where unemployment rose to 20 percent, someone shot a spotted owl and nailed it to a sign (risking a $20,000 fine and one year in prison). In Oregon, loggers had bumper stickers that read: "IF IT'S HOOTIN', I'M SHOOTIN'," "SAVE A LOGGER/EAT AN OWL," and "I LIKE SPOTTED OWLS . . . FRIED." Northern California suffered too. In Happy Camp, all four sawmills closed and the town collapsed as area timber harvests declined from 50 million board feet to 8 million. The population fell from 2,500 to 1,100, and more than half those remaining were on public assistance.[14]

By now, those trying to save the spotted owl and its old-growth habitat were locked in bitter scientific, legal, political, and personal conflict with those whose

[10] For an overview of the history, philosophy, and evolution of this statute, see Robert L. Fischman, "Predictions and Prescriptions for the Endangered Species Act," *Environmental Law,* March 2004.

[11] Department of the Interior, Threatened and Endangered Species System database, http://ecos.fws.gov/tess_public/, accessed December 2, 2004.

[12] "Determination of Threatened Status for the Northern Spotted Owl," 55 FR 21623, June 26, 1990.

[13] Department of the Interior memorandum in *The Administration's Response to the Spotted Owl Crisis: Joint Oversight Hearing before the Subcommittee on National Parks and Public Lands of the Committee on Interior and Insular Affairs,* U.S. House of Representatives, March 24, 1992, p. 167.

[14] Richard C. Paddock, "Town's Decline Rivals That of the Spotted Owl," *Los Angeles Times,* October 23, 1995, p. A3.

livelihood depended on the productivity of national forests. In 1993 then newly elected President Bill Clinton fulfilled a campaign promise by presiding over a "timber summit" in Portland, Oregon, where he listened to the strong and polarized views of scientists, environmentalists, and timber industry representatives. As a result, early in 1994 the Clinton administration introduced the Northwest Forest Plan (NWFP) designed to resolve the impasse and move forward.

The NWFP attempted to appease both environmentalists and industry. It covered 24.4 million forest acres. Logging was proscribed in 80 percent of this area. This was thought to be sufficient to permit recovery of the spotted owl. The remaining 20 percent of the area in the NWFP was to be managed for timber production based on guidelines set up to protect the owl and other endangered species. For example, no logging would be permitted in "owl circles" having a radius of 2.7 miles extending from known owl nests.

The plan permitted logging 1.2 billion board feet annually in mature and old-growth forests.[15] This harvest level was nearly double that of years since the injunction but was still almost 90 percent less than the year before the injunction. The NWFP spelled permanent loss of tens of thousands of timber jobs, so it committed $1.2 billion over five years to retrain workers, help small businesses, and compensate for lost tax revenues in timber towns.

Despite the broad recovery plan and paltry timber harvest authorized by the NWFP, environmentalists sued to block it. However, it was upheld by a federal court. Even so, little timber cutting took place. At first, delay was caused by convoluted, bureaucratic Forest Service procedures for setting up timber auctions. Later, environmentalists began to challenge timber auctions, suing the agency at every turn to block action.

THE ENDANGERED SPECIES ACT ATTACKED

The political climate in this battle changed in the early 1990s when Republicans gained a congressional majority and began to attack environmental laws. They reserved special ire for the Endangered Species Act. By this time, a storm of protest swirled around

the statute, much of it generated by the rising property rights movement. This movement represents property owners hurt by regulations that reduce the value of their land. Both corporations that owned expanses of timber and small landowners with only a few acres were hurt when they could not harvest the trees they owned. They demanded compensation by government when this occurred.

A clause in the Fifth Amendment, known as the *takings clause,* protects property owners. It reads: "nor shall private property be taken for public use without just compensation." In the past, the takings clause had been interpreted as requiring compensation only when government takes over property through eminent domain or when the owner is wholly deprived of its use. Except in unusual circumstances, it has never been held to require payment for land-use restrictions incidental to enforcement of environmental laws.

Opponents of regulation seized on the takings clause to argue that landowners deserved compensation when regulators reduced property values. Eventually, this position achieved some success in the courtroom. In 1997 an Oregon jury awarded Boise Cascade Corp. more than $2 million for the value of 56 acres of timberland that it was unable to harvest because of a spotted owl nest.[16] However, this precedent never took hold. Other courts held that endangered species restrictions were not a taking for public use in the same sense as when the government seized entire properties using eminent domain.[17]

Nevertheless, the assault on the Endangered Species Act continued. The government, reinforced by federal judges, pursued a relatively inflexible enforcement policy. As anger about the statute's role in reducing timber harvests rose, sentiment in Congress for changing it grew. To ease pressures for weakening the act, the Clinton administration discovered new flexibility in a provision of the law that permitted *habitat conservation plans* negotiated between the government and private landowners. These plans are

[15] Report of the Forest Ecosystem Management Assessment Team, *Forest Ecosystem Management: An Ecological, Economic, and Social Assessment* (Washington, DC: U.S. Department of Agriculture et al., July 1993).

[16] Kate Freedlander, "Timber Firm Wins Judgment on State's Logging Limits," *The Oregonian,* November 23, 1997, p. 1.

[17] In 1988, President Ronald Reagan issued Executive Order 12630 setting forth guidelines for the Department of the Interior and the Fish and Wildlife Service when their actions affected the use of private property. See *Regulatory Takings: Agency Compliance with Executive Order on Government Actions Affecting Private Property Use,* GAO–04–120T, October 16, 2003.

binding agreements, entered voluntarily, in which a landowner agrees to take conservation measures, usually beyond the letter of the law, and in return receives permission to log or otherwise use property, even if it means harm to an endangered species or critical habitat in the process.

An early example of one of the plans came in 1995 when the Murray Pacific Company, which owned a 53,000-acre tree farm in Washington populated by spotted owls, agreed to preserve 43 percent of the property as habitat for the owl and four other endangered species. The agreement was detailed and specific; for example, the company was to leave trees outside five cave openings to protect a bat species and had to monitor the temperature of streams and leave more trees standing on their banks to shade them if readings began to rise. In exchange, Murray Pacific received an "incidental take permit" absolving it from blame if, in logging the rest of the property, any members of an endangered species were harassed or killed. Without the plan, Murray Pacific probably would have been denied the right to log its land at all.

By 2004 there were 16 habitat conservation plans for private forest lands in the range of the northern spotted owl. The agreements have "no-surprise" clauses, guarantees that even if new evidence about an endangered species emerges years later, no additional conservation measures will be required.[18] They also include a "baseline" policy so that if the numbers of an endangered species increase, the landowner is not required to take additional measures to protect them. This removes an incentive for private landowners to drive out or kill endangered species before their presence is reported and the land rendered useless for development or timber harvest.

Environmental groups oppose habitat conservation plans, incidental take permits, and the no-surprises policy, all of which they see as compromising the survival chances of species on the borderline. Incidental take permits allow logging companies to destroy some owl habitat. And the no-surprises policy may turn out to be foolish. Science is just beginning to understand certain species and complex ecosystems. Yet habitat conservation plans are locked into place for decades—some for as long as 100 years. Even if new information about causes of extinction is discovered, landowners cannot be forced to alter their activities.

ENVIRONMENTALISTS BLOCK TIMBER HARVESTS

Habitat conservation plans have facilitated logging on some timberland owned by individuals and forest products companies, but logging in federal forests covered by the NWFP has fallen far short of the promised 1.2 billion board feet annually. Timber harvests never reached that level, and in 2003 only 162 million board feet came out of the woods, just 20 percent of what had been promised. The main roadblocks are set by environmentalists, who use both the law and tactics of civil disobedience to stop logging.

The Endangered Species Act allows citizen suits to prod federal agencies when they fail to meet statutory obligations. Environmental activists have brought hundreds of citizen suits over the last decade challenging timber harvests. Most of these actions are based on the presence of endangered species in areas to be logged. Others claim that timber auctions have been inadequately surveyed for the presence of species. Still others press for listing of new species or compliance with legal deadlines to complete recovery plans for previously listed species.

Several environmental groups specialize in this litigation. The Center for Biological Diversity, for example, averaged one new lawsuit every 32 days for years following the adoption of the NWFP.[19] The lawsuits tie down government agencies, forcing them to put more resources into litigation and leaving less energy for managing species. The overworked agencies miss so many deadlines that one environmental lawyer says bringing "[a] missed deadline case is like shooting fish in a barrel."[20] Craig Manson, the assistant secretary in the Department of the Interior who oversees species programs, says that the Endangered Species Act is "broken," making this analogy: "Imagine an emergency room where lawsuits force the doctors to treat sprained ankles while patients with heart attacks expire in the waiting room and you've got a good picture of our endangered species program right now."[21]

The purpose of the lawsuits is to preserve the forests. Zero harvest is the goal. After a forest fire in

---

[18] "Habitat Conservation Plan Assurances ('No Surprises') Rule," 63 FR 8859, February 23, 1998.

[19] Tom Knudson, "A Flood of Costly Lawsuits Raises Questions about Motive," *Sacramento Bee*, April 24, 2001, p. A1.

[20] Ibid., p. A1.

[21] U.S. Department of the Interior, "Endangered Species Act 'Broken'—Flood of Litigation over Critical Habitat Hinders Species Conservation," *News Release*, May 28, 2003, p. 1.

the Ochoco National Forest near Prineville, Oregon, environmental litigators filed a 104-page appeal when the Forest Service tried to sell 54 trees that had been cut to create a fire break—even though the trees had been lying on the ground for almost a year.[22] They argued that the trees should be allowed to decay on the forest floor, returning their nutrients to the soil. A California environmental group developed software enabling it to create so many timber sale appeals that it blocked or slowed the sale of almost 500 million board feet.[23]

Activists also use a wide range of protest tactics. In the national forests, they sit in trees, lie in front of logging trucks, and put metal spikes in trees scheduled for harvest so that saw blades will shatter if the logs are milled. On private timberland, they trespass and occupy sites slated for logging.

All this is illegal once a stand of trees is clear of appeals and ready for logging under government rules. However, activists feel justified by the ethical duty to protect species and forests. "It's against the law to trespass," says one, "but we feel there's a higher law."[24]

The George W. Bush administration pledged to increase timber yields and move them up close to the 1.2 billion board feet allowed by the NWFP. It has been unable to accomplish this because even where the forest plan permits cutting, courts have agreed with environmentalists that the strict habitat conservation protections in the Endangered Species Act prevent it.[25]

A TENUOUS EXISTENCE FOR BOTH OWLS AND LOGGERS

In 2002 a timber industry group, the American Forest Resources Council, sued the Department of the Interior to force a review of the northern spotted owl's status and remove its Endangered Species Act protection if that was no longer justified by scientific

evidence.[26] To settle the case, the agency set up an expert review panel that thoroughly evaluated scientific evidence about the risk of extinction.

The panel found no scientific basis for estimating the total owl population. Instead, it focused on long-term studies of owl reproduction and adult survival in 14 areas of Washington, Oregon, and California. As indicated in Exhibit 1, the populations in 9 of the 14 areas are declining. The other five areas were stable. Nowhere was a studied population increasing. The panel found it difficult to estimate change in the size of critical habitat. It noted that 515,000 acres, or 2.11 percent of the habitat covered by the Northwest Forest Plan, had been lost to logging over a decade. It also estimated that over the same period that loss was offset by the ingrowth of 600,000 acres of late-successional (old growth) habitat within the same area.[27]

Overall, the panel decided that the owl was still threatened with extinction. It no longer faced habitat loss because of logging, but growth of new habitat was insufficient to compensate for losses that had occurred before it was given Endangered Species Act protection in 1990. In addition, the owl faced several new threats, including habitat destruction from massive forest fires, increased competition from more aggressive barred owls, and the arrival of West Nile virus.

The panel concluded that the evidence did not warrant elevating the status of the northern spotted owl from threatened to endangered. However, slow declines in owl populations, lack of critical habitat expansion, and uncertainties posed by emerging threats suggested that the species was still threatened. So the owl still needed Endangered Species Act protection.

The review panel's conclusion was bad news for the forest products industry, and timber interests continue to argue that turning forests into species preserves is bad policy.[28] Owl protection hurts the

---

[22] Steve Lundgren, "End of the Line," *The Oregonian,* July 29, 2001, p. A17.

[23] William Wade Keye, "Mill Towns Subsist on Logs from Afar," *Sacramento Bee,* October 28, 2001, p. B6.

[24] Eric Bailey, "Two Sides Firmly Rooted over Logging Battle," *Los Angeles Times,* May 29, 2001, p. B8.

[25] See, for example, *Gifford Pinchot Task Force v. U.S. Fish & Wildlife Service,* 378 F.3d 1059, striking down six biological opinions that owl population survival would not be threatened by timber sales in critical habitat.

[26] *American Forest Resources Council v. Secretary of the Interior,* Civil No. 02–6100–AA (D. Oregon).

[27] U.S. Fish and Wildlife Service, *Northern Spotted Owl Five-Year Review: Summary and Evaluation* (Portland, OR: USFWS, November 2004), pp. 24–26.

[28] See, for example, testimony of Jason Spadaro, president of SDS Lumber Company in Bingen, Washington, and a representative of the American Forest Resources Council, before the Subcommittee on Public Lands and Forests, Senate Energy and Natural Resources Committee (180th Congress, 2nd Session, September 14, 2004), considering S.2709.

EXHIBIT 1
Trends in
Northern
Spotted Owl
Demography
in 14 Areas of
Population
Study in
Washington,
Oregon, and
California

Source: Adapted
from U.S. Fish and
Wildlife Service,
*Northern Spotted Owl
Five-Year Review:
Summary and Evalua-
tion* (Portland, OR:
USFWS, November
2004), Table 1.

Owl Population Study Area	Reproduction	Adult Survival	Annual Rate of Change*	Population Change
Washington				
Wenatchee	Stable	Declining	0.917	Declining
Cle Elum	Declining	Declining	0.938	Declining
Rainier	Stable	Declining	0.896	Declining
Olympic	Stable	Declining	0.956	Declining
Oregon				
Coast Ranges	Declining	Stable	0.968	Declining
H. J. Andrews	Stable	Stable	0.978	Declining
Warm Springs	Stable	Stable	0.908	Declining
Tyee	Increasing	Stable	1.005	Stationary
Klamath	Stable	Stable	0.997	Stationary
South Cascades	Declining	Stable	0.974	Stationary
California				
NW California	Declining	Declining	0.985	Declining
Hoopa	Declining	Stable	0.980	Stationary
Simpson	Increasing	Stable	0.970	Declining
Marin	Stable	Stable	NA[†]	NA

*Estimates of <1 represent a decrease in the number of owls; estimates of >1 represent an increase.
[†]Sample size too small to make an estimate.

Pacific Northwest economy. It pushes along the trend of mill closings and job losses in small towns throughout the owl's range.[29] In addition, secondary manufacturers in the Pacific Northwest, unable to supply their need for wood locally, increasingly rely on imported timber from countries such as Canada, Brazil, and Chile. Logs, planks, and chips arrive by ship and are trucked to the region's small factories. There, within sight of some of the world's great forests, they substitute for locally grown wood in porch posts, door frames, and garden furniture. The irony would be no greater if Saudi Arabian refineries depended on imported oil or Hawaiian canneries on pineapples from the mainland.

There is a second irony. Because there are fewer environmental safeguards on wood production in other countries than in the United States environmentalists have, in effect, made species extinction and damage to forest ecosystems an export item.

The exact price of protecting the spotted owl is elusive, but high. One study looked at projections of wood prices, consumption and production trends in the United States, and estimated changes in wood products revenues, incomes, and costs to consumers caused by owl protection. The authors concluded that measures to raise the survival odds of the owl to 91 percent would lead to a $33 billion reduction in economic welfare, most of which would come out of the pockets of workers and businesses in the Pacific Northwest. Enforcing the Endangered Species Act in a way that would raise the owl's survival odds to 95 percent would push the economic sacrifice up to $46 billion.[30] If this is the case, assuming a spotted owl population of 5,000, a number in the high range of recent estimates, the price tag on each owl is $6.6 to $9.9 million.

[29] Hal Bernton, "Loggers in Oregon, Washington State Work in Waning Field," *The Seattle Times,* April 12, 2004, p. A1; Bryan Denson, "Cut Out of the Picture," *The Oregonian,* April 11, 2004, p. A15; and Erik Robinson, "A Decade of Compromise: Timber Towns Struggle under Forest Plan," *The Columbian,* April 13, 2004, p. A1.

[30] C. Montgomery et al., "The Marginal Cost of Species Preservation: The Northern Spotted Owl," *Journal of Environmental Economics and Management* 26 (1994), p. 11.

The timber conflict is rooted in opposing values. Environmentalists want to save species. A species such as the northern spotted owl takes millions of years to evolve. Its loss would be irretrievable in the span of time that constitutes human historical consciousness. One more element would be removed from the profusion of life on earth. And humanity would be impoverished for that subtraction from its biological inheritance, a subtraction made all the worse because perhaps avoidable. On the other side, there is no more eloquent exponent than Neal Korpela, a forklift driver who is jobless after 25 years at the Ochoco Lumbermill in Prineville. "Tough decisions have to be made . . . about how we're going to value people over animals and plants," he says. "Most of the economy of Crook County is an endangered species, and no one seems to have a habitat recovery program for us."[31]

---

[31] Quoted in "Machines Quiet at Newly Closed Mill," Associated Press, August 1, 2001.

Questions

1. Are you in favor of using the national forests of the Pacific Northwest to preserve the northern spotted owl, even if it means catastrophic loss of jobs, mill closures, depleted tax revenues, underfunded schools, and growing reliance on imported lumber?

2. When government prohibits logging near spotted owl nests, does this violate rights given the landowners by the takings clause of the Fifth Amendment? Should owners of private timberland be compensated by the government for their losses? Would it be fair to shift the burden of species protection to taxpayers?

3. Evaluate the actions of environmental groups. Are the values of activists correct? Do they have an ethical duty to natural law? Are environmental litigators abusing the privilege of citizen suits?

4. Should enforcement of the Endangered Species Act continue to become more flexible? Or should it tighten to protect spotted owls and other endangered species more? What changes, if any, should be made in the Endangered Species Act?

Chapter Fifteen

Managing Environmental Quality

Louisiana-Pacific Corporation

Arthur and Margaret Orjias settled on 50 acres of land in an eastern Colorado valley. They had almost finished building their house in 1984, when a new Louisiana-Pacific Corporation (LP) plant started operating nearby. The Montrose Plant, as it was called, turned out waferboard, a type of paneling made by mixing aspen chips in a glue-like resin, pressing them into wafers, and baking them in an oven. The oven was heated by burning wood. Inside it, hot exhaust gases from the fire cured the board. These gases emerged from the oven containing formaldehyde, isocyanates, and tiny wood particles.

Immediately after production began, nearby residents were bothered by smoke so dense that cars going through the valley sometimes turned on their headlights during the day. The Orjias suffered from coughing, headaches, earaches, swollen glands, and nausea. After three years of medical problems and unresolved complaints to the company, the couple abandoned their home and moved.

A year later, Colorado regulators finally issued a permit to the Montrose Plant mandating the use of air pollution controls and setting emission levels. A continuous monitor that recorded an opacity reading on a graph every six minutes was also required (see Figure 15.1).

For the next two years, the plant repeatedly violated its permit and, in 1990, it was fined $80,000 by the Colorado Department of Public Health. A new and more stringent permit was then issued, placing an hourly limit on wood fuel for the oven and limiting the plant to production of 210,000 square board feet of finished panels per 12-hour shift. These limits were intended to improve air quality in the valley.

The plant manager, however, ordered employees to tamper with the opacity monitor. When permit limits were likely to be exceeded, the workers put reflective tape near the light beam to trick the device, and they wedged wood chips in the recording pen to stop it from going past the 20 percent limit. After a fired employee exposed what was going on, the EPA raided the plant, seizing 23 boxes of records. It took investigators three years to figure out how the scheme worked.

FIGURE 15.1 An Opacity Monitor

Factories and power plants are given permits by the EPA or state regulators mandating the use of mechanical or chemical devices to remove gases, particles, and odors. To reduce smoke, the Montrose Plant was required to run exhaust gases through an electrified filter. Positively charged soot particles in the oven exhaust smoke were run through negatively charged filters that attracted and retained them. Filtered exhaust streams were to have an opacity reading of 20 percent or less, that is, no more than 20 percent of the light passing through the air in the exhaust stream could be reflected by particles. This 20 percent opacity limit was to be achieved 95 percent of the time. The diagram illustrates how an opacity monitor works. A light beam from the left passes through exhaust gases and any loss of light is measured by the detector at right.

Source: General Accounting Office.

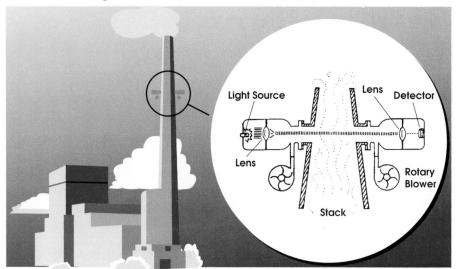

Meanwhile, the Montrose Plant documents so alarmed the EPA that even before their full review, it launched an investigation of LP facilities nationwide. What it found was a corporate culture of disrespect for environmental rules. "[I]n the structure of an organization like this you don't need to tell people to violate the law," said a federal prosecutor. "You tell them 'we need so much production' and people know what they're going to have to do."[1] In 1993, the agency fined LP $11 million and forced it to install $70 million of new pollution control equipment.

In 1995 the EPA brought a criminal indictment against LP and two employees in the Montrose Plant matter.[2] The firm's three highest executives resigned and a new management team came in, determined to improve environmental performance. The Montrose Plant case was settled in 1998 when the company agreed to a $37 million fine and five years' probation. The plant superintendent was fined $10,000 and given

[1] Quoted in Mark Eddy, "Judge Fines Timber Firm $37 Million," *Denver Post,* May 28, 1998, p. A1.
[2] *United States v. Louisiana Pacific Corp.,* 908 F.Supp 835 (1995); 925 F.Supp. 1484 (1995); and 106 F.34d 345 (1997).

six months' home detention, and a supervisor was sentenced to five months in prison, both for criminal conspiracy to violate the Clean Air Act. LP's new CEO Mark A. Suwyn appeared in the courtroom to apologize for the corporation. He announced that the Montrose Plant would be a "model of environmental compliance."[3]

Louisiana-Pacific is a large building materials maker with 40 mills and manufacturing plants. Strict enforcement of environmental laws taught the company a lesson, so it began to "green" itself. Adopting a new environmental policy, it pledged to "meet or surpass the requirements of environmental laws and regulations and to improve the environment."[4] It set up special environmental management systems at each facility. Employees received thousands of hours of environmental training. At waferboard mills costly ceramic thermal units that reduce formaldehyde emissions by heating exhaust gases to high temperatures were installed.

The company is making progress. In 1999 it was fined $100,000 when a California particleboard plant polluted a stream. However, that may be the last vestige of the bad LP. Since its indictment it reports that notices of violation from regulatory agencies have steadily declined from almost 80 in 1995 to only 3 in 2004.[5] In 2002 the reformed LP won an EPA award for waste reduction and by 2005, five of its plants had won environmental awards from state regulators and the EPA.

Command-and-control enforcement of the kind that cracked the knuckles of Louisiana-Pacific is critical in environmental regulation. It forced the company to move beyond an obsession with maximum output to a focus on compliance. Yet, as important as strict regulation is, broad progress toward nonpolluting, sustainable manufacturing requires corporations to go beyond compliance.

In this chapter we begin by explaining how pollution risks are assessed to determine which are most important to regulate. We then discuss alternative approaches to regulation with emphasis on new, more flexible initiatives. Finally, we show how many companies are now managed differently so they can move beyond simple legal compliance.

REGULATING ENVIRONMENTAL RISK

Environmental regulation is very expensive. The cost to the nation of complying with environmental regulations is greater than the cost of complying with all other forms of social and economic regulation combined.[6] In 2000 total environmental compliance costs were estimated at $148 billion.[7] This is a large sum. Is the money well spent? It seems to be. According to a government study, for the decade of 1993

---

[3] Quoted in Nina Siegal, "If I Believed in Hell, This Could Be No Worse," *The Progressive,* December 1998, p. 30.

[4] "Corporate Policy on Protection of the Environment," www.lpcorp.com/environment/e_policy.jsp.

[5] *Building Our Vision: Louisiana-Pacific Corporation's Sustainability Report, 2004* (Portland, OR: Louisiana-Pacific Corporation, 2004), p. 29.

[6] Based on the Congressional Budget Office's 1997 estimate that environmental compliance costs were 52 percent of overall compliance costs and its 1998 estimate of between 70 to 74 percent. See General Accounting Office, *Regulatory Accounting: Analysis of OMB's Reports on the Costs and Benefits of Federal Regulation,* GAO/GGD–99–59, April 20, 1999, pp. 32–33.

[7] See General Accounting Office, *Environmental Protection Agency: Status of Achieving Key Outcomes,* GAO–01–774, June 2001, p. 5.

to 2003 major environmental rules were "responsible for the majority of costs and benefits generated" by all federal regulation.[8] The benefits of Environmental Protection Agency rules were estimated at between $38 and $132 billion, while their costs were estimated at $34 to $39 billion. This means that for every dollar spent on environmental regulation the nation got between $1 and $4 in benefits.

If environmental expenditures are to bring maximum benefit, they must be focused on the highest risks to human health and nature. *Risk* is a probability existing somewhere between zero and absolute certainty that a harm will occur. The probability of any pollution risk can be studied scientifically; then regulators, politicians, and the public must decide what, if anything, should be done to mitigate it.

Congress has added about 30 provisions in environmental laws requiring that regulatory decisions be based on risk assessments. The goal of these provisions is to focus limited dollars on the greatest hazards. The EPA does many risk assessments, and they have great significance for business. If they show that a pollutant or activity poses relatively high risks, laws can require enormous expenditures to reduce it.

risk
A probability existing somewhere between zero and 100 percent that a harm will occur.

ANALYZING HUMAN HEALTH RISKS

The basic model for analyzing human health risks is shown in Figure 15.2. It separates risk analysis into two parts represented by two circles. In circle A are the elements of *risk assessment,* the largely scientific process of discovering and weighing the dangers posed by a pollutant. In circle B are the elements of *risk management,* the process of deciding which actions to take (or not take) regarding specific risks. We will explain the nature and interaction of these elements.

risk assessment
The largely scientific process of discovering and weighing dangers posed by a pollutant.

Risk Assessment

The four basic risk assessment steps shown in circle A in Figure 15.2 have become standard at the EPA and other agencies that sometimes evaluate the dangers of pollutants. In fact, they are now the standard worldwide.[9] In theory, risk assessment is a scientific process leading to an objective, quantitative measure of the risks posed by any substance. As we will see, however, science often falls short of this goal. So the EPA and other agencies make a series of precautionary assumptions based on the fear that scientific data, which are often ambiguous or inconclusive, might understate risks to human health. As the precautionary assumptions are piled one on top of another, the process grows less rigorous and, in the view of some critics, begins to overstate risks. When risks are overstated regulation of

risk management
The process of deciding which regulatory action to take (or not take) to protect the public from the risk posed by a pollutant.

---

[8] Office of Management and Budget, *Informing Regulatory Decisions: 2004 Draft Report to Congress on the Costs and Benefits of Federal Regulations* (Washington, DC: OMB, February 20, 2004), p. 5.

[9] The standards evolve with growing scientific understanding. Risk assessment guidelines for carcinogens were first issued by the Environmental Protection Agency in 1986. In 2001, the agency announced that it was following a revised set of guidelines. Currently, the agency is considering another draft revision for adoption; see EPA, *Draft Final Guidelines for Carcinogen Risk Assessment* (Washington, DC: EPA, Risk Assessment Forum, March 2003, NCEA–F–0644A).

FIGURE 15.2
Elements
of Risk
Assessment
and Risk
Management
and Their
Sequence

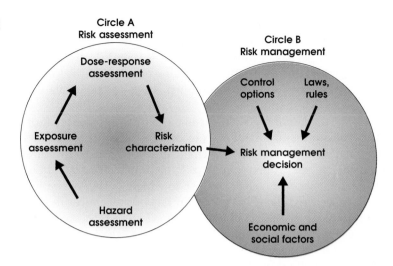

business becomes more expensive and the nation's environmental regulation dollars are not well spent. Nevertheless, risks are often overstated to ensure that public health is protected with a margin of safety.

Hazard Assessment

hazard assessment
The process of establishing a link between a substance, such as a chemical, and human disease. The link is established primarily by animal tests and epidemiological studies.

Hazard assessment establishes a link between a substance, such as a chemical, and human disease. When a substance is thought to pose a risk, the two basic methods of proving it dangerous are animal testing and epidemiological studies.

In animal tests, species such as mice and rats are exposed to high levels of the substance through diet, inhalation, or other means for an appreciable part of their life span. In a cancer study, as many as 1,000 animals may be divided into three groups with different exposure levels. One group is exposed to the maximum dose that the animals can tolerate without dying. The second group receives half this dose. The third group is a control group receiving no exposure. At the end of the test, the animals are dissected and tumors and other abnormalities in organs are counted. If the exposed animals have many tumors, the assumption is that the chemical is an animal carcinogen, and regulators tend then to make the precautionary assumption that it is a human carcinogen as well.

Several problems cast doubt on the validity of animal tests. First, scientists rely heavily on strains of rats and mice genetically disposed to high rates of tumor production.[10] This predisposition raises doubts about whether a substance is a complete carcinogen or simply a tumor promoter in an otherwise susceptible species. EPA guidelines call for adding benign and malignant tumors and basing the assumption of carcinogenicity on the total rather than only on the number of malignant tumors. This is an additional precautionary assumption that may exaggerate risk.

Second, in animals exposed to large amounts of a chemical, tumors can arise from tissue irritation rather than normal carcinogenesis. For example, rats forced to breathe extreme concentrations of formaldehyde exhibit nasal inflammation.

[10] Tracy Lyon, "Carcinogenesis in Transgenic Mouse Models," *Environmental Health Perspectives,* September 1997, pp. 912–13.

Tumors appear in their noses, but some or all of them result from abnormally rapid cell division that magnifies chromosomal abnormalities, not from the carcinogenic properties of formaldehyde. It is scientifically uncertain if a substance that promotes cancer in high doses also promotes it in low doses. Humans, of course, have lower environmental exposures to chemicals than the prodigious doses given to test animals.

And third, animal physiology can be so different from that of humans that disease processes are unique. For example, gasoline vapor causes kidney tumors in male rats, but the biological mechanism causing these tumors is unique to rats; humans lack one protein involved. Even animals differ in their susceptibility to disease. Inhalation of cadmium dust, to which workers in battery factories are exposed, causes high levels of cancer in rats but no cancer in mice. Which result is appropriate for assessing risk to workers? Here EPA guidelines call for making the precautionary assumption that human risk calculations should be based on the reaction of the most sensitive species.

epidemio-logical study A statistical survey designed to show a relationship between human mortality (death) and morbidity (sickness) and environmental factors such as chemicals or radiation.

A second method of identifying hazards is the *epidemiological study,* a statistical survey of human mortality (death) and morbidity (sickness) in a sample population. Epidemiological studies can establish a link between industrial pollutants and health problems. To illustrate, recent studies show the following associations.

- Excess hearing loss in workers exposed to carbon disulfide (CS_2) and noise in a viscose rayon plant. This hearing loss was not found in workers exposed to the same noise levels but not CS_2.[11]
- Elevated risk of loss of color vision among workers exposed to styrene in factories making fiberglass-reinforced plastics.[12]
- Reduction in head circumference in babies born to mothers with exposure to chlorpyrifos and pyrethroids, ingredients in household pesticides.[13]
- Elevated mortality from lymphatic cancers among workers exposed to 1,3-butadiene at synthetic rubber plants.[14]

Epidemiological studies have the advantage of measuring real human illness, but they have low statistical power and are riddled with uncertainties. In particular, people are exposed to literally thousands of substances, and individual exposures vary. For example, the study of synthetic rubber plant workers, noted above, showed four lymphatic cancers among 364 workers, more in a group that size than the 0.69 predicted by mortality tables for the general population. All 364 workers had been exposed to the chemical 1,3-butadiene (bue-ta-DIE-een) by working for

[11] Shu-Ju Chang et al., "Hearing Loss in Workers Exposed to Carbon Disulfide and Noise," *Environmental Health Perspectives,* October 2003.

[12] Fabriziomaria Gobba et al., "Acquired Dyschromatopsia among Styrene-Exposed Workers," *Journal of Occupational Medicine,* July 1991.

[13] Gertrud S. Berkowitz, "*In Utero* Pesticide Exposure, Maternal Paraoxonase Activity, and Head Circumference," *Environmental Health Perspectives,* March 2004. Paraoxonase is an enzyme that appears in the blood as a result of pesticide exposure.

[14] Elizabeth Ward et al., "Mortality Study of Workers in 1,3-Butadiene Production Units Identified from a Chemical Workers Cohort," *Environmental Health Perspectives,* June 1995.

at least six months at three Union Carbide synthetic rubber plants in West Virginia. The four lymphatic cancers are statistically significant but still a small number. Could exposure to multiple chemicals over the 39-year period covered by the study have caused these cancers?

There are difficulties with epidemiological studies beyond multiple, confounding exposures. Because lung tumors and other cancers have latency periods of up to 40 years, these studies may not detect harm done by recent exposures. Death certificates and diagnoses of disease are frequently inaccurate. Multiple diseases contribute to many deaths. In addition, data from one population may not predict risk for another population. For example, worker populations, on which many epidemiological studies are based, are healthier than the general population, which contains more sensitive older and younger people. In the study at the Union Carbide butadiene units, for example, only 185 of the 365 workers died over the 39 years, compared with 202 deaths that would have been expected in the general population. However, though their accuracy is subject to doubt, the results of epidemiological tests can be valuable. Arsenic, for instance, does not cause cancer in lab animals; only epidemiology shows it to be a human carcinogen.

Dose-Response Assessment

dose-response assessment
A quantitative estimate of how toxic a substance is to humans or animals at varying exposure levels.

A *dose-response assessment* is a quantitative estimate of how toxic a substance is to humans or animals at increasing levels of exposure. The potency of carcinogens, for example, varies widely. Formaldehyde is a strong carcinogen that causes tumors in 50 percent of exposed lab animals at a dose of 15 parts per million (ppm). Vinyl chloride, on the other hand, is a very weak carcinogen that is benign at less than 50 ppm and, even at the much higher dose of 600 ppm, causes tumors in less than 25 percent of animals.[15]

extrapolation
To infer the value of an unknown state from the value of another state that is known.

Public exposures to toxic substances are usually well below the exposures of workers. And the exposures of both workers and the public are far lower than the extreme exposures of animals in high-dose tests. For most chemicals, in fact, regulators use *extrapolation* from high doses to predict the effects on human populations at much lower doses. For many years, the EPA has used a model that assumes a *linear dose-response rate*—that is, that there will be a proportionate decrease in cancers from large exposures to small ones (if, for example, exposure decreases by 25 percent, then cancers will decrease by 25 percent).

linear dose-response rate
A relationship in which adverse health affects increase or decrease proportionately with the amount of exposure to a toxic substance.

Figure 15.3 illustrates the theory of extrapolation from high to low doses with respect to carcinogens. The shaded area covers an observed range of responses at relatively high doses. Epidemiological studies on workers and laboratory experiments with rodents typically produce such data in high-dose ranges. The linear extension extended down to zero from the observed range is a prediction made in the absence of experimental data, one that is conservative in protecting public health. It suggests that risks rise substantially over the range of exposure to a human population. Many carcinogens, on the other hand, are less dangerous at low doses, as represented by the sublinear curve extending from the observed range.

[15] Louis A. Cox Jr. and Paolo F. Ricci, "Dealing with Uncertainty: From Health Risk Assessment to Environmental Decision Making," *Journal of Energy Engineering*, August 1992, p. 79.

FIGURE 15.3
Alternative Assumptions for Extrapolating the Effects of High Doses to Lower Dose Levels

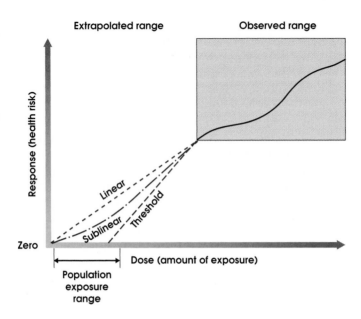

threshold
An exposure point greater than zero at which a substance begins to pose a health risk. Until this point, or threshold, is reached, exposure to the substance poses no health risk.

And still other carcinogens have a *threshold,* that is, they do not produce tumors at very low exposure levels and pose no risk until some threshold exposure amount is exceeded. If the hypothetical substance in Figure 15.3 responded based on the threshold curve as illustrated, there would be little risk of harm to public health within the exposure range shown.

The EPA makes the precautionary assumption that, in the absence of rigorous low-dose data, risk estimates in high-to-low-dose extrapolation should be based on the linear curve. This invites cautious risk estimates suggesting more regulation to limit human exposure than would be called for based on a sublinear or threshold curve. The higher the inferred risk, the more justification there is for high expenditures to control polluting emissions.

Environmentalists who favor more regulation approve of the linear model. However, industry, which dislikes the expensive regulations it spawns, favors the use of sublinear and threshold models that support less regulation. The EPA has recently suggested willingness to depart from the linear model when rigorous evidence supports the validity of an alternative assumption. Since many toxic chemicals are as yet incompletely studied, such evidence is frequently lacking. For example, data on human exposure are available on only 6 percent of 1,456 toxic chemicals of concern to the EPA.[16]

exposure assessment
The study of how much of a substance humans absorb through inhalation, ingestion, or skin absorption.

Exposure Assessment

Exposure assessment is the study of how much of a substance humans absorb through inhalation, ingestion, or skin absorption. The level of a substance in one of the three media—air, water, and land—does not indicate how much of that

[16] General Accounting Office, *Environmental Information: EPA Needs Better Information to Manage Risks and Measure Results,* GAO–01–97T, October 3, 2000, p. 4.

substance is taken in by humans. Further study is needed to verify intake and concentrations in body tissues.

An example is a study of people pumping gasoline. Gasoline contains five toxic organic compounds that evaporate easily.[17] Pumping gas displaces air in fuel tanks, exposing people to them. To measure this exposure, researchers took blood samples of 60 motorists, both before and after refueling. They found that blood concentrations of all five compounds rose after gas pumping. Benzene, for instance, rose from 0.19 parts per billion (ppb) to 0.54 ppb and toluene (TOL-you-een) from 0.38 ppb to 0.74 ppb. The higher concentrations lasted no longer than 10 minutes. This study confirms that motorists have short-term exposure to carcinogens when they pump gas.

To make exposure assessments, researchers measure activities that bring individuals in contact with toxic substances, including such things as how much water people drink, their length of skin contact with water, amounts of soil eaten by children at play, inhalation rates, and consumption of various foods. Because movements and activities differ among people in studied populations, regulators present their estimates as a distribution of individual exposures. The estimates include both a central estimate (based on mean or median exposure) of the average person's exposure and an upper-end estimate for the most highly exposed persons.[18]

Risk Characterization

risk characterization
A written statement about a substance summarizing the evidence from prior stages of the risk assessment process to reach an overall conclusion about its risk. It includes discussion of the strengths and weaknesses of data and, if the data support it, a quantitative estimate of risk.

Risk characterization is an overall conclusion about the dangers of a substance. It is a detailed, written narrative describing the scientific evidence, including areas of ambiguity. A risk characterization for a carcinogen, for example, discusses the kinds of tumors promoted, human and animal data that suggest cancer causation for pertinent routes of exposure (oral, inhalation, skin absorption), and dose-response levels. Based on the discussion, the narrative ultimately characterizes the risks in quantitative terms.

For example, the EPA estimates the lifetime risk of leukemia from inhalation of benzene in a range from 2.2 to 7.8 in one million for a person exposed to 1 $\mu g/m^3$ (one microgram per cubic meter). That is, in a population of one million people exposed to very low levels of airborne benzene over the 75 years that the EPA calculates as an average lifetime, there will be two to eight extra cases of leukemia.

Such quantitative risk estimates then help to decide what level of abatement should be required of industry. There is no agreement about how high a risk should be before regulators must act to reduce it. In 1980 the Supreme Court, in a case that required OSHA to prove significant health risks to workers before requiring expensive worker protective measures, addressed the subject of "significant" risk.

[17] These are benzene, ethyl benzene, *m-/p*-xylene, *o*-oxylene, and toluene. Lorraine C. Backer et al., "Exposure to Regular Gasoline and Ethanol Oxyfuel during Refueling in Alaska," *Environmental Health Perspectives,* August 1997, p. 850.

[18] For the EPA, the highest exposed groups are those above the 90th percentile. General Accounting Office, *Chemical Risk Assessment: Selected Federal Agencies' Procedures, Assumptions, and Policies,* GAO–01–810, August 2001, p. 80.

Some risks are plainly acceptable and others are plainly unacceptable. If, for example, the odds are one in a billion that a person will die from cancer by taking a drink of chlorinated water, the risk clearly could not be considered significant. On the other hand, if the odds are one in a thousand that regular inhalation of gasoline vapors that are 2 percent benzene will be fatal, a reasonable person might well consider the risk significant and take the appropriate steps to decrease or eliminate it.[19]

At the EPA, a lifetime risk of contracting cancer from a chemical substance or radiation source greater than 1 in 10,000 is generally considered excessive and subject to regulation. The goal of regulation is to reduce such risks to 1 in a million or lower. However, risks that fall between 1 in 10,000 and 1 in a million are usually considered acceptable.[20] With benzene, the EPA estimates that long-term exposures to air concentrations of 0.13 to 0.45 $\mu g/m^3$ pose a 1 in 1,000,000 risk, but when concentrations rise to 13 to 45 $\mu g/m^3$ exposed individuals face a 1 in 10,000 risk.[21] Therefore, if populations living near an oil refinery or a chemical plant were exposed to concentrations above 45 $\mu g/m^3$ the EPA would be inclined to force the facility to reduce air emissions.

Policy guidelines developed from quantitative risk estimates enrage some environmental activists. Asks one: "Would you let me shoot into a crowd of 100,000 people and kill one of them? No? Well, how come Dow Chemical can do it? It's okay for the corporations to do it, but the little guy with a gun goes to jail."[22] However, the alternative to a policy of accepting pollution risks between 1 in 10,000 and 1 in 1,000,000 is to decide that virtually no level of risk is acceptable. Eliminating infinitesimal risks from chemicals in an industrial society is not possible. Efforts to reduce them much below the EPA's acceptable range are often prohibitively expensive. Law enforcement to protect citizens from killers costs far less.

Risk characterizations are built on a series of calculations about toxicity, potency, and exposure that, as we have noted, are made using scientific method. Yet because of the limits of science in this area, research findings are adulterated by a series of precautionary assumptions. So risk characterizations may not be accurate, and when they are not they tend to overestimate risks, requiring more expensive pollution controls. With benzene, for example, the EPA's risk estimates are based on linear extrapolation to low doses because there are no data on human exposures in the range of 1 to 45 $\mu g/m^3$. The resulting 1 in 10,000 to 1 in 1,000,000 risk estimates are, therefore, conservative, likely to overstate risk, and likely to impose higher than necessary control costs on business.

[19] *Industrial Union Department, AFL-CIO v. American Petroleum Institute,* 488 U.S. 655 (1989).

[20] General Accounting Office, *Radiation Standards: Scientific Basis Inconclusive,* GAO/RCED–00–152, p. 9 and fn. 23.

[21] EPA, Integrated Risk Information System, "Benzene: CASRN 71–43–2," April 17, 2003, II, C.1.2.

[22] Quoted in John A. Hird, *Superfund: The Political Economy of Environmental Risk* (Baltimore: Johns Hopkins University Press, 1994), p. 200.

Risk Management

Risk management (see again Figure 15.2, circle B) encompasses regulation of pollutants and health risks. Whereas risk assessment in circle A in Figure 15.2 is nominally hard science, risk management decisions are based on the social sciences—law, economics, politics, and ethics. We will discuss the elements of risk management.

Control Options

These are alternative methods for reducing most risks. For example, hazardous wastes can be stored in a landfill or broken down into harmless substances by high-temperature incineration. A spectrum of regulatory options also exists, ranging from strict enforcement to voluntary request. Later in the chapter these options are discussed at more length.

Legal Considerations

Many environmental laws are specific about risk reduction required and methods of achieving it. The Clean Air Act directs the EPA to set standards for control of hazardous air pollutants based on levels that can be achieved by the best control devices on the market. The Food Quality Protection Act of 1996 directs the EPA to set standards for pesticide residues in fruits and vegetables at levels where "there is a reasonable certainty of no harm." Then, because Congress considered children especially vulnerable to pesticides, it required that the EPA further reduce the risk by a multiple of 10. The Endangered Species Act prohibits consideration of economic factors in the decision to list a species as endangered.

In general, environmental laws so often dictate regulatory decisions that one observer calls them "Congressional handcuffs."[23] However, there is always some latitude for regulators when they set up the specific rules to carry out congressional requirements. An example occurred when the EPA defined the best technology standard for hazardous air pollutant emissions as the level of control achieved by the best-controlled 12 percent of industry sites. This percentage does not appear in the statute, only in the rule developed by the EPA.

Other Economic and Social Factors

Risk decisions cannot always be based solely on scientific findings. Technical data, such as control device engineering, may open or limit options. Public opinion polls or interviews may define politically acceptable options. Cost–benefit studies can illuminate economic consequences of alternative regulatory approaches. We will now discuss cost–benefit analysis at greater length.

[23] Kenneth W. Chilton, *Enhancing Environmental Protection While Fostering Economic Growth*, Policy Study No. 151 (St. Louis: Washington University, Center for the Study of American Business, March 1999), p. 22.

COST–BENEFIT ANALYSIS

cost–benefit analysis
The systematic calculation and comparison of the costs and benefits of a proposed action. Costs and benefits are assigned common unit values, such as dollar amounts, so they can be directly compared.

Cost–benefit analysis is the systematic calculation and comparison of the costs and benefits of a proposed action. If benefits exceed costs, the action is desirable, other things being equal. Rigorous cost–benefit studies assign common values, such as dollar amounts, to all costs and benefits so that they can be compared using a common denominator.

Cost calculations typically include such factors as enforcement costs, capital and compliance costs to industry, foregone net benefits such as lowered crop yields or the costs of substitution for a banned substance, potential job losses, and inflation. Benefits can include lives saved, reduced absenteeism from work, lower health care expenditures, rising property values, increased tourism, and heightened aesthetic appeal. The accounting can be detailed. For example, if a regulation is expected to reduce public exposure to a toxic chemical, the benefits could include the predicted number of illnesses or deaths avoided as calculated from risk data. The economic benefits of avoiding these illnesses could then be calculated by setting forth the expected age distribution of their victims, disabilities likely to result, their length, medical costs, lost productivity, foregone wages, and amounts of compensable pain and suffering.

Regulators must submit to the Office of Management and Budget a cost–benefit study to justify any proposed rule that imposes compliance costs of $100 million or more on the U.S. economy. These studies are recondite and costly.[24] Their scientific and economic assumptions are frequently questioned by affected industries. In practice, the requirement that they be done complicates and slows regulation.

Advantages of Cost–Benefit Analysis

Cost–benefit analysis has several advantages. First, it forces methodical consideration of each economic impact a policy will have on society. It disciplines thinking, though it does not always result in clear choices. Cost–benefit studies show which alternative is optimal in economic terms, but they do not show which alternative is best in terms of noneconomic criteria such as ethical duty or political consequences.

A second advantage of cost–benefit analysis is to inject rational calculation into emotional arguments. Environmental risks are not always proportionate to the public alarm that arises upon their discovery. When the public is fired up over a new menace, politicians, responding to the alarm, can be hasty to legislate. In some laws Congress has required that public health be protected without consideration of cost and this invites rules that impose greater costs than the benefits they yield. Emotional decisions are not necessarily wrong, but dispassionate ones may better match risks and limited dollars.

Third, cost–benefit analysis that reveals marginal abatement costs can help regulators find the most efficient level of regulation. Figure 15.4 illustrates the typical

---

[24] Guidelines for preparing cost–benefit studies are in Office of Management and Budget, "Draft 2003 Report to Congress on the Costs and Benefits of Federal Regulations," 68 FR 5492, February 2, 2003, at 5517–5527.

FIGURE 15.4 Relationship between Extent of Regulation, Costs, and Benefits in Environmental Regulation

Source: Adapted from Kenneth W. Chilton, *Enhancing Environmental Protection while Fostering Economic Growth,* Policy Study No. 151 (St. Louis: Washington University, Center for the Study of American Business, March 1999), p. 8.

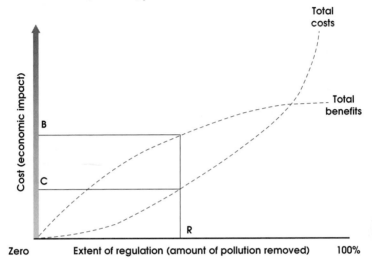

relationship between environmental regulation and changes in costs and benefits. Initially, at or near zero, pollution controls are very cost-effective. Control equipment rapidly cuts emissions and reduces risks to public health, creating rising benefits. However, as higher levels of control are reached, it is increasingly expensive to remove each additional increment. More complex control equipment must be purchased. More energy will be consumed by its operation. New control technologies may have to be invented. Yet even as this money is spent, the risk to public health is reduced less and less because falling concentrations of toxics pose fewer dangers. Costs begin to rise more rapidly than benefits, ultimately exceeding them and eventually rising exponentially as 100 percent cleanup, a quixotic goal, is neared.

The ideal level of regulation is at point R in Figure 15.4, the point where benefits most exceed costs (B minus C). At this point, each dollar spent produces maximum benefit. In theory, dollars spent for regulation after point R could be better spent on reducing other, less-regulated environmental risks. In cases such as this, cost–benefit analysis can identify efficient regulatory goals to prevent skyrocketing expenditures for trivial benefits. It provides an artificial but valuable test of efficient resource allocation for regulators not subject to a market mechanism.

Criticisms of Cost–Benefit Analysis

As attractive as cost–benefit analysis seems, it has critics. Here are a few of their concerns.

First, fixing precise values of costs and benefits is difficult and controversial. For cost–benefit analysis to work, costs and benefits must be measured using a common metric. But how can the value of a clear sky, fish in a stream, fragrant air, extra years of life, or preserving species for a future generation be priced? Their worth is subjective. Assigning dollar amounts to untraded goods such as scenic beauty or human life invites discord. There are ways to do it, but the critics dispute their accuracy.

contingent valuation
A method for assigning monetary worth to features of the natural environment.

One method of measuring the monetary worth of natural features is *contingent valuation,* a polling process in which people are asked to put a dollar amount on nature. A sample of people are asked what sum they are willing to pay to protect a natural feature. The average monetary response is multiplied by the number of American households to arrive at a specific dollar value. The EPA recently issued a rule requiring that the gargantuan Navajo Generating Station, a coal-burning power plant in Arizona, cut sulfur dioxide emissions by 90 percent at an annual cost of $89.6 million. The plant is only 12 miles north of Grand Canyon National Park. The ecological benefit of the rule is a 7 percent improvement of winter visibility in the Grand Canyon, meaning that a person can see about 133 miles instead of only 124. Is this worth $89.6 million annually? Yes, said the EPA, based on a survey in which a sample of the public was asked how much money their households would be willing to pay each year for cleaner Grand Canyon air. This turned out to be from $1.30 to $2.50 per year per household. The EPA multiplied these figures by the number of American households, making the visibility improvement worth $90 million to $200 million.[25]

Methods of calculating the value of human life are controversial because they clash with public values of fairness and equity. At first, environmental regulators estimated the value of a life based on future lifetime earnings. This method was attacked as unfair, because the lives of the poor or those with little income, for example, homemakers or retirees, had less value than the lives of the rich and those of younger wage earners. The method was quickly abandoned. One critic noted that such calculations run "directly contrary to the egalitarian principle, with origins deep in the Judeo-Christian heritage, that all persons are equal before the law and God."[26] However, no subsequent method for calculating the value of a life evades this basic shortcoming.

Today, the EPA uses a "willingness to pay" method that values a statistical life at $6.1 million. It arrives at this figure by combining data from surveys that ask people how much they are willing to pay for reducing the risk of early death and data from studies of the wage premium that workers accept to face the risks in dangerous jobs.[27] Critics attack this approach as flawed because workers are not always well informed about risks they face. And women, who are more risk averse than men, are underrepresented in dangerous jobs.[28] Recently the Bush administration instructed the EPA to use the statistic "life year saved" to value benefits of

[25] General Accounting Office, *Navajo Generating Station's Emissions Limit,* GAO/RCED–98–28, January 1998, pp. 1–3 and app. III.

[26] Thomas O. McGarity, "Health Benefits Analysis for Air Pollution Control: An Overview," in John Blodgett, ed., *Health Benefits of Air Pollution Control: A Discussion* (Washington, DC: Library of Congress, Congressional Research Service, February 27, 1989), p. 55.

[27] Charles W. Schmidt, "$ubjective $cience: Environmental Cost–Benefit Analysis," *Environmental Health Perspectives,* August 2003, p. A532.

[28] Frank Ackerman and Lisa Heinzerling, *Priceless: On Knowing the Price of Everything and the Value of Nothing* (New York: The New Press, 2004), p. 75.

environmental regulation. However, this metric was dropped after senior citizen groups objected that it discounted the value of their lives. Reducing risk for a 20-year-old would save more life years than for a 70-year-old.[29] Some opponents of life valuation reject all approaches, arguing that the very process of pricing human life mocks its extraordinary and sacred dignity.

Related criticisms come from environmentalists who dislike cost–benefit approaches because they invite trade-off of environmental quality. To them, pristine nature has an intrinsic value transcending money. In American history, the Bill of Rights and the Emancipation Proclamation were never subject to cost–benefit study; the moral rights they set forth were considered absolute.[30] Now we have a duty to respect nature as we respect humanity, apart from money considerations. Such objections reject the importance of efficiency in policy decisions. For many, maximum efficiency is not a test of the Good Society. Although cost–benefit analysis seems objective and neutral, it implies that ethical duties can be balanced against utilitarian benefits to society.

Another difficulty with cost–benefit analysis is that the benefits and costs of a program often fall to separate parties. Purifying factory wastewater raises costs to the business and to consumers of its product. Yet benefits from clean water accrue to shoreline property owners, realtors, individuals with lower medical bills, and fish. In such cases, weighing diverse cost–benefit effects raises questions of justice.

In sum, there is validity in criticisms of cost–benefit analysis, but it may nonetheless bring more efficient regulation. It is a hard reality that dollars for pollution abatement are limited. Decisions about where to spend them are required. One defender of the practice of monetizing human life puts it this way: "It's clearly not a winner when it comes to making yourself look good at public meetings, but it's the right thing to do from a public-safety standpoint."[31]

REGULATORY OPTIONS FOR MANAGING ENVIRONMENTAL RISKS

Regulators and legislators have many options for reducing risks to health and the environment. Figure 15.5 illustrates the range of choices. Most regulatory activity takes place on the far left of the spectrum. However, there is growing use of options to the right based on evidence that some balance between control and freedom is often more effective.

command-and-control regulation
The practice of regulating by setting uniform standards, strictly enforcing rules, and using penalties to force compliance.

Command-and-Control Regulation

One cause of high pollution-abatement costs is heavy reliance on *command-and-control regulation.* Most federal statutes ask regulators to set uniform standards across industries, apply rigid rules to individual pollution sources, specify cleanup

---

[29] John J. Fialka, "EPA to Stop 'Death Discount' to Value New Regulations," *The Wall Street Journal,* May 8, 2003, p. D3.

[30] Steven Kelman, "Cost–Benefit Analysis: An Ethical Critique," *Regulation,* January–February 1981, p. 31.

[31] W. Kip Viscusi, Harvard Law School, quoted in John J. Fialka, "Balancing Act: Lives vs. Regulations," *The Wall Street Journal,* May 30, 2003, p. A4.

FIGURE 15.5
The Spectrum of Regulatory Options

Command and control	Flexible enforcement	Market incentives	Required disclosure	Voluntary compliance

CONTROL   **FREEDOM**

technology, set strict timetables for action, issue permits, and enforce compliance, all with limited or no consideration of costs.

There are advantages to command-and-control regulation. It enforces predictable and uniform standards. There is great equity in applying the same rules to all firms in an industry. The record proves that it produces abatements and it comforts the public to know that the EPA is there like an old-fashioned schoolmarm, watching companies like a hawk, slapping wrists, and putting unregenerate polluters in the dunce's chair.

However, this approach can be inefficient and increase costs without commensurate increases in benefits. A study done by the EPA and Amoco Corporation showed how typical regulation worked at a single Amoco refinery. A key finding was that under the EPA's command-and-control regimen, cuts in air emissions cost an average $2,100 per ton, but if the refinery were given more flexibility, 90 percent of reductions would cost only $500 per ton.[32] This study was a major stimulus for the introduction of new methods for controlling pollution either by using market incentives or by making regulation more flexible.

Market Incentive Regulation

Market mechanisms give polluters financial motives to control pollution while also giving them flexibility in how reductions are to be achieved. The market forces this approach unleashes usually bring abatement more efficiently and creatively than traditional command-and-control regulation. In the past decade market incentives have grown in popularity, most of all in Europe, much less in the United States. There are many varieties of *market incentive regulation*.

market incentive regulation
The practice of harnessing market forces to motivate compliance with regulatory goals.

Taxes and Fees

Taxes and fees can be imposed on polluting emissions or products. Taxes and fees are widely used in Europe, where, for example, many countries tax air emissions. Italy puts a tax of 53 euros per ton per year on SO_2 emissions and 105 euros on NO_x emissions.[33] The United States has some similar taxes. Most states charge an annual fee of about $35 a ton, authorized in the Clean Air Act, for permits to emit criteria pollutants.[34] Product taxes are a variant. An Austrian tax on fertilizers and pesticides reduced their use by 30 percent within two years.

Sometimes taxes are coupled with incentives. The largest such scheme is in China, where the State Environmental Protection Administration applies a

[32] Caleb Solomon, "What Really Pollutes? Study of a Refinery Proves an Eye-Opener," *The Wall Street Journal*, March 29, 1993, p. A1.

[33] Organisation for Economic Co-operation and Development, *Economic Instruments for Pollution Control and Natural Resources Management in OECD Countries: A Survey* (Paris: OECD, October 1999), p. 16.

[34] Environmental Protection Agency, *The United States Experience with Economic Incentives for Protecting the Environment*, 240–R–01–001, January 2001, pp. 37–38.

combination of emission charges and pollution abatement subsidies along with traditional command-and-control regulation. Polluting firms pay charges based on wastewater discharges, air emissions, solid waste generation, and noise creation. Then up to 80 percent of the charge can be refunded to the firm for investment in pollution control. More than half a million companies in China are harnessed in this system and a World Bank study determined that it is highly effective in abating pollution.[35] Another example of a tax-subsidy tandem is the Swedish government's tax on NO_x emissions by electric power plants. The tax is collected from all electric companies, then rebated based on emissions per unit of energy produced. In this way the most efficient companies are subsidized by the least efficient ones.

environmental tax reform
The substitution of revenues from taxes on pollution for revenues from taxes on productivity.

More broadly, some countries are experimenting with *environmental tax reform,* or the substitution of revenues from taxes on pollution for revenues from taxes on productivity. Traditionally, the bulk of government revenues comes from income, sales, revenue, and payroll taxes. Advocates of environmental tax reform argue that substituting revenue from pollution taxes for revenue from taxes on productivity pays a double dividend. First, it reduces ecological harm. And second, it reduces the deadweight of taxation on activities that create wealth. European countries are the most aggressive with environmental tax reform. Germany began to substitute energy use taxes for taxes on labor in 1999. Norway has imposed taxes on electricity generation, fertilizers, pesticides, lubricating oil, gasoline, and other sources of pollution, and 4.9 percent of its revenue now comes from environmental levies.[36]

Deposit-and-Refund Laws

Deposit-and-refund laws require consumers of products that degrade the environment to pay an extra, refundable charge at the time of purchase, giving them an incentive to recycle the products after use. Only 10 states have laws providing redemption values for beverage containers, and the number is not growing. A similar device, the product take-back program, is designed to shift responsibility for pollution or waste creation from the end user to the manufacturer. These programs are most widespread in Europe. Manufacturers are required to take back or recycle their products, for example, car batteries and heavy applicances such as refrigerators, at the end of their lives. Sometimes the manufacturer is charged a fee for future disposal costs.

Emission Trading Programs

Emission trading programs, sometimes called cap-and-trade programs, work by setting an overall limit on emissions of a pollutant. Then total emissions are divided among individual sources by giving each source permits allowing the amount of pollution currently emitted. After that, sources are allowed to release only amounts they can cover with permits or suffer heavy fines. Each permit equals a unit of pollution, for example, one pound or one ton, and sources are

---

[35] Hua Wang and Ming Chen, *How the Chinese System of Charges and Subsidies Affects Pollution Control Efforts by China's Top Industrial Polluters* (Washington, DC: World Bank, Working Paper No. 2198, October 1, 1999).

[36] Ministry of Finance, "The History of Green Taxes in Norway," http://odin.dep.no/fin/engelsk/p4500279/p4500285/006041-990406/dok-bn.html, accessed November 2004.

allowed to trade them at a market price. Total emission reduction comes when, at scheduled intervals, the government retires permits from the market. Companies have a financial incentive to reduce emissions. By lowering emissions faster than required by permit reductions they can sell unused permits to other firms. And they must lower emissions as permits are retired or face the cost of buying additional ones at rising market rates.

Emission trading results in sources with low abatement costs taking out more of the pollution than sources with higher costs. It costs some companies less to abate pollution for many reasons, including the kind of fuel used, type of industrial process, age of equipment, and level of control already reached. Thus, the same net reduction is achieved at much lower cost than under a command-and-control system that ignores differences in marginal abatement costs from firm to firm.

The premier example of emission trading is the sulfur emissions trading program among coal-burning utilities in the United States. National emissions have been capped. On an auction market, or with each other, utilities now buy and sell one-ton permits to release SO_2. To reduce pollution, the EPA is retiring permits, in effect lowering the nationwide cap and clearing the nation's skies. It is estimated that the program has reduced SO_2 emissions at a cost savings of $700 million annually over traditional enforcement methods.[37] Its success has led to imitation by other governments. Now the Kyoto Protocol contains an elaborate trading mechanism for the exchange of greenhouse gas emission allowances.

Under the Kyoto Protocol, governments distribute allowances to emissions sources. Then, allowances are reduced so that reductions mandated in the treaty are met by each nation. As the number of allowances falls, companies have a range of options. They can simply reduce their emissions, and if they go below their targeted allowance, they can sell the difference to other emitters at a market price. They can offset above-allowance emissions by planting trees to absorb carbon. This may be done anywhere in the world, since carbon emissions are a global atmospheric problem. Or they can offset their over-allowance emissions by funding low-emissions technology in developing nations (which initially are not required to make cuts). Given these choices companies can pick the least costly way to comply with mandatory cuts in their emissions of warming gases.

Information Disclosure

Information disclosure about environmental performance is a form of regulation having the potential to harness market forces by affecting consumer perceptions and equity prices. An example is the Toxics Release Inventory (TRI) compiled by the EPA. Each year industrial facilities releasing any of 650 pollutants must report the amount of those emissions. The information is published, and citizens can search it to learn what substances they are exposed to by nearby businesses.[38] In 2002 reported toxic releases were 4.8 billion pounds. Since the TRI started in 1987, total releases have declined by 49 percent. Corporations dislike being listed as leading polluters by volume and there are many examples of reductions exceeding

---

[37] "Emissions Impossible?" *The Wall Street Journal,* July 23, 2001, p. A14.

[38] The Toxics Release Inventory home page is at www.epa.gov/tri.

those required by law just to avoid attracting attention. William K. Reilly, former head of the EPA, tells the story of Monsanto's chairman, who, after seeing the company's TRI data, realized for the first time how high the volume really was. He set a goal of reducing emissions by 90 percent over the next four years.[39]

Voluntary Regulation

Although they remain far less prevalent than command and control, market incentive approaches are growing in importance. Another way that regulation is made more flexible is the voluntary program. When industry complaints about suffocating enforcement rose in the 1980s, the EPA adopted a series of voluntary programs. Project XL (eXellence and Leadership) is an example.

In Project XL, the EPA collaborates with companies, relaxing rules to allow innovative, lower-cost ways of protecting the environment. Participating firms agree to reduce pollution beyond levels set by existing standards. A Georgia-Pacific pulp and paper mill at Big Island, Virginia, uses a chemical fluid to make pulp from hardwood. When the fluid is spent, it is evaporated and the residue incinerated, releasing hazardous air pollutants. To meet impending EPA emission standards it would have been necessary to spend millions of dollars rebuilding or retrofitting the incinerator. Instead, the company proposed to install an untried but promising new steam gasification technology. If it worked, it not only would cut toxic air emissions well below those achieved using existing technology, but would produce energy. However, it might not work. To encourage the company, the EPA put a special rule in the *Federal Register* delaying compliance deadlines so the new technology could be tried.[40]

Project XL is one of about 20 voluntary programs started by the EPA. AgSTAR promotes manure-handling practices that lower methane emissions from dairy and swine farms; Green Lights encourages energy-saving lighting; and National Environmental Performance Track enrolls companies with outstanding environmental records, then reduces their reporting requirements, lessens frequency of inspections, and allows them more flexible rule compliance.

When a company signs up for a voluntary program, there are often reporting requirements, but no enforcement actions are taken for failure to meet goals. Companies have many motives for participating. They get regulatory relief and there can be cost savings. The EPA freely hands out awards that have public relations value. Eastman Kodak entered the WasteWise program's Hall of Fame for recycling 650 million one-time-use cameras, taking almost 25 million pounds of plastics and printed circuit boards out of the waste stream. And companies can also create a competitive advantage. Improved environmental performance can raise costs for a firm's competitors if it signals to the EPA that other companies in the industry can reasonably be required to show similar performance.[41]

[39] William K. Reilly, "Private Enterprises and Public Obligations: Achieving Sustainable Development," *California Management Review,* Summer 1999, p. 22.

[40] "Amendments to Project XL Site-Specific Rulemaking for Georgia-Pacific Corporation's Facility in Big Island, VA," 68 FR 46102, August 5, 2003.

[41] Thomas P. Lyon, "'Green' Firms Bearing Gifts," *Regulation,* Fall 2003, p. 38.

Core Elements of an Environmental Management System

- An environmental policy
- Planning and strategy that include environmental factors
- Identification of impacts on the environment
- Development of goals and performance measures

- Monitoring and corrective action
- Formal stakeholder involvement
- Employee awards, incentives, and training
- A philosophy of continuous improvement

MANAGING ENVIRONMENTAL QUALITY

environmental management system
A set of methods and procedures for aligning corporate strategies, policies, and operations with principles that protect ecosystems.

In the 1970s corporations passed over a great divide, leaving an era of freedom in which they were subject to few environmental constraints and entering an era of strict rules and limits. At first, managers saw the new rules as cost burdens. A few resented regulators, hid problems, and resisted the laws. Most found regulation to be expensive, adversarial, and sometimes irrational, but they complied. Although resistance and grudging compliance remain, many companies have moved away from this, adopting management systems that protect the environment, often beyond regulatory requirements. This new thinking is not altruistic. As in the past, corporate alignment with social values is mainly a response to market pressures. Some of the most important market and nonmarket pressures are summarized in Table 15.1.

Environmental Management Systems

ISO 14001
A standard for an environmental management system that sets forth the basic elements of management action required in a competent effort.

The most proactive companies establish an *environmental management system* (EMS), which is a set of methods and procedures for aligning corporate strategies, policies, and operations with principles that protect ecosystems. The leading international model for such systems is *ISO 14001*, a standard for environmental management developed by the International Organization for Standardization. The letters ISO refer to the international body that created it, the International Organization for Standardization. The number 14001 indicates its place in the ISO 14000 family, a series of environmental standards including environmental labeling (ISO 14020), product life-cycle assessment (ISO 14040), and product design (ISO 14062). Some companies, for instance, ExxonMobil, design their own EMSs, but typically firms base them on ISO 14001 and apply for certification by trained third-party auditors. This is done because there is a trend for corporations to require suppliers and vendors to have a working EMS, and ISO 14001 certification verifies this. Matsushita Electrical Industries (Panasonic), for instance, has a procurement policy to consider a supplier's environmental record along with cost, quality, and delivery and gives priority to companies certified

TABLE 15.1 **Inducements to Higher Environmental Performance**

Consumer demands	Consumers increasingly favor less-polluting, resource-conserving products.
Insurance premiums	Insurers lower premiums for companies when they face less risk of liability for pollution damage.
Disclosure requirements	Government agencies require considerable public disclosure of environmental information. Toxics Release Inventory data is one example. Another is disclosure to investors of potential environmental liabilities in Form 10Ks required by the Securities and Exchange Commission.
Access to international markets	Nations vary in environmental requirements. European standards for recycling and packaging, for example, are often more strict than those in the United States.
Activist pressures	Environmental groups are vigilant and aggressive. They collect and distribute information about corporate performance. Some groups have developed performance standards and successfully pressured companies to adopt them. There are many partnerships between companies and activists.*
Regulatory relief	Companies in the EPA's flexible regulation projects that reduce compliance costs and pressures must have excellent compliance records and promise to exceed legal requirements in the future.
Legal liabilities	The law now has a tight grip on polluters. The EPA fines companies for violating laws. Managers have been imprisoned for criminal violations.
U.S. Sentencing Commission Guidelines	When criminal offenses occur, sentencing guidelines reduce penalties for companies and their managers if management controls to ensure compliance with environmental laws were in place.
Profit and cost reduction potential	Many companies find ways to convert former wastes into salable products or raw material for production processes. Changing production processes to reduce emissions often lowers costs. And studies suggest that firms with better environmental performance tend to be more profitable.†
Industry standards	Many industries, sometimes in cooperation with environmental groups, have created environmental management codes and systems. Two examples are the Sustainable Forestry Initiative of the pulp and paper industry and the Responsible Care Program of the chemical industry. Most industry codes require auditing to certify companies as in compliance.
Cross-industry standards	A set of standards named ISO 14000, developed by the International Standards Organization, sets up universal standards for managing environmental aspects of manufacturing. To be certified under these standards, companies must go through a rigorous inspection and auditing process. The Global Reporting Initiative requires reporting of a "triple bottom line" that includes information about environmental impacts. Increasingly, companies and governments around the world are requiring that suppliers be certified under some of these green codes.

*Dennis A. Rondinelli and Ted London, "How Corporations and Environmental Groups Cooperate: Assessing Cross-Sector Alliances and Collaborations," *Academy of Management Executive*, February 2003.
†For example, Glen Dowell, Stuart Hart, and Bernard Yeung, "Do Corporate Global Environmental Standards Create or Destroy Market Value?" *Management Science*, August 2000.

under ISO 14001.[42] The green procurement trend is responsible for an explosion in worldwide ISO certifications from 257 facilities in 1995 to more than 66,000 in 2003.[43] Many certifications are in developing economies. More facilities in China have adopted ISO 14001 than in the United States.

CAPITALISM EVOLVING

The spread of environmental management suggests that the business community is rethinking old assumptions about its relationship to nature. We cannot predict how far this rethinking will go, but a recent book, *Natural Capitalism,* offers a vision of sustainable activity that stands in contrast to the exploitation of nature in traditional industrial capitalism.[44] Its authors argue that four major shifts are required to create a new paradigm of "natural capitalism."

First, companies must become much more productive with resources and be far more conserving of energy and material.

Second, there must be a shift to biologically inspired production models in which the waste is not released as pollution but becomes an input for another process. This mimics nature where, for example, waste of one species is food for another. In fact, industrial facilities can be connected in a web of materials exchange. At Kalundborg, an industrial park in Denmark, some facilities feed off each other this way. One plant makes plasterboard using surplus gas from a refinery and gypsum from a coal-burning power plant. The power plant also sends excess steam to a pharmaceutical plant and warm water to a fish farm.

Third, strategy must move to new business models emphasizing services rather than the sale of goods. The authors illustrate this with the story of a carpet company that redefined its business from making and selling new carpet to the service of providing floor covering. After once installing carpets, it later replaces only worn areas and recycles old carpeting into new. This service and recycling approach reduces the extraction of virgin resources from nature.

Fourth, business must reinvest in natural capital by finding ways to create value from maintenance and restoration of ecosystems.

Capitalism, as practiced now, conforms little to this nature-friendly vision. Nevertheless, companies are taking a broad range of actions to reduce adverse environmental impacts. What follows are some illustrations, often from the vanguard, of these actions.

precautionary principle
As a general rule, when industrial activity poses a risk to human health or ecosystems, if that risk is poorly understood, then prudence calls for restraint.

- *Precautionary action.* An idea called the *precautionary principle,* which has taken root among environmentalists, holds that when industrial activity poses a risk to human health or ecosystems, even if that threat is as yet poorly understood, prudence calls for restraint. Recently, advances in methods for detecting

[42] Matsushita Electric Group, *Green Procurement Standards,* rev. ed., ver. 3 (Osaka: Matsushita Electric Industrial Co., Ltd., August 27, 2003), p. 3.

[43] International Organization for Standardization, *2003 ISO Survey* (Geneva: International Organization for Standardization, December 2003), p. 22.

[44] Amory B. Lovins, L. Hunter Lovins, and Paul Hawken, *Natural Capitalism: Creating the Next Industrial Revolution* (Boston: Little Brown, 1999).

chemicals in living tissue led scientists to discover tiny amounts of the substance perfluorooctane sulfonate (PFO), as little as 0.5 parts per million, in human blood and animal tissue around the world. The source is 3M Co., which began using the chemical in Scotchgard fabric protector in the late 1950s. Learning this, 3M scientists expressed surprise and disbelief. They examined health data on workers at Scotchgard plants exposed to PFO over many years and found no adverse effects. However, 3M decided to take the product off the market in 2000 to avert any possible harm to life. Since it had no substitute for PFO, it lost a $500 million-a-year business.[45] Of course, the company anticipated government action and it was petrified by the lawsuit potential. These pressures enforced the precautionary principle, illustrating once again that environmental responsibility by business is most often an adaptation to compelling forces.

pollution prevention
The modification of industrial processes to eliminate contaminants before they are created. In contrast, end-of-pipe control methods trap pollutants after their creation.

- *Pollution prevention.* End-of-the-pipe control technologies isolate or neutralize pollutants after they are generated. Pollution prevention is the modification of industrial processes to eliminate contaminants before they are created. For example, many companies have stopped using solvents to clean production equipment, substituting soap or isopropyl alcohol in their place. This eliminates evaporation of hazardous compounds in solvents and often works just as well and at lower cost. Simple forms of pollution prevention, such as putting a lid on a tank to stop evaporation or tightening valves to stop leaks, are used by many companies. After such easy steps, however, pollution prevention requires complex redesigns of processes and products. These projects are expensive and raise technical barriers. At many firms, pollution prevention projects will not be approved, even if they reduce harmful emissions or reduce costs, unless they will bring a return on capital invested equal to or greater than alternative investments.

- *Product analysis.* Products can be examined from an environmental standpoint. Eastman Kodak uses life-cycle assessment to gauge the environmental impact of a product from manufacturing through lifetime use to disposal. The company looks at factors such as raw materials used, energy consumed, emissions, and potential for recycling. Hewlett-Packard has a network of more than 70 "product stewards," each in charge of the environmental impact of a specific product line.[46]

- *Environmental metrics.* Companies are innovating to find better ways of measuring environmental costs and performance. In the past, costs such as record keeping for hazardous substances or excess energy consumption have been hidden in overhead accounts. External costs that companies impose on society by damaging the environment have gone unmeasured and are not incorporated into management accounting. Some companies are experimenting with accounting methods that reveal such formerly obscured costs and are developing innovative ways to measure environmental performance. SC Johnson uses a "greenlist" to rate ingredients for its household products. Its chemists have

[45] Joseph Weber, "3M's Big Cleanup," *BusinessWeek,* June 5, 2000, pp. 96–97.
[46] Lynelle Preston, "Sustainability at Hewlett-Packard: From Theory to Practice," *California Management Review,* Spring 2001, p. 27.

many raw material choices for the surfactants, solvents, propellants, fragrances, and other ingredients that go into insecticides, waxes, and cleaners. Before choosing, they look at a scorecard that ranks substances from 0 to 3 based on an overall rating of human and environmental toxicity. A 0 means "restricted use" and requires higher management approval, 1 is "acceptable," 2 is "better," and 3 is "best." Chemists try to achieve higher scores as they formulate products. After the scorecard appeared in 2001, the company set a goal of raising ingredient scores by 8 percent in two years across all brands and tied employee and team compensation to that objective. By 2003 brand scores had improved an average 12.5 percent.[47]

CONCLUDING OBSERVATIONS

Global economic growth carries with it many threats to the thin, fragile biosphere in which human life exists. As such threats are recognized, societies adopt regulations to control the danger. However, regulation that only commands is inadequate to the ultimate task, which is the creation of industrial activity that harmonizes with natural cycles.

In this chapter we explained interim progress that is making regulation more flexible and focused on the greatest risks to human health. Then we enumerated forces in the business environment that create incentives in industry to operate more sustainably. These forces have led to the adoption of more eco-efficient management styles. The trend is clearly toward less-polluting, less-resource-intensive economic activity. The reality, however, is that while leading corporations are more environmentally proactive, sustainability is as yet a remote ideal.

[47] World Business Council for Sustainable Development, *SC Johnson: Easing Our Ecological Footprint* (Geneva: WBCSD, September 14, 2004), www.wbcsd.org.

Johns Manville Corporation and the Asbestos Nightmare

Like a cinema character who falls from glory to misfortune but eventually recovers the Good Life, Johns Manville Corporation has a story to tell. Founded in 1901, it was the world's largest asbestos company and it prospered until the 1970s, when growing fear of disease wilted demand for the substance. Then, injured workers sued the company, throwing it into bankruptcy.

While sheltered in bankruptcy during the 1980s, it set up a special trust arrangement to compensate asbestos victims. It also stopped making asbestos products. Emerging from bankruptcy, the company returned to profitability and was bought by Warren Buffett in 2001. As a member of Buffett's Berkshire Hathaway family of companies, and free of all responsibility for paying asbestos victims, it now prospers again.

This is a happy ending, but only because Johns Manville escaped the turbulence in its wake, a vortex that has since pulled other companies into bankruptcy and threatens to swallow more.

ASBESTOS

Asbestos is a generic term for a family of fibrous minerals found mainly in underground rock formations. The asbestos most widely used in industrial society is chrysotile (KRIS-ah-till); among other kinds, only

An old photograph showing spray application of LIMPET asbestos, a product of the Keasbey and Mattison Company. The two unprotected workmen at right are feeding lumps of asbestos into mixing machines. Source: *American Journal of Public Health* 81, no. 6 (June 1991), p. 796. © American Journal of Public Health.

amosite (AM-ah-site) and crocidolite (crow-SID-alight) have seen commercial application and only in very small amounts.[1]

To get asbestos, ore is mined and put through a manufacturing process. Rocks are crushed to free asbestos fibers, and a blowing process separates them from the debris. These fibers are then combined with other materials to make commercial products. For instance, fibers longer than 1 centimeter (about 4/10 inch) can be spun with cotton into yarn for fireproof clothing. Short fibers of 5 micrometers or less can be matted with wool to create felt insulation for boiler pipes. Asbestos easily blends with other materials and has been used in a wide range of products, including ceiling tile, roofing, cement, gaskets, and plastics. It has phenomenal strength, does not

burn, resists heat conduction and dampens sound. So it adds these useful qualities to any material with which it is joined. Over the years, asbestos has brought great benefits to society. Its fire-proofing quality has saved uncounted lives. In brake linings, it has increased motor vehicle safety. Its use in paint, roofing, and insulation has added comfort to living.

Workers are exposed to asbestos when they breathe air containing fibers the size of tiny motes of dust. Even the largest chrysotile fibers have a diameter only one-twenty-fifth that of a human hair, so they are easily inhaled. Being sharp, the fibers tend to stick in the lungs. Inhalation exposures lead to characteristic medical conditions. The least serious are pleural plaques, or thickening of the membranes lining the lungs that cause no impairment and do not lead to additional illness. Asbestosis is an irreversible scarring of the lungs that in mild cases causes no symptoms, but leads to shortness of breath

[1] All types of asbestos are inorganic chemical compounds; chrysotile, for example, is composed of magnesium, silicon, oxygen, and hydrogen $(3MgO \bullet 2SiO_2 \bullet 2H_2O)$.

in moderate cases and to progressive breathing impairment in severe cases. The fibers also initiate cellular changes leading to lung cancer and to mesothelioma, a fatal cancer of the abdominal wall. Because of long latency periods after exposure, at least 10 years and as many as 40 years can pass before the onset of illness.

Chrysotile is less dangerous than other kinds of asbestos. Within weeks to months after inhalation, the lungs expel most chrysotile fibers. Amosite and crocidolite fibers, on the other hand, remain embedded for many years. Chrysotile fibers, because of their curled shape, do not penetrate as deeply into lung tissue and, because of their chemical composition, break up more easily. Nevertheless, prolonged exposure to chrysotile dust is extremely dangerous. An epidemiological study of 17,800 insulation workers revealed it to be a potent carcinogen. In a 10-year period, these workers had 486 lung cancers, 460 percent more than the 105.6 cases predicted for a general population.[2]

Even low exposures to asbestos are dangerous. Illness has been found among family members of asbestos workers whose only exposure was the dust that came into the home on the breadwinner's clothes at the end of the day.[3] Years ago, in asbestos towns, where sons followed fathers into dusty plants, the ranks of families were decimated. Because of widespread use, the general population in developed countries is still exposed to asbestos. Autopsy results show that most people have less than 50 asbestos fibers per gram of dry lung, however. Heavy occupational exposures can create a burden of more than four million fibers per gram of dry lung.[4]

[2] Irving J. Selikoff et al., "Mortality Experience of Insulation Workers in the United States and Canada, 1943–1976," *Annals of the New York Academy of Sciences* 330 (1976), pp. 91–116.

[3] Henry A. Anderson et al., "Asbestosis among Household Contacts of Asbestos Factory Workers," in Irving J. Selikoff and E. Cuyler Hammond, eds., *Health Hazards of Asbestos Exposure* (New York: New York Academy of Sciences, 1979), p. 387.

[4] Hiroyuki Yamada et al., "Talc and Amosite/Crocidolite Preferentially Deposited in the Lungs of Nonoccupational Female Lung Cancer Cases in Urban Areas of Japan," *Environmental Health Perspectives,* May 1997, pp. 505–6; and Andrew Churg et al., Correspondence, *The New England Journal of Medicine,* October 1, 1998, p. 999.

THE ASBESTOS GIANT

Johns Manville Corporation was created in the merger of two roofing and insulating companies in 1901. It grew over the years, and by the 1960s it had 33 plants and mines and turned out more than 500 asbestos-bearing products. And it was extremely profitable. Management applied heavy pressure on business units to make quarterly and yearly performance numbers.

Johns Manville workers and managers knew that asbestos dust caused serious illness. As early as the 1940s, the company installed advanced dust collection and filtration machinery to protect workers. But in many plants where profit pressure existed, operation of this equipment was considered a cost unrelated to productivity, and so repair and maintenance were deferred.

Bill Sells, a Johns Manville manager in the 1960s, told of acquiring a new vocabulary after taking over the Waukegan, Illinois, plant. A worker who had serious asbestosis was said to be "dusted." When the company physician took X rays and discovered workers with pathological lung changes, these "red cases" had to be assigned to lower-exposure areas. Sells installed better ventilation systems and saw improvement in companywide practice, but it came too late. "During the 1970s and 1980s," he writes, "I had to say good-bye to every member of my Waukegan administrative staff. They had become my friends and now, one by one, they contracted mesothelioma and died."[5]

Sells blames the failure to protect workers on a corporate culture that reinforced an attitude of denial. Managers believed that asbestos was a terrific product and that the company was doing what it could to reduce exposure. In fact, Johns Manville had set an exposure limit of 6 f/cm^3 (fibers per cubic centimeter) in its plants, half the standard of 12 f/cm^3 recommended in the 1960s by an industry trade association and well below the probable 100 f/cm^3 or more exposures that occurred years before in uncontrolled plants. This was commendable, but the company went no further. It did not, for example, aggressively fund research to confirm the safety of any exposure level. Today the standard set as safe by the Occupational Safety and Health Administration

[5] Bill Sells, "What Asbestos Taught Me about Managing Risk," *Harvard Business Review,* March–April 1994, p. 82.

is 0.2 f/cm^3, only 3 percent of Johns Manville's 1960s standard.[6]

BANKRUPTCY

Johns Manville's culture of denial got a rude shock in the 1970s when injured workers began to sue and received large awards from juries. Two important changes in the law were responsible. First, courts permitted workers to bring tort actions, or suits alleging wrongful acts, against asbestos makers. Previously, they had been restricted to low-paying state worker-compensation claims. Second, there were major changes in products liability law, or the body of common law that requires manufacturers such as Johns Manville to compensate persons who are injured by their products.

Before the 1960s, manufacturer liability was based on the idea of *negligent conduct.* For an injured person to win in court, a manufacturer had to be proven negligent, that is, shown to have acted without reasonable care in making a product. But by the time asbestos cases arose, product liability law had begun to incorporate a theory of *strict liability,* under which manufacturers could be found legally responsible for injuring consumers even if they had not been negligent.[7] The rise of strict liability made it much harder for Johns Manville to win cases. A landmark defeat for the company came in 1982, when a court accepted the argument that it was liable for asbestos injury even without the plaintiff proving that management knew asbestos was dangerous.[8] This decision turned the tide of litigation against Johns Manville, making bankruptcy inevitable.

In other cases, attorneys proved that the firm's executives engaged in a conspiracy to hide the dangers of asbestos. They learned that in the 1920s

Raybestos-Manhattan, a brake-lining manufacturer, had requested that Metropolitan Life Insurance Co. undertake health surveys of its workers. Metropolitan reported in 1931 that there was a high incidence of asbestosis among Raybestos-Manhattan workers and issued a strong warning about asbestos. The report was discussed at a meeting between top executives of Johns Manville and Raybestos-Manhattan, and those present agreed to keep the information secret to avoid lawsuits. The minutes of the meeting were locked in a vault at Raybestos-Manhattan until the executive keeping them died; then they were given to the man's relatives, who kept them in storage for many years. After asbestos litigation appeared, a family member chose to give the secret meeting minutes to an attorney for asbestos victims.

With the conspiracy revealed, Johns Manville could no longer convince juries that management had been unaware of asbestos dangers in the past. Juries that heard about the secret meeting set records awarding punitive damages to sick workers. Punitive damages are sums awarded in excess of due compensation for injury to punish a corporation for flagrant misbehavior.

Another breakthrough was the testimony of Dr. Kenneth W. Smith, a former company doctor at a Johns Manville plant in Canada. Smith stated that in 1949 he grew concerned about employees and sent a report to management stating that of 708 workers he had X-rayed, only 4 had normal, healthy lungs. To avoid upsetting the workers and lowering their productivity, he withheld his findings from them. Dr. Smith documented the fact that top company officers—including a future Johns Manville president—had seen his report but did not act on it.

The growth curve in the number of suits was rapid. The first came in 1968, and by 1973 there were only 13; but by 1980 there were 5,000 and by 1982 there were 16,500. Most of the plaintiffs were not Johns Manville employees. They had worked at shipyards, factories, and construction companies using the company's products. Ultimately, the beleaguered firm could no longer hold back the deluge. Another 36,000 claims were predicted for a total liability of at least $2 billion and probably much more. In fact, this would turn out to be a gross underestimate. However, at the time, even $2 billion was unaffordable.

On August 26, 1982, Johns Manville filed a voluntary petition to reorganize under Chapter 11 of the

---

[6] The permissible exposure limit is a time-weighted average of 0.2 fibers > 5 mm/cm^3, eight hours per day, 40 hours per week.

[7] See American Law Institute, *Restatement of the Law of Torts, 2d,* vol. 2 (Washington, DC: American Law Institute Publishers, 1965), sec. 402A, pp. 347–48. Section 402A imposes liability for damages on anyone who sells a product in defective condition unreasonably dangerous to the consumer where the product reaches the consumer without substantial change and causes the consumer injury even though the seller has exercised all possible care in the manufacture and distribution of the product.

[8] *Beshada v. Johns-Manville Products Corp.,* 90 N.J. 191, 447 A.2d 539 (1982).

Bankruptcy Reform Act of 1978. Chapter 11 allows companies that might become bankrupt to restructure their debts before insolvency occurs.

THE BANKRUPTCY PERIOD

The day after the bankruptcy, Johns Manville published a letter in leading newspapers trying to explain its action to creditors, investors, and the public.

> To avoid Chapter 11, we would have had to strangle the company slowly, by deferring maintenance and postponing capital expenditures. We would also have had to cannibalize our good business just to keep going. If recent trends had continued, we would have had to mortgage our plants and properties and new credit would be most difficult and expensive to obtain. This is no way to go forward.

However, controversy followed. A *Fortune* magazine writer called it "a particularly daring example of the new uses of bankruptcy,"[9] and a Harvard law professor admired it as "pretty creative."[10] A former asbestos worker accused the firm of "cold-hearted profit motives" and "murder."[11]

Johns Manville continued normal business operations but was protected from creditors. Payments to suppliers, banks, and victorious plaintiffs stopped. Lawsuits were frozen. The company's assets were sequestered until it negotiated with its creditors a reorganization agreement, or a plan to pay its debts, and had the plan approved by a bankruptcy court.

Six years passed as the company negotiated such a plan with attorneys for asbestos victims and other creditors. During this time, more than 2,000 claimants died while their lawsuits were stalled by the bickering.

A TRUST IS BORN

In late 1988 Johns Manville emerged from Chapter 11. The court-approved reorganization plan required putting $2.5 billion into a trust fund that would be run independently of the company and from which payments to all present and future victims would be made.

To fund the Manville Personal Injury Settlement Trust, as it was officially named, the company did a one-for-eight reverse split of common shares and turned over 80 percent of them to the trust. If, for example, you had held 800 shares of Johns Manville before the split, you owned only 100 afterward. The other 700 went to the trust to pay asbestos victims. Thus, common shareholders—including many former asbestos-plant employees—were the biggest financial losers under the reorganization plan. Ironically, Johns Manville's victims became its new owners because the trust, owning most of the common shares, had effective control of the company.

There was more. Johns Manville also had to pay into the trust 20 percent of its adjusted net earnings (a measure of profit) beginning in 1992 and for as long as needed to pay all injury claims. In return, the plan gave current and former company executives permanent immunity from lawsuits and shielded the company from further asbestos suits.

Sick workers who had waited six years to resolve their cases now could only apply to the trust for compensation. Under the trust's rules, Johns Manville's payout to asbestos victims was limited and far lower than it would have been had the pre–Chapter 11 lawsuits gone forward. This was the key to the company's survival. The trust would pay scheduled amounts; there would be no more crushing punitive damages awarded.

The company's CEO, W. Thomas Stephens, argued that the reorganization plan was fair and noted that most of the managers who had made mistakes in years past were now dead. "I get a little hot under the collar when people say that [Johns] Manville entered Chapter 11 to evade its legal responsibilities," he said. "Giving up $2.5 billion, 20 percent of your profits, and 80 percent of your stock is not exactly walking away from the right solution."[12]

---

[9] Anna Cifelli, "Management in Bankruptcy," *Fortune,* October 31, 1983, p.18.

[10] Quote in Clemens P. Work, "Bankruptcy: An Escape Hatch for Ailing Firms," *U.S. News & World Report,* August 22, 1983, p. 66.

[11] Quoted in Ben Sherwood, Gary Geipel, "Asbestos Lawsuits Paralyzed, House Panel Told," *Los Angeles Times,* February 11, 1983.

[12] Quoted in George Melloan, "A Company Held Captive by the Plaintiff Bar," *The Wall Street Journal,* October 4, 1988, p. A29.

THE REBIRTH OF JOHNS MANVILLE

During its six years in Chapter 11, Johns Manville ended all asbestos operations. On emerging from bankruptcy, it no longer sold any asbestos-bearing products, but it had other problems. Its reputation had suffered. Eventually, it tried to escape the asbestos stigma with a short-lived name change to Shuller Corporation in 1996.[13] However, because the Johns Manville brand name was so well established, a new CEO reversed this decision a year later.

Another major problem was making its common shares attractive again to investors. Although Johns Manville showed annual profits throughout the bankruptcy years (except for three years when extraordinary charges related to reorganization occurred) and remained profitable, investors were frightened away by its future obligation to pay 20 percent of its profits to the trust. To make the stock more attractive, the company and the trust negotiated an agreement in 1994 in which the company gave the trust an additional 32.5 million shares and, in return, the annual profit payment to the trust was eliminated.

PROBLEMS WITH THE TRUST

The goal of the trust is to pay fair compensation to all asbestos victims over time. Each is to receive "as equivalent a share as possible of their claims' values" no matter what year their claim is made.[14] When it was created in 1988, epidemiologists and statisticians predicted about 100,000 asbestos-injury claims would be settled for an average of $25,000 each. However, both claims and settlements soon swelled far beyond expectations. By 1990 the trust had settled 23,867 claims at an average $43,231 each, and an additional 157,000 claims existed. More were predicted. Based on these numbers, the trust could not pay existing claims, let alone future ones.[15]

When this shortfall became apparent, a federal judge ordered the trust to suspend payments until revised payout guidelines could be set up. It took 4½ years of legal wrangling before operations resumed. The solution was to pay only 10 percent of the value of all current and future claims and to reduce the fees of lawyers representing victims to 25 percent of their awards. So, for example, a former shipyard worker with mesothelioma, entitled to receive $200,000 for the illness under the original payout schedule, got only $20,000 and might owe a lawyer $5,000, netting only $15,000 in the end. The bankruptcy court judged this plan fair since all present and future claimants would be equally paid.[16] But victims felt anger and disappointment.

Part of the problem was that most of the trust's assets were its holdings of Johns Manville stock. By the mid-1990s, the trust still held approximately 80 percent of Johns Manville shares. Since the stock remained under a cloud because of uncertainty about the obligations of the company to the trust, share price did not appreciate. Eventually, the trust decided that the best way to raise cash was to sell the company.[17] In early 2001 it sold all its shares to Berkshire Hathaway, which purchased Johns Manville for approximately $1.8 billion and began to operate it as a wholly owned subsidiary.[18]

The company continues to be a leading manufacturer of insulation and building materials. Today it has about 10,000 employees and revenues of more than $2 billion. It no longer carries any legal obligation to help asbestos victims. That burden now falls entirely on the trust.

Unfortunately for the trust, the Johns Manville sale failed to remedy its long-term underfunding. The number of claims continued to rise beyond those anticipated, and in mid-2001 the trust cut the pro rata amount it pays on claims from 10 percent to only 5 percent. As claims continued to rise another cut to

[13] Over the years, the company has had the following name changes: H. W. Johns-Manville Company (1901), Johns-Manville Corporation (1926), Manville Corporation (1981), Schuller Corporation (1996), and Johns Manville Corporation (1997).

[14] Manville Personal Injury Settlement Trust, *2002 Trust Distribution Process*, www.mantrust.org, p. 1, accessed November 28, 2004.

[15] *Ocsek v. Manville Corp. Asbestos Compensation Fund,* 956 F.2d 152 (7th Cir. 1992) at 154.

[16] *In re Johns-Manville Corporation,* 876 F. Supp. 473 (E. & S.D.N.Y. 1995).

[17] Daniel Gross, "Recovery Lessons from an Industrial Phoenix," *New York Times,* April 29, 2001, p. C4.

[18] Berkshire Hathaway Inc., Form 10K, March 30, 2001, p. 9.

EXHIBIT 1

Source: Manville Personal Injury Settlement Trust, *2002 Trust Distribution Process* (Bedford, NY: MPIST, September 12, 2002), pp. 7–10.

The Manville Personal Injury Settlement Trust pays claims for eight levels of asbestos disease. The amount it pays is called the scheduled value, which is based on a review of historical settlements and current court awards.

As the levels rise the injury is more serious and to get compensation claimants must present more evidence of exposure to Johns Manville asbestos products. Level I, other asbestos disease, includes primarily cases of pleural plaques or pleural thickening and requires proof of some exposure to Manville asbestos. Levels II, III, and IV require proof of at least six months of occupational exposure to Manville asbestos and medical documentation showing progressively more serious incapacity. Level V includes colorectal, laryngeal, esophageal, pharyngeal, or stomach cancers associated with asbestos exposure. Levels VI and VII include lung cancers in persons with occupational exposure to asbestos, but those who also have pleural plaques or asbestosis are placed in the higher level. Finally, Level VIII includes those who provide evidence of asbestos exposure and a diagnosis of mesothelioma.

Current rules permit the trust to pay only 5 percent of the scheduled value in each category.

Level	Scheduled Disease	Scheduled Value
I	Other Asbestos Disease	$600
II	Asbestosis/Pleural Disease	$12,000
III	Asbestosis/Pleural Disease	$25,000
IV	Severe Asbestosis Disease	$95,000
V	Other Cancer	$45,000
VI	Lung Cancer (One)	$95,000
VII	Lung Cancer (Two)	$95,000
VIII	Mesothelioma	$350,000

2.5 percent seemed imminent. The major problem was that law firms were submitting large numbers of claims for unimpaired workers with X-ray anomalies that had been interpreted as asbestos injury. These workers had no health problems and their lung abnormalities were not necessarily caused by asbestos. Areas of lung abnormality have multiple causes and appear in about one-quarter of the working-age population. Moreover, when the trust audited a sample of X rays it found that 41 percent of them showed either no injury or less injury than the submitting law firm claimed.[19]

In 2002, a bankruptcy court judge allowed the trust to require more medical evidence and to lower its payments in the disease categories where the unimpaired claims fell. This led to a decline in claims, but the trust is still paying only 5 percent of the scheduled value for the eight categories of asbestos

disease shown in Exhibit 1. Although about 100,000 claims to be settled at an average of $25,000 each had been expected in 1988, by 2004 the trust had paid out $3.2 billion to settle 623,391 claims at an average of only $5,153 each.[20] Its net worth was $1.6 billion, but with more than 6,000 claims arriving each month it was unable to increase its payout, even to seriously ill victims.

THE ASBESTOS NIGHTMARE

After the Johns Manville bankruptcy, lawyers moved against other asbestos companies. Law firms specializing in asbestos exposure cases organized large numbers of claims, forcing the companies one by one to enter Chapter 11. Twenty-five of them set up trusts similar to the Johns Manville trust, and these too

[19] Lester Brickman, "On the Theory Class's Theories of Asbestos Litigation: The Disconnect between Scholarship and Reality," *Pepperdine Law Review* 31, no. 33 (2003), p. 132.

[20] Manville Personal Injury Trust, *Financial Statements and Report of Manville Personal Injury Settlement Trust for the Period Ending June 30, 2004*, exhibit III, at www.mantrust.org.

have been inadequately funded to handle the number of new claims submitted to them. When the assets of asbestos makers had been depleted, entrepreneurial law firms began to sue companies in other industries where workers had been exposed to asbestos products. So far, more than 70 companies have been driven into bankruptcy and about 8,400 others have been sued.

The cases now target companies in 44 of the 82 standard industrial categories.[21] Automakers Daimler-Chrysler, Ford Motor, and General Motors face suits over exposure from asbestos in brake linings. Others include Campbell Soup, Dow Chemical, General Electric, Georgia-Pacific, IBM, Procter & Gamble, and Sears. The drug company Pfizer was hit with 171,611 lawsuits because one of its subsidiaries had made asbestos-containing coatings for industrial equipment before it was acquired in 1968.[22] Overall, it is estimated that industry has paid as much as $54 billion for asbestos claims, about $20 billion of which has gone to attorneys' fees. As many as 50,000 jobs have been lost as a consequence of bankruptcies.[23]

Heavy workplace exposures to asbestos ended by the mid-1970s. Asbestos cancer mortality is declining. Since asbestosis usually appears about 10 years after exposure, new cases should be in steep decline. Yet the number of asbestos claims continues to rise. The reason is that attorneys, who typically get 25 to 40 percent of monetary awards, are recruiting new litigants. In addition, asbestos lawsuits have overwhelmed American courts, leading to a series of procedural changes and rulings designed to process cases more efficiently by relaxing standards. These alterations have made it easier to get awards and have encouraged more lawsuits.

Plaintiffs are now recruited by screening companies. These for-profit entities take mobile X-ray units from town to town, stopping at union halls, hotels, motels, and mall parking lots to conduct mass screenings for asbestos injury. Before X rays are given, the person being screened must sign a form agreeing to let a sponsoring law firm represent him or her. The X rays are often read on the spot and if an abnormality exists the person may be given further medical examination.

There is considerable subjectivity in the reading of chest X rays. Opaque spots on the lungs may indicate asbestos injury, but there are as many as 150 other conditions that could cause them. Since the screening companies are paid based on the number of litigants they generate, there is an incentive to interpret abnormalities as consistent with asbestos damage. Workers come for the screenings in the hope of getting money they would not otherwise have had. "The lawyers said I could get $10,000 or $12,000 if the shadow is big enough, and I know just the fishing boat I'd buy with that," said one worker.[24]

Almost all claims from mass recruitment efforts are claims for pleural plaques or asbestosis based on interpretation of abnormalities in X rays. Anyone with a lung abnormality and an occupational history of working near asbestos is a potential litigant. If workers do not remember what asbestos products they were around, they are coached. A paralegal who worked with asbestos litigants explains how it worked. "I'd go through page by page and encourage the client to recall the products they used. It would be pretty strong encouragement. Most of the time when I left, I had ID [identification] for every manufacturer that we needed to get ID for."[25] The result of these tactics is that 90 percent of asbestos claims facing companies today are for people who are unimpaired. They are not sick and may never get sick.

More than 610,000 asbestos claims are currently before the courts. Some judges resort to a wholesale approach for settling cases. In so-called inventory settlements, lawyers demand that companies pay aggregate sums in the millions of dollars to large groups of claimants. If the companies refuse, the attorneys threaten to take the cases before juries one by one. Most companies are unwilling to risk large punitive damage awards from juries sympathetic to sick

[21] Roger Parloff, "Welcome to the New Asbestos Scandal," *Fortune,* September 6, 2004, p. 190.

[22] "Pfizer Settles Asbestos Litigation," *Los Angeles Times,* September 4, 2004, p. C3.

[23] Michelle J. White, "Resolving the 'Elephantine Mass,'" *Regulation,* Summer 2003, p. 48.

[24] Quoted in Andrew Schneider, "Asbestos Lawsuits Anger Critics," *St. Louis Post Dispatch,* February 9, 2003, p. A1; cited in Brickman, "On the Theory Class's Theories of Asbestos Litigation," n. 105.

[25] Quoted in Christine Biederman, "Toxic Justice," *Dallas Observer,* August 13, 1998, p. 12; cited in Brickman, "On the Theory Class's Theories of Asbestos Litigation," n. 393.

workers, so they cave in.[26] However, as a consequence they wind up paying large sums to people who are not sick and who they may not have harmed, since the only evidence of exposure to their asbestos product decades earlier may be the coached statements of recall by workers.

Another form of asbestos bankruptcy is the prepackaged bankruptcy. Here the company negotiates outside of court with law firms representing large numbers of injury claims. Before entering bankruptcy, the company agrees to turn over to the claimants a sum of assets and the rights to all proceeds from its insurance policies. It then goes through only a brief bankruptcy period because the arrangements for settling its debts have already been worked out.

The winners in this arrangement are the corporation, the mass of unimpaired claimants, and their attorneys, who collect up to 40 percent of the compensation in contingency fees. There are two losers. Insurance companies are forced to pay once the company concedes liability and enters bankruptcy. Courts have ruled that insurers that covered companies when workers were exposed to asbestos are responsible for settlements years, even decades, later when asbestos illness becomes manifest. Because of the vulnerability of insurers, many asbestos attorneys have sued very small companies with no assets just to milk their old insurance policies. Seriously ill asbestos victims also lose. Because so much money is handed out to healthy claimants and in attorney fees, less remains to compensate them. Former Attorney General Griffin B. Bell has called it "an injustice that lawyers routinely receive 33% to 40% of each recovery, often aggregating to millions of dollars, while sick and needy claimants receive less than they deserve."[27]

Asbestos compensation is an intractable problem. The work of plaintiffs' attorneys has been called scandalous, fraudulent, and corrupt. For years *The Wall Street Journal* has editorially cursed the "asbestos legal blob" engulfing the courts and industry.[28] No device or arrangement for compensating victims has worked well. The tort system and the courts are overwhelmed. The Johns Manville trust model is characterized by underfunding leading to inadequate and falling compensation of victims. Mass litigation with recruited litigants is a form of legal blackmail that the courts are unable to prevent. It misallocates money to not-ill and least-ill victims. The U.S. Supreme Court has twice refused to let lawyers consolidate asbestos cases into large class actions, ruling that future claimants were not adequately considered. Instead, the justices called on Congress to take action.[29]

In 1999 Republicans in Congress, with the support of industry, introduced a bill that would end lawsuits, set up a trust fund to pay all victim compensation, establish strict medical criteria, limit payments, end punitive damage awards, and reduce the fees taken by plaintiffs' attorneys. Money in the fund would come from defendant companies, their insurers, and private trusts such as the Manville trust. The bill failed to pass. It was opposed by labor unions, which thought workers would not get enough compensation, and by asbestos attorneys, who stood to gain from the status quo. These forces have killed the bill in every legislative session since its introduction in 1999.[30]

With the failure of a political solution there is no end in sight to the asbestos nightmare. And the American story is only part of a world epidemic. Between 1900 and 2000 approximately 30 million tons of asbestos were put into commerce, and about

---

[26] This fear is very real. In 2003, a jury ordered U.S. Steel Corp. to pay $250 million to a former employee with mesothelioma. The man had been exposed to asbestos in fire retardant insulation between 1950 and 1981 at the company's Gary, Indiana, steel plant. The jury was angry because management had known that asbestos was a carcinogen, but failed to warn or protect workers. So in addition to $50 million in compensatory damages, it awarded $200 million in punitive damages to the 70-year-old man with a terminal illness. See *Whittington v. U.S. Steel*, No. 12-L1113 (Madison Co., Ill., Cir. Ct.) 2003.

[27] Griffin B. Bell, *Asbestos Litigation and Judicial Leadership: The Courts' Duty to Help Solve the Asbestos Litigation Crisis* (Washington, DC: National Legal Center for the Public Interest, June 2002), p. 43.

[28] See, for example, "The Latest Asbestos Scam," June 1, 2004, p. A16.

[29] See *Amchem Prods. v. Windsor*, 117 S.Ct. 2503 (1997), and *Ortiz v. Fiberboard Corp.*, 199 S.Ct. 2295 (1999). In *Norfolk & Western Railway v. Ayers*, 123 S.Ct. 1210 (2003), the Court allowed railroad workers with asbestosis to recover damages based on mental anguish from the fear of developing cancer. It elected not to change liability rules to prevent such lawsuits even though they would add to the torrent of asbestos cases and called once again on Congress to create a national dispute resolution mechanism.

[30] The most recent version is a $140 billion trust fund in the Fairness in Asbestos Injury Resolution Act, S.2290, introduced by Sen. Orrin Hatch (R-Utah) in 2004.

2 million tons are still mined and shipped each year. Although use is decreasing in industrialized countries, it is increasing in Eastern Europe, Russia, Brazil, China, and some developing economies elsewhere. Since transnational asbestos corporations are bankrupt, the business is carried out by national companies. A handful of countries now ban asbestos. The only international effort to curtail its use is a weak 1986 Asbestos Convention sponsored by the United Nations but ratified by only 27 nations. Canada is the world's largest asbestos producer and the leading exponent of its use. It is estimated that 100,000 to 140,000 workers now die annually from asbestos disease. It has been suggested that the Canadian government close its asbestos mines and pension the 1,500 miners who work in them.[31]

[31] Figures in this paragraph are from Joseph LaDou, "The Asbestos Cancer Epidemic," *Environmental Health Perspectives,* March 2004, pp. 285–89.

Questions

1. Did Johns Manville make responsible use of bankruptcy law? What were the advantages and disadvantages of the Chapter 11 filing?

2. Was the reorganization plan fair to the company's stakeholders, including asbestos victims, shareholders, creditors, and employees? Was the trust fund the best alternative for compensating injured asbestos workers?

3. Was Johns Manville adequately punished for its actions? Should it have been permitted to reorganize and resume normal operations? Is it fair that the company has no current obligation to asbestos victims?

4. Is there a better solution for compensating asbestos victims than the current trust fund arrangement? Are current victims, who receive only 5 percent of planned settlement amounts, being fairly treated?

Chapter **Sixteen**

Consumerism

Harvey W. Wiley

On a spring day in 1863 a tall, thin boy of 18 left the farm where he had grown up, walking five miles over dirt roads to a nearby town. There he would be the first in his family to attend college. Like the restless America of his era, he was leaving rural roots behind in a journey of hope and ambition. His name was Harvey Washington Wiley. He would become the first modern consumer crusader.

The example of his parents molded Young Harvey's character. His father was a farmer who through self-learning became an evangelical minister and part-time school teacher. A man of Christian virtue, principle, and independent mind, he stood against slavery despite the open anger of neighbors. His mother taught herself to read. Knowledge was so important in the Wiley home that the latest works of science, literature, and commentary were mail-ordered and read aloud to little Harvey.

Harvey got a bachelor's degree from Hanover College, then attended Indiana Medical College, graduating as a physician in 1871. Still hungry for formal education, he enrolled at Harvard and graduated in less than two years with a chemistry degree. For a year in Germany he studied with the world's most renowned chemists. Returning to Indiana he became a professor at the new Purdue University and set up its chemistry labs. Soon he was absorbed in food chemistry and began working with Indiana state officials to detect adulteration in food products.

With industrialization the nation's food supply was changing. As people moved from farms to cities they depended on businesses to prepare, can, bottle, package, and distribute edibles. It was a time of major advances in science, and the Victorian era had a childlike faith in the powers of modern chemistry. A large, highly competitive food industry applied new food chemistries using preservatives, colorings, flavorings, texturizers, and other additives. With few laws to police dishonorable operators, dangerous, fraudulent, and cheapened products made their way to market. Canned beef was preserved with formaldehyde. Strawberry jam was made from pulped apple skins, hayseeds, and glucose. Ground pepper was sometimes mostly nutshells.[1]

Working in his campus lab, Wiley pioneered experimental science in the study of food adulteration. Using techniques he had learned in Germany, he detected widespread fraud and his reports attracted attention. His reputation grew and soon he was considered for the presidency at Purdue. However, the trustees frowned on his

[1] W. E. Mason, "Food Adulterations," *North American Review*, April 1900, pp. 548–53.

extended bachelorhood and noted that he exhibited undignified behavior for a professor. His main infractions were riding a bicycle around town and playing baseball with students. They passed him over. So when he was offered the position of Chief Chemist at the Department of Agriculture in 1883, he accepted.

Arriving in Washington, DC, Wiley, now 39, took charge of the Bureau of Chemistry. This small entity had been set up in 1862 to hunt for contaminated agricultural commodities. He worked tirelessly, uncovering danger, dilution, mislabeling, and cheating in the nation's groceries. Yet he lacked the means to protect public health. Fewer than half the states had pure food laws and those were often contradictory—what was legal in one state was banned in another. Worse, no federal law existed to regulate foodstuffs in interstate commerce.

Wiley began to agitate for a national pure food law. For more than two decades he worked tirelessly, giving speeches, writing reports, convening meetings of scientists and food producers, and lobbying legislators.

Strong support came from civic groups, physicians, state officials, and food companies that saw a competitive advantage in legislating standards. Devious rivals who mixed cheap ingredients into cans and jars would have to meet the standards or leave the market.[2] The Heinz Company, for example, adopted food purity as an advertising theme. To reassure the public it introduced glass jars and factory tours. Founder H. J. Heinz was intensely religious and often framed business decisions in moral terms. He created a production technique to eliminate preservatives. It required quality ingredients, sterilization, and vacuum seal technology. Although his avowed motive was to safeguard public health, he knew that unscrupulous competitors could not afford his manufacturing method.

Principled opposition to food regulation came from states' rights advocates opposed to any expansion of federal power, no matter how benign of intent. Less honorable opposition came from companies that profited by adulteration. They worked in the shadows of Capitol Hill, buying influence to obstruct passage.

As Wiley labored, 190 protective measures were introduced in Congress. None passed, but support was growing. Wiley himself drafted a bill introduced in 1902. Then he departed from scientific routine, staging a melodramatic experiment that captured the country's imagination. He believed that chemical preservatives harmed consumers, but lacked scientific proof. He designed a study in which young men would be fed suspect preservatives and monitored for signs of distress, then talked Congress into appropriating $5,000 for "hygienic table trials."

Wiley set up a kitchen, dining room, and laboratory in the basement of the Bureau of Chemistry building and advertised for volunteers. A dozen young men, all civil service employees from the Department of Agriculture, signed up. They pledged "on their honor" to eat every meal in the basement dining room, to eat or drink nothing (except water) that was not given as part of the trial, to carry around jars for collection of urine and feces to be submitted for lab analysis, to pursue their regular work and sleep schedules, and to submit to weekly doctors' exams.

---

[2] See Donna J. Wood, *Strategic Uses of Public Policy: Business and Government in the Progressive Era* (Marshfield, MA: Pittman, 1986), chapter 5.

Members of the "poison squad" dining in the basement of the old Bureau of Chemistry building. The Civil Service chef hired to cook their meals had once been chef to the Queen of Bavaria. Source: Courtesy of the FDA History Office.

Wiley first fed the men borax, a then-common preservative. He began by adding half a gram a day to their food. Over two years, he gradually added more. The routine was 10 days of healthy food followed by 20 days of food dosed with borax. At two grams appetites dropped off and some subjects had bowel problems. At four grams more serious problems emerged. The men had headaches and abdominal pain. Three took to their beds. Wiley stopped the test, believing he had evidence that borax was a human poison.[3]

A *Washington Post* reporter discovered Wiley's experiment, nicknamed the men the "poison squad," and wrote regularly about them. Whether or not Wiley intended the trials as partly grandstanding, the public was captivated. They inspired considerable levity, becoming the grist for comedians and minstrel shows. Yet they also put growing pressure on Congress to pass Wiley's pure food bill.

For five years Wiley tested other preservatives on new ranks of volunteers. He found signs of ill health caused by salicylic acid, formaldehyde, and copper sulfate, none of which are used as preservatives today. Years later, Wiley believed that the experiments had permanently damaged the health of several poison squad members.

In 1906, even as the poison squad continued its work, Congress finally passed the Pure Food and Drug Act "preventing the manufacture, sale, or transportation of adulterated or misbranded or poisonous or deleterious foods, drugs, medicines, and liquors."[4] The dam of obstruction had finally broken under pressure of the acute public

[3] Harvey W. Wiley, *The History of a Crime Against the Food Law* (Milwaukee: Lee Foundation for Nutritional Research, 1955), chapter II. Originally published in 1929.

[4] Pure Food and Drug Act of 1906, Sec. 1.

Harvey W. Wiley (1845–1930). Source: Courtesy of Univ. of Iowa Library Special Collections Department, Redpath Chautauqua Collection.

indignation about meat packing plants described in Upton Sinclair's novel *The Jungle.* Wiley's years of hard work and the theater of his poison squad, however, had prepared the ground. Recognizing this, Congress gave Wiley's Bureau of Chemistry the power to examine foods for adulteration or misbranding.

The press called the new law the Wiley Act. Its passage seemed to be the final victory in his crusade for public health. Yet appearance deceived. Wiley attempted vigorous enforcement, but his perfectionist standards often dictated strict rules. He was uneasy with compromise. Food makers resisted his authority and outflanked him by appealing to his boss, Secretary of Agriculture James Wilson, and to President Theodore Roosevelt. Both grew exasperated with him. Roosevelt thought him a vexing nag. At a White House meeting with Wiley and food manufacturers on the use of saccharine the president became furious with the stubborn chemist. Only an idiot, he told Wiley, would be against all use of saccharine in food.

With time, Wiley's enforcement ability eroded. Secretary Wilson, with Roosevelt's approval, undermined Wiley's independence. Wilson appointed an assistant to Wiley who reported directly to him, not to Wiley. Then he set up a panel of scientists to look over Wiley's shoulder and review his decisions. Defeated and bitter, the aging warrior resigned his post in 1912. Yet he could not leave the field. He continued lecturing and writing about consumer causes. His new bride, a suffragette whom he had married in 1911 at age 66, was active in women's groups such as the Housekeepers' Alliance that fought for consumer causes. He wrote about food for *Good Housekeeping* magazine and set up the Good Housekeeping Seal of Approval standard. He died in 1930.[5]

Harvey Wiley's campaign for pure food came at the time when small, local markets for goods and services were expanding to national size. It was in this era that the idea of a class of people with a well-defined interest in safe, pure, and honest commodities emerged. This class came to be called consumers. Wiley's distinction is to have been its first national champion. Unlike Ralph Nader, he had no basic distrust of big companies and the capitalist system. He believed in fighting for honest firms by driving out shady competition. But he shared with later consumer advocates the goal of using government power to protect consumers from predatory corporations.

America's memory of Dr. Wiley has dimmed, but his work still touches our lives. The law he fought for is the foundation of modern food and drug regulation. The Bureau of Chemistry, by enforcing its provisions, evolved into the current Food and Drug Administration, a powerful agency that protects public health.

---

[5] "Dr. H. W. Wiley Dies; Pure-Food Expert," *New York Times*, July 1, 1930, p. 24.

In this chapter we begin by defining and discussing the idea of consumerism. Then we describe the protective shield of statutes, regulations, and consumer law that has risen to protect consumers since Harvey Wiley's era.

CONSUMERISM

consumer
A person who uses products and services in a commercial economy.

consumerism
A term denoting (1) a movement to promote the rights and powers of consumers in relation to sellers and (2) a powerful ideology in which the pursuit of material goods beyond subsistence shapes social conduct.

A *consumer* is a person who uses products and services in a commercial economy. *Consumerism* is a word with two meanings. In common usage it refers to a movement to promote the rights and powers of consumers in relation to sellers of products and services. It also denotes an exceptionally powerful ideology of pursuit of material goods that shapes social conduct. We will discuss both these themes.

Consumerism as an Ideology

Consumerism describes a society in which people define their identities by acquiring and displaying material goods beyond what they need for subsistence. Although small pockets of consumerism existed in the distant past, its widespread suffusion through large populations is a relatively recent phenomenon, appearing for the first time in Western Europe only about 300 years ago and spreading from there.[6] Its appearance is explained by the rise of supportive conditions.

Economic progress set the stage. By the eighteenth century, commercial economies based on currency exchange had replaced systems of subsistence living and bartering in Western Europe. As economies grew, modest affluence spread in classes below the aristocracy. Expanding overseas trade in colonial empires brought new products, including sugar from the West Indies, porcelain from China, and cotton fabrics from India. People began to spend more for goods and services beyond what they needed for basic survival. The apparatus and institutions necessary to support consumerism quickly appeared. Small shops selling a wide range of goods sprang up in cities. Shopkeepers discovered that their customers' needs were not limited to necessities, but were infinitely expandable. Innovations such as window displays, sale pricing, loss leaders, and print advertising arose. The merchants encouraged producers to create a flow of new products, including toys, furniture, books, watches, perfumes, and household objects.

The full emergence of consumerism came as these economic changes interacted with cultural and social developments. One important development was the declining influence of religion. From the time of its rise in ancient Rome, Christianity had sanctified the dignity of the poor and encouraged followers to forsake the life of this world for the goal of otherworldly salvation. This doctrine made no room for any soul whose life was based on the ostentatious display of worldly pleasure. It could have suffocated rising consumerism. But now this stricture was loosened by the great philosophical current of the Enlightenment, which elevated the importance of human reason above the dogma of Christianity and led to the rise of individualism. The world of human relationships assumed greater importance and consumers could focus on material things with less guilt.

[6] Peter N. Stearns, *Consumerism in World History: The Global Transformation of Desire* (London: Routledge, 2001), pp. ix–x.

And then, the industrial revolution put societies in flux. This was the final element in the alchemy of consumerism. Populations grew. People left ancestral homes in the country to live beside strangers in cities. New occupations emerged. Some merchants and traders became wealthy. Centuries-old class and status boundaries wore down and as they faded people began to display material goods to establish their identity and standing in the social hierarchy. If a man no longer wore the insignia of a trade or guild, he could adorn himself with expensively made, colorfully dyed cotton garments and show that his occupation made him affluent. A newly rich merchant could emulate the aristocracy by building a manor house of his own. People spent more time "shopping." The acquisition of material objects had achieved a new centrality in their lives.

The Rise of Consumerism in America

Consumerism appeared in America when the time was right for forces similar to those in Europe to interact. It took about a century for the process to work. Beginning in the early 1800s, a commercial economy began to appear. The ascetic Puritan theology that had oppressed individualism in the northern colonies was fading. The lure of business success in the new land leapt over the boundaries of the tight, authoritarian communities in which it could not flourish. Wealth accumulated from expanding international trade and in the last half of the century industrial development spread growing affluence.

The spark for the ascendency of consumerism in America came with a confluence of events at the turn of the twentieth century. The railroads were knitting territory together, forming national markets. The great merger wave of 1896–1904 created businesses with the reach to serve these expanded markets. Machines and assembly lines made mass production of consumer goods possible. Electricity and other new technologies led to a steady stream of new consumer products, for example, autos, watches, refrigerators, vacuum cleaners, toasters, and radios. Simultaneously, in large numbers people left cramped small-town societies and moved to cities with more fluid social currents. Waves of immigrants, people newly adrift from their cultural moorings, arrived.

In this open society characterized by loose social ties, high mobility, and cultural variation, people began to express role and status through the products they consumed. Immigrants imbibed American culture when they drank Coca-Cola or ate a Baby Ruth candy bar, the latter named for the widely loved infant daughter of President Grover Cleveland.[7] Their children declared their participation when they displayed clothing styles appropriate to the New World. Advertising facilitated this social communication through products. It created new national brands and endowed them with social significance, allowing people to declare their membership in groups, their status, and their values by the goods they displayed (see Figure 16.1). The ads endowed products with meanings that were widely shared and understood, even by strangers, in a large and mobile population.

---

[7] Ruth Cleveland was born in 1891 when Grover Cleveland was out of office between his two nonconsecutive terms. The popular Democrat ran for the presidency three times, elected in 1884, defeated in 1888, and elected again in 1892. The brand was created by the Curtiss Candy Company after his daughter was born on October 3, 1891.

FIGURE 16.1   Immigrants and others could display and feel a connection with American culture by using consumer products. This collage of tobacco packaging and advertising images from the late 1800s and early 1900s illustrates powerful symbolism for ideals of liberty and freedom in American culture. Liberty Tobacco was an American Tobacco Company brand, George Washington Greatest American Cut Plug was made by R. J. Reynolds Tobacco Co., and Golden Eagle was made by T. C. Williams Co.

Source: Rare Book, Manuscript, and Special Collections Library, Duke University.

Gary Cross, a historian of American commercial culture, defines consumerism as "the belief that goods give meaning to individuals and their roles in society."[8] According to Cross, consumerism, which has never been a formal philosophy, is now the dominant ideology in America. "Americans," says Cross, "define themselves and their relationships with others through the exchange and use of goods."[9] He believes that consumerism expresses a more powerful worldview than political ideologies, religions, or class and ethnic distinctions. If we are unable to appreciate this fully, it is because of its pervasiveness and the lack of a visible alternative.

Voices have long been raised against a focus on consumption. One early critic of emergent consumerism was the economist Thorstein Veblen. In his 1899 book *The Theory of the Leisure Class*, he challenged conventional economic wisdom that the purpose of buying goods was to use them for the functional utility they provided. Veblen argued that in the new industrial society people no longer

[8] Gary Cross, *An All Consuming Society: Why Commercialism Won in Modern America* (New York: Columbia University Press, 2000), p. 1.

[9] Ibid., p. 4.

earned their status in warfare or by successful hunting, for instance. Instead, they acquired property to create what he called "invidious comparison" between themselves and their less successful neighbors.[10] They displayed their status through "conspicuous consumption," or the "unremitting demonstration of the ability to pay."[11] When the book appeared, it was received as only a satire, which disappointed Veblen. It outraged the economists of his era. Now, a century later its core insights seem correct.

Criticism of the values in modern consumerism persists.[12] Ralph Nader and other leaders of the consumer movement exhort Americans to be practical in their expenditures, to be vigilant against advertising that tempts them into extravagance, and to put function ahead of excitement in their purchases. Such appeals produce few converts. The alternative of simplified, utilitarian living in the mold of the Puritans, Benjamin Franklin, or Henry David Thoreau is perhaps now an impractical vision.

Attempts to create sanctuaries from consumerism in American society have also been losing efforts. Blue laws prohibiting stores from opening on Sundays, once pervasive, were an effort to rope off one day of the week and free it of commercialism. Such laws now hold little sway. When radio was new, pioneers of broadcasting such as David Sarnoff of RCA were afraid to air commercials. For the first time, the voices and ideas of outsiders came right into the sheltered retreat of the family living room. Would commercials offend? Quickly, the answer came. The vast majority felt no affront.

More recently, consumer advocates have tried to fence off childhood from the blandishments of materialism. Battles have been fought over ads on children's television programs, ads in schools, and ads for tobacco and alcohol suspected of appealing to underage starters. Although there have been some victories with respect to specific products and policies, it is far too late to sequester children from advertising.

Around the globe, the formula for consumerism has been activated in one nation after another over the last century. With economic growth and social change the ideology has risen in Russia, Asia, Latin America, the Middle East, and Africa. One historian speculates that it is "the most successful Western influence in world history."[13] It may, on the other hand, be less a Western than a universal phenomenon, rising more like a fire started when lightning strikes under the right conditions. It may emerge from the spontaneous interaction of human nature, economic progress, and cultural change occurring at a certain moment in the historical development of every society.

Consumerism, once it takes hold, seems irrepressible, but resistance continues. Western colonialism in Africa left a persistent disdain for Western values and lifestyles, including consumerism. The spread of an Islamic fundamentalism that rejects Western materialism has divided populations in the Middle East. And

---

[10] Thorstein Veblen, *The Theory of the Leisure Class* (New York: Penguin Books, 1979), p. 27. Originally published in 1899.

[11] Ibid., p. 87.

[12] See, for example, David A. Crocker and Toby Linden, eds., *Ethics of Consumption: The Good Life, Justice, and Global Stewardship* (Lanham, MD: Rowman & Littlefield, 1998).

[13] Stearns, *Consumerism in World History*, p. 73.

Catholicism still resists a material focus. Pope John Paul II has called the consumer life "improper" and "damaging" because it is directed toward "having rather than being" and it subordinates "interior and spiritual" dimensions of human life to "material and instinctive dimensions."[14]

Consumerism as a Protective Movement

Fraud, deception, and greed are universal in consumer markets. The idea of a collective interest in protecting consumers dates back to the earliest transactions between merchants and customers. In the United States an organized social movement to protect consumers sprang to life in the 1870s when Populist farmers attacked railroads for unfair rates and bad service. In the early years of the twentieth century, Progressives in both parties capitalized on the political power of consumers as a class of citizens with similar interests and grievances. The result was passage of a range of consumer protection laws, including the Food and Drug Act of 1906. Then consumer protection languished until a new era of progressive activism in the 1960s and 1970s prompted another wave of legislation to protect consumers and expand their rights.[15]

There were several triggers for this modern movement. Popular critics accused business of manipulating consumers. In *The Waste Makers*, for example, Vance Packard attacked corporations for everything from using annual model changes to make automobiles obsolete to designing potato peelers that blended in with the peelings and got thrown away, thereby creating a need for another purchase.[16] Ralph Nader aroused the public about automobile safety in his book *Unsafe at Any Speed* and emerged as the leader of a national movement.[17] President John F. Kennedy responded to rising, widespread consumer discontent with a special message to Congress in 1962 in which he said that consumers had basic rights and these rights had been widely abridged.[18] He listed the rights to make intelligent choices among products and services, to have access to accurate information, to register complaints and be heard, to be offered fair prices and acceptable quality, to have safe and healthful products, and to receive adequate service.

Congress responded to President Kennedy's speech, over the next decade passing more than a dozen consumer protection statutes and setting up four new federal agencies—the Federal Highway Administration (1966) to set highway safety standards, the Federal Railroad Administration (1966) to regulate rail safety, the National Highway Traffic Safety Administration (1970) to protect the public from unsafe automobiles, and the Consumer Product Safety Commission (1972) to guard against unsafe products.

[14] Ioannes Paulus PP.II, Encyclical Letter, *Centesimus annus* (May 1, 1991).

[15] According to Elizabeth Cohen in *A Consumer's Republic* (New York: Knopf, 2003), after the Great Depression, politicians elevated the importance of consumers by defining consumer demand as the key to American prosperity.

[16] Vance Packard, *The Waste Makers* (New York: David McKay, 1960), pp. 40–41.

[17] Ralph Nader, *Unsafe at Any Speed* (New York: Pocket Books, 1966).

[18] See "Text of Kennedy's Message to Congress on Protections for Consumers," *New York Times*, March 16, 1962.

These legislative successes marked the peak of the modern consumer movement. By the mid-1970s the business community had mobilized to block the great dream of the movement's activists, which was to consolidate enforcement of consumer laws, then scattered among many agencies, into one superagency named the Consumer Protection Agency. The inspiration for these activists was creation of the Environmental Protection Agency in 1970. The EPA centralized enforcement of environmental regulations previously dispersed among many agencies. Its coordinated effort strengthened environmental regulation.

Consumer activists longed for a comparable agency in their field. By 1976, however, conservatives and business lobbies had won a battle for public opinion, convincing Americans that their government was growing too powerful. They claimed that the rising tide of regulatory red tape created costs out of all proportion to benefits and crippled corporations in international competition. In the changed political climate shaped by these views, the Consumer Protection Agency bill was decisively defeated in 1976 despite the support of President Jimmy Carter. Never again was it seriously advanced.

Since then, Congress has not been predisposed to enact many new laws and has not set up another new consumer agency. Nevertheless, there have been some new statutes, and federal agencies have steadily minted rules pursuant to existing authority. The result has been continuous growth in consumer regulation. Figure 16.2 shows the expansion of spending (in constant 2000 dollars) by agencies that protect consumer health and safety. In fiscal year 1960, existing agencies spent $485 million, but that rose over the years until by fiscal year 2005 it was estimated that the agencies would spend $4.7 billion over the same range of programs. State and local governments have also significantly expanded their regulatory activity. Consumer protection is today a major function of government.

FIGURE 16.2   **Spending on Consumer Health and Safety by Federal Regulatory Agencies: 1960–2005**
Figures are in constant (2000) dollars and include spending on a range of consumer protection programs by six departments and agencies. Excluded are workplace safety, environmental, and antitrust regulation.

Source: Susan Dudley and Melinda Warren, *Regulator's Budget Continues to Rise: An Analysis of the U.S. Budget for Fiscal Years 2004 and 2005* (Arlington, VA, and St. Louis, MO: Mercatus Center and Weidenbaum Center, 2004), Table A-2.

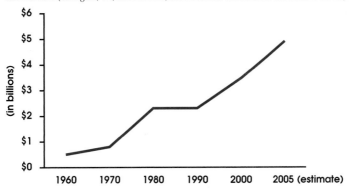

THE CONSUMER'S PROTECTIVE SHIELD

We now turn to an examination of the massive statutory shield that protects consumers from abuses, real and imagined. Besides federal laws and regulations, there are significant protections at the state and local level. Every state and local government has extensive consumer protection laws, ranging from requirements for uniform electrical connections to protections from fraudulent billing. An important protection also exists in the dissemination of information to the mass media.

More than 50 federal agencies and bureaus are active in consumer affairs. Our focus here will be on a few of the dominant federal agencies. We begin by describing the responsibilities of three major agencies: the Consumer Product Safety Commission (CPSC), the National Highway Traffic Safety Administration (NHTSA), and the Food and Drug Administration (FDA). This description reveals the awesome responsibilities Congress has placed on these agencies. While each is in need of moderate reforms it is astonishing how effective they have been despite changing ideologies in administrations, powerful critics, budget restraints, and too little staff to meet all their statutory requirements.

The Consumer Product Safety Commission (CPSC)

This agency, created by Congress in 1972, is directed by six major statutes. These laws mandate it to

1. Protect the public against unreasonable risks of injury and death associated with consumer products.
2. Assist consumers to evaluate the comparative safety of products.
3. Develop uniform safety standards for consumer products and minimize conflicting state and local regulations.
4. Promote research and investigation into the causes and prevention of product-related deaths, illnesses, and injuries.

Much of the effort of the agency in saving lives and making homes safer is undertaken in cooperation with business. This arrangement has resulted in voluntary standards established by industries and the CPSC staff. From 1990 through 2004 there were 276 voluntary safety standards created. While the Commission has authority to issue mandatory orders, only 35 were issued in that period. In 2004 the Commission completed 354 cooperative recalls involving 216 million product units. These recalls involved consumer products that either violated mandatory standards or presented substantial risks to the public.[19] The voluntary safety standards covered products such as bicycles, bunk beds, toys, lawn mowers, cigarette lighters, swimming pool covers, spas, and thousands of other products.

---

[19] Consumer Product Safety Commission, *Performance and Accountability Report, Fiscal Year 2004* (Washington, DC: CPSC, November 2004), p. 4.

One of the latest and largest recalls is 150 million pieces of rings, necklaces, and bracelets made in India, because they contain toxic levels of lead.[20] Other recent recalls included heavy duty swing seats, Suzuki and Kawasaki off-road motorcycles, fluorescent light bulbs, table saws, and riding lawn mowers. Children's safety has been a prime concern of the agency. To protect children it has recalled products violating prescribed standards inluding toys using lead paint, children's furniture, and playground equipment.

The CPSC regulates every consumer product except guns, boats, planes, cars, trucks, foods, drugs, cosmetics, tobacco, and pesticides, which are in the province of other agencies. Even with these exclusions, its mandate is enormous, since it must oversee 15,000 classes of products, work with thousands of manufacturers, and address millions of consumer complaints.

From its creation by the Nixon administration in 1972, the agency has faced serious barriers to achieving its mandated goals. The political environment has been difficult. Nixon was unenthusiastic about it. In both the Ford and Carter administrations it became embroiled in political battles. President Reagan wanted to abolish it but could not. Instead, he drastically cut its budget. Its budget has improved in the past two administrations.

The National Highway Traffic Safety Administration (NHTSA)

This agency was created by Congress in 1966 and has authority to

1. Mandate minimum safety standards for automobiles, trucks, and their accessories.
2. Establish fuel economy standards.
3. Administer grant programs that promote highway safety.
4. Conduct research on and development and demonstration of new vehicle safety techniques.

Regulations of this agency cover virtually every feature of the automobile. No other agency has such extensive controls over a single product. A short list of programs just to protect occupants of an automobile would include air bags, safety belts, energy-absorbing or collapsible steering columns, penetrating-resistance windshields, recessed door handles, breakaway rearview mirrors, padded dashboards, crushable front ends, passenger compartment designs to resist crushing, and tire standards.

The agency has power to mandate recall of defective products. A highly publicized recall initiated by the agency was the joint announcement of Bridgestone/Firestone and Ford Motor Co., in 2000, to recall 14.4 million tires that contained safety-related defects. Most of the tires in question were original equipment on Ford vehicles, primarily the Ford Explorer. The decision was based on evidence that defects caused the tires' treads to shred at high speeds and vehicles to roll over.

Automobile companies have complained about the costs of many of the agency's mandates, but there is no doubt that the regulations have saved thousands of lives. Some industry critics claim that its programs cost too much and that

---

[20] Amelia Neufeld, "Toy Jewelry Recalled over Lead Concerns," *Los Angeles Times*, July 9, 2004, p. 3.

Under strict liability an injured plaintiff must prove only that the manufacturer made a product in a defective condition that made it unreasonably dangerous to the user, that the seller was in the business of selling such products, and that it was unchanged from its manufactured condition when purchased. The "defect" can exist because of poor design, insufficient warning, or even hazards unknown to the manufacturer. It is an inherent danger not anticipated by the buyer and may exist even though the product was carefully manufactured.

This is the legal doctrine that dismantled the asbestos industry. When strict liability was accepted by the courts, sick asbestos workers no longer had to prove that Johns Manville or other companies were negligent because they knew about asbestos hazards. All they had to prove was that asbestos was "defective," that is, that it contained an inherently dangerous quality. The asbestos companies were then liable to compensate workers with asbestos disease. As the court stated in *Greenman v. Yuba Power Products*, "The purpose of [strict] liability is to insure that the costs of injuries resulting from defective products are borne by the manufacturers that put such products on the market rather than by the injured persons who are powerless to protect themselves."[33] This idea, now embedded in the law, was another big step away from *caveat emptor*.

AN ASSESSMENT OF PRODUCT LIABILITY SUITS

Product liability law has attracted controversy. Supporters, including consumer advocates and plaintiffs' attorneys, argue that it fulfills its purpose to compensate victims and to deter future corporate wrongdoing. They point to products such as the Dalkon Shield and flammable children's pajamas taken off the market following litigation. Because of lawsuits, tobacco companies had to release documents that confirmed knowledge about the dangers of smoking.[34]

Corporations, on the other hand, see a legal doctrine in need of reform. They argue that product liability law has moved beyond straightforward victim compensation to become a system of insurance against the risks posed by products in modern life. The economic effects are pernicious. Manufacturers price damage awards into product prices, forcing consumers to subsidize product liability costs. Large jury awards compensate injured consumers, but as much as 40 percent may go to attorneys. And productivity in entire industries has been crippled.

The general aviation industry is an example. Accident rates for civil aircraft began a steady, uninterrupted decline in the 1940s that has now continued for more than 60 years. Manufacturers worked to design and build safer aircraft because of market forces. No company could survive if buyers believed that its planes were more dangerous than those of its competitors. Then, in the 1960s, product liability law changed to permit strict liability and by the 1970s a striking rise in airplane crash lawsuits and liability awards had occurred. Sometimes, crash victims and their relatives prevailed when accidents were caused by defects unknown or unknowable when the airplanes were made.

[33] Ibid., at 63.
[34] "Justice for the Injured: An Interview with Joanne Doroshow," *Multinational Monitor*, March 2003, p. 23.

- *Improving quality.* There are many cost advantages to reducing product flaws. One is liability reduction. Quality programs include a chain of actions to prevent flawed products from reaching markets, including reliability testing and inspections. One manufacturer sold clocks that could catch on fire after only four hours of operation—a product with disastrously high potential liability. It had installed the wrong electronic component in them because it looked similar to the right component. Better quality control could have prevented the error.
- *Instructions and warning labels.* Instructions are opportunities to teach consumers how to use a product safely. Warning labels are pointed advisories about dangers of which consumers may not be aware. Courts have held that warning labels are not necessary for such obvious, commonsense dangers as putting fingers in a rotating lawn mower blade. However, in the current litigious climate many manufacturers take no chances. One company put a label on its hair dryer reading: "Do not use while sleeping." Another put a warning on a Superman costume stating: "Wearing this outfit does not enable you to fly."[48]
- *Product recalls.* When reports come in that a product defect poses a risk of harm, manufacturers can conduct recalls. Recalls are extremely expensive, and may be prohibitively expensive for very small manufacturers, but they eliminate or reduce liability. Large companies, such as auto companies, have recall procedures in place so that they can react quickly to news of problems.

Such actions as these reduce, but cannot eliminate, product liability exposure. The U.S. legal system makes it easier for plaintiffs to win large damage awards from product makers than do the systems of other countries. In Europe, attorneys do not work on a contingency basis and most European countries require losers to pay court costs. This discourages low-merit cases. Except in the United Kingdom, lawyers are not permitted to advertise for clients as do American lawyers. And, in addition, awards tend to be much lower, particularly since punitive damages are usually not allowed. In Asia, product liability is a relatively new idea. Chinese product liability laws were introduced only in 1993. And in Japan, only since 1995 have consumers been allowed to sue manufacturers. In short, nowhere else in the world has the legal system created such a favorable environment for product lawsuits as in the United States.

CLUDING OBSERVATIONS

Consumerism is a word with two meanings. It refers both to a kind of society and to a protective movement. In this chapter we discuss trends related to both meanings. First, consumerism as a way of life is spreading around the world because the conditions that support it are becoming more common. Where it is already established, it is strengthening its grip. Second, consumers in the United States are now more protected from injury, fraud, and other abuses than in the past because of stronger government regulation and more consumer-friendly common law doctrines. Protections are also growing in other industrialized nations.

[48] Ibid., p. 119.

Damage to the industry was extensive. One company went bankrupt and others were in financial trouble. The introduction of newer planes that might have been safer by design was delayed. In 1994, Congress passed a law exempting civil aircraft more than 18 years old from product liability claims and this has led to some revival of the industry.[35] In the end, neither the spike in damage awards nor the legislation affected the number of fatal accidents. The rate of decline remained steady and constant. Strict liability rules served only to transfer money from aircraft makers to accident victims and their attorneys and to reduce industry productivity.[36]

Another complaint of industry is that many product liability lawsuits are frivolous and jury awards are capricious. Two well-known cases against McDonald's permit critical analysis of the industry perspective. In *Pelman v. McDonald's Corp.* the guardians of two obese children filed a lawsuit seeking to hold McDonald's responsible for the children's weight under doctrines of negligence, warranty, and strict liability.[37] They argued that McDonald's products were inherently dangerous because they contained high levels of sugar, salt, fat, and cholesterol. By selling them, McDonald's breached an implied warranty that its food was safe to eat. They claimed that McDonald's was negligent for failing to warn consumers about the dangers of its foods. The court granted McDonald's motion to dismiss the case before trial, holding that consumers could reasonably be assumed to know the health effects of McDonald's foods and the company had no duty to warn them of the need for a healthy diet.

In *Liebeck v. McDonald's Restaurants*, the company was sued by Stella Liebeck, a 79-year-old woman who bought a cup of coffee at a McDonald's in Albuquerque.[38] In the passenger seat of a car, she put the cup between her thighs and tried to pull the lid off. But the cup tipped and the scalding hot coffee burned her. Liebeck sued, arguing that McDonald's had breached an implied warranty of fitness because its coffee, as sold, was simply too hot for consumption. A jury awarded her $160,000 in compensatory damages and hit McDonald's with $2.7 million in punitive damages. Commentators seized on the case as an example of a runaway jury award.

In the first case, the court recognized the obesity lawsuit as frivolous and without merit under the law. It allowed the children's guardians to amend and refile the suit, giving them every chance to present claims of substance, but in the end they could not. Courts most often reject claims without merit. In this regard, there is more merit to the second case than meets the eye. Liebeck had a major injury. She suffered third-degree burns over 6 percent of her body, spent eight days in the hospital and had high medical costs. Testimony revealed that McDonald's sold its coffee at a temperature of 180° F., much higher than the 135° to 140° that consumers serve coffee in their homes. At temperatures that high, third-degree burns can occur

[35] The General Aviation Act of 1994, P.L. 103–298.

[36] *Economic Report of the President and The Annual Report of the Council of Economic Advisors, 2004* (Washington, DC: U.S. Government Printing Office, 2004), pp. 212–14.

[37] 237 F. Supp. 2d 512 (S.D.N.Y. 2003). See Samuel J. Romero, "Obesity Liability: A Super-Sized Problem or a Small Fry in the Inevitable Development of Product Liability?" *Chapman Law Review*, Spring 2004.

[38] CV 93-02419 (D.N.M. August 18, 1994). The jury held Liebeck 20 percent accountable for causing her injuries.

in as little as 2 seconds, compared to more than 60 seconds at temperatures below about 160°. Moreover, McDonald's was forced to release documents showing more than 700 previous burn claims from customers. In court, a company representative stated that the coffee tasted better when held at high temperature and that the number of customer burns was so small relative to the number of cups served it did not plan to lower the temperature. This may have angered jurors. The $2.7 million in punitive damages awarded by the jury was less than two days' revenue from coffee sales at McDonald's.[39] Subsequently, the judge reduced the punitive award to $480,000, or three times the compensatory award. So, contrary to the popular supposition of a runaway jury, the *Liebeck* case reveals a basis for judgment against the corporation and a reasonably limited award.

Business Wants Product Liability Reform

Product liability suits are filed in every state and in federal courts, and there is no central reporting of them. Therefore, comprehensive and up-to-date statistics about their number, disposition, and jury awards are elusive.[40] In raw numbers, they seem to be no more than 3 to 5 percent of all tort cases, or 9,000 to 15,000 per year, but this figure is uninformative because it includes massive asbestos, tobacco, and breast implant *class action* lawsuits, each with tens of thousands of individual plaintiffs.[41] Class actions support the cost of litigating when individual losses are small, but aggregate losses are large.

What is known is that corporations see the costs of product liability suits as excessive. A 2004 survey of CEOs reported that 80 percent believed tort costs, of which product liability awards are a major part, gave foreign competitors an advantage.[42] The National Association of Manufacturers estimated that this cost advantage was 3.2 percent.[43] Another survey asked corporate counsel to name their foremost litigation concern. Product liability was ranked first by 26 percent, first among manufacturing company counsel, and fourth among counsel from all industries.[44]

The business community, stung by product liability suits, rising liability insurance costs, bankruptcies of some corporations and industries because of large awards over defective products (for example, Johns Manville, A. H. Robins, Dow Corning), and looming threats of bankruptcy to companies in other industries

class action
A legal procedure that joins individual plaintiffs into a group to litigate a case in which they share a common interest and agree to be bound by a common judgment.

[39] S. Reed Morgan, "McDonald's Burned Itself," *Legal Times,* September 19, 1994, p. 26.

[40] The Congressional Budget Office reports that in 1996 product liability cases decided by jury trial, excluding asbestos cases, the plaintiff won in 37 percent of the cases, the median award was $177,000, and only 16 percent of awards exceeded $1 million. See *Economic Report of the President and The Annual Report of the Council of Economic Advisors, 2004,* Table 11-1.

[41] See National Center for State Courts, "National State Court Caseload Trends," *Caseload Highlights,* vol. 1, no. 1, August 1995, p. 2; National Council on State Courts, *Examining the Work of State Courts, 2003* (Williamsburg, VA: NCSC, 2004), p. 26; and "Jury Awards Rise Sharply in Defective-Product Cases," *New York Times,* January 30, 2001, p. C1.

[42] "Tort Costs Kill Our Competitive Edge," *Crain's Detroit Business,* July 26, 2004, p. 9.

[43] Ibid.

[44] "Fulbright & Jaworski Takes Pulse of 300 Corporate Counsel for Survey of U.S. Litigation Trends," *The Corporate Counsellor,* September 11, 2004, p. 3.

(for example, tobacco and firearms), has pressed to pass reforms, including the following.

- Establish uniform federal product liability stand
- Move product liability cases to federal courts t shopping among state jurisdictions for courts wi gressional action, the Chamber of Commerce a millions of dollars into campaigns to defeat jud corporate defendants.[45]
- Eliminate strict liability for products that cause in not reasonably have been foreseen when the prodt
- Limit punitive damages in product liability case moved in this direction, most recently suggesting th not exceed four times actual compensation.[46] Som necticut and Michigan, have capped damage awards lawsuits.
- Immunize industries through legislation. Recently, industries have asked Congress to change the law to more difficult. Drug and vaccine makers have also s lawsuits. The Mississippi state legislature prohibitec against tobacco companies.

IMPACTS ON OPERATIONS

Consumer advocates and trial attorneys claim that trends in forced more responsibility on manufacturers. Expensive la companies to drop high-risk products, including asbestos, o ical implants, football helmets, and vaccines. Others have introduction of new products, depriving consumers of a of innovations. And many firms have learned that the fo important for preventing lawsuits.

- *Attention to design.* Products can be scrutinized in the desi hazards and risks that might be avoided with modification. some product liability suits. For example, the manufacturer o sued after a boy fighting with his brother in a kitchen fell an jured by the hood's sharp edge. Although there was no adu boys, the manufacturer lost the case because under questionin designing a rounded edge would not have been more expensi have impaired the range hood's function.[47]

[45] "Robert Lenzner and Matthew Miller, "Buying Justice," *Forbes,* July 21, 2003, p. 6
[46] *State Farm Mutual Automobile Insurance Company v. Campbell,* 123 S. Ct. 1513 (2 discussion in Chapter 7.
[47] Randall L. Goodden, *Product Liability Prevention: A Strategic Guide* (Milwaukee, WI: 2000), p. 100.

These trends seem likely to continue. As the ideology of consumerism tightens its grip, responsive governments will expend more resources on issues raised by shopping for, purchasing, using, and displaying material objects. These issues will be more complex as populations grow, product choices expand, technology changes the nature of products, and marketing becomes more sophisticated.

Advertising Alcohol

In 2004 NASCAR announced that it would allow liquor brands to sponsor race cars. In explaining the decision to reverse a long-standing ban, its President Mike Helton said "the biggest thing is that the spirits companies have proven themselves as leaders in responsibility and are encouraging adults who choose to drink to do so responsibly."[1] This reasoning seemed wrong to the American Medical Association, which called on NASCAR "not to endanger the lives and health of youth through the glamorization of liquor."[2]

Immediately, the world's largest spirits seller, the Anglo-French transnational Diageo PLC, announced that its Crown Royal Canadian whisky would sponsor a car painted in the label's purple and gold colors. A company spokesman said that putting its brand logo on the hood would allow it "to connect with millions of adult consumers . . . and remind them about the importance of responsible drinking."[3] Again, not everyone agreed. George Hacker, of the Center for Science in the Public Interest, a consumer organization that fights what it considers to be inappropriate alcohol advertising, stated that having liquor companies teach responsible drinking was "like having Ronald McDonald promote healthy eating or Joe Camel promote smoking cessation."[4]

Such disagreement reflects a long-standing divergence of values about alcohol in American culture. In the late 1800s temperance groups began a great crusade against the evils of alcohol. Eventually, they led the nation into a brief era of prohibition. In 1919 the Eighteenth Amendment to the U.S. Constitution banned production and sale of alcohol, but the Twenty-First Amendment repealed it in 1933. Prohibition attitudes have faded but not vanished.

The first poll on alcohol consumption in 1939 revealed that most of American adults, 60 percent, drank, and the number has remained approximately that ever since.[5] However, about 20 percent of Americans still believe that making and selling alcohol is immoral.[6] And many more retain a prohibition-era belief that liquor is a more potent and risky alcoholic beverage than beer or wine.

Since the 1930s broadcasters have been unwilling to offend public attitudes by airing liquor ads. The prejudice against liquor extends also to taxation and distribution. Compared with beer and wine, spirits are more heavily taxed and state and local laws put more restrictions on how and when they can be sold. These market barriers hurt liquor sales.

The alcoholic beverage industry is a mature and stagnant business. Per capita consumption has slowly declined by about 10 percent over the past 25 years.[7] Fierce competition exists among the three segments for market share, which is a driving force behind the industry's emphasis on clever advertising. Beer now has 57 percent, distilled spirits 29 percent, and wine

[1] Quoted in Rick Minter, "NASCAR Lifts Ban on Alcohol Ads," *The Atlanta Journal-Constitution*, November 11, 2004, p. 3D.

[2] Shav Glick, "Dramatic Changes Put NASCAR on a Roll," *Los Angeles Times*, November 28, 2004, p. D5.

[3] Quoted in "Mark Kreidler Says Drinking and Driving (Advertisements) a Good Mix," *Pittsburgh Post-Gazette*, November 16, 2004, p. C2.

[4] Ibid.

[5] "Vices: Smoking, Drinking, and Gambling," *The American Enterprise*, October–November 2001, p. 62.

[6] International Communications Research, "Drinking and Driving Survey," July 13–17, 2001, sponsored by the Harvard School of Public Health, question 26.

[7] U.S. Bureau of the Census, *Statistical Abstract of the United States: 2003*, 123rd ed. (Washington, DC, 2003), table 216.

14 percent.[8] One reason for the dominance of beer is that brewers advertise heavily on network television, a venue closed to distillers.

In the 1980s, when the introduction of light beers drove beer sales higher and liquor sales began to decline, distiller Seagrams & Sons decided to push for "equalization," or the equal treatment of liquor. It developed television ads explaining that the alcohol in distilled spirits was the same as the alcohol in beer and wine and that standard servings of all three contained about the same amount of alcohol—1.5 ounces. American networks rejected these ads in keeping with their voluntary policy of not accepting liquor ads. A decade later, in 1996, Seagrams decided to try advertising liquor on cable channels and local stations, but a public outcry caused the project to fail. Seeing little potential growth from its liquor brands, the company sold them to Diageo.

Diageo continued the fight for equalization. In 2001 it marketed Smirnoff Ice, the first flavored malt beverage. It was brewed like beer, but flavored like vodka though it contained no vodka. Smirnoff Ice could be advertised on television and it turned into a $1 billion-a-year brand for Diageo. Having made an inroad with Smirnoff Ice, Diageo pressed the television networks to take ads for its liquor brands.

In late 2001 NBC agreed to run Smirnoff Vodka ads if they were preceded by four months of public service spots. Diageo began to run these spots, but before the four months were over, NBC rescinded the agreement, citing public opposition and criticism by lawmakers in Congress who planned to hold hearings about televising liquor ads. Cynics discounted these reasons as pretexts and believed that NBC was afraid of alienating Anheuser-Busch, which was a gold mine of beer ads and not at all enamored about the idea of equivalency.

When NASCAR announced its race cars would carry liquor brand names Diageo clearly won a round. Even as the television networks refused to sell commercial time to the company, they would fill their screens with rolling liquor billboards for its products. The liquor industry trade association, the Distilled Spirits Council of the United States (DISCUS), thought it was "only fair," that such advertising

appear on the second-most-watched sport because beer companies could sponsor baseball and football telecasts.[9]

THE ATTACK ON ALCOHOL ADVERTISING

The NASCAR episode is a window into the broader attack on alcohol advertising. Although prohibition is a moribund idea, a strong anti-alcohol movement still exists. Its leaders are activists in church, health, consumer, and citizens' groups such as Mothers Against Drunk Driving (MADD). Its greatest successes have been getting all states to raise the legal drinking age to 21 and establishing a national drunken-driving standard of .08 blood alcohol content.[10] It also wants to ban or restrict alcoholic beverage advertising. The movement's indictment against alcohol ads is based on four beliefs.

First, advertising increases consumption. Many ads are designed to attract new drinkers and promote additional drinking. Miller Lite's classic "Tastes Great—Less Filling" spots attempted to reposition beer as a competitor to soft drinks, telling consumers that light beer is a low-calorie drink that can be consumed more often than regular beer. The Michelob beer campaign based on the slogan "Put a little weekend in your week" encouraged weekend social drinkers to think of all days of the week as drinking occasions. A recent campaign by the Wine Marketing Council suggests that wine goes with television viewing.

Studies of the effect of advertising on consumption have generated mixed evidence. Generally, national studies find no correlation between overall spending for alcohol ads and consumption. But some studies of local areas show that increased advertising does raise consumption and that advertising bans reduce it.[11] No firm conclusion is yet

[8] Deborah Ball and Christopher Lawton, "In Its Long War with Brewers, Liquor Industry Gets Aggressive," *The Wall Street Journal*, May 24, 2004, p. A10.

[9] DISCUS President Peter Cressy, quoted in David Wharton and Martin Henderson, "Next for NASCAR: Hard Liquor Ads," *Los Angeles Times*, November 11, 2004, p. D1.

[10] Mark Murray, "Unbottling the 0.8 Percent Solution," *National Journal*, November 4, 2000, p. 3488.

[11] For an overview of this research, see Henry Saffer, "Studying the Effects of Alcohol Advertising on Consumption," *Alcohol Health & Research World*, vol. 20, no. 4 (1996), and Hae-Kyong Bang, "Analyzing the Impact of the Liquor Industry's Lifting of the Ban on Broadcast Advertising," *Journal of Public Policy & Marketing,* Spring 1998.

possible. This does not deter critics who believe that when alcohol ads saturate the media, they create a climate of undeserved social approval for drinking. George Hacker of the Center for Science in the Public Interest prefers to rely on plain, unscientific common sense.

> To pretend, as alcohol marketers do, that the advertisements do not have any effect on consumption is disingenuous at best. . . . [C]onsider that [companies] spend hundreds of millions of dollars advertising their products. One would think they have some faith in that investment. Try finding an advertising agency modest enough to confess that marketers have been wasting all (or even some of) that money. . . . [T]o suggest that it does not help bring in new consumers and encourage current users to consume more begs credulity. Trusting one's eyes and ears makes more sense.[12]

Second, ads encourage children and teenagers to start drinking. The underage audience is bombarded with ads for beer, wine, and liquor. Youths see as many as 2,000 beer and wine commercials on television every year.[13] And advertisers are purposely or inadvertently careless about placement. One study found that in 2003, 69,054 ads were run on programs where they were more likely to be seen by viewers ages 12 to 20 than by adults of legal age.[14] The cumulative mass of alcohol ads is an irresistible lesson that drinking is fun and leads to social acceptance. Researchers report that fifth- and sixth-grade children who can describe alcohol ads have more positive attitudes toward drinking than less knowledgeable children.[15] And many ads are popular with children. For example, one survey found that Budweiser spots

featuring the lizards Frankie and Louie were the favorites of children aged six to seventeen.[16] Alcohol ads seep in at very early ages. Millie Webb is a former president of MADD. Two of her children were killed in a drunken-driving accident. One day she noticed a frog on her patio and showed it to her three-year-old nephew, who knew its name. "He said 'Budweiser,'" she recalls. "It broke my heart."[17]

Underage consumption is significant. There are about 12 million drinkers between 12 and 20 years old, creating a market estimated at $10 billion.[18] By the eighth grade, 44 percent of children have used alcohol and 20 percent have been drunk. By the twelfth grade, 77 percent have used alcohol and 60 percent have been drunk, more than half of them once a month or more.[19] Activists claim that the alcoholic beverage industry targets underage drinkers not only with advertising but with specialty products designed to attract youth. These include flavored malt beverages, sometimes called "alcopops," single-serving vodka and tequila cocktails with names such as Yellin Melon Balls and Blu-Dacious Kamikaze, and novelty products such as cups of strawberry gelatin containing vodka.[20] Although the industry denies targeting under-21 drinkers, it makes no difference to critics. "Whether alcohol producers intentionally target 15- and 16-year-olds is irrelevant," argues Hacker; "[t]hat they reach them with the most sophisticated means and the most seductive messages creates enough of a problem."[21]

[12] George A. Hacker, "Liquor Advertisements on Television: Just Say No," *Journal of Public Policy & Marketing,* Spring 1998, p. 139.

[13] Center for Science in the Public Interest, "Stop Liquor Ads on TV: Talking Points," www.cspinet.org/booze/liquorads/liquor-talkingpoints.htm.

[14] "Report: Youth Exposure to TV Ads Continues to Increase," *Alcoholism & Drug Abuse Weekly,* October 18, 2004, p. 3.

[15] Joel W. Grube, "Television Beer Advertising and Drinking Knowledge, Beliefs, and Intentions among Schoolchildren," *American Journal of Public Health,* February 1994. See also Erica W. Austin and Christopher Knaus, "Predicting the Potential for Risky Behavior among Those 'Too Young' to Drink as the Result of Appealing Advertising," *Journal of Health Communication,* January–March 2000.

[16] Kathy DeSalvo, "FTC Investigates Alcohol Company's Ad Practices," *SHOOT,* September 25, 1998, p. 39.

[17] Mark O'Keefe, "Critics Take Aim at NBC Plan to Air Liquor Ads," *Family Living,* January 14, 2002, p. D8.

[18] The estimate is by Joseph Califano Jr., director of the National Center on Addiction and Substance Abuse at Columbia University. Quoted by Cal Thomas, "Congress Must Ban Liquor Ads from TV," *Baltimore Sun,* December 20, 2001, p. A23.

[19] "2004 Data from In-School Surveys of 8th, 10th, and 12th Grade Students," the Monitoring the Future Study, Institute for Survey Research, University of Michigan, table 1.

[20] Alejandro Bodipo-Memba, "'Shooters' and Other Alcoholic Novelties Face Scrutiny," *The Wall Street Journal,* April 14, 1999, p. B1.

[21] George A. Hacker, "Alcohol Advertising: Are Our Kids Collateral or Intended Targets?" speech to the Leadership to Keep Children Alcohol Free Conference, January 10, 2002, p. 3.

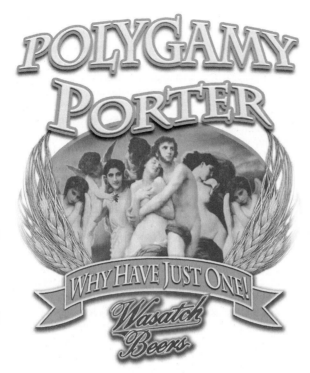

Polygamy Porter, a brand marketed by Wasatch Brewing Co., is a parody of the Mormon custom, now banned, of taking multiple wives. The ad campaign features the slogan "Why have just one!" This kind of appeal is condemned by the anti-alcohol movement for encouraging more consumption. Source: Photo courtesy of Wasatch Brewing Company.

Third, sophisticated lifestyle advertising used by alcohol makers is manipulative because it locks into inner drives. Informational advertising presents details about a product, for example, its price, availability, and quality. In contrast, lifestyle advertising positions a product to fulfill emotional needs. Pictures and copy associate alcohol with fulfillment of desires for popularity, success, sophistication, rebellion, romance, and sexual conquest. The ads endow commodity products such as vodka or lager beer with brand images. Then, by drinking that brand, the consumer adopts and projects the brand image. These ads may convey little or no objective information about the beverage, only an emotional theme. Sexual images are a staple of alcohol marketing. However, one study of alcohol ads in magazines during a 14-year period found that other appeals predominated over sexual imagery. In *Life,* for example, prestige and social acceptance were more frequent themes.[22] Whatever the image, critics believe that

lifestyle ads are highly manipulative because they play on emotions. If consumers respond to them they are being tricked into fulfilling inner needs by drinking.

Fourth, alcohol advertising is targeted not only at young drinkers but, sometimes inappropriately, at other groups too. An example of objectionable targeting is the heavy advertising of malt liquors in inner-city black neighborhoods and in black media. Malt liquor has a higher alcohol content than regular beer, and advertisements for it appeal to drinkers looking for a high. Recently, United States Beverage Company introduced a malt liquor called Phat Boy. "Phat" is a slang word used by teens for something hip, cool, or exciting. Phat Boy was marketed with graffiti-style ads as "the new malt liquor with an attitude." It came in 40-ounce bottles, each having nearly as much alcohol as a six-pack of regular beer. After an outcry by activists, the company dropped the brand, although the reason it cited was poor sales.[23] Hispanics are also targeted. For example, alcohol companies stage parties, promotions, concerts, and happy hours with

[22] Geng Cui, "Advertising of Alcoholic Beverages in African-American and Women's Magazines: Implications for Health Communication," *Howard Journal of Communications,* October 2000, p. 288.

[23] Melanie Wells, "Phat Boy Brew on Way Out," *USA Today,* September 14, 1998, p. 12B.

Cinco de Mayo themes. One critic laments that "[t]he alcohol industry has managed to erase all reference to this day as a historical event, one that Latino youth and their families should take pride in, and transformed it into a major marketing time of year."[24] Joseph E. Seagram & Sons changed the picture of the captain on bottles of Captain Morgan Spiced Rum when focus groups revealed that a less cartoon-like image attracted more male Hispanic drinkers.[25]

ALCOHOL MARKETERS DEFEND THEIR ADVERTISING

The industry defends its ads. First, it says, ads are not the cause of alcohol abuse. As noted, studies fail to show that advertising increases consumption. So commercials and billboards cannot be blamed for car accidents, teen suicides, sexual aggression, spouse abuse, binge drinking, and alcoholism. Alcoholism, for example, is a complex disease caused by personality, family, genetic, and physiological factors rather than by viewing ads. So the main result of restraints would be to deprive moderate drinkers of product information, not to ameliorate social problems. As one advertising executive notes, trying to stop problem drinking with an ad ban "makes as little sense as trying to control the Ku Klux Klan by outlawing bed linens."[26] Ad restrictions would also muzzle a competitive weapon. Because of stagnating demand, most alcohol ads are aimed not at expanding demand but at getting consumers to switch brands. Without advertising, starting a new national brand would be almost impossible and established brands would have an insurmountable advantage. Innovative products such as ice beers would be hard to introduce.

Second, anti-alcohol groups assume that the public is too stupid to make responsible decisions. The idea of curbing ads is condescending. Consumers are intelligent and skeptical. They are not duped by the association of alcohol with attractive images. Does anyone expect brewers and vintners to associate their products with root canals, traffic congestion, or income taxes? The rejection of lifestyle advertising is also condescending. If a consumer uses an alcohol brand to feel more sophisticated, popular, or sexual, who is to say that this method of satisfying the person's inner need is wrong? No one would criticize a woman for feeling glamorous while she is wearing perfume, even though the perfume is simply a chemical, nonessential to healthy life, and the glamour was created by ad imagery. If advertising endows alcoholic beverages with a quality that satisfies emotional needs in responsible drinkers, it bestows a legitimate benefit. The critics assume there is no merit to a product beyond its utilitarian qualities. What a dull world it would be if all products were marketed and used on this basis.

Third, the beer, wine, and spirits industries have voluntary codes of advertising behavior. The policies in these codes are extensive and specific. For example, the Beer Institute's *Advertising & Marketing Code* prohibits depictions of excessive consumption, intoxication, and drinking while driving. Models in beer ads must be over 25 and "reasonably appear" to be over 21 years old. No ads should be placed in media where the audience is primarily under 21 years old, and beer ads should never show "any symbol, language, music, gesture, or cartoon character that is intended to appeal primarily to persons below the legal purchase age." No depictions of Santa Claus or sexual promiscuity are permitted.[27] The Wine Institute's *Code of Advertising Standards* has similar guidelines. It prohibits showing the Easter bunny.[28] The Distilled Spirits Council of the United States *Code of Good Practice for Distilled Spirits Advertising and Marketing* is the most detailed and in its Preamble claims to "ensure responsible, tasteful, and dignified advertising . . . to adult consumers." Its provisions are similar to the two other codes. It allows "depictions of persons in a social or romantic setting" but forbids advertisers to "depict sexual prowess as a result of beverage alcohol consumption."[29] Each code sets a standard of advertising only on television programs where at least 70 percent of the audience is 21 years of age or older.

Compliance with industry self-regulation is voluntary. The DISCUS code is the only one with a formal review process. A five-member review board considers

[24] Juana Mora, "A Day of Pride, Prey to an Ad Blitz," *Los Angeles Times,* April 23, 2000, p. B17.

[25] Shelly Branch, "Seagram's Captain Morgan Gets Allied Domecq's Attention," *The Wall Street Journal,* November 20, 2000, p. B4.

[26] Eric Clark, *The Want Makers* (New York: Viking Press, 1988), p. 285.

[27] At www.beerinstitute.org/admarkcode.htm.

[28] At www.wineinstitute.org/communications/statistics/Code_of_Advertising.htm.

[29] At www.discus.org/industry/code/code.htm.

This ad associates Bud Dry with fun, companionship, and sexuality.
Source: © Joel Gordon.

complaints about ads and decides whether they meet code standards. It then notifies companies. The results are not made public, but the Federal Trade Commission reported that between 2000 and 2003 the review board considered 26 complaints and decided that 19 of the ads violated the DISCUS code. All member companies discontinued or revised their ads in response.[30] The Beer Institute and the Wine Institute codes have no similar compliance mechanisms. They simply pass on complaints to member companies with no recommendations or follow-up.

Fourth, alcohol makers deflect critics by broadcasting public service announcements that preach moderation and by setting up education and community-action projects such as designated-driver programs. There are many such programs. The Distilled Spirits Council of the United States sponsors college campus programs in which students teach each other about moderation, and it has a program for training bartenders to serve drinks responsibly. Anheuser-Busch, Inc., has six public service programs that promote responsible drinking. Alert Cab, for instance, gives free taxi rides to restaurant and bar patrons who have been drinking.

[30] Federal Trade Commission, *Alcohol Marketing and Advertising: A Report to Congress* (Washington, DC: FTC, September 2003), p. 10.

Finally, the industry does not deny targeting younger drinkers, minorities, women, and other groups with advertising themes. The puzzle faced by companies is that the critical young age group of consumers shares many interests and behaviors with teenagers below the legal drinking age. With respect to ads aimed at minorities, the industry believes this practice is legitimate. Market segmentation and the targeted advertising that makes it work are standard in many industries. When toy companies make black or Latina dolls, social critics applaud, but when alcohol companies make products that appeal to minority communities, critics argue that these consumers are too gullible and naive to withstand manipulation, implying that minority consumers are not as astute as white consumers. The real problem is that the product is alcohol, not that the ads have ethnic or racial appeal.

RESTRICTING ALCOHOL ADVERTISING

Today there is little government regulation of alcohol ads, and, in recent years, federal courts have weakened that which does exist and raised barriers to added restrictions. Two federal agencies have some power over the claims that companies make.

Under a 1935 law, the Bureau of Alcohol, Tobacco and Firearms regulates container labels to prevent false claims, obscene images, and the use of words such as "strong" and "extra strength." Originally, the law prohibited statements of alcohol content on labels so that companies could not start strength wars. However, in 1995 the Supreme Court held that censoring this information violated bottlers' speech rights, so alcohol content can now be printed on labels.[31] A second agency, the Federal Trade Commission, has the power to stop "deceptive" and "unfair" advertising claims, and now and then it flexes its muscles regarding alcohol ads.

Altogether, the body of government regulation covering alcohol advertising imposes few restraints. Critics want stronger measures. In the 1990s several bills were introduced in Congress to limit alcohol ads, for example, by banning them near schools and playgrounds, in publications with large youth readerships, on college campuses, and during prime-time television hours.[32] The prospect for such measures faded after a 1999 Supreme Court decision that struck down a federal ban on broadcast ads by casinos.[33]

The court has also chipped away at other restrictions. Until 1996 Rhode Island banned price advertising for alcoholic beverages, claiming it was justified in doing so to promote temperance. However, the Supreme Court struck the ban down, saying that price advertising is protected by the First Amendment's free-speech guarantee.[34]

ARE RESTRICTIONS ON ALCOHOL AND TOBACCO ADS CONSTITUTIONAL?

Images and statements in advertising are speech. Therefore, proposals for muzzling liquor, beer, and wine companies raise constitutional issues. The First Amendment protects all speech from government-imposed curbs, but courts have distinguished *non-*

commercial speech from *commercial* speech. The former is speech in the broad marketplace of ideas, encompassing political, scientific, and artistic expression. Such speech is broadly protected. The latter is speech intended to stimulate business transactions, including advertising. This kind of speech receives less protection.

The right of free speech is assumed to be a fundamental barrier against tyranny and is not restricted lightly. Courts will not permit censorship of noncommercial speech unless it poses an imminent threat to public welfare, as it would, for example, if a speaker incited violence or a writer tried to publish military secrets.

With respect to commercial speech, however, various restrictions are allowed. For example, ads for securities offerings can appear only in the austere format of a legal notice and tobacco ads are barred on radio and TV. Would courts approve additional restrictions on alcoholic beverage advertising?

The most important legal guidelines for weighing restraints on commercial speech are those set forth by the Supreme Court in 1980 in the *Central Hudson* case.[35] Here the Court struck down a New York regulation banning advertising by public utilities, a regulation intended to help conserve energy. Justice Lewis Powell, writing for the majority, set forth a four-part test to decide when commercial speech could be restricted.

- The ad in question should promote a lawful product and must be accurate. If an ad is misleading or suggests illegal activity, it does not merit protection.
- The government interest in restricting the particular commercial speech must be substantial, not trivial or unimportant.
- The advertising restriction must directly further the interest of the government. In other words, it should demonstrably help the government reach its public policy goal.
- The suppression of commercial speech must not be more extensive than is necessary to achieve the government's purpose.

All government actions to ban or restrict alcohol ads could be challenged by industry and would have to pass the four-part *Central Hudson* test to survive.

---

[31] *Rubin v. Coors Brewing Company,* 514 U.S. 618 (1995).

[32] See, for example, the "Voluntary Alcohol Advertising Standards for Children Act," H.R. 1292, 105th Congress., 1st Sess. (1997), introduced by Representative Joseph P. Kennedy II (D-Massachusetts).

[33] *Greater New Orleans Broadcasting Association, Inc. v. U.S.,* 527 U.S. 173 (1999).

[34] *44 Liquormart v. Rhode Island,* 517 U.S. 484 (1996).

[35] *Central Hudson Gas & Electric Corp. v. Public Service Commission,* 447 U.S. 557.

LAWSUITS

A new approach to limiting alcohol advertising is the use of class action lawsuits. In 2003, Dr. Ayman R. Hakki, a plastic surgeon in Washington, DC, sued alcohol companies for a class of parents with children under the age of 21 whom advertising and promotional practices had lured into underage drinking. Hakki believes that Adolph Coors, Bacardi USA, Heineken USA, Brown-Forman Corporation, Diageo, and six other companies engaged in "a long-running, sophisticated, and deceptive scheme . . . to market alcoholic beverages to children and other underage consumers" to "generate billions of dollars a year in unlawful revenue."[36] The suit claims that the companies were negligent because they knowingly employed unreasonable marketing to reach and appeal to children. In doing so, they violated a duty to safeguard the interests of parents in guarding their children against the dangers of underage drinking. A second claim is that the companies engaged in fraud and deception by misrepresenting alcohol as having certain uses, characteristics, and benefits that it does not have. Hakki seeks an injunction to stop ads that target underage drinkers and to have the companies disgorge "billions of dollars in ill-gotten profits" from illegal purchase of alcoholic beverages.

A second class action has been prepared in California for parents Lynne and Reed Goodwin, whose 20-year-old daughter Casey was killed by an 18-year-old drunk driver in 2003.[37] The Goodwins are suing Anheuser-Busch and Miller Brewing alleging that the company's youth-oriented ads violate state laws against underage drinking and lure minors into the unlawful purchase and consumption of beer. The class of plaintiffs includes parties harmed by drunk drivers who were exposed to the brewers' ads. The Goodwins also accuse the companies of violating California consumer laws prohibiting deceptive, unfair, and misleading advertising.

These and similar lawsuits come from the same law firms that brought tort and product liability suits against the tobacco companies. They rely on novel and untested legal theories of intentional tort, negligence, breach of warranty, and fraud. None of them have yet come to trial. Even if they stall, they could still affect advertising practice.

A PERSPECTIVE ON ALCOHOL ADVERTISING

Alcohol advertising is controversial. The Prohibition Party argument that it promotes an immoral, sinful, and unhealthy habit has few advocates today. However, underage drinking is an important social problem and sometimes leads to unnecessary tragedy. The mainstream campaign to limit alcohol advertising is focused on protecting children and teenagers. Its activists believe that appeals in alcohol ads intentionally or negligently spill over to influence underage drinkers. Evidence is strong that children and teenagers are attracted to some alcohol ads. But proof of cause and effect between advertising and underage consumption eludes researchers.

Critics believe that the alcohol companies intentionally target underage drinkers to gain revenue and to lock in brand loyalty at an early age. They make a circumstantial case based on appearance. For example, the plaintiff's brief in the *Hakki* lawsuit points to messages on a Bacardi Web site accessible to persons under the legal drinking age. The site advises how to "avoid any dirty looks from mom as you reach for the Bacardi bottle at 8 AM" and lists a recipe for "breakfast with a bang" with the ingredients rum, grapefruit, and sugar for use when "your mom still persistently nags you about having fruit with breakfast."[38]

Such unmistakable appeals to a potential underage audience are not typical. Most advertising targets legitimate age groups. When the Federal Trade Commission studied advertising for flavored malt beverages, it required nine large alcohol companies to produce documents describing the research, creation, and development of ads. It found that "99% of the dollars spent to advertise FMBs on television, radio, and in print media were expended in compliance" with the industry code.[39]

[36] *Hakki v. Zima Company et al.,* Civ. No. 03-0009183 (Superior Court, District of Columbia, CD, 2003), *Complaint,* November 14, 2003, p. 3.

[37] *Goodwin v. Anheuser-Busch Co.s, Inc.; Miller Brewing Co.,* Superior Court of the State of California, County of Los Angeles (2004).

[38] *Hakki v. Zima Company et al., Complaint,* pp. 8–9.

[39] Federal Trade Commission, *Alcohol Marketing and Advertising: A Report to Congress,* p. 4.

Critics believe that alcohol marketers are so sophisticated they could precisely limit appeals to drinkers age 21 and over without any spillover to underage drinkers. Belief in this much command of an audience is perhaps wishful. Skepticism about the ability of alcohol ads to influence anyone may be equally reasonable. Miller Brewing developed a series of "Catfight" commercials for Miller Lite that won the 2003 grand prize for sexism from the Advertising Women of New York, but Miller Lite sales fell 2.5 percent while the commercials were running.[40] When Allied Domecq tried to reposition its Kahlúa brand with drinkers aged 21 to 29 it ran youth-oriented print ads with brazen sexual imagery. The effort was a complete failure.[41]

In fact, advertising is rarely the powerful force it is made out to be.[42] It is often ignored by consumers, undermined by competitors, and drowned in a flood of commercial stimuli. Still, the alcohol industry surely has an ethical duty to reduce potential harm. It may or may not be meeting this duty now.

Questions

1. Do you support liquor advertising on network television? Is it fair to restrict advertising for liquor advertising more than advertising for other alcoholic beverages?

2. Do alcoholic beverage companies fulfill their ethical duty to be informative and truthful in advertising? Do they generally uphold their ethical duty to minimize potential harm to society from underage drinking?

3. Are some beer, wine, or spirits ads misleading? What examples can you give? What is misleading in them? Do some ads contain images and themes that go too far in appealing to an audience under the legal drinking age? Can you give examples?

4. Do you believe there is a need for more restrictions on alcohol advertising? If so, what limits are needed? Explain how a ban or any restrictions could be argued to meet the *Central Hudson* guidelines.

5. Should alcohol advertisers be held liable for wrongdoing under product liability theories of negligence, breach of warranty, or strict liability? Explain why or why not.

[40] See Christopher Lawton, "Miller, Coors Still Bet Sex Sells Beer," *The Wall Street Journal*, June 6, 2003, p. B3; and Suzanne Vranica, "Sirius Ad Is Best Bet for Most Sexist," *The Wall Street Journal*, April 1, 2004, p. B6.

[41] Robert Guy Matthews, "Spirits Makers Aim to Juice Up Their Old-School Beverages," *The Wall Street Journal*, November 11, 2004, p. B5.

[42] Gerard J. Tellis, *Effective Advertising: Understanding When, How, and Why Advertising Works* (Thousand Oaks, CA: Sage, 2004), pp. 11–12.

Chapter **Seventeen**

The Changing Workplace

Ford Motor Company

The history of the Ford Motor Company is told in the changing experiences of its workers. Their story illustrates how powerful forces discussed in this chapter act to change the workplace.

Henry Ford (1863–1947) was a brilliant inventor. After incorporating the Ford Motor Company in 1903, he designed one car after another, naming each chassis after a letter of the alphabet. In 1908, he began selling the Model T, a utilitarian, crank-started auto that came only in black. An early Model T cost $850, but Ford introduced the first moving auto assembly line and, by 1924, mass output lowered the price to $290. The assembly line was a new, revolutionary technology that changed work at Ford, turning assemblers from craftsmen into interchangeable parts like those in the cars they assembled.

Ford sold 15.5 million Model Ts before production ended in 1927. Despite a warning in the form of fast-dropping market share in the mid-1920s, Ford failed utterly to anticipate a sea change in the auto market. The company clung to the spartan Model T even as consumers turned to the styling changes, closed body design, and brand hierarchy offered by General Motors. Finally, Ford had to suspend production, stilling its great River Rouge assembly plant for seven months while the Model A was hurriedly designed. More than 100,000 idled workers felt the sting of hardship that came from competition not well met.

Henry Ford was an obstinate man, obsessed with power, iron-willed, dictatorial, and cynical about human nature. He spied on his employees in their homes to see if they smoked or drank. Believing that workers were motivated by fear, he created a tense atmosphere marked by arbitrary and capricious dismissals. Managers knew they had been fired when they arrived at work to find their desks chopped to pieces. Sometimes two managers were given the same duties and the one failing to thrive in the competition was fired. In his autobiography, Ford wrote that a "great business is really too big to be human."[1] As the firm grew, his authoritarian style became embedded in its informal culture. Independent managers left, and he was surrounded by

[1] Henry Ford, *My Life and Work* (Garden City, NY: Doubleday, 1923), p. 263.

Model Ts pass along the first moving assembly line at Ford Motor Company's Highland Avenue plant in Detroit. The photograph was taken in 1913. Source: © National Archives/ CORBIS.

sycophants who would have jumped into the Detroit River if he had asked. They, in turn, were ruthless and autocratic with their subordinates.[2]

This atmosphere made conditions attractive for early labor organizers. The first efforts came in 1913. Ford fought unions, calling them "the worst things that ever struck the earth."[3] He hired thugs and underworld figures to work at his plants, spying on workers and intimidating anyone who abetted the union cause. This strategy was successful until Congress passed the landmark National Labor Relations Act in 1935, protecting the right of unions to organize. Under the new law, Ford Motor Company was found guilty of unfair labor practices at nine plants. Ford's lawyers delayed the inevitable for a few years, but in 1941 its workers, by a vote of 97 percent to 3 percent, voted to unionize. Federal regulation had been too powerful a force for Ford's campaign of fear to overcome.

Even after the unions, authoritarianism remained firmly entrenched. In 1945 Henry Ford himself felt its barb when he was ousted in a coup engineered by family members. He was replaced by his grandson, Henry Ford II, who also proved to be an autocrat.

In the early 1980s Ford again suffered the harsh discipline of the market. Three years of disastrous losses awakened it to heightened international competition. Japanese auto companies had captured 20 percent of American sales. The company studied Japanese management and decided to emulate its focus on work teams and continuous quality improvement. It set out to make a world-class sedan using methods similar to those used by Japanese car makers.

[2] Anne Jardim, *The First Henry Ford: A Study in Personality and Business Leadership* (Cambridge, MA: MIT Press, 1970), pp. 114–15.

[3] Quoted in Keith Sward, *The Legend of Henry Ford* (New York: Rinehart & Company, 1948), p. 370.

In Japanese management philosophy, competing personalities and individualism are thought to hamper productivity. So Ford tried to change its corporate culture. Over the years, it had tended to select autocrats for management positions. A study of 2,000 Ford managers classified 76 percent as "noncreative types who are comfortable with strong authority" (as compared with about 38 percent of the population).[4] To bring change, thousands of managers went to workshops on participative management.

Ford was rewarded for its efforts when the new Taurus sedan appeared in 1985. It was a quick success and became the best-selling car in America between 1993 and 1995. In 1994 the company made an extraordinary profit of $5.3 billion. Yet in that year, a new Ford chairman, Alexander Trotman, started Ford 2000, a radical change program to prepare the company for an even more competitive global car market.

Ford 2000 reorganized the way work was done. It revised the company's organization chart. It tore apart bureaucracy and instilled a new team philosophy. Layers of middle managers disappeared. Tasks were defined in meetings instead of by superiors. Committees decided on promotions and did performance reviews. More than 25,000 managers left hierarchical slots and moved into teams. Jobs were eliminated and early retirements encouraged. Workers felt considerable anxiety over these changes.

Although Ford's profit performance was strong, the Ford 2000 upheaval failed to make it a more dominant competitor. Its global market share for cars and trucks once again started to slip away. Competition in the global automobile industry is relentless. Inroads against rivals are excruciatingly difficult because of worldwide production overcapacity. The potential for oversupply means that car companies cannot easily raise output to increase revenue. Because brand loyalty among customers is declining, they cannot inflate prices. The only way to create profits in this situation is to cut costs and increase net income on each car sold. Leaner organizations save money. So does new technology. As part of Ford 2000, the company invested in new computers that not only design cars but automatically cut the tools and dies used to make them.

In 1999 a new CEO, Jacques Nasser, took over. Nasser, a man of relentless energy who functioned on three hours of sleep, had visions of turning Ford into a high-flying company like General Electric. He pushed methods that paralleled those used at GE, vowing to remake Ford's culture yet again. Nasser is of Lebanese descent and wanted to diversify Ford's workforce so others would not experience forms of bias he had felt over the years. In a speech, he said: "There are too many middle-aged white Anglo-Saxon males running the company."[5] The statement created animosity, and when he introduced a GE-like forced ranking system to evaluate managers, it led to lawsuits by low-ranked white-male managers claiming age discrimination. They argued that they were being unfairly pushed out to create a diverse workforce.

---

[4] Melinda G. Builes and Paul Ingrassia, "Ford's Leaders Push Radical Shift in Culture as Competition Grows," *The Wall Street Journal,* December 3, 1985, p. A1.

[5] Quoted in Joseph B. White and Norihiko Shirouzu, "A Stalled Revolution by Nasser Puts a Ford in the Driver's Seat," *The Wall Street Journal,* October 31, 2001, p. A1.

Ford earned a record profit in 1999, but trouble soon appeared again. Ford's quality and its market share were eroding. Then disaster hit in 2000 when tire failures on Ford Explorers caused hundreds of deaths and injuries. Nasser did not survive the crisis and in 2001 William Clay Ford, Jr., the great grandson of Henry Ford, took over. Early in 2002 he announced still another restructuring. Despite Ford 2000 and the Nasser initiatives, the company had failed to get its costs under control. Toyota made vehicles for $1,800 less than Ford. Quality problems persisted. Ford needed to cut closer to the bone.

Four car models were dropped, and over the next three years 35,000 positions were eliminated. Suppliers were pressured to cut their prices. Many laid off employees and outsourced work to low-wage factories in Mexico and China.[6] Then Ford began sending engineering work to India, where automotive design can be done for $60 an hour instead of up to $800 an hour in Detroit.[7] Many white-collar employees now fear that their jobs will be outsourced.

This short history of Ford Motor Company illustrates how forces in the business environment have shaped the work lives of Ford employees. In this chapter we take a systematic look at these forces.

EXTERNAL FORCES CHANGING THE WORKPLACE

Those who work today are swept up in turbulence caused by six environmental forces: (1) demographic change, (2) technological change, (3) structural change, (4) competitive pressures, (5) reorganization of work, and (6) government intervention. These forces often interact, magnifying their power. A discussion of each follows.

Demographic Change

Population dynamics slowly but continuously alter labor forces. Out of a 2002 population of 289 million Americans, about half, or 145 million, make up the civilian labor force as either working or unemployed (the rest are retired, disabled, students, homemakers, children under age 16, or not counted because they received unreported wages). This is the third-largest labor force in the world, though it pales in comparison to China's 840 million and India's 644 million.[8]

Historically, the American labor force has grown rapidly and continuously. It continues to grow, but more slowly, at a rate expected to be about 1.1 percent a year through 2012.[9] Amid this slower overall workforce expansion, however, the number of workers in some demographic categories is growing faster than in others, producing incremental but significant changes. Table 17.1 shows data for the 2002 labor force and projects current trends to the year 2012.

[6] Tom Murphy, "Low Cost, High Anxiety," *Ward's Auto Week,* August 1, 2004, p. 8.

[7] "Second Wave: Design Outsourcing Set to Hit Indian Shores," *Financial Express,* December 28, 2004, p. 1.

[8] Figures are from the U.S. Bureau of Labor Statistics and the World Bank, *World Development Indicators 2000,* p. 46, table 2.3. Figures for China and India are 2002 estimates based on predicted growth rates.

[9] Mitra Toossi, "Labor Force Projections to 2012: The Graying of the U.S. Workforce," *Monthly Labor Review,* February 2004, table 1.

TABLE 17.1
The American Labor Force: 2002–2012 (in thousands)

Source: Bureau of Labor Statistics.

Demographic Component	2002	Percent in 2002	2012	Percent in 2012	Percent Change
Men	77,500	53.5%	85,252	52.5%	−1.0%
Women	67,363	46.5	77,017	47.5	1.0
White	120,150	82.9	130,358	80.3	−2.6
Black	16,564	11.4	19,765	12.2	0.8
Hispanic	17,942	12.4	23,785	14.7	2.3
Asian	5,949	4.1	8,971	5.5	1.4
Other groups*	2,200	1.5	3,175	2.0	0.5
Total labor force†	**144,863**	**100.0%**	**162,269**	**100.0%**	**12.0%**

*Includes American Indians, Alaska Natives, Native Hawaiians, Pacific Islanders, and those reporting two or more races.
†Numerical and percentage totals exceed 100 percent because Hispanics may also be classified in other racial categories.

Table 17.1 shows that, proportionately, Hispanics and Asians are increasing their numbers faster than whites and blacks are. By 2012, Hispanics will have replaced blacks as the second-largest ethnic group. Asians are the fastest growing group, increasing in number by 51 percent over the decade in the table. But because their overall numbers are small, they will remain a relatively small proportion of the labor force. Since the 1970s women have increased their participation more rapidly than men, and although this trend is slowing, it will continue through 2012.

These changes mean that the workforce continues to grow more diverse in gender and ethnicity. In percentage terms, however, the changes are slight. By 2012 whites will decline by 2.6 percent, Hispanics will increase by 2.3 percent, Asians, despite their rapid rise in numbers, will increase by only 1.4 percent, women will increase by 1 percent, and blacks will increase by less than 1 percent. These are modest shifts. However, they represent only one decade of a steady, long-term trend toward diversity that has brought major change since the 1950s. Businesses in cosmopolitan areas experience even more rapid diversity increases than these national figures suggest.

The workforce is also aging. High fertility rates following World War II created a baby boom generation born between 1946 and 1964. As this generation entered the labor market in the 1970s, the median age of the workforce dropped, reaching a low of 34.6 years in 1980. The baby boomers are now a bulge of workers in their early 40s to late 50s. As they age, the median age of the workforce rises, and it is predicted to reach 41.4 years in 2012. This would be the oldest ever recorded, surpassing the previous high of 40.5 in 1962. Because the nation's fertility rate has declined since the baby boom years, generational cohorts of workers following the baby boomers are smaller. As these aging mainstays of the labor force retire in large numbers over the next two decades, a shortage of skilled and experienced workers may arise.

Graying of the workforce is more rapid in other developed nations. It is caused by increases in life expectancy combined with declines in fertility. Life expectancy has increased markedly in most nations. In the United States it rose from 47 in 1900 to 77 in 2002.[10] Birth rates have fallen in the developed world and are now below replacement rates in many nations. In Germany and Japan, for example, the fertility rate of 1.4 births per woman is far below the replacement rate of 2.1. The populations of these nations are predicted to begin a period of long-term decline. Because fewer young workers will arrive in the next 10 to 20 years, low-fertility countries face a challenge in filling entry and lower-level jobs.

While many developed nations confront population declines and all have aging workforces, many developing nations have explosively growing, youthful populations. Since the 1970s the United States has absorbed a huge wave of immigrants, most from these nations. It currently takes in about 1 million legal immigrants each year and an estimated 500,000 undocumented immigrants. About 9.3 million undocumented immigrants reside in the United States and 6 million of these are estimated to be in the workforce.[11] The influx of immigrants shapes the American labor force by accelerating its growth, increasing the number of Hispanics and Asians, and slowing the rise in average age.

Since the fertility rate in the United States has fallen to 2.1, equal to the replacement rate, continued immigration will prevent the population declines facing Europe and Japan. Immigration gives the United States a long-run competitive advantage in labor costs. Japan and some European countries have tight immigration laws. The Japanese want to preserve racial purity and have difficulty integrating non-Japanese into their workplaces. Many European nations are strongly ethnocentric and tightly restrict immigration. Immigration, however, brings an influx of younger workers who are less costly and more adaptable.

Technological Change

When the United States was an agrarian nation fall harvests absorbed enormous amounts of labor. Gangs of men crossed grain fields swinging sickles and scythes. Behind them came women and children to bundle the cuttings. In the 1850s Cyrus McCormick began to manufacture a line of horse-drawn mechanical harvesters, each ridden by a single farmer, that mowed and mechanically baled tall crops. Over the last three harvests of the Civil War, farmers bought 160,000 of McCormick's harvesters. The Commissioner of Agriculture estimated that each reaper freed five men for service in the Union Army, a factor in its victory.[12] With the war over, the men returned to work in factories, not fields, a sudden, unprecedented conversion of 7.6 percent of the labor force that stimulated industrial growth.[13]

Technological change has many impacts on work. It affects the number and type of jobs available. Invention of the airplane, for example, created new job titles such as pilot and flight attendant. Webmasters, or employees who design and

[10] Robert A. Rosenblatt, "U.S. Not as Gray as 31 Other Countries," *Los Angeles Times,* December 15, 2001, p. A17; and United Nations Development Programme, *Human Development Report: 2004* (New York: UNDP, 2004), table 1, p. 139.

[11] General Accounting Office, *Workforce Challenges and Opportunities for the 21st Century: Changing Labor Force Dynamics and the Role of Government Policies,* GAO–04–845SP, June 2004, p. 5.

[12] T. A. Heppenheimer, "Cyrus H. McCormick and Company," *American Heritage,* June 2001, p. 10.

[13] Based on an estimate of 800,000 agricultural workers as a percentage of the 1860 labor force of 10,532,750.

update Web sites, emerged with the rise of the Internet. New machines are used by management to raise productivity and reduce costs. Robots in auto manufacturing made American companies more competitive in cost and quality with Japanese automakers. Computers have reduced the need for clerical workers and middle managers who existed primarily to collect, analyze, and report information.

Automation has a turbulent impact on employment. It has long been feared. When running for president in 1960, John F. Kennedy warned that automation posed "the dark menace of industrial dislocation."[14] Two years later an industry–labor group compared its effects on the economy to that of a hydrogen bomb. It displaces jobs in traditional occupations. Yet, the number of jobs available in the United States has continuously increased, absorbing new entrants in the growing labor force. This is projected to continue.

Automation causes significant job loss in less-skilled manufacturing and service occupations. In coal mining, for example, mechanization has eliminated 344,000 pick-and-shovel jobs, 83 percent, since 1950. The movement to robotics in the 1980s put almost 40,000 robots on U.S. assembly lines and eliminated two-thirds of all assembly-line jobs by 1990. In service industries, the blows have been equally telling. Automated phones have eliminated 239,000 telephone operators, 67 percent, since 1950.[15] Between 1987 and 1998, 20 percent of these jobs were lost, even as the average number of daily conversations increased by more than 600 percent.[16]

Structural Change

structural change
Any shift in the proportions of agricultural, goods-producing, and service occupations in an economy.

Structural change is caused by processes of job creation and job destruction that continuously alter the mix of productive work in every economy. The American job landscape is shaped by the three long-term structural trends shown in Figure 17.1. Their action is similar in all industrialized nations.

First, the *agricultural sector* has declined from predominance to near insignificance as an occupation. In early colonial America, farming occupied 90 percent of Americans. By 2002 it employed only 1.6 percent as fewer and larger farms delivered the nation's food supply using automated methods to grow crops and raise animals.[17] The Bureau of Labor Statistics predicts that the number of agricultural workers will fall a little more, to 1.2 percent of the labor force, by 2012.

agricultural sector
The economic sector that includes farming, fishing, and forestry occupations.

Second, the percentage of workers employed in the *goods-producing sector*, which rose through most of the nation's early history, is now in long-term decline. In 1950

goods-producing sector
The economic sector that includes manufacturing, mining, and construction.

[14] Quoted in Brink Lindsey, "10 Truths about Trade," *Reason*, July 2004, p. 31.

[15] Figures for coal mining and telephone operator employment are for the years 1950 to 2002, from U.S. Census Bureau, *Statistical Abstract of the United States: 1956*, 77th ed., and *2003*, 123rd ed. (Washington, DC, 1956 and 2003); for 1950, tables 910 and 257; for 2003, tables 889 and 615.

[16] Stephen Franklin, "Telephone Operators Are among Those Being Displaced by Technology," *San Jose Mercury News*, September 6, 1998; U.S. Census Bureau, *Statistical Abstract of the United States: 2000*, 120th ed. (Washington, DC, 2000), table 917.

[17] Sector employment figures in this section are from Jay M. Berman, "Industry Output and Employment Projections to 2012," *Monthly Labor Review*, February 2004, table 1; and from various editions of the *Statistical Abstract of the United States*. Sector employment percentages for 2002 do not total 100 percent; the missing increment of 7.6 percent includes private household wage and salary earners and nonagricultural self-employed.

FIGURE 17.1   Historical Trend Lines for Employment by Major Industry Sector, 1800 to 2012 (Projection)

Sources: Bureau of Labor Statistics, U.S. Census Bureau; and Herman E. Kroose, *American Economic Development* 2nd ed. (Englewood Cliffs, NJ: Prentice Hall, 1966), p. 27. Post-1985 figures reflect some reclassification of industries.

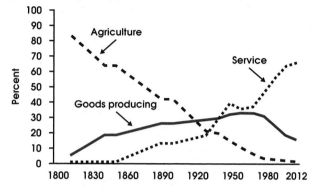

industry jobs occupied 34 percent of workers, but by 2002 this kind of employment had declined to only 15.7 percent of the labor force. By 2012 these occupations are predicted to slump further to 14.1 percent. There are many reasons for the fall of manufacturing work, but the two most significant are productivity growth, primarily through automation, and relocation of assembly to lower-wage countries. In steel production, for example, foreign competition caused a loss of 518,400 U.S. jobs, from a peak of 620,400 jobs in 1953 to only 102,000 in 2001.[18] However, since 1970, the amount of steel made per hour by each U.S. worker has more than doubled because of automation. Goods-producing jobs have declined only as a percentage of the overall labor force. In absolute numbers, employment in this sector has held steady since 1950, while manufacturing output in the United States has continually risen, soaring from $89 billion in 1950 to $1.9 trillion in 2001.

service sector
The sector of occupations that add value to manufactured goods.

Third, there is explosive growth in the *service sector,* which includes jobs in retailing, transportation, health care, and other occupations that add value to manufactured goods. For example, a surgeon adds value to a scalpel, a desk clerk to the mattress in a hotel room. Growth in this sector is caused by growth in goods production and trade. Service jobs have risen from 40 percent of the workforce in 1950 to 75 percent in 2002 and are predicted to rise to 78 percent in 2012. The nation's fastest-growing occupation, business computer services, exemplifies this explosive growth. It employed 271,000 people in 1979, then grew by 773 percent to employ 2.1 million in 2000.

The direction of these three trends is remarkably similar in all developed nations. Table 17.2 shows how they have shaped occupational structures elsewhere. The seven nations in the table all experienced long-term job losses in agriculture and industry and steep growth in service sector employment. Nations that have

[18] U.S. Bureau of the Census, *Statistical Abstract of the United States: 2003,* table 987.

TABLE 17.2
Comparative
Occupational
Structures
of Seven
Developed
Nations: 2003

Source: World Bank,
*World Development
Report 2005,* table 3.
Copyright © 2004
by World Bank.
Reproduced by
permission of World
Bank via Copyright
Clearance Center.

	Agriculture	Industry	Services
Australia	4%	26%	71%
France	3	25	72
Germany	1	30	69
Italy	3	29	69
Japan	1	31	68
Sweden	2	28	70
United Kingdom	1	26	73

not yet industrialized tend to have large agricultural sectors. Some developing nations are dominated by their industrial sectors. For example, industry is 53 percent of GDP in China, 49 percent in Malaysia, and 44 percent in Indonesia.[19]

Structural change is a critical factor in the decline of labor unions. Before the wave of protective legislation passed in the 1930s, unions represented only 5 percent of industrial workers, but this tripled to 15 percent by 1940 and reached a zenith of 25 percent in the 1950s.[20] Unions raised wages and increased benefits for blue-collar workers. These improvements rippled through the entire manufacturing sector because nonunionized companies had to approximate the welfare levels of union workers if they wished to prevent unionization.

In the 1970s, however, union membership in the private sector began a long slide as structural change eroded its base of factory workers. Employment shifted to service industries and to industries employing knowledge workers, who are difficult for industrial unions to organize, and to low-wage countries where unions are illegal or weak. By 2002 unions represented less than 9 percent of private sector employees in the United States. The upward push on wages and benefits that unions provide for both members and nonmembers has weakened commensurately.

Today, the United States has lower union representation of the private labor force than most other developed economies. In Western Europe, although union membership has declined for two decades, roughly a third to a half of all workers remain unionized. An exception is France, where union membership is only slightly larger than in the United States.[21] This is one reason that labor costs are much higher in many European nations than in the United States.

Competitive Pressures

Recent trends have intensified competition for American companies. Customers demand higher quality, better service, and faster new-product development. In the United States deregulation of large industries such as airlines, telecommunications,

[19] World Bank, *World Development Report 2005* (Washington, DC: World Bank, 2004), table 3, p. 260.

[20] U.S. Bureau of the Census, *Statistical Abstract of the United States: 1956* (Washington, DC: U.S. Government Printing Office, 1956), table 271.

[21] Znoelle Knox, "Unions Begin to Struggle in Europe," *USA Today,* November 11, 2004, p. B1; and Greg J. Bamber, Russell D. Lansbury, and Nick Wailes, eds., *International & Comparative Employment Relations,* 4th ed. (London: Sage, 2004), chapter 1.

TABLE 17.3   International Wage Comparison
The table shows hourly compensation for manufacturing workers in U.S. dollars based on currency exchange rates. Compensation includes wages, insurance, labor taxes, and paid leave.

Source: Bureau of Labor Statistics; and Peter Coy, "Just How Cheap Is Chinese Labor?" *BusinessWeek,* December 13, 2004, p. 46. Figures are for 2003, except Cambodia, China, and Vietnam, which are for 2002.

Cambodia	$0.45	Singapore	$7.41
Sri Lanka	0.49	Korea	10.29
China	0.64	Japan	20.09
Vietnam	1.22	United Kingdom	20.37
Mexico	2.48	France	21.13
Brazil	2.67	United States	21.97
Taiwan	5.84	Germany	29.91

trucking, and electric utilities has stirred formerly complacent rivals. In both domestic and overseas markets, corporations are increasingly challenged by foreign competitors. Foreign trade grew from just 9 percent of the U.S. economy in 1960 to 28 percent in 2002 and is predicted to rise to 34 percent by 2012.[22] Foreign competitors have many advantages, including lower labor costs, a strong dollar, and, sometimes, higher worker productivity.

In a global labor market workers in developed nations are exposed to competition from pools of low-cost workers. In less affluent, less industrialized countries, wages are lower for many reasons, including oversupply of labor compared with demand, low living standards, local currency valuations, labor policies of regimes where workers have limited political power, and wage competition among countries seeking to attract jobs.

By global standards, American workers are extremely expensive. In 2003 the average hourly compensation for a manufacturing worker in the United States was $21.97 an hour. This was not the highest in the world. That distinction went to heavily unionized workers in Denmark making $32.18 an hour.[23] Average compensation in the original 15 European Union nations was $24.05. However, because of the weakening euro, compensation costs in the highest-paying European nations have fallen closer to American levels. And in the newly industrializing economies of Asia and Latin America an hour of labor costs far less. Table 17.3 shows the huge wage gap between developed and developing economies.

Given this wage variation, companies in some industries can no longer afford to do low-skilled manufacturing in the United States and contract to have it done in a foreign country. Or they find ways to increase productivity of domestic labor by reducing employees to a minimum and applying technology to enlarge their

[22] Betty W. Su, "The U.S. Economy to 2012: Signs of Growth," *Monthly Labor Review,* February 2004, p. 23.

[23] Figures in this paragraph are from Bureau of Labor Statistics, "International Comparisons of Hourly Compensation Costs for Production Workers in Manufacturing, 1975–2003," November 2004, table 2, at www.bls.gov.

output. Either way, there are generally fewer jobs for American workers in the occupation affected. Similar wage competition now exists in globalizing service industries.

Reorganization of Work

Corporations alter business processes—the work that they do—as they adjust to environmental changes, primarily competition. A key driver of competition and, therefore, change in business processes, is a changing relationship with time and space. Communication is faster and transport is cheaper. Both factors lead companies to reorganize and cause workforce turbulence. This turbulence, which is the creative force of the economy on display, is widely feared by workers who lose jobs.

For most of the twentieth century manufacturing occurred near markets for products. As transport costs have fallen, manufacturers more often separate production from consumption by sending their manufacturing to low-cost countries, then shipping products back to customers. There are many examples. A recent story is how the prime contractor on the new six-story Salt Lake City public library underbid its competitors by sending part of the construction work to Mexico. It hired a Mexico City company to manufacture 2,000 massive concrete panels that make up the building, saving $1 million even though the panels had to be trucked 2,350 miles to the job site.[24]

Because of abundant and inexpensive bandwidth through fiber-optic cable and the Internet, service work that formerly had to be done within companies can now also be sent to low-cost locations. This has led to the outsourcing of white-collar work in information technology, customer service, telemarketing, accounting, and document management. The annual salary of a software engineer in the United States is $60,000 a year or more, but only $4,800 in Hungary and $5,800 in India.[25] So software costs dramatically less when it is designed in Budapest or Bangalore and consumed at the end of a fiber-optic line in Silicone Valley. This means that white-collar jobs in the United States, Europe, and Japan will migrate to India, China, and Russia, which are emerging as hubs for service production, just as low-wage Asian nations emerged in the 1950s as manufacturing hubs.

outsourcing
The transfer of work from within a company to an outside supplier.

offshoring
The transfer of work from within a company to a supplier in another country.

Trade in services between nations is growing, creating fears about job loss from *outsourcing*. Outsourcing, a word that has taken on emotional overtones, occurs when a company sends work of any kind to an outside supplier rather than pay its own employees to do it. It may be manufacturing or service work. Usually, outsourcing is done to cut labor costs, although outside suppliers may have expertise or achieve economies of scale that a company would find expensive to duplicate. Outsourcing may move work to either a domestic or a foreign contractor. When work moves to a foreign country this is sometimes called *offshoring*.

[24] Joel Millman, "Blueprint for Outsourcing," *The Wall Street Journal*, March 3, 2004, p. B1.
[25] Bruce Stokes, "And Away They Go," *National Journal*, March 27, 2004, p. 942.

FIGURE 17.2
Job Gains and
Job Losses in
the American
Labor Force:
1993–2004

Source: Bureau of
Labor Statistics,
"Business
Employment
Dynamics," series
extracted
December 30, 2004.

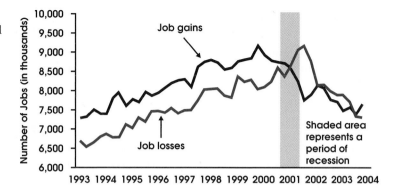

Outsourcing has fueled attacks on corporations for destroying well-paying jobs in developed nations out of greed.[26] Statistics on outsourcing are imprecise. A widely cited estimate is that American firms will outsource 3.3 million jobs to foreign countries by 2015.[27] Only in 2004 did the Bureau of Labor Statistics begin to measure outsourcing. Its initial calculation was that in the first quarter of 2004, out of 239,000 workers who lost their jobs in mass layoffs, only 4,600 were unemployed because their work left the country.[28] This is a small fraction of job loss and affects a microscopic element of the labor force.

Overall, outsourcing is only a small eddy in the churning tides of job gain and job loss that sweep over American workers. Figure 17.2 shows that between 1993 and 2004, except for a period of recession in 2001, each year more jobs were created than lost. During this period, the economy created an average of 32.5 million new jobs every year while eliminating 30.9 million, for a net average annual gain of 1.6 million. These figures reflect the dynamic of reorganization that is a central force reshaping the structure of the economy and the nature of work.

For corporations, outsourcing cuts costs, raises margins, and promotes growth. When costs of production fall, profits increase and prices drop. This stimulates innovation as companies invest in improving old products and creating new ones. With lower prices, consumers can afford to buy more and inflation is lower, creating new demand for goods and services. Traditional manufacturing and service jobs may fly across the oceans, but other domestic jobs arise in new sectors as the economy grows. Although economically beneficial, outsourcing is politically volatile. The creation of new jobs always lags behind the destruction of old ones. Whereas the benefits of outsourcing are widely distributed, its temporary pains are intensely felt by redundant workers who ask politicians for protection.

[26] See, for example, Lou Dobbs, *Exporting America: Why Corporate Greed Is Shipping American Jobs Overseas* (New York: Warner Business Books, 2004).

[27] By Forrester Research in 2002, cited in Stokes, "And Away They Go," p. 943.

[28] Bureau of Labor Statistics, News Release, "Extended Mass Layoffs Associated with Domestic and Overseas Relocations, First Quarter 2004," p. 1. Only 10,000 lost work because of domestic outsourcing.

GOVERNMENT INTERVENTION

All governments intervene in labor markets, but there is wide variation. We first discuss how labor regulation has developed in the United States. Then we explain the alternative model in Japan and Europe. Last, we explain the trade-offs in labor regulation that all governments face.

Development of Labor Regulation in the United States

employment contract
The agreement by which an employee exchanges his or her labor in return for specific pay and working conditions. It is an abstract concept, but may also be set forth in writing.

Historically, a strong laissez-faire current in American economic philosophy made governments at all levels reluctant to interfere with the *employment contract,* or the agreement by which an employee exchanges his or her labor in return for specific pay and working conditions. Today, government intervention is extensive and growing, but this is a twentieth-century trend.

Before 1860, the number of persons employed as wage earners in factories, mines, railroads, and other workplaces was relatively small. With industrialization, the number rapidly grew. Between 1860 and 1890, the number of wage earners rose from 1.33 million to 4.25 million, a 320 percent increase.[29] This rise, which would continue into the 1930s, created a new class interest, and it was an aggrieved one. In the hardhearted wisdom of the day, employers treated workers as simply production costs to be minimized; there was relentless downward pressure on wages and reluctance to improve working conditions.

Liberty of Contract

liberty of contract
The freedom of employers and workers to negotiate the employment contract—including wages, hours, duties, and conditions—without government interference.

Before the 1930s, government intervention on behalf of workers was very limited, consisting mostly of feeble state safety regulations and laws to limit working hours. In the late 1800s and early 1900s, strong majorities on the Supreme Court upheld the *liberty of contract* doctrine. This doctrine held that employers and workers should be free of government intervention to negotiate all aspects of the employment contract, including wages, hours, duties, and conditions.[30] For many years, the Court struck down state and federal laws that interfered with this theoretical freedom. Such laws were regarded as "meddlesome interferences with the rights of the individual."[31]

The great flaw in the liberty of contract doctrine was that it assumed equal bargaining power for all parties, whereas employers unquestionably predominated. For employers, liberty of contract was the liberty to exploit. Employees could be fired at will and had to accept virtually any working conditions. Unchallenged

---

[29] Arthur M. Schlesinger, *Political and Social Growth of the United States: 1852–1933* (New York: Macmillan, 1935), p. 203.

[30] The liberty of contract majority first emerged in *Allgeyer v. Louisiana,* 106 U.S. 578 (1897), where Justice Rufus W. Peckham grounded it in the due process clause of the Fourteenth Amendment, which says that no state can "deprive any person of life, liberty, or property, without due process of law."

[31] Justice Peckham, writing for a 5–4 majority in *Lockner v. New York,* 198 U.S. 61 (1905). The decision struck down an 1897 New York State law limiting bakery employees to 60-hour weeks.

Turn-of-the-century cartoonist Art Young drew this cynical view of the lopsided employment contract in the days before labor unions and laws protecting worker rights. Source: Cartoon by Art Young.

dominion of employers opened the door to the negligent treatment of workers that fueled the labor union movement, a social movement to empower workers. Employers resisted demands for kinder treatment of workers and bitterly fought the rise of unions.

Waves of Regulation

It was not until the 1930s that government regulation of the workplace began to redress the huge power imbalance favoring employers. One major step was the Norris-LaGuardia Anti-Injunction Act of 1932, which struck down a type of employer–employee agreement called, in the colorful language of unionists, a "yellow dog contract." These were agreements that workers would not join unions. Employers virtually extorted signatures on them when workers were hired, and hapless applicants had little choice but to sign if they wanted the job—and jobs were scarce in the 1930s. If union organizing began, companies went to court, where judges enforced the agreements. The Norris-LaGuardia Act outlawed yellow dog contracts, overturning a 1908 Supreme Court decision that upheld them under the liberty of contract doctrine.[32]

The new law encouraged unions. It was soon followed by the National Labor Relations Act of 1935, which guaranteed union organizing and bargaining rights, and by other laws that fleshed out a body of rules for labor relations. After the 1930s, employers still dominated the employment contract, but unions increasingly checked company power over wages and working conditions.

Figure 17.3 shows how this first wave of federal workplace regulation in the 1930s, which established union rights, was followed by two subsequent waves. A second wave, between 1963 and 1974, moved federal law into new areas, protecting civil rights, worker health and safety, and pension rights. A third wave, between 1986 and 1996, again broadened federal authority to address additional, and somewhat narrower, employment issues. During this period, Congress enacted the following laws.

- A provision in the Comprehensive Omnibus Budget Reconciliation Act of 1986 allows separated workers to continue in group health plans for up to 18 months at their own expense.
- The Immigrant Reform and Control Act of 1986 protects work rights of legal aliens and prohibits hiring illegal aliens.
- The Worker Adjustment and Retraining Act of 1988 requires companies with more than 100 workers to give 60 days' notice prior to plant closings or large layoffs.
- The Employee Polygraph Protection Act of 1988 prohibits the use of lie detectors to screen job applicants and narrows grounds for using the tests to detect employee theft or sabotage.
- The Drug-Free Workplace Act of 1988 requires companies with federal contracts to take measures against drug abuse.
- The Americans with Disabilities Act of 1990 prohibits discrimination against the disabled and requires employers to make reasonable accommodations for people with substantial physical or mental impairments.
- The Family and Medical Leave Act of 1993 gives workers the right to take up to 12 weeks of unpaid leave for family reasons such as childbirth or illness.
- The Health Insurance Portability and Accountability Act of 1996 guarantees that preexisting medical problems will continue to be covered by health insurance when workers switch jobs.

Altogether, approximately 200 federal laws have been enacted since the 1930s, including amendments to original statutes, so only the major ones are shown in Figure 17.3. These laws have been based on the dominant perspective of 1930s reformers that the relationship between labor and management is antagonistic. Based on this model, a broad and complex regulatory structure has been created over more than 75 years to counterbalance the perceived weakness of workers in the employment contract with corporations. It has greatly improved the lives of

---

[32] *Adair v. United States*, 291 U.S. 293 (1908).

FIGURE 17.3   A Chronology of Major Workplace Regulations

This figure shows the historical march of major statutes (and one executive order) regulating labor–management and employer–employee relations. Note the existence of three rough clusters or waves of intervention.

Source: Adapted from General Accounting Office, "Testimony: Rethinking the Federal Role in Worker Protection and Workforce Development," 1995, p. 5.

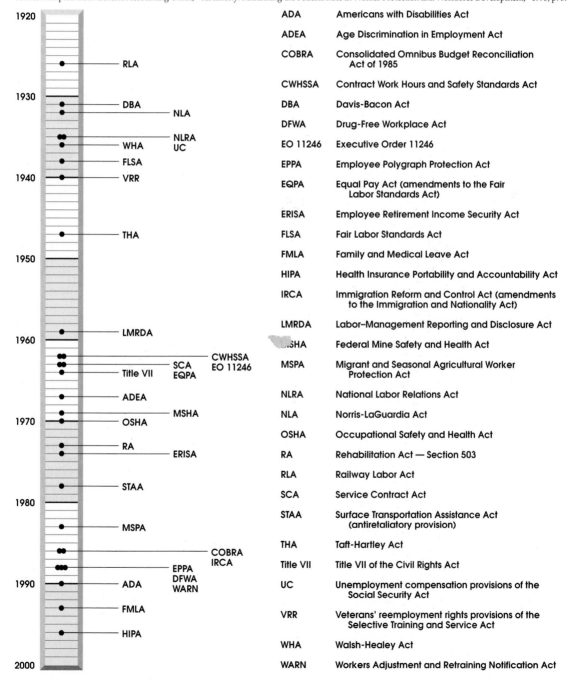

ADA	Americans with Disabilities Act
ADEA	Age Discrimination in Employment Act
COBRA	Consolidated Omnibus Budget Reconciliation Act of 1985
CWHSSA	Contract Work Hours and Safety Standards Act
DBA	Davis-Bacon Act
DFWA	Drug-Free Workplace Act
EO 11246	Executive Order 11246
EPPA	Employee Polygraph Protection Act
EQPA	Equal Pay Act (amendments to the Fair Labor Standards Act)
ERISA	Employee Retirement Income Security Act
FLSA	Fair Labor Standards Act
FMLA	Family and Medical Leave Act
HIPA	Health Insurance Portability and Accountability Act
IRCA	Immigration Reform and Control Act (amendments to the Immigration and Nationality Act)
LMRDA	Labor–Management Reporting and Disclosure Act
MSHA	Federal Mine Safety and Health Act
MSPA	Migrant and Seasonal Agricultural Worker Protection Act
NLRA	National Labor Relations Act
NLA	Norris-LaGuardia Act
OSHA	Occupational Safety and Health Act
RA	Rehabilitation Act — Section 503
RLA	Railway Labor Act
SCA	Service Contract Act
STAA	Surface Transportation Assistance Act (antiretaliatory provision)
THA	Taft-Hartley Act
Title VII	Title VII of the Civil Rights Act
UC	Unemployment compensation provisions of the Social Security Act
VRR	Veterans' reemployment rights provisions of the Selective Training and Service Act
WHA	Walsh-Healey Act
WARN	Workers Adjustment and Retraining Notification Act

FIGURE 17.4
After OSHA:
Declining
Workplace
Fatalities,
Rising Labor
Force

Sources: Bureau of
Labor Statistics,
Occupational
Safety and Health
Administration.

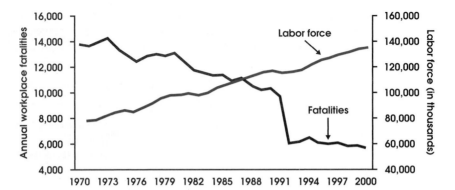

workers. No more dramatic example of a beneficial regulation exists than the decline in workplace fatalities after creation of the Occupational Safety and Health Administration in 1970. Through the 1950s and the 1960s the number of injuries and deaths for workers was slowly rising.[33] As Figure 17.4 shows, since 1970 the number of fatalities has dropped markedly even as the size of the labor force increased by 75 percent.

Federal regulations are only part of the growing web of regulation that fetters employers. State courts and legislatures have created additional rules. Legislatures in many states enact laws that go beyond federal requirements, turning the states into "policy laboratories" that experiment with the cutting edges of employment law.[34] For example, Vermont gives workers 24 hours of leave to attend school functions and go to medical appointments. Louisiana bans employment discrimination based on the sickle cell trait. Each year more states adopt laws banning discrimination based on genetic test results.

Federal laws typically apply only to firms with more than a specified number of employees—often as many as 50 or 100. Many states enact laws that extend the same employee protections to smaller firms. The federal Family and Medical Leave Act, for example, entitles employees of firms with 50 or more workers to take as long as 12 weeks of unpaid leave for family matters such as adoption, illness, or birth. But Oregon lowers the size of the company to 25 workers and Vermont to 15. The federal law requiring 60-day advance notification of plant closings applies only to companies with 100 or more workers, but in Hawaii, employers with 50 or more workers must give 45-day notice. These state actions enhance worker protections.

State courts have added additional worker protections. While federal courts often decide issues of constitutionality and statutory interpretation, they have not expanded workplace rights beyond the statutes. State courts, on the other hand, have used doctrines of common law to establish new employee rights in the

---

[33] Charles Noble, *Liberalism at Work: The Rise and Fall of OSHA* (Philadelphia: Temple University Press, 1986), pp. 61–63.

[34] Kirstin Downey Grimsley, "Where Congress Fears to Tread," *Washington Post National Weekly Edition,* August 21, 2000, p. 18.

absence of legislation. A leading example of the power of state courts is how, in recent years, they have revised the doctrine of employment-at-will, shriveling perhaps the most fundamental right of an employer—the right to hire and fire.

Erosion of the Employment-at-Will Doctrine

In the United States, there is a body of common law, or law derived from judicial decisions, that governs employer–employee relationships. In general, this law holds that employers and employees may enter voluntary employment contracts and that either party may freely end these agreements anytime.

While employed, an employee must act "solely and entirely" for the employer's benefit in all work-related matters or be liable for termination and damages. Furthermore, when a conflict arises between an employee and an employer, the employee must conform to the employer's rules. The common law in this area is derived from paternalistic English common law that, in turn, was influenced by Roman law that framed employment in terms of a master–servant relationship. Under this body of law, employers have had extensive rights to restrict employee freedom and arbitrarily fire workers.

Until recently, an extreme interpretation of the employment contract prevailed. It resounds in the oft-quoted statement by a Tennessee judge in 1884: "All may dismiss their employees at will be they many or few, for good cause, for no cause, or even for cause morally wrong without being thereby guilty of legal wrong."[35] *Employment-at-will*, therefore, was traditionally defined as an employment contract that could be ended by either party without notice and for any reason—or for no reason.

employment-at-will
A theory in law that an employment contract can be ended by either the employer or the employee without notice and for any reason.

With the rise of government intervention since the 1930s, absolute discharge rights have been eroded. Federal and state laws take away the right to fire employees for many reasons, including union activity, pregnancy, physical disability, race, sex, national origin, and religious belief. In addition, state courts have introduced three common-law exceptions to firing at will.

First, employees cannot be fired for complying with public policy. In *Petermann v. International Brotherhood of Teamsters,* a supervisor requested a California worker to dissemble in testimony before a legislative committee probing unions.[36] The worker answered questions honestly anyway and was fired. The court struck down the firing, declaring an overriding public interest in ensuring truthful testimony to lawmakers. In another case, *Sabine Pilot Service, Inc. v. Hauck,* a deck hand was ordered to pump oily bilge water into the ocean off the Texas coast. The worker read a placard posted on the ship stating that this was illegal, phoned the Coast Guard for confirmation, and refused to do it any more. He was fired. A Texas court held that an employer could not fire a worker for refusing to disobey the law.[37] This exception to firing at will is recognized in 43 states.[38]

[35] *Payne v. Western & Atlantic R.R. Co.,* 81 Tenn. 507 (1884).
[36] 344 Cal. App. 2d 25 (1959).
[37] 687 S.W.2d 733 (Tex. 1985).
[38] Charles J. Muhl, "The Employment-at-Will Doctrine: Three Major Exceptions," *Monthly Labor Review,* January 2001, p. 4.

A second check on freedom to fire is recognized where an implied contract exists. Daniel Foley worked at Chase Manhattan Bank, and his superiors made oral statements that his job was secure. For seven years he got regular promotions and raises. One day, Foley learned that the FBI was investigating his supervisor for embezzling money at a former job, so he told a vice president. Shortly, the supervisor fired Foley. However, a California court ruled that Foley had been promised permanent employment if his performance was satisfactory. It held, in *Foley v. Interactive Data Corp.,* that the company had violated an implied contract.[39] Following this decision, companies began to avoid hinted promises of job tenure, such as references to "permanent" employees in brochures and handbooks. Courts in 38 states have adopted this exception.

Third, courts in 11 states limit the employer's ability to fire when an implied covenant of good faith is breached. These courts accept that such a covenant is present in all employer–employee relations. The test of any firing is whether it meets an implied duty to be fair and just. Unfair and malicious dismissals fail to pass. In *Cleary v. American Airlines,* for example, the company fired an 18-year employee, giving no reason.[40] Although company policy contained a statement that the firm reserved the right to fire an employee for any reason, a California court was convinced that the purpose of the firing was to avoid paying Cleary a sales commission. It awarded him punitive damages.

Of the three exceptions to employment-at-will, the implied covenant of good faith exception departs most from the vision of unrestricted dismissal. Indeed, it defies the amoral core of employment-at-will. Those courts adopting it reject the old notion of employer–employee equality, believing that employers overmatch the power of employees and have a duty of fairness in actions that determine the livelihoods of their workers. In a case where Kmart Corporation fired an employee to avoid paying retirement benefits, a Nevada court, holding the firing in "bad faith," noted that:

> We have become a nation of employees. We are dependent upon others for our means of livelihood, and most of our people have become completely dependent upon wages. If they lose their jobs they lose every resource except for the relief supplied by the various forms of social security. Such dependence of the mass of the people upon others for all of their income is something new in the world. For our generation, the substance of life is in another man's hands.[41]

Only three states fail to take up any of the new exceptions, and only six states embrace all of them. The great majority have adopted one or two, and the overall trend is toward greater restriction on the employer's ability to fire. One state, Montana, now has a law that permits employers to discharge workers only for "good cause."

Work and Worker Protection in Japan and Europe

The level of benefits and protections in the United States is high but not exceptional. Elsewhere in the developed world, workers benefit from similar and even

---

[39] 205 Cal. App. 3d 344 (1985).

[40] 168 Cal. Reptr. 722 (1980).

[41] Quoted in Muhl, "The Employment-at-Will Doctrine: Three Major Exceptions," p. 10, citing 103 Nev. 49, 732 P.2d 1364 (1987).

greater welfare guarantees. Cultural differences are evident in how worker rights are supported, but in every nation where strong welfare measures are in place, labor costs are high.

Japanese workers are among the world's most expensive. In 2003 average hourly compensation for a manufacturing worker in Japan was $20.09, or just $1.88 less than an American counterpart. The fringe benefits of regular employees in the large companies that employ about 40 percent of the Japanese workforce typically include company housing, meals, child education expenses, and paid vacations. Japanese males, called salarymen, enjoy virtual lifetime employment in major firms. Protection against job loss is not, however, extended to women. These benefits are provided voluntarily by paternalistic Japanese companies.

Japanese history and culture in part explain why companies are so generous. Japan's long feudal period shaped cultural patterns based on values derived from the spread of ancient Chinese culture to the islands, including belief in rigid status hierarchies, strong duties of loyalty owed to rulers, emphasis on group rather than individual welfare, and the belief that a paternalistic government should provide for citizen welfare. Later, these values molded the relationship between modern workers and the industrial corporation. Just as the feudal Japanese vassal owed fealty to a lord, workers were asked to give loyalty to their company and place work group interests above individual interests.

Japanese workers are very committed. They work long hours. Most salarymen will not leave the office at night until their boss does and the boss is reluctant to leave before his subordinates. Vacations are often neglected and holiday credits accumulate. Sick leave is seldom used. One explanation for this hard work, in addition to cultural values, is that career ladders in large corporations have frequent small promotion and salary steps.[42]

Japanese salarymen sometimes work themselves to illness or death. A stereotypical case is that of Kazumi Kanaya, a Toyota Motors manager who crumpled at the office one day and lapsed into a permanent coma. Kanaya worked 12 hours a day every day, seldom taking a day off in spite of gout so painful that he needed a cane to walk. Although his wife pushed him to get medical attention, he argued that his work schedule precluded it. Near the end, he was in charge of an important sales office at Toyota, and the company culture dictated extraordinary efforts. He worked seven days a week, often staying until after 10:00 P.M. His collapse was caused by untreated meningitis.[43] Such overwork is not blamed on unreasonable employers. It is regarded as exceptional dedication and as a duty called forth by the beneficence of the company toward its workers.

karoshi
A Japanese word denoting death from the stress of overwork.

Estimates of incidents of mortality from working too hard range from 10,000 to 30,000 each year. Such deaths are so common that a word, *karoshi*, appeared in the Japanese language to denote death from the pressure and fatigue of overwork.

[42] Toyohiro Kono and Stewart Clegg, *Trends in Japanese Management: Continuing Strengths, Current Problems and Changing Priorities* (New York: Palgrave, 2001), p. 280.

[43] Darius Mehri, "Death by Overwork: Corporate Pressure on Employees Takes a Fatal Toll in Japan," *Multinational Monitor*, June 2000, p. 26.

In 1986 the Japanese worker compensation system recognized karoshi as a syndrome marked by emotional and physical stress accumulated during six months or more of overwork. However, few claims are filed—only 819 in 2002, of which just 160 were compensated.[44]

In the United States, worker rights and social protections were wrested from employers by pugnacious and politically active labor unions. In Japan, however, the centuries-old Confucian tradition of harmony in relationships prevented a similar labor–management fissure from developing. Unions never grew strong and unified. Most today are company unions, and they rarely strike or make strident demands. Likewise, no adversarial relationship arises between companies and government agencies enforcing worker rights in Japan as often happens in the United States. Japanese workers have far fewer legislated rights than U.S. and European workers.

Industrialized nations in northern Europe also give high wages and comprehensive benefits to workers. This is reflected in average hourly compensation for manufacturing workers of $32.18 in Denmark, $31.55 in Norway, $29.91 in Germany, $21.13 in France, and $18.35 in Italy. In the aftermath of World War II, these countries adopted, in similar versions, a *social welfare model* of industrial relations to protect their populations against any repeat of the ravages of depression and unemployment experienced in the 1930s. Governments took over major industries and ran them to ensure full employment. Lavish welfare packages for workers were legislated in European parliaments. Socialist parties supported the creation of powerful unions that could negotiate wages and benefits over entire industries.

social welfare model
A form of industry–labor–government relationship in which government heavily regulates the labor market to secure strong rights and high benefits for workers.

Forces of global competition now strain this social welfare model. European workers are so expensive to employ that job-creating investments go elsewhere. Germany is an example. The benefits and protections achieved by German workers are exceptional. That is why Germany has one of the highest labor costs in the world and has struggled for more than a decade to get unemployment below 10 percent. A complex network of laws, union agreements, and customs makes its labor market relatively inflexible. Workers are entitled to generous government pensions, health insurance, annual sick leave of up to four weeks, unemployment checks of up to 67 percent of previous income for 32 months, 30 paid vacation days, and a six-month notice before termination. This is average for the social welfare nations of Europe, but it far exceeds worker benefits and protections in the United States.

Employers fund much of this. German companies must pay taxes and contributions equaling 49 percent of each worker's direct wages, including 27 percent in employment taxes, 12 percent for pensions, and 10 percent for health insurance.[45] In addition, German laws tightly regulate much business activity, for example, by prescribing the hours when factory machines can run and prohibiting most labor during an official Sunday "pause." The average German works 22 percent fewer hours each year than the average American.[46]

[44] "Record 160 Karoshi Cases Recognized in FY02," *The Daily Yomiuri* (Tokyo), June 11, 2003, p. 2.

[45] Grace Sung, "Europe's Job Woes Bogged Down by Reform Inaction," *The Straits Times,* January 22, 2002, p. 4.

[46] Niall Ferguson, "Bone-Tired? You Need a Job in Europe," *Los Angeles Times,* August 11, 2004, p. B11.

Such expensive labor discourages investments that create more jobs. Over the decade of 1994 to 2004 unemployment averaged 9.2 percent in the European Union as opposed to only 4.6 percent in the United States.[47] As a result, there are many proposals for reform. European governments have reprivatized industries, but they have had less success rolling back social supports for workers in the face of opposition by large unions and socialist parties. Recently, German unions, fearing loss of jobs to low-wage Eastern European countries, have reluctantly negotiated contracts extending weekly working hours from 35 to 40. The German government ended the practice of allowing older workers to collect unemployment compensation even when they were not looking for a job and has proposed scaling back social benefits, including pensions and sick pay.

Despite industry opposition, some European governments continue to take actions that raise labor costs. France, like Germany, suffers from chronic unemployment near 10 percent. In 1998 its socialist government, over the objections of employers, implemented a 35-hour workweek law. Its purpose was to create more jobs by mandating shorter hours, assuming that companies would be forced to hire more people to maintain output. Like their German counterparts, French employees are expensive. Employers pay similarly high social taxes to provide for their security and benefits. And the new law, renewed in 2002, makes it even more expensive by requiring that laid-off workers be paid for nine months while they seek new jobs. The unintended, but logical, result of the 35-hour law has been rising productivity in French industry as employers choose to invest in automation instead of hiring more workers. Unemployment remains close to 10 percent.

In much of Europe, the results of lavish social safety nets and protections for workers are persistent, high unemployment and slowed economic growth. In Germany, France, and elsewhere, only gradual and modest rollbacks of entitlements for workers are likely.

Observations about Labor Regulation

The bare minimum for labor market regulation is compliance with four core labor standards set forth in international labor conventions. They call on nations at any stage of economic development to (1) eliminate all types of forced labor, (2) abolish child labor, (3) ensure equal opportunity and nondiscrimination, and (4) guarantee collective bargaining.[48] These standards are widely accepted, though not yet universally enforced. Most nations move beyond them and provide added rights and protections for workers. Worker welfare is an important goal, but experience proves that striking the right balance between too much and too little is difficult.

Workers must be protected, but they are hurt in the long run if companies cannot allocate labor to its most productive uses. Firms must respond quickly to changing technologies and competition. If they are slowed by restrictive work rules that obstruct the reorganization of work they grow less competitive and, in the end, hire fewer workers at lower wages. Figure 17.5 illustrates trade-offs in labor regulation and suggests that a balance must be struck between worker

---

[47] Ibid.

[48] World Bank, *World Development Report 2005* (Washington, DC: World Bank, 2004), box 7.4.

FIGURE 17.5
The Trade-off in Labor Regulation

Worker Protection Goals

- Job security
- Collective bargaining
- High wages
- Limited hours
- Pensions
- Health and safety
- Nondiscrimination

Competitiveness Goals

- Create jobs
- Allow restructuring
- Adopt new technology
- Adjust to changing demand
- Encourage investment
- Allow turnover
- Reduce regulatory burden

INFLEXIBLE   FLEXIBLE

welfare and competitiveness. When a nation puts more weight on the left side of the balance by indulging workers, its labor market becomes relatively inflexible. When it moves to the right, by loosening constraints on the treatment of workers, its labor market turns more flexible.

Trade-offs are unavoidable. If a nation tries to create good jobs for low-skilled workers by adopting a high minimum wage, employers will hire fewer unskilled workers, leaving many without any job. As the minimum wage moves lower, more jobs appear, but the worker's standard of living is lower. In some nations expensive safety regulations discourage hiring and leave many workers in the informal sector where they are not protected by any rules at all. If rules are too strict, they will be bypassed, frustrating both workers and employers. Regulations that restrict firing are an example. The Netherlands requires companies to consult with unions before laying off more than 20 employees. These consultations take several months with uncertain results. So when a large software company needed to lay off 700 workers quickly it went through a complicated sleight of hand by laying off groups of 19 in regions around the country. It reorganized its workforce, but avoiding the thicket of rules made the adjustment inefficient. And the workers still lost their jobs.[49]

Similar trade-offs are present with rules that set work hours, limit dismissals, mandate union participation in company decisions, and tax employers for social benefits provided by government. Research suggests that in heavily regulated labor markets job growth is slower, unemployment lasts longer, companies invest less in new technology, firm size is smaller, and the labor force is less skilled.[50] The World Bank recently ranked the United States as one of the most flexible labor markets in the world.[51]

[49] Dan Bilefsky, "The Dutch Way of Firing," *The Wall Street Journal,* July 8, 2003, p. A14.

[50] World Bank, *Doing Business 2004: Understanding Regulation* (New York: Oxford University Press, 2004), chapter 3.

[51] Ibid., p. 35.

CONCLUDING OBSERVATIONS

The combined impact of the six forces changing the workplace—demography, technology, competition, structural shift, reorganization of work, and government regulation—creates both uncertainty and opportunity. These forces vary in the degree to which they can be managed. Demographic and structural changes are uncontrollable but also slow and predictable. Technological change, which is often rapid and unpredictable, is a radical and disruptive force but a long-run source of new jobs. The importance of competition and work reorganization is elevated now in developed nations, where great corporations, expanding into global markets, rush to automate and send their work to low-wage countries. Finally, the importance of government regulation cannot be underestimated.

Perhaps the most critical factor in determining both the experience of workers and the success of economies is the balance a government strikes between protecting labor and allowing adjustment to competitive forces. Globalization of production and labor markets makes the accumulated workers' protections of the last half of the twentieth century a cost burden on companies, governments, and consumers where flexibility is absent. In these nations there is pressure to revise labor laws, weakening protections and social welfare for workers.

How will workers fare in the currents of change? Experience suggests that fortunes will be mixed. Yet it is likely that if the global economy prospers, the benefits of rising prosperity will allow more protections and long-run job gains will outweigh the costs of short-term occupational dislocations.

Workplace Drug Testing

There is a long record in the United States of drug use in the workplace. However, it was not until the 1980s that drug testing by employers began. The initiative came from the federal government.

The U.S. Navy began the first random drug testing as a result of its discovery of widespread drug use following an accident on the *USS Nimitz* in 1982. Other branches of the federal government quickly followed. In 1986 President Reagan issued Executive Order 12564 requiring all federal agencies to develop a "drug-free workplace" by establishing a program to test for the use of illegal drugs by employees in sensitive positions.

A Conrail engineer who had been smoking marijuana rolled his string of locomotives past a warning light and into the same track as a high-speed train carrying 500 people. The collision, in 1987, killed 16 people and injured 176. In 1989 the *Exxon Valdez*, a large oil tanker, struck a rock formation and spilled millions of gallons of crude oil in the pristine waters of Prince William Sound in Alaska. There was enormous loss of animal life and destruction to the economic and social fabric of the area. Alcohol was partly responsible for this disaster. Such accidents resulted in the passage of the Omnibus Transportation Employee Testing Act of 1991, requiring the Department of Transportation to test employees in safety sensitive transportation jobs for drug and alcohol use.

The Department of Energy, the Department of Defense, and the Nuclear Regulatory Commission all require private sector drug-testing. The Occupational Safety and Health Act requires employers to provide safe working environments. The Drug-Free Workplace Act of 1988 requires companies to maintain drug-free workplaces if they want to get contracts from federal agencies. In addition, there are state laws covering this subject. In sum, there are a thicket of laws that employers must follow in any drug testing program.

Following this combination of conspicuous accidents and new laws there was rapid expansion of drug testing in public and private workplaces. In 1983 there were only six firms in the Fortune 500 companies that were testing their workers for drugs. During 2003 there were 55 million drug tests performed in the United States of which 90 percent were urine tests.[1]

The Department of Health and Human Services in 1988 published guidelines for urine tests of federal employees and government contractors. In 2004 a proposed set of guidelines was announced that would permit testing, in addition to urine, of hair, saliva, and sweat. At this writing (January 2005) a final rule has not been published.

The issue of drug testing is complex and has scientific, economic, social, ethical, and legal dimensions. The major questions of the subject are simple to state. The answers can be highly controversial. For example, Why are drug tests needed? Who should be tested? What tests should be given? How should the tests be conducted? The fundamental issue is the conflict between the right of employers to protect their property and the right of employees to be free of unwarranted intrusions of their privacy. In any particular company how should the balance be determined?

THE COSTS OF DRUG ABUSE

The behavior of drug-using employees imposes costs. For example, lost productivity, higher insurance premiums, excessive absentee and sick leave rates, the loss of trained workers who are fired or die, the administrative costs of anti-drug programs, extra plant security, property damage, declines in employee morale, tarnished company images, lawsuits, and thefts of property. The overall cost to employers of drug use in the workplace has been estimated to be from $75 to $100 billion annually in lost time, accidents, and worker compensation and health care costs,

according to Department of Labor estimates.[2] OHS Inc., one of the largest drug testing companies in the United States, says it charges from a low of $25 per urine drug test to a high of $65. The range is determined by the volume of business a company does with OHS Inc. The company estimates that the average price per drug test in the entire country, including the cost of collection and laboratory analysis, is $44.[3]

BEHAVIOR OF DRUG-ABUSING EMPLOYEES

Drug addicted employees tend to exhibit one or both of two pernicious effects. The first is distortion of time, which is seen in the inability of the employee to follow normal time patterns for job activities. The second is lack of motivation, which is seen as lack of interest in normal performance standards. Both effects stem from imbalances of brain chemistry caused by the chronic presence of marijuana, cocaine, or other drugs in the bloodstream.[4] Supervisors are trained to suspect drug abuse when employees show patterns of behavior such as these:

- Frequent tardiness and absences from work, especially on Mondays and Fridays and near holidays.
- Poor concentration, forgetfulness, missed deadlines and frequent mistakes.
- Mood changes, including a wide range of states that interfere with personal relationships such as depression, withdrawal, hostility, and over excitability.
- Risk taking and frequent accidents.

DRUG-TESTING PROGRAMS

Companies must choose what kind of testing to use. There are a variety of drug-testing methods, including the following:

Employee searches may include searches of lockers, workstations, desks, and purses. They seldom include bodily searches, which anger workers and create

---

[1] OHS, Inc., "Drug Testing Employees in Your Workplace Is Our Core Business," http//www.ohsincl.com/DRUG-TESTING_COST.htm.

[2] Reported by Joy Davia, "Worker Drug Use Harder to Mask," *Democrat and Chronicle,* Rochester, New York, January 3, 2005.

[3] Ibid, p. 2.

[4] William F. Banta and Forest Tennant, Jr., *Complete Handbook for Combating Substance Abuse in the Workplace* (Lexington, MA: Lexington Books, 1989), p. 45.

litigation. Drug-sniffing dogs are extremely effective in locating contraband. But searches are often ineffective. For example, drugs can be secreted in common areas so that individual ownership is concealed.

Surveillance can detect drug use, but has many pitfalls. It is difficult to keep undercover agents a secret. Spying can shatter employee morale. Surveillance agents can make mistakes, such as striking an employee, that can result in expensive lawsuits.

Written drug tests are available from a dozen or more vendors of employment tests. They ask job applicants and employees whether they have used drugs, what kind, and how often. The validity of these tests is unproven, but they are the least expensive type of drug test.

Polygraphs, or lie detectors, were used frequently in the past, but no more. The accuracy of the results is open to question. Furthermore, the Employee Polygraph Protection Act of 1988 so severely limits their use that most employers no longer use them for drug testing.

Fitness-for-duty exams, sometimes called performance tests, detect impaired acuity. In one test, for example, workers sit in front of a computer screen and turn a knob to keep a moving point centered between two lines. Such tests measure impairment but they do not show the cause, which may be drugs, alcohol, fatigue from staying up with a sick baby all night, or emotional upset. Advocates of performance tests believe they are less physically intrusive than other forms of testing. Critics argue that poor performance invites an employer to ask intrusive questions about private off-work behavior.

Blood tests are useful primarily for alcohol abuse testing. They are expensive and exceptionally intrusive and, because of legal challenges, are rarely used by employers. Their main advantage is that they can determine the approximate time a drug was used.

Saliva tests test for marijuana use but are unreliable. They are useful only up to three hours after marijuana is smoked, and rinsing the mouth can remove detectable residues.

Hair analysis tests can detect use of cocaine, marijuana, or other illegal drugs for as long as three months prior to removing a 1½-inch growth of hair for testing. However, it takes about seven days for substances indicative of drug use to appear in the hair. Few companies use it.

Urinalysis is the most commonly employed testing method. Before discussing urinalysis in some detail, the options about whom to test and the drugs to be tested for should be noted.

EMPLOYEES WHO MIGHT BE TESTED

Employers have many options as to whom to test. Here are some of the major ones.

- *Those in safety-sensitive positions.* This might refer to national security but also could include those who could jeopardize the safety of themselves or other employees or the public at large. Included also would be people handling substantial amounts of money or carrying firearms.

- *Those who provide cause.* When employees are frequently absent on Mondays or take periodic unexpected absences, have frequent accidents, display erratic behavior, or show inconsistent job performance, they may be singled out for drug testing.

- *Those who have gone through rehabilitation.* When employees have gone through a drug rehabilitation program, they may be subject to periodic drug testing.

- *Those who apply for employment.* Job applicants, especially for sensitive positions, may be tested.

- *Random testing of all employees.* Random testing makes it harder for employees who use drugs to escape detection, since they cannot arrange to be free of drugs for irregular tests that come by surprise.

DRUGS OF ABUSE TESTED BY EMPLOYERS

In 1988 the National Institute for Drug Abuse (NIDA) issued guidelines on drug-abuse programs for public sector employees. Five drugs were identified for testing: tetrahydrocannabinol, the psychoactive ingredient in marijuana; cocaine; opiates; amphetamines; and phencyclidine. Many employers added other drugs to this list, including barbiturates, benzodiazepines, methadone, methaqualone, and propoxyphene. Some routinely test for alcohol, a legal drug and the most commonly abused. Many now test for ecstasy, a drug in the amphetamine and methamphetamine family that has become more widely abused. Ira A. Lipman, chairman and president of Guardsmark, a security and drug-testing firm, notes that ecstasy "is dangerous both to the user and to workers . . . [and] can create an unsafe work environment."[5]

URINALYSIS

There are several basic types of urine tests. The first is the *immunoassay test.* This is an inexpensive test costing about $20 to $25 that can be done quickly with modest laboratory equipment and technician training. However, this test is not always 100 percent accurate. For example, it may register positive if a person has recently used any of 10 common over-the-counter drugs.

If the test is positive, a second and much more accurate test may be used to confirm. It involves a different chemical process called *chromatography.* It is more time-consuming and more expensive (about $50 per test) and requires a highly trained technician to interpret results. It is not, therefore, used for mass screening but is held in reserve to double-check a positive result on an immunoassay test.

A third test may be done with a *mass spectrometer.* It is the most accurate test, and the most expensive. Gas chromatography/mass spectrometer tests are so sensitive they have detected cocaine and a by-product, cinnamolycocaine, in the urine of people who have drunk one or two cups of coca leaf teas imported from Peru.

One shortcoming of urine tests is that they can be thwarted by employees who tamper with a sample. A small amount of table salt, bleach, laundry soap, ammonia, or vinegar causes screening tests to miss drug residues in the urine. Consequently, employees giving urine samples must be closely supervised.

There is a cottage industry of companies selling methods to pass drug tests. They have colorfully named Web sites, such as ezklean.com, urineluck.com, and passyourdrugtest.com. They sell masking products including synthetic urine, herbal concoctions, chemically treated shampoos (for passing hair tests), and specialty gadgets.[6] Drug-testing companies buy and study these products trying to stay one step ahead of the cheating. Many, of course, do not work as advertised.

A significant problem with urine testing is that it cannot show whether an employee is "high" or impaired. Cocaine and heroin can be detected up to three days after last use and marijuana up to two months after last use. This means that a person who used cocaine at a party Saturday night could be nailed by a drug test Tuesday morning when feeling hale and working productively. But if a colleague had taken LSD that morning and was hallucinating and dangerous, the LSD could not be detected with a simple screening test. An immunoassay test cannot detect hallucinogens such as LSD.

STARTING A DRUG-FREE WORKPLACE PROGRAM

Once a company has chosen from among the options, the Institute for a Drug-Free Workplace recommends the following steps:

1. Identify any federal or state laws with which you must comply.
2. Write a clear, consistent, and fair policy that includes the conditions under which drug testing is to be conducted and the consequences of a "positive" drug test result.
3. If applicable, consult with union representatives and bargain in good faith on the terms and conditions of the drug-testing program.
4. Identify and contact a certified laboratory to set up a drug-testing contract. If possible, go for a visit.
5. Contract with a collection site to receive testing samples.
6. Develop and implement a system to protect the confidentiality of employee drug test records.
7. Designate the person who will receive the test results from the laboratory, and make sure that person is aware of confidentiality issues.
8. Have your policy reviewed by legal counsel.

[5] PR Newswire, "Guardsmark, Inc., Expands 100% Drug Testing Program to Include 'Ecstasy,' " July 18, 2001.

[6] Marianne Costantinou, "The American Way," *San Francisco Chronicle,* August 12, 2001, p. 3.

9. Notify employees 30 to 180 days before testing starts.
10. Establish procedures for review of all positive drug test results by a medical review officer.
11. Communicate to employees that management also is fully subject to the policy, the specifics of the testing program, what is expected of them as employees, the company's reasons for promoting a drug-free workforce, and the adverse employment consequences of a policy violation.[7]

WHY CORPORATIONS FAVOR DRUG TESTING

First, it is needed to comply with certain laws and contract requirements. Federal and state laws require drug tests for certain workers and companies. As noted before, the Drug-Free Workplace Act of 1988 requires private employers with federal contracts over $25,000 to have comprehensive policies designed to prevent drug abuse. Most states and some cities have laws concerning drug testing. Thus, complying with the law is a major reason for drug testing.

Second, drug testing has beneficial results. Insurance costs will be reduced, productivity will increase, and a number of other benefits noted above will accrue to both the workers and the company.

Third, corporate drug testers argue that urinalysis is a practical method of testing for drug use. Although urine tests are intrusive, they are less so than some alternatives such as drug-sniffing dogs, polygraphs, searches through handbags and desks, undercover investigations, entry and exit searches, and closed-circuit TV monitors in restrooms. When done correctly, urine tests are reliable. Good programs follow the Rule of Two, in which two positive tests are required before action is taken. The first test, an inexpensive screening test, is followed by a second, more sophisticated confirming test on the same vial of urine. Cutoff levels for positive results can be set reasonably high to avoid unnecessarily stigmatizing innocent employees. Errors can also be minimized by using

proper procedures for specimen collection and laboratory analysis.

Fourth, there is a social responsibility argument for drug testing. As employers screen applicants and employees, it becomes harder for drug abusers to make a living. Employees have no right to use marijuana, cocaine, hallucinogens, PCP, heroin, and designer drugs. Their use is illegal and creates crime, illness, broken families, and broken lives. Thus business is helping society by combating drug use. From an individual standpoint, if companies can catch a drug-using employee early, it might save his or her career. Many companies refer employees who test positive to assistance programs for treatment rather than terminate them.

Fifth, competitors have drug-testing programs. Hewlett-Packard, for instance, started drug testing because its competitors did. If Hewlett-Packard had not done so, its applicant pool would have filled with drug users unable to get jobs elsewhere.[8]

WHY SOME EMPLOYEES OPPOSE DRUG TESTING

As compelling as these arguments are, drug testing in general and urine testing in particular raise difficult questions. Critics point out that the right of an employer to protect assets and property must be balanced against the rights of individual employees to a reasonable amount of privacy. Opponents make telling points.

First, urine testing is intrusive and an invasion of privacy. To avoid false positive results based on the presence of other drugs in the urine, employees are asked to list all prescription and over-the-counter drugs taken in the last 30 days. This reveals their private, off-duty lives and medical histories. Also, chemical analysis of urine (or blood) can reveal more than drug use. Employers could test it and discover medical conditions such as pregnancy, clinical depression, diabetes, and epilepsy. For all these reasons, civil libertarians believe urine testing smacks of Big Brother.

Second, urine testing is inherently demeaning whether a sample is taken with visual or passive supervision. An author of a law journal article put it this way: "[I]n our culture the excretory functions are

[7] *Annual Corporate Membership Survey,* cited in Marc A. de Bernardo, *Workplace Drug Testing: An Employer's Development & Implementation Guide* (Washington, DC: Institute for a Drug-Free Workplace, 1994), pp.51–52.

[8] Costantinou, "The American Way," p. 4.

shielded by more or less absolute privacy, so much so that situations in which this privacy is violated are experienced as extremely distressing, as detracting from one's dignity and self-esteem."[9]

Third, the tests are unjust because they violate ethical standards of fair treatment. Testing is a dragnet; many innocent people are tested for each drug user detected. A presumption of guilt is placed on everyone, and workers must prove their innocence. If there is an overriding safety justification to prohibit drug abuse—for example, among bus drivers or railroad engineers—then it may be prudent. But indiscriminate testing of applicants and employees who are not in critical safety-related positions is an evil greater than the drug abuse it seeks to remedy.

Fourth, urine tests are imperfect. Inaccuracies arise from lab errors, mixed-up specimens, and false positives that are due to legal drugs in the body. Errors are too frequent and cast suspicion on employees or cost them their jobs. If scrupulous collection and laboratory procedures are followed, testing is very accurate. But not all companies and labs are that scrupulous. For example, follow-up confirmatory tests after a positive on a simple screening test are expensive, and not every firm is willing to undertake the extra expense for job applicants.

Fifth, drug tests can be misleading and cannot meet reasonable evidentiary standards. The ACLU says "they cannot detect impairment and, thus, in no way enhance an employer's ability to evaluate or predict job performance."[10] The ACLU adds, "Even a confirmed 'positive' provides no evidence of present intoxication or impairment; it merely indicates that a person may have taken a drug at some time in the past.[11] Emphasis should be placed on employee assistance programs and not drug testing, says the ACLU.

Finally, drug testing is not cost-effective. For drug testing to be cost-effective it would be necessary, says the ACLU, for it to identify a significant number of drug abusers. In 1990 the federal government spent $11.7 million to test workers in 38 agencies. Of approximately 29,000 tests made, only 153 (.5 percent) were positive. The cost of finding one positive was estimated to be $77,000 per user.[12]

DRUG TESTING AND THE LAW

Legal precedent on drug testing is relatively new and still developing, but the clear trend is to uphold it where it is part of a previously announced and carefully formulated policy. Here is a short briefing on legal issues.

Since the Bill of Rights in the U.S. Constitution restrains only government actions, public employees are protected by these provisions, but employees in private businesses are not. This is a major legal difference; public employers must meet stricter guidelines for testing. The Fourth Amendment guarantees protection to public employees against "unreasonable searches and seizures," and courts have generally held that urine tests and other forms of testing, such as blood tests for HIV antibodies, are a form of search and seizure. The Fifth Amendment guarantees due process of law and protects against self-incrimination. Public employers must guard against firings that violate these rights.[13] Since 1988 federal agencies have adhered to testing guidelines issued by the Department of Health and Human Services. These guidelines attempt to elevate due process for government employees to an impeccable level and stipulate testing procedures in detail.[14]

There have been many court challenges to federal urine-testing programs, but those programs that have reached the Supreme Court have been upheld. Yet the decisions also show that some of the justices have grave misgivings about drug testing and do not believe it is permitted by the Fourth Amendment.

In *Skinner v. Railway Labor Executives' Association,* the Court was asked to decide whether railroad workers could be forced to submit to mandatory urine and blood tests for drugs.[15] In a 7–2 decision, the Court held that the clear public interest in railroad safety outweighed the privacy rights of

---

[9] Charles Fried, "Privacy," *Yale Law Journal,* January 1968, p. 487.

[10] American Civil Liberties Union, *Drug Testing in the Workplace,* Briefing Paper No. 5, undated.

[11] Ibid.

[12] "Focus on Federal Drug Testing," *Individual Employment Rights,* BNA, April 9, 1991, reported in *Drug Testing: A Bad Investment,* ACLU, undated.

[13] These rights are extended to state, county, and local employees through the Fourteenth Amendment.

[14] National Institute on Drug Abuse, *Comprehensive Procedure for Drug Testing in the Workplace.*

[15] 57 LW 4324 (1989).

employees. But in a strong dissent, Justice Thurgood Marshall compared the decision with the Court's 1940s decisions upholding the assignment of Japanese to relocation camps during World War II and noted that "when we allow fundamental freedoms to be sacrificed in the name of real or perceived exigency, we invariably come to regret it."[16]

A second case decided by the Supreme Court, *National Treasury Employees Union v. Von Raab,* involved a urine-testing program of the U.S. Customs Service.[17] It required applicants for positions in which they would interdict drugs, carry guns, or work with classified material of interest to criminals to submit to urine tests. In a 5–4 decision, the majority argued that the national drug crisis, together with the special gravity of drug enforcement work, justified weighing the public interest in drug-free customs agents more heavily than the interference with the agents' civil liberties. Thus, testing was "reasonable" under the Fourth Amendment. Justice Antonin Scalia, writing in dissent, warned that the Court was too cavalier in sacrificing basic constitutional privacy rights. He quoted these famous lines written by Justice Louis Brandeis in 1928: "The greatest dangers to liberty lurk in insidious encroachment by men of zeal, well-meaning but without understanding."[18]

In 1995 the Court decided a third case and remained divided about the issue. In a 6–3 decision in *Vernonia School District v. Acton,* it upheld the requirement that all student athletes in an Oregon high school submit to urine testing. The majority in *Vernonia* was willing to balance the privacy right of individuals against the legitimate needs of government agencies, in this case, the "substantial need of teachers and administrators for freedom to maintain order in the schools."[19] Writing in dissent, however, Justice Sandra Day O'Connor argued that random drug testing such as that on the high school athletes intruded on privacy where individual grounds for suspicion of wrongdoing did not exist. The Founding Fathers, she stated, clearly intended the Fourth Amendment to prohibit general searches of the population such as this and, therefore, such random drug tests were unconstitutional.

These three cases reveal an undercurrent of discomfort and opposition even though the Court approved testing in all three situations that came before it.[20]

Although the Fourth Amendment applies only to government as an employer, the discretion of private sector employers is limited by other legal guidelines. First, many state and local governments have adopted laws that regulate drug testing. These laws vary considerably. For instance, San Francisco prohibits drug testing under most circumstances but permits tests for pre-employment, for suspicion of use, and after accidents. Florida permits testing of job applicants and employees, but if they are tested, the employer must follow specific procedures set forth in the Florida Drug-Free Workplace Act. Many states prescribe mandatory precise testing procedures. Second, private employers are open to common-law actions by employees based on doctrines such as negligence, defamation, assault and battery, emotional distress, invasion of privacy, or wrongful discharge. Employees have sued over drug testing using all these legal theories. Some have won in court, but there is no overall trend to prohibit drug testing programs. Union contracts also may circumscribe drug testing.

In the end, however, private employers are generally free to test, provided they have a well-written company policy that conforms to federal regulations and the laws of states and cities in which they operate.[21] However, there is such a bramble bush of rules on testing and privacy that compliance is a

---

[16] At 57 LW 4324 (1989); the relocation camp cases are *Hirabayashi v. United States,* 320 U.S. 81 (1943); and *Korematsu v. United States,* 320 U.S. 323 U.S. 214 (1944).

[17] 49 U.S. 656 (1989).

[18] In *Olmstead v. United States,* 227 U.S. 479 (1928).

[19] *Vernonia School District v. Acton,* 115 S.Ct. 2391 (1995).

[20] In 2000 the Supreme Court decided a case in which a truck driver for Eastern Associated Coal Corp. had been discharged after his urine test came out positive for marijuana in random testing. The employee filed a grievance and was reinstated, but he then tested positive for marijuana use a second time and was fired again. However, once again a union arbitrator reinstated the driver. The company argued that rehiring such an employee violated public policy, specifically Department of Transportation regulations that required companies to maintain programs guarding against drug use by drivers. In its decision, the Supreme Court upheld the arbitration agreement on the narrow grounds that Department of Transportation regulations did not forbid employing drivers who had tested positive. The justices did not reach the conduct of the drug-testing program in their decision. The case is *Eastern Associated Coal Corp. v. United Mine Workers of America,* 531 U.S. 57.

[21] Lee Fletcher, "Employer Drug Testing Has Pitfalls," *Business Insurance,* October 23, 2000.

complex problem for corporations that operate in many locations. According to Gerald L. Maltman Jr., chairman of Baker & McKenzie, a global employment law firm:

> It's a real tough nut to crack for employers with sites in multiple states, because you end up having to tailor the intrusiveness of your policy depending on the state in which you're doing your testing. Illinois, for example, is a state that is very pro-employer, whereas California is a state that is very pro-employee on the issue of privacy. Because there is no federal law that governs the privacy issue, you, in essence, have employers subject to very much a patchwork quilt of common law claims.[22]

In 2002 in *Board of Education v. Earls* the Supreme Court upheld the widespread use of random drug testing of public school students. This was a significant expansion of its ruling in the *Vernonia* case. In a split decision the Court upheld a program in the Tecumseh School District in Oklahoma which required all middle and high school students to consent to random urinalysis testing for drugs if they participated in any extracurricular activity. This was a category which included the Future Homemakers of America, the band, the cheerleading squad, and the choir. Students who were found to be using drugs were barred from their activities and referred to counseling. They were not disciplined in any other way.

The drug testing policy was challenged by Lindsay Earls, an honor student. She lost her case in the federal district court in Oklahoma City but won it in the United States Court of Appeals for the 10th Circuit in Denver. The court concluded that the Supreme Court decision in the Vernonia School District case which established the athletes-only precedent did not validate the broader Tecumseh policy. The court said the Tecumseh policy, however, violated the Fourth Amendment's prohibition against unreasonable searches.

The Supreme Court overturned that decision. Justice Clarence Thomas, who wrote the decision for the majority, said the Tecumseh policy was permissible as a means for the School District to prevent drug use among its students and did not violate the Fourth Amendment. He said the policy was entirely reasonable in light of the spread of drug use among school age students. He added that although the Tecumseh

School District did not at the time seem to have a serious problem ". . . it would make little sense to require a school district to wait for a substantial portion of its students to begin using drugs before it was allowed to institute a drug testing program designed to deter drug use."[23]

BASEBALL OWNERS AND PLAYERS APPROVE NEW DRUG TESTING RULES

In January 2005 the owners and players approved a new drug testing program for major league baseball. There was a program in effect since 2002 but everyone agreed it was toothless. The new program was prompted by pressure from fans, owners, politicians, some of the players, and acknowledgment of several prominent players that they used performance enhancing drugs. The new program covered a wide range of banned substances and imposed harsher penalties for their use by a player.

Included, for example, are human growth hormones, agents that mask steroids in tests, THG, ephedra, and substances that act as precursors to steroids. Furthermore, the agreement includes a provision that any new substance named by the federal government as performance enhancing will also be included. The main focus of the agreement was to ban muscle-building drugs. Critics of the program said they were disappointed that the list of banned substances did not include amphetamines which, many say, are more widespread than the muscle-building drugs.

The agreement provides for random sampling throughout the year. Penalties for testing positive are severe but not as tough as in some sports, as shown in the attached exhibit.

Senator John McCain (R-Ariz), a prominent critic of drug use in major sports, was asked how he felt about the decision. "No, it's not everything that I had wanted, but it's certainly significant progress," he said.[24] He had threatened to introduce legislation to deal with the issue but now said he would not do so. Some critics said the penalties were too lenient and they should be comparable to those used in the Olympics.

[22] Ibid. p. 1.

[23] *Board of Education v. Earls,* 122 S.Ct. 2559 (2002).

[24] Tim Brown, "Baseball Toughens Policy on Steroids," *Los Angeles Times,* January 14, 2005, p. A1.

Baseball Pumps Up the Penalties
Major League Baseball announced a stricter steroid-testing program to deal with health and integrity issues. The agreement runs until December 2008.

Penalties for positive tests for steroid use in various sports

	First Offense	Second	Third	Fourth	Fifth
Major League Baseball					
New	10 days	30 days	60 days	1 year	League decision
Old	Counseling	15 days	25 days	50 days	1 year
Other Sports					
Minor league baseball	15 games	30 games	60 games	1 year	Lifetime
NFL	4 games	6 games	1 year	1 year	1 year
NBA	5 games	10 games	25 games	25 games	25 games
Olympics	2 years	Lifetime			

Source: Tim Brown, "Baseball Toughens Policy on Steroids," *Los Angeles Times*, January 14, 2005, p. A20. Copyright, 2005, *Los Angeles Times*. Reprinted with permission.

Questions

1. Should urine testing, or other types of testing, be permitted among public and private employees to prevent drug abuse? Why or why not?
2. If you believe that urine testing in some form might be acceptable, write down the outlines of a sound testing program. Who should be tested? Employees? Job applicants? Should there be random testing? Should people in all job categories be tested?
3. As a manager with responsibility for conducting a testing program, what would be your response to the following situations?

   a. An employee who tests positive for marijuana on a Monday morning but has a spotless 10-year work record.
   b. An airline pilot who refuses a random test.
   c. A job applicant who tests positive for cocaine use.
   d. An employee who tests positive for cocaine use.
   e. An employee who comes to your office the night before an announced urinalysis and admits that he regularly uses a hallucinogenic drug off the job.
   f. A productive worker who gives no outward sign of drug use but who is named as a drug abuser at work in an anonymous tip.
   g. An employee involved in a serious work accident who refuses to take an immunoassay test based on her belief in the right to privacy.
   h. The recommendation of the union that management be given the same tests as workers.

4. Why should there be any difference in drug testing between a government office worker and a professional athlete?
5. Do you believe the major league baseball agreement of 2005 was too lenient or too stringent?

Chapter **Eighteen**

Civil Rights at Work

Johnson Controls, Inc.

Johnson Controls, Inc., of Milwaukee was founded in 1885 by Professor Warren Johnson to manufacture his new invention—the electric room thermostat. The company grew into a large multinational with factories on every continent.

Over the years, the company diversified by moving into auto components. It makes seats, instrument panels, consoles, and other parts and delivers them just-in-time to the assembly lines of the big auto firms. In addition, it is the largest manufacturer of lead-acid batteries in the United States. It was battery making that got the company into a landmark legal fight.

Medical research in the 1980s found that small amounts of lead that were harmless to adults could damage a fetus and cause stillbirth, low birth weight, and retardation. In response, Johnson Controls banned fertile women from certain battery-making jobs where workers inhaled lead particles. Ending a woman's exposure when pregnancy was discovered was not prudent because lead stays in the body a long time—it takes five to seven years for just half of it to be excreted.

Unless women proved that they were infertile, Johnson Controls moved them to other jobs. But sometimes the new jobs paid less and women voluntarily sterilized themselves to avoid losing income. For example, Gloyce Qualls, age 34, was removed from a job welding auto battery posts and given a safer job putting vents in motorcycle batteries. She elected to have a tubal ligation to regain her old job. Elsie Nason, age 50, also chose sterilization after being transferred to a lower-paid job.

What happened at Johnson Controls was typical in firms with so-called fetal protection policies. Many companies, including General Motors, Ford, Dow Chemical, DuPont, and Monsanto, had them. It was believed that if impaired children were born, they could sue corporations for exposing them to lead in the womb. So the policies protected stockholders along with fetal health.

Some women workers thought that rules barring them from battery line jobs were sexist. Eight women at Johnson Controls, joined by their union, filed a legal challenge. They argued that Johnson Controls's policy violated Title VII of the Civil Rights Act of 1964, which bans employment discrimination based on sex.

The company responded that it was a "business necessity" to keep fertile women away from lead to prevent future lawsuits. In addition, the company argued, Title VII allowed exceptions to its general rule against sex discrimination. These exceptions,

bona fide occupational qualification
A legal exception that lets employers consider sex, race, or other usually prohibited factors when these become essential job qualifications.

called *bona fide occupational qualifications* (BFOQs), exist when workers of one or the other sex cannot do a job the right way precisely because of their sex. An advertising agency, for example, can screen out men applying for a job modeling women's bathing suits. Johnson Controls felt that infertility should qualify as a BFOQ in battery making.

Two lower courts agreed with the company.[1] But in 1991, a unanimous Supreme Court held that the fetal protection policy caused illegal sex discrimination.[2] Women could not be excluded from any battery-making job. Its opinion said that excluding women from work based on their ability to get pregnant violated Title VII, which had been amended some years before to make job actions based on pregnancy illegal. No BFOQ exception existed either, because pregnancy did not hinder a woman's ability to make batteries as efficiently as men. Johnson Controls should inform women of risks and then let them decide.

The Court also stated that for Johnson Controls, obeying federal civil rights law was a defense against future lawsuits by children impaired in the womb. *The Wall Street Journal* challenged this assertion, asking: "Is there a jury in the land that would tell an injured child who sues a corporation that, sorry, your mother decided to risk it and you must pay the price?"[3]

Before the decision, Johnson Controls had acted to lower lead exposure in its factories but no available technology eliminated it. It returned to a voluntary fetal protection policy. Feminist groups were elated; women could chart their own destinies. Gloyce Qualls, however, had married and regretted that she could not have children.

This story illustrates the strong protections available in federal civil rights law for women—and for other groups—who claim discrimination in the workplace. In this chapter we discuss employment discrimination and explain the evolution of laws and methods used to fight it over the years.

A SHORT HISTORY OF WORKPLACE CIVIL RIGHTS

The American nation was founded on noble ideals of justice, liberty, and human rights. Yet for most of the country's history, business practice openly diverged from these ideals and discrimination on the basis of race, color, sex, national origin, religion, and other grounds was common and widespread. Significant protection from employment discrimination has existed for little more than 40 years of the 230 years since independence.

The Colonial Era

Employment discrimination in America can be dated from 1619 when European slave traders first brought African natives to the later-to-be nation's shores. When the colonies declared their independence from England in 1776, there were 500,000 slaves, mostly in the southern colonies. In the northern colonies, there was considerable anguish about slavery because it clashed with the ideals of those who had

---

[1] See 680 F.Supp. 309 (DC–EDW 1988) and 886 F.2d 871 (7th Cir. 1989).
[2] *Automobile Workers v. Johnson Controls, Inc.*, 111 S.Ct. 1196. There were three concurring opinions.
[3] "Justices Adopt Fetal Position," *The Wall Street Journal*, March 22, 1991, p. A8.

recently escaped from religious persecution and government tyranny in Europe. The Declaration of Independence expresses the founders' ideals.

> We hold these truths to be self-evident, that all men are created equal, that they are endowed by their Creator with certain unalienable Rights, that among these are Life, Liberty, and the pursuit of Happiness.

natural rights
Rights to which all human beings are entitled. Governments cannot grant them or take them away.

civil rights
Rights bestowed by governments on their citizens.

The "unalienable" rights are *natural rights,* that is, rights to which a person is entitled simply because he or she is human and that cannot be taken away by government. Natural rights exist on a higher plane than *civil rights,* which are rights bestowed by governments on their citizens. Natural rights are a standard against which the actions of governments and employers must be measured and can be found wanting.

This statement in the Declaration distills a body of doctrine known as the American Creed, which historian Arthur M. Schlesinger, Jr., defines as incorporating "the ideals of the essential dignity and equality of all human beings, of inalienable rights to freedom, justice, and opportunity."[4] In the language of the time, the phrase "all men" was a reference to free, white males. Thomas Jefferson included in the original draft a strong statement condemning slavery as a "cruel war against human nature itself, violating its most sacred rights of life & liberty."[5] But this offended slave owners and had to be deleted to preserve unity in the coming revolution against England.

Despite the limited inclusiveness of the Declaration's language, its statement of natural rights, notes Schlesinger, challenged whites to live up to its ideals and, if anything, "meant even more to blacks than to whites, since it was the great means of pleading their unfulfilled rights."[6]

The U.S. Constitution reflected this bifurcated view of civil rights. When it was ratified in 1789, it sanctioned the practice of slavery in five clauses. Article 1, section 2, for example, counted slaves as three-fifths of a person for purposes of apportioning seats in the House of Representatives.[7] Yet the Bill of Rights contained ringing phrases protecting a wide range of fundamental rights.

Civil War and Reconstruction

Beginning at about the time the Constitution was ratified, an antislavery movement originated in a small sect within the Church of England. This movement grew rapidly, and in a century's time, its moral arguments largely swept slavery from the world stage.[8] In the United States, the issue of slavery rose to a crisis in the Civil War fought between 1861 and 1865. In 1863 President Abraham Lincoln issued the Emancipation Proclamation that freed an estimated 4 million slaves.

[4] Arthur M. Schlesinger, Jr., *The Disuniting of America* (New York: Norton, 1992), p. 27.

[5] Edward S. Corwin and J. W. Peltason, *Understanding the Constitution,* 4th ed. (New York: Holt, Rinehart and Winston, 1967), p. 4.

[6] Schlesinger, *The Disuniting of America,* p. 39.

[7] See also Article I, section 9, limiting taxation of slaves; Article I, section 9, prohibiting Congress from ending the slave trade before 1808; Article IV, section 2, requiring return of fugitive slaves to owners; and Article V, prohibiting amendment of Article 1, section 9, before 1808.

[8] Thomas Sowell, *Race and Culture: A World View* (New York: Basic Books, 1994), pp. 210–14.

Following the war, Congress passed three constitutional amendments designed to protect the rights of former slaves especially in the South.

- The *Thirteenth Amendment* in 1865 abolished slavery.
- The *Fourteenth Amendment* in 1868 was intended to prevent southern states from passing discriminatory laws. It reads, in part: "No State shall make or enforce any law which shall abridge the privileges or immunities of citizens of the United States; nor shall any State deprive any person of life, liberty, or property, without due process of law; nor deny to any person within its jurisdiction the equal protection of the laws."
- The *Fifteenth Amendment* in 1870 prohibited race discrimination in voting.

These amendments were supplemented by a series of civil rights acts passed by Congress, most notably one in 1866 to protect blacks against employment discrimination and another in 1875 to protect them from discrimination in transportation and accommodations. Altogether, these amendments and statutes created a formidable legal machinery to implement the rights to which blacks were entitled under the American Creed. If this machinery had been allowed to function, a century of painful employment discrimination against blacks and other groups might have been prevented. But it was not to be.

racism
The belief that each race has distinctive cultural characteristics and that one's own race is superior to other races.

There was tremendous resistance to the new laws in the South, but at first much enforcement was possible because of the continuing presence of the Union Army, an occupying force that kept a temporary lid on southern resistance to black rights, which was formidable and violent. Because the troops protected voting rights, for example, 16 blacks were elected to Congress and about 600 to state legislatures. But the presidential election of 1876 ended the era of southern rehabilitation.

In the race, the Republican candidate Rutherford B. Hayes lost the popular vote to his Democratic opponent Samuel J. Tilden, but the vote was close in the electoral college and returns from three southern states were contested. Hayes agreed to an "understanding" that if the electoral votes from these southern states were cast for him, he would withdraw the remaining federal troops. History records that Hayes won the election and the soldiers left. An important check on racism went with them.

Jim Crow laws
Measures enacted in the South from 1877 to the 1950s legalizing segregation in public places, buses, trains, restaurants, schools, and businesses. The term *Jim Crow,* taken from a song in a nineteenth-century minstrel show, came to stand for the practice of discrimination or segregation.

White racism reasserted itself in the South in many ways. *Racism,* defined broadly, is the belief that each race has distinctive cultural characteristics and that one's own race is superior to other races. It persists when myths and stereotypes about inferiorities are expressed in institutions of education, government, religion, and business. Racism leads to social discrimination, or the apportioning of resources based on group membership rather than individual merit. It insulates the power of a privileged group—for example, white Americans—from challenge.

Southern states adopted segregationist statutes called *Jim Crow laws.* These laws institutionalized the idea that whites were superior to blacks by creating segregated schools, restrooms, and water fountains; in literacy tests that disenfranchised blacks; in restrictive covenants, or deeds, that prevented whites from selling property to blacks in certain neighborhoods; and in discriminatory hiring that kept blacks in menial occupations.

Other Groups Face Employment Discrimination

Other groups in the United States faced extensive and institutionalized employment discrimination as well. Native Americans were widely treated as an inferior race. In the nineteenth century, the federal government spent uncounted millions of dollars to destroy their societies and segregate them on reservations.

A large population of roughly 90,000 Hispanics suddenly became residents of United States territory when Mexico ceded Texas in 1845 and other tracts of southwestern land in 1848. Soon these Mexican Americans were victims of a range of discriminatory actions. They were legally stripped of extensive land holdings and exploited in a labor market where discrimination confined them to lesser occupations. They suffered great violence; more Hispanics were killed in the Southwest between 1850 and 1930 than blacks were lynched in the South.[9]

Beginning in 1851, Chinese laborers began to enter the country. They settled in western states and many owned placer mines. In 1863 several thousand began working on the construction of the Central Pacific Railroad. Some started businesses such as laundries and restaurants. By the 1870s there were 100,000 Chinese in western states; in California there were 75,000, about 10 percent of the population. Although they faced prejudice, their presence was tolerated until economic depression set in and the white majority felt they were competing for jobs and customers. Then economic and racial discrimination began in earnest.

Special taxes passed by state legislatures were used to confiscate their mines and ruin their commercial businesses. Some towns ordered all Chinese to leave. San Francisco passed an ordinance requiring city licenses for all laundries, then denied licenses to Chinese laundries.[10] The California state constitution, adopted in 1874, prohibited Chinese from voting and made it illegal for corporations to hire them. Finally, Congress banned the immigration of Chinese laborers in 1882.

The earliest Japanese immigrants found similar inhospitality. By 1880 there were only 124 Japanese in the United States, but their numbers increased rapidly as employers sought replacements for the cheap Chinese labor supply that had been cut off. By 1890 about 100,000 Japanese immigrants had arrived, most in California. Japanese laborers were typically paid 7 to 10 cents an hour less than whites. Like the Chinese, they ultimately threatened white labor and soon faced violent prejudice in cities. They turned to agricultural work in California's fertile inland valleys, but powerful white farmers resented their presence. California passed laws prohibiting Japanese land ownership, and in 1924 Congress banned further Japanese immigration.

Although employers wanted to utilize Japanese labor, social attitudes frequently made this impossible. For example, in 1925 Pacific Spruce Corporation brought 35 Japanese to the small lumber town of Toledo, Oregon, to work in its sawmill. A mob of 500 men, women, and children swarmed the mill and the company had to load the Japanese on trucks that took them to Portland.[11]

[9] John P. Fernandez, *Managing a Diverse Work Force* (Lexington, MA: Lexington Books, 1991), p. 165.

[10] In *Yick Wo v. Hopkins,* 118 U.S. 356 (1886), the Supreme Court struck down the ordinance as a violation of the equal protection clause of the Fourteenth Amendment. Had the Court followed up on this precedent, it could have struck down Jim Crow laws in the South.

[11] Herman Feldman, *Racial Factors in American Industry* (New York: Harper, 1931), pp. 89–90.

As this brief sketch on nineteenth- and early twentieth-century employment discrimination shows, neither the American Creed nor the fine legal mechanism put in place after the Civil War worked to stop racism. Why not? The former was eclipsed by broad public prejudice. The latter had to be enforced against the grain of southern racism and was, in any case, soon dismantled by the Supreme Court in two landmark cases—the *Civil Rights Cases* and *Plessy v. Ferguson.*

The *Civil Rights Cases*

The Civil Rights Act of 1875 was passed to prevent racial discrimination in "inns, public conveyances on land or water, theaters and other places of public amusement."[12] The law set a fine of up to $1,000 or imprisonment up to one year for violation. Still, there was widespread discrimination against freed slaves by business and soon a series of cases reached the Supreme Court. Two cases involved inns in Kansas and Missouri that had refused rooms to blacks. And in one case, the Memphis and Charleston Railroad Company in Tennessee had refused to allow a woman "of African descent" to ride in the ladies' car of a train. These cases were consolidated into one opinion by the Supreme Court in 1883 and called the *Civil Rights Cases.*[13]

The Civil Rights Act of 1875 was based on the Fourteenth Amendment, and in the Court's opinion, Justice Joseph P. Bradley focused on its wording. Because the amendment reads that "no state" shall discriminate, Bradley held that it did not prohibit what he referred to as a "private wrong." If race discrimination was not supported by state laws, it was a private matter between companies and their customers or employees and the Fourteenth Amendment did not prohibit it. For this reason, Congress lacked the authority to regulate race bias among private parties; therefore, the Civil Rights Act of 1875 was unconstitutional.

The *Civil Rights Cases* so narrowed the meaning of the Fourteenth Amendment that it became irrelevant to a broad range of economic and social bias. Congress and the courts could no longer use it to strike down much of the most brazen race discrimination. It was not necessarily a wrong decision; in fact, many constitutional scholars believe that the Court made a reasonable decision for that day given the clear reference to state action in the Fourteenth Amendment. But in dissent, Justice John Marshall Harlan argued that "the substance and spirit of the recent Amendments of the Constitution have been sacrificed by a subtle and ingenious verbal criticism."[14]

Plessy v. Ferguson

Southern states had passed so-called Jim Crow laws that sanctioned race segregation. If the Fourteenth Amendment could not prohibit private individuals from depriving each other of basic rights, did it not still clearly prohibit states from enacting laws that abused the former slaves? The answer was no.

One such law was the Separate Car Act passed by Louisiana in 1890. This statute required all Louisiana railroads to "provide equal but separate accommodations

---

[12] An Act to Protect all Citizens in their Civil and Legal Rights, 18 Stat. At L., 335, section 1.

[13] 109 U.S. 835 (1883).

[14] 109 U.S. 844.

for the white, and colored races, by providing two or more passenger coaches for each passenger train, or by dividing the passenger coaches by a partition so as to secure separate accommodations."[15] This law, like other Jim Crow laws, was based on the *police power* of the state, a presumed power inherent in the sovereignty of every government, to protect citizens from nuisances and dangers that might harm public safety, health, and morals.

police power
An inherent power of state governments to regulate economic and social relationships for the welfare of all citizens.

On June 7, 1892, Homer Plessy, who was seven-eighths Caucasian and one-eighth African, bought a first-class ticket on the East Louisiana railroad to travel from New Orleans to Covington. Boarding the train, he took a vacant seat in the white coach. He was asked by the conductor to move to the "nonwhite" coach. Plessy refused and was taken to a New Orleans jail.

Plessy brought suit, claiming he was entitled to "equal protection of the laws" as stated in the Fourteenth Amendment. In 1896, in *Plessy v. Ferguson,* the Supreme Court disagreed, holding that as long as separate accommodations for blacks were equal to those of whites, blacks were not deprived of any rights. Justice Henry B. Brown, writing for the majority, argued that laws requiring race separation "do not necessarily imply the inferiority of either race to the other" and were a valid exercise of police power by state legislatures because they enhanced "comfort, and the preservation of the public peace and good order."[16]

This ruling completed the destruction of the Fourteenth Amendment as a mechanism to guarantee civil rights. The Court's interpretation legitimized the *separate but equal* doctrine, or the belief that segregation of races was not inherently unequal. The separate but equal doctrine, which became the foundation for legal apartheid in the South, stood for 58 years until reversed in 1954 by the Court in its famous school desegregation case, *Brown v. Board of Education.*[17]

separate but equal
The belief, prevalent in the South, that racially segregated facilities were not inherently unequal.

Plessy is in retrospect notorious and some say one of the worst decisions ever made by the Court because of its consequences. The justices missed an opportunity to read the Fourteenth Amendment in a way that would protect blacks from the schemes of white racists. They must have thought that a decision striking down Jim Crow would be unpopular and widely disobeyed and may have sought to prevent the Court from being weakened by disregard for its opinions. As in the *Civil Rights Cases,* Justice Harlan was a lone dissenter who kept the light of the American Creed flickering by lecturing the majority. He wrote:

> Our Constitution is color-blind and neither knows nor tolerates classes among citizens. In respect of civil rights, all citizens are equal before the law. The humblest is the peer of the most powerful. The law regards man as man, and takes no account of his . . . color when his civil rights as guaranteed by the supreme law of the land are involved.[18]

[15] Act 111 of 1890, quoted in Richard Epstein, *Forbidden Grounds: The Case Against Employment Discrimination Laws* (Cambridge, MA: Harvard University Press, 1992), pp. 99–100.

[16] *Plessy v. Ferguson,* 163 U.S. 540 (1896), at 544 and 550. John H. Ferguson was the judge who denied Plessy's constitutional claim in the New Orleans Criminal Court.

[17] 347 U.S. 483.

[18] 163 U.S. 537.

After the *Plessy* decision, Jim Crow laws became entrenched throughout the South. The water fountains in this photograph taken in North Carolina in 1950 symbolize a much larger universe of discrimination, including employment discrimination. Source: © Elliott Erwitt/ Magnum Photos.

Long Years of Discrimination

The nation's civil rights laws were now hopelessly crippled. Southern legislatures were emboldened by *Plessy.* Now needing no special moral justification, Jim Crow laws spread. Black workers faced the most blatant discrimination. They were not allowed to hold jobs such as streetcar conductor or cashier where they would have any authority over whites. Labor unions refused to admit blacks, and a few that did limited them to low-pay occupations. The Brotherhood of Locomotive Engineers, for example, barred blacks from being locomotive engineers. In South Carolina, a law prohibited blacks and whites from working in the same room or using the same plant entrances in the cotton textile industry. Such custom spread to the North. A study of economic opportunity for blacks in Buffalo, New York, told the following tale.

> A [black] man tells of being made a moulder in a foundry, later to be replaced by a white worker and reduced to the grade of moulder's helper, and finally dismissed when he made a complaint. Another man was given a chance to try out for a skilled-labor job in a stone-cutting concern and, having made good, was given the position temporarily, losing it, however, a few days later when the superintendent "came down through the shop" and, seeing him so employed, told the foreman to put another man on the work.[19]

[19] Quoted in Feldman, *Racial Factors in American Industry,* p. 36.

THE CIVIL RIGHTS ACT OF 1964

This kind of open discrimination continued in the South. A study of 175 firms in New Orleans in 1943 found that almost all of them hired blacks, but then 93 percent segregated their workforces and 79 percent segregated job categories.[20] In the North, many companies refused to hire blacks at all. A study of 14 plants in Chicago in 1952, for example, found that 10 of them, or 71 percent, excluded blacks.[21]

In the late 1950s and early 1960s, a new civil rights movement arose. Under the leadership of blacks such as Martin Luther King, this movement was nonviolent and again focused on making America live up to the ideals in the American Creed. "The American people are infected with racism—that is the peril," said King. "Paradoxically, they are also infected with democratic ideals—that is the hope."[22]

The pressures of this movement led to many social reforms, among them passage of the Civil Rights Act of 1964, which is today the cornerstone of the structure of laws and regulations enforcing equal opportunity. Its Title VII prohibits discrimination in any aspect of employment. It reads, in part:

It shall be an unlawful employment practice for an employer:

1. To fail or refuse to hire or to discharge any individual, or otherwise to discriminate against any individual with respect to his compensation, terms, conditions, or privileges of employment, because of such individual's race, color, religion, sex, or national origin.
2. To limit or classify his employees or applicants for employment in any way which would deprive any individual of employment opportunities or otherwise adversely affect his status as an employee, because of such individual's race, color, religion, sex, or national origin. [Section 703(a)]

Title VII also created the Equal Employment Opportunity Commission (EEOC), an independent regulatory commission, to enforce its provisions. All companies with 15 or more employees fall under the jurisdiction of Title VII and must report annually to the EEOC the number of minorities and women in various job categories.[23] If bias exists, employees can file charges with the EEOC. The agency then attempts to resolve charges through conciliation or voluntary settlement, but if that fails, it can sue in a federal court. In 2004 there were 58,328 charges filed under Title VII leading to the recovery of $139 million in monetary benefits to workers suffering discrimination.[24]

---

[20] Logan Wilson and Harlan Gilmore, "White Employers and Negro Workers," *American Sociological Review,* December 1943, pp. 698–700.

[21] Lewis M. Killian, "The Effects of Southern White Workers on Race Relations in Northern Plants," *American Sociological Review,* June 1952, p. 329.

[22] Quoted in Lani Guinier, "[E]racing Democracy: The Voting Rights Cases," *Harvard Law Review,* November 1994, p. 109.

[23] A 1972 law extended coverage of Title VII to federal, state, and local government employees, so today Title VII covers most workers. Workers at firms with fewer than 15 employees can sue under state and local civil rights laws or, for race discrimination, may seek remedy under the Civil Rights Act of 1866.

[24] U.S. Equal Employment Opportunity Commission, "Title VII of the Civil Rights Act of 1964 Charges: FY 1992–FY 2004," www.eeoc.gov/stats/vii.html, accessed February 2005.

The overall purpose of Title VII, which is clear from the congressional debates that preceded its passage, was to remove discriminatory barriers to hiring and advancement and create a level playing field for all workers. As originally enacted, it did not require that minority workers be hired simply because they belonged to protected groups. It did not require employers to redress racially imbalanced workforces or change established seniority systems. No whites would be fired, lose their seniority, or be adversely affected. Simply put, from the day the law went into effect, all bias was to end. Job decisions could be made only on merit.

Disparate Treatment and Disparate Impact

disparate treatment Unequal treatment of employees based on race, color, religion, sex, or national origin.

Title VII made overt, blatant employment discrimination illegal. It enforced a legal theory of *disparate treatment.* Disparate treatment exists if an employer gives less favorable treatment to employees because of their race, color, religion, sex, or national origin. For example, a retail store that refused to promote black warehouse workers to sales positions, preferring white salespeople to serve predominantly white customers, would be guilty of this kind of discrimination. Disparate treatment violates the plain meaning of Title VII.

Although the intention of Title VII was to create a level playing field by prohibiting all discrimination, given the entrenched prejudices of employers in the 1960s, expecting that bigotry would instantly vanish was futile. The statute would need to evolve, and it did.

disparate impact Discrimination caused by policies that apply to everyone and seem neutral but have the effect of disadvantaging a protected group. Such policies are illegal unless strongly job-related and indispensable to conduct of the business.

When Title VII went into effect, employers could no longer engage in outwardly visible displays of discrimination. "Whites only" signs came down from windows and discrimination went underground where it was disguised but just as invidious. Instead of openly revealing prejudicial motives, employers hid them. Minority job applicants were simply rejected without comment or were found less qualified in some way. Or employers introduced job requirements that appeared merit based but were in fact pretexts for discrimination. Female applicants had to meet height, weight, and strength requirements that favored men. Southern blacks were given tests that favored better-educated whites.

This kind of discrimination was hard to eradicate under the existing provisions of Title VII because employers would not admit a discriminatory motive and claimed that their job criteria were neutral and merit based. The flaw in Title VII was that it contained no weapon to fight *disparate impact.* Disparate impact exists where an employment policy is apparently neutral in its impact on all employees but, in fact, is not job related and prevents individuals in protected categories from being hired or from advancing.

business necessity A legal defense a company can use to fight a disparate impact charge. It must show the practice in question was job-related and essential. To rebut this defense, a plaintiff can show that another practice was equally good and less discriminatory.

To combat disparate impact, the court initially used a case-by-case judicial test for discrimination. First, the applicant or employee made a charge alleging bias. Then the employer had to set forth a reason why it was a *business necessity* to engage in the practice. Then the burden of proof shifted back to the employee to prove that the employer's reason was phony, which was frequently hard to do.[25] This back-and-forth dance in which each individual case was separately considered was awkward and time consuming for the courts and placed the difficult

[25] This sequence was set up in *McDonnell Douglas v. Green*, 411 U.S. 792 (1973).

burden of proving the employer's secret motive on individual plaintiffs who lacked the legal resources of corporations. Some other way to fight hidden employer racism was needed. The Supreme Court would create it.

The *Griggs* Case

The Duke Power Company had a steam-generating plant in Draper, North Carolina, where workers had been segregated by race for many years. The plant was organized into five divisions and blacks had been allowed to work only in the lowest-paying labor department. The company had openly discriminated, but when Title VII took effect, it rescinded its race-based policies and opened all jobs to blacks.

However, it also instituted a new policy that required a high school diploma to move up from the labor department to the coal-handling, operations, maintenance, or laboratory and test departments. Now black workers could apply for formerly white-only jobs that paid more only if they had finished high school. Alternatively, they could take an intelligence test and a mechanical aptitude test, and if they scored at the same level as the average high school graduate, they could meet the high school diploma requirement. But since blacks in the area were less educated, this requirement frustrated their ambitions. Instead of rejecting blacks for being black, Duke Power now rejected them for lacking education. Black workers filed suit, alleging that the education and testing requirements had the effect of screening them out and were, in any case, unrelated to the ability, for example, to shovel coal in the coal-handling department.

In *Griggs v. Duke Power,* decided in 1971, the Supreme Court held that diploma requirements and tests that screened out blacks or other protected classes were illegal unless employers could show that they were related to job performance or justified by business necessity. They were unlawful even if no discrimination was intended. The *Griggs* decision, and the legal theory of disparate impact it created, was necessary for Title VII to work. If employers had been permitted to use sinuous evasions and substitute proxies for direct racial bias, Title VII would have been ineffective.

In 1978 the EEOC defined illegal disparate impact for employers with a guideline known as the *80 percent rule.*

80 percent rule
A statistical test for disparate impact. The test is failed when, for example, blacks or women are selected at a rate less than 80 percent of the rate at which white male applicants are selected.

> A selection rate for any race, sex, or ethnic group which is less than four-fifths (4/5) or (eighty percent) of the rate for the group with the highest rate will generally be regarded . . . as evidence of adverse impact.[26]

This rule is met if a company has hired minorities at the rate of at least 80 percent of the rate at which it hires from the demographic group (usually white males) that provides most of its employees. If, for example, it hires 20 percent of all white applicants, it must then hire at least 16 percent (80 percent of 20 percent) of black applicants. If it hires less than 16 percent of blacks, this statistical evidence defines unlawful disparate impact. The company is now on the defensive. It must show that the employment practices it uses, such as tests or applicant screening

[26] 29 CFR 1607.4 D (1989).

criteria, are a business necessity. Using the business necessity defense, it must prove that the test or practice is "essential," and the need for it is "compelling."[27]

With the addition of the theory of disparate impact by the judiciary, Title VII had evolved beyond its original meaning and could be used to strike down a broader range of discrimination. Title VII finally gave blacks and others a potent legal mechanism to get the civil rights on the job that Congress had tried to give them during the Reconstruction era. In a sense, broken promises were repaired. There is little in Title VII that would have been needed if, a century before, the Supreme Court had given good-faith construction to Reconstruction-era laws.

AFFIRMATIVE ACTION

affirmative action
Policies that seek out, encourage, and sometimes give preferential treatment to employees in groups protected by Title VII.

Affirmative action is a phrase describing a range of policies to seek out, encourage, and sometimes give preferential treatment to employees in the groups protected by Title VII. The broad use of affirmative action was rejected when Title VII was drafted and its congressional backers assured the business community that blacks and others would not have to be given preference over whites. Title VII was designed as a stop sign to end discrimination, not as a green light to engineer racially balanced workforces. Yet no sooner had President Lyndon Johnson signed it than civil rights groups argued that its philosophy of equal opportunity was too weak; blacks and others were so disadvantaged by past rejection that they lacked the seniority and credentials of whites. They could not compete equally in a merit system, and preferential treatment was needed to get justice.

Executive Order 11246

The origin of most affirmative action in corporations is Executive Order 11246, issued by President Johnson in 1965.[28] As originally written, the order simply required federal contractors to refrain from discrimination. It imposed penalties for noncompliance and established an agency in the Department of Labor, the Office of Federal Contract Compliance Programs (OFCCP), to enforce its provisions.

However, in 1971, the Labor Department issued Order No. 4, which requires federal contractors to analyze major job categories—especially officials and managers, professionals, technicians, sales workers, office and clerical workers, and skilled crafts workers—to find out if they are using women and minorities in the same proportion as they are present in the area labor force. If protected groups are underrepresented, companies must set up goals and timetables for hiring, retention, and promotion. About 200,000 corporations, employing 22 percent of the labor force and including nearly all of America's largest firms, have contracts to supply goods and services to government. So in effect, Executive Order 11246, as revised by Order No. 4, imposes widespread affirmative action.

The OFCCP, with one exception, does not establish rigid hiring goals for companies. The exception is in the construction industry, where, since 1980 it has

---

[27] Epstein, *Forbidden Grounds*, p. 212, citing *Williams v. Colorado Springs School District*, 641 F.2d 835 at 842.

[28] Now codified as 41 CFR 60–30.1 (2001).

mandated a goal of 6.9 percent females. In other industries, however, it requires contractors to set hiring goals and make a "good faith" effort to achieve them. Adequate progress is usually defined as a final hiring total that meets the 80 percent rule.

The OFCCP conducts zealous compliance reviews. Teams descend on a contractor, looking around, interviewing employees and managers, and auditing all kinds of records from interview notes to payroll slips. Each year the agency does nearly 4,000 such audits. At the San Diego Marriott Hotel & Marina, OFCCP team members walked around restaurants, banquet halls, and the front desk and failed to see a single black woman working in a visible position. A look at job applications soon revealed that most black women had been rejected for positions where they would interact with hotel guests. Some were better qualified than whites who were hired. Once this information surfaced, the hotel gave job offers, back pay, and benefits—a package worth $670,000—to 34 black women.[29] In extreme cases, the OFCCP can disqualify corporations from receiving federal contracts. This is rare. However, it is common for inspections to uncover violations of antidiscrimination guidelines.

THE SUPREME COURT CHANGES TITLE VII

From the beginning, affirmative action was controversial. Philosophically, it challenges the American Creed in several ways. It affronts the ideal of equality of opportunity by substituting equality of result. It affronts the ideal of achievement based on merit. And it affronts the ideal of individual rights before the law by substituting group preferences. When affirmative action first started, it posed more than a philosophical problem. Corporations were alarmed by its potential for generating lawsuits. If they failed to remedy race and sex imbalances in their workforces, they faced penalties for violating federal laws. If they used affirmative action to increase numbers of minorities and women, they feared reverse discrimination suits by white males.

Affirmative action was bound to provoke fierce legal challenges, and the Supreme Court used these attacks to read revolutionary changes into Title VII. The first high-profile challenge came from Allan Bakke, a white male denied admission to the medical school at the University of California at Davis. In the entering class, 16 places out of 100 had been reserved for minority students. Bakke argued that he was better qualified than some minority students admitted and he had suffered illegal race discrimination under Title VII because he was white. In *Regents of the University of California v. Bakke,* the Supreme Court ruled in his favor.[30] In a muddled, divided, and verbose opinion, the justices forbade strict quotas. Yet they also held that race and ethnicity could be one factor considered in admissions. This kept affirmative action alive but failed to resolve the dilemma of employers, who still feared reverse discrimination lawsuits.

[29] Office of Federal Contract Compliance Programs, "OFCCP Egregious Discrimination Cases," www.dol.gov/dol/esa/public/media/reports/ofccp/egregis.htm.
[30] 438 U.S. 265 (1978).

Then a second case arose from a Kaiser Aluminum and Chemical Corporation plant in Louisiana. The Kaiser plant was near New Orleans where 39 percent of the workforce was black. Few blacks worked at the plant before passage of Title VII, and even with it, by 1974, only 18 percent of the plant's workers were black. Moreover, less than 2 percent of skilled crafts workers were black because Kaiser required previous craft experience and seniority. Blacks had little of either since crafts unions excluded them. Kaiser had federal contracts and, to comply with Executive Order 11246, it adopted an affirmative action plan in 1974 to raise percentages of black workers. One goal was to bring blacks into skilled craft positions, so the plan reserved 50 percent of crafts-training openings for them. This was clearly a race-based quota.

In 1974 a white laboratory analyst, Brian Weber, who had worked for Kaiser for 10 years, applied for a crafts-training program that would place him in a more skilled job and raise his yearly pay from $17,000 to $25,000. To pick the trainees, Kaiser set up dual seniority ladders—one for blacks and another for whites. Names were picked alternately in descending order from the top of each ladder, starting with the black ladder, until positions were filled, with the result that seven blacks and six whites were chosen. Weber was too low on the white ladder and was not selected, whereas two blacks with less seniority than Weber were chosen (see Figure 18.1). This was a classic case of reverse discrimination.

Weber brought suit, claiming that the selection procedure violated the clear language in Title VII that prohibited making employment decisions based on race. He

FIGURE 18.1
Selection of Crafts Trainees at Kaiser
Kaiser and the union selected 13 crafts trainees. All candidates met minimum qualifications, but black applicants number 6 and 7 had less seniority than whites number 7, 8, and 9.

claimed that his Fourteenth Amendment rights to equal treatment under the law had been abridged. Justice William J. Brennan delivered the opinion of the Court in 1979 in *United Steelworkers of America v. Weber,* ruling that Kaiser's affirmative action plan embodied the "spirit of the law," which was to overcome the effects of past discrimination against blacks.[31]

The Court also established important criteria for judging the legality of affirmative action programs that it would frequently use in later years. First, a plan must be designed to break down historic patterns of race or sex discrimination. Second, the plan must not create an absolute bar to the advance of white employees. In the *Weber* case, for example, some whites were still admitted to training. Third, the plan must not require the discharge of white workers. And finally, the plan should be flexible and temporary, so that it ends when goals are met.

The *Weber* decision added an entirely new meaning to Title VII. Henceforth, Title VII no longer stood guard over a neutral playing field. Now, it permitted the very thing that its drafters assured the nation it would not do—it permitted race-conscious preferential treatment for members of protected groups. A strong dissent in *Weber* by future Chief Justice William Rehnquist attacked the majority for adding this meaning to Title VII in contravention of its language, which clearly forbade *all* race discrimination, including that against whites. He referred to Brennan's opinion as "a tour de force reminiscent not of jurists such as Hale, Holmes, or Hughes, but of escape artists such as Houdini."[32]

The *Weber* case squarely raised the issue of reverse discrimination and confirmed that affirmative action plans were legal even if they adversely affected whites. After *Weber,* companies no longer worried about lawsuits by angry white workers. Affirmative action spread.

One year after *Weber,* the Supreme Court upheld race-conscious "set-aside" programs in *Fullilove v. Klutznick.*[33] To spur the economy, Congress in 1977 established a $4 billion fund for public works construction. Ten percent of the fund was reserved, or set aside, for minority contractors, who had to get some contracts even when they were not low bidders. When white contractors challenged the set-asides, the Court ruled that they were an appropriate remedy for past discrimination against minority contractors.

The *Bakke, Weber,* and *Fullilove* cases showed that a majority on the Supreme Court supported affirmative action. Yet in each case, there were strong dissents. And even among the justices who supported affirmative action, there was disagreement about its legitimate scope. Thus began many years of contentious jurisprudence in which the Court defined the limits of affirmative action, then began to restrict it.

In the 1980s a liberal majority on the Court established generous boundaries for affirmative action. It held, for example, that seniority systems could not be overridden during layoffs to retain recently hired blacks.[34] In several other cases, it

---

[31] 443 U.S. 193.

[32] 47 LW 4859.

[33] 448 U.S. 448 (1980).

[34] *Firefighters Local Union No. 178 v. Stotts,* 467 U.S. 561 (1984); and *Wygant v. Jackson Board of Education,* 476 U.S. 267 (1986).

confirmed its decision in *Weber* by upholding affirmative action plans with hiring quotas for blacks.[35] It also upheld affirmative action to increase percentages of women in skilled crafts work.[36] Throughout, a minority of conservative justices vigorously dissented from the opinions of the liberal majority.

By 1988, however, President Ronald Reagan, an opponent of affirmative action, had appointed three new associate justices and a conservative bloc of five justices emerged to dominate the liberals on affirmative action cases.[37] As cases came before the court, this group began to whittle away at race-conscious preferences, making affirmative action more difficult to carry out.[38] Its advocates were infuriated, and soon Congress sent a clear message to the Supreme Court by passing the Civil Rights Act of 1991. This statute reversed a number of decisions to restore broad grounds for affirmative action.

Since 1991, through retirements and appointments, a majority of justices have in one case or another declared an inclination to end affirmative action on constitutional grounds. Yet the policy has survived every major test. In *Adarand v. Peña,* a cobbled-together majority saved the day by setting up a "strict scrutiny" test that made affirmative action programs more difficult to justify.[39] In *Grutter v. Bollinger,* a bare five-to-four majority agreed that the University of Michigan Law School's affirmative action program met this test.[40] The future is uncertain, but if the conservative bloc retains its strength, new tests of affirmative action are likely to result in a decision that racial preferences in employment violate the equal protection clause in the Fourteenth Amendment.

The Affirmative Action Debate

The legal debate about affirmative action parallels a broader debate in society. This debate revolves around three basic ethical considerations.

First, there are *utilitarian* considerations. Utilitarian ethics require calculations about the overall benefit to society, as opposed to the costs, of affirmative action. Advocates argue that preferential treatment policies benefit everyone by making fuller use of talent. Critics say that affirmative action has been ineffective or that its meager benefits are outweighed by the fairness problems it raises.

Pinning down the overall effect of affirmative action is difficult. For example, three studies of the impact on blacks when federal contractors changed their hiring

---

[35] *Local 28 v. EEOC,* 478 U.S. 421 (1986); *Local No. 93 v. City of Cleveland,* 478 U.S. 450 (1986); and *United States v. Paradise,* 480 U.S. 149 (1987).

[36] *Johnson v. Transportation Agency, Santa Clara County, California,* 480 U.S. 616 (1987).

[37] This bloc included Chief Justice William Rehnquist and Justices Anthony Kennedy, Sandra Day O'Connor, Antonin Scalia, and Byron White. These five joined to dominate the liberals William Brennan, Thurgood Marshall, Harry Blackmun, and John Paul Stevens. Kennedy, O'Connor, and Scalia were Reagan appointees.

[38] See, for example, *City of Richmond v. J. A. Croson Co.,* 488 U.S. 469 (1989) requiring more proof of past discrimination to justify affirmative action; *Wards Cove Packing Company v. Atonio,* 490 U.S. 642 (1989), raising the burden of proof in disparate impact cases; and *Martin v. Wilks,* 490 U.S. 755 (1989), allowing whites passed over for promotion because of affirmative action to bring discrimination lawsuits.

[39] 132 L.Ed.2d 158 (1995).

[40] 59 U.S. 306 (2003).

TABLE 18.1
The 10 Occupations with the Largest and the 10 with the Smallest Percentages of Women

Source: U.S. Department of Labor, *Women in the Labor Force: A Databook,* table 11. Figures are for 2002.

Most Women	Percent*	Fewest Women	Percent*
Preschool and kindergarten teacher	98%	Heavy equipment mechanic	0.4%
Secretary	96	Brickmason, stonemason	0.4
Child care worker	95	Crane operator	0.4
Receptionist	94	Heating/AC mechanic	0.6
Registered nurse	93	Bus and truck mechanic	0.7
Teacher assistant	93	Excavating machine operator	1.0
Bookkeeper	92	Concrete finisher	1.2
Hairdresser	91	Pest control worker	1.4
Nursing aide	91	Structural metalworker	1.4
Maid	89	Plumber	1.5

*Refers to women as a percentage of all workers in the occupation.

20 percent of all women working full time. The 10 jobs on the right are the least feminized among almost 50 traditionally male occupations in manufacturing, construction, and precision craft work with fewer than 5 percent women. Although women are moving into nontraditional occupations, they do so in small numbers.

The largest number of women work as executives, managers, and administrators, where they make up 46 percent of the broad occupational category. Yet they have not moved into the highest paying, most prestigious positions. Within all corporations, women are only 23 percent of chief executives and 26 percent of general managers.[63] Even this limited upper echelon presence falls precipitously within the aristocracies of the Fortune 500. There, in 2003, women were only 15.7 percent of officers (up from 8.7 percent in 1995), held only 13.6 percent of the seats on boards of directors, constituted only 5.2 percent of top earning executives, and held only 1.2 percent of CEO positions.[64] These numbers lead some to say that women have hit a *glass ceiling,* or an invisible barrier of sex discrimination thwarting career advancement to the highest levels. Women are also 55 percent of professionals. They hold the majority of positions in lower-paying professions such as registered nurse, however, and are moving only slowly into some traditionally prestigious and higher paying jobs. They are, for example, just 31 percent of physicians, 29 percent of lawyers, 19 percent of dentists, and 11 percent of engineers.

glass ceiling
An invisible barrier of discrimination thwarting the advance of women to top corporate positions.

Subtle Discrimination

Women face discriminatory male attitudes. Many workplace cultures are based on masculine values. In them, the expectation is that women will behave according to traditional male–female stereotypes. Men holding these stereotypes are

---

[63] Bureau of Labor Statistics, *Highlights of Women's Earnings in 2003* (Washington, DC: BLS, September 2004), table 2.

[64] Carol Hymowitz, "Women Put Noses to the Grindstone, and Miss Opportunities," *The Wall Street Journal,* February 3, 2004, p. B1.

conditioned to see women in the role of lovers, wives, or daughters; they subconsciously expect female co-workers to act similarly and be supportive and submissive.

In blue-collar settings, sexism may be blatant; some men will openly express biases. In managerial settings, sex discrimination is usually subtle, even unintentional. Men may assume that women are secretaries. In groups, men address other men first. They discount or ignore women's ideas. They make women uncomfortable with locker-room humor. They fail to include women in after-hour socializing. A female bond trader at Morgan Stanley Dean Witter in New York tells of hosting a dinner for her clients, all male, and some male co-workers. Afterward, the men politely called a taxi for her safe return home, then went to a club with topless dancing, where they spent the rest of the evening. The following day, the men recounted stories of revelry with her clients.[65]

Masculine cultures underlie many kinds of differential treatment. The norms in these cultures are usually not openly sexist. They can be nearly invisible, manifest only as practices that seem innocent and neutral. The problems they cause for women are often unintended. At one global retailing corporation dominated by men in the top ranks, a culture of flexible operations had grown up in which meetings were held spontaneously, often at the last minute or late in the day. Important decisions were made quickly. This culture was highly successful because it facilitated fast reaction to markets and minimized bureaucratic inefficiencies. However, it was hard on women who bore heavier responsibilities for households and children than the men. When a meeting suddenly materialized for the early evening, some women could not stay, and if they did not they were left out of critical decisions and unable to defend their turf.[66]

Deborah Tannen studied the linguistic styles of men and women at work.[67] According to Tannen, men and women learn different ways of speaking in childhood. Boys are taught by peers and cultural cues to use words in ways that build status and emphasize power over other boys. Girls, on the other hand, use language to build rapport and empathy with their playmates. Unlike boys, girls will ostracize a playmate who brags and asserts superiority in a group.

Later in life, these conversation styles carry over into the workplace, where they can place women at a disadvantage. In meetings, women may be reluctant to interrupt or criticize the ideas of another, whereas men push themselves into the conversation and engage in ritual challenges over the validity of ideas. Men hear women make self-effacing or apologetic remarks and conclude that they lack self-confidence. Tannen thinks that the female linguistic style makes it harder to make a firm impression in male-dominated groups, so they are more often interrupted in meetings and their ideas may be pushed aside. "I have yet to talk to any woman

[65] Patrick McGeehan, "Wall Street Highflier to Outcast: A Woman's Story," *New York Times,* February 10, 2002, p. 1.

[66] Debra E. Meyerson and Joyce K. Fletcher, "A Modest Manifesto for Shattering the Glass Ceiling," *Harvard Business Review,* January–February 2000, pp. 128–29.

[67] Deborah Tannen, "The Power of Talk: Who Gets Heard and Why," *Harvard Business Review,* September–October 1995.

FIGURE 18.2
The Narrowing Gap between Men's and Women's Weekly Earnings

Source: Bureau of Labor Statistics, *Highlights of Women's Earnings in 2003* (Washington, DC: BLS, September 2004), table 13.

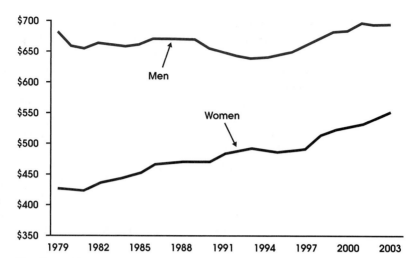

Note: The trend lines represent median weekly earnings of full-time wage and salary workers between 1979 and 2003 (in constant 2003 dollars).

who doesn't report an anecdote about this issue," she says.[68] Tannen recommends demonstrative speech, but many women report that men react negatively to aggressive behavior.

Compensation

Women earn less than men. Before the Equal Pay Act was signed in 1963, newspapers openly ran help-wanted ads with separate male and female pay scales for identical jobs, and in that year, across all occupations, the average woman earned only 59 cents for every dollar earned by a man. The Equal Pay Act, which forbids pay differences based on sex, has been effective in narrowing the earnings gap. Since its passage the gap has steadily narrowed and by 2003 women earned 80 cents for every dollar earned by a man.[69]

As the gap has narrowed, women's earnings have steadily grown, while men's have remained relatively stagnant. Figure 18.2 shows the trend in average weekly earnings in all occupations for both men and women over the past quarter century. Over these years, men's earnings rose a negligible 1.4 percent, while women's earnings improved by 29 percent.[70] An underlying factor that explains the better fortune of women is long-term structural change in the economy. Women hold a higher percentage of jobs in rapidly growing service occupations, while men predominate in the static manufacturing sector where there has been no job growth. Another factor is the progress toward equal opportunity made by women because of new laws and declining sexist bias.

---

[68] Quoted in Ralph D. Ward, *Improving Corporate Boards* (New York: John Wiley & Sons, 2000), p. 215.

[69] Bureau of Labor Statistics, *Highlights of Women's Earnings in 2003,* table 13. The exact figure is 79.5 percent.

[70] Men's earnings were $685 in 1979 and $695 in 2003; women's were $428 in 1979 and $552 in 2003.

Although women are moving closer to men, the gender gap is persistent. There are three reasons. First, occupational segregation places women in female-dominated occupations that tend to be lower paying than male-dominated ones. One study found that in occupations where more than 90 percent of jobs were held by women, the women earned 29 percent less than women in predominantly male occupations. The disadvantage fell to 21 percent if the occupation was only 50 percent female and fell to only 14 percent, well below the average 20 percent wage gap for all women, if the occupation was only 30 percent female.[71] Women continue to choose female-dominated occupations because they see other women in them, because cultural stereotyping feminizes certain occupational roles, because some traditionally female jobs better accommodate career interruptions, and because barriers to entry are low.

Second, women pay a heavy earnings penalty for child bearing and child rearing, activities that interrupt careers by leading women into part-time work and intermittent exits from the labor force. Because women in their 20s and 30s often leave work, employers sometimes hesitate to invest heavily in training them, their seniority lags, and men leap ahead. The statistic cited above, that women now make 80 percent of men's earnings, is based on comparisons of earnings for men and women working full time for a year. It does not account for women who work only part time or part of the year. An analysis of the actual earnings histories for a group of 2,826 similar men and women aged 26 to 59 who were followed for 15 years revealed that the women made only 38 percent of what the men did.[72] So the estimate that women's earnings are 20 percent lower than men's is probably an underestimate—and likely a big one.

Third, the earnings gap reflects elements of discrimination. It narrows when women and men of similar age, occupational experience, and educational background are compared. Still, it does not disappear. In one study of men and women holding degrees in 130 professional fields, women were paid equally with or made more than men in only 11 fields employing just 2 percent of the women. In all the remaining fields, women averaged only 73 percent of men's pay.[73] Nothing in the statistical analysis of men's and women's characteristics, besides sex, accounts for this shortfall.

Its cause defies statistical explanation and is either discrimination or another, unmeasured factor, for example the hesitance of women, found in some studies, to engage in competition, show ambition, or negotiate for salary.[74] Even in the most heavily female occupations men still earn more than women. For example, women's earnings are 93 percent of men's for secretaries, 90 percent for elementary and middle school teachers, and 81 percent for teacher assistants.[75] No

---

[71] Stephanie Boraas and William M. Rodgers III, "How Does Gender Play a Role in the Earnings Gap? An Update," *Monthly Labor Review,* March 2003, p. 10.

[72] Stephen J. Rose and Heidi Hartmann, *Still a Man's Labor Market: The Long-Term Earnings Gap* (Washington, DC: Institute for Women's Policy Research, 2004), p. 10.

[73] Daniel E. Hecker, "Earnings of College Graduates: Women Compared with Men," *Monthly Labor Review,* March 1998, p. 63.

[74] See references to studies in footnotes 53–55.

[75] Bureau of Labor Statistics, *Highlights of Women's Earnings in 2003,* table 2.

research documents causes for these discrepancies apart from biased treatment of women. The exact weight of this treatment on women's earnings is elusive.

The pay gap between men and women is worldwide, although in most other nations it is lower than in the United States. The International Labor Office reports that "in most economies women still earn 90 percent or less of what their male co-workers earn" because they "often hold low-level, low-paying positions in female-dominated occupations."[76] Wage gaps are the highest in rich, developed nations because high-paying occupations dominated by men have expanded. The largest gap is in Japan. The gaps are smallest in developing nations where men and women still crowd into low-wage and agricultural occupations. One cross-national study estimated that after weighing all other factors, about 20 percent of the wage gap in 64 countries was unexplained by any factor other than "significant bias in the labor market treatment (discrimination) of women."[77]

Sexual Harassment

sexual harassment
Annoying or persecuting behavior in the workplace that asserts power over a person because of their sexual identity. It is illegal under Title VII of the Civil Rights Act of 1964.

quid pro quo
A situation, defined as illegal, when submission to sexual activity is required to get or keep a job.

hostile environment
A situation, defined as illegal, where sexually offensive conduct is pervasive in a workplace, making work unreasonably difficult for an affected individual.

Many women experience *sexual harassment* at some time in their careers. In a recent survey, 34 percent of employees in six industries stated that they had observed some form of it in the past year.[78] Various forms of harassment exist, and same-sex harassment is prohibited by the same laws that bar male–female harassment; however, the major workplace problem is harassment of women by men. In a landmark book, *Sexual Shakedown*, Lin Farley defined this form of harassment as "unsolicited nonreciprocal male behavior that asserts a woman's sex role over her function as a worker."[79]

Sexual harassment of women encompasses a wide range of behavior. It can be very subtle, as when older men treat younger women like daughters, an approach that diminishes the authority of a female manager. More direct forms of harassment are staring, touching, joking, and gratuitous discussions of sex. The most serious forms include demands for sexual favors or physical assaults. These behaviors reinforce male power in work settings. By treating a woman as a sex object, a man places her in the stereotyped role of submissive female, thereby subordinating and marginalizing her. The message is, "You're only a woman, that's the way I see you. And at that level you're vulnerable to me and any man."[80]

In 1980 the EEOC issued guidelines (see Figure 18.3) making sexual harassment a form of sex discrimination under Title VII. The guidelines define two situations where harassment is illegal. One is the *quid pro quo*, when submission to sexual activity is required to get or keep a job. The other is a *hostile environment*, where sexually offensive conduct is so pervasive that it becomes unreasonably difficult to

[76] International Labour Office, *Global Employment Trends for Women 2004* (Geneva: ILO, March 2004), p. 14.
[77] Ibid., p. 13.
[78] KPMG Integrity Management Services, *2000 Organizational Integrity Survey: A Summary* (New York: KPMG, 2000), p. 2.
[79] Lin Farley, *Sexual Shakedown* (New York: McGraw-Hill, 1978), pp. 14–15.
[80] Cynthia Cockburn, *In the Way of Women: Men's Resistance to Sex Equality in Organizations* (Ithaca, NY: ILR Press, 1991), p. 142.

FIGURE 18.3
The EEOC Guidelines on Sexual Harassment

Source: 29 CFR 1604.11(a).

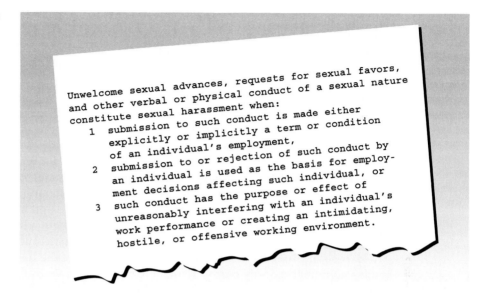

Unwelcome sexual advances, requests for sexual favors, and other verbal or physical conduct of a sexual nature constitute sexual harassment when:

1 submission to such conduct is made either explicitly or implicitly a term or condition of an individual's employment,

2 submission to or rejection of such conduct by an individual is used as the basis for employment decisions affecting such individual, or

3 such conduct has the purpose or effect of unreasonably interfering with an individual's work performance or creating an intimidating, hostile, or offensive working environment.

work. The range of conduct that can create a hostile environment has expanded to become very broad, but is not subject to precise definition. At first, courts often held that coarse language, innuendo, and pinups were part of some work environments and that Title VII could not magically dignify the manners of male workers throughout America.[81] Then, in a landmark case, a female welder named Lois Robinson, one of only seven women among 1,010 skilled craftsworkers in a Florida shipyard, complained that suggestive and lewd pinups, drawings, and cartoons created a hostile working environment. A Florida court agreed with her, holding that even if men enjoyed this decor, it nevertheless created an abusive climate for Robinson.[82]

In 1993 the Supreme Court set up a test for hostile environments. Teresa Harris, a manager in a Nashville company that rented forklifts, filed an EEOC complaint about the behavior of the company president, Charles Hardy. Over several years, Hardy had engaged in a pattern of vulgar and demeaning behavior that targeted Harris as a woman. He made derogatory remarks such as "You're a woman, what do you know?" and "We need a man as the rental manager." He made her serve coffee in meetings. He asked Harris and other female employees to fish coins out of his front pants pockets and sometimes threw objects on the floor, asking the women to pick them up while he commented on their breasts and clothing. He proposed negotiating Harris's raise at a Holiday Inn and suggested that she try giving sexual favors to get forklift rentals. When Harris complained and threatened to quit, Hardy apologized and she stayed, but his boorishness resumed.

[81] See, for example, *Rabidue v. Osceola Refinery Co.,* 805 F.2d 611 (CA–6 1986).
[82] *Robinson v. Jacksonville Shipyards,* 760 F.Supp. 1486 (M.D. Fla. 1991), at 1524.

Other women at the company testified that Hardy's behavior was all part of a ribald, joking atmosphere that everyone understood and enjoyed. Did Forklift Systems contain a hostile working environment? A lower court did not think so, ruling that although it was a close call and Hardy was a vulgar man, there was no proof that his conduct created a situation so intimidating that it interfered with Harris's ability to do her job.[83] However, when the case reached the Supreme Court, the justices created new criteria for defining a hostile environment.

In *Harris v. Forklift Systems,* they held that the guideline was whether sexual harassment created "an environment that a reasonable person would find hostile or abusive." There was no "mathematically precise test" for what constituted a hostile environment, but harassing conduct should be examined with respect to its "frequency" and "severity," whether it is "physically threatening or humiliating," and whether it "unreasonably interferes" with work.[84] The Supreme Court sent the *Harris* case back to a lower court for rehearing based on these criteria, and, a year later, that court ordered the company to set up a sexual harassment policy and to pay Harris's attorney fees. Forklift Systems appealed, but the litigants ultimately made a nonpublic, out-of-court settlement to end the case.

Since the *Harris* decision, the Supreme Court has expanded the law of sexual harassment. In two 1998 decisions it made corporations liable for damages when their employees create a hostile environment.[85] They can escape liability only if management proves that it tried hard to prevent and remedy harassment and, in addition, that the aggrieved employee neglected to make a complaint.[86] Now, most companies have formal policies prohibiting sexual harassment and have set up complaint channels.

CORPORATE EFFORTS TO PROMOTE DIVERSITY

diversity management
Programs to increase worker heterogeneity and make corporate cultures more friendly to employees of any race, ethnicity, gender, age, religion, sexual orientation, or disability.

Employers are now heavily regulated. While most companies, particularly small ones, simply try to comply with all the laws and regulations, many large firms go beyond compliance to promote workforce diversity. *Diversity management* refers to programs that increase worker heterogeneity and change corporate cultures, making them hospitable to employees regardless of race, ethnicity, gender, age, religion, sexual orientation, or disability.

Diversity management is a broader effort than affirmative action. Affirmative action is compliance-oriented hiring of individuals from a narrow range of racial and ethnic categories. Once hired, the law requires nondiscrimination and, sometimes, promotion to fill quotas, but there is no requirement that people's differences

[83] *Harris v. Forklift Systems, Inc.,* No. 3–89–0557 (M.D. Tenn. 1990).

[84] 510 U.S. 23 (1993).

[85] See *Burlington Industries v. Ellerth,* 524 U.S. 742 (1998) and *Faragher v. City of Boca Raton,* 524 U.S. 775 (1998). As a result of these cases, the EEOC issued new guidelines for employers. See EEOC, "Enforcement Guidance: Vicarious Employer Liability for Unlawful Harassment by Supervisors," Notice 915.002, June 18, 1999. These guidelines cover all forms of harassment prohibited under Title VII, including that based on race, ethnicity, national origin, and religion as well as sexual harassment.

[86] See *Pennsylvania State Police v. Suders,* 124 S. Ct. 2342 (2004).

be indulged. Women and minorities must often assimilate into white and male corporate cultures that have limited tolerance for differences. Protected individuals get in, but to prosper and advance they must mirror the values and behavior of the dominant group.

Diversity management, on the other hand, is based on the belief that people in a wide range of identity groupings have dissimilar backgrounds and social experiences. Their behavior does not always conform to the norms of a single corporate culture. Corporations should recognize these differences and change to accommodate them. There are countless identity groupings. Federated Department Stores, for instance, recognizes 26 groups in its diversity program, including racial and ethnic categories and, among others, disabled, atheist, devout, homosexual, married, single, and older employees.[87]

A commitment to diversity can be an intoxicating force. Sodexho is the largest provider of outsourced food and management services in North America. In the 1990s it decided to combine affirmative action with strong diversity management. It introduced new practices, including training, managerial bonuses based on diversity, and a public "diversity scorecard" to exhibit results. The results were striking. In five years, between 1998 and 2003, the number of whites in Sodexho North America's workforce of 110,000 dropped from 75 percent to 55 percent.[88] Individuals from categories of humanity defined as diverse surged in to replace them.

Advocates promote diversity management using two arguments. They say it is an ethical action needing no justification beyond its inherent goodness. And they say that it can strengthen businesses in ways such as the following.

- *It lowers costs of recruiting, turnover, absenteeism, and lawsuits.* Minorities and women have higher turnover and absenteeism than whites and males because of the presence of hurdles the corporation fails to see and remove. Less frustration raises both tenure and productivity and can prevent discrimination charges.

- *It improves understanding of markets and customers.* At Merck, an anticoagulant drug sold poorly in Hispanic markets until a Hispanic manager noticed that the package insert was written only in English. After translation into Spanish, sales rose. The idea was simple, but nobody else had thought of it.[89]

- *It reduces friction and leads to creativity and better decisions in groups and teams.* Research does not confirm this. There is some evidence that diverse teams make better decisions because they consider more perspectives.[90] However, team members may have more trouble learning to work together.[91] Some studies

[87] Cora Daniels, "Too Diverse for Our Own Good?" *Fortune,* July 9, 2001, p. 116.

[88] Rohini Anand, "Sodexho: Strategic Imperative to Set the Benchmark for Corporate America," *Across the Board,* Special Advertising Section, November–December 2003, unnumbered page.

[89] Margaret A. Hart, *Managing Diversity for Sustained Competitiveness* (New York: The Conference Board, 1997), p. 5.

[90] Faye Rice, "How to Make Diversity Pay," *Fortune,* August 8, 1994, p. 79.

[91] Jennifer A. Chatman and Francis J. Flynn, "The Influence of Demographic Heterogeneity on the Emergence and Consequences of Cooperative Norms in Work Teams," *Academy of Management Journal,* October 2001.

have associated diversity with better corporate performance.[92] But others have found little effect, leading one group of researchers to conclude that "the simplistic 'business case' for diversity . . . does not work."[93]

To succeed, a diversity management program must be part of the corporate management system.

- *Leadership* is critical. Without it, diversity efforts will not be seen as central to business strategy. Taylor Cox, Jr., a diversity management consultant, tells how leaders go wrong. Managers commit to attending meetings about diversity tasks but change their plans when operations make competing demands on their time. A manager picked to open a diversity training session welcomed attendees and then said, "I'm sorry you have to be here today and sit through all of this."[94] When asked at a diversity meeting whether anyone in the company had been promoted or passed over because of performance on diversity, a senior vice president of human resources could not think of anyone. Glen Hiner of Owens Corning, Inc., set a different example. When he came into the company, he stated in the first meeting with senior executives, "We are too white and too male, and that will change." He followed this by taking large and small actions, from appointing women and minorities to high positions to requiring a statement about the dignity of individuals printed on all business cards.[95]

- *Change in the organization structure* creates focal points for diversity efforts. Many companies have corporate diversity officers. In large companies, coordinators in business units often support these staff executives. Sometimes a steering committee of top managers runs the program. Coordinating committees are common in divisions of large firms. An example is the Diversity Leadership Council at Lockheed Martin's Missiles & Space Division, which consists of diversity coordinators, managers from the division's business units, and representatives of six formally recognized employee groups. Among these groups a gay, lesbian, or bisexual group with 30 members helps employees to "feel more free to be 'out.'"[96] An Asian American and Pacific Islander group promotes training to combat the stereotype that Asians are not assertive.

- *Training programs* sensitize employees to prejudices and cultural differences. A recent study found that 73 percent of 108 companies surveyed conducted diversity training. The typical training course averaged 25 people and lasted 10 hours. Topics covered, in order of frequency, were workplace discrimination,

[92] Orlando C. Richard, "Racial Diversity, Business Strategy, and Firm Performance: A Resource-Based View," *Academy of Management Journal,* April 2000.

[93] Melissa Master, "Limits to Diversity?" *Across the Board,* November–December 2003, p. 36.

[94] Taylor Cox, Jr., *Creating the Multicultural Organization* (San Francisco: Jossey-Bass, 2001), p. 41.

[95] Marc Bendick, Jr., Mary Lou Egan, and Suzanne M. Lofhjelm, "Workforce Diversity Training: From Antidiscrimination Compliance to Organizational Development," *Human Resource Planning,* January 2001, p. 10.

[96] *Lockheed Martin Today,* "Common Ground: Workplace Evolving to Support Increased Employee Diversity," 2000, www.lockheedmartin.com/diversity/common.html.

stereotypes, ways of making people from diverse groups welcome, the contribution of diversity to productivity, nondiscriminatory promotions and evaluations, white-male resistance, and the cultures of a range of groups.[97]

- *Mentors* can be assigned to women and minorities to overcome isolation in firms where the hierarchy is predominantly white and male. A recent study of successful managers in large companies found that high-potential minorities were often discouraged by mid-career. They tended to move up more slowly than high-potential whites, who were put on fast tracks earlier. As whites got key assignments and promotions, the minority managers often felt discouraged. A key to their ultimate success was the support of mentors who opened doors for them.[98]

- *Data collection* is needed to define issues and measure progress. Many companies conduct surveys. Twice a year, for example, Allstate Insurance Co. surveys its employees to learn how they feel they are being treated.[99] Related to data collection is measurement. Because of the pervasive philosophy in business that what gets measured gets done, many companies quantify diversity goals. The Quaker Oats Company created a statistic called the "best-practices index" that registers points for every program and action taken in each of its plants. Its diversity administrator argues: "Most CEOs may not know a lot about diversity, but they understand numbers. They can tell the difference between a facility with 1,000 points on the best-practices index, and a facility with 500 points."[100]

- *Policy changes* establish new rules. Following a public relations disaster when tapes of executives making racially biased remarks were leaked to the press and a $115 million settlement of a race discrimination lawsuit, Texaco set up a program to reform its corporate culture. Many policies changed as a result. One example is a new rule that no human resource committee meeting can take place unless attended by a minority or a woman. If such a person is sick or delayed, the meeting is postponed.[101]

- *Reward systems* encourage managers to achieve diversity goals. Diversity can be one element of performance reviews. Division managers at ExxonMobil are required at annual reviews to present career development plans for 10 females and 10 minority males. At Coca-Cola 25 percent of each manager's compensation is based on achieving diversity goals.[102]

Resistance to diversity projects comes from white males who feel blamed for problems and perceive a losing game in which the advance of others precludes their success and from some women and minorities hoping to deemphasize their

[97] Bendick, Egan, and Lofhjelm, "Workforce Diversity Training," p. 10.

[98] David A. Thomas, "The Truth about Mentoring Minorities: Race Matters," *Harvard Business Review,* April 2001, pp. 99–107.

[99] Louisa Wah, "Diversity at Allstate: A Competitive Weapon," *Management Review,* July–August 1999, p. 28.

[100] Hart, *Managing Diversity for Sustained Competitiveness,* p. 8, citing I. Charles Mathews, vice president of diversity management.

[101] Kenneth Labich, "No More Crude at Texaco," *Fortune,* September 6, 1999, p. 208.

[102] Betsy McKay, "Coke CEO to Tie Pay to Diversity Goals, Create Post on Promotion of Minorities," *The Wall Street Journal,* March 10, 2000, p. B7.

differences and assimilate into the dominant company culture. Yet, growing diversity in workforces and markets ensures that these programs will remain strong because there is a business rationale for them. Nondiscrimination has moved from a social responsibility, to a legal duty, to a business imperative. In the end, it may be the latter consideration that closes any remaining gap between the promises of natural rights in the Declaration of Independence and the neglect of them in practice.

CONCLUDING OBSERVATIONS

Workplace discrimination has existed throughout American history. The first national effort to end it began during the Civil War, with the Emancipation Proclamation freeing slaves, and included constitutional amendments and civil rights laws passed after the war. This effort floundered because societal values hindered enforcement of the laws.

In the 1960s, a second effort to eradicate discrimination began with passage of the Civil Rights Act of 1964. Since then, more laws and thousands of agency and court decisions have greatly reduced, but not eliminated, job bias against minorities and women. Today, the accumulated corpus of antidiscrimination law is massive, complex, and controversial where it embodies preferential treatment. But overall, and unlike the reconstruction-era effort, it works. Along with government, corporations are taking many actions—both voluntary and legally mandated—to make progress.

Yet more needs to be done. There is widespread evidence of continuing discrimination. Research on wage gaps, studies of job applications, and the continued existence of many discrimination suits attest to it.

Adarand v. Peña

This is the story of an affirmative action case that made its way to the U.S. Supreme Court. When the Court announced that it would hear *Adarand v. Peña*, there was considerable speculation about the outcome. The plaintiff, a white male, argued that preferential treatment for minority and female contractors was unconstitutional. Would the justices agree?

In due course, the nine-member Court issued a lengthy (21,800 words) split decision, showing itself to be as fractured as the public in its thinking. It divided 5 to 4, with six separate opinions—a majority opinion, two concurring opinions, and three dissents. The result? Affirmative action lived on but became harder to justify. With the support of affirmative action foes in the legal community, Adarand Constructors tried to carry the case farther, refusing to give up until the Court killed affirmative action in

all its forms. The case bounced around the federal court system for another six years until fizzling out in 2001 when the Supreme Court dismissed it.

THE GUARDRAIL SUBCONTRACT

In 1987 Congress appropriated a huge sum, more than $16 billion, to the Department of Transportation (DOT) for highway construction across the nation.[1] Ten percent, or $1.6 billion, was earmarked for small businesses run by "socially and economically disadvantaged individuals."[2]

[1] The Surface Transportation and Uniform Relocation Assistance Act of 1987, P.L. 100–17.

[2] Section 106(c)(1).

Socially disadvantaged persons were defined as "those who have been subjected to racial or ethnic prejudice or cultural bias" and *economically disadvantaged persons* were defined as those "whose ability to compete in the free enterprise system has been impaired due to diminished capital and credit opportunites as compared to others in the same business area who are not socially disadvantaged."[3]

It was to be presumed that black, Hispanic, Asian Pacific, subcontinent Asian, and Native American persons and women were both socially and economically handicapped. Any small business with 51 percent or greater ownership by persons in these categories could be certified as a *disadvantaged business enterprise,* or DBE. Then, Congress put monetary incentives to hire DBEs into the highway construction law. The story here illustrates how these incentives worked.

In 1989 Mountain Gravel & Construction Company received a $1 million prime contract to build highways in the San Juan National Forest of southwest Colorado. It requested bids from subcontractors to install 4.7 miles of guardrails. Two small companies that specialize in guardrail installation

[3] Section 106(c)(2)(B).

responded. Adarand Constructors, Inc., a white-owned company, submitted the low bid, and Gonzales Construction Company, a firm certified as a DBE, submitted a bid that was $1,700 higher.

Ordinarily, Mountain Gravel would have chosen the low bidder, but the prime contract provided that it would be paid a bonus, up to 10 percent of the guardrail subcontract, if it picked a DBE.

On this subcontract, the bonus payment was approximately $10,000, so even by accepting a bid $1,700 above the low bid, Mountain Gravel came out $8,300 ahead. Gonzales Construction, the high bidder, got the nod.

The part of the prime contract that caused Mountain Gravel to reject Adarand Constructors's low bid was called a *subcontractor compensation clause.* It provided that a sum equal to 10 percent of the subcontract would be paid to Mountain Gravel, up to a maximum of 1.5 percent of the dollar amount of the prime contract, if one DBE subcontractor was used. If two DBE subcontractors had been used, the extra payment could have been as much as 2 percent of the prime contract.

Losing the guardrail job angered Randy Pech, the white male co-owner and general manager of Adarand Constructors. "It was very discouraging to

Randy Pech of Adarand Constructors.
Source: © Gaylor Wampler/Sygma CORBIS.

run a legitimate, honest business," said Pech, "to go to a lot of trouble of bidding on a project—to know you did a great job and come in the low bid—and then find out they can't use you because they have to meet their 'goals.'"[4] Pech's lawyer, William Pendley, spoke more bluntly about the subcontractor compensation clause. "It works like a bribe," he said.[5]

This was not the first time Adarand Constructors had faced this situation. It was one of only five Colorado contractors specializing in guardrails. The other four, Cruz Construction, Ideal Fencing, C&K, and Gonzales Construction, were minority-owned and, by virtue of that, designated as DBEs. These four competitors were all stable businesses at least 10 years old, and on nonfederal highway projects, they sometimes beat Adarand Constructors with lower bids. Yet when federal highway dollars were being spent, Adarand Constructors frequently lost—even with the lowest bid.

Later it would be documented that because of the subcontractor compensation clause, prime contractors had rejected the company's low bids five times to favor its DBE competitors. Mountain Gravel's bid estimator verified that Adarand Constructors's low bid on the 4.7 mile guardrail job would have been accepted if the extra payment had not existed. Fed up, Randy Pech sued the federal government.

In his suit, Pech claimed that the subcontractor compensation clause violated his constitutional right to equal treatment under the law. This right is found in the Fifth Amendment of the Constitution, which reads: "No person shall . . . be deprived of life, liberty, or property, without due process of law." Although this wording does not literally state that citizens are entitled to equal treatment, the Supreme Court has held that its meaning protects citizens from arbitrary or unequal treatment by the federal government in the same way that the Fourteenth Amendment prohibits states fom denying "equal protection of the laws" to their citizens. Pech did not seek monetary damages, but requested an injunction, or a court-ordered halt, to any future use of contract clauses providing extra payments on subcontracts given to DBEs.

Things got off to a bad start for Pech when the U.S. District Court for the District of Colorado ruled against him.[6] The court held that it was within the power of Congress, when it enacted the highway bill, to use race- and gender-based preferences to compensate for the harmful effects of past discrimination. Pech appealed to the Tenth Circuit Court of Appeals, but, two years later, it affirmed the district court's decision.[7] Pech then took the next step and appealed to the Supreme Court, which agreed to decide the case. Because the lawsuit named Transportation Secretary Federico Peña as a defendant, it was entitled *Adarand v. Peña.*

THE CONSTITUTION AND RACE

The Court was being asked to decide whether classifying citizens by race in order to treat them differently was constitutionally respectable. This was not a new question; neither was it one that has ever been resolved with clarity. Affirmative action has deeply divided the Court, but it is not the first race-based classification scheme to raise constitutional problems.

Between 1884 and 1893, the Court decided a series of challenges to exclusionary laws passed by Congress stopping the immigration of Chinese laborers and restricting the civil rights of resident Chinese. At first, the justices struck down laws that treated Chinese differently from American citizens.[8] Eventually, however, the Court went along with a wave of public hysteria over the Chinese and in key decisions upheld laws that denied them equal treatment.[9]

A few years later, in 1896, the Court had an opportunity to strike down the Jim Crow laws of the old South in *Plessy v. Ferguson* but failed to do so. Instead, it upheld the Louisiana statute requiring segregation of whites and nonwhites in separate railroad cars and fixed in place the infamous "separate but equal" doctrine. In a lone dissent that rang across decades,

---

[4] Marlene Cimons, "Businessman Who Brought Lawsuit Praises Ruling by Justices," *Los Angeles Times,* June 13, 1995, p. A15.

[5] David G. Savage, "'Colorblind' Constitution Faces a New Test," *Los Angeles Times,* January 16, 1995, p. A17.

[6] *Adarand Constructors, Inc. v. Samuel K. Skinner,* 790 F.Supp. 240 (D.Colo. 1992). Then-Secretary of Transportation Skinner was named as the defendant.

[7] *Adarand Constructors, Inc. v. Federico Peña,* 16 F.3d 1537 (10th Cir. 1994). By this time, Peña was Secretary of Transportation.

[8] *Chew Heong v. United States,* 112 U.S. 536 (1884); and *United States v. Jung Ah Lung,* 124 U.S. 621 (1888).

[9] *Lee Joe v. United States,* 149 U.S. 698 (1893).

Justice John Marshall Harlan called the Constitution "color blind" and said that race was not a valid criterion for making law.

> In respect of civil rights, common to all citizens, the Constitution of the United States does not, I think, permit any public authority to know the race of those entitled to be protected in the enjoyment of such rights. . . . [T]he common government of all shall not permit the seeds of race hate to be planted under the sanction of law.[10]

During World War II, the Court was once again called upon to decide the question of a race-based government action. In early 1942, President Franklin Roosevelt issued an executive order, which Congress ratified, requiring the relocation of 70,000 persons of Japanese descent, both American citizens and resident aliens, from homes on the West Coast to inland evacuation camps.

This policy was challenged as depriving the Japanese Americans of their Fifth Amendment guarantee of equal protection of the laws. However, the Court once again upheld a racial classification scheme. In the majority opinion, Justice Black conceded that "all legal restrictions which curtail the civil rights of a single racial group are immediately suspect" and must be subjected "to the most rigid scrutiny."[11] Nevertheless, the evacuation order passed this "rigid scrutiny," because the president and Congress were taking emergency actions in time of war to prevent sabotage and avert grave danger. In dissent, Justice Frank Murphy argued that the evacuation "goes over 'the very brink of constitutional power' and falls into the ugly abyss of racism."[12]

In 1954 the Court finally reversed its decision in *Plessy.* In the landmark school desegregation case *Brown v. Board of Education,* it agreed that under the "separate but equal" doctrine, the states had provided grossly unequal schools for blacks.[13] During oral arguments in the case, Thurgood Marshall, destined to be the first black Supreme Court justice, invoked the principle of a color-blind Constitution. A unanimous Court struck down "separate but equal" as a violation of the equal protection clause in the Fourteenth Amendment.

---

[10] 163 U.S. 554, 560.

[11] *Korematsu v. United States,* 323 U.S. 214.

[12] 323 U.S. 242.

[13] 347 U.S. 483.

The *Brown* decision, however, did not mean that the Court saw a completely color-blind Constitution. In the 1970s, suits by whites who had suffered reverse discrimination as a result of affirmative action began to reach its docket. In the first such cases, a divided Court upheld affirmative action, but was obviously troubled by it and tried to define its limits. There was also an ideological split among the justices, with a liberal bloc condoning race-based affirmative action and a conservative bloc inclined to severely limit or prohibit it.

THE FULLILOVE CASE

In 1980 the Court heard for the first time a challenge to a set-aside program for minority businesses. In the Public Works Employment Act of 1977, Congress authorized $4 billion for public works projects such as dams, bridges, and highways. At least 10 percent of this sum was set aside for businesses owned by "minority group members," who were defined as "Negroes, Spanish-speaking, Orientals, Indians, Eskimos, and Aleuts."[14]

The law was challenged by several associations of white contractors, who claimed to have lost business and argued that the set-aside violated their constitutional rights to equal protection. But in *Fullilove v. Klutznick,* the Court held that Congress could use racial classification schemes to strike at racist practices used by prime contractors on federal projects.[15]

Over the years, courts have developed standards for testing the constitutional validity of laws that classify citizens. All such laws must withstand one of three levels of scrutiny by a skeptical judiciary.

The lowest level is *ordinary scrutiny,* which requires that government prove its classification scheme is "reasonably" related to a "legitimate interest." For example, classifying citizens by income for purposes of tax collection would pass this minimum test.

The second level is *intermediate scrutiny,* a heightened standard requiring that the law be "substantially related" to an "important government objective." In the past, intermediate scrutiny was typically used for laws related to gender, for example, the law drafting men for military service but not women.

---

[14] Section 103(f)(2).

[15] 448 U.S. 448.

The final, and most exacting, level of scrutiny, called *strict scrutiny,* is reserved for racial classifications regarded as pernicious and undesirable. When strict scrutiny is used, it is presumed that the law in question is unconstitutional unless it passes a specific two-part test. The government must prove that it serves a "compelling" government interest and is "narrowly tailored," that is, not more extensive than it needs to be to serve its purpose. There are no fixed definitions of the words "reasonably," "substantially related," and "compelling," but they represent an escalating standard of proof.

The majority opinion in *Fullilove* showed that neither Chief Justice Warren Burger nor the five other justices who joined and concurred with him were particularly alarmed about race-based set-asides for minority contractors. The chief justice subjected the minority business program in the Public Works Employment Act to only an intermediate level of scrutiny.

THE CROSON AND METRO CASES

After *Fullilove,* nine years passed before the Court looked at set-asides again. In 1989 the Court struck down an affirmative action plan used by the city of Richmond, Virginia, requiring that 30 percent of construction work be awarded to minority contractors. In *Richmond v. Croson,* the Court held that because the city's plan was a suspect racial classification, it should be subject to strict scrutiny.[16] And when the two tests required by strict scrutiny were applied, the plan could not pass constitutional muster.

First, although the population of Richmond was 50 percent black and less than 1 percent of city contracts were awarded to black firms, the city had not proved a "compelling" interest because it had never conducted studies to show that this statistical discrepancy was caused by race discrimination. Without proof of past discrimination, no "compelling" justification for raced-based remedial action existed.

And second, the plan was not "narrowly tailored"; in addition to giving preference to black contractors, it entitled Hispanic, Asian, Native American, Eskimo,

and Aleut contractors located anywhere in the United States to take advantage of preferential bidding rules. This scheme of inclusion was too broad. The Court ruled that for white contractors, the Richmond plan violated the Fourteenth Amendment guarantee of equal protection under the law.[17]

In the wake of the *Croson* decision, more than 200 set-aside plans around the country were dropped or changed for fear that they would be challenged and struck down. In Richmond, the percentage of contract dollars awarded to minority businesses plummeted from 30 percent to "the low single digits."[18]

A year later, in 1990, the Court confronted a case in which white-owned broadcasters challenged a congressional statute requiring that the Federal Communications Commission give certain preferences to minority radio and television companies when it issued broadcast licenses. Congress declared that its purpose was to promote diversity in programming. In *Metro Broadcasting v. FCC,* a five-member majority of the Court composed of four remaining liberals and the usually conservative Justice Byron White held that "benign race-conscious measures" undertaken by Congress to compensate victims of discrimination need be subject only to the standard of "intermediate scrutiny."[19] Creating diversity in broadcasting was an "important governmental objective," and preferences for nonwhite and female broadcasters were "substantially related" to achieving this objective. In dissent, Justice Anthony M. Kennedy sought to refocus the Court on the mistake made in the *Plessy* case. "I regret," he wrote, "that after a century of judicial opinions we interpret the Constitution to do no more than move us from 'separate but equal' to 'unequal but benign.'"[20]

---

[16] *City of Richmond v. J. A. Croson Co.,* 488 U.S. 469 (1989).

[17] The Fourteenth Amendment protects American citizens from unjust actions by state governments. It reads: "No State shall . . . deny to any person within its jurisdiction the equal protection of the laws." The City of Richmond, being chartered by the state of Virginia, was therefore a governmental actor falling under the reach of the Fourteenth Amendment.

[18] Paul M. Barrett and Michael K. Frisby, "Affirmative-Action Advocates Seeking Lessons from States to Help Preserve Federal Programs," *The Wall Street Journal,* December 7, 1994, p. A18.

[19] 497 U.S. 547.

[20] 497 U.S. 637–38.

TWO LINES OF PRECEDENT

This was where matters stood until 1994, when *Adarand* came before the Court. The Supreme Court likes to follow precedent and generally adheres to the rule of *stare decisis* (STARE-ray da-SEE-sis), a Latin term meaning to stand as decided. The judicial system is based on the principle that once a matter of law is settled, courts should follow the established path. Judges believe that this should be the case even though a court would decide the question differently if it were new. *Stare decisis* preserves one of the law's primary virtues, its predictability.

However, two different precedents had been established for minority preferences in contracting. In *Croson,* the Court had applied strict scrutiny to a city plan and declared it unconstitutional. But *Adarand* was not about a city plan; it involved a plan enacted by Congress. Traditionally, the Supreme Court recognizes that Congress represents the will of the American people and thus its actions deserve great deference. The line of precedent closest to the issue in *Adarand* was that emerging from *Fullilove* and *Metro.* In both cases, the Court had applied only intermediate scrutiny to congressional affirmative action plans and in both cases the plans were upheld. This result was consistent with the Court's studied deference toward Congress.

THE DECISION

Attorneys for each side in *Adarand v. Peña* presented 30 minutes of oral argument before the nine justices on January 17, 1995.[21] On June 12, 1995, the Supreme Court released a 5–4 decision in favor of Adarand Constructors.[22] The majority opinion, written by Justice Sandra Day O'Connor, departed from the line of precedent running from *Fullilove* and *Metro* and instead returned to *Croson* and ruled that the Department of Transportation plan giving preferences in bidding to minority subcontractors would have to withstand the test of strict scrutiny. It held that the plan was a race classification and presumed to be unconstitutional unless it was "narrowly tailored" to

meet a "compelling government interest." Justice O'Connor wrote as follows.

> [W]e hold today that all racial classifications, imposed by whatever federal, state, or local governmental actor, must be analyzed by a reviewing court under strict scrutiny. In other words, such classifications are constitutional only if they are narrowly tailored measures that further compelling governmental interests. To the extent that *Metro Broadcasting* is inconsistent with that holding it is overruled.[23]

She justified departing from the *Fullilove* and *Metro* precedents by citing Justice Felix Frankfurter, who 55 years earlier had written that *"stare decisis* is . . . not a mechanical formula of adherence to the latest decision, however recent and questionable, when such adherence involves collision with a prior doctrine more embracing in its scope, intrinsically sounder, and verified by experience."[24] The Court's longstanding, deep suspicion of any race classification, wrote O'Connor, should override the recent efforts of some liberal justices to apply more lax scrutiny to forms of discrimination they called "benign."

However, the majority was unwilling to say that no scheme of race-conscious preferences could withstand strict scrutiny. Using affirmative action might still be possible for the government. O'Connor wrote:

> Finally, we wish to dispel the notion that strict scrutiny is "strict in theory, but fatal in fact. . . ." The unhappy persistence of both the practice and the lingering effects of racial discrimination against minority groups in this country is an unfortunate reality, and government is not disqualified from acting in response to it.[25]

This completed the majority opinion. The Court did not uphold or strike down the Transportation Department's subcontractor bidding clauses. Instead, it remanded, or returned, the case to the Tenth Circuit Court of Appeals to be redecided using the strict scrutiny test instead of the lesser test of intermediate scrutiny.[26] The result of this tougher

---

[21] This oral argument can be heard in CSPAN's recorded archives at www.cspan.org/guide/courts/historic/oa072598.htm.

[22] 132 L. Ed. 2d 158, 515 U.S. 200 (1995).

[23] 132 L. Ed. 2d 182.

[24] 132 L. Ed. 2d 184, citing *Helvering v. Hallock,* 390 U.S. 106, at 119.

[25] 132 L. Ed. 2d 188.

[26] 16 F.3d 1537, vacated and remanded.

review would determine whether the equal protection rights of Randy Pech at Adarand Constructors had been violated. Thus, as in many cases that come before the high court, the justices avoided deciding the specific question and decided only matters of law.

JUSTICE SCALIA CONCURS

Justice Antonin Scalia, a conservative and longtime foe of affirmative action, wrote a concurring opinion in which he agreed with the application of strict scrutiny but took the extreme position that "government can never have a 'compelling interest' in discriminating on the basis of race in order to 'make up' for past racial discrimination in the opposite direction."[27] He elaborated:

> Individuals who have been wronged by unlawful racial discrimination should be made whole; but under our Constitution there can be no such thing as either a creditor or a debtor race. The concept of racial entitlement—even for the most admirable and benign of purposes—is to reinforce and reserve for future mischief the way of thinking that produced race slavery, race privilege and race hatred. In the eyes of government, we are just one race here. It is American.[28]

Justice Scalia concluded that it was very unlikely and probably impossible that the Department of Transportation program could pass the strict scrutiny test.

JUSTICE THOMAS CONCURS

Justice Clarence Thomas, the Court's only black member, agreed with the majority opinion, but wrote separately to underscore the principle that the Constitution requires all races to be treated equally. In his eyes, there was no moral difference between a law designed to subjugate a race and a law passed to give it benefits.

> That these programs may have been motivated, in part, by good intentions cannot provide refuge from the principle that under our Constitution, the government may not make distinctions on the basis of race. As far as the Constitution is concerned, it is

irrelevant whether a government's racial classifications are drawn by those who wish to oppress a race or by those who have a sincere desire to help those thought to be disadvantaged.[29]

Thomas also argued that affirmative action degrades the very individuals it tries to help.

> So-called "benign" discrimination teaches many that because of chronic and apparently immutable handicaps, minorities cannot compete with them without their patronizing indulgence. Inevitably such programs engender attitudes of superiority or, alternatively, provoke resentment among those who believe that they have been wronged by the government's use of race. These programs stamp minorities with a badge of inferiority and may cause them to develop dependencies or to adopt an attitude that they are "entitled" to preferences.[30]

THE DISSENTERS

Three separate dissenting opinions were written, joined in by four justices. In the first, Justice Stevens, joined by Justice Ginsburg, objected to the departure of the majority from established precedent and argued that the Court had a duty to uphold the intermediate scrutiny standard. Stevens also disagreed with the majority that all discrimination was the same in principle.

> There is no moral or constitutional equivalence between a policy that is designed to perpetuate a caste system and one that seeks to eradicate racial subordination. Invidious discrimination is an engine of oppression, subjugating a disfavored group to enhance or maintain the power of the majority. Remedial race-based preferences reflect the opposite impulse: a desire to foster equality in society. No sensible conception of the Government's constitutional obligation to "govern impartially" . . . should ignore this distinction. . . . The consistency that the Court espouses would disregard the difference between a "No Trespassing" sign and a welcome mat.[31]

A second dissent by Justice Souter, in which Justices Ginsburg and Breyer joined, objected to the Court's departure from the *Fullilove* and *Metro*

---

27 132 L. Ed. 2d 190.

28 Ibid.

29 Ibid.

30 132 L. Ed. 2d 191.

31 132 L. Ed. 2d 192, 193.

precedents. He argued that more deference was owed to Congress and affirmed his approval for laws that try to redress persistent racism.

The third dissenting opinion came from Justice Ginsburg, joined by Justice Breyer. She wrote to underscore the lingering effects of "a system of racial cast" in American life. According to Ginsburg:

> White and African-American consumers still encounter different deals. People of color looking for housing still face discriminatory treatment by landlords, real estate agents, and mortgage lenders. Minority entrepreneurs sometimes fail to gain contracts though they are the low bidders, and they are sometimes refused work even after winning contracts. Bias both conscious and unconscious, reflecting traditional and unexamined habits of thought, keeps up barriers that must come down if equal opportunity and nondiscrimination are ever genuinely to become this country's law and practice.
>
> Given this history and its practical consequences, Congress surely can conclude that a carefully designed affirmative action program may help to realize, finally, the "equal protection of the laws" the Fourteenth Amendment has promised since 1868.[32]

THE CASE MOVES ON

The Supreme Court elected to decide principles of law. It declined to settle the specific question of whether the subcontractor compensation clause was constitutional. Therefore, it sent the case back to the Tenth Circuit, with instructions to decide the constitutionality question. The Tenth Circuit, in turn, sent the case down to the U.S. District Court in Colorado where it had originated in 1992.

In 1997, almost two years after the Supreme Court's decision, the district court issued an opinion. Judge John L. Kane Jr. applied the strict scrutiny test to the subcontractor compensation clause, and the result invalidated the clause. The clause passed the part of the test requiring the government to show a compelling interest. Judge Kane stated that there was sufficient evidence of bias in contracting before Congress when it passed the law.

However, the clause failed the test of narrow tailoring. Judge Kane held that basing social and economic disadvantage solely on race was unfair. Under the existing criteria for selecting DBEs, a multimillionaire who immigrated from Hong

Kong and became a U.S. citizen one day before applying would automatically qualify, but a poor white man who had lived in the United States his entire life could not. So the set-aside program was overinclusive and unconstitutional. Since Colorado was administering the program for the federal government, Judge Kane issued an injunction ordering the state to stop using the objectionable regulation.[33]

Pech and his company had won, but defenders of affirmative action wanted to put up a fight. The Department of Transportation appealed the decision back to the Tenth Circuit. Then Colorado refused to comply with Judge Kane's ruling. Governor Roy Romer argued, disingenuously, that a federal court order did not apply to a state government.

Adarand Constructors immediately sued the state to force its obedience. When the case came before Judge Kane, Colorado argued that it had changed its contracting program. It no longer used the subcontractor compensation clause, and it allowed all contractors, including white males, to get DBE status if they could show disadvantage.

Judge Kane was furious at the recalcitrance of Colorado officials. Instead of retrying the entire issue, he declared that Adarand Constructors had suffered years of discrimination and financial hardship at the hands of a government enforcing an unfair, unconstitutional law. He decreed that the company was eligible for DBE status.[34] Pech applied for it, and it was granted by Colorado in 1998.

Meanwhile, the *Adarand* decision had sparked a national debate. The federal government had approximately 160 preference programs for businesses certified as disadvantaged. In the year that *Adarand* was decided, $10 billion in contracts earmarked for minority and female vendors was distributed through various preference schemes. Opponents of affirmative action felt that, because of the decision, such practices should cease.

There was no doubt that *Adarand* cast a shadow over these arrangements, but their supporters had no intention of conceding defeat. Instead, President Clinton promised to "mend, not end" affirmative action. What he had in mind was revising preferential

---

[32] 132 L. Ed. 2d 212.

[33] *Adarand Constructors, Inc. v. Peña,* 965 F. Supp. 1556 (D. Colo. 1997).

[34] *Adarand Constructors, Inc. v. Romer,* Civ. No. 97–K–1351 (June 26, 1997).

Who Is Disadvantaged?

Any person who is a citizen and falls into one of the following categories is presumed to be socially and economically disadvantaged (beginning in 1999, persons with a net worth of $750,000 or more were disqualified). If the person has 51 percent ownership or greater in a company applying for a federal highway construction contract, that company qualifies as a "disadvantaged business enterprise" and can receive preferential treatment on federal highway contracts.

Black. Includes persons having origins in any black racial groups in Africa.

Hispanic. Includes persons of Mexican, Puerto Rican, Cuban, Dominican, Central or South American, or other Spanish or Portuguese culture or origin, regardless of race.

Native American. Includes American Indians, Eskimos, Aleuts, or Native Hawaiians.

Asian-Pacific Americans. Includes persons whose origins are Japan, China, Taiwan, Korea, Burma (Myanmar), Vietnam, Laos, Cambodia (Kampuchea), Thailand, Malaysia, Indonesia, the Philippines, Brunei, Samoa, Guam, the U.S. Trust Territories of the Pacific Islands (Republic of Palau), the Commonwealth of the Northern Marianas Islands, Macao, Fiji, Tonga, Kirbati, Juvalu, Nauru, Federated States of Micronesia, or Hong Kong.

Women. All women are included.

Source: 49 CFR §26.1 (2000); 64 FR 5128 (1999).

treatment rules so that the programs would withstand legal challenge.

Congressional opponents of affirmative action started a floor fight trying to kill a 10 percent set-aside provision in a new highway funding bill. In March 1998 strident debate erupted in the Senate over an amendment to delete the set-aside, but the amendment was defeated, leaving more than $17 billion of new highway funds earmarked for DBEs.[35]

In 1999 the Department of Transportation issued revised rules for awarding federal highway contracts to DBEs.[36] They stated that the 10 percent of highway funding reserved for DBEs was not a "quota" or a "set-aside" but an "aspirational goal at the national level." The DBE participation level in each state receiving highway funds could be higher or lower. To meet DBE goals, the states were required to first use "race-neutral" measures, that is, to do things to help all small businesses, including both DBEs and white-male-owned companies.

[35] Amendment No. 1708, 144 Cong. Rec. S1395.

[36] Department of Transportation, "Participation by Disadvantaged Business Enterprises in Department of Transportation Program," 64 FR 5096–5148.

These measures did not require race–gender classifications and included, for example, training and advice in bidding and contract work, bonding assistance, and breaking large contracts into pieces that small businesses could more easily handle. However, if such methods did not fully achieve DBE goals and "egregious" discrimination existed, then "race-conscious" methods that gave preferences to DBEs, including set-asides on which only DBEs could bid, could be used.

The states were required to do studies pinpointing discrimination, so that there would be a compelling rationale for race-conscious actions if they were needed. The rules also tightened qualifications for persons designated as "economically disadvantaged." This status was from now on denied to persons with a net worth of $750,000 or more (calculated as personal net worth minus the value of a primary residence and the ownership interest in the contracting business). The rules allowed white males to apply for socially or economically disadvantaged status. However, unlike minorities and women who are still automatically included (unless worth more than $750,000), the burden is on white males to prove that they have suffered financial hardship from discrimination.

These changes significantly scaled back affirmative action in highway programs. Later, President Clinton issued an executive order that introduced similarly constricted affirmative action methods in all federal contracting.[37]

ADARAND KEEPS GOING

Although the use of preferences was being scaled back, through it all Pech persisted in the belief that any race- and sex-based preferences at all were unconstitutional. The case continued its odyssey through the federal courts.

The Department of Transportation had appealed Judge Kane's 1997 ruling that the subcontractor compensation clause was unconstitutional. In 1999 the Tenth Circuit ruled that the case was now moot because Colorado had changed its contracting guidelines and no longer used the bonus clause. In addition, the court noted that Colorado had classified Adarand Constructors as a DBE.[38] Adarand, which argued that the Colorado guidelines were still unconstitutional, appealed to the Supreme Court. In 2000 the Supreme Court reversed the Tenth Circuit's decision and sent the case back with instructions to decide the constitutionality of the Colorado contracting guidelines.[39]

Later that year, the Tenth Circuit responded, deciding that although the original Colorado highway contracting rules had been unconstitutional, the states' new rules were narrowly tailored to meet a compelling government interest, and therefore, constitutional. Again, Adarand Constructors appealed the decision to the Supreme Court, which took the case under review. It argued that the Tenth Circuit had erred in its constitutional analysis because no rules that used race or sex as a criterion for awarding government funds could pass the strict scrutiny standard. In its brief, it argued the arbitrariness of the rules:

> [E]very single legally admitted permanent resident or citizen of the United States who happens to be female or who can trace his origins to any of 42 specifically designated countries is automatically presumed to have attempted to enter the American

highway construction business and to have experienced racial prejudice that somehow hindered that attempt.[40]

Adarand Constructors urged the Court to adopt the position of Justice John Marshall Harlan that the Constitution is color-blind. It believed that both Congress and the states continued to "trample the constitutional rights of countless innocent individuals."[41] Conservative foes of affirmative action cheered the case on. John O'Sullivan, writing in the *National Review,* articulated their view.

> Today, . . . preferences bestow benefits on something like 65 percent of Americans by extracting a sacrifice from the remaining 35 percent who happen to be white males. Their injustice is now real and concentrated. In other words, they are now plainly and undeniably [victims of] an official program of negative discrimination against a minority: the sole remaining example of institutionalized racism in the United States.[42]

Adarand was a major challenge to affirmative action, but there would be no decision on it. In late 2001 the Supreme Court, after hearing oral arguments, dismissed the case without a decision, saying that it should never have accepted it in the first place. The reason was something of a technicality. In an unsigned opinion, a unanimous Court explained that in the case Adarand Constructors was not challenging the Tenth Circuit's decision about Colorado's contracting rules. Instead, it was arguing that federal guidelines were unconstitutional. The Tenth Circuit decision had not addressed federal guidelines. Therefore, since the Supreme Court was "a court of final review and not first review," it declined to take up the merits of Adarand's arguments and the case was "dismissed as improvidently granted."[43]

With this dismissal the litigation epic of the *Adarand* case, shown in Exhibit 1, came to sudden end. The merits of its final appeal are still up for debate, if not for a formal decision.

---

[37] Executive Order 13170, "Increasing Opportunities and Access for Disadvantaged Businesses," October 6, 2000.

[38] *Adarand Constructors, Inc. v. Slater,* 169 F.3d 1292 (10th Cir. 1999).

[39] *Adarand Constructors, Inc. v. Slater,* 528 U.S. 216 (2000).

[40] Petitioner's Brief on the Merits, June 11, 2001, p. 11.

[41] Ibid., pp. 19–20.

[42] John O'Sullivan, "Preferred Members," *National Review,* September 3, 2001, p. 20.

[43] *Adarand Constructors, Inc. v. Mineta,* 122 S. Ct. 511, at 514 and 515. Norman Mineta, a new Secretary of Transportation, was now the respondent.

EXHIBIT 1 The *Adarand* Odyssey.
This diagram shows the path of the case as it moved through levels of the federal court system over nine years. Twice the Supreme Court remanded the case, that is, sent it back to a lower court for deliberation consistent with legal principles it set forth. Name changes occurred as each new Secretary of Transportation was named as the defendant.

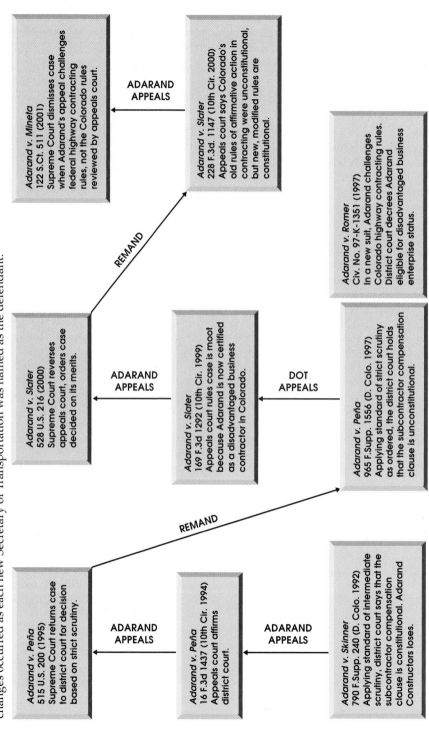

Adarand v. Mineta
122 S.Ct. 511 (2001)
Supreme Court dismisses case when Adarand's appeal challenges federal highway contracting rules, not the Colorado rules reviewed by appeals court.

ADARAND APPEALS

Adarand v. Slater
228 F.3d. 1147 (10th Cir. 2000)
Appeals court says Colorado's old rules of affirmative action in contracting were unconstitutional, but new, modified rules are constitutional.

Adarand v. Romer
Civ. No. 97-K-1351 (1997)
In a new suit, Adarand challenges Colorado highway contracting rules. District court decrees Adarand eligible for disadvantaged business enterprise status.

REMAND

Adarand v. Slater
528 U.S. 216 (2000)
Supreme Court reverses appeals court, orders case decided on its merits.

ADARAND APPEALS

Adarand v. Slater
169 F.3d 1292 (10th Cir. 1999)
Appeals court rules case is moot because Adarand is now certified as a disadvantaged business contractor in Colorado.

DOT APPEALS

Adarand v. Peña
965 F.Supp. 1556 (D. Colo. 1997)
Applying standard of strict scrutiny as ordered, the district court holds that the subcontractor compensation clause is unconstitutional.

Adarand v. Peña
515 U.S. 200 (1995)
Supreme Court returns case to district court for decision based on strict scrutiny.

REMAND

ADARAND APPEALS

Adarand v. Peña
16 F.3d 1437 (10th Cir. 1994)
Appeals court affirms district court.

ADARAND APPEALS

Adarand v. Skinner
790 F.Supp. 240 (D. Colo. 1992)
Applying standard of intermediate scrutiny, district court says that the subcontractor compensation clause is constitutional. Adarand Constructors loses.

Questions

1. What constitutional issue is raised in the *Adarand* litigation?
2. After the Supreme Court's 1995 decision in *Adarand v. Peña* what requirements did an affirmative action program have to meet to be constitutional?
3. Was the decision of the Court majority correct? Why or why not?
4. In a concurring opinion, Justice Scalia said that race classifications by government were never legitimate. In dissenting opinions, Justices Stevens, Souter, and Ginsburg argued that race-conscious remedies were justified. What were their arguments? With whom do you agree? Why?
5. Following *Adarand v. Peña,* the district court held that the affirmative action program in federal highway contracts was unconstitutional. Do you agree with this decision? Why or why not?
6. Do you believe that the Department of Transportation's current rules for helping DBEs get highway construction contracts pass the strict scrutiny requirement?

Chapter **Nineteen**

Corporate Governance

Enron's Governance Debacle

Enron Corp. for years was a favorite of stockholders who enjoyed the rise of its stock price from a low of $19.10 at the beginning of 1999 to a high of $90.80 in 2000. Until the 1990s the company was one of the world's largest natural gas, oil, and electricity producers. Then, in that decade, the company's business model changed radically as it evolved into the world's largest energy-trading company. It also created an unknown but large number of limited partnerships and other financial entities, numbering in the hundreds, perhaps in the thousands, dealing with commodities and services.

In its 2000 *Annual Report,* the company said its revenues had increased from $13.2 billion in 1996 to $100.8 billion in 2000, with a growth of profits from $1 million in 1996 to $1.1 billion in 2000. This bright picture clouded in October 2001, when Enron announced a $544 million after-tax charge against earnings related to the transactions of some partnerships. A month later the company said it was revising its financial statements from 1997 to 2001 to reduce net income by more than $1 billion. The reason was that it had been reporting income from some of its trading arrangements that was not real. And billions of dollars in debt had been hidden in so-called off-the-books accounts. Investors lost confidence in Enron, and cash flow declined to the point where the company could not meet its debt obligations. Finally, on December 2, 2001, the company filed for bankruptcy. It was the largest bankruptcy in U.S. history.

What happened? A swarm of congressional committees announced hearings to discover the answer, but they were frustrated by top Enron executives who chose to exercise their Fifth Amendment right to remain silent rather than incriminate themselves. Faced with a complex investigative task, those needing reasons could at least agree with Arthur Levitt, Jr., a former SEC chairman, who offered the sweeping explanation that "all systems failed in the Enron debacle."[1] In all likelihood he had in mind the board of directors, top management, internal auditors, outside auditors and lawyers, investment analysts, the SEC, and business journalists. As Nora Brownell, commissioner of the Federal Energy Regulatory Commission put it, "Everyone who has touched Enron should be looking in the mirror."[2] In this brief introductory story we cannot unravel the failures of all these parties. Instead, we focus on the massive

---

[1] Arthur Levitt, Jr., "All Systems Failed in the Enron Debacle," *Los Angeles Times,* January 24, 2002.

[2] John R. Emshwiller and Rebecca Smith, "Murky Waters: A Primer on Enron Partnerships," *The Wall Street Journal,* January 21, 2002, p. C14.

failure of corporate governance, primarily by the board of directors and to a lesser degree top managers.

The Board of Directors and Top Management

Enron's board was composed of individuals with distinguished backgrounds (see the next page). This board obviously had enough collective acumen that its oversight should have prevented the ignominious collapse of its charge. In October 2001, a Special Committee was created by the board to look at transactions between Enron and investment partnerships created and managed by Andrew S. Fastow, the company's chief financial officer. This action was triggered by huge losses in these partnerships contributing to the escalating financial problems of the company.

The Special Committee submitted its 218-page report to the board of directors on February 1, 2002.[3] In reviewing the extremely complex world of Enron's partnerships, it cast a critical eye on the governance structure of the company beginning with the board of directors.

The board had approved Fastow's partnerships even though, in some cases, they created a conflict of interest. The problem was that in some of the partnerships he was both a manager for Enron and an investor in an outside entity that engaged in financial transactions, such as the buying and selling of assets, with Enron. Which interest would be his priority, Enron's or his own? The rules of the Financial Accounting Standards Board (FASB), an organization that sets guidelines for accounting practices, are that if an outside investor puts in 3 percent or more of the capital in a partnership, the corporation, even if it provides the other 97 percent, does not have to declare the partnership as a subsidiary. Therefore, assets and debt in the partnership can be withheld from the corporation's balance sheet. Using this device, Enron was able to hide losses and debt totaling hundreds of millions of dollars.[4]

The directors recognized that it was a conflict of interest for Fastow to be an outside investor but defined it as a modest problem in light of the great potential gain for Enron, and they thought that it could be handled by certain controls specified by the board. These controls required the approval of top executives and the board on partnership deals. This policy was a mistake. The approval requirement gave a green light to expansion of the partnerships beyond anything envisioned by the board.

The controls on Fastow were never properly implemented. The Special Committee found that board committees, such as the audit committee, "were severely hampered by the fact that significant information was withheld from them."[5] Observers outside the company have not been as charitable, placing much of the blame for Enron's failure on the audit committee.[6] The Special Committee reached the obvious conclusion

---

[3] William C. Powers, Jr., chair; Raymond S. Trobh; and Herbert S. Winokur, Jr., *Report of Investigation by the Special Investigative Committee of the Board of Directors of Enron Corp.,* February 1, 2002. Powers was chair of the committee and dean of the University of Texas School of Law. Powers and Trobh were admitted to the board after the committee was formed. Winokur had been a member of the board for some time.

[4] Emshwiller and Smith, "Murky Waters," p. C1.

[5] Powers, Trobh, and Winokur, *Report of Investigation,* p. 159.

[6] Louis Lavelle, "Enron: How Governance Rules Failed," *BusinessWeek,* January 21, 2002, p. 28.

Enron's Board of Directors

ROBERT A. BELFER
New York, New York
Chairman, Belco Oil & Gas Corp.

NORMAN P. BLAKE, JR.
Colorado Springs, Colorado
Chairman, President and CEO, Comdisco, Inc.,
and Former CEO and Secretary General, United
States Olympic Committee

RONNIE C. CHAN
Hong Kong
Chairman, Hang Lung Group

JOHN H. DUNCAN
Houston, Texas
Former Chairman of the Executive Committee of
Gulf & Western Industries, Inc.

WENDY L. GRAMM
Washington, D.C.
Director of the Regulatory Studies Program of
the Mercatus Center at George Mason University
Former Chairman, U.S. Commodity Futures
Trading Commission

KEN L. HARRISON
Portland, Oregon
Former Chairman and CEO, Portland General
Electric Company

ROBERT K. JAEDICKE
Stanford, California
Professor of Accounting (Emeritus) and Former
Dean, Graduate School of Business, Stanford
University

KENNETH L. LAY
Houston, Texas
Chairman, Enron Corp.

CHARLES A. LEMAISTRE
San Antonio, Texas
President Emeritus, University of Texas M.D.
Anderson Cancer Center

JOHN MENDELSOHN
Houston, Texas
President, University of Texas M.D. Anderson
Cancer Center

JEROME J. MEYER
Wilsonville, Oregon
Chairman, Tektronix, Inc.

PAULO V. FERRAZ PEREIRA
Rio de Janeiro, Brazil
Executive Vice President of Group Bozano
Former President and COO, Meridional Financial
Group, and Former President and CEO, State Bank
of Rio de Janeiro, Brazil

FRANK SAVAGE
Stamford, Connecticut
Chairman, Alliance Capital Management
International (a division of Alliance Capital
Management L.P.)

JEFFREY K. SKILLING
Houston, Texas
President and CEO, Enron Corp.

JOHN A. URQUHART
Fairfield, Connecticut
Senior Advisor to the Chairman, Enron Corp.,
President, John A. Urquhart Associates, and
Former Senior Vice President of Industrial and
Power Systems, General Electric Company

JOHN WAKEHAM
London, England
Former U.K. Secretary of State for Energy and
Leader of the Houses of Lords and Commons

HERBERT S. WINOKUR, JR.
Greenwich, Connecticut
President, Winokur Holdings, Inc., and Former
Senior Executive Vice President, Penn Central
Corporation

Source: Enron *Annual Report* 2000, pp. 54–55.

that proliferation of the partnerships had exposed the company to enormous risks. At the same time, Fastow had been able to orchestrate side deals netting him more than $30 million as an individual.

The Special Committee did not place sole blame for Enron's failure on its directors, but it accused the board of failing to exercise its oversight responsibility. The committee said: "The Board of Directors was denied important information that might have led it to take action, but the Board also did not fully appreciate the significance of some of the specific information that came before it."[7] Some partnership arrangements were presented to the board that involved substantial sums of money and risk and the board failed to give them the scrutiny they deserved. Some of these intricate deals had received only 10 or 15 minutes of attention at board meetings. The board cannot be faulted, said the Special Committee, for not acting if it had no or insufficient information. It could be faulted, however, for limited scrutiny and probing.

The board had also approved procedures for management appraisal of partnerships and other, similarly arcane, arrangements such as limited-liability companies set up by Enron. For example, it directed its audit committee to conduct annual reviews of all partnership transactions. The committee, however, failed to probe deeply into the intricate transactions being generated. The board charged the chief accounting officer with the responsibility of reviewing and approving all transactions between Enron and its partnerships. Here again, the review was inadequate. What it all amounted to, said the Special Committee, was that top management was not "watching the store."

Financial Impacts

Enron's collapse resulted in mass layoffs. That, of course, was devastating to those who lost a job. To compound that disaster, many employees whose 401(k) retirement accounts were heavily invested in Enron stock saw their savings disappear. Janice Farmer of Orlando, Florida, for example, an Enron retiree, told the Senate Commerce Committee she at one time had $700,000 in her employee stock plan but now had only $4,000.[8]

In contrast, top managers were enriched by tens of millions of dollars as the financial fortunes of Enron declined. Days before it filed for bankruptcy, the company disbursed $55 million in bonuses to about 500 employees.[9] Michael Kopper, who worked for Fastow, invested $125,000 in one partnership and received more than $10 million in return. Throughout 2001, managers sold millions of shares of Enron stock at relatively high prices. Kenneth Lay, Enron's chairman, sold over $123 million of Enron stock in 2000 and $23 million in 2001.[10] Other top managers also made tens of millions of dollars in capital gains by selling before the fall.

[7] Ibid., p. 148.

[8] Robert L. Jackson, "Tearful Tales of Investors' Losses Fill Senate Panel Hearing on Enron," *New York Times,* December 19, 2001, p. C3.

[9] Richard A. Opell, Jr., and Kurt Eichenwald, "Enron Paid $55 Million for Bonuses," *New York Times,* December 6, 2001, p. 81.

[10] Marianne Lavelle and Matthew Benjamin, "The Biggest Bust," *U.S. News & World Report,* December 10, 2001, p. 34.

FIGURE 19.2   **Implementation and Ongoing Costs of Sarbanes-Oxley (Accounting, Audit, Consulting, Legal, New Hires, Others)**

Source: From *31st Annual Board of Directors Study, 2004*, p. 36. Courtesy of Korn/Ferry International.

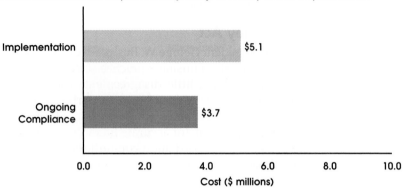

In addition to the new Sarbanes-Oxley regulations, the New York Stock Exchange has issued new corporate governance rules. For example, listed companies must publish ethics codes and corporate governance guidelines. Independent directors must approve director nominations and CEO compensation. Boards must have a majority of independent directors. Audit committees have the responsibility to hire and fire outside auditors.

A number of influential organizations are concerned with corporate activities. The Securities and Exchange Commission is the most prominent. The National Association of Corporate Directors has considerable influence upon corporate directors' activities. The Financial Accounting Standards Board has influence on standards for accounting records. The major pension funds have significant impact on corporate activities and we will discuss them later.

Many corporate managers accept and welcome these reforms. Robert Eckert, chairman and CEO of Mattel, is one (see the accompanying box). But Eckert, along with many other corporate executives, complains about the costs of the new reforms. As shown in Figure 19.2, executives have said that the average cost of installing Sarbanes-Oxley reforms is $5.1 million and that it takes $3.7 million each year to maintain them.[18]

Robert F. Felton, a director at McKinsey & Company, noted in 2004: "Arguably, the past few years have seen more corporate-governance reform than the previous several decades. Yet recent McKinsey surveys show that many directors and institutional investors clearly agree that too little reform has taken place to meaningfully improve board governance."[19] Others disagree. John A. Thain, CEO of the

---

[18] *Korn/Ferry International, 31st Annual Board of Directors Study, 2004*, p. 6. This is a poll of 1,000 directors and chief executives in 14 nations. Virtually all the reporting companies were large.

[19] Robert F. Felton, "A New Era in Corporate Governance Reform," *McKinsey Quarterly,* Summer 2004, p. 6.

Robert Eckert, Chairman and CEO, Mattel, Inc., Los Angeles, California

"The Sarbanes-Oxley (and new NYSE) provisions have added a level of rigor to financial reviews by both senior management and the board. That's all to the good. The drawback is that they have also added a level of bureaucracy, and in the end, the way we run the company, close the books, gather reporting data and disseminate it hasn't really changed all that much. But the process takes longer and at the same time we must report to the public faster. The combination places a great burden on the system. It takes up more of the time of our outside resources, including auditing and law firms, and for insiders it means working more hours than before. There is no question that our costs have gone up as a result. I'm not going to say how much, but enough so that I've noticed. But it is understandable that we all have to pay the price for the mistakes and bad faith of others. Had there been only one bad apple, I would say that the government had gone overboard with the new regulations. But the fact is that there wasn't just one."

Source: From *31st Annual Board of Directors Study, 2004*, pp. 22–23. Courtesy of Korn/Ferry International.

New York Stock Exchange, told the Economic Club of New York that reform had "gone far enough."[20] In general, business executives welcome the new regulation while feeling that its costs are excessive.

CORPORATE GOVERNANCE DEFINED

corporate governance
The legal checks and balances that define the rights and limit the powers of shareholders, boards of directors, and managers.

Corporate governance is the overall control of activities in a corporation. It is concerned with the formulation of long-term objectives, strategies, and plans and the proper management structure (organization, systems, and people) to achieve them. Also, it entails making sure that the structure functions to maintain the corporation's integrity, reputation, and responsibility to its various stakeholders.

In this definition, governance is the concern of the board of directors, who have authority to see that the CEO performs the operational activities of the corporation. The flow of authority, as shown in Figure 19.3, is from the powers granted in the charter to stockholders, then to directors, and then to the CEO. In reality, in many corporations the flow of authority is from the charter to the CEO, who exercises power over directors. Shareholders and the public have limited ability to influence activities of directors or the CEO.

[20] Louis Lavelle, "Governance: Backlash in the Executive Suite," *BusinessWeek*, June 14, 2004, p. 36.

FIGURE 19.3 Flow of Authority in Corporate Governance

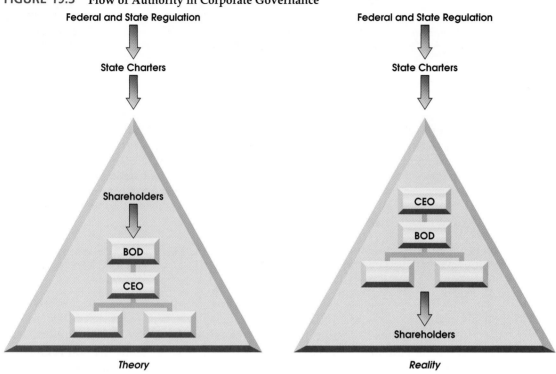

THE CORPORATE CHARTER

corporate charter
A document issued by a government that brings a corporation into being and defines its scope of authority. In the United States charters are issued by states.

The *corporate charter* is the legal authority for corporate managers and directors to function in conformance with the definition of corporate governance given above. All American corporations except a few quasi-public enterprises chartered by the federal government (for example, the Tennessee Valley Authority) are chartered by the state in which they incorporate. At the Constitutional Convention of 1787, the Founders debated a federal chartering power but decided that existing state controls were adequate to regulate corporate activity.

All states have general incorporation laws and compete with one another to attract the tax revenues of large corporations. Delaware is the longtime victor in this competition and charters almost half the largest industrial corporations in the United States. The attraction of Delaware, despite the fact that costs of incorporation there are higher than in most states, is the business-friendly corporate laws in the state. It has been said that Delaware will not be underregulated, meaning that its laws are less restricting of corporate activities. Also, its Chancery Court, which handles only business cases, is very accommodating to corporate interests.

Corporate charters specify the rights and responsibilities of stockholders, directors, and officers. Fundamentally, they lodge control over the property of the enterprise in stockholders who own shares in the assets of the company and vote those shares in naming a board of directors to run the firm. The directors have a fiduciary responsibility to protect the interests of the shareholders. They are responsible for appointing officers to run the day-to-day affairs of the company. The legal line of power runs from the state, to shareholders, to directors, to managers.

The charters also include detailed provisions about such matters as annual meetings, methods of choosing directors, and the authority of directors to issue stock. For instance, charters are specific about calling meetings of shareholders, declaring dividends, electing and removing officers, proposing amendments of the articles of incorporation, and so on. Such charter provisions are meant to protect the interests of shareholders. A vast body of law that seeks to do the same thing has also been created over time.

THE COMPOSITION AND SIZE OF BOARDS

In 2004 the average corporate board had 11 members, according to a comprehensive study by Korn/Ferry International.[21] The number varies by industry. Banks, for example, have 14 members. Most industries have 10 to 12 members. These numbers would be excessive for Giovanni Agnelli, the founder of Italy's huge Turin-based Fiat conglomerate. He once observed: "Only an odd number of directors can run a company, and three are too many."[22] This is an extreme position, of course, but most small firms and many large ones do have small boards. The trend in recent years has been to smaller size.

The number of outside directors on boards has grown until today the average corporate board has 8 outside directors and 2 inside directors. Eighty-two percent of the boards have at least one woman director, as compared with 69 percent in 1995. Seventy-six percent have one or more ethnic minority directors, compared with 47 percent in 1995. Fifteen percent of the boards studied have noncitizens as members, compared with 17 percent in 1995.

In the past, board members were usually suggested by the CEO to the board for approval. This is still the procedure in many companies, especially smaller ones. But more boards now have nominating committees or corporate governance committees that take on this responsibility. CEOs, however, still play a prominent role in selection. Once selected, the names of the nominees are presented to the shareholders for their approval or disapproval at the annual stockholder meeting.

Boards are divided into committees. The committees most frequently found on boards as reported by Korn/Ferry are: audit (100 percent), compensation (100 percent), nominating (96 percent), corporate governance (90 percent), stock options

---

[21] *Korn/Ferry International, 31st Annual Board of Directors Study, 2004,* p.10. The average board experience of respondents is seven years.

[22] Quoted in Pal Betts, "Heads Begin to Roll at Fiat," *Paris Financial Times,* June 18, 1990.

(80 percent), executive (49 percent), director's compensation (41 percent), succession planning (35 percent), finance (30 percent), corporate responsibility (17 percent), and investment (15 percent).[23] Other committees sometimes found on boards are public affairs, corporate ethics, employee pensions and benefits, human resources, environment, science and technology, corporate contributions, and legal affairs. Specific committee responsibilities vary from company to company.

Board Structures in Foreign Countries

German companies have "two-tier" boards that consist of an upper supervisory board and a lower management board. The supervisory board exercises broad control over the company. Its members, which include representatives of banks, major shareholders, trade unions, and suppliers, are appointed at an annual meeting of stockholders. This board supervises the management board. It elects members of the management board whom it can remove anytime. The lower board manages the detailed operations of the company. The EU has debated whether this model should be mandated in a European Community statute, but no decision has been made.

The structure of most European boards is not too different from that in the United States, except in Germany. Boards in the United Kingdom are a little smaller, namely 9. The supervisory board in Germany averages 16 members. In France, 81 percent of the boards require directors to own shares in the company they serve. In Germany there is no such requirement. Only 30 percent of the boards in France have succession plans. In the United Kingdom it is 70 percent. Most boards in the United Kingdom have written guidelines on corporate governance, compared with 36 percent in France. Most directors in Japan (81 percent of the companies) have pension plans. Far fewer boards in other countries have these plans. Most French public companies have a single structure like American companies but a few use the German model.[24]

The Korn/Ferry report concluded: "While most boards around the world are now in compliance with respective regulations, directors have not become complacent. . . . They are dealing head-on with core responsibilities such as CEO compensation and performance, management succession, and strategic positioning."[25]

The Duties of Directors

The Sarbanes-Oxley Act alters some duties of corporate directors. A far more comprehensive definition of board duties is incorporated in the report of a Commission on Public Trust and Private Enterprise created by the Conference Board. The Commission was asked to make specific recommendations for boards concerning executive compensation, corporate governance, and audit and accounting oversight.[26]

---

[23] *Korn/Ferry International, 31st Annual Board of Directors Study, 2004,* p. 13.

[24] Ibid., pp. 22–54.

[25] Ibid., p. 66.

[26] The Conference Board, *Commission on Public Trust and Private Enterprise* (New York: The Conference Board, 2002 and 2003).

Peter G. Peterson, chairman of The Blackstone Group, former U.S. Secretary of Commerce, and chairman of the Federal Reserve Bank of New York, chaired this commission whose members included prominent executives such as Paul Volcker, former chairman of the Board of Governors of the Federal Reserve System, Andy Grove, chairman of Intel, and John W. Snow, then chairman and CEO of CSX Corporation and now Secretary of the Treasury. They said, "The ultimate responsibility for good corporate governance rests with the board of directors. Only a strong, diligent and independent board of directors that understands the key issues, provides wise counsel and asks management the tough questions is capable of ensuring that the interests of share owners as well as other constituencies are being properly served."[27]

The commission dealt at length with the characteristics needed for strong boards. It said that directors should:

1. Exercise objectivity and autonomy to make independent, informed decisions;
2. Develop the knowledge and expertise to provide effective board oversight;
3. Display the character, integrity, and will to assert their points of view, and demonstrate loyalty exclusively to the corporation and its shareowners;
4. Devote the time necessary to fulfill the legal, regulatory and stock exchange requirements imposed upon them; and
5. Have the ability to retain, to the extent they deem necessary, advisors and independent staff support.[28]

The commission also made specific recommendations. It duplicated many of the rules of the Sarbanes-Oxley Act, the New York Stock Exchange, and the Securities and Exchange Commission. However, there were some additions, such as the following.

- Each corporation should carefully consider separating the offices of the chairman of the board and the chief executive officer. Where there is no separation, a presiding director should be established.
- A core responsibility of the board is to understand and approve the corporation's central, long-term strategies.
- The nominating/governance committee has many duties, such as recommending to the board an appropriate organization, determining qualifications for membership, presenting a slate of nominees, creating orientation and training for new members, formulating corporate governance principles for board approval, and evaluating candidates for CEO succession.
- The board should plan to evaluate itself, its committees, and the CEO.
- The board should oversee corporate ethics.

For each of the above policies (the commission called them principles) there were precise specifications of duties. The depth, detail, and completeness of the commission's recommendations eludes this brief summary. The commission's work represents a major new specification of the corporate board of directors' role, duties, organization, and performance.

[27] Ibid., p. 18.
[28] Ibid., p. 21.

INSTITUTIONAL INVESTORS AND GOVERNANCE

The growth of pension and mutual fund assets has given institutional investors new power in corporate governance. Their total assets rose from $70 billion in 1980 to more than $11 trillion in 2004. The equity investments of these funds rose from $258 billion in 1980 to $6.5 trillion in the third quarter of 2004. At that time, the total value of corporate equities on the market was, according to the Federal Reserve System, $13.5 trillion. The proportion of equities held by institutions has sharply increased since the 1950s, as shown in Figure 19.4. The stock holdings of these institutions give them a majority of the common shares in many companies, which gives them power to influence corporate governance, and they have used it.

Before the mid-1980s, pension fund managers were passive investors and usually went along with the decisions of corporate managers. Jesse Unruh, treasurer of the State of California and manager of the state's two largest pension funds, decided it was time for institutional investors to exert their power over governance issues. The immediate factor that energized him was that his funds had lost money when managers of Disney and Texaco paid corporate raiders to go away. He said, "Up to this point we have all been used and generally abused by

FIGURE 19.4 **Percent of Equity Held by Institutions**

Source: Board of Governors of the Federal Reserve System.

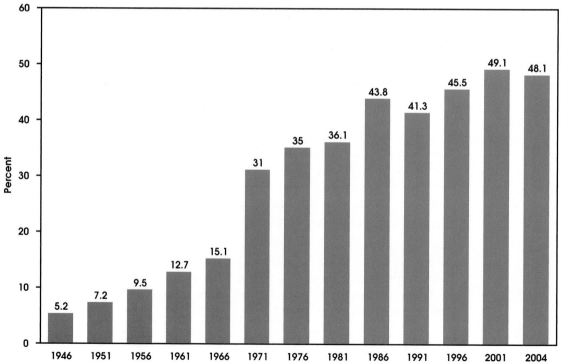

everybody—corporate raiders, arbitragers (takeover speculators) and management—because we are all so ignorant and ineffective in these situations."[29]

Unruh's ire led to the formation of the Council of Institutional Investors (CII) by 31 pension fund managers who controlled approximately $200 billion of assets, most of which was invested in equities. The CII endorsed a Shareholders Bill of Rights demanding a voice in "fundamental decisions which could affect corporate performance and growth."[30] Since then, institutional investors have been more active in corporate governance issues.

Should pension fund managers seek to influence corporations? If not, why not? If so, in what way? The interest of many pension fund managers is essentially short-term improvement in the value of the portfolios they manage. If they are not satisfied with the management of the companies whose stock they hold, the shares can be sold. This is possible when the shares owned in any single corporation are few. But when a pension fund such as the California Public Employees' Retirement System (CalPERS), whose assets in 2004 were more than $178 billion, owns a large percentage of any company's stock, it is essentially an owner-investor. In this light, it makes sense to seek to influence companies whose performance is deficient but whose long-term promise is bright.

CalPERS

CalPERS is a leader in governance activism among pension funds. Its initiatives have evolved over time. Its first efforts were aimed at actions of companies to ward off corporate raiders. Then, beginning in 1993, the fund identified each year a list of companies in its portfolio whose stocks underperformed stock market indexes. CalPERS urges the boards of these companies, sometimes privately and sometimes publicly, to improve governance and enhance long-term stock performance.

In 1998 the fund issued a list of standards for a model corporate board called the "Corporate Governance Core Principles and Guidelines." The document contains two sections—core principles and guidelines. The core principles, says CalPERS, represent the foundation for accountability between a corporation's management and its owners. Most of the core principles are incorporated in standards established by others, as we have noted. The guidelines represent additional features that further advance accountability. Each recommendation is accompanied by an explanation of meaning and CalPERS's reason for including it. A detailed definition of an independent director and his or her duties appears in the document's appendix.

CalPERS combs its portfolio of more than 1,800 companies to identify companies with poor financial and corporate governance performance. Four companies were identified in 2004 for its annual so-called "Focus List." They were Emerson Electric, Maytag, Royal Dutch Shell Petroleum, and The Walt Disney Company. Sean Harrigan, president of CalPERS, said, "Corporate governance reforms are needed for these companies to restore long-term profitability and investor confidence."[31]

[29] In Debra Whitefield, "Unruh Calls for Pension Funds to Flex Muscles," *Los Angeles Times*, February 3, 1985, p. E3.

[30] Council of Institutional Investors (New York: Council of Institutional Investors, undated).

[31] CalPERS, "CalPERS Releases 2004 Corporate Governance Focus List," Press Release, June 9, 2004.

The fund specified why each of these companies was targeted. For example, it said Emerson Electric stock had lost more than 40 percent of its value over five years and its debt levels had drastically increased. Also, its board had given an excessive retirement package to its chairman and the fund wanted it to reconsider the terms of this commitment. The pension fund also wanted Emerson to reduce insider representation on its board.

In November 2004, CalPERS announced plans to focus on abusive executive compensation systems and hold boards of directors more accountable for unwarranted generosity. The plans call for reform on a national level by addressing the issue with the Securities and Exchange Commission, the financial exchanges, and the compensation consulting industry. CalPERS points to a widening gap between the pay of top executives and that of average workers. Quoting *BusinessWeek,* the fund said that salaries of top executives grew to be 535 times the average worker's salary in 2000 compared with 42 times in 1980.[32]

CalPERS has a program to withhold proxy support for directors. The object is to improve corporate governance by focusing attention on the makeup of corporate boards of companies whose stock the fund owns. In 2004 the fund said it would withhold votes for directors at nearly 20 companies, including AT&T, Sears, and Ford. One reason was that their audit committees permitted outside auditors to provide nonaudit services. In one firm, the director was a senior advisor to an investment company that provided banking services for the company.[33] In another case the fund said it would withhold voting for Warren Buffett, who serves on the board of Coca-Cola. He also serves on the audit committee, and since one subsidiary of a company that Berkshire Hathaway (Buffett's holding company) owns provides services to Coca-Cola, Buffett has a conflict of interest.

CalPERS has examined the impact of its focused attention on stock prices and found that between 1992 and 2001 companies on the list showed an average return of 46 percent in the year after their listing.[34] Independent studies have confirmed the positive impact of share price on underachieving companies that find their way onto CalPERS's list.

Activism, of course, stimulates critics. For example, *The Wall Street Journal* criticized the fund for taking its program to withhold votes at the annual stockholder meetings to absurd lengths. The editors said: "Consider its recent campaign against Warren Buffett, the legendary stock picker and something of a corporate governance scold himself. CalPERS wants him off the Coca-Cola board because he sat on the committee that voted to allow the company's outside auditor (Ernst & Young) to perform some nonaudit services for Coke also."[35] Votes for eight other directors at Coca-Cola were to be withheld by CalPERS. A representative for Coca-Cola said that the directors targeted were talented and respected executives and held large amounts of the company's stock. According to a company

[32] CalPERS, "CalPERS Adopts Plan to Tackle Abusive Compensation Systems," Press Release, November 15, 2004.

[33] CalPERS, "CalPERS Targets AT&T, Sears, Ford," Press Release, May 10, 2004.

[34] CalPERS, "CalPERS Releases 2004 Corporate Governance Focus List," June 9, 2004.

[35] "Conflict in California," *The Wall Street Journal,* May 11, 2004, p. A18.

representative, "[T]here are few people more closely aligned with the interests of our shareholders."[36]

CalPERS and its president Sean Harrigan came under increasing criticism for "overreaching." He has been too aggressive said many corporate executives and politicians. Harrigan was accused of pushing an agenda that often had little to do with advancing shareholder values. As a former union leader, he was accused of favoring workers over business management. Finally, the five-member State Personnel Board failed to reappoint him as its representative to CalPERS and CalPERS's 13-member governing board failed to reappoint him as president. He left CalPERS at the end of 2004, after two years in office. Many observers predict the fund will continue its activism but be a little less aggressive than under Harrigan. We shall see.

COMPENSATION

A principle reason behind demands for corporate reform is that many people consider the compensation of CEOs to be excessive. In a Gallup poll, 79 percent of the respondents said that executives of a large corporation take improper actions to help themselves at the expense of the corporation.[37]

How Much Are CEOs Paid?

First, accurately calculating the exact pay and benefits of a chief executive is difficult. The publicly reported salary of a CEO, as well as any annual bonus, is clear enough. Problems arise in calculating the value of stock options, which are a large part of most CEO compensation, benefits such as deferred compensation, perquisites, and pensions. A *stock option* is a right to buy the company's stock at a fixed price and under conditions determined by the board of directors. Usually the price is set at or close to the current price and there is a limit on the time granted to the receiver to buy the stock, usually 10 years. Thus, if the stock of XYZ corporation today is $10 and rises to $50 dollars within the time limit, say 10 years, the CEO can buy that stock at $10 and reap the gain between this price and the future market price. If the stock does not rise above $10, the option is worthless. See page 612, footnote 6 for more on options.

stock option
Right to purchase a specified number of shares in a company's stock for a specified price at a future date.

Nearly all corporations have compensation committees that set the pay and benefits of top executives. Perceptions of excessively generous pay and benefits for CEOs inspire widespread outrage. This is an old story. In 1939 President Franklin D. Roosevelt railed against the "entrenched greed" of corporation executives, and the criticism has periodically arisen since. By today's standards, CEO pay in President Roosevelt's era was modest. Eugene G. Grace, president of Bethlehem Steel, was the highest paid executive in 1929. He received a salary of $12,000 and a bonus of $1.6 million. In 1949 the highest paid executive was Louis B. Mayer, first vice president of Lowe's Inc., who got $509,622. This contrasted with the average

---

[36] "CalPERS to Withhold Votes at Citigroup, Coke," *Los Angeles Times,* April 13, 2004, p. C4.

[37] In The Conference Board, *Commission on Public Trust and Private Enterprise,* p.17.

Cendant Shareholders Attack Executive Pay

On April 20, 2004, Cendant Corporation held its annual stockholder meeting at the Grand Hyatt New York. Among the shareholders attending was Daniel Steininger, chairman of The Catholic Funds. Steininger would present a resolution asking Cendant's board of directors to seek shareholder approval before paying CEO Henry R. Silverman more than 100 times the pay of the average Cendant worker.

The Catholic Funds manages an equity mutual fund named the Catholic Equity Fund with two purposes. First, as an index fund it tries to match the investment return of the Standard & Poor's 500 list of companies. Second, it advocates Catholic values. It refuses to invest in corporations with hospitals that allow abortions. It follows Catholic social teaching that each person is created in the likeness of God and is entitled to dignity and fair treatment. And it believes that according to the teachings of Jesus, everyone will be judged by their treatment of the least privileged.[1] This has led it to focus on the perceived evil of immoderate executive pay. According to Theodore Zimmer, the Fund's president, "We believe that a chief executive who demands excessive compensation is likely to have a value structure that devalues the contributions of workers and a mindset that undervalues the importance of treating workers with dignity and justice."[2]

In the past, the fund simply screened out companies that offended its principles, but its leadership decided to take a more active role. Instead of selling its holdings in firms such as Cendant it now chooses to advocate change. Besides Cendant, it was bringing proposals to reform executive pay before the shareholders of seven other companies.[3]

---

[1] Edward M. Welch, "Justice in Executive Compensation," *America Magazine,* May 19, 2003, p. 8.

[2] Quoted in William Baue, "The Value of Transformation: The Catholic Equity Fund," August 11, 2004, at www.socialfunds.com/news/pring.cgi?sfArticleID+1492.

[3] These companies were Alcoa, Delta Airlines, Compuware, International Paper, J. P. Morgan Chase, MetLife, and Time Warner.

CENDANT'S CREATOR: HENRY SILVERMAN

At the age of 15, Henry R. Silverman took his first business trip, traveling to a meeting where his father, the CEO of a finance company, gave a presentation to stock analysts. Afterwards, Henry amazed his father with intense questions about the meeting. If this was an augury that young Henry would one day build a great company, it was not discernible by 1961, when he graduated from Williams College with a degree in art history. Nor was it plain three years later, when he received a law degree from the University of Pennsylvania. But he soon moved toward business again.

Through the influence of his father, he became an assistant to Steve Ross, a brilliant deal maker who was then building what would become Warner Communications. Later, he assisted Saul Steinberg, a corporate takeover artist. Then he struck out on his own. Applying lessons learned from the masters, he started a company named HFS Incorporated in 1991. Silverman built HFS through a frenzy of acquisitions including real estate brokerage Century 21, hotels such as Ramada and Howard Johnson, and the Avis Rent-a-Car system. His acquisitions were usually winners and the company grew. He was adept at integrating new businesses into the company and raising their profit margins.

In 1998 Silverman seized an opportunity to combine HFS with a direct marketing firm named CUC International. He envisioned a strategic fit between the two companies in which people patronizing HFS franchises could be thrown into the CUC International marketing machine. It was an $11 billion merger. The new company was named Cendant Corporation.

Cendant's promise lured investors and by the spring of 1998 its stock reached a new high of 41⅜. Silverman was its largest stockholder. His stake was worth about $1.1 billion.[4] He was a winner, but he

---

[4] Amy Barrett, "Henry Silverman's Long Road Back," *BusinessWeek,* February 28, 2000.

EXHIBIT 1   **Cendant Corporation Quarterly Share Price 1998–2005**

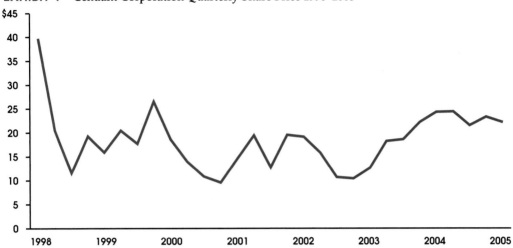

was about to become a victim. That April auditors noticed accounting irregularities in CUC International earnings reports between 1995 and 1997, the years immediately preceding the merger. When Cendant announced a restatement of earnings for those years its shares fell to 19¹⁄₁₆ on the next trading day. In the following months they would fall as low as 7½. Further investigation revealed pervasive fraud at CUC International.[5] Silverman sought the help of a psychiatrist to control his rage.

Every senior manager who had been with CUC International left Cendant. Some shareholders felt that Silverman should have closely investigated the books before the merger and they brought more than two dozen lawsuits. Eventually these would be settled for $2.8 billion without Cendant admitting any liability. But Cendant was badly wounded. With its stock price down and billions lost to shareholder lawsuits, Silverman could not continue his strategy of building revenues through acquisition. Investors

were wary. Determined to regain his reputation, he shifted Cendant's strategy.

Over the next two years, he propped up the share price by selling 18 businesses and using the funds in a massive stock buyback. Exhibit 1 shows quarterly share prices for Cendant. By mid-1998 these actions halted the free fall started by the accounting problems and then brought steady share price recovery lasting until the shares were caught in the downdraft of overall stock market decline in 2000 and 2001. Cendant's profit performance remained strong. Exhibit 2 shows a steady rise in net profit after 2000. This sustained net profit performance led to share price recovery during 2001. As net profit continued to rise through 2004, the share price rose with it to more than double the lows of 2000. However, the price did not recover to the highs achieved before revelations of accounting fraud.

Thanks to Silverman's determination, Cendant regained a sound footing. With the rise in its share price and a strong balance sheet, it weathered the loss of investor confidence. In 2004 it ranked 106 on the Fortune 500 with revenues of $18.2 billion, making it slightly larger than McDonald's and Anheuser Busch. Its market value of $23.5 billion was equal to that of Ford Motor. It employed about 90,000 people.

---

[5] Former top executives at CUC have been indicted on fraud and conspiracy charges. See *Securities and Exchange Commission v. Cosmo Corigliano et al.*, C.A. No. 00–2873 (KSH–PS) (D.N.J. filed June 14, 2000); and Superceding Indictment, *United States v. Walter A. Forbes and E. Kirk Shelton*, No. 3:02CR00264 (U.S.D.C., Dist. of Conn., filed December 11, 2002).

EXHIBIT 2
Net Profit of Cendant Corporation 1998–2005 (projected)

Source: Andre J. Costanza, "Cendant," *Value Line,* October 29, 2001.

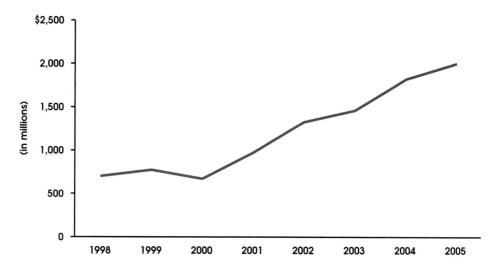

HENRY SILVERMAN'S COMPENSATION

In the post-merger years of 1998 to 2003, Henry Silverman's annual compensation, including his salary, bonus, and the value of stock options ranged from a high of $42 million to a low of $14.8 million. In most years he made more by exercising

Henry R. Silverman, Chairman and Chief Executive Officer, Cendant Corporation. Source: © James Leynse/ CORBIS.

options.[6] In 2000 his annual compensation was $42 million, but by selling options worth $129 million, he increased his total income to $171.4 million. Exhibit 3 shows the details of his annual compensation, option sales, and total compensation. In addition, by 2003 Silverman owned 41.6 million Cendant shares, approximately 4 percent of the total outstanding. He also held another 33.6 million shares of exercisable options worth about $287 million.

Under Cendant Corporation bylaws its 15-member board of directors determines the compensation of senior executives, including Henry Silverman. The board set up a 3-member compensation committee to develop a compensation strategy that would attract and retain talented executives, be competitive with pay at similar companies, and fairly compensate them for their performance. The compensation committee approves the details of executive pay packages

[6] Stock options give the holder the right to buy from the company a specified number of common shares for a specified price at a future date. On this date the options *vest,* that is, the person who holds them may buy the stock at the *exercise price,* or the market price of the shares on the day the options were granted. Options have an *expiration date.* They can no longer be exercised at some point, typically 1 to 10 years, after they vest. The options must be taken advantage of during an *exercise period,* or a period of years between vesting and expiration. If the market price of the shares is higher than the exercise price anytime during the exercise period, the holder can *exercise* the options, that is, buy shares at the exercise price. If the market price is lower than the exercise price when the options vest, they are worthless.

EXHIBIT 3   Annual Compensation of Henry Silverman 1998–2003

Source: Cendant Corporation definitive proxy statements 1999–2004, Securities and Exchange Commission, EDGAR database, forms DEF 14-A.

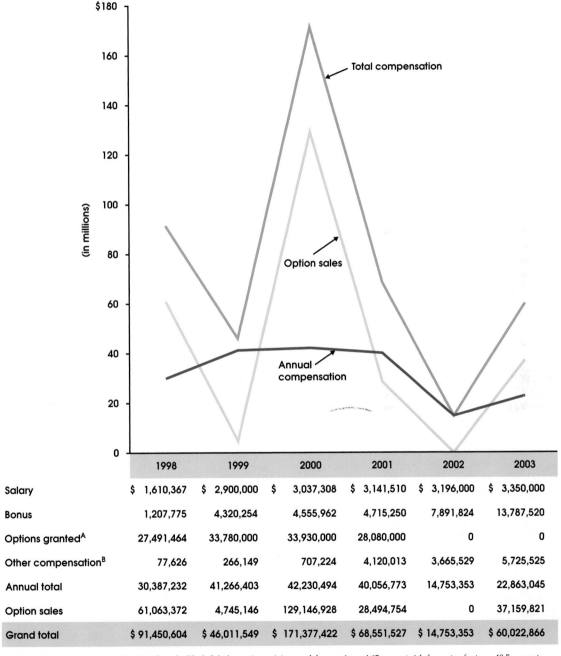

	1998	1999	2000	2001	2002	2003
Salary	$ 1,610,367	$ 2,900,000	$ 3,037,308	$ 3,141,510	$ 3,196,000	$ 3,350,000
Bonus	1,207,775	4,320,254	4,555,962	4,715,250	7,891,824	13,787,520
Options granted[A]	27,491,464	33,780,000	33,930,000	28,080,000	0	0
Other compensation[B]	77,626	266,149	707,224	4,120,013	3,665,529	5,725,525
Annual total	30,387,232	41,266,403	42,230,494	40,056,773	14,753,353	22,863,045
Option sales	61,063,372	4,745,146	129,146,928	28,494,754	0	37,159,821
Grand total	$ 91,450,604	$ 46,011,549	$ 171,377,422	$ 68,551,527	$ 14,753,353	$ 60,022,866

[A]Option totals are theoretical values based on the Black-Scholes option pricing model assuming a 4.65 percent risk-free rate of return, 49.5 percent volatility, no dividend payout, and a 5.27 year expected life.
[B]Other compensation includes, *inter alia,* use of company aircraft ($59,825 in 2003), matching contributions to a deferred compensation plan ($1,025,251 in 2003), premium payments on a $100,000,000 life insurance policy ($4,574,473 in 2003), and medical benefits ($4,800 in 2003).

spelled out in written agreements. All three members of the committee are outside directors.

Between 1998 and 2002, Silverman was compensated according to the terms of an employment contract signed in 1991. Among its provisions was an annual option grant of 2 million common shares. After accounting fraud scandals in companies where executives received large option grants and then manipulated earnings to inflate stock prices, shareholders pressured companies to reduce or eliminate options as a form of executive compensation. In 2002 Cendant's board and Silverman agreed to eliminate options from his pay package. This required negotiation of a new agreement.

Working with the human resources staff at Cendant and an outside law firm, Silverman created a proposal, then submitted it for approval to the board compensation committee. It was accepted without any change. It called for a base salary of $3.3 million, a bonus of 0.60 percent of pretax income, a $100 million life insurance policy, and perquisites that included use of company aircraft and cars. If he left the company for any reason, he would be entitled to a payment of his base salary plus his target bonus multiplied by the number of years remaining in the agreement or 2.99, whichever was greater. He would also have lifetime employment as a company consultant making $83,000 a month, continued payments on the insurance policy for the rest of his life, and lifetime medical coverage for his entire family. These severance payments were owed to Silverman even if he were fired for cause, including for gross negligence or even the commission of a felony against the company. The agreement would remain in force through 2012.

While negotiating the agreement, Silverman paid legal fees of $203,113. The board of directors agreed to reimburse him this amount plus an amount equal to his taxes on the reimbursement payment.

CHALLENGES ARISE

It was to this compensation package that the Catholic Funds objected. Other shareholders did too. One of them, Leonard Loventhal, sued Silverman and the entire board of directors for what he called "exorbitant and illegal payments" that "breached their fiduciary duties of loyalty, due care, good faith, and candor" to all stockholders.[7] Loventhal claimed that

the agreement was excessive because it failed to tie Silverman's bonus to performance goals and the severance payments were astonishingly generous, being owed even if Silverman were fired for malfeasance. He also argued that the Sarbanes-Oxley Act prohibited company loans to executives and the payments on Silverman's $100 million life insurance policy were, therefore, illegal. If Silverman died, the proceeds would repay Cendant and the rest would go to his family. It amounted to a loan.

Cendant announced a settlement of the Loventhal lawsuit the day before the annual shareholders meeting.[8] Rather than contest it, the board of directors made four changes in Silverman's compensation. Its expiration was moved up five years to 2007. Potential severance payments were reduced to 2.99 times his previous year's compensation. His bonus would be conditioned on "specified earnings growth targets." And if he left Cendant his $83,000 monthly retainer was limited to five years.[9] New arrangements for insuring his life would be sought. Although these changes were known to managers of the Catholic Equity Fund, they decided that Silverman's pay was still excessive and that its shareholder proposal should go forward. Accordingly, what follows is the text of the resolution as it was introduced at the meeting.

STOCKHOLDER PROPOSAL

The Catholic Equity Fund, 1100 West Wells Street, Milwaukee, Wisconsin 53233, owner of approximately 2,900 shares of the Company's common stock, has given notice of its intention to present the following resolution at the 2004 Annual Meeting. CRISTUS Health, 2600 North Loop West, Houston, Texas 77092, Congregation of the Divine Providence, P.O. Box 37345, San Antonio, Texas 78237, Providence Trust, 515 SW 24th Street, San Antonio, Texas 78297 and Congregation of the Sisters of Charity of the Incarnate Word, P.O. Box 230969, 6510 Lawndale, Houston, Texas 77223 have indicated their intention to co-sponsor this proposal.

WHEREAS:

U.S. CEO compensation is often excessive (1) and often tempts CEOs to undertake self-serving ventures (2) and often degrades long-term stock performance. (3) The ratio of average CEO pay to

---

[7] *Leonard Loventhal Account v. Henry R. Silverman et al.,* C.A. 20565, Court of Chancery of the State of Delaware, March 10, 2004, p. 1 and para. 54.

[8] The settlement was accepted by the Delaware court on August 19, 2004.

[9] Cendant Corporation, Form 8-K, August 24, 2004, exhibit 9.01.

average-worker pay has skyrocketed from about 40 in 1980 to at least several hundred currently. (4)

Both *BusinessWeek* and *Forbes* gave the Company their worst rankings in their studies of CEO compensation versus stock performance. (5) Another study shows the Company's 2002 CEO compensation to be 578 times the pay of an average U.S. worker. (6)

We believe that the system for compensating CEOs would markedly improve if companies would take three steps. First, restore a reasonable relationship to average-worker pay. Second, include company stock or options in the CEO's compensation only if the company provides that same type of compensation to all fulltime workers on a basis that would avoid increasing the pay gap. Third, link CEO compensation to meeting specific performance requirements that would mainly reflect the contributions of the CEO rather than of the work force or the economy in general.

In our opinion, a huge CEO-to-worker pay gap not only degrades worker and therefore company performance but also violates the dignity and worth of every human being that is the foundation of Catholic social teaching and common moral principles.

RESOLVED: The shareholders urge the Board of Directors:

- To limit the Compensation paid to the CEO in any fiscal year to no more than 100 times the average Compensation paid to the company's Non-Managerial Workers in the prior fiscal year, unless the shareholders have approved paying the CEO a greater amount;

- In any proposal for shareholder approval, to provide that the CEO can receive more than the 100-times amount only if the company achieves one or more goals that would mainly reflect the CEO's contributions; and

- In that proposal, to provide for grants to the CEO of stock options or other equity only if the company provides equity compensation to all fulltime employees such that they would participate proportionally in stock performance.

This proposal does not apply to compensation agreements presently in effect.

"Compensation" means salary, bonus, the grant-date present value of stock options, the grant-date present value of restricted stock, payments under long-term incentive plans, and "other annual" and "all other compensation" as those categories are defined for proxy statement purposes.

"Non-Managerial Workers" means those employees of the company worldwide whose

work would put them into the categories of Blue-Collar Occupations or Service Occupations or the Sales and Administrative Support components of White-Collar Occupations as used by the Bureau of Labor Statistics in its National Compensation Surveys.

Notes:
1. Conference Board, 9/17/02 (quoting Greenspan: "infectious greed"), *BusinessWeek* 4/22/02 ("simply out of hand").
2. Edward M. Welch, "Justice In Executive Compensation," America 5/19/03.
3. United For a Fair Economy, "The Bigger They Come, The Harder They Fall," http://www.ufenet.org/press/2001/Bigger_They_Come.pdf.
4. Economist.com, Executive Pay, 10/9/03.
5. http://bwnt.businessweek.com/exec_comp/2003/index.asp; http://www.forbes.com/2003/04/23/ceoland.html.
6. AFL/CIO Executive Paywatch, www.aflcio.org.[10]

SHAREHOLDER PROPOSALS

Common shareholders are entitled to one vote for each share they own. Under the laws of most states, including Delaware, where Cendant is incorporated, shareholders have the right to vote on certain matters. They can come to the annual meeting to vote in person. But most cast their votes before the meeting on a ballot mailed out by management called a proxy (voting can also be done by telephone or on the Internet).

At the Cendant annual meeting, shareholders were asked by the company's management to elect five nominees to the board of directors, to ratify a change in company bylaws requiring all directors to be reelected annually, and to approve the choice of Deloitte & Touche as its auditor. Besides the shareholder proposal from the Catholic Equity Fund, one other shareholder proposal was presented.[11]

Shareholder proposals are allowed by the Securities and Exchange Commission (SEC) if certain

[10] Cendant Corporation, *Proxy Statement,* March 1, 2004, pp. 44–45.

[11] The other proposal, sponsored by Joseph Grogan, an individual owning 1,000 shares of Cendant, recommended separation of the CEO and chairman of the board positions and the appointment of an independent director as board chair. Cendant's management opposed the resolution. It received 18.6 percent of the votes cast.

conditions are met.[12] The shareholder must own $2,000 or more of the company's securities for at least one year. The proposal cannot exceed 500 words. Its submission must comply with a few formal procedures and deadlines. And the shareholder must be at the annual meeting to present it.

Each year, hundreds of such proposals are advanced. Many come from public and union pension funds owning large blocs of a company's securities. The Catholic Equity Fund proposal was one of 414 proposals submitted in 2004 seeking to change some aspect of corporate governance.[13] Of these, 141 focused on executive compensation. The rest sought to change methods of electing directors, director tenure, takeover defenses, and auditing practices.

Many other proposals came from progressive activists, religious groups, and miscellaneous critics of business. Proposals from these parties typically raise corporate social responsibility issues.[14] They lack any chance of approval; not one has ever passed when opposed by the company. But they are useful for broadcasting the political and ideological views of their sponsors.

Management can petition the SEC to exclude proposals on certain grounds. If, for example, they relate to a trivial aspect of the company's operations, bring a personal grievance against the company, contain false statements, or would require breaking a law, they can be left out. Otherwise, they must be put before the stockholders. This can be expensive for a corporation. One estimate is that a shareholder resolution costs an average of $87,000 for legal counsel, administrative work, printing, distribution, and vote counting.[15]

---

[12] 17 C.F.R. 240.14a-8 (2000). The regulations were created by the SEC under authority found in the Securities and Exchange Act of 1934. They have been revised many times by the Commission, most recently in 1998. See Release No. 34040018 dated May 21, 1998, at www.sec.gov/rules/final/34-40018.htm.

[13] Georgeson Shareholder, *Annual Corporate Governance Review 2004* (New York: Georgeson Shareholder, 2004), figure 2.

[14] For background on the rise of social responsibility shareholder proposals, see David Vogel, *Lobbying the Corporation: Citizen Challenges to Business Authority* (New York: Basic Books, 1976).

[15] Roberta Romano, "Less Is More: Making Institutional Investor Activism a Valuable Mechanism of Corporate Governance," *Yale Journal on Regulation*, Summer 2001, p. 174. This estimate is based on a 1997 survey of corporations by the SEC.

CENDANT OPPOSES THE CATHOLIC EQUITY FUND PROPOSAL

The SEC permits companies to make written statements of opposition. Cendant responded to the Catholic Equity Fund proposal by printing this rejoinder in the proxy statement sent to all shareholders.

Board of Directors' Position

The Board of Directors recommends a vote "AGAINST" the above proposal. The Board believes that adoption of this proposal would severely limit the Company's ability to attract, motivate, and retain the best leadership talent in today's competitive environment and in the future by capping the compensation that may be paid to the Chief Executive Officer. The Company must be able to offer integrated compensation programs that pay competitively and consistently with comparable companies, align executive compensation with stockholder interest, and link total compensation to Company and individual performance.

The proposal would limit the Chief Executive Officer's compensation based on an arbitrary and formalistic mathematical formula that does not take into account the complex factors and analysis that must be considered in determining the appropriate compensation of a Chief Executive Officer. Such factors and analysis considered in arriving at a compensation amount include financial and other business goals of the Company as well as individual contributions and performance. The Compensation Committee, which is composed entirely of independent, non-employee directors, recognizes its responsibility to recommend executive compensation decisions that are in the best interest of the Company and the long-term interests of the Company's stockholders. The Board, which reviews and approves such compensation recommendations and the terms of any employment agreement entered into between the Company and its executive officers, agrees that executive compensation must be carefully evaluated. In entering into the amended and restated employment agreement with the current Chief Executive Officer (described more fully in the Compensation Committee Report on Executive Compensation contained in this proxy statement), the Compensation Committee and the Board devoted significant time and effort to assess the performance of the Company's Chief Executive Officer, and considered the Company's goals and objectives, performance and relative stockholder return, the value of similar incentive awards to executive officers at comparable companies, and awards made to the Chief

Executive Officer in prior years to formulating the appropriate compensation terms of the Company's Chief Executive Officer.

The Board believes that it is ultimately in our stockholders' best interest that this process not be subject to the limitations set forth in the proposed resolution. The proponent's arbitrary and formalistic pay cap proposal would restrict the Compensation Committee's role in engaging in the complex analysis necessary to determine appropriate compensation levels and remove from the Compensation Committee the flexibility to recognize significant accomplishments of an individual that may be critical to ensuring the long-term success of the Company. The proponent's restriction on granting the Chief Executive Officer equity awards would deprive the Company of needed flexibility in designing effective incentives to retain and properly incentivize the Chief Executive Officer. The Board believes that equity awards provide effective incentives to management and such awards are designed to align the interests of the Company's management and stockholders. Under the current employment agreement with the Chief Executive Officer, any award of stock options or other equity incentive award is in the discretion of the Compensation Committee. Under the previous employment agreement with the Chief Executive Officer, he had a contractual right to such awards. The Board believes that the elimination of such right in the current employment agreement demonstrates that the Board and the Company's management are continually evaluating and taking appropriate action with respect to executive compensation without the need for an arbitrary and formalistic mathematical formula to determine executive compensation levels.[16]

THE BOARD OF DIRECTORS UNANIMOUSLY RECOMMENDS THAT YOU VOTE "AGAINST" THIS PROPOSAL.

DEFEAT, BUT THE CAUSE LIVES ON

When all the votes were counted, the Catholic Equity Fund proposal was defeated. Of the approximately 1.02 billion outstanding shares of Cendant common

stock, about 879 million shares, or 85.9 percent, were voted. The recommendation to limit Henry Silverman's pay received only 6.1 percent of the votes cast.[17]

Five of the Fund's seven proposals to limit executive pay at other companies came to a vote and support was uniformly low. The highest vote was 12.1 percent at Alcoa. Elsewhere it was 8.26 percent at Time Warner, 8.22 percent at J. P. Morgan Chase, 3.66 percent at International Paper, and 2.04 percent at MetLife. The fund had withdrawn its Compuware and Delta Airlines proposals before a vote because it felt that those companies had improved their compensation policies. Because the proposals at Cendant and three other companies got more than 3 percent of the vote, under SEC rules they are eligible for reintroduction at the next year's annual meetings.

Out of the 141 proposals on executive compensation introduced in the 2004 proxy season, only 21 passed—all seeking to have companies expense options at the time they are granted. The average vote on 12 proposals to restrict the pay of executives, including the Catholic Funds proposals, was only 10 percent.[18]

Questions

1. Is the core recommendation of the Catholic Equity Fund shareholder proposal, to limit executive pay to 100 times the pay of average nonmanagement workers in a company, sound? Why or why not?

2. If you owned shares of Cendant Corporation, would you have voted for the Catholic Equity Fund proposal? What are your reasons?

3. Is Henry Silverman paid too much? If so, what would be a more reasonable level of compensation?

4. What changes, if any, should be made in Henry Silverman's compensation agreement?

---

[16] Cendant Corp., *Proxy Statement,* pp. 45–56.

[17] To be precise, of the shares voted, 6.1 percent were for the proposal, 92.7 percent against, and 1.2 percent abstained. Because 14.1 percent of shares were not voted, the proposal was supported by only 4.2 percent of shares outstanding.

[18] Georgeson Shareholder, *Annual Corporate Governance Review 2004,* figure 8.

Index